CHARLES WESLEY

A Reader

Edited by

JOHN R. TYSON

OXFORD
UNIVERSITY PRESS

OXFORD
UNIVERSITY PRESS

Oxford   New York
Athens   Auckland   Bangkok   Bogotá   Buenos Aires   Calcutta
Cape Town   Chennai   Dar es Salaam   Delhi   Florence   Hong Kong   Istanbul
Karachi   Kuala Lumpur   Madrid   Melbourne   Mexico City   Mumbai
Nairobi   Paris   São Paulo   Singapore   Taipei   Tokyo   Toronto   Warsaw

and associated companies in
Berlin   Ibadan

Copyright © 1989 by Oxford University Press Inc.

First published in 1989 by Oxford University Press, Inc.
198 Madison Avenue, New York, New York 10016

First issued as an Oxford University Press paperback, 2000

Oxford is a registered trademark of Oxford University Press

Library of Congress Cataloging-in-Publication Data
Wesley, Charles, 1707–1788.
   Charles Wesley–a reader.
   Includes indexes.
   ISBN 0-19-503959-9; 0-19-513485-0 (pbk)
   1. Wesley, Charles, 1707–1788.   2. Methodist Church—
Clergy—Biography.   3. Theology—Addresses, essays,
lectures.   I. Tyson, John R.   II. Title.
BX8495.W4A33   1989   287'.092'4   [B]   85-29787

9 8 7 6 5 4 3 2 1

Printed in the United States of America
on acid-free paper

CHARLES WESLEY

Preface

Charles Wesley: A Reader was born during the research for my Ph.D. dissertation, "Charles Wesley's Theology of the Cross" (Drew University, 1983). One of the most startling results of that inquiry was the recognition that, with a few notable exceptions, very little had been written about the co-founder of Methodism. The irony of this literary silence was enhanced by the tremendous quantity of generally unknown and often unpublished manuscript materials by Charles Wesley that I found. The analysis of his literary corpus became a necessary and laborious preliminary undertaking to addressing the larger question of Charles's theology of redemption. In response to the paucity of Charles's writings available to the public, I felt compelled to construct an anthology that would present Wesley's life and thought through his own words.

This *Reader* uses the writings of Charles Wesley to construct a documentary life of Charles Wesley, weaving a sort of autobiographical tapestry out of Charles's journal, hymns, letters, and sermons. Much of the material is unknown or previously unpublished; in some instances, more familiar hymns and sermons have been given in their fuller form and original context. Wesley's words and ideas are set in the life situations that gave them occasion, and yet Charles Wesley reaches beyond his own time to delineate and invigorate the faith of contemporary Christians.

I am grateful to Reverend William Leary and the Methodist Church Archives and History Committee in England for permission to publish from their massive manuscript holdings at the John Rylands Library of the University of Manchester, Manchester, England. With but a few important exceptions, all the rare manuscript material collected in this anthology comes from that collection. My heartfelt thanks are also extended to Mr. David Riley and his colleague Mr. John Tuck for their diligence in locating and copying manuscript materials for me.

Additional manuscript support came from the Methodist Church, Overseas Division (Methodist Missionary Society), England; I am grateful for their permission to publish Charles Wesley's letter on the Atlantic crossing. My thanks to Mrs. M. J. Fox for supplying me with a copy of that important piece of correspondence, and also to Dr. Frank Baker for his help in locating and transcribing that letter. Two of Charles's hymns were published from "Ms. Cheshunt" held in the Cheshunt College Foundation, Westminster College, Cambridge University. I am grateful to Dr. S. H. Mayor for supplying me with a copy of that manuscript, and to the Cheshunt Foundation for the kind permission to publish the hymns from it. I have endeavored to preserve Charles Wesley's own spelling, punctuation, and form when materials are printed from his manuscripts.

I am especially pleased to have the opportunity to print two hitherto unpublished sermons, which were only recently transcribed from Wesley's shorthand by Reverend Thomas Albin and Reverend Oliver A. Beckerlegge. I am grateful to Mr. Albin for contributing these two sermons to this collection.

Several important published materials have also been reprinted in this *Reader*. My thanks to the Methodist Publishing House of England, Epworth Press, for permission to publish two of John Wesley's letters from John Telford's edition of *The Letters of John Wesley* (London: Epworth, 1931), and for permission to reprint the hymn "Yokefellows" from Frank Baker's *The Representative Verse of Charles Wesley* (London: Epworth, 1962). My thanks to Mr. Charles Cole, editor of the *Methodist Quarterly Review* (*QR*), and the United Methodist Publishing House for permission to reprint portions of my article "Charles Wesley, Pastor," which appeared in *QR* 4, no. 1 (Spring 1984): 9–22. Unless otherwise indicated, the selections from Charles's journal are taken from the 1849 *Journal of Charles Wesley, M.A.* (London: John Mason), edited by Thomas Jackson.

Thanks are also due to Dr. Bard Thompson and Dr. Kenneth Rowe of Drew University, Madison, New Jersey, for their insightful comments on portions of this material when they served on my dissertation committee. I am particularly indebted to Kenneth Rowe for his careful reading of my manuscript.

I am richly blessed with a wife, Beth, family, and friends whose concern and support saw this project through to completion. I am grateful to Mr. and Mrs. Douglas Lister of Leigh-on-Sea, Essex, for their hospitality when I visited England, and for Douglas's invaluable assistance in rendering Charles Wesley's shorthand journal fragment into English. I am also indebted to my friends and colleagues Dr. David Howard and Dr. Gordon Stockin. Dr. Howard, professor of history, Houghton College, New York, performed the heroic task of proofreading parts of my manuscript; Dr. Stockin, professor emeritus of classics, Houghton College, identified and translated most of the Latin phrases appearing in this *Reader*. My thanks are also extended to Dr. Leonard I. Sweet, president of United Theological Seminary, Dayton, Ohio, for his comments on the research behind my introduction to Chapter 12, and to the able staff of Willard Houghton Memorial Library, Houghton College, for their kind assistance and frequent use of materials from the Wesleyana Room. I am grateful to Cynthia Read and the staff at Oxford University Press for their assistance in preparing this manuscript for publication.

Finally, I extend my gratitude to Dr. James H. Pain, Henry and Annie M. Pfeiffer Professor of Religion at Drew University, whose insistence (nearly a decade ago) that I look into Charles, *the other Wesley*, gave this project its inception. My thanks to him for his leadership and encouragement in my dissertation research, and for his staunch insistence that this project would be a useful contribution to scholarship and to the life and faith of the church. Hence, in token of my affection and admiration for him, I dedicate this book to James Pain, my mentor and my friend.

Houghton, N.Y.   J.R.T.
September 1988

Contents

CHARLES WESLEY

Introduction

CHARLES WESLEY—THE MAN

Charles Wesley stood in the shadow of his more famous (and more forward) brother John. John's overshadowing, which characterized to some degree their relationship in life, has been exaggerated by history's forgetfulness about Charles Wesley. Methodists in particular and Protestants in general have venerated John Wesley as one of the brightest lights of eighteenth-century Christianity, but the deeds of Charles have not often come to the forefront. History's preference for John over Charles has reflected, in part, the temperaments of the two men; Charles shunned the limelight, John was attracted toward it. In addition, Charles's lifelong allegiance to the Church of England caused Methodists of his own day to treat him with suspicion, and suggests why their more modern descendants turned toward the other Wesley as their hero, champion, and patriarch.

The youngest Wesley brother had an inauspicious beginning. He was born two months prematurely, and thereby began a pattern of frailty and illness that would plague him all his life. But there was also an air of Divine destiny about the Wesley household. Charles's father, Samuel Wesley, felt it; as he lay on his own deathbed he confided to his youngest son: "Be steady, the Christian faith will surely revive in the Kingdom; you shall see it though I shall not."[1] From this household would come a religious revival to shake England and the New World.

The Epworth manse where Charles Wesley spent his childhood was a bustling place where Christian faith, hard work, and education were esteemed. His father, Samuel Wesley Sr., an avid Anglican and a scholar, was a bit of an overmatch for his somewhat brutish parishioners. His mother, Susanna, was also a person of rare talents who served as primary school teacher and spiritual director to an ever-increasing brood of children. Pastor Wesley, overemployed in pastoral work, publication, and ecclesiastical office, found time only for the weightier issues of life, like finance (trying to get out of debt) and theology. He left the day-to-day course of affairs to Susanna and the older children. Samuel was, however, the boys' (and sister Hetty's) instructor in classics and theology.

On his fifth birthday Charles learned the alphabet in that "little school in the

3

house." The next day he was able to read the first verse of Genesis. Much to the credit of their mother, all three sons acquitted themselves well at important second-ary schools, won royal preferments toward their education and went on to pres-tigious Oxford. The Wesley sisters did not fare as well. Despite their native ability and promise, eighteenth-century society denied them the opportunities for personal development that were afforded their brothers. Without dowries to commend them to polite society, and yet with education, refinement and Christian diligence that set them above their neighbors, the Wesley sisters could not find suitable matches in isolated Epworth. Their lot was the drudgery of the household and, where marriage occurred, unhappy matches.[2]

The Wesleys (also spelled Westleys in earlier days) had a distinguished heritage in Christian leadership, reaching back through three generations of preachers. On the maternal side, Susanna's father, Dr. William Annesley, was an important Pu-ritan, as Charles's great-grandfather, Bartholomew Westley, had been. The streams of Anglican churchmanship and Puritan piety were well mingled among the Wesleys.

They were also a family of poets. Samuel Wesley Sr. spent much of his life composing religious verse and died just short of completing his *magnum opus* on Job. One of his hymns was published in John's 1739 edition of *Hymns and Sacred Poems,* "Behold the Savior of Mankind," and it still survives in the modern Methodist hymnals.[3] According to Mabel Brailsford, in this penchant for poetry Samuel Wesley, Jr., both followed and eclipsed his father, "whose working hours from cradle to grave were largely devoted to pounding out the heroic couplets which he expected, against all evidence, would eventually bring him riches."[4] But the son possessed what his father so sorely lacked, a lively wit, which "won him a perma-nent place amongst the English epigrammatists."[5] In addition to the two younger brothers, John and Charles, sister Hetty (Mehetabel) and her mother also showed a proclivity toward poetry; and it is said, though there are few extant examples, that Hetty's poetry was the finest of all.[6]

In terms of emotional makeup Charles seemed to be more his father's son, impetuous, short-tempered, and given to outbursts of feeling, whereas John's mea-sured reserve and quiet persistence emulated that of their mother. At the age of eight Charles left Epworth and attended Westminster school through the benevolence of his older brother Samuel; his home became Charles's and Samuel Jr. became a sort of foster-father to his young brother. Although the influence of the two Samuels must be taken together in each instance, it seems certain that Charles's brother Samuel molded his staunch Anglicanism, his love for the classics and his poetical muse.[7]

Upon arriving at Oxford to further his studies Charles resisted what he termed "the gloomy and mechanical piety" of the place. His success at the popular diver-sions aroused some concern back at Epworth, and John—who was serving as his father's curate—was dispatched to Oxford for an on-site investigation. He would later describe Charles's frame of mind in the following way: "He pursued his studies diligently, and led a regular, harmless life; but if I spoke to him about religion he would warmly [i.e. "heatedly"] answer, 'What! would you have me be a saint all at once?' and would hear no more.''[8] Yet, by the time he wrote his letter of January 22, 1729, Charles intimated to John that he hoped not to "relapse into my former state of insensibility.''[9] Reviewing that first year at Oxford and the transformation that had begun during the second year, Charles recalled: "My first year at college I lost in diversions. The next I set myself to study. Diligence led me into serious thinking. I went to the weekly Sacrament, and persuaded two or three young scholars to accompany me, and to observe the method of study prescribed by the Statutes of the University. This gained me the harmless nickname of a Methodist.''[10]

Thus, it was Charles Wesley who began that "Holy Club" where Methodist piety started to take shape.[11] It was he who first earned the title of derision, "Methodist," and turned it into a badge of honor. His warmth and devotion quickly drew other students around him in fellowship. One of that group, John Gambold, described Charles as "a man made for friendship; who by his cheerfulness and vivacity, would refresh his friend's heart, with attentive consideration, and would enter into and settle all his concerns. . . .''[12] John Wesley soon resumed his residency as a fellow at the university and, as Charles said, "came to our assistance. We then proceeded regularly in our studies, and in doing what good we could to the bodies and souls of men.''[13] Two important elements of character are revealed in the smooth transition in leadership of the Holy Club: the first is Charles's deference to John Wesley, and the second John's talent for organization and leadership. Under John's leadership the rather informal "Club" evolved into a religious society with carefully prescribed disciplines and regulations.

The changes that the Holy Club had inspired in Charles Wesley were apparent to his brother Samuel when the younger brother spent the summer of 1729 with him. In a letter to John, Charles confided: "They wonder here I'm so strangely dull (as indeed mirth and I have shook hands and parted) and at the same time pay me the compliment of saying I grow extremely like you.''[14] This "compliment" was a product of Charles's wit, for it was no compliment from Samuel, who had shaped the young Charles after his own image. John Wesley's Oxford diaries, only now being transcribed by Richard Heitzenrater, describe Charles as a man who "merits emulation—in meekness, tenderness, and learning.''[15] Each of these qualities would become a hallmark of Charles Wesley.

In many ways the piety of the Oxford Methodists was an extension of the Epworth manse; the practical and devotional authors preferred by Susanna were augmented with classical studies of the sort the sons received from Samuel. Their "method" included close study of the Bible, spiritual classics like Henry Scougal's *Life of God in the Soul of Man* and Thomas à Kempis's *Imitation of Christ,* along with contemporary practical works by English authors like Jeremy Taylor (*Holy Living and Holy Dying*) and William Law (*A Serious Call to a Devout and Holy Life* and *Christian Perfection*). Added to this blend was a discovery of the spiritual riches to be found in the Church Fathers; especially formative were writers of the Eastern Church. Theirs was a "method" that was to be lived, lived in periods of prayer and fasting, frequent communion, alms giving and visits with the condemned felons at Newgate prison. The theoretical was wedded to the practical, as the theological and devotional dimensions of the faith had as their goal the development of inner purity.[16] When news about the Oxford endeavor reached the rector at Epworth he recognized its roots and expressed his pride in his sons' undertaking: "I hear my son, John, has the honour of being styled 'the Father of the Holy Club'; if it be so, I must be the grandfather of it and I need not say that I had rather any of my sons should be so dignified and distinguished than to have the title of his Holiness."[17] For the father, like his sons, personal piety was esteemed above the highest ecclesiastical position.

Much has been written about the contrasting personalities of John and Charles Wesley, and while it is difficult to characterize them at a distance of so many years, it seems that Thomas Jackson appropriately styles Charles as "the child of feeling and emotion; John of intellect, who demanded a reason for everything."[18] Yet it will not do to picture Charles as a naive emotionalist (or an "enthusiast," in the eighteenth-century parlance). He was a shrewd judge of character, who quipped that brother John was "born for the benefit of knaves."[19] And Charles was far less willing to entertain emotional extravagance, pretentious perfections, and feigned miracles among the Methodists than was his more logical brother. The younger Wesley had an uncanny ability to size up a situation quickly, and acted more on intuition than by the force of sheer logic.

John Wesley recognized that he and his brother were men of very different temperament, and in a letter of 1766 he appealed to Charles to use their different gifts to complement and not impede each other: "If I am (in some sense) the head and you the heart of the work, may it not be said, 'the whole head is sick and the whole heart faint'? Come, in the name of God, let us arise and shake ourselves from the dust! Let us strengthen each other's hands in God, and that without delay."[20] This same distinction between the "head" and "heart" was evident in the Wesleys' evangelistic styles. One of John's letters to Charles urges, "O insist everywhere on *full* redemption, receivable by *faith alone!* Consequently to be looked for *now* You are *made* as it were, for this very thing. Just here you are in your element. In connection I beat you, but in strong, pointed sentences you beat me."[21] John's preachments came with compelling logic, but Charles's were packed with wholehearted directness.

Charles Wesley, as we meet him in his hymns and sundry writings, was a man who could hit the whole scale of human emotions. He could soar to heights of joy and ecstasy, and drop deep into dungeons of despair. Tradition has characterized John Wesley as a humorless man, whereas, whether or not that is true of his older brother, Charles possessed a lively wit and used it to take command of a situation through a pregnant pun or subtle turn of phrase. He was a man of warmth, capable of deep and lasting relationships. Unlike John, Charles invested himself in his marriage and family, and his *Hymns for Families* reveal the joy he knew as father and husband. If there was often warmth with him, there was also occasional heat. Charles could be explosive and impetuous. A few of John's letters remonstrate with his brother for Charles's rough handling of the Methodist lay preachers, and it was Charles who stormed out of the 1755 Methodist Conference when it seemed to him that separation from the Church of England was impending.[22]

Charles also had an iron will. It was a tremendous feat for that frail, undersized, sensitive lad to become captain of his school at Westminster. Even as a child he had shown character. He certainly was no coward, thrashing the school bully in defense of a smaller boy. While caught in the grasp of grinding poverty he refused an offer from a distant and wealthy relative—Garret Wesley—to become his heir, since that improvement would cost him life at Epworth and Westminster. In Georgia only a visit from his brother John softened Charles's resolve to starve to death rather than accept aid from people he considered his antagonists.[23] Later in life he openly opposed John's ill-conceived engagement to Grace Murray, a young woman already betrothed to one of the Methodist preachers. Charles quickly took the situation into his own hands and solved it by marrying the girl off to her former suitor while John Wesley was out of town. And it was Charles Wesley who, almost single-handedly, kept Methodism from leaving the Church of England—so long as he lived.

Charles was a man of the heart, not only in temperament but also—and supremely— in matters of religion. Throughout his Christian pilgrimage he used his own sense of peace and acceptance as a spiritual barometer for measuring the vitality of his faith. In his later years this reliance upon inner experience and a sense of assurance would send Charles on a quest for an unqualified sort of Christian Perfection; in May of 1738 his inward odyssey sent him (as he said) ". . . seeking Christ, as in an agony."[24] In his introspection and reliance upon religious experience Charles stood closer to the mystical tradition than did his brother John. Although Charles renounced the mystics' doctrinal errors, John was not convinced that he ever really got "the poison" of mysticism out of his system. John wrote that some of Charles's later hymns "savour a little of Mysticism," and he added, "I have rather corrected or expunged them. . . ."[25] But Charles's mysticism, while sharing some similarities with that of William Law and his other early mentors, was reshaped by his intensive study of the Scriptures. His was a mysticism of the Pauline union with Christ, "I in Christ" and "Christ in mé"; it meditated on the Johannine theology of love as the essence of God and the force of renovation in the life of the believer; and it sought the holiness of the Epistle to the Hebrews—"without which no man shall see God." As we shall see in our examination of his theology, aspiration overcame introspection in Charles's thought and the Christian Perfection that stood at the apex of his soteriology came only as a complete renovation of the inner person by the surrender of self to an invasion of love and purification by the Holy Spirit. Sanctification was nothing less than having the *imago Dei* restored through Christ.

Charles's intuitive approach to religion gave his doctrine vitality and depth, but also had debilitating effects that became evident in his hymns. The almost constant illness of his later life caused Charles to peer more deeply into the problem of pain than most poets have dared. Likewise, his sense of dread and god-forsakenness caused him to try to find therapeutic value in the dark night of the soul. He occasionally despaired of the pain of this life, seeking "release" or "discharge" through the victory of the Christian's death. These influences gave some of Charles's poetry a morbid cast, which John Wesley edited out of the published hymns. Charles's frail health and oscillating moods merged with the literary climate that produced such works as Gray's *Elegy Written in a Country Churchyard*, Wharton's *The Pleasures of Melancholy* and Young's *Night Thoughts,* and a spate of morbid poetry at the mid-point of the eighteenth century; each of these elements must be taken into any consideration of his melancholy.[26]

The brothers Wesley experienced the usual complications met in sibling relationships. Charles was, as John Gambold styled him, "a man made for friendship": gregarious, open, humble, self-effacing. Mabel Brailsford suggested that "Charles' genius was derivative, and took its color from the associate with whom he was most in sympathy at the moment."[27] Thus, a scenario can be created that depicts him as an excessively pliable sort, "swayed hither and thither" first by brother Samuel, then John, and finally "governed" by his wife Sally.[28] John Gambold recorded some surprise at the degree of Charles's deference to John during their Oxford career: "I never observed any person have a more real deference for another, than [Charles] had for his brother. . . . He followed his brother entirely. Could I describe one of them, I should describe both."[29] From the distance of his declining years, Charles saw this same deference to John as the real basis of his own Divine "call" to the New World.[30] General Oglethorpe, observing the growing depression of young Charles Wesley during his Georgia mission, diagnosed his case this way: "On many accounts I should recommend to you marriage, rather than celibacy. You are of a social temper, and would find in a married state the difficulties of working out your salvation exceedingly lessened and your helps increased."[31] Charles was "of a social temper," he had a deep affection for people (especially his family), and he would go a long way to avoid conflict or disharmony. He often played the role of peacemaker between John and figures like William Law, George Whitefield, and the Countess of Huntingdon.[32]

A letter from John Wesley to Charles, written at the height of the perfectionist schism raging in the London Methodist Society (July 9, 1766), sets the younger brother's deference in its proper context. "How apt you are," lamented John, "to take the colour of your company! When you and I [talked] together you *seemed* at least to be of the same mind with me, and now you are all off the hooks again! . . . unless you only talk because you are in the humour of contradiction; if so, I may as well blow against the wind as talk with you."[33] The letter is especially revealing since it sets Charles's "humour of contradiction" alongside his changeability as facets of character to be considered in understanding Charles and his relationship with his brother John.

It seems that Charles was an easygoing sort, who out of genuine affection for his brother and others often chose compliance over conflict. Yet, like all siblings, he occasionally sought to establish his independence from his brother, even in the context of close fraternal relationship: consider his intervention in John's proposed marriage to Grace Murray, his persistent refusal to forsake his family in Bristol in the face of John's urgent pleas for help in the itineracy, his unqualified conception of Christian Perfection (which, John said, was "set *too* high"), and his almost single-minded efforts to keep Methodism from separating from the Church of England—even going so far as to publish an open letter to John to force his hand to pen in support of the same cause.[34]

An interesting example of the two-sidedness of Charles's relationship with his brother emerges through Charles's practice of annotating his correspondence as he read and filed it. Receiving an urgent letter from John, pleading for concerted action in the evangelistic work, Charles filed it with the note: "Trying to bring me under his yoke."[35] He would not or could not trade his frail health or family obligations for John's itinerant ministry. On the other hand, a letter from Selina, Countess of Huntingdon—a staunch friend of Charles and his wife—was filed with a note that signaled the end of their relationship since she urged Charles to publicly denounce his brother: "Lady Huntingdon's last. UNANSWERED BY JOHN WESLEY'S BROTHER."[36] Theirs was the natural rivalry among brothers (and sisters); it was complicated by their differences in temperament and theology, but it stood on the larger foundation of their love and respect for each other.

The most significant, single evaluation of Charles Wesley's character appears in the 1816 edition of his sermons. The remembrance is especially important since it comes to us from his widow, and provides a clue to Charles's puzzling deference to John and others:

It has been remarked that public men do not often shine in private life. Though he regarded "all the world as his parish," and every man as his brother, [Charles] was amiable in his domestic circle, and kind to his relations, especially to those who were dependent upon him, or whom he thought neglected and oppressed. Charles was full of sensibility and fire; his patience and meekness were neither the effect of temperament or reason, but of divine principles. John affectionately discharged the social duties, but Charles seemed formed by nature to repose in the bosom of his family. Tender, indulgent, kind, as a brother, a husband, a father, and a master; warmly and unalienably devoted to his friend; he was a striking instance that general benevolence did not weaken particular attachments, discerning in the character of men, incapable of disguise, and eminently grateful. The peculiar virtue of John was forgiveness of enemies. He has been frequently known to receive even into his confidence those who had betrayed it, and basely injured him. They not only subsisted on his bounty, but shared his affection; nor was it easy to convince him that any one had wilfully deceived him; or, if it were attested to by facts, he would only allow it had been so in that single instance.

Equally generous and kind was his brother respecting enemies, and capable of an entire reconciliation; but he could not replace his confidence where he had experienced treachery. This formed some variation in their conduct, as also the higher church principles of Charles, who manifested them to the last, by desiring to be buried in consecrated ground.

His most striking excellence was humility; it extended to his talents as well as virtues; he not only acknowledged and pointed out but *delighted* in the superiority of another, and if there ever was a human being who disliked power, avoided pre-eminence, and shrunk from praise, it was Charles Wesley.

"In their lives they were lovely, and in their deaths they were not divided."

His poetical talents were confined to sacred subjects; he wrote short hymns on the most remarkable passages of the Old and New Testament. There is not a point of divinity, doctrinal, experimental, or practical, which he has not illustrated in verse. His funeral hymns breathe not only the spirit of poetry, but the extreme susceptibility of the pious author, and the religion of the heart.

As a preacher he was impassioned and energetic, and expressed the most important truths with simplicity, brevity, and force.

Most of these sermons were delivered in his early youth, when he was in America:

the thirteenth sermon, by the Rev. John Wesley, was never published amongst his
works. They are presented to the public by his WIDOW.[37]

There was in Charles Wesley's humility and zest for finding the Divine in the
regular things of life an openness that makes him accessible to the modern reader.
His struggles and pathos, as well as pride as father and husband, shine through. He
appears as a person like ourselves; a pilgrim, genuine and vulnerable—yet also
actuated by exemplary faith and infectious love. It is this quality in Charles Wesley
that caused Rattenbury to call him a "simple" and "ordinary" man, while acknowledging that his gift of verse was "the greatest single gift which either brother
possessed."[38] As we shall see in the succeeding sections, Charles's contributions
were extraordinary; they were many and diverse. Yet, he had that same self-
effacing, servant attitude Wesley observed in Jesus; in a sense Wesley's humility
was a part of his "greatness" since, like the hero of Kipling's poem, "he talked
with crowds and kept his virtue, and walked with kings—nor lost the common
touch." No small part of history's forgetfulness about Charles Wesley is a product
of his own propensity to shun praise and the limelight. He did not bother to collect
and publish his popular sermons, his journal makes rare report of his own accom-
plishments, and he repressed over one third of the hymns he wrote—probably
because they were controversial and would attract undue attention to himself, or set
his brother and the Methodist movement in an unfavorable light.

In the anthology that follows this introduction selections from Charles Wesley's
huge literary production are presented as windows into his life and thought. Charles
will tell his own story from the Georgia mission onwards. The salient events of his
life will be represented by selections of his writings; likewise, the shape of his mind
and theology will be illustrated by snatches from important portions of his literary
corpus.

WESLEY'S WRITINGS

The Journal

Charles Wesley began keeping his journal during his college years at Oxford. Like
his brother and other young men of his time, Wesley undertook the task as a way of
regulating his life and enhancing his own spiritual development. It was John Wesley
who had begun to write a journal, but he quickly convinced Charles to join him in
the practice. Charles's letter to John, dated May 5, 1729, probably marks the
beginning of his efforts at keeping a journal. He lamented: "I would willingly write
a diary of my actions, but don't know how to go about it. . . . I'm fully convinced
of the usefulness of such an undertaking. I shall be at a standstill till I hear from
you."[1] This decision to follow his elder brother's example in keeping a "diary"
was an important step for Charles. It signaled his growing seriousness about religious matters and a willingness to examine himself and his actions from that same
perspective.

Although Charles began keeping a journal in 1729, his early diary has not
survived. His published journal, first issued in 1849 and reprinted only recently,

commences with Charles's entry for March 9, 1736—the day the Wesleys and their two comrades from the Holy Club arrived in Georgia. The early entries are comparatively full, but as the journal moves toward the pivotal year of 1738 and the Herculean efforts of the Methodist revival that followed, Charles's entries become more terse and irregular. Hence, Frank Baker finds Charles's journal "very uneven," an understatement worthy of Wesley himself.[2]

In its mature form the journal is a series of compact entries that dwell more upon the author's activities than upon his inner thoughts and reflections. Charles had another avenue of expression for exploring the depths of the inner person: his hymns. This lack of introspection in Charles's journal becomes especially obvious when it is compared to the journals of brother John. Furthermore, while Charles's journal gives an apt (but truncated) picture of the man and his ministry, it gives few hints of the writer's reading habits and theological quests. What we do find there is an adequate account of Wesley's life pilgrimage from one faith-straining situation to another. Thus his journal provides the background that sets Charles's hymns in their historical context; it likewise evidences many of the same theological terms and concerns which were later formative in the more popular Wesleyan hymns.

Perhaps even more important than these benefits (and these *are* important elements) is the way in which Charles's journal provides a strong and almost untapped source for examining his preaching ministry. Charles Wesley is well remembered in popular piety as "the sweet singer of Methodism," and clearly with some justification since his hymns were his most enduring contribution; but he was remembered by his brother and those who recorded his death in the minutes of the 1788 Methodist Conference as a man of many excellent gifts. "His *least* praise," read the minutes, "was his talent for poetry. . . ."[3] He was also a prominent preacher and itinerant minister who followed his brother John into the work of the Methodist revival and societies—as Thomas Jackson says—"with equal steps."[4] In many instances Charles's journal represents little more than an annotated sermon log recording his harried steps across the British Isles. It discloses to even the casual reader that Wesley's itinerant ministry was both sustained and vigorous. In a close analysis of the sermon texts reported and the occasions addressed one finds in the journal the substance his hymns were made of—the real-life situations of a busy pastor, preacher, evangelist. There is also an impatience about his journal, as though there were many other duties that Charles preferred to keeping his diary.

Much of Charles's published journal was received and collected in installments as he mailed them home in letters to his wife, Sally, or brother John. Huge sections of the record are missing and it is easily assumed that portions were simply lost in transit or mislaid prior to being bound into a collection. Thomas Jackson also recalled a gross mishandling of Charles's journal even after it was collected and bound, though prior to its publication:

> A little while before it was published [the journal] was in great danger of being irrevocably lost. It was found among some loose straw on the floor of a public house in London, where the furniture of the owner was for a time deposited; several leaves in the volume being cut from the binding, and yet not removed.[5]

Charles Wesley may have destroyed portions of his own journal. These deletions may have pertained to Charles's interest in the emotional extravagances that occurred in the early years of the revival. It is also likely that some of the more pointed polemical material was expunged.[6] But neither of these conjectures completely accounts for the gaps and omissions in Wesley's published journal. A number of factors conspired to obscure Wesley's activities, and among these were Charles's own modesty, his difficult shorthand, and the unwillingness of his family to provide the written resources that might have done justice to his memory. John Wesley's journal entry for September 3, 1788, says: "I made a little beginning of some account of my brother's life. Perhaps I may not live to finish it."[7] His "account" never appeared, and what became of it remains an open question.

Certainly a portion of the blame for the scanty record on Charles must also rest with Thomas Jackson, the editor of the 1849 edition of Charles Wesley's journal. While it is true that sections of the record were lost, destroyed, or withheld, it is also clear that Jackson failed to use all the manuscript material that was available to him. Because of Charles's personal penchant for privacy and the unreliable state of the mails, Wesley occasionally wrote the most personal or revealing portions of his letters and journal in the (then) new shorthand system of Dr. John Byrom.[8] A close comparison of the published journal with the manuscript sources of Charles's diary indicates that none of the shorthand material was included in the edition prepared by Thomas Jackson, though much of it was later transcribed by Nehemiah Curnock.[9] One might conclude from this that Jackson did not read Byrom's shorthand and failed to consult with someone who could, and hence some of the most important portions of the journal were simply omitted. An obvious example of this problem can be seen in the 1753 Ms. "Shorthand Journal Fragment" (carried here in Chapter Ten).[10]

The Letters

Charles Wesley's letters are a second important and virtually unutilized source for examining the man and his ministry. Thomas Jackson found them to be "artless epistles," probably because Charles's letters lack the pastoral polish of John Wesley's published correspondence.[11] But John had high regard for Charles's literary skills: "I am very sensible," he wrote, "that writing letters is my brother's talent rather than mine."[12]

The letters of Charles Wesley are important windows into the private side of the man; likewise, they often fill gaps in his published journal by supplying tidbits of information about the silent years of his life. Of particular interest in this regard are Charles's domestic letters; most of the one hundred and six letters appended to Jackson's edition of the journal are of this type. They show Charles Wesley as a family man and supply a private side to balance the public record of his life. The majority of those published letters are addressed to Sally, Sarah Wesley, Charles's wife. They were composed while Wesley was away from their home in Bristol, fulfilling ministerial duties in London, or as far away as Ireland or Wales. In these letters we glimpse the emotions and events that caused him to write hymns such as

"On the Death of a Child."[13] We also see the warmth of a man who could turn love poems written to his wife during their courtship into hymns of Christian love.[14] In these same letters we meet a man whose family life is so permeated by Christian faith that he is even able to write a hymn "For a Child Cutting His Teeth"![15] No portion of Charles Wesley's life was so insignificant or mundane that it could not become an avenue for praising God. As Thomas Jackson concluded, these "domestic letters bespeak the hand and heart of the husband and of the father, and convey a favourable impression of the writer in both these sacred relations."[16]

The critical state of Charles Wesley's correspondence is rather problematic.[17] But the value of Charles Wesley's letters becomes obvious when they are merged with the journal to produce a fuller picture of the man and his work. The correspondence is especially helpful in filling some of the gaps in the journal, and likewise it shows us more of the inner man than does much of the journal material. Charles's letters are also important resources for establishing the date and authorship of a few of his hymns. They are helpful in examining his treatment of certain theological themes or issues. What is most startling about Charles Wesley's correspondence is that it lacks the strong (formally) theological note that is often found in the letters of John Wesley; there are, for example, no counterparts to John's polemical letters to "Mr. Smith" or Dr. Middleton.[18] Charles's letters are, by and large, personal letters, and when they venture beyond the personal toward the theological, their emphasis is strongly pastoral, not theoretical or doctrinaire. The usefulness here will be seen in the way they fill in the gaps between Charles's journal, hymns, and sermons.

The Sermons

Charles Wesley has not been remembered as a great preacher-evangelist. His success at hymn writing and partial retirement from itinerant preaching in the 1750s caused his contributions as an evangelist to be forgotten. Even prior to his conversion (1738) Charles had thrown himself wholeheartedly into the ministry of proclamation. He was tireless in his efforts. As John Telford recalled, "Charles Wesley never spared his strength, five services a day were by no means unusual."[19] His journal betrays a few self-conscious hints of Charles's success and popularity as a preacher, preaching, for example, to well over 4,000 people at Hanham on September 23, 1739.[20] The early Methodists demonstrated their appreciation for Wesley's work by making his sermon "Awake Thou That Sleepest" the most frequently published and purchased tract among the Methodists during the lifetime of the Wesleys.[21]

Like his brother John, Charles was a reluctant evangelist, particularly so when called upon to enter that new mode of preaching, open-air evangelism. Initially, Anglican churches and the Methodist societies were the chief locations of his labors; but on June 24, 1739, he "broke down the bridge" and "became desperate" by embarking on that innovation, field preaching; thereafter Charles used streets, fields, and gardens, as well as established churches and Methodist meeting rooms.[22]

Despite Charles's personal reticence, field preaching was a most appropriate medium. His fine voice and poet's way with words made his sermons extremely effective. As he described in a letter from Runwick in August 1739, song and sermon worked together in a Charles Wesley preaching service: "God enabled me to lift up my voice like a trumpet so that all distinctly heard me. I concluded with singing an invitation to the sinners."

After his marriage on April 8, 1749, with increasing family responsibilities, Charles Wesley gradually disengaged himself from the incessant itinerant ministry that had dominated so much of his earlier life. During that same period increased bouts with illness limited his efforts more and more to the cities of the Methodist triangle: London, Bristol, and Newcastle. His journal entry for Friday, August 9, 1751, reveals Charles's growing awareness of his limitations regarding the preaching ministry:

> I preached, but very feebly, on "the third part I will bring through the fire." *Preaching I perceive is not my principal business.* God knoweth my heart, and all its burdens. O that He would take the matter into His own hand, though He lay me aside as a broken vessel.[23]

The letter represents the beginning of a ministerial transition that occurred in the early 1750s; henceforth the main focus of Charles's work would not be found in preaching but rather in the "making" of hymns. Formerly those two tasks had been of equal importance to him.

An observable change also occurred, some years earlier, in Charles's method of sermon preparation. It can be demonstrated both chronologically and linguistically. Examined linguistically, it is clear that between March 9, 1736, and October 20, 1738, Wesley relied rather heavily upon written sermons and often upon sermons written by other preachers. In his own parlance these sermons could be said to be "preached" or sometimes they were "read." After October 20, 1738, Charles increasingly depended upon spontaneous exposition as his main sermon technique; during this period the term "expounded" appeared in the journal as a description of his pulpit style. A journal entry for June 21, 1738, exactly one month after his conversion, shows Charles using one of John Wesley's sermons: "The Lord gave us more matter for thanksgiving at Blendon, where I *read* my brother's sermon on faith."[24] This sermon "on faith" was very likely John's Standard Sermon #1, "Salvation by Faith," which he had preached at St. Mary's Oxford only ten days before. The next day, June 22, 1738, Charles wrote: "In the evening we had a meeting at Mr. Pier's and *read* my brother's sermon."[25] Presumably Charles was referring back to the same sermon he had utilized the day before. He concluded his record for June 22 by noting that the hearers were "purified by faith," his phraseology reflecting the title of John's standard sermon.[26] The journal entry for July 9, 1738, finds Charles once again preaching his "brother's sermon on faith"; indeed, he preached it twice.[27]

During this same July 1738, his journal explicitly states that Charles Wesley was writing his own sermons: "Mon., July 31. I began writing a sermon upon Gal. 3:22 ('But the Scriptures hath concluded all under sin'), that the promise by faith in Jesus might be given."[28] On Wednesday, August 16, 1738, Charles reported that he "*read* the Homily on Justification."[29] Perhaps his own sermon on Gal. 3:22 was not finished: at any rate, Wesley relied on the Anglican Homily when lecturing at "Jeph. Harris's Religious Society." By August 20, Wesley returned to the Galatians 3:22 passage when he preached at Islington, but his journal gives no indication of whether Charles's message was from a "written sermon" or not.[30] By August 31, 1738, he was clearly preaching his own sermon; Charles wrote, "At the society I *read my sermon,* 'the scripture hath concluded all under sin,' and urged my usual question: 'do you deserve to be damned?' "[31] In another interesting entry, for the day of September 5, 1738, Charles recorded, "Read *my sermon";* his phraseology suggests, perhaps, that this homily on Gal. 3:22 was the only written sermon Wesley possessed that was *his own.*[32]

By October of 1738 a second important transition was also taking place in Charles Wesley's preaching. His journal entry for October 15, 1738, locates him at Islington, where Charles "preached on the 'one thing needful'; and *added much extempore* [*sic*]."[33] The sermon he preached was probably Sermon #5 from the 1816 collection; but even more significant than that identification were the closing words of Wesley's report: "added much extempore." They mark the beginning of a new direction in Charles's preaching. By October 20, 1738, Charles was preaching with complete spontaneity:

> Seeing so few present at St. Antholin's, I thought of preaching extempore, afraid; yet ventured on the promise: 'Lo, I am with you always'; and spake on justification from Rom. 1:15, for three quarters of an hour, without hesitation. Glory be to God, who keepeth his promise for ever.[34]

After this journal entry Charles more and more often described his own pulpit style as "expounding." For the balance of 1738 and the entire year of 1739 he recorded "expounded" more than "preached."[35] While on the surface of the matter this preference in terminology might not seem significant, prior to October 20, 1738, Charles rarely used the term "expounded" to describe his preaching. The shift of terminology that his journal used to describe his pulpit work signals a corresponding shift in pulpit style. The earlier application of "reading" pointed to Charles's dependence upon written sermons (his own and others'), whereas the later term— "expounded"—signaled his movement to a free-flowing style of presentation, which he characterized as being "extempore" and which did not depend upon formal notes or written preparation. It marked a movement away from formal Anglican preaching toward the more spontaneous expositions of the Wesleyan revival.

A similar shift of style can be seen in the sermons of Charles Wesley that have survived from this period. The transition is best seen in the difference between the published sermons of the 1816 edition and the shorthand manuscript sermons, housed in the Methodist Archives and Research Centre, The John Rylands University Library of Manchester, Oxford Road, Manchester, England.[36] The published sermons follow the form of the standard homilies; they are tightly reasoned and argued, and in this regard they resemble the published sermons of John Wesley. The shorthand sermons, especially the later ones, are quite different in their form. Often they simply cite a line of Bible text, and then give a paragraph (or so) of exposition and application. The sermon simply alternates between text and exposition until the entire Bible passage under consideration has been "expounded."[37] In view of the shift in terminology examined above one would expect that the published sermons of the 1816 edition were products of the earliest years of Charles's ministry, the more formal shorthand manuscript sermons came from the period of transition, and his shorthand "expositions" were produced in the more harried years of the Wesleyan revival. But October 24, 1738, did not mark a continental divide for Charles Wesley's mode of preaching; on February 26, 1739, and July 11, 1750, his journal reports him preaching a "written sermon."[38] In spite of these few instances, the basic pattern of Charles's later preaching had been set and he turned more and more toward extemporaneous exposition.

After 1738 Charles began preaching by simply opening the Bible and expounding on the first verse that presented itself. This approach was first attested in Charles's letter to his brother John, dated March 1740: "I was greatly disturbed by an unusual unnecessary premeditating what to preach upon. . . . In the pulpit, I opened the Book and found the place where it was written 'the Spirit of the Lord is upon me, because He hath anointed me to preach the gospel to the poor, &c.' I explained our Lord's prophetic office, and described the persons on whom alone He could perform it. I found as did others that He owned me."[39] By May 20, 1743, this method of selecting a sermon text by opening the Bible and picking a passage at random had become noticeable in Charles's journal. In his entry on May 20 Charles wrote, "I preached on the first words I met."[40] On the next day his record was roughly the same, "preached on the first presented words."[41] This method became rather common for Charles, and it is reported with a degree of regularity in his terse journal entries.[42] However odd this process of selecting a sermon text might seem to the modern reader, it must have also seemed irregular to a man like Charles Wesley. Wesley was a classicist with a Master's Degree from Oxford. His education included classical languages and rhetoric, and each of these disciplines would naturally bias him toward careful exegesis and formal sermon preparation. But two years of almost continuous preaching and perpetual study of the Scriptures added a dimension to Charles Wesley's preaching that Oxford did not. His regimen left him thoroughly saturated with the Bible; he was as well suited as any preacher has been for this spontaneous method of exposition. And there is an obvious link between Charles's growing interest in spontaneity and the rather sparse collection of his sermons that has survived.[43] Wesley committed few of his later sermons to paper, so it is scarcely surprising that so few of them appeared in print. Apart from his formally prepared "Awake, Thou That Sleepest," which he wrote in 1742 and preached "before the University at Oxford" on April 4 of that year, the recently discovered shorthand manuscript sermons are the only extant examples of his mature homiletical work.

Charles was conscious of his own penchant for "preaching Christ,"[44] "preaching faith,"[45] or "preaching the Gospel."[46] For him these were roughly synonymous terms for describing the core of the New Testament faith—framed in the language of personal appeals and response. But a formal consideration of a theology

of proclamation was rather late in appearing among Charles's writings, and even
that late occurrence is implicit and indirect. Charles's journal entry for September
11, 1748, records with glowing approval this "charge," which the bishop of Exeter
gave his clergy:

> My brethren I beg you will rise up with me against only moral preaching. We have
> been long attempting the reformation of the Nation by discourses of this kind. With
> what success? Why, none at all. On the contrary, we have very dexterously preached
> the people into downright infidelity. We must change our voice; we must preach Christ
> and Him crucified. Nothing but the Gospel is, nothing will be found to be, the power
> of God unto salvation, besides. Let me, therefore, again and again request, may I add,
> *let me charge you*, to preach Jesus and salvation through his name; preach the Lord
> who brought the saying of the Great High Priest, 'He that believeth shall be saved.'
> Preach repentance towards God, and faith in our Lord Jesus Christ.[47]

The bishop's "charge to the clergy" echoes Charles Wesley's own sentiments
about preaching the transforming message of the Gospel. Charles intimated he was
"much refreshed by reading it," adding that this charge "deserves to be written in
letters of gold."[48] Charles's preaching, like his hymns, centered upon themes of
redemption and reconciliation through faith in Christ. His journal entry for January
4, 1747, recorded: "I preached at the Cross as usual."[49] While this "cross" may
refer to a geographic location, such as Kennington-cross, it is as likely a theological
reference; it is a terse summation of the focal point of Charles's proclamation, the
cross of Christ, and redemption through faith in His saving death and resurrection.
Redemption through Christ *was* Charles's theology of proclamation; he seemed
intent upon following the Pauline pattern of preaching "Christ and Him crucified."

Unfortunately, the extant corpus of Charles Wesley's sermons is sparse. The
main resources amount to three types of material: (1) the collection of sermons
attributed to Charles Wesley and published in 1816, (2) a collection of six manuscript sermons, written in the difficult shorthand of Dr. John Byrom, which has only
recently been discovered and is now being transcribed, and (3) those few sermons
that appear in other published material. Each of these sources will be utilized in the
anthology that follows this introduction.

Richard Heitzenrater has indicated that the sermons attributed to Charles Wesley
by the author of the 1816 collection were probably not actually written by Charles.
Apparently those who prepared the sermons for publication misread a shorthand
note, scrawled on the back of the manuscript of Sermon IX, which reported that
Charles had "transcribed" the sermons "from my brother's copies."[50] The younger brother had been ordained a few weeks prior to embarking upon the Georgia
mission, and he might quite naturally rely on John's experience and sermon files;
the elder brother had been writing sermons since 1726, when he was curate for his
father at Wroot and Epworth. The Wesleys lived in an age that had few of our
modern scruples about plagiarism, and preachers, even more then than now, flat-
tered each other with a rather direct borrowing of material. The Wesleys were
certainly a part of this milieu, and as was noted above, Charles continued to preach
both the standard homilies and John's sermons even after returning to England. But

Charles made these sermons his own by his use of them. While they initially came from the pen of the older Wesley, they have survived only in Charles's copies; certainly his application of John's early sermons not only signals Charles's approval, but also suggests that they come to us as a reflection of the shape of his own mind and faith.

The second important collection of Charles Wesley's sermons has only recently come to light.[51] Eight small manuscript booklets have been discovered in the Methodist Archives, and Research Centre, The John Rylands University Library of Manchester, Manchester England. The booklets contain six unpublished, shorthand sermons by Charles Wesley; in two instances the manuscripts carry a first and second draft of the same sermon (hence there are eight items but only six sermons in the collection).

A third source for examining Charles Wesley's pulpit work is found in two sermons that he wrote and preached, but that were carried among the published works of John Wesley. The first of these, "Awake, Thou That Sleepest," is carried in all the Wesleyan collections as Standard Sermon #3, occasionally with a note attributing it to Charles.[52] The sermon is a mosaic of biblical words and phrases, a characteristic even more reminiscent of Charles's hymns than John Wesley's sermons. Charles's sermons are reputed to have been full of emotion, and this element is also found in "Awake, Thou That Sleepest"; it is peppered with exclamation points. The second sermon that may have been written by Charles Wesley and is included in John Wesley's *Works* is published sermon #129, "The Cause and Cure of Earthquakes."[53]

A final, though indirect, source for Charles's sermonic work is found in the short annotations that appear in his journal; these give brief glimpses into the content and effects of many of his favorite sermons. He had a central core of favorite sermons, and perhaps considered having them published, but that publication never materialized. Yet, a close examination of Charles's journal and hymns not only suggests the identity of these favorites, but also allows the reader to discover how Wesley preached them. Although the journal record of Charles's sermons is not complete—since a sizable portion of the record has simply slipped out of existence—a close examination of those texts and their connection with Charles's journal and hymns is particularly instructive (see Appendix A).

The numerous texts that are simply said to have been "expounded" give little clue to Wesley's application of those biblical passages. But the remaining dozen of frequently preached passages do shed some light on our modern darkness about Charles Wesley's evangelism. He consistently expounded the entire gospel in each passage, but there was also a particular sense in which certain of Charles's sermons were more christocentric than others. Of the sixteen sermons that head the "most frequently preached" list, four were decidedly christological in character: "The Good Samaritan," "All Ye Who Passed By," "Thou Shalt Call His Name Jesus," and "Behold the Lamb of God."

Charles preached "The Good Samaritan" at least eighteen times and it was one of his more dramatic sermons. In his reconstruction of the biblical drama the hearer of the sermon or singer of the hymn becomes the wounded traveler, beset by thieves; in the same symbolic way Jesus is the Good Samaritan who brings the healing and redemption. Wesley's journal indicates that he preached this sermon to between three and four thousand eager listeners, and it was clearly one of his more popular homilies.[54] Healing became Charles's metaphor for redemption in his exposition of the parable, as his journal recorded: "I showed them their case and their Physician in the wounded traveler and good samaritan."[55] Sin, for Wesley, was frequently symbolized by illness, with healing as its counterpoint in redemption; hence, the recovery of the wounded traveler proclaimed the gospel of redemption. Charles generally described the healing process as "the pouring of oil,"[56] though on a few occasions the pouring was of "oil and wine."[57] The result of these healing libations was that the wounded are "made whole" and their wounds are "bound up."[58] The effects of this sermon among Wesley's hearers were sometimes quite radical. Charles's journal entry for Sunday 16, 1739, recalled: "I expounded the Good Samaritan to between three and four thousand, with power, . . . A woman fell down under the stroke of it."[59] This seems to be an example of what later revivalists would call "being smitten in the Spirit," and it is one of the few examples of emotional extravagance that remain in Charles's (perhaps sanitized) journal. The same sermon evoked moving testimonies of redemption or wholeness.[60]

Charles Wesley could preach "Christ and Him crucified" from virtually any Bible text. A second of these christological sermons, possessing a distinctively dramatic emphasis, was based on Lam. 1:12: "Is it nothing to you, all ye that pass by? behold, see if there be any sorrow like unto my sorrow, which is done unto me, wherewith the Lord hath afflicted me in the day of his fierce anger." The Old Testament text became a springboard that propelled the reader to Golgotha: Wesley made his hearers contemporaries of Christ's death, forcing them to "look upon Him whom they have pierced."[61] This mythopoetic experience was so real that the listeners "had close fellowship with Him in His sufferings."[62] In Charles Wesley's hands the Lam. 1:12 passage becomes Christ's own call for evangelistic decision as He hangs ever before us on His cross: "At Biddicks we had close fellowship with Him in His Sufferings, while He cried, 'Is it nothing to you, all ye that pass by?' "[63]

Other examples from the list of Charles's favorite sermons isolated the theme of redemption as the centerpole of the sermon. "Repent and Believe the Gospel," "All Under Sin," "Ho, Everyone That Thirsteth," and "Lazarus Raised" were sermons of this sort. Of these Charles's journal particularly illuminates the preaching of the John 11 text: "At the Foundry I discoursed on Lazarus raised. . . . then I strongly recommended the use of the means [of grace] from the words 'take away the stone'; and showed the weakness of faith from those words, 'He that was dead came forth, bound hand and foot.' "[64] The movement from death to life was a prominent metaphor in Charles's sermons and hymns, its image marking a movement from being dead in sin toward being alive through faith in Christ. Likewise, faith is constantly presented as the force that breaks one's bonds and effects liberation.

The third type of sermon, which Charles frequently preached, called for inner renewal of the whole person. "The One Thing Needful" and "Wrestling Jacob" were the most frequently attested examples of this category of sermon. Inner renewal and restoration of the *imago Dei* (image of God within a person) was that *one thing needful.*[65] In "Wrestling Jacob" the hearer of the sermon and the singers of the hymn are transformed into Jacob wrestling with the Christ-Angel for "the Blessing."[66] Owing at least in part to the popularity of this sermon, "the Blessing" became an important Wesleyan epigram for sanctification or Christian Perfection. For Charles Wesley the restoration of the paradisiacal image was to be received as a purifying work of the Holy Spirit Who made Christ present in the human heart; it was to be anticipated—indeed longed for—in this life but was most characteristically considered to be consummated on the threshold between this life and the life to come.

The final grouping of sermons from this list of Charles's favorites dealt with the themes of persecution and comfort: "These Are They Which Come Out of the Great Tribulation" and "Come All Ye That Labour and Are Heavy Laden" were among the sermons of this sort. "Comfort" was an important theological concern in Charles Wesley's thinking: it was the focus of at least eight sermons based on Isa. 40:1f—"Comfort Ye my people"—and repeatedly emerged as an important theme in his hymns.[67] The early Methodists frequently knew physical persecution for their faith, and Charles urged them to seek the path of purification (like metal tried by fire) in the midst of their trials. "Comfort" also formed an important connection with the Wesleyan doctrine of assurance, since both brothers taught that Christians can have an inward and "sensible" knowledge of their acceptance by God.

The extant sermon sources in the Charles Wesley literary corpus are interesting both from the historical and from the literary-critical point of view. Much of the material traditionally attributed to Charles Wesley was not written by him; while other genuine sermons are only now coming to light. A few of Charles's more popular sermons have been reprinted among John Wesley's works, often without any indication of his authorship. And the connection between Charles's journal and hymns as a means for examining his preaching is only now being examined. Yet his sermons, however significant in their own day, now play a supportive role; Charles Wesley's heart and mind are most directly found in his hymns, and it is to that source we must turn our fullest attention.

THE HYMNS

Charles Wesley's poetical muse was astonishing; not only in terms of the quality of his verse, but also in its sheer quantity. Although Wesley wrote a huge corpus of hymns, over four hundred of which still adorn the worship of various Christian groups, there is no clear consensus as to the exact number of hymns composed by him, since several important issues complicate the ascription of authorship.

The first matter is the general question of authorship. Was a particular hymn composed by John or Charles? Since the brothers seemed to have had a gentlemen's agreement about not designating the composer of the separate hymns, the inquirer is

faced by what Frank Baker has aptly called "the vexed problem of joint authorship."[1] A second question, more easily dispatched than the first, has to do with
what constitutes a "hymn"; do we mean "published hymns," or hymns that were
actually sung, or are Charles's manuscripts and *Short Hymns on Select Passages of
Scripture* (1762) also to be taken into account even though they were almost never
sung? The brothers were willing to consider their productions "Hymns and Sacred
Poems" without ever formally distinguishing between those two categories, and
that phrase aptly titled four of their most influential hymnals. Since neither of the
founders of Methodism composed music (though Charles's sons did), the distinction between "hymn" and "poem" was found largely in the application and not the
shape the compositions were given.

The numerical calculation of Charles's hymns runs from a high of 9,000[2] down to
a low of 3,000—if one excludes the lyric poems.[3] The median estimate reaches
about 7,300 hymns.[4] It is clear that Charles wrote regularly and often. He has been
laughingly called "an evangelical centaur," half man and half horse, and perhaps,
as Mabel Brailsford suggests, the rhythm of the Methodist hymns "to this day
enshrines the steady jog-trot of their horses' hooves."[5] Charles's hymns also took
their tone from the bouncy, dance-hall music of his day. When a crew of drunken
sailors from West Cornwall loudly greeted Wesley's preaching with their ditty
"Nancy Dawson," Charles remarked that he liked their tune but not their lewd
lyrics. He invited his detractors to return again later in the day, promising to have a
song for them all to sing together; a huge crowd gathered for his second service and
Charles passed out his apology for Christian hymnody, "On the True Use of
Musick" (carried here as No. 56), written to the same tune the sailors had shouted
at him earlier in that day.[6]

His own journal gives a few hints at Charles's habits in making hymns. Most
often we read there about the occasions that spawned his hymns. At one point his
recollection of a serious fall revealed how naturally the day-to-day work of writing
hymns had become a part of Charles's life; "Near Ripley," he wrote, "my horse
threw and fell upon me. My companion thought I had broken my neck; but my leg
was only bruised, my hand sprained, and my head stunned: *which spoiled my
making of hymns,* or thinking at all, till the next day, when the Lord brought us to
New Castle."[7] Wesley measured the severity of his injury by his inability to
compose hymns for an entire day. Clearly, this break in his hymn writing was
something Charles was not accustomed to; if, in fact, he wrote 9,000 hymns,
Charles Wesley composed a hymn a day every day for nearly twenty-five years of
his adult life. Often his journal reports that he wrote verse as he rode to his next
preaching post: "I crept on, singing or making hymns, till I got unawares to
Canterbury."[8]

The Methodist hymns were composed out of the life experiences of their author's
ministry and they were also tools of his ministry. As Charles wrote in a letter of
August 26, 1739, "I concluded with singing an invitation to the sinners."[9] The
hymns were often a portion of the fellowship between Charles and his Christian
friends: "I dined at Mr. Brockman's and we administered to one another in Psalms
and hymns and spiritual songs."[10] The hymns were also aids in Charles's personal

devotions: "We sang together and prayed as in the months that are past."[11] And wearisome travel by horse, coach, or on foot was made more pleasant by bellowing Methodist hymns: "We sang and shouted all the way to Oxford."[12]

It is generally assumed that Charles's hymn-writing career began with his conversion experience in May 1738. Actually, Charles may have begun to write poetry in Georgia. His "Hymn for Seriousness," for example, has geographical and emotional references that seem to link it to Charles's American adventure.[13] While it is unclear how many of Charles's hymns survived the Georgia mission, some of the songs included in his *Hymns and Sacred Poems* (1749)—for example, "A Hymn for Midnight"—come from that earlier period.[14]

The Methodist hymnbooks, beginning with the 1739 *Hymns and Sacred Poems* and running up to the 1749 two-volume edition with the same title, were published either solely under John Wesley's name or jointly carrying the names of both brothers. *Hymns and Sacred Poems* of 1749 was hastily constructed out of older material from Charles's notebooks. It was published to convince his future mother-in-law that the young Methodist preacher could raise the sort of money necessary to wed and support the fair Sally Gwynne. Beginning with this "bride-price" hymnal and excluding the standard *Collection of Hymns for the Use of the People Called Methodists* (London: J. Paramore, 1780), the hymnbooks published after 1749 were the work of Charles Wesley.

The Methodist hymnbook of 1780 was a joint project, and its preface seems to clearly indicate how the Wesleys' hymn-writing partnership worked: Charles wrote, and John edited. But that simplistic attribution is not completely accurate, since John wrote: "But a small part of these hymns is of *my own composing*, I do not think it inconsistent with modesty to declare, that I am persuaded no such Hymn Book has yet been published in the English language."[15] What portion of these hymns were of John's "composing" and whether or not that phrase refers to translations or original compositions are questions that shall be treated more directly below, but here in the latest—as in the earliest Methodist hymnbooks—the "vexed problem of joint authorship" emerges with force.

The traditional solution to the problem of identifying the author of the various hymns has been to attribute all the translations (from German mainly, though also from French and Spanish), as well as all the adaptations of hymns by other writers like George Herbert or Isaac Watts, to John Wesley. There is some basis to this approach since the first Methodist hymnal, *A Collection of Psalms and Hymns* (Charles-town [*sic*]: Lewis Timothy, 1737), was solely the work of John and was composed entirely of translations and adaptations. A few original compositions were also attributed to John on the basis of their inferior literary style; but by and large, John Wesley's contribution was considered to be rather small.

This approach to the question of authorship, pioneered by early Methodist hymnologists like David Creamer,[16] was followed by standard sources like John Julian's *A Dictionary of Hymnology*.[17] Yet it combines the double danger of being both simplistic and inaccurate by assuming that John's poems would necessarily be inferior to Charles's and also that Charles was incapable of making any of the translations carried in the Methodist hymnbooks. The first assumption is made without a shred of proof, whereas the second flies in the face of clear manuscript evidence. There is strong indication that Charles was involved with at least three of the Methodist hymns translated from the Moravian (German) hymnbook.[18] The only clear occasion of John Wesley erupting into verse after 1749 was during the Grace Murray affair, when the love of his life (or so it seemed) was wrenched from him (with the complicity of brother Charles). Thus, it does seem that John Wesley wrote little poetry after 1749, but how much or how little must remain an open question.

The Later Hymns

Charles's *Hymns and Sacred Poems* of 1749 is a watershed in the Wesleyan hymnological corpus. It is clear that the two-volume edition was entirely Charles's own composition, since John Wesley claimed to know nothing of the books prior to their publication: "In the year 1749," John wrote, "my brother printed two volumes of 'hymns and sacred poems.' As I did not see these before they were published, there were some things in them I did not approve of."[19] While John probably did not see these hymnals prior to publication, it is certain that he saw *some* of the hymns therein; both "An Act of Devotion"[20] and "Jesus, from whom all blessings flow"[21] were first published by him before the appearance of the *Hymns and Sacred Poems* of 1749. The former hymn was first carried at the conclusion of John's *A Farther Appeal.*[22] The latter selection first appeared at the end of John Wesley's *Earnest Appeal to Men of Reason and Religion.*[23] Hence, it is certain that John saw a few of the hymns in the 1749 collection; yet his denial certainly suggests that he had not seen the completed hymnbook.

John Wesley's disclaimer for the 1749 hymnal points to a second thorny issue in the Wesleys' hymns—the extent of John's editorial control over Charles's compositions. One must seriously question how much the published hymns reflect Charles's undiluted verse, and how extensively John's editorial polish affected the *form and content* of those hymns.

Many of John's editorial emendations were purely of the literary sort. Most of the editorial changes that John made in Charles's hymns had to do with John's dislike for some of his brother's favorite words and phrases. The first hint of this editorial struggle emerges in John's printed sermon #117, where he intimates: "Some will think I have been over-scrupulous with regard to one particular word, which I never use myself either in verse or in prose, in praying or in preaching, though it is very frequently used by modern divines. . . . It is the word *dear.*"[24] John then argued against the use of this term since it takes "too much familiarity with the great Lord of heaven and earth" and is not found so applied in any portion of the Bible.[25] From this admission we can conclude that a Wesley hymn which addresses the Deity as "Dear" was not from John Wesley's pen and probably also escaped his editorial work.

Another indication of John's preference in word choice came to light in a spirited discussion over the *Nativity Hymns* (1746), which Charles published without John's editorial examination. In a letter to Charles, dated December 26, 1761, John laments further problems with a reprint edition of the same hymnal: "Pray tell brother Sheen I am largely displeased at his reprinting the *Nativity Hymns* and omitting the very best in the collection. . . . Omit one or two more and I will thank you. They are *namby-pambical.*"[26] Precisely what John disapproved of among the *Nativity Hymns* is open to conjecture; if, however, his remarks above are taken seriously it is very likely that John found verses like this one rather offensive: "He comes from above, / In manifest love, / The Desire of our eyes, / The meek Lamb of God / in a manger He lies."[27]

This matter of maudlin or "namby-pambical" language was not confined to the nativity hymns; in fact, it appears in most of John Wesley's emendations of Charles's hymns. For example, the third verse from Charles's *Short Hymns on Select Passages of Scripture* (1762) was omitted from John's *A Collection of Hymns for the Use of the People Called Methodists* (1780), although all the other verses of the hymn were used:

3   Bears transform'd with oxen graze,
        Their young together feed,
   With the calf the lion plays,
        Nor rends the dandled kid;
   Harshest natures reconciled
        with *soft* and fierce with *meek* agree,
   gentle, tractable, and *mild*
        As *harmless* infancy.[28]

Eric Sharp's recent article, "Gentle Jesus, Meek and Mild—Variations on a Nursery Theme, for Congregation and Critic," has called for a reexamination of this phraseology, which John Wesley found so offensive.[29] Today, the effect of words like "gentle, meek, and mild" cause one to think of someone or something "insipid," but in their biblical application and eighteenth-century currency they presented a far different picture: "they are strong, positive, and above all biblical."[30] "Gentle" in Wesley's day characterized a person of culture and breeding—a *gentle*man. "Mild" was Charles's way of discussing the motives involved in Christ's incarnation, a term suggesting a *kenotic* Christology and the love of a self-emptying God. "Meek" referred to Jesus' acceptance of the necessity of his own suffering; it is the language of the way of the Cross, for Christ and for Christians. While Eric Sharp properly suggests what might have been the connotations these "namby-pambical" terms carried for Charles Wesley, it is quite clear that John did not like the language of sentimentality and edited it out of Charles's hymns with the same vigor that he avoided it in his own translations of the Moravians' hymns.[31]

Other editorial changes were even more substantial. Charles, due in part to his own emotional makeup and frail health, came to see mourning and suffering as purifying agents in the pilgrim's quest for Christian Perfection. John, when using Charles's later hymns in his own hymnbooks, generally omitted verses that present-

ed mourning, weeping, and physical suffering as positive agents or purifying devices. The following verses, for example, were first published in Charles' *Funeral
Hymns* of 1746:

5   Thou know'st in the Spirit of prayer
       I groan for a speedy release,
    And long have pined to be there,
       Where sorrow and misery cease;
    Where all temptation is past,
       And loss and affliction are o'er,
    And anguish is ended at last,
       And trouble and death are no more.

6   Come thou to my cure I pray
       For this, and for nothing beside,
    Make ready, and bear me away,
       Thy weary, disconsolate bride;
    The days of my mourning and pain,
       Cut short, and in pity set free,
    And give me to rest and to reign,
       For ever and ever in Thee.[32]

In subsequent editions of the Wesleyan hymnbooks this hymn remained a favorite,
but these two verses emphasizing suffering and mourning were not reprinted.

Charles's later hymns evidenced a second emphasis, which John apparently
considered to be a theological aberration and sought to "correct." The 1760s saw a
great controversy arise within Methodism over the doctrine of sanctification, and
more specifically as it pertained to Christian Perfection. While Charles's understanding of Christian Perfection had always shared a large common ground with that
of his brother, it is also clear that from the very outset his explication was somewhat
different from John's. The brothers differed on the definition, nature, and timing of
perfection. Charles's basic definition was that Christian Perfection or sanctification
meant a restoration of the image of God (*imago Dei*) within a person; it meant
undoing the effects of the Edenic fall and restoration of a person's paradisiacal
identity. His view, then, was by its very nature an unqualified conception of what
this "perfection" meant. It meant nothing less than a recovery of the original
relationship with God and its concomitant righteousness. John Wesley had a more
qualified conception of Christian Perfection. For him, it was more a matter of purity
of motive or will; and so emerged his famous distinction between sin "properly"
and "improperly so-called." "Sin properly so-called" was willful transgression of
a known law of God, and John believed that the love of God operative within the
Christian could eradicate these willful, knowledgeable sins.[33] It was admittedly a
high ideal, but John also found himself forced to chide Charles for "setting perfection *too* high."[34] The younger brother seemed to see John's qualified conception of
perfection, based on this doctrine of sin, as an equivocation and he would have none
of it. Both brothers preached and sought perfection as a possibility in this life, and
both (at least initially) understood it as an event that could come instantaneously
upon a person in one divine moment. After 1749, as Charles and John each—

increasingly—followed his own path, Charles came to emphasize the gradual growth of holiness or perfection over the instantaneous reception of it. This development was radicalized by his opposition to the pretenders of perfection who divided and damaged the London Methodist Society with their talk of being instantaneously made "as perfect as Angels." Hence, Charles's later hymns also broke with John's timetable for perfection; he not only increasingly emphasized the gradual growth in sanctity, but also (as an obvious corollary to his unqualified conception) came to believe that Christian Perfection was generally realized only on the threshold between this life and the life to come. As we shall see below, John's editorial hand corrected each of these developments, which he viewed as aberrations, in Charles's later hymns. Other editorial changes occurred because Charles occasionally used phraseology that could easily be misconstrued if taken out of its Wesleyan-Arminian context. Consider, for example, the following verse:

6   The *unchangeable decree is past,*
      The sure predestinating word.
    That I, who on my Lord am cast,
      I shall be like my sinless Lord:
    'T was fix'd from all eternity;
      All things are possible to me.[35]

In the larger context of the Wesleys' thought "the unchangeable decree" referred to the *means* of redemption; what had been decreed was that those who are redeemed will be reconciled to God through faith in Christ. In a similar way, what was "predestined" for the Methodists was that the redeemed must be *conformed to the image of Christ.* Hence, theological language that to the Wesleys was a call to "the two great truths of the everlasting Gospel, universal redemption and Christian Perfection," might have certainly sounded (to the uninitiated) like double predestination and particular election in its Calvinistic form.[36] This hymn was first published in Charles's *Hymns and Sacred Poems* (1749), and later was reissued in John's 1780 *A Collection of Hymns for the Use of the People Called Methodists*; in John's application verse six was carefully omitted.[37]

Thus from the historical and critical standpoint Charles's later hymns, which are relatively unknown, are of vast significance. Not only can they assuredly be traced to the younger brother's hand, thereby solving a bit of the "vexed problem" of authorship; but also in these later hymns we meet the unretouched thought of Charles Wesley. In the later hymns he steps out from under John Wesley's editorial control and, to that degree, also from under John's ideological shadow.

The largest single contribution of Charles's career as a hymnologist was his *Short Hymns on Select Passages of Scripture,* which appeared in 1762. The title is sufficiently explanatory, since the work was a poetic commentary on selected Bible verses. It included more than 5,100 hymns. These volumes, along with the almost six books of material left in manuscript, form the most extensive and perhaps most enlightening portion of Charles's literary corpus. The hymns, especially the unpublished ones, reveal the evolving views of Charles Wesley. The differences with John on the matter of sanctification as an instantaneous work and Charles's own emphasis upon a theology of suffering both become more pronounced. Hence, in a letter to Dorothy Furly, John Wesley warned the woman, "take care you are not hurt by anything in the *Short Hymns* contrary to the doctrines you have received."[38] Charles's unpublished hymns on "Four Gospels and Acts" are even more controversial items. In the face of a heretical conception of Christian Perfection that was dividing Methodism in London, Charles set forth his own views more forcefully and attacked the "boasters of Perfection." Further, in these same hymns we meet Charles Wesley as a great expositor of Scripture, a privilege normally denied us because so few of his sermons have survived. There are over 1,200 "Short Hymns on Select Passages of Scripture" that exist only in manuscript form, written or edited in Charles's own hand.

The Early Hymns

The first Methodist hymnbook was published in 1737, by John Wesley. It was the product of his ministerial endeavors during the ill-fated Georgia mission. The contents of the 1737 *Psalms and Hymns* were adaptations from the great English hymnologists (especially Herbert and Watts) or translations (mostly from the German Moravian Hymnbook).[39] None of Charles's own hymns appeared in the earliest collection and the stirring, original compositions for which Methodism would become famous began appearing only after the brothers returned to England. In the earliest years of the revival the brothers published five hymnals jointly (1739–1745), and a sixth, *Moral and Sacred Poems* (1744), appeared under John's name alone. Since it was a policy of the Wesleys not to identify the author of the various hymns, it is particularly difficult for the modern investigator to identify the hymns of John and Charles in these earliest collections.

The consensus among hymnologists on the limited extent of John Wesley's contribution to the early hymnals (between 50 and 100 hymns) could hardly be more solid.[40] The traditional assumption has been that John wrote few, if any, original hymns; it is further assumed that Charles read no German and translated none of the hymns from foreign languages. Where "proof" has been offered on behalf of the authorship of a specific hymn it has often come forward in the form of prosodic or internal evidence, touching upon the style or mode of expression in the hymn. There is some substance to each of these avenues of approach, but neither of them seems as conclusive as historical connection or manuscript evidence. Recent discoveries make it clear that Charles was involved in the production of at least three of the Wesleyan renditions of German hymns, hence a part of the foundation of the older consensus is crumbling.[41]

Much attention has also been given to the meter, foot, and rhyme utilized in the Wesleyan hymns. The later hymns, those published after 1749, which can assuredly be attributed to Charles, evidence an unbelievable variety of meter, foot, and rhyme. Charles's standard tool, in terms of foot, was iambic. Yet, even in that foot Charles's versatility was astonishing; he used no fewer than forty-five different iambic meters.[42] His favorite form, by far, was the six-eights (8.8.8.8.8.8), six lines of eight poetic feet, which Charles generally rhymed ABABCC. It is the rhyme scheme of the classic sonnet. Although he seemed most at home with iambic, Charles also ventured into the rhythmic rage of his day—the anapestic foot. The bounces of the three-foot line gave Wesley's hymns a joyous attitude; they reflected the popular "jigs" of the day and produced in their hearers a natural desire to keep time with hands or feet. Updating the eighteenth-century's musical medium a bit, one might imagine that the impact of Charles's anapestic hymns could have had the potential effect of introducing jazz or rock and roll into otherwise staid contemporary worship. Charles also showed himself to be quite versatile in trochaic feet, composing over 1,000 poems in sixteen trochaic meters.[43]

An examination of Charles Wesley's rhymes evidences the same versatility met in the other aspects of his poetry. It is especially instructive to observe his application of the so-called "imperfect" or "half-rhymes." These are rhymes that find harmony in the eye but not in the ear. George Vallins (among others) has suggested that Charles's imperfect rhymes fall into such well-defined patterns that they can be used as evidence for ascribing authorship of the Wesleyan hymns.[44] Since Charles's imperfect rhymes are consistent throughout his work, they do seem to be helpful in distinguishing his compositions from those by John Wesley. It has been traditionally argued that Charles did not rhyme in a "defective manner"; that is to say, it was thought that he did not rhyme in patterns that were asymmetrical. Thus the authorship of the hymn "O Sun of Righteousness" had often been attributed to John Wesley since it has a "defective" rhyme.[45] In point of fact, Charles Wesley was in the habit of trying new rhymes, many of which were not symmetrical. These experimentations occur quite prominently in the unpublished "Short Hymns on Select Passages of Scripture." In a like manner, it could be argued that John's orderly editorial tastes would eschew the sort of innovations that are apparent in "O Sun of Righteousness." Here we sense a bit of the dilemma of those who seek to identify the author of these hymns on the basis of prosody. The problem amounts to this: in the hymn in question do we detect the innovative Charles or the less adept John? The very same piece of evidence could be construed to argue for opposite solutions to the problem of authorship.

These expeditions into meter, foot, and rhyme in the Wesleyan hymns have produced significant patterns and interesting observations about Charles's characteristics as a poet. The prosodic features, when wedded to considerations like vocabulary, word choice, and content analysis, begin to form a set of criteria by which one might ascribe the authorship of various Wesley hymns through internal analysis. Henry Bett was one of the first hymnologists to suggest that it was possible to use these internal criteria to go beyond the more traditional and uncritical approach to authorship.[46] J. E. Rattenbury tested Bett's canons and accepted them virtually intact.[47] Yet, as Frank Baker suggests, "We should be on much safer ground if we were able to formulate canons based on ascertained work of Charles Wesley, particularly if this is done in such a way as to reveal the variations brought by maturity and age."[48] Baker's suggestion was a proper and provocative one, but one that was also difficult to bring to fruition. It formed the foundation of the methodology this writer sought to apply to the Wesleyan hymns in his dissertation research.[49] From a wealth of earlier scholarship and through thorough original research in the later Charles Wesley hymns I developed a profile of thirty-one points of internal and external criteria for identifying the authorship in the earlier hymnological corpus.[50] In testing and applying these canons to the ascertained hymns of Charles Wesley it became clear that in many instances the internal criteria were simply too subjective to be determinative.

The leading role in my own approach to the process of identification was then transferred to the external evidence. This shift in emphasis grounded the ascription of the early hymns in historical documentation, and lessened a bit of the subjectivity that seemed inherent in many of the internal criteria. Hence, the internal (prosodic) evidence is important, but it should play a role supportive and secondary to external (historical) evidence. This same process of ascription has been used to identify the early hymns carried in this anthology; they have been selected *chiefly* on the basis of manuscript evidence, references in Charles's own writings, or clear connections with his biography. Where this sort of evidence is lacking the question of ascription must remain an open one.

SOURCES OF WESLEY'S POETIC DICTION

Charles Wesley's formal education shaped his work; his Oxford M.A. in classical literature and languages served him well as poet and biblical exegete. He drew heavily upon this classical preparation and upon his contemporary context as he developed and articulated his theology. Charles often interacted with the luminaries of the day, writers both religious and secular, using what vehicles seemed most suitable to communicate his message in the eighteenth-century idiom. It was in this sense that Henry Bett described the Wesleys as "great plagiarists" though in "an honorable sense."[1] Yet it is obvious from a close reading of Charles's journal and letters that he was not an omnivorous reader like John Wesley. He was, perhaps even more completely than his brother John, *homo unius libri* (a man of one book). He wrote in a literary style that shared characteristics with those of the leading poets of his day. Yet Wesley's style was also uniquely his own—tailored to fit the specific tasks of a poet who was also a Methodist evangelist.

His poetry was written at an important junction in the history of English literature. The giants of English poetry, including Shakespeare and Milton, were still, of course, extremely influential. A host of equally important "neoclassicists" or "Augustans" were coming into prominence. The rule of the classicists began roughly with the writings of John Dryden in the mid-seventeenth century and extended toward the end of the eighteenth century, with the work of Samuel Johnson.[2] Many of the poets who were Charles Wesley's contemporaries are still studied as molders of the English language and poetic expression. Nor is it surprising that echoes of these literary luminaries found their way into Charles's compositions.

The leading element that Charles shared with his poetic contemporaries was his "classicism."[3] Donald Davie has suggested that Wesley's classical training and thorough biblical study combined to give his work a "purity of poetic diction."[4]

Not only did Charles possess formal training in the classics, but classical forms and expressions commonly occured in his own literary style. As Davie observed, "In Wesley, as in [Samuel] Johnson, the blunted or blurred metaphor comes sharper and lives again in a sort of a latinate pun. . . ."[5] Charles's application of words like "seerer," "signify," "cancelled," "sealed," "meritorious," "virtue," "meek," and "balmy" stands as a monument to his ability to remake the ordinary with the classical root in mind. He refurbished terms of everyday currency by looking, with the clarity of an Oxford linguist, to their root meaning. His hymns also reflect the literary structures of the Augustan age; Maldwyn Edwards, for example, has identified eight structural reminiscences of John Dryden's poems in Charles's poetical rendition of the Psalms.[6]

To this "classicism" must be added Wesley's sense of wit and liveliness—these emerged in the hymns through puns, hyperbole, or exaggeration. James Dale identified this same dimension when he described the "strength" of Charles's verse: ". . . its delight in paradox and in the pithy epigrammatic phrase are aspects of his 'strength.' "[7] Oxymoron, one of Wesley's favorite devices, emerged naturally and powerfully throughout his phraseology: "Impassive, He suffers; immortal, He dies." E. M. Hodgson described the impact of Charles's poetic diction in an oxymoron of her own: "Charles makes the classic popular and the popular classic."[8] What George Lawton wrote concerning John Wesley's prose is certainly true of Charles's poetry: it ". . . is a stout threefold cord having Scriptural, Classical and Colloquial strands interwoven, and flecked with other colourful threads."[9] We shall take each of these "strands" as an avenue for examining the sources of Charles Wesley's thought and imagery; having by that method set his work in historical context, we shall then close with an examination of his theological method.

Eighteenth-Century Literature

As was the custom of his day, Charles Wesley did not provide the reader with notes or any form of citation to indicate the sources that influenced his thinking or style as he prepared his hymns. Hence, most of the identifications of the influence of other authors come to us in the form of "echoes" or veiled allusions to other works. Henry Bett's *The Hymns of Methodism in their Literary Relations,* first issued in 1901, remains the standard summary of this detective work behind the form of Charles's hymns.[10]

Bett laments the loss of Wesley's own annotated volume of Shakespeare. The volume was destroyed by the devoted Methodist John Pawson, so that "godly" readers would not be unduly scandalized by Charles's high regard for the bard of Stratford. But Bett was able to identify only a few reminiscences of Shakespeare's phraseology in Charles's "Preparation for Death."[11] In a similar way Bett heard a few echoes of John Dryden, one of the fathers of eighteenth-century neoclassicism, and also of Joseph Addison, one of Dryden's able successors.[12] A few "unmistakable allusions to Milton," the Wesleys' great precursor in Christian verse, and the more contemporary Abraham Cowley can be identified.[13]

Charles's flexibility of style and meter may be an indication of a debt he owed to Matthew Prior, and contrariwise, the more staid and formal verses of Alexander Pope seem to have had little effect upon him.[14] Pope was one of Wesley's most influential literary contemporaries, but Henry Bett discerned only "two or three slight allusions" to Pope's *Essay on Man,* and a few "extraordinary" echoes of his *Eloisa to Abelard* in Charles's poems.[15] Charles's letters report his admiration for many of the same poets identified by inference in his hymns; Cowley, Spenser, Milton, Prior, and Young are among those writers mentioned directly in Wesley's correspondence.[16]

Much has been written about the morbid cast of the poetry of the mid-eighteenth century, including Young's *Night Thoughts* (1743–1745) as well as Thomas Gray's *Elegy Written in a Country Churchyard* (1751) and by implication Charles Wesley's later hymns.[17] While this penchant for "the spleen" (as the Augustans termed it) had some foundation in the biography of authors like Young and Wesley, it was also a sort of literary rebellion against the emotional strictures of an earlier Augustan poetic form. In Edward Young melancholy also merged with his apology for Christian faith. This connection was set forth most clearly in the author's self-conscious admission in the introduction to "Night Six: The Infidel Reclaimed. In Two Parts, Containing the Nature, Proof, and Importance, of Immortality."[18] Young intended to convince his reader of the importance of immortality (and by implication Christian faith as the way to that end) by confronting his audience with the inevitability of death. It is small wonder that Charles Wesley enjoyed reading the poetry of Edward Young. In Young he met a cobelligerent in the common cause of the Gospel, who was also a poet who utilized scriptural, classical, and colloquial language, as well as vital experience, to frame the Christian message in an eighteenth-century idiom.

The journal and correspondence of Charles Wesley give few indications of the writer's reading habits, and commentators as diverse as J. Ernest Rattenbury and Henry Moore have taken the paucity of these connections with secular literature as proof that Charles read little—beyond the Bible—after he left the university.[19] While this conclusion seems hardly tenable in view of the echoes that contemporary literature sent through Charles's hymns, it is clear that the primary source and shape of his poetic diction was not drawn from his contemporaries. Rattenbury estimated that Charles's application of secular sources amounted to about one allusion for every 2,000 lines of poetry; hence, ". . . the influence of secular writers, and also religious, though obvious is really no more conspicuous than might be the tang of erudition to a kind of poetry in which it is often missing."[20]

The Classics

Charles Wesley's hymns were written during a literary renaissance that was determined to recover the poetical riches of the old Augustan age. James Johnson, who has written one of the standard treatments of the literature of the period, has identified the application of classical forms, philology, and resources as leading factors in the "neoclassicism" of the English eighteenth century.[21] An obvious indication of this renaissance of classical study can be found in the extensive reprinting of the important books from antiquity. Even more significant, perhaps, was the way in which important eighteenth-century poets consciously patterned themselves after the form and diction of the classics. Charles's contemporary Alexander Pope provides a clear example of this attempt to recover classical style. He first edited and published Homer's *Iliad* in several installments between 1715 and 1720. Upon completion of that project, Pope turned to *The Odyssey*—which appeared in two parts in 1725 and 1726; by 1733 Pope felt sufficiently schooled in classical literature and forms to publish a volume of fine poems entitled *Imitations of Horace*. Similar developments can be traced in the works of Dryden, Prior, Addison, and other leading poets of the age.

Charles Wesley was a classical scholar of some distinction. His talents probably exceeded John's in this area, hence Charles drew the assignment of "correcting" or "enlarging" his brother's famous *Notes on the New Testament*. Latinisms and classical phraseology are apparent in Charles's hymns, but in comparison to John Milton (1604–1674) and other precursors in religious poetry, Wesley's dependence upon classical constructions seems relatively slight.[22] He was, in this sense, a "neo"-classicist—struggling to weave the classical into the colloquial—and may even be located on the leading edge of an important literary transition that was taking shape in the mid-eighteenth century.

There are numerous reminiscences of classical poetry and literature in Charles's hymns and journal; allusions to Vergil's *Aeneid* and to Horace, Homer, and Plato (among others) were a rather natural part of his writings.[23] At college both Wesleys assumed classical nicknames that they used when corresponding with Sally Kirham and the Granville sisters (Mary and Anne); John was "Cyrus," and Charles "Araspes"; the young women became "Varanese," "Aspasia," and "Selima." It indicated that the five enjoyed the cozy communication of the Augustan age, when polite parlor conversation led naturally to topics literary, religious, and (perhaps in a *double* sense) Romantic.[24]

An anecdote shows how close to the surface Charles's classicism lay: tradition suggests he once defended himself against the abuse of that virago, his brother's wife, by reciting Vergil at the top of his voice. Vergil seems to have been Charles's favorite Latin poet, as Horace was his brother John's.[25] His hymnological echoes of classical poetry were certainly not orchestrated applications; they flowed naturally from the mind and pen of a man who was himself a student of antiquity. Yet this classicism did not dominate or weigh down Wesley's verse; he used classical phrases and etymology sparingly, like rare spices that added a pleasant flavor to colloquial forms. Thus on the one hand it is clear that both by formal training and historical context Charles Wesley participated in the larger world of the eighteenth-century literary milieu, and yet on the other hand, Wesley was not *bound* by his classicism as Milton, Dryden, and others before him had been.

Christian Tradition

James Johnson described an "organic unity" that was formed out of Greco-Roman and Judeo-Christian elements and welded into eighteenth-century neoclassical thought. The synthesis was, in basis at least, a literary one, and included men as diverse as Shaftesbury, Bolingbroke, and Gibbon, who found Christian beliefs unacceptable, as well as writers like Dryden, Swift, Pope, and Addison, for whom "the whole cloth of the mind was the weaving of a Christian warp with the woof of classical knowledge."[26] The neoclassicists' intellectual milieu tied these authors, whether religious or not, to pagan and patristic sources.

William Cave's *Apostolici or Lives of the Primitive Fathers* (1677) and Edward Stillingfleet's *Origines sacrae* (1662) were two very popular collections of patrology that enjoyed wide circulation among the Augustans.[27] The Wesleys also knew and used Cave's *Apostolici*; John even abridged and published it in his *Christian Library* of 1753.[28] Readings in the creeds, liturgy, and doctrine of the ancient church were also a part of the regimen of the Oxford Holy Club.[29]

Charles Wesley's own writings make few direct references to the Church Fathers. "Ms. Luke" gives the most explicit citation found in his hymns; in that instance the author actually announces that he is introducing "a saying of Chrysostom."[30] Henry Bett has identified allusions to most of the major Fathers (and a few of the minor ones) in Charles's hymns; Tertullian's *De carne*, Ignatius's *Epistle to the Romans*, and Augustine's *Confessions* were among the patristic standards contributing to Wesley's poetic diction.[31] His shorthand journal entry for December 5, 1753, looks to the sufferings of Ignatius of Antioch for a parallel to Charles's trials with the demented John Hutchinson (cf. No. 124).

The vitality of Charles's Anglican heritage is easily seen in his use of the Anglican doctrinal standards and *Book of Common Prayer*. Twice his journal shows Wesley defending himself against the charge of doctrinal innovation ("justification by faith alone") by appealing to the Anglican articles and homilies.[32] Charles's own sermons indicate that he occasionally cited the Anglican doctrinal standards in his own preaching, but he more typically appealed to them when in dialogue with clergy who might be expected to both know and affirm them.[33] The Homilies were included in his own devotional life, his study, and in his ministry among the Methodists.[34]

The *Book of Common Prayer* was a second segment of the Christian tradition that Charles Wesley inherited through his attachment to the Church of England. His journal indicates that he utilized the Prayer Book both in private devotions and public worship.[35] There was a brief period, running through late 1739 and much of 1740, when Charles's journal is silent about prayers that were "read" (e.g. from the Prayer Book). But a major controversy over the practice of "stillness" with the so-called "Moravian Brethren"—who were in part dissident Methodists who would not adhere to the ordinances of the Church of England—drove Charles back to the *Book of Common Prayer*. Charles also used the Prayer Book sporadically in his mature years.[36] He apparently felt free to use or not use it as seemed most appropriate in a given situation.

Charles's *Short Hymns on Select Passages of Scripture*, first published in 1762 but composed and revised from the 1750s until the time of his death in the 1780s, reveal that the *Book of Common Prayer* continued to be a resource for Wesley's personal reflection and poetical diction. Many of his *Short Hymns* based on the Psalms show Charles's preference for the Prayer Book rendition over the text of the Authorized Version, which he used throughout the rest of the collection.[37] Hence, it seems appropriate—both in the shape of his life and in his poetry—to consider Charles Wesley as one of those eighteenth-century figures in whom the classical and Christian traditions happily merged. His appreciation for and application of the patristic and Anglican standards is well documented in Wesley's writings, and was formative for his faith as well as his hymns.

The Bible

J. E. Rattenbury has wryly suggested that "a skillful man, if the Bible were lost, might extract it from Wesley's hymns. They contain the Bible in solution."[38] Charles's language in poem, pulpit, and everyday speech was both shaped and informed by biblical expressions. His hymns are veritable mosaics of biblical allusions. Wesley selected, shaped, and polished biblical words, phrases, and allusions and then cemented them together to construct image-laden works of art. Wesley's hymns and sacred poems are "biblical" not only in the sense that they accurately communicate the Bible's doctrines and principles, but also in a more primary sense. The hymns are patchworks of biblical materials; words, phrases, and allusions were cut from the fabric of the Authorized Version and sewn into a new pattern that was tailored by the poet-theologian of the Methodist revival.

Various attempts have been made to uncover the source of the various Bible fragments that Charles united in his hymns.[39] In his manual, John W. Waterhouse put eight popular Wesley hymns under close scrutiny in an attempt to uncover the source and application of the biblical themes that Charles used with such familiarity. Looking at the line, "O for a thousand tongues to sing / My great Redeemer's praise, / The glories of my God and King, / The triumphs of His grace," Waterhouse heard echoes of over a dozen scriptural applications.[40] In fact it is not unusual to find over a dozen biblical passages fused together in one of Charles's verses.

Charles's favorite description for the Bible was "the oracles," a designation which emphasized the revelatory impact that Charles felt in the Scriptures.[41] It was his habit to use the Bible as the foundation for his religious and theological expression, hence Charles also called the Scriptures his "rule of faith."[42] Doctrine, creed, and religious experience were all evaluated by the "sacred standard."[43] While Charles had an unambiguous confidence in the accuracy of the biblical record, his doctrine of Scripture had its basis in the connection between the Word and Spirit of God. For him the Bible was the enlivened Word because of the way God's Spirit bears witness to the Incarnate Word through the vehicle of the written Word; the Spirit of Christ—more often than the Bible per se—was said to be infallible in the revelatory event.[44]

It was precisely this emphasis upon the revelatory function of the Bible, expressed theologically in the dynamic relation of Word and Spirit, that gave Charles Wesley's hymns a direction which was so essentially biblical, and also so fresh and lively. He had an acute reverence for the Bible; for Charles it was a means of grace, a channel through which communion with Christ flows by the power of His Spirit. The following verse from Wesley's hymn based on Mat. 9:20–21 expresses well his deep appreciation for the Scriptures ("I blush and tremble to draw near"), and yet also his willingness to use the Bible as "a garment" through which to "touch my Lord":

> Unclean of life and heart unclean,
>   How shall I in His sight appear!
> Conscious of my inveterate sin
>   I blush and tremble to draw near;
> Yet through the garment of His Word
>   I humbly seek to touch my Lord.[45]

Charles Wesley, like many commentators before him, including Augustine and Luther, was stoutly christocentric in his approach to the Bible. Barbara Welch, examining Wesley's poetry from a literary standpoint, pointed to this Christocentrism as a characteristic that distinguished Charles from both the Augustan poets of his own age and his hymnological precursors like George Herbert and Isaac Watts.[46] The Augustan mood meditated upon the wonders of nature in order to contemplate the greatness of God, "but in Wesley that is only holy, it seems, which was raised on the Cross; Christ redeemed men, not creation. This habit in Wesley of envisaging the world almost exclusively from a supernatural viewpoint marks a central difference between him and that group of fashionable poets."[47] Bernard Manning, in his classic *Hymns of Wesley and Watts*, followed this theme as a way of distinguishing those two great poets of Scriptural material: "Watts, time and time again, set the faith of the incarnation, the passion, and resurrection, against its cosmic background. He surveys the solar system, the planets, the fixed stars, the animal creation, from the beginning to the end of time."[48] Where Watts seemed to follow the more traditional poetic form of the neo-classicists, Charles Wesley refined that poetic diction by restructuring it around Christ and other central biblical themes (like redemption, atonement, and self-giving), thereby making the poetic approach more directly serve his biblical agenda.

Isaac Watts was a pioneer in the art of paraphrasing the Psalms and other biblical texts. His ideal was to follow the biblical text as closely as possible and restate its message in the best (Miltonesque) poetic diction he could muster. Charles Wesley "paraphrases" (if that is even an appropriate word to use to describe his approach) the Bible by weaving biblical words, phrases, and images together to form a new interpretative fabric. Thus, Charles Wesley not only paraphrased, but commented as he framed his poetic expositions of Scripture. The boldness apparent in Wesley's style was the poet's willingness to grapple with biblical passages artistically, shaping them into a hymn of his own theological expression—formed along the lines of the Bible's central themes.

CHARLES WESLEY'S THEOLOGY

Although Wesley has left us his journal, letters, and a few important sermons—and each of these provides important information about his life and thought—his hymns remain his most enduring contribution and the single most important source for studying his theology. As George Findlay suggests, ". . . there is no better introduction to Methodist theology than the Wesley hymns."[1] The hymns are theological pieces, but they are not—to use the Wesleyan term—"speculative divinity"; rather, they represent a marriage of theological doctrine and living religious experience. Charles's hymns are the "Pilgrim's Progress" of the eighteenth century: they consider all the stages along life's way, opening all of life to Christian reflection and celebration. There is virtually no aspect of human existence that is not treated in Charles's verse! The hymns complement Charles's journal: the latter gives the outward life of the man, and the former reveal his inward reflections upon his life. But to say that these hymns communicate "experience" is not to suggest that they are, as Donald Davie characterized so many of the Romantic hymns of the era, "geysers of warm feelings."[2] Charles's hymns are full of feeling, and yet they remain rooted in the Lockean age with Wesley's interest in an "experimental" or "practical divinity" that links experience with its occasion in life.[3]

Several of Charles's hymnbooks were more directly theological than the others. The most distinctively doctrinal collections were *Hymns of God's Everlasting Love* (1741), which direct strong polemics against the Calvinists, *Hymns on the Lord's Supper* (1745), and *Hymns on the Trinity* (1767); though all of Charles's work combined astute theology with Augustan poetical diction. But poetry is not syllogism or diatribe; the words convey meaning, to be sure, but also rhyme, rhythm, and mood. There is thus solid theological content communicated through a medium that is fluid—theologically speaking. It was this combination that Rattenbury had in mind when he described Charles Wesley as "an artist, not a scientist."[4] The artist's medium was verse and vivid imagery; while each poem carries its payload, the issues under consideration must fit between the lines or they might not be sung or said. Charles Wesley the poetic theologian worked by a different set of rules than "divines" of a more formal sort.

Poetry is a picture-painting device. Words and images are layered upon each other and blended to create an overall mood or effect. Theology is also an image-building enterprise. The basic images may have come from the marketplace, or lawcourt, but religious language (and Scripture itself) sanctifies those pictures and turns them into vehicles of theological communication. Both theology and poetry are bridges built from the human side of the divine-human chasm. They are transitory and impressionistic at best, communicating in broad brush strokes and borrowed images.

Classical Christian theology shaped its theology of redemption around four basic images: (1) those using purchase language, borrowed from the marketplace and commercial transaction, (2) the language of pardon, acquittal, and justification, framed in a courtroom motif, (3) cleansing and purification ideas, based in the imagery of sacrifice or ritual cleansings, and (4) allusions to armed conflict, which carried connotations of victory and liberation. Each of these foundational, scriptural images is a "poetic" expression, in the sense that it is a word-picture applied as a vehicle of theological reflection. What better way is there to approximate the biblical expressions than to wrap the theology of redemption in its own poetic images, as Wesley did in his hymns? In this sense, poetry may be one of the best vehicles of theological expression since it captures so well the original image-building process that is so central to theological communication. Add to poetry the music that transforms it into a hymn and the poem becomes both a catechism and an affirmation for congregations and crowds. This was precisely the role played by Wesleyan hymnody: it took essentially biblical words, phrases, and images, and framed them into theological statements that sang in the hearts and on the lips of the common folk of England.

It is to this wedding of poetic and theological imagery that we must turn to consider Charles Wesley's theological contribution. He constantly used the language of sacrifice and the forms of the penal substitution theory of the atonement to convey his theology of redemption. "Blood" became one of his favorite redemption words, appearing nearly 800 times in his later hymns alone! The application had its heritage in the sacrifices of Leviticus, but its primary focus was to be found in "the Blood of Christ." Throughout the hymnological corpus "blood" stood for Christ's death and its saving significance.[5] But there is no "theory" of the atonement presented here! The biblical past blends with present experience: Christ who died "for me" becomes—through faith and renovation—"Christ in me."

Anselmic imagery dominates in Wesley's theology of redemption, with substitution as one of his major categories. But Charles also connected the atonement with inner cleansing, finding in Christ both the pattern and power for living a life of self-giving. He used traditional "penal" language in ways that overflowed traditional categories and broke through juridical transaction. In his poetic vistas "blood" transports us to Golgotha and Christ's death, but the "blood" of Wesley's hymns not only "reconciles" and "cleanses," it becomes personified to "plead" our case before the Divine tribunal and then "speaks" assurance of forgiveness into our hearts. In a similar way Wesley's legal language ("pardon," "acquittal," "justification") overflowed the courtroom to link up with liberation and imagery of the reconciled family. Price-paying expressions surpassed "debt" to speak also of victory and sanctification. Even when phraseology suggesting the pacification of the wrath of an angry God was occasionally employed, the intention of the author seemed not so much to drive frightened sinners into the Kingdom as to lure them by the display of the sheer costliness of forgiveness.

If one were pressed to identify the heart of Charles Wesley's theology, it may be found in his own estimation of the center of the Gospel. His journal entry for Sunday, July 12, 1741, offers two key elements as a point of departure: "I declared," Charles wrote, "the two great truths of the everlasting gospel, universal redemption and Christian Perfection."[6] From this point of entry we move toward other salient features that characterized Charles Wesley's theology.

Universal Redemption

The Wesleyan "universalism" was bounded on the one side by Charles's emphasis on his doctrine of an unlimited atonement and by his preaching of the "universal call" of the Christ on the other. In his journal he recalled, "I enforced His [Christ's] universal call, 'look unto me, and be saved, *all* the ends of the earth.' "[7] The same theme was woven deeply into the tapestry of his hymns. The gospel "all" was directly mentioned over three hundred times in Charles's later hymns alone, and the affirmation of the universal effectiveness of Christ's death emerged with incalculable frequency. Generally his statement of this doctrine was simple and direct: "Know every child of Adam's race, / Thy Saviour died for Thee!"[8] The foundational element in the unlimited atonement was found in the life-giving efficacy of Christ's death: "The man who lived for *all* to die, / Who died in *all* to live."[9]

An important corollary to Charles's affirmation of the "universal call" was his Arminian conception of the doctrines of election and predestination. He believed that in Christ's death all people are elected to salvation, hence those who cannot come to God must look within themselves to find the hindrance to God's reconciling grace:

1   Will they not? Alas for them,
    Dead in sin who Christ refuse!
        He did all the world redeem,
    All unto salvation choose;
        Sinners come, with me receive,
    All the grace He waits to give.

2   In ourselves the hindrance lies,
    Stopp'd by our own stubborn will;
        He His love to none denies,
    He with love pursues us still;
        Sinners come, and find with me
    Only heaven in His decree.[10]

The last two lines, framed in the language of invitation, are also a polemic against the Calvinistic "horrible decree," which prescribed election of some people unto damnation; there is, says Wesley, "only heaven" in God's decree, though even God's plans go awry because of the perverseness of "fallen" human will.

Charles Wesley strongly emphasized the doctrine of original sin. He had a color-ful collection of clichés for describing it: "the sinful nature," "my bosom sin," and "inbred stains" were among them. In each case, however, it was clear that Charles made no permanent distinction between "sin" in the original sense, and personal, actual "sins." In his mind the former invariably led to the latter; hence, he wrote, "My double sin I grieve."[11] And while Wesley was quite concerned about "Christ's blood washing my sins away," his constant focus was upon the renewal of the inner, sinful human nature.[12] Charles's conception of redemption emphasized freedom from past guilt and from the present power of sin; it meant a liberation that took the original and actual aspects of sin together. Salvation, to use a few of Wesley's favorite words, was "full Salvation," or "complete," "Salvation to the uttermost"; each term implied freedom from both "the guilt and power of sin."[13] The effects of this redemptive process could as easily be described as "canceling" past sin, or "breaking the chains of sin."[14] Each of these phrases spoke of his tremendous optimism about God's grace, grace which had as its final goal "perfect love":

Jesus, the first and the last,
   On thee my soul is cast;
Thou didst thy work begin
   By blotting out my sin;
Thou wilt the root remove,
   And *perfect* me in *love*.[15]

Christian Perfection

Sanctification was the heart of Charles Wesley's gospel; it was the logical and theological completion of justification by faith in Christ. Several of his favorite redemption words suggest this connection between the outset and the culmination of one's Christian faith: "full salvation," or "complete redemption," for example, were terms for sanctification that defined it as fruit of the life of faith. The numerical predominance of sanctification terms in his hymns is overpowering. Holiness and perfection words occur in excess of six hundred times in Charles's late hymns alone, and this count does not include those many times in which the doctrine was implied or stated without the application of distinct sanctification terms. His conception of Christian Perfection was formed on the pattern of the First Epistle of John and the Epistle to the Hebrews; it emphasized the filling of the believer with the *agape* ("selfless" or "other-directed") love of God—the ensuing renovation of will and person created the "holiness without which no one will see God." For John Wesley this "perfection" was a matter of uniformity of will and willful conformity to the Divine intention; it meant freedom from willful sin, but not infirmity, mistake, or error. Unlike brother John's, Charles Wesley's conception of perfection maintained an unqualified vision; in his mind the completion (*telos*) of the faithful life pilgrimage was nothing less than the restoration of the paradisiacal *imago Dei* (image of God) within a person. This was the same as saying that the image or mind of Christ was formed within the Christian. The constructive thrust of Charles's view was expressed in images of cleansing and renewal, but the ultimate goal of perfection was wholeness. This wholeness meant holiness, perfect love, or finding the fullness of Christ within. As Charles wrote in one of his many hymns describing those "Waiting for Full Redemption":

4   He shed His blood to wash us clean
From all unrighteousness, and sin,
   To save from all iniquity;
Jesus hath died for us; for me.

5   He died that we might be made whole,
Holy in body, spirit, soul;
   Might do His will like there above,
Renew'd in all the life of love.

6   Lay the foundation then no more,
Reach forth unto the things before,
   On to the prize undaunted press,
And seize the crown of righteousness.

9   His nature to our souls make known,
        And write the name in the white stone,
            We all shall His fullness prove,
        And find the pearl of perfect love.[16]

The Methodist doctrine of Christian Perfection was easily misunderstood, or transformed into an eighteenth-century form of antinomianism which claimed that the
believer could be as perfect as the angels. The doctrine was particularly volatile
when John's strong insistence upon perfection as a present reality was blended with
Charles's unqualified conception of the nature of perfection; the London Methodist
Society produced just this sort of concoction under the influence of the "angelic"
perfection of Thomas Maxfield and George Bell in the 1760s. Charles opposed their
presumptuous claims and heretical teaching by increasingly emphasizing the process or pilgrimage aspect of sanctification. In his hymns "the blessing" was gained
only in "wrestling" with God; it came only through struggle, living through a sense
of godforsakenness, and the purifying effects of Christ's Cross and our own. This
perfection defied pride, and Charles Wesley's affirmations were framed in characteristic humility, "not as one who has attained." It came with a dialectical impact;
like the parabolic descriptions of the kingdom of God, it was both a "treasure to be
hidden in a field" and yeast that would quietly leaven the whole bushel.[17]

Christology

Charles Wesley's hymns persistently present a robust Christology. He often strung
Old and New Testament titles together, heaping one affirmation on top of another,
in order to create an elaborate and compelling statement of Christ's Deity. Yet, even
his most elaborate constructions found their final realization "in me":

1   Jesus, the infinite I am,
        With God essentially the same,
            With Him enthroned above all height,
        As God of God, and Light of Light,
            Thou are by Thy great Father known,
        From all eternity His Son.

2   Thou only dost the Father know,
        And wilt to all thy followers show,
            Who cannot doubt Thy gracious will
        His glorious Godhead to reveal;
            Reveal Him now, if thou art He,
        And live, Eternal Life, in me.[18]

Charles employed the traditional devices for describing the person and work of
Christ; he used, for example, the "threefold office" (Prophet, Priest, and King)
with great effectiveness.[19] Yet, his hymns also demonstrate Wesley's creativity and
versatility; over fifty different christological titles appear in the later hymns alone.[20]
The incarnation and atonement dominated his hymnological landscape. Wesley
affirmed, like Anselm before him, that the focus and motive of the incarnation were

located in the atonement of Christ: "Who man became for man to die."[21] Charles often turned to the language of the Suffering Servant Songs (especially Isa. 52:12–53:13) to describe the work of the incarnate Christ:

> The Son of Man, the Man of woe,
>   Why did He leave the sky?
> T'was all His business here below,
>   To serve us, and to die![22]

The "business" of Christ was completed in His resurrection: "He died for our sins, and He liveth again!"[23] But the goal of the Christ event was not the celestial rule of Christ at the right hand of God the Father; for Charles Wesley the incarnation continues as Christ is formed in Christians. The culmination of the Christ-event, while including the heavenly session, is more directly found in perfect love:

> 1   He did; the King invisible,
> Jehovah, once on earth did dwell,
>   And laid His majesty aside;
> Whom all His heavens cannot contain,
>   For us He lived, a mournful man,
> For us a painful death He died!
>
> 2   Still the great God resides below,
> (And all His faithful people know
>   He will not from His church depart)
> The Father, Son and Spirit dwells,
>   His kingdom in the poor reveals,
> And fills with heaven the humble heart.[24]

Recapitulation

The structure of Charles Wesley's theology of redemption bears a strong resemblance to the patristic doctrine of recapitulation. Irenaeus (d. 198?) is generally considered to be the first exponent of this posture, though through him and his successors the redemption theme became rather common in the early eastern church. His point of departure came from the connection between creation and redemption suggested in the Pauline pairing of the First and Second Adams.[25] The original righteousness of the *imago Dei* bestowed in creation and then lost in the paradisiacal fall anticipates a return to perfection as the goal of the incarnation and redemption of Christ. Irenaeus, therefore, understood restitution of the Divine image within as the central feature of the Christ-event: ". . . our Lord Jesus Christ," he wrote, "Who did through His transcendent love, become what we are that He might bring us to be even as He is Himself."[26] From the earliest years of his preaching Charles Wesley pointed to Christian Perfection (the restoration of the *imago Dei*) as the "one thing needful" for Christians. His sermon by that title made sanctification the constitutive characteristic of Christian faith, and described perfection in the language of recapitulation: "To recover the first estate from which we are fallen is *the one thing needful;* to re-exchange the image of Satan for the image of God, bondage for freedom, sickness for health! Our one great business is to erase out of our souls the likeness of our destroyer, and to be born again, to be formed anew after the likeness of our Creator."[27] In this preconversion sermon (which was later also preached during the revival) the foundation of Charles's unqualified conception of Christian Perfection was laid, and Charles clung to it tenaciously—even through the debates of the 1760s and through his own feelings of godforsakenness.

Charles's application of imitation themes forms another important connection between his theology of redemption and the patristic doctrine of recapitulation. Imitation of Christ is an important impetus behind Irenaeus's conception of recapitulation; and for Wesley, too, imitation of Christ marked out the path of Christian discipleship. Christ's servant posture and *kenotic* ("self-emptying") life-style demanded emulation (even though the connotations of Wesley's "meek" and "mild" terminology are sometimes lost on a modern readership).[28] Charles's theology of the Cross did not stop with a doctrine of atonement; it resolutely pushed toward "the way of the cross" (*via cruxis*) and a theology of suffering (*via dolorosa*).

Charles's conception of the atonement took Golgotha with the utmost historical and theological significance; yet, there is also a contemporary element at work. Christ's cross demanded a cross for those who would follow Him. The atonement, though complete or "finished" from the perspective of putting sin away in a potential way, also needed to be completed by the response of faith and deeds of faithfulness. The latent effectiveness of Christ's death was affirmed in dramatic terms; yet, the present effectiveness of the cross enters the life of the Christian through faith and the demands of costly discipleship.

Wesley used the term "atonement" to describe both the finished and unfinished work of Christ. Presented in his poetic, dramatic format, this idea meant that Christ hung ever before the seeker to elicit the response of faith. This approach was not found only in his hymns, but also emerged in Charles's journal.[29] The "finished-unfinished" dialectic was also present in Charles's theology of suffering—"the school of the cross," as he termed it. The Christian, he urged, is to be "conformed to an expiring God."[30] The creative thrust of Wesley's "school of the cross" was not located in an imitation of the life of the humble Galilean. The focus of our imitation of Christ is to be found, more specifically, in the suffering and cross-bearing Christ. Wesley urged the Christian, therefore, to conform to "the pattern" of the suffering Christ, and this conformity to Christ has as its goal the re-creation of Christ's character:

5   While I thus my Pattern view,
     I shall bleed and suffer too,
         With the Man of sorrow join'd
     One become in heart and mind.

6   More and more like Jesus grow,
     Till the Finisher I know,
         Gain the final Victor's wreath,
     Perfect love in perfect death.[31]

Charles insisted that "bearing the cross" was a heavy burden, one which in this world meant suffering would be a portion of the Christian's life. Yet he found in that same suffering a purification of the will and intentions that made the way of the cross part of the path to perfection. This emphasis was graphically demonstrated in his application of the Lukan phrase "daily dying." In Charles's hands bearing the cross daily became an explanation of the process of self-renunciation that laid aside selfishness.[32] In a similar way, the "cross" was preparatory to receiving the "crown."[33] Charles's poetic commentary on Mark 8:34 (parallel Matt. 16:24) combined all of these themes:

> The man that will Thy Follower be,
>   Thou bidd'st him still himself deny,
> Take up his daily cross with Thee,
>   Thy shameful death rejoice to die,
> And choose a momentary pain,
>   A crown of endless life to gain.[34]

Many commentators, including Charles's brother John, have found Charles's theology of suffering somewhat extreme; few will link suffering and purification as directly as he did.[35] Yet, through his own unique blend of a profound concern for Christian Perfection, his own ill health and accompanying melancholy, and awareness of the inner harmony of Holy Writ, Charles Wesley extended the atonement into the daily life of Christians as few Protestant theologians have dared.

If the suffering servant image became one of Charles's main metaphors for describing the Christian's life, he never lost sight of the "servant" side of that identification. The follower of Christ, bearing the cross, is called to "fill my Lord's afflictions up."[36] Wesley's application of that Pauline phraseology had its basis in seeing Christ reflected in the face of the outcast, oppressed, or one's neighbor, and alleviating their affliction as a portion of the reconciling effects of the cross. Charles's hymns and sermons on "The Good Samaritan" were particularly powerful explications of the connection between the cross and Christian service.[37]

The Holy Spirit

Recent scholarship has drawn attention to the importance of the role of the Holy Spirit in the Wesleys' soteriology; "they were working," as Albert Outler has written, "with a distinctive *pneumatology* that has no exact equivalent in 'Western Spirituality' up to their time."[38] This pneumatology set Wesleyan soteriology in the context of a dialogical interaction between the Holy Spirit and human spirits. The presence of the Spirit is the operative principle in Charles Wesley's conception of sanctification.[39] This emphasis is well documented in the hymnological corpus, both before and after the hymns for Pentecost (*Waiting for the Promise of the Father*, 1746), and can be established in Wesley's unpublished hymns of later vintage:

> Sinners, the Promise is for you,
>   Who'er believe that God is true,

> And will to man his Spirit give;
>   Your day of Pentecost is near;
> And while the joyful news ye hear,
>   You shall the Holy Ghost receive;
> Impower'd of Christ to testify,
>   The Saviour-Prince, the Lord most high,
> The great omnipotent I am,
>   The glorious God of Truth and grace,
> The Friend of all our pardon'd race,
>   Ye shall in life and death proclaim.[40]

The "Promise" offered in this hymn, and many of those in the hymnal of similar title, was the bestowal of God's Spirit. The imagery was based on the events of the early chapters of the book of Acts, and in Charles's hands it often became a shorthand expression for sanctification since he linked a cessation of "inbred sin" with an accompanying visitation by the Spirit:

> Thy blood can save from inbred sin
>   And make my leprous nature clean;
> If thou Thy Spirit impart,
>   Anger, concupiscence and pride
> Shall never with Thy Spirit reside,
>   Or lodge within my heart.
>
> No evil thought shall there remain
>   Pass through thy temple or profane
> The place of thy abode
>   (Where all thy glory is reveal'd),
> With the majestic presence fill'd,
>   Of an indwelling God.[41]

The imagery paralleling the indwelling of the Spirit with the filling of the temple of our bodies (based on 1 Cor. 3:17) was a useful way of describing the renovation worked by the Holy Spirit within a Christian. But the "Promise" and Pentecostal imagery were not—univocally—sanctification categories for Charles; since his own conversion had occurred on Whitsuntide (Pentecost), he could also use these elements to sing of justification by faith.[42]

The Johannine texts, upon which Charles based his hymns *Waiting for the Promise of the Father*, hold the clue to his pneumatology. Those texts, drawn chiefly from the fourteenth and sixteenth chapters of the Fourth Gospel, identified the function of the Holy Spirit as being one of making the ascended and physically *absent* Christ *present* and active in the lives of the disciples. Through these passages, and the hymns formed on them, Charles's pneumatology was tied to both Christology and Christian Perfection.

From Charles's earliest sermons (e.g. "One Thing Needful"), the balance point of his literary corpus and his theology was invariably christocentric. Sanctification for him meant (alternately) having Christ formed within, or having the *imago Dei* restored through the grace of Christ and the presence of the Holy Spirit. These were synonymous descriptions of sanctification for Charles, and each found its efficacy in Christ's death. This same connection was firmly established in Charles's published and manuscript (unpublished) "Short Hymns on Select Passages of Scripture." These hymns of 1762 and thereafter are especially significant for understanding Charles's development because they escaped the editorial pen of John Wesley. They show a virtually complete transition from his earlier emphasis upon sanctification as a distinct or crisis experience toward a conception that emphasized growth or maturation as the dominant theme. These later hymns continue Wesley's earlier soteriological connection between the Holy Spirit and Christ, and press pilgrimage as the way of Christian Perfection.[43] Many of Charles's "Short Hymns" wove these two theological elements into one unified fabric:

1   Unless we faith receive
     And still to Jesus cleave,
         Our God we cannot please
     By fruits or righteousness,
         Or work a work, or speak a word,
     Or think a thought, without the Lord.

2   But freely justified
     In Jesus we abide,
         The Spirit's fruits we show,
     In true experience grow;
         Daily the sap of grace receive,
     And more and more like Jesus live.[44]

Union with Christ and the presence of the Spirit become functional equivalents; the vine-branches imagery (John 15) became an apt analogy for describing the Christian's reception of the grace of Christ and perfection in His image. Charles's most pervasive thrust in pneumatology was one that tied his interest in the Holy Spirit to Christian Perfection and Christ-likeness. Hence, the constructive (and innovative) thrust of Charles's doctrine of the Holy Spirit was to be found in his definition of sanctification under the impact of the doctrine of the Trinity. For Wesley, sanctification meant having God's image formed within; it was a recapitulation of the *imago Dei,* and an undoing of the effects of Eden's Fall. Since this renewal was synonymous with having Christ (his "image" or "mind") formed within the Christian, the Holy Spirit—as One who "calls to mind the things of Christ" and "convicts of sin and righteousness"—is identified as the agent of renovation. Charles, therefore, connected terms like "blood," "virtue," and "grace" with the work of the Holy Spirit.[45] The office of the Spirit was to apply the effectiveness ("virtue," "merits," or "blood") of Christ's life and death to the Christian—by faith. This approach clearly encompasses his doctrine of sanctification, but it sets Christian Perfection in the context of Wesley's entire soteriology and effectively undercuts the "enthusiastic" (heretical) perfectionism that threatened Methodism in the 1760s.

What was most distinctive about Charles's pneumatology was the way in which it became a feature of his attempt to describe a perfection that was both a present power and a lifelong quest. In a similar way Wesley's christocentric approach to the pneumatic images of Pentecost drew his doctrine of sanctification deeply into the structure of his theology of redemption through an application of the doctrine of the Trinity; this approach distinguished Charles's Christian Perfection from that of "enthusiasts," later Revivalists, and Pentecostals, who operated with a "pneu-matocentric" conception of Christian Perfection and anticipated a sanctification that arrived as a singular, "second blessing."[46] In contrast to those developments, Charles's doctrine of sanctification was fundamentally christocentric, and—in its most mature form—described sanctification in images of growth or maturation.

The Trinity

The doctrine of the Trinity was a vital consideration in Charles Wesley's theology of redemption. The inner communion of the triune God was crucial to the very structure of Wesley's soteriology. Redemption, in its fullest sense, was deemed a triune work:

1   The sacred three conspire
   In love to fallen man,
        T' exalt the creature higher,
   And turn his loss to gain;
        Still in the new creation
   The persons all agree,
        Joint causes of salvation,
   To raise and perfect me.

2   The Father's grace allures me,
   And to my Saviour gives;
        The Saviour's blood assures me,
   That God His child receives;
        The Comforter bears witness
   That I am truly His,
        And brings my soul its fitness
   For everlasting bliss.

3   The Father, Son and Spirit
   Himself to me makes known,
        And I in Him inherit
        One God, forever One:
   Jehovah's purest essence
        My raptured spirit seals;
   And all His blissful presence
        In all His people dwells.[47]

The doctrine of the Trinity was not merely an artifact of theological tradition in Charles Wesley's soteriology; it was, rather, a dynamic principle that cemented his theology of redemption together at several important points. Redemption as re-capitulation takes its impetus from changing roles within the Trinity. Christian Perfection, in its various descriptions, was characteristically presented as a work of the Triune God; sanctification as "Perfect Love" looked to "Love" as the Divine essence to explain how God or Christ was formed within the Christian through the workings of the Holy Spirit. Perfection as restoration of the *imago Dei* also took a trinitarian starting point; the "image of God" becomes "the mind of Christ" formed within by the indwelling Spirit.

The dilemma of the atonement, with the tension between the juridical wrath and Son-sending love of God, was resolved in the intertrinitarian communion; as Wesley wrote: "My Saviour in my Judge I meet."[48] The imagery of the lawcourt plays a vital role in Wesley's hymns; but in his application strict judgement and legal reparations are not the final word in this lawcourt. The judge is also the Father of our Lord Jesus Christ, and because of the trinitarian equality of the Father and Son the stern judge dissolves into the friendly advocate: "And in the judge our Brother find, / Our Advocate and Friend."[49] Thus, the relationship between Father and Son explains the situation of the Christian before the "bar" of God's eschatological tribunal: "The men who freely pardon'd here / On Jesus' death depend, / Shall boldly at the bar appear, / And find the Judge their Friend."[50] The doctrine of the Trinity pervaded Charles Wesley's theology; the Trinity emerged as a principle of integration and coherence throughout his thought.

Churchmanship

One of the distinctive elements of Charles Wesley's theology, and one which increasingly distinguished his views from those of his brother John, was Charles's strong attachment to the Church of England. Rattenbury went so far as to conclude that Charles's ". . . love for the Church was his deepest human loyalty"; it certainly tested his loyalty to his brother and to the Methodist revival.[51] The younger Wesley's affection for the established church can be easily traced to the Epworth manse and the early influence of the two Samuel Wesleys.[52] Thomas Jackson erred in his estimation that Charles's attachment "consisted in the bare use of the liturgy."[53] Wesley was deeply attached to the Anglican communion; he affirmed its doctrinal standards, adhered to its practices and imbibed its piety through the *Book of Common Prayer* and the Homilies. He continued to understand Methodism as a renewal movement within the Church of England (as it had been at its inception at Oxford), even when all others—including John Wesley—were willing to concede that it was becoming a separate sect. Charles was cognizant of his greater degree of commitment to the Church of England; at the height of his controversies with the Methodist lay preachers he intimated to his wife: "My chief concern upon earth . . . was the prosperity of the Church of England; my next that of the Methodists, my third of the preachers."[54] As Frank Baker aptly observed, "the attempt to keep Methodism within the Anglican Church was Charles' life-work."[55]

Yet Charles Wesley's attachment to the Church of England was not a rigid or inflexible sort of affection. There was, in fact, a high degree of "irregularity" in his Anglicanism.[56] Charles preached in the open air and in the bounds of other ministers' parishes without the degree of hesitation we hear from John—who described his first attempts at field preaching as submitting "to be more vile."[57] Charles never served a parish and was not a link in the church's chain of authority. He preached during hours of stated worship in the established churches, and administered the sacraments in Methodist preaching houses. Each of these practices constituted a degree of ecclesiastical irregularity, and each of these innovations seemed to have been born out of the necessity of bringing renewal to England and the English Church.

In Charles Wesley the sympathies of a high churchman and the pragmatism of a Methodist evangelist met and struggled for equilibrium. His creative synthesis of Anglican churchmanship and revivalist methodologies placed Charles in an ecclesiastical "no man's land." The Anglicans, with some justification, regarded the Methodists with suspicion since their irregularities seemed to be signs of an impending schism. Charles, perhaps even more than John Wesley, was sensitive to this criticism, and as the years seemed to confirm the critics' prophecies he labored tirelessly to keep the Methodists in the Church of England. But many of the Methodists, including even John Wesley, saw practical reasons for separation from the Church of England. The societies in England and abroad needed sacramental service; the lay preachers clamored for the right of administration and were resentful of Charles's attempts to bar them from that function. Thus, Charles stood between the conforming Anglicans and dissenting Methodists; with the former he shared a common heritage and sacramental theology, and with the latter a common cause in revival. This dilemma made the issue of Methodism's relation to the Church of England a tremendous burden for Charles, and a significant cause of tension between him and his brother.

As we shall see below, from 1744 onward Charles began a one-man campaign to keep the Methodists "regular" (from the Anglican point of view). His hymns styled the lay preachers (who sought sacramental authority) "priests of Molock" and "vile deceivers"; nor was John Wesley immune to his brother's polemical poems. Immediately after John's ordination of Dr. Coke for service in America, in 1784, Charles produced verses that seemed to cancel the partnership of a half century. In the end, however, the brothers remained "partners in reproach," and a final breach between them was averted. Through much prayer, and in the face of Charles's declining health, they were able to (as George Whitefield had earlier said) "agree to disagree." Their final years together were passed in the comradeship they had known all their lives. Charles, like the patriarch Joseph, left a commandment regarding his bones: he is interred in the graveyard of his Anglican parish church at Marylebone. John would later be buried in the yard behind his Methodist Chapel on City-Road. Their last resting places thus became an acted parable of their differing approaches to churchmanship.

NOTES

CHARLES WESLEY—THE MAN

1. Maldwyn Edwards, *Family Circle* (London: Epworth Press, 1949), p. 37.
2. *Ibid.* Edwards's account remains the best modern treatment of the entire Wesley family. Adam

Clark's *Memoirs of the Wesley Family* (New York: J. Collord, 1832) preserves primary source material from each member of the clan.

3. George Osborn, ed. *The Poetical Works of John and Charles Wesley*, 13 vols. (London: Wesleyan-Methodist Conference, 1868–1872), I, p. 117 [hereafter: *P.W.*]. The same hymn is carried in the *Book of Hymns* of the United Methodist Church (1964), #428.

4. Mabel Brailsford, *A Tale of Two Brothers* (London: Hart–Davis, 1954), p. 30.

5. *Ibid.*

6. Mehetabel (Hetty) Wesley (1697–1750) was one of the notable daughters born to Samuel and Susanna. She had a quick mind, learning to read the Greek New Testament before her eighth birthday. She also had a quick wit and pleasant manner, as was attested by her many suitors. In 1724 she eloped with a dashing young "unprincipled" lawyer, who then refused to marry her. Hetty returned to the Epworth manse, where her humiliation was met by her father's wrath. She married one William Wright, an unlettered traveling plumber, as a way of escaping her unhappy circumstances. Curnock described her husband as being "far below her mentally, morally, and religiously." Cf. John Telford, ed., *The Journal of the Rev. Charles Wesley, A.M.: The Early Journal, 1736–1739* (London: Hazel, Watson, and Viney, 1910), p. 318 [hereafter: Telford, *CW Journal*], and Edwards, *Family Circle, op. cit.* John Julian, *A Dictionary of Hymnology* (London: John Murray, 1915), contains an apt discussion on the Wesleys as a family of poets and preserves one of Hetty's poems, "A Mother's Address to her Dying Infant," pp. 1258–1259. Over a dozen of her compositions appear in Adam Clark's *Memoirs, op. cit.*, pp. 315–330.

7. John E. Rattenbury, *The Evangelical Doctrines of Charles Wesley's Hymns* (London: Epworth Press, 1941), pp. 90, 107, 112.

8. Frank Baker, *Charles Wesley as Revealed by His Letters* (London: Epworth Press, 1948), p. 10.

9. *Ibid.*

10. Charles Wesley's Letter to Dr. Chandler, headed "London, April 28th, 1785." Held by the Methodist Archives and Research Centre, The John Rylands University Library of Manchester, Manchester, England [cf. No. 1].

11. The inception of Oxford Methodism is a matter of some debate, due at least in part to the fragmentary and conflicting reports that have come down to us from the Wesleys and their earliest biographers. Charles's letter to William Chandler [No. 1 below] indicates that the young Wesley brother remembered himself as first being dubbed a "Methodist" while John was away from the university. The unsigned editor of Charles's published sermons, thought to be his wife, followed the same line of identification. Cf. Charles Wesley, *Sermons by the Late Charles Wesley* (London: Baldwin, Cradock, and Joy, 1816), p. xi [hereafter: *CW Sermons*].

More recently, Frederick Gill, in his *Charles Wesley the First Methodist* (London: Epworth Press, 1964), has continued the traditional ascription, although Richard Heitzenrater disputes it in his *The Elusive Mr. Wesley* (Nashville: Abingdon Press, 1984), II, p. 206.

Charles's recollection of the attachment of the name "Methodist" is probably accurate. John Wesley's earliest statements about the Holy Club are found in his painful letter to William Morgan, written in November 1729, which sought to explain the circumstances surrounding the death of Morgan's son. At that point a group made up of the two Wesleys, the younger Morgan, and "one more, agreed to spend three or four evenings a week together." John Telford, ed., *The Letters of John Wesley*, 8 vols. (London: Epworth Press, 1931), I, p. 124 [hereafter: *JW Letters*]. Certainly, it was the practical piety of that little fellowship—perhaps even more than the ascription of their name—that was the constitutive feature of Oxford Methodism.

12. Frederick Gill, *Charles Wesley, op. cit.*, p. 38.

13. Charles's Letter to Dr. Chandler [No. 1].

14. Baker, *Charles Wesley, op. cit.*, p. 16.

15. Richard Heitzenrater, "John Wesley and the Oxford Methodists, 1725–1735" (Ph.D. disserta-

tion, the Divinity School, Duke University, 1971). The citation is from John's Oxford Diary, I, p. 57, June 25, 1726.

16. Cf. *ibid.;* Robert Tuttle, *John Wesley: His Life and Theology* (Grand Rapids: Zondervan, 1978), pp. 113–126, and Heitzenrater, *The Elusive Mr. Wesley, op. cit.,* pp. 63–74, for discussion of the piety of the Oxford Methodists.

17. Edwards, *Family Circle, op, cit.,* p. 35.

18. Thomas Jackson, *The Life of the Rev. Charles Wesley,* 2 vols. (London: J. Mason, 1841), II, p. 24.

19. Brailsford, *Two Brothers, op. cit.,* p. 165.

20. *JW Letters,* IV, p. 322.

21. *Ibid.,* V, p. 16.

22. *Ibid.,* III, p. 128f; John Wesley, *The Works of John Wesley,* 14 vols. (London: The Wesleyan-Methodist Conference, 1872, and later reprints), XII, p. 131 [hereafter: *JW Works*].

23. Thomas Jackson, ed., *The Journal of Charles Wesley,* 2 vols. (London: John Mason, 1849), I, p. 18 [hereafter: Jackson, *CW Journal.*].

24. *Ibid.,* p. 85.

25. *JW Letters,* VIII, p. 122.

26. Frank Baker, in *Charles Wesley, op. cit.,* p. 104, catalogues Charles's illnesses for the later period of his life, which emerged in his correspondence: "pleurisy, neuralgia, lumbago, dysentery, piles, rheumatism, gout, scurvy—and a host of ailments." Cf. John Butt, *The Augustan Age* (London: Hutchinson University Press, 1965); Ralph Cohen, "The Augustan Mode," *Eighteenth Century Studies,* I (1967–1968), pp. 3–32; Donald Davie, *The Purity of Diction* (London: Chatto and Windus, 1952); Northrop Frye, "Towards Defining an Age of Sensibility," *English Literary History,* Vol. 23 (1956), pp. 144–152; James Johnson, *The Formation of English Neo-Classical Thought* (Princeton: Princeton University Press, 1967); David Morris, *The Religious Sublime* (Lexington: University of Kentucky Press, 1972); John Sitter, *Literary Loneliness in Mid-Eighteenth-Century England* (Ithaca and London: Cornell University Press, 1982); James Sutherland, *A Preface to Eighteenth-Century Poetry* (London: Oxford University Press, 1948); and Donald Wesling, "Augustan Form: Justification and Breakup of a Period Form," *Texas Studies in Literature and Language,* Vol. 22, No. 3 (Fall 1980), pp. 394–428, for background on the literary tenor of Wesley's day. See Henry Bett, *The Hymns of Methodism* (London: Epworth Press, 1913); James Dale, "The Theological and Literary Qualities of the Poetry of Charles Wesley in Relation to the Standards of His Age" (Ph.D. dissertation, Cambridge University, 1960); Martha England and John Sparrow, *Hymns Unbidden* (New York: The New York Public Library, 1966); and Barbara Ann Welch, "Charles Wesley and the Celebrations of Evangelical Experience" (Ph.D. dissertation, University of Michigan, 1971), for helpful examinations of Charles's poetry in its larger literary context.

27. Brailsford, *Two Brothers, op. cit.,* p. 130.

28. *Ibid.* -

29. *Ibid.,* pp. 73–74.

30. Charles Wesley's Letter to Dr. Chandler [No. 1].

31. Jackson, *CW Journal,* I, p. 35.

32. *Ibid.,* I, p. 159; II, pp. 81, 129.

33. *JW Letters,* V, p. 19.

34. Cf. *P.W.,* VI, pp. 53–65, "An Epistle to the Rev. John Wesley" (1755).

35. *JW Works,* XII, 116; *JW Letters,* III, p. 113.

36. Gill, *Charles Wesley, op. cit.,* p. 176.

37. *CW Sermons,* pp. xxxii–xxxiv.

38. John E. Rattenbury, *The Conversions of the Wesleys: A Critical Study* (London: Epworth Press, 1938), p. 84.

WESLEY'S WRITINGS

1. Baker, *Charles Wesley, op. cit.*, p. 13.

2. *Ibid.*, p. 3.

3. *JW Works*, XIII, p. 514 [emphasis added].

4. Jackson, *CW Journal*, I, p. iv.

5. *Ibid.*, I, p. v.

6. *Ibid.*, p. iv.

7. Nehemiah Curnock, ed., *The Journal of the Rev. John Wesley* (London, 1909–1916, 8 vols.), VII, p. 432 [hereafter *JW Journal*].

8. John Byrom, *The Universal Shorthand* (Manchester: John Hanop, 1776). The system was first sold through private lessons from the 1720s onward.

9. Telford, *CW Journal*.

10. The shorthand manuscript is located in the Methodist Archives and Research Centre, The John Rylands University Library of Manchester, Manchester, England. It was first published in my article "Charles Wesley Pastor: A Glimpse Inside the Shorthand Journal," *QR: The Methodist Quarterly Review*, Vol. 4, No. 1 (Spring 1984), pp. 9–21. It is reprinted here as Nos. 118–121, with the kind permission of Mr. Cole and the *QR*.

11. Jackson, *CW Journal*, I, p. xli.

12. Frederick Luke Wiseman, *Charles Wesley, Evangelist and Poet* (New York: Abingdon Press, 1932), p. 202.

13. *P.W.*, V, pp. 80–82.

14. *Ibid.*, "Hymns for Christian Friends," pp. 403–558, may have been born this way.

15. *P.W.*, VII, "Hymns for Families" (1757), p. 89.

16. Jackson, *CW Journal*, I, p. xlii.

17. Baker, *Charles Wesley, op. cit.*, p. 3.

18. *JW Works*, XII, pp. 56–105.

19. John Telford, *The Life of Charles Wesley* (London: The Wesleyan Book Room, 1900), p. 124.

20. Jackson, *CW Journal*, I, p. 178.

21. *JW Works*, V, pp. 25–37. The sermon is reprinted as No. 55 of this anthology; cf. Baker, *Charles Wesley Letters, op. cit.*, p. 35.

22. Jackson, *CW Journal*, I, pp. 155–156, 283–305, 306–307. Cf. Chapter Four, No. 24, June 23d.

23. *Ibid.*, II, p. 91 [emphasis added].

24. *Ibid.*, I, p. 107 [emphasis added].

25. *Ibid.*, p. 108 [emphasis added].

26. *Ibid.*

27. *Ibid.*, p. 117.

28. *Ibid.*, p. 125.

29. *Ibid.*, p. 126 [emphasis added].

30. *Ibid.*, p. 127 [emphasis added].

31. *Ibid.*, p. 129 [emphasis added].

32. *Ibid.*, p. 130 [emphasis added].

33. *Ibid.*, p. 132 [emphasis added].

34. *Ibid.*, p. 133.

35. "Expounded" appears 39 times, and "preached" 31.

36. Thomas Albin, "Charles Wesley's Earliest Evangelical Sermons," *Methodist History*, Vol. 21, No. 1 (Oct. 1982), pp. 60–63, gives an account of the discovery of these sermons; a process in which the present writer played a small role. The text of all of these sermons will be printed as an occasional publication of the Wesley Historical Society (England), under the title *Charles Wesley's Earliest Ser-*

mons: Six Manuscript Shorthand Sermons Hitherto Unpublished and Now Deciphered and Edited by Thomas R. Albin and Oliver A. Beckerlegge [hereafter: *CW Shorthand Sermons*].

37. Methodist Archives and Research Centre, The John Rylands University Library of Manchester, Manchester, England, "Charles Wesley Ms. Shorthand Sermon Booklets," six in number. The sermon on John 8, offered below as No. 38, is a good example of this method of preaching.

38. Jackson, *CW Journal*, I, pp. 114, 144.

39. Baker, *Charles Wesley, op. cit.*, p. 30; Jackson, *CW Journal*, I, p. 204.

40. Jackson, *CW Journal*, I, p. 307.

41. *Ibid.*

42. *Ibid.*, pp. 325, 387; II, p. 98.

43. Baker, *Charles Wesley, op. cit.*, pp. 38–39.

44. Jackson, *CW Journal*, I, pp. 117, 120, 125, etc.

45. *Ibid.*, pp. 124, 125, 126, 127, etc.

46. *Ibid.*, pp. 104, 142, etc.

47. *Ibid.*, II, pp. 31–32.

48. *Ibid.*, p. 31.

49. *Ibid.*, I, pp. 438, 439.

50. Richard P. Heitzenrater, "John Wesley's Early Sermons," *Proceedings of the Wesley Historical Society*, Vol. 36, pt. 4 (Feb. 1970), p. 113, n. 13.

51. Albin, "Charles Wesley's Early Sermons," *op. cit.*, pp. 60–63.

52. *JW Works*, V, pp. 25–37, without identification; cf. N. Burwash, ed., *Wesley's Doctrinal Standards*, Part I, *The Sermons with Introduction* (Salem, Ohio: Schmul Publication, 1967 reprint of the 1881 edition) [hereafter: Burwash, *Standards*]. The text of this sermon is carried as No. 56 below.

53. *JW Works*, VII, pp. 386–400; cf. Jackson, *CW Journal*, II, pp. 68–69; *P.W.*, VI, pp. 17–52.

54. Jackson, *CW Journal*, I, p. 173.

55. *Ibid.*, II, p. 5; cf. No. 29 below for the text of his hymn based on the parable.

56. *Ibid.*, I, p. 173.

57. *Ibid.*, I, p. 335.

58. *Ibid.*, I, p. 173; II, p. 6.

59. *Ibid.*, I, p. 173.

60. *Ibid.*, I, p. 173, II, p. 6.

61. *Ibid.*, I, p. 351; cf. No. 64 below for the text of a hymn using this phraseology.

62. *Ibid.*

63. *Ibid.*

64. *Ibid.*, I, p. 220.

65. *CW Sermons*, pp. 84–85.

66. Jackson, *CW Journal*, I, pp. 278, 336. The hymn is reprinted as No. 48 below.

67. *P.W.*, II, pp. 49–57; cf. No. 33 below.

THE HYMNS

1. Frank Baker, ed., *The Representative Verse of Charles Wesley* (London: Epworth Press, 1962), p. lviii.

2. *Ibid.*, p. xi.

3. *Ibid.*, p. liii.

4. Rattenbury, *Evangelical Doctrines, op. cit.*, pp. 19–20.

5. Brailsford, *op. cit., Two Brothers*, p. 117.

6. Cf. *P.W.*, V., pp. 397f, and Wiseman, *Charles Wesley*, pp. 91–92.

7. Jackson, *CW Journal*, I, p. 313 [emphasis added].

8. *Ibid.*, II, p. 214.

9. *Ibid.*, I, p. 165; cf. pp. 145, 166.

10. *Ibid.*, p. 131; cf. pp. 134, 139.

11. *Ibid.*, p. 150; cf. pp. 138, 140, 142, 146, 154, and 161.

12. *Ibid.*, p. 131; cf. p. 145.

13. Telford, *Life of Charles Wesley*, pp. 244–245; "Lo! on a narrow neck of land," *P.W.* IV, p. 316.

14. *P.W.*, I, pp. 49–59. Baker, *Representative Verse, op. cit.*, p. 153, detects connections between this hymn and the letters Charles wrote in November of 1735 and February 1736, suggesting that the hymn was also composed during that period of Wesley's ministry. See notes 13 and 18.

15. *JW Works*, XIV, p. 340 [emphasis added].

16. David Creamer, *Methodist Hymnology* (New York: Joseph Longking, 19848).

17. John Julian, *Dictionary of Hymnology, op. cit.*

18. Baker, *Representative Verse, op. cit.*, pp. 167–172; and John R. Tyson, "Charles Wesley and the German Hymns," *The Hymn*, Vol. 35, No. 3 (July 1984), pp. 153–158.

19. *JW Works*, XI, p. 391.

20. *P.W.*, V, pp. 10–11.

21. *P.W.*, V, pp. 481f.

22. *P.W.*, V, p. 10.

23. *P.W.*, V, p. 481.

24. *JW Works*, VII, pp. 293–294 [emphasis added].

25. *Ibid.*

26. *JW Letters*, IV, p. 166 [emphasis added].

27. *P.W.*, IV, p. 113.

28. *P.W.*, IX, pp. 385–386 [emphasis added]. Compare with John Wesley, ed., *A Collection of Hymns for the Use of the People Called Methodists* (London: J. Paramore, 1780) [hereafter, *M.H.B.*], p. 420, where the hymn is carried but this particular verse is omitted.

29. Eric Sharpe, "Gentle Jesus, Meek and Mild—Variations on a Nursery Theme for Congregation and Critic," *The Evangelical Quarterly*, Vol. 53, No. 3 (July–Sept., 1981), p. 151.

30. *Ibid.*

31. John R. Tyson, "Charles Wesley's Sentimental Language," *Evangelical Quarterly*, 57, No. 3 (July 1985), pp. 269–275.

32. *P.W.*, VI, p. 191.

33. *JW Works*, V, pp. 223–233, "The Great Privilege of those that are born of God"; and *JW Letters*, V, p. 322. Colin Williams, *John Wesley's Theology Today* (Nashville: Abingdon Press, 1960), pp. 126–130, offers a useful discussion of John's doctrine of sin.

34. *JW Letters*, V, p. 20; John summarizes his own understanding of Christian Perfection (in dialogue with Charles) in *JW Letters*, IV, pp. 187f. Cf. John R. Tyson, *Charles Wesley on Sanctification: A Biographical and Theological Study* (Grand Rapids: Francis Asbury Press, 1986), for a full discussion of Charles's view of Christian Perfection as distinguished from that of John Wesley.

35. *P.W.*, V, p. 301 [emphasis added].

36. Jackson, *CW Journal*, I, p. 286.

37. *M.H.B.*, pp. 381–382.

38. *JW Letters*, IV, p. 189.

39. Henry Bett, *Hymns of Methodism* (London: Epworth Press, 1912), pp. 13–20.

40. *Ibid.*, pp. 21–34; Rattenbury, *Evangelical Doctrines, op. cit.*, pp. 21–25, 58–89; Baker, *Representative Verse, op. cit.*, pp. lviii–lxi.

41. See note 18 above.

42. Baker, *Representative Verse, op. cit.*, pp. xliv–xlvi.

43. *Ibid.*

44. George H. Vallins, *The Wesleys and the English Language* (London: Epworth Press, 1954), pp. 81–83, offers six summary statements about Charles's half rhymes.

45. John Telford, *The Methodist Hymn Book Illustrated* (London: Charles Kelly, n.d.), p. 310.

46. Bett, *Hymns of Methodism, op. cit.*

47. Rattenbury, *Evangelical Doctrines, op. cit.*, pp. 22–23.

48. Baker, *Representative Verse, op. cit.*, p. lx.

49. John R. Tyson, "Charles Wesley's Theology of the Cross: An Examination of the Theology and Method of Charles Wesley as seen in his doctrine of the Atonement" (Ph.D. dissertation, The Graduate School, Drew University, 1983).

50. *Ibid.*, pp. 115–123.

SOURCES OF WESLEY'S POETIC DICTION

1. Bett, *Hymns of Methodism, op. cit.*, pp. 168–169.

2. These boundaries are a matter of convenience; they are, of course, the focus of lively debate. Until recently the scholarly consensus supported a schema using Dryden and Johnson as parameters for a neoclassical or Augustan period in English poetry; cf. Emilie Legouis and Louis Cazaamian, *A History of English Literature* (New York: Macmillian, reprint, 1957), pp. 690–870; Hugh C. Holman, *A Handbook of Literature*, 4th edition (Indianapolis: Bobbs-Merrill, 1980), pp. 83–84. Recent literature, like Donald Wesling's article, "Augustan Form: Justification and Breakup of a Period Style," *Texas Studies in Literature and Language*, Vol. 22 (Fall 1980), pp. 394–428, have reopened the whole question of "Augustan form."

3. Donald Davie, *Purity of Diction in English Verse* (London: Chatto and Windus, 1952), pp. 70–81. Of particular interest is his Chapter V, "The Classicism of Charles Wesley," in which the author demolishes the wall between "lyrical" and "didactic" or "secular" and "religious" poetry and sets Wesley's verse in its larger contemporary context.

4. *Ibid.*, p. 70.

5. *Ibid.*, p. 79.

6. Maldwyn Edwards, "Charles Wesley's Poetical Version of the Psalms," *Proceedings of the Wesley Historical Society*, Vol. 31, No. 3 (Sept. 1957), pp. 62–64.

7. James Dale, "The Theological and Literary Qualities of the Poetry of Charles Wesley in Relation to the Standards of His Age" (Ph.D. dissertation, Cambridge University, England, 1960), p. 136.

8. E. M. Hodgson, "Poetry in the Hymns of John and Charles Wesley," *Proceedings of the Wesley Historical Society*, Vol. 38, Nos. 2 and 3 (Aug. 1971 and Jan. 1972), p. 133.

9. George Lawton, *John Wesley's English: A Study of His Literary Style* (London: George Allen and Unwin, Ltd., 1962), p. 14.

10. James Dale, in his Ph.D. dissertation (*op. cit.*), treats this topic without moving far beyond the identifications established by Henry Bett over fifty years ago. Barbara Welch, in her Ph.D. dissertation, "Charles Wesley and the Celebrations of Evangelical Experience" (University of Michigan, 1971), locates Charles's poetry in an Augustan context, as did Donald Davie in his fine work *Purity of Diction*, *op. cit.*, pp. 70–82. Yet contemporary scholarship has not identified a significant number of eighteenth-century allusions beyond those noted by Bett.

11. Bett, *Hymns of Methodism, op. cit.*, pp. 130–131.

12. *Ibid.*, pp. 140–146.

13. *Ibid.*, pp. 133–137, 143–144.

14. *Ibid.*, pp. 159–160.

15. *Ibid.*, p. 160.

16. Baker, *Charles Wesley Letters, op. cit.*, pp. 129, 142.

17. Isabel St. John Bliss, "Young's Night Thoughts In Relation to Contemporary Christian Apologetics," *Publications of the Modern Language Association*, Vol. 49 (1934), pp. 37f. This treatment has been enhanced by recent scholarship: Daniel Odell, "Young's Night Thoughts as an Answer to Pope's Essay on Man," *Studies in English Literature*, Vol. 12 (1972), pp. 481–501. Others, like John Sitter, have compared the Anglican Young with the Jansenist Blaise Pascal, "Theodicy at Mid-Century: Young, Akenside, and Hume," *Eighteenth Century Studies*, Vol. 12, No. 1 (Fall 1978), pp. 90–106; Martin Price, *To the Palace of Wisdom* (Southern Illinois University Press: Feffer and Sons, 1964), pp. 335–351; and R. D. Stock, *The Holy and Daemonic from Sir Thomas Browne to William Blake* (Princeton: Princeton University Press, 1982), pp. 188–200. Stock suggests that Young writes in literary connection with Pope, but with the apologetic agenda of Pascal.

18. Donald French, ed., *Minor Poets of 1660–1780*, Vol. V (London: Benjamin Blum, 1961), p. 160.

19. Rattenbury, *Evangelical Doctrines, op. cit.*, p. 48.

20. Rattenbury, *Evangelical Doctrines, op. cit.*, p. 47.

21. James William Johnson, *The Formation of English Neo-Classical Thought* (Princeton: Princeton University Press, 1967), p. 87. Johnson presents an excellent survey of the various segments of classical literature applied in the contemporary (eighteenth-century) literature: Greek antiquity, pp. 69–90, Roman antiquity, pp. 91–105; and Christian antiquity, pp. 106–121.

22. Bett, *Hymns of Methodism, op. cit.*, pp. 35–56.

23. *Ibid.*, pp. 124–127.

24. *JW Journal*, I, pp. 16–27.

25. Bett, *Hymns of Methodism, op. cit.*, pp. 124–125.

26. Johnson, *English Neo-classical Thought, op. cit.*, pp. 120–121.

27. *Ibid.*, pp. 111–112.

28. *JW Journal*, III, p. 392; cf. p. 499.

29. Cf. Richard P. Heitzenrater, "John Wesley and The Oxford Methodists, 1725–1735" (Ph.D. dissertation, Department of Religion, Duke University, 1972), pp. 25–151, is the best treatment of Oxford Methodism currently available.

30. "Ms. Luke," an unpublished hymn based on Luke. 21:2, p. 296 in the manuscript, located at the Methodist Archives and Research Centre, The John Rylands University Library of Manchester, Manchester, England.

31. Bett, *Hymns of Methodism, op. cit.*, pp. 98–107.

32. Jackson, *CW Journal*, I, pp. 178, 126.

33. *CW Shorthand sermons*, sermon based on Rom. 8:23–24 top of ms. page 9, for example.

34. Jackson, *CW Journal*, I, pp. 88, 128, etc.

35. *Ibid.*, pp. 104, 111, 120, 121, 123, 125, 127, 130, 131, etc.

36. *Ibid.*, I, pp. 201, 250, 287 (twice), 289, 298; II, p. 254.

37. *P.W.*, IX, pp. 274–293, where "Short Hymns" Nos. 819, 821, 828, 832, 835, 836, 837, 840, 844, 848, 851, 852, 853, among many others, follow the Prayer Book version of the Psalms instead of the Authorized Version (KJV).

38. Rattenbury, *Evangelical Doctrines, op. cit.*, p. 48.

39. *Ibid.*, cf. David Creamer, *Methodist Hymnology, op. cit.*, Emory Bucke, ed., *Companion to the Hymnal* (Nashville: Abingdon Press, 1970); John Julian, *A Dictionary of Hymnology, op. cit.*; Bernard Manning, *The Hymns of Wesley and Watts* (London: Epworth Press, 1943); Robert McMuthan, *Our Hymnody: A Manual of the Methodist Hymnal* (New York: The Methodist Book Concern, 1937); George J. Stevenson, *The Methodist Hymn Book and its Literary Associations* (London: Hamilton, Adams, and Co., 1870); John Telford, *The Methodist Hymn Book Illustrated* (London: Charles Kelly, 1906).

40. John W. Waterhouse, *The Bible in Charles Wesley's Hymns* (London: Epworth Press, 1957), pp. 5–9.

41. *P.W.*, XII, p. 411, #2934; *P.W.*, IX, p. 380, #1074; cf. Chapter 12: "Expositor of Scripture."

42. *P.W.*, XII, p. 411, #2934.
43. *P.W.*, IX, p. 380, #1074; cf. *P.W.*, X, pp. 24–25, #1314.
44. *P.W.*, XIII, p. 183, #3372.
45. *P.W.*, X, pp. 224–225, #216.
46. Barbara Welch, "Charles Wesley and the Celebrations of Evangelical Experience," *op. cit.*, pp. 113–114.
47. *Ibid.*
48. Bernard Manning, *The Hymns of Wesley and Watts*, *op. cit.*, pp. 42–43.

CHARLES WESLEY'S THEOLOGY

1. George Findlay, *Christ's Standard Bearer* (London: Epworth Press, 1956), p. 9.
2. Davie, *Purity of Diction*, *op. cit.*, p. 79.
3. *JW Works*, XIV, p. 340. Preface to the 1780 *M.H.B.*
4. Rattenbury, *Evangelical Doctrines*, *op. cit.*, p. 86.
5. *P.W.*, V, p. 317, #215.
6. Jackson, *CW Journal*, I, p. 286.
7. *Ibid.*, p. 268; cf. p. 254.
8. *P.W.*, XI, p. 346, #1668.
9. *P.W.*, XI, p. 381, #1756 [emphasis added].
10. *Ibid.*, pp. 374–375.
11. *P.W.*, X, p. 3; cf. *P.W.*, V, p. 48.
12. *P.W.*, IV, pp. 272f, "Redemption Hymns," #49.
13. *P.W.*, XII, p. 152.
14. "Ms. Luke," pp. 71–72, an unpublished hymn based on Luke 5:21; cf. *P.W.*, XII, p. 224.
15. *P.W.*, XIII, p. 221 [emphasis added].
16. *P.W.*, V, p. 317, #215.
17. "Ms. Matthew," an unpublished hymn based on Matt. 13:44.
18. *P.W.*, X, pp. 252–253, #289.
19. *P.W.*, V, p. 323, #130; *ibid.*, p. 325; X, p. 118, #1554; *ibid.*, p. 139, #4; *ibid.*, p. 141, #7.
20. Cf. Appendix B, "Christological Titles in Charles Wesley's Later Hymns."
21. *P.W.*, XI, p. 305, #1584.
22. *Ibid.*, p. 37, #999.
23. *Ibid.*, p. 306, #1587.
24. *P.W.*, IX, p. 175, #550; cf. *ibid.*, p. 160, #500.
25. Cf. 1 Cor. 15:20, 45; Rom. 5:14, 15.
26. Irenaeus, "Against Heresies," from Alexander Roberts and James Donaldson, *Ante-Nicean Fathers*, Vol. I (Grand Rapids: William B. Eerdmans, reprinted 1977), p. 527.
27. *CW Sermons*, p. 86 [emphasis added]. For the text of this sermon, see No. 6 below.
28. Erich Sharpe, "Gentle Jesus, Meek and Mild," *op. cit.*, pp. 149–165.
29. Jackson, *CW Journal*, II, p. 7; *P.W.*, IX, pp. 362–363, 387–388; *P.W.*, VII, pp. 341–342.
30. "Ms. Luke," p. 34, an unpublished hymn based on Luke 2:34.
31. *P.W.*, XIII, pp. 153–154, #3313.
32. *P.W.*, IV, p. 34; *P.W.*, V, p. 143; *P.W.*, VII, p. 99.
33. "Ms. Luke," p. 78, an unpublished hymn on Luke 6:11; *ibid.*, p. 276, an unpublished hymn based on Luke 19:11; *P.W.*, III, p. 331; *P.W.*, IV, pp. 32, 39; *P.W.*, V, pp. 154, 163, 169, 177, 196, 209 , etc.
34. *P.W.*, V, pp. 153–154.
35. Cf. Rattenbury, *Evangelical Doctrines*, *op. cit.*, pp. 288–290, for a discussion of this aspect of

Charles's thought; also *P.W.*, IX, pp. 100, 158; *P.W.*, XIII, pp. 157, 181, for examples in his hymns and for instances of John Wesley's editorial reaction.

36. *P.W.*, V, p. 20.

37. *P.W.*, XI, p. 1961; *P.W.*, II, pp. 156–158; Baker, *Charles Wesley, op. cit.*, p. 39.

38. Albert Outler, "Preface," to Frank Whaling, ed., *John and Charles Wesley* (New York: Paulist Press, 1981), pp. xv–xvi.

39. Timothy Smith, "The Holy Spirit in the Hymns of the Wesleys," *Wesleyan Theological Journal*, Vol. 16, No. 2 (Fall 1981), pp. 20–48; cf. T. Crichton Mitchell, "Response to Dr. Timothy Smith on the Wesleys' Hymns," *ibid.*, pp. 49–58.

40. "Ms. Acts," p. 5, an unpublished hymn on Acts 1:8.

41. *P.W.*, X, p. 13, #1292.

42. *P.W.*, XII, p. 40, #2152.

43. *P.W.*, XII, pp. 18–19, #2105; p. 19, #2106, #2107; p. 20, #2109, #2110; p. 36, #2145; p. 38, #2148, #2149; for examples of maturation language: *P.W.*, XII, pp. 19–20, #2108; p. 20, #2109; #2110; p. 21–22, #2112; p. 39, #2151; etc.

44. *P.W.*, XII, pp. 19–20, #2108.

45. Cf. Tyson, "Charles Wesley's Theology of the Cross," *op. cit.*, Chapter 2, "Redemption Language," pp. 125–362.

46. Cf. Donald Dayton, "The Doctrine of the Baptism of the Holy Spirit: Its Emergence and Significance," *Wesleyan Theological Journal*, Vol. 13, No. 1 (Spring 1978), pp. 114–126; Thomas Langford, *Practical Divinity* (Nashville: Abingdon, 1983), pp. 134f; Timothy Smith, "The Holy Spirit," *op. cit.*, seems to suggest that Charles Wesley's pneumatology was similar to that of the later revivalists (such as Asa Mahan), whereas it is my opinion that it is not. Dayton's article contains an excellent discussion of the transition that took place in the Wesleyan theology of the Holy Spirit, using Asa Mahan as an example. In Charles Wesley's application pneumatology expressed a christocentric renovation in the believer, and generally was not isolated from his larger theology of redemption.

47. *P.W.*, VII, pp. 338–339.

48. *P.W.*, XI, p. 417, #1893.

49. *P.W.*, VII, p. 224, #31.

50. *P.W.*, X, p. 264, #316.

51. Rattenbury, *Evangelical Doctrines, op. cit.*, p. 228.

52. John Bowmer, "The Churchmanship of Charles Wesley," *Proceedings of the Wesley Historical Society*, Vol. 31 (1957–1958), pp. 78f.

53. Jackson, *Life, op. cit.*, II, pp. 472–473.

54. Baker, *Charles Wesley Letters, op. cit.*, p. 103.

55. *Ibid.*, p. 131.

56. Rattenbury, *Evangelical Doctrines, op. cit.*, p. 230; Jackson, *Life, op. cit.*, II, pp. 472–473.

57. *JW Journal*, II, pp. 172–173. April 2, 1739.

1 / Georgia and the Making
of a Minister

Charles's development at Oxford, through the academics of the university and the regimen of the Holy Club, was soon put to the test. Initially, his practical piety led to service in the environs of Oxford (including Newgate prison), but soon he, his brother, and two of their friends went on a bold adventure in the New World.

No. 1   Letter to Dr. Chandler

Charles's most comprehensive autobiographical statement is found in his letter to Dr. Chandler. The recipient was an Anglican clergyman, about to embark for the New World. Written late in Charles's life (April 28, 1785), the epistle gives an overview of its author's life pilgrimage, with special emphasis upon Methodism's ties to the Church of England. Charles wrote the letter soon after John Wesley ordained Dr. Coke as bishop for the Methodists in America, hence his letter concludes with a lament over the impending separation from the Mother Church. It is full of the author's "dread of separation" and is tinged with sadness at his brother's ordinations which—for Charles at least—signaled the beginning of that end. His staunch Anglicanism and his attempts at vindicating himself in the days of growing distance between the Methodists and the Church of England did nothing to endear the younger Wesley to the Methodists and their lay preachers. The letter is also particularly important for considering Charles's early ministry since it offers his own report of the motives that took him to America, and offers his own estimation of his ministry in Georgia and thereafter.

The letter is reprinted here from the manuscript, with the permission of the Methodist Archives and History Committee, England.

London, April 28th, 1785.
Rev. and dear Sir,—As you are setting out for America, and I for a more distant country, I think it needful to leave you some account of myself, and of my companions through life. At eight years old, in 1716, I was sent by

my Father, Rector of Epworth, to Westminster School, and placed under the care of my eldest brother Samuel, a strict Churchman, who brought me up in his own principles. My Brother John, five years older than me, was then at the Charter-house [School]. From Westminster College, in 1727, I was elected Student of Christ-Church [Oxford University]. My brother John was then a Fellow of Lincoln.

My first year at College I lost in diversions. The next I set myself to study. Diligence led me into serious thinking. I went to the weekly sacrament, and persuaded two or three young scholars to accompany me, and to observe the method of study prescribed by the statutes of the University. This gained me the harmless nickname of Methodist. In half a year my Brother left his curacy at Epworth, and came to our assistance. We then proceeded regularly in our studies, and in doing what good we could to the bodies and souls of men.

I took my Master's Degree, and only thought of spending all my days at Oxford. But my brother, who always had the ascendant over me, persuaded me to accompany him and Mr. Oglethorpe to Georgia. I exceedingly dreaded entering into holy orders: but he overruled me here also, and I was ordained Deacon by the Bishop of Oxford, Dr. Potter, and the next Sunday, Priest, by the Bishop of London, Dr. Gibson.

Our only design was, to do all the good we could, as Ministers of the Church of England, to which we were firmly attached, both by education and by principle. (My brother still thinks her the best-constituted national Church in the world.)

In 1736 we arrived, as Missionaries, in Georgia. My Brother took charge of Savannah (and I of Frederica), waiting for an opportunity of preaching to the Indians. I was, in the meantime, Secretary to Mr. Oglethorpe, and also Secretary for Indian Affairs.

The hardship of lying on the ground, &c., soon threw me into a Fever and Dysentery, which in half a year forced me to return to England. My Brother returned the next year. Still we had no plan, but to serve God, and the Church of England. The lost sheep of this fold were our principal care, not excluding any Christians, of whatever denomination, who were willing to add the power of godliness to their own particular form.

Our Eldest Brother, Samuel, was alarmed at our going on, and strongly expressed his fears of its ending in a separation from the Church [of England]. All our enemies prophesied the same. This confirmed us the more in our resolution to continue in our calling; which we constantly avowed, both in public and private; by conservation, and preaching, and writing; exhorting all our hearers to follow our example.

My Brother drew up rules for our societies, one of which was, constantly to attend the Church prayers, and sacrament. We both signed them, and likewise our hymn-books.

When we were no longer permitted to preach in the churches, we preached (but never in church hours) in houses, or fields, and sent, or rather carried, from thence multitudes to church, who had never been there before. Our society in most places made the bulk of the congregation, both at prayers and sacrament.

I never lost my Dread of Separation, or ceased to guard our societies against it. I frequently told them, "I am your servant as long as you remain in the Church of England; but no longer. Should you forsake her, you would renounce me."

Some of the Lay-Preachers very early discovered an inclination to separate, which induced my brother to print his "Reasons Against Separation."[1] As soon as it appeared, we beat down the schismatical spirit. If any one did leave the Church, at the same time he left our society. For nearly fifty years we kept the sheep in the fold; and having filled the number of our days, only waited to depart in peace.

After our having continued friends for above seventy years, and fellow-labourers for above fifty, can anything but death part us? I can scarcely yet believe it, that, in his eighty-second year, my Brother, my old, intimate friend and companion, *should have assumed* the Episcopal Character, ordained Elders, Consecrated a Bishop, and sent him to ordain our lay-Preachers in America! I was then in Bristol, at his Elbow; yet he never gave me the least hint of his Intention. How was he surprised into so rash an action? He certainly persuaded himself that it was right.

Lord Mansfield told me last year, that "ordination was separation." This my Brother does not and will not see; or that he has renounced the Principles and Practice of his whole life; that he has acted contrary to all his Declarations, Protestations, and Writings, robbed his friends of their boasting,[2] realized the Nag's head ordination, and left an indelible blot on his name, as long as it shall be remembered!

Thus our Partnership here is dissolved, but not our Friendship. I have taken him for better or worse, till death do us part; or rather, re-unite us in love inseparable. I have lived on earth a little too long—who have lived to see this evil day. But I shall very soon be taken from it, in steadfast faith that the Lord will maintain his own cause, and carry on his own work, and fulfill his promise to his church, "Lo, I am with you always, even to the end!"

Permit me to subscribe myself, Rev. and dear Sir,

Your faithful and obliged servant and brother.

P.S. What will become of those poor sheep in the wilderness, the American Methodists? How have they been betrayed into a separation from the Church of England! Which their Preachers and they no more intended than the Methodists here! Had they had patience a little longer, they would have seen a real Primative Bishop in America, consecrated by three Scotch Bishops, who have their consecration from the English Bishops, and are acknowledged by them as the same as themselves. There is therefore not the least difference between the members of Bishop Seabury's Church, and the members of the Church of England. *You know I had the happiness of conversing with that truly Apostolic man, who is esteemed by all that know him as much as by you and me.*[3] [The preceding sentence in italics was a shorthand insertion in the manuscript.] He told me, he looked upon the Methodists in America as sound members of the Church, and was ready to ordain any of their Preachers whom he should find duly qualified. *His* Ordinations would be indeed genuine, valid and episcopal.

But what are your poor Methodists now? Only a new sect of Presbyterians! And after my brother's death, which is now so near, what will be their End? They will lose all their influence and importance; they will turn aside to vain janglings; they will settle again upon their lees; and, like other Sects of Dissenters, come to nothing!

No. 2   Letter of the Atlantic Crossing

This letter, written while the Wesleys' ship lay off the American coast, shows that Charles's spirits had sunk low during the crossing. It foreshadows the moods which would later haunt him in Georgia, and offers important insights into his psychological state just prior to the mission. Written in Charles's own hand, the letter was addressed to "V," his friend "Varanese," Sally Kirkham. The "Selima" mentioned in the first paragraph is Anne Granville; "Cyrus" was John Wesley's pen name.[4] Charles's advice to Sally Kirkham strikes a familiar note; "the single eye," his metaphor for describing undivided intentions and Christian Perfection, would emerge again in sermon and in song. In the midst of describing the vital religion of his correspondents Wesley lost his melancholy. His third paragraph, as Charles recognized, is not consistent with his original tone; "I cannot myself account for the strange expansion of heart which I feel in the midst of my wishes for your welfare." The letter lifts his mood, hence he pleads for further correspondence from his "best friends."

The letter is reprinted here from the manuscript with the permission of the Methodist Church, Overseas Division (Methodist Missionary Society), England. The manuscript has several holes in it, apparently due to the frailty of the paper at its folds, hence a complete transcription is not possible. The portions of the letter which are missing are presented in the following form [. . .]. Several portions of the letter are lined out as Charles edited it while writing. Where possible these stricken sections have been carried alongside his final reading. I am grateful to Dr. Frank Baker for help in locating this manuscript letter, and for his notes, which assisted me in deciphering Charles Wesley's scrawl. Charles's original abbreviations have been translated in the text below in order to make it more readable.[5]

On Board the Simmonds off the island of Tibey in Georgia.
Feb. 5, 1736.

God has brought an unhappy, unthankful wretch hither, through a thousand dangers, to renew his complaints, and loathe the Life which has been preserved by a series of Miracles. I take the moment of my arrival to

inform you of it, because I know you will thank Him, tho'[ugh] I cannot. I
cannot, for I yet feel myself. In vain have I fled from myself to America; I
still groan under the intolerable weight of inherent misery! If I have never
yet repented of my undertaking, it is because I c[oul]d hope for nothing
better in England—or Paradise. Go where I will, I carry my Hell about me;
nor have I the least ease in anything, unless in thinking of S[elima] and
you! This very night conversing with, tho'[ugh] but in a dream, I quite
forgot that I was miserable but alas—
    "I woke to all the woes I left behind"
and am now fled from the Reproaches of my Friends for irresignation to
you for refuse [sic, "refuge"]. To you only I can complain tho'[ugh] I have
wearied out all my Friends beside. And tis well for them that a few hours
or days will place them out of hearing. It gives me Concern while that I
must so soon be separated from ye few that were are still dear to me. Their
Example is reproach but no Encouragement; their advice a pain of but
not an Help to me. Yours and the thoughts and words of S[elima] (could
you but prevail upon her to send them) would not and thou only, would
surely alleviate if not remove my Trouble. For h[er] this [letter] is intended
equally with you, for I know h[er] soul is heart is as your heart; all
gentleness and pity—O that you both might profit by my loss and never
know the misery of Divided Affections. I feel [. . . .] little good will towards
you, such [. . . .] that [. . . .]
    Besides you Two I have no Relations, no Friends in England, who I have
either write to, or find any ease in thinking of. And if for you I do pray
[preceding word inserted with a caret] continually with an earnestness like
that of Dives [Luke 16:19f] that ye may never come into this state of torment.—I cannot follow my own Advice; but yet I advise you—Give GOD
your hearts: Love Him with all your souls; serve Him with all your
strength. Forget those things that are behind; Riches, Pleasure, Honour—
in a Word, whatever does not lead to GOD. From this Hour let your eye be
single. Whatever ye speak, or think, or do, let God be your Aim, and God
only! Let your One End be to please and love God! In all your Business, all
your Refreshments, all your Diversions, all your Conversations as well in
all those which are commonly called Religious Duties, let your Eye be strait
forward to God. Have One Design, One Desire, One Hope! Even that the
God whom ye served may be your GOD and your all in time and in
eternity! O be not of a double heart! Think of nothing else—seek nothing
else! To love God and to be beloved of Him is enough. Be your eye first on
this One Point, and your whole bodies shall be full of light. GOD shall
continually lift up, and that more and more, the light of His Countenance
upon you. His H[oly] Spirit shall dwell in you and shine more and more
upon your souls unto your Perfect Day. He shall purify your Hearts by
Faith from every Earthly Thought, every unholy Affection. He shall
[e]stablish your Souls with so lively a hope as already lays hold on the prize

of your High Calling. He shall fill you with Peace and Joy and Love. Love, the Brightness of his glory, and the express image of H[is] Person! Love which never rusts, never fadeth, but still spreads its flame, still goeth on conquering and to conquer, till what was but now a weak foolish, wavering, sinful Creature, be filled with all the Fullness of GOD!

I cannot myself account for the strange Expansion of Heart which I feel in the midst of my wishes for your Welfare. It is not Charity; for that arises from your love of GOD, a Principle I am utterly ignorant of. If it springs from ought else it is of no worth,—and yet tis [all?] I have to rest my Soul upon. I know no Pleasure but in [full?] consciousness that I Love you, or rather, in contemplating something[?] lovely in you.

> "And shall I doat on your scattered pieces of a [unclear?] and imperfect picture, and never be afflicted with [. . .] ginal[?] beauty[?]? Ought I not to conclude that if there be so much sweetness in a drop there must be infinitely more in the fountain; if there be so much splendor in a ray, what must the sun be in its glory?"

I herewith send you C[yrus]'s Journal, which may possibly make you some amends for the Pain I put you to in reading this. He is indeed Devoted—but I cannot bear to think of his Happiness! And find a preposterous sort of Joy, that I am going to be removed from the sight of it. Could I hide me from Myself too in these vast impervious Forests, how gladly would I fly to 'em as my last asylum, and lose myself for ever in a Blessed Insensibility and Forgetfulness!—But it is a fruitless wish, and that salutation of Satan better becomes me—

Hail horrors, hail, and thou profoundest gloom
Receive thy new possessor—one who brings
A mind not to be changed by place or time![6]

Feb. 14, off Peeper's Island.

My Friends will rejoice with me in the Interval of ~~peace~~ ease I at present enjoy. I look with horror back on the Desperate spirit ~~which~~ that dictated those Words above, but shall let them stand as the naked picture of a Soul which can never know reserve toward you.—I will still call myself a *Prisoner of Hope*. God is able to save to the uttermost, to break my bonds in sunder, and ~~give~~ bring Deliverance to the Captive!—"To what I am resigned?" is a question I am continually asking myself tho' God alone can answer it. This ~~will~~ I am persuaded, will now be ~~yet~~ soon determined; for I am come to a crisis.—The work I see immediately before me is the care of 50 poor families; (alas for them that they should be so cared for!). Some few of whom are not far from the Kingdom of God. Among these I shall either be Converted or Lost. I need not ask your prayers; you both make mention of me in them continually. Obstinate pride, Invincible Sensuality stand betwixt God and me. The whole Bent of my Soul is to be afflicted. My

Office calls for an ardent love of souls, a desire to spend and to be spent for them, and Earnestness to lay down my Life for the Brethren. May the Spirit that maketh intercession for us, direct you how to intercede for me!

I have a thousand things to say. Many[,] many dear named[?] friends would be remembered. Particularly that ~~good~~ Best of men [her father] whose parting Tears I can never forget. Has God in pity to you withheld him longer from his Reward? Or do you find by his increasing Desire to be Dissolved, that he is just going to be taken from your hand? Let [that be?] the Death of the Righteous and let my last end be li[ke] his. You are cut off from wishing my Regard to some whom I will shortly challenge for my friends in the presence of GOD and his angels.

Be pleased to let no one see your Journal except whom you yourself could trust with every thing. It is not Impossible but I may one day tell you the Reason for my request. But this I submit. [. . .] [Meet] you I surely shall when [we?] shall part no more!

If there be Time for transcribing them I will s[end yo]u my brother's Reasons (O that I could say they were mine too) for coming hither. I long to hear from you—Both; (take notice S[elima]!). And that for this very plain Reason, that I may love you better. Nothing increases our love like prayer for each other, and I am never so near the Spirit of Intercession as when I am reading the Letter of my friend. Therefore, S[elima], write. It is my greatest Happiness on Earth to love you both for GOD's sake, and will be part of my Happiness in Heaven. Methinks I anticipate the freedom of that blessed place, where they neither Marry, nor are given in Marriage.—My heart is now full of you,—O that I were such as that my Prayer might avail much for you! [i.e. a righteous man as in James 5:16] I earnestly recommend you both to GOD, and trust He will conduct us to All rejoice together in Him!

No. 3   Hymn: "Written for Midnight"

The hymn first appeared in *Hymns and Sacred Poems* (1739). It carried various titles in subsequent editions, including: "A Midnight Hymn for one under the Law"—reflecting its pre-conversion character—and "A Midnight Hymn for one convinced of Sin"—reflecting John Wesley's emendations for the 1780 *Collection of Hymns for the Use of the People Called Methodists*, which transformed it into a more evangelical hymn.[7]

The song seems to have been written during Charles's Atlantic crossing, a time when its author was traversing the "Bosom of the Deep."[8] Charles's spirits had sunk low during the long voyage; he was filled with self-doubt and spiritual despair. Several of his lines lament his plight and ask for release through death or a Divine visitation—a desire that received censure from brother John. The hymn moves from despair of the author's present circumstances toward an eschatological hope phrased in the Pauline *Maranatha* ("Come quickly Lord!") and the Johannine language of renewal—"Light," "Life," and "Love." Charles's original lines are carried below. The manuscript version of the hymn carries an emphatic "No" penned in by John Wesley at the point of the asterisk.

1 While Midnight Shades the Earth o'erspread,
       And veil the Bosom of the Deep,
   Nature reclines her weary Head,
       And Care respires and Sorrows sleep:
   My Soul still aims at Nobler Rest,
   Aspiring to her Saviour's Breast.

2 Aid me, ye hov'ring Spirits near,
       Angels and Ministers of Grace;
   Who ever, while you guard us here,
       Behold your Heav'nly Father's Face!
   Gently my raptur'd Soul convey
   To Regions of Eternal Day.

3 Fain would I leave this Earth below,
       Of Pain and Sin the dark Abode;
   Where shadowy Joy, or solid Woe
       Allures, or tears me from my GOD:
   Doubtful and Insecure of Bliss,
   Since Death alone confirms me His. [NO!]*

4 Till then, to Sorrow born, I sigh,
       And gasp, and languish after Home;
   Upward I send my streaming Eye,
       Expecting till the Bridegroom come:
   Come quickly, Lord! Thy own receive,
   Now let me see thy Face, and live.

5 Absent from Thee, my exil'd Soul
       Deep in a Fleshly Dungeon groans;
   Around me Clouds of Darkness roll,
       And lab'ring Silence speaks my Moans:
   Come quickly, Lord! Thy Face display,
   And look my Midnight into Day.

6 Error and Sin, and Death are o'er
       If Thou reverse the Creature's Doom;
   Sad, *Rachel* weeps her Loss no more,
       If Thou the GOD, the Saviour come:

---

*John Wesley's editorial "NO!" indicated his rejection of Charles's notion that death *alone* would free his soul from "pain and sin" and then secure "Bliss." Cf. *P.W.*, I, pp. 49–50; Baker, *Representative Verse, op. cit.*, pp. 153–154.

Of Thee possest, in Thee we prove
The Light, the Life, the Heav'n of Love.

No. 4 Journal Selections: March 9–December 4, 1736
(Jackson, *The Journal of Charles Wesley*, 1849, and Telford,
The Early Journal, 1810)

Charles's Georgia experience was even more dismal than that of his brother John.
The desolation of Frederica and his double duties as secretary and pastor did not
wear well on Charles. The rough conditions of his rustic parish undermined his frail
health as quickly as malevolent parishioners sapped his initial fervor. He disem-
barked on March 9 with renewed vigor but village gossip and his high church
proclivities soon alienated him from most of the settlement. The vindictive Mrs.
Hawkins set herself to the task of severing the relationship between General
Oglethorpe (leader of the expedition) and Charles Wesley, since she believed
Wesley had had her husband—the company's physician—jailed for shooting his
gun on the Sabbath. The gossip ran rife; to the general she whispered of Wesley's
traitorous attitudes, and to the pastor she revealed the general's reputed adulteries.
After less than three weeks in the country Charles's parishioners avoided him on the
town's only street, and the servants returned his linen unwashed. John came down
from Savannah on a lightning visit to dissuade Charles from his resolution to starve
to death rather than accept the aid of his tormentors. The breach between
Oglethorpe and the younger Wesley was somewhat repaired, but his mission was
irrevocably lost in Charles's sickness and depression; he resigned his post on July
25, and began the long voyage home to England. Oglethorpe,[9] for his part, sent
Wesley home as a courier, giving a cloak of honor to his withdrawal and an
opportunity to reconsider his resignation.

The selections below are (for the most part) given in their entirety, but interven-
ing entries have been omitted between the dates presented. Wesley developed
abbreviations for the people who appeared in the journal frequently; for example
M.H. was Mrs. Hawkins. In the accounts below Charles's abbreviations have been
converted into their fuller form.

Tues., March 9th, 1736, about three in the afternoon, I first set foot on St.
Simon's island, and immediately my spirit revived. No sooner did I enter
upon my ministry, than God gave me, like Saul, another heart. So true is
that [remark] of Bishop Hall: "The calling of God never leaves a man
unchanged; neither did God ever employ any one in His service, whom He
did not enable to the work He set him; especially those whom He raises up
to the supply of His place, and the representation of Himself." The people,
with Mr. Oglethorpe, were all arrived the day before.

The first who saluted me on my landing was honest Mr. Ingham,[10] and
that with his usual heartiness. Never did I more rejoice at the sight of him;
especially when he told me the treatment he has met with for vindicating

the Lord's day: such as every Minister of Christ must meet with. The people seemed overjoyed to see me: Mr. Oglethorpe in particular received me very kindly.

I spent the afternoon in conference with my parishioners. (With what trembling ought I to call them mine!) At seven we had evening prayers, in the open air, at which Mr. Oglethorpe was present. The lesson gave me the fullest direction, and greatest encouragement: "Continue instant in prayer, and watch in the same with thanksgiving; withal praying also for us, that God would open unto us a door of utterance, to speak the mystery of Christ; that I may make it manifest, as I ought to speak. Walk in wisdom toward them that are without, redeeming the time. Let your speech be always with grace, seasoned with salt, that ye may know how ye ought to answer every man.' Say to Archippus, Take heed to the ministry which thou hast received of the Lord, that thou fulfill it." [Col. 4:2–6, 17] At nine I returned, and lay in the boat.

Thur., March 11th. At ten this morning I began the full service, to about a dozen women, whom I had got together; intending to continue it, and only to read a few prayers to the men before they went to work. I also expounded the second lesson with some boldness, as I had a few times before.

After prayers I met Mrs. Hawkins's maid, in a great passion of tears, at being struck by her mistress. She seemed resolved to make away with herself, to escape her Egyptian bondage. With much difficulty I prevailed upon her to return, and carried her back to her mistress. Upon my asking Mrs. Hawkins to forgive her, she refused me with the utmost roughness, rage, and almost reviling.

Mr. Tackner, whom I talked with next, made me full amends. He was in an excellent temper; resolved to strive not with his wife, but himself, in putting off the old man and putting on the new.

In the evening I heard the first harsh word from Mr. Oglethorpe, when I asked for something for a poor woman. The next day I was surprised by a rougher answer, in a matter that deserved still greater encouragement. I know not how to account for his increasing coldness.

My encouragement was the same in speaking with Mrs. Welch, whom I found all storm and tempest. The meek, the teachable Mrs. Welch (that *was* in the ship) was now so wilful, so untractable, so fierce, that I could not bear to stay near her. I did not mend my self by stumbling again upon Mr. Oglethorpe, who was with the men under arms, in expectation of an enemy. I stayed as long as I could, however, *"unsave within the wind / Of such commotion"*; but at last the hurricane of his passion drove me away.

Sun., March 14th. We had prayers under a great tree. In the Epistle I was plainly shown what I ought to be, and what to expect. . . . [2 Cor. 6:3–10]

I preached with boldness, on singleness of intention [cf. No. 5, a sermon entitled "The Single Eye"], to about twenty people, among whom was Mr. Oglethorpe. Soon after, as he was in M.H.'s hut, a bullet (through the carelessness of one of the people, who were exercising today) flew through the wall, close by him.

Mrs. Germain now retracted her consent for having her child baptized: however, Mrs. Colwell's I did baptize by trine [*sic.*] immersion, before a numerous congregation.

At night I found myself exceeding faint, but had no better bed than the ground; on which I slept very comfortably, before a great fire, and waked the next morning perfectly well.

Tues., March 16th. I was wholly spent in writing letters for Mr. Oglethorpe. I would not spend six days more in the same manner for all Georgia.

Thurs., March 18th. To-day Mr. Oglethorpe set out with the Indians, to hunt the buffalo upon the main, and to see the utmost limits of what they claimed. In the afternoon Mrs. Welch discovered to me the whole mystery of iniquity.

I went to my myrtle-walk, where, as I was repeating, "I will thank thee, for thou hast heard me, and art become my salvation," a gun was fired from the other side of the bushes. Providence had that moment turned me from that end of the walk, which the shot flew through; but I heard them pass close by me.

Sun., March 21st. Mr. Oglethorpe had ordered, oftener than once, that no man should shoot on a Sunday. Germain had been committed to the guard-room for it in the morning, but was, upon his submission, released. In the midst of the sermon a gun was fired. Davidson, the constable, ran out, and found it was the Doctor; told him it was contrary to orders, and he was obliged to desire him to come to the officer. Upon this the Doctor flew into a great passion, and said, "What, do not you know I am not to be looked upon as a common fellow?" Not knowing what to do, the constable went, and returned, after consulting with Hermsdorf, with two centinels, and brought him to the guard-room. Hereupon Mrs. Hawkins charged and fired a gun; and then ran thither, like a mad woman, crying she had shot, and would be confined too. The constable and Hermsdorf persuaded her to go away. She cursed and swore in the utmost transport of passion, threatening to kill the first man that should come near her. Alas, my brother! what has become of thy hopeful convert?[11]

In the afternoon, while I was talking in the street with poor Catherine [Mrs. Hawkins's maid], her mistress came up to us, and fell upon me with the utmost bitterness and scurrility; said she would blow me up, and my brother, whom she once thought honest, but was now undeceived: that I was the cause of her husband's confinement; but she would be revenged, and expose my d—d hypocrisy, my prayers four times a day by the beat of a drum, and abundance more, which I cannot write, and thought no woman, though taken from Drurylane, could have spoken. I only said, I pitied her, but defied all she or the devil could do; for she could not hurt me. I was strangely preserved from passion [anger], and at parting told her, I hoped she would soon come to a better mind.

In the evening hour or retirement I resigned myself to God, in my brother's prayer for conformity to a suffering Saviour.[12]

Faint and weary with the day's fatigue, I found my want [lack] of true holiness, and begged God to give me comfort from his word. I then read, in the evening lesson, "But thou, O man of God, flee these things; and follow after righteousness, godliness, faith, love, patience, meekness. Fight the good fight of faith, lay hold on eternal life, whereunto thou art called, and hast professed a good profession before many witnesses." [1 Tim. 6:11,12] Before prayers I took a walk with Mr. Ingham, who was surprised that I should not think innocence a sufficient protection. I had not indeed acquainted him with what Mrs. Welch had told me [i.e. the lie of Oglethorpe's seduction]. At night I was forced to exchange my usual bed, the ground, for a chest, being almost speechless through a violent cold.

Wed., March 24th. I was enabled to pray earnestly for my enemies, particularly Mr. Oglethorpe, whom I now looked upon as the chief of them. Then I gave myself up entirely to God's disposal, desiring I might not now want power to pray, when I most of all needed it. Mr. Ingham then came, and read the thirty-seventh Psalm: a glorious exhortation to patience, and confidence in God, from the different estate of the good and wicked. After breakfast I again betook myself to intercession, particularly for M[rs.] W[elch], that Satan, in the shape of that other bad woman [Hawkins], might not stand at her right hand. Doubting whether I should not interpose for the prisoners, I consulted the oracle [Bible], and met Jer. 44:16, 17: "As for the word which thou has spoken to us in the name of the Lord, we will not hearken unto it: but we will certainly do whatsoever thing goeth forth out of our own mouth." This determined me not to meddle with them at all.

At eleven I met Mrs. Perkins, who told me of the infamy Mrs. Hawkins has brought upon Mr. Oglethorpe, the utter discouragement it will be to the people, if she is supported. Farther she informed me that Mrs. Welch begins to repent of having engaged so far with her, confessing she has done it through cowardice, as thinking Mr. Oglethorpe will bear her out against all the world.

Soon after I talked with Mrs. Welch and with the last degree of astonishment heard her accuse herself. Horror of horrors! Never did I feel such excess of pity. I gave myself up to prayer for her. Mr. Ingham soon joined me. All the prayers expressed a full confidence in God: when notice was given us of Mr. Oglethorpe's landing. Mrs. Hawkins, Mr. Ingham, and myself were sent for. We found him in his tent, with the people round it; Mr. and Mrs. Hawkins within. After a short hearing the officers were reprimanded, and the prisoners dismissed. At going out Mrs. Hawkins modestly told me, she had something more to say against me, but would take another time. I only answered "You know, Madam, it is impossible for *me* to fear *you*." When they were gone, Mr. Oglethorpe said he was convinced, and was glad I had had no hand in all this. I told him I had something to impart, of the last importance, when he was at leisure. He took no notice, but read his letters; and I walked away with Mr. Ingham, who was utterly astonished. The issue is just what I expected. [. . .]

Thur., March 25th. . . . At half an hour past seven Mr. Oglethorpe called me out of my hut. I looked up to God, and went. He charged me with mutiny and sedition; with stirring up the people to desert the colony. Accordingly he said they had had a meeting last night, and sent a message to him this morning, desiring leave to go; that their speaker had informed against them, and me the spring of it all; that the men were such as constantly came to prayers, therefore I must have instigated them; that he should not scruple shooting half-a-dozen of them at once; but that he had, out of kindness, *first* spoke to me. My answer was, "I desire, Sir, you would have no regard to my brothers, my friends, or the love you had for me, if anything of this is made out against me. I know nothing of their meeting or designs. Of those you mentioned, not one comes constantly to prayers, or sacrament. I never incited any one to leave the colony. I desire to answer my accuser face to face." He told me, my accuser was Mr. Lawley, whom he would bring, if I would wait here. I added, "Mr. Lawley is a man who has declared he knows no reason for keeping fair with any man, but a design to get all he can by him: but there was nothing to be got by the poor Parsons." I asked whether he himself was not assured that there were enough men in Frederica to say or swear anything against any man that should be in disgrace: whether, if he himself was removed, or succeeded ill, the whole stream of the people would be turned against him; even this Lawley, who was of all others the most violent in condemning the prisoners, and justifying the officers. I observed, this was the old cry, "Away with the Christians to the lions"; mentioned Hawkins and his wife's scandalizing my brother and me yesterday even in his presence. I asked what redress or satisfaction was due my character; and what good I could do my present parish, if cut off by their calumnies from ever seeing one half of it. I ended with assuring him, I had and should still make it my business to promote peace among all. I felt no disturbance while speaking, but lifted up my heart to God, and found him present with me. While Mr. Oglethorpe was fetching Lawley, I thought of our Lord's words, "Ye shall be brought before Governors and Kings for my sake. But when they deliver you up, take no thought how or what ye shall speak: for it shall be given you in that same hour what ye shall speak" [Matt. 10:18, 19]; and applied to Him for help, and words to make my defense.

Before Mr. Oglethorpe returned I called upon Mr. Ingham, and desired him to pray for me: then walked, and musing on the event, opened the book on Acts 15:31–33: "Which when they had read, they rejoiced for the consolation; and . . . exhorted the brethren with many words, and confirmed them. And after they had tarried there a space, they were let go in peace." Mr. Ingham coming, I related all that had passed. On sight of Mr. Oglethorpe and Lawley, he retired.

Mr. Oglethorpe observed, the place was too public. I offered to carry him to my usual walk in the woods. On our way God put it into my heart to say, "Show only the least disinclination to find me guilty, and you shall see what a turn it will give the accusation." He took the hint, and instead of calling upon Lawley to make good his charge, began with the quarrel in general; but did not show himself angry with me, or desirous to find me to blame. Lawley, who appeared full of guilt and fear, upon this dropped his accusation, or shrunk from it into my "forcing the people to prayers." I replied, that the people themselves would acquit me of that; and as to the officers' quarrel, I appealed to the officers for the truth of my assertion, that I had had no hand at all in it; professed my desire and resolution of promoting peace and obedience: and as to the people, I was persuaded their desire of leaving the colony arose from mistake, not malice. Here Mr. Oglethorpe spoke of reconciling matters; bade Lawley tell the petitioners, he would not so much ask who they were, if they were but quiet for the future. "I hope," added he, "they will be so; and Mr. Wesley here hopes so too," "Yes sir," says Lawley, "I really believe it of Mr. Wesley, and had always a very great respect for him." I turned, and said to Mr. Oglethorpe, "Did not I tell you it would be so?" He replied to Lawley, "Yes; you had always a very great respect for Mr. Wesley. You told me he was a stirrer-up of sedition, and at the bottom of all this disturbance." With this gentle reproof he dismissed him; and I thanked him for having first spoken to me of what I was accused of, begging he would always do so. This he promised, and then I walked with him to Mrs. Hawkins's door. She came out aghast to see me with him. He there left me, "and I was delivered out of the mouth of the lion."

Fri., March 26th. "My soul is always in my hand; therefore I will not forget thy law." This morning, early, Mr. Oglethorpe called me out to tell me of Mrs. Lawley's miscarriage, by being denied access to the Doctor for bleeding.[13] He seemed very angry, and to charge me with it; saying he should be a tryant if he passed by such intolerable injuries. I answered, I knew nothing of the matter, and it was hard it should be imputed to me; that from the first Hermsdorf told the Doctor he might visit whom of his patients he pleased; but the Doctor would not. I denied my having the least hand in the whole business, as Hermsdorf himself had declared. He [Oglethorpe] said, "Hermsdorf assured me, what he did, he did by your advice." I answered, "You must mistake his imperfect English; for many have heard him say the contradictory of this. Yet I must be charged with all the mischief." "How else can it be," said he, "that there should be no love, no meekness, no true religion among the people? but instead of that, mere formal prayers." "As to that I can answer for them, that they have no more of the form of godliness than the power. I have seldom seen above six of them at public service. . . ."

Mr. Oglethorpe, meeting me in the evening, asked when I had prayers. I said, I waited his pleasure. While the people came slowly, "You see, Sir," said I, "they do not lay too great a stress on forms." "The reason of that is, because others idolize them." "I believe few stay away for that reason." "I don't know that." Mr. Oglethorpe stood over against me, and joined audibly in the prayers. The chapter was designed for me, and I read it with great boldness, as follows:—"I charge thee before God, and the Lord Jesus Christ, who shall judge the quick and the dead at his appearing. . . ." [2 Tim. 4:1–3, 5, 16–18]

Sat., March 27th. This morning we began our Lord's last discourses to his disciples: every word was providentially directed to my comfort, but particularly those: "Let not your heart be troubled: ye believe in God, believe also in me." "I will not leave you comfortless: I will come to you." "Peace I leave with you, my peace I give unto you. Let not your heart be troubled, neither let it be afraid." (John 14:1, 18, 27)

I was sensibly concerned this afternoon at hearing that Mrs. Welch is growing more and more like Mrs. Hawkins, declares she will no longer be priest-ridden, jests upon prayers, and talks in the loose, scandalous dialect of her friend. In the evening a thought came into my mind of sending Mr. Ingham for my brother. He was much adverse to leaving me in my trials, but was at last persuaded to go.

Sun., March 28th. I went to the storehouse (our tabernacle at present) to hearken what the Lord would say concerning me. Both myself and the congregation were struck with the first lesson: Joseph and Potiphar's wife. The second was still more animating: "If the world hate you, ye know that it hated Me before it hated you. If ye were of the world, the world would love its own." (John 15:18, 19) After the prayers poor Mr. Davidson stayed behind to take his leave of Mr. Ingham. He burst into tears, and said: "One good man is leaving us already. I can foresee nothing but desolation. Must my poor children be brought up like these savages?" We endeavoured to comfort him by showing him his calling. At ten Mr. Ingham preached an alarming sermon on the day of judgement, and joined me in offering up the Christian sacrifice [the Eucharist].

In my walk at noon I was full of heaviness; complained to God that I had no friend but Him; and even in Him could now find no comfort. Immediately I received power to pray; then, opening my Bible, read as follows: "Hearken unto Me, ye that seek the Lord; look unto the rock whence ye are hewn." "Fear ye not the reproach of men, neither be ye afraid of their revilings." "Who art thou, that thou shouldst be afraid of a man that shall die; . . . and has feared continually every day because of the fury of the oppressor? and where is the fury of the oppressor?" [Isa. 51:1, 2, 12, 13] After reading this, no wonder that I found myself renewed with confidence.

While Mr. Ingham waited for the boat, I took a turn with Mr. Horton. He fully convinced me of Mrs. Hawkins's true character: ungrateful in the highest degree, a common prostitute, a complete hypocrite. He told me her husband and she had begged him upon their knees to intercede with Mr. Oglethorpe not to turn them out of the ship, which would be their utter ruin. This he accordingly did; though Mr. Oglethorpe at first assured him he had rather given one hundred pounds than take them. The first person she fell upon [attacked], after this, was Mr. Horton himself, whom she abused as she has since me. From him I hastened to the water-side, where I found Mr. Ingham just put off. O happy, happy friend! *Abiit, erupit, evasit!* [Latin: He departed, he burst forth, he escaped!]¹⁴ But woe is me, that I am still constrained to dwell with Meshech!¹⁵ I languished to bear him company, followed him with my eyes till out of sight, and then sunk into deeper dejection than I had known before.

Mon., March 29th. I was revived by those words of our Lord: "These things have I spoken unto you, that you should not be offended. They shall put you out of the synagogues: yea, the time cometh, that whosoever killeth you will think that he doeth God service. And these things will they do unto you, because they have not known the Father, nor me." "In the world ye shall have tribulation: but be of good cheer; I have overcome the world." (John 16:1–3, 33)

Knowing I was to live with Mr. Oglethorpe, I had brought nothing with me from England, except my clothes and books; but this morning, asking a servant for something I wanted (I think a tea-kettle), I was told Mr. Oglethorpe had given orders that no one should use any of his things. I answered, that order, I supposed, did not extend to me. "Yes, Sir," says she, "you was excepted by name." Thanks be to God, that it is not yet made capital [crime] to give me a morsel of bread.

Tues., March 30th. Having laid hitherto on the ground, in a corner of Mr. Reed's hut, and hearing some boards were to be disposed of, I attempted in vain to get some of them to lie upon. They were given to all besides. The Minister of Frederica must be *aphirator, athemistos, anestios* [Greek: incorruptible, lawless, relaxed]. Yet are we not hereunto called, *astatein, kakopathein* [Greek: homeless, afflicted].Even the Son of man had not where [*sic.*] to lay his head! [Matt. 8:20]

I find the Scripture an inexhaustible fund of comfort. 'Is my hand shortened at all, that it cannot save? or have I no power to deliver? I gave my back to the smiters, and my cheeks to them that plucked off the hair. I hid not my face from shame and spitting. For the Lord God will help me, therefore shall I not be confounded. Therefore I have set my face like a flint; and I know that I shall not be ashamed. He is near that justifieth me; who will contend with me? Let us stand together. Who is mine adversary? let him come near to me. Behold, the Lord God will help me: who is he that shall condemn me?"

Wed., March 31st. I begin now to be abused and slighted into an opinion of my own considerableness. I could not be more trampled upon, was I a fallen Minister of state. The people have found out that I am in disgrace, and all the cry is

Curramus praecipites, et
Dum jacit in ripa calcemus Caesaris hostem

[Latin: Let's run headlong, and while he lies upon the bank, let's trample the enemy of Caesar].[16]

My few well-wishers are afraid to speak to me. Some have turned out of the way to avoid me. Others desired I would not take it ill, if they seemed not to know me when we should meet. The servant that used to wash my linen sent it back unwashed. It was a great cause of triumph my being forbid the use of Mr. Oglethorpe's things, and in effect debarred of most of the conveniences, if not necessaries, of life. I sometimes pitied, and sometimes diverted myself with, the odd expressions of their contempt; but found the benefit of having undergone a much lower degree of obloquy at Oxford.

Thur., April 1st. . . . Hitherto I have been borne up by a spirit not my own; but exhausted nature at last prevails. It is amazing she held out so long. My outward hardships and inward conflicts, the bitterness of reproach from the only man I wished to please,

> At last have borne my boasted courage down

Accordingly, this afternoon, I was forced by a friendly fever to take to my bed. My sickness, I knew, could not be of long continuance; but, as I was in want of every help and convenience, must either shortly leave me, or release me from farther [sic.] suffering.

In the evening Mrs. Hird and Mrs. Robinson called to see me, and offered me all the assistance in their power. I thanked them, but desired they would not prejudice themselves by taking this notice of me. . . .

Sat., April 3d. Nature I found endeavoured to throw off the disease by excessive sweats: I therefore drank whatever my women brought me.

Sun., April 4th. Many of the people had been ill of the bloody flux. I escaped hitherto by my vegetable diet; but now my fever brought it. Notwithstanding this, I was obliged to go abroad, and preach, and administer the sacrament. My sermon on, "Keep innocency, and take heed to the thing that is right, for this shall bring a man peace at the last," was deciphered into a satire against Mrs. Hawkins. At night I got an old bedstead to lie on, being that on which the scout-boat man had died.

Mon., April 5th. At one this morning the sandflies forced me to rise, and smoke them out of the hut. The whole town was employed in the same manner. My congregation in the evening consisted of two Presbyterians and a Papist. I went home in great pain, my distemper being much increased with the little duty I could discharge.

Tues., April 6th. I found myself so faint and weak, that with the utmost difficulty I got through the prayers. Mr. Davidson, my good Samaritan, would often call, or send his wife to tend me: and to their care, under God, I owe my life.

To-day Mr. Oglethorpe gave away my bedstead from under me, and refused to spare one of the carpenters to mend me up another.

Fri., April 16th. My brother brought me off a resolution, which honor and indignation had formed, of starving rather than ask for necessaries. Accordingly I went to Mr. Oglethorpe, in his tent, to ask for some little things I wanted. He sent for me back again, and said, "Pray Sir, sit down. I have something to say to you. I hear you have spread several reports about [the following material was written in shorthand][17] *me and Mrs. Hawkins. In this you are the author of them. There is a great difference in telling such things to another and to me. In you who told it your brother, 'tis scandal; in him who repeated it to me, 'tis friendship. My religion does not, like the Pharisees', consist in long prayers, but in forgiving injuries, as I do this of yours, not but that the thing is in itself a trifle and hardly deserves a serious answer; though I gave one to your brother because he believed the report true. 'Tis not such things as these which hurt my character. They would pass for gallantries and rather commend me to the world."*

Here he made slight of the matter, at the same time vindicating himself from the imputations, and went on: "I know many suppose a thirst for fame the motive of all my actions, but they are mistaken. I have had more than my share of it, and my fortune is now, I believe, on the turn."

After lifting my heart up to God I replied: "I come first [i.e. to the point]; *as you suppose me guilty, 'tis the greatest kindness that you can forgive me. I shall only speak the truth and leave you to judge of it. I absolutely deny the whole charge. I have neither raised nor spread this report, but wherever I heard it, checked it immediately. Some who themselves spoke it in my hearing have, I suppose, gone, and fathered their own words upon me. I had myself mentioned this to you, had I still continued in your favour. I did mention it to my brother, that he might tell it to you. Suppose I myself believed it, I should never have propagated* [it], *because I am not to speak evil of the ruler of my people. The ground of the people's suspicion was Mrs. Hawkins's great assurance during her confinement. All they say of you they say of my brother and her. She said so herself, at first, but has since eaten her words. The letter she intercepted was wrote before this report was heard of. I own, to suffer thus as an evildoer, and from you, is the severest trial I have ever known. My shyness was caused by yours. As I shall always think it my duty to please you to the utmost of my power, I hope you will look upon me as you used to do. I know your unforgiving temper, and that if you once entertain a suspicion or dislike, it is next to impossible to remove it." He promised to be the same to me as before.*]. . . .

The next day my brother and Mr. Delamotte set out in an open boat for Savannah. I preached in the afternoon on "He that now goeth on his way weeping, and beareth forth good seed, shall doubtless come again with joy and bring his sheaves with him."

Easter Eve, April 24th. At ten I was sent for by Mr. Oglethorpe. He began: "Mr. Wesley, you know what has passed between us. I took some pains to satisfy your brother about the reports concerning me, but in vain. He here renews his suspicions in writing. I did desire to convince him, because I had an esteem for him; and he is just so considerable to me as my esteem makes him. I could clear up all, but it matters not. You will soon see the reason of my actions.

I am now going to death. You will see me no more. Take this ring, and carry it from me to Mr. V[ernon, one of the trustees of the colony]. If there is a friend to be depended upon, he is the one. His interest is next to Sir Robert's. Whatever you ask, within his power, he will do for you, your brother, and your family. I have expected death for some days. These letters show that the Spaniards have long been seducing our allies, and intend to cut us off at a blow. I fall by my friends;—Gascoin, whom I have made; the Carolina people, whom I depended upon to send their promised succours. But death is to me nothing. Towers will pursue all my designs; and to him I recommend them and you."

He then gave me a diamond ring: I took it, and said: "If, as I believe, *Postremum fato, quod te alloquor, hoc est* [Latin: Last of all it is by this fate that I address you],[18] hear what you will quickly know to be true, as soon as you are entered upon the separate state. This ring I shall never make any use of for myself. I have no worldly hopes. I have renounced the world. Life is bitterness to me. I came hither to lay it down. You have been deceived, as well as I. I protest my innocence as to the crimes I am charged with; and take myself to be now at liberty to tell you what I thought never to have uttered. [The following is in shorthand.] *Mrs. Welch excited in me the first suspicion of you after we were come here. She afterwards told you her own words as if they had been mine. This she confessed both to my brother and me, as likewise that she had falsely accused me to you of making love to her. She was put upon it by Mrs. Hawkins saying, "Let us supplant those parsons, and we shall have Mr. Oglethorpe to ourselves."*[19]

When I had finished this relation he seemed entirely changed, full of his old love and confidence in me. . . .

Thur., April 29th. About half-hour past eight I went down to the bluff, to see a boat coming up. At nine it arrived with Mr. Oglethorpe. I blessed God for still holding his soul in life. In the evening we took a walk together, and he informed me more particularly of our past danger. . . . I gave him back his ring, and said, "I need not, Sir, and indeed cannot, tell you how joyfully and thankful I return this. . . ."

Wed., July 21st. I heard by my brother that I was to set sail in a few days for England.

Sun., July 25th. I resigned my Secretary's place, in a letter to Mr. Oglethorpe. After prayers he took me aside, and asked me whether all I had said was not summed up in the line he showed me on my letter:— *Magis apta tuis tua dona relinquo* [Latin: I leave as gifts things more suitable to yours]. "Sir, to yourself your slighted gifts I leave, / Less fit for me to take than you to give."

I answered, I desired not to lose his esteem, but could not preserve it with the loss of my soul. He answered, he was satisfied of my regard for him; owned my argument drawn from the heart unanswerable; and yet, said he, "I would desire you not to let the Trustees know your resolution of resigning. There are many hungry fellows ready to catch at the office; and in my absence I cannot put in one of my own choosing. The best I can hope for is an honest Presbyterian, as many of the Trustees are such. Perhaps they may send me a bad man; and how far such a one may influence the traders, and obstruct the reception of the Gospel among the Heathen, you know. I shall be in England before you leave it. Then you may either put in a deputy or resign.

You need not be detained in London above three days; and only speak to some of my particular friends (Vernon, Hutchinson, and Towers), to the Board of Trustees, when called upon, and the Board of Trade.

On many accounts I should recommend to you marriage, rather than celibacy. You are of a social temper, and would find in a married state the difficulties of working out your salvation exceedingly lessened, and your helps as much increased."

Mon., July 26th. The words which concluded the lesson and my stay in Georgia, were, "Arise, let us go hence." Accordingly at twelve I took my final leave of Savannah. When the boat put off I was surprised that I felt no more joy in leaving such a scene of sorrows.

[Sat.], July 31st. I arrived with my brother at Charlestown. I lay the night at an inn. Next morning I was much rejoiced at hearing Mr. Appee was still in town, waiting for my company to England. His ingenuous, open temper, and disengagement from the world, made me promise myself a very improving and agreeable voyage: especially as I doubted not but the sudden death of his mistress had taken off that appearance of lightness, which I attributed rather to his youth and education, than any natural inconstancy. After breakfasting with Mr. Eveley, a merchant who had bespoke lodgings for us, I went in quest of my friend. We met with equal satisfaction on both sides: but I did not observe those deep traces of sorrow and seriousness which I expected. I asked him whether his loss had had its due effect, in making his heart more tender, and susceptible of divine impressions. By his answer I concluded his heart was right, and its uppermost desire was to recover the divine image.

Something of this desire I felt myself at the holy sacrament, and found myself encouraged, by an unusual hope of pardon, to strive against sin.

Mon., August 2d. I had observed much, and heard more, of the cruelty of masters towards their negros; but now I received an authentic account of some horrid instances thereof. The giving a child a slave of its own age to tyrannize over, to beat and abuse out of sport, was, I myself saw, a common practice. Nor is it strange, being thus trained up in cruelty, they should afterwards arrive at so great perfection in it; that Mr. Star, a gentleman I often met at Mr. Lasserre's, should, as he himself informed L[asserre], first nail up a negro by his ears, then order him to be whipped in the severest manner, and then to have scalding water thrown over him, so that the poor creature could not stir for months after. Another much-applauded punishment is, drawing their slaves' teeth. One Colonel Lynch is universally known to have cut off a poor negro's legs; and to kill several of them every year by his barbarities.

It were endless to recount all the shocking instances of diabolical cruelty these men (as they call themselves) daily practice upon their fellow-creatures; and that on the most trivial occasions. I shall only mention one more, related to me by a Swiss gentleman, Mr. Zouberbuhler, an eye-witness, of Mr. Hill, a dancing-master in Charlestown. He whipped a she-slave so long, that she fell down at his feet for dead. When, by the help of a physician, she was so far recovered as to show signs of life, he repeated the whipping with equal rigour, and concluded with dropping hot sealing-wax upon her flesh. Her crime was over-filling a tea-cup.

These horrid cruelties are the less to be wondered at, because the government itself countenances and allows them to kill their slaves, by the ridiculous penalty appointed for it, of about eleven pounds sterling, half of which is usually saved by the criminal's informing on himself. This I can look upon as no other than a public act [statute] to indemnify murder.

Wed., August 11th. Coming on board our ship, I found the honest Captain had let my cabin to another. My flux and fever that has hung upon me, forced me for some nights past to go into a bed; but now my only bed was a chest, on which I threw my self in my boots, and was not over much troubled with sleep till morning. What was still worse, I then had no asylum to fly from the Captain; the most beastly man I ever saw; a lewd, drunken quarrelsome fool; praying, and yet swearing continually. The first sight I had of him was upon the cabin-floor, stark naked, and dead drunk.

Fri., August 13th. The wind was still contrary; so that we were forced to lie off the bar, about five miles from Charlestown.

Mon., August 16th. A faint breeze springing up, the pilot, weary of waiting a week to no purpose, said he would venture over the bar, though he feared there was not water enough. Accordingly we attempted it, and got above half of the two miles between us and the sea, when a violent squall arose, and drove the ship before it with incredible swiftness. Before it began we were almost becalmed, so that it saved the ship, at least, from being aground, though with the immediate hazard both of that and our lives. The sailors were in great consternation, expecting to be stranded every moment. The pilot cursed the ship most heartily, and the hour he set foot on her. Having scraped along the ground for some minutes before, the ship at last stuck. She got clear, and stuck fast a second time; immediately fell into seven fathom of water.

The Mate afterwards told me, it was one thousand to one but she had been lost by the Captain's folly and ignorance, in letting fly the mainsail, while we were struck [sic] on the bar; which was the surest way to fix her there; as it must have done had we not been on the very edge of it.

Tues., August 17th. We were much surprised (the passengers, I mean) at finding, as soon as over the bar, that two of our twelve sailors were obliged to pump every half-hour.

Sat., August 28th. After a restless, tempestuous night, I hardly rose at eight. Our happier Captain, having got his dose, could sleep a day and a night upon the stretch, and defy either pumps or squall to wake him.

Mon., August 30th. At noon we were alarmed by an outcry of the sailors, at their having continued pumping several hours, without being able to keep the water under. They desired the Captain to put into some port, before they were got out to sea too far for returning; but he was too drunk to regard them. At five the sailors came down in a body to the great cabin, waked, and told him it was as much as their lives were worth to proceed on the voyage, unless their leaks were stopped; that he remembered it was as much as they could do to keep the ship above water in their passage from Boston, being forced to pump without ceasing; that the turpentine fell down upon, and choked up the pumps continually: nor was it possible to get at it, or to hold it out in such continual labour; which made them so thirsty, they could not live on their allowance of water; that they must come to shorter still, through his neglect to take in five more hogsheads of water, as his Mate advised him; that he owned they had no candles for half the voyage: on all which accounts they begged him to consider whether their common safety did not require them to put in at some land, for more water and candles, and, above all, to stop their leaks. The Captain, having now slept out his rum, replied, "To be sure, the men talked reason," and without consulting any of his officers, immediately gave orders to stand away for Boston.

Wed., September 22d. Having sailed for some hours without discovering land, we began to think the light which the Mate had seen was of some ship, and not the lighthouse. At two we made land; which the men found to be Cape Cod, about eighteen leagues from Boston. The wind blew from shore, yet we kept our course. At midnight the storm gave place to a calm. These have constantly succeeded each other since our leaving Charlestown.

Fri., September 24th. Being within sight of the lighthouse, at nine in the morning, the pilot came on board us. At two I gladly obeyed his hasty summons, and went into his boat with the other passengers, bidding an hearty farewell to our wretched ship, and more wretched Captain, who for the last two days had, most happily for us, lain dead drunk on the floor, without sense or motion.

I was at leisure now to contemplate a prospect entirely new, beautiful beyond all I had ever seen. We sailed smoothly on, in a vast basin, as it seemed, bounded on all sides with small innumerable islands. Some of these were entire rock, in height and colour not unlike Dover cliffs: others steep, and covered with woods. Here and there lay a round hill, entirely clothed with green; and all at such equal distances, that the passages seemed artificially made, to admit the narrow streams between.

Having passed one of these passages, we were presented with a new set of hills, and rocks, and woods, in endless variety; till we came to the castle, three miles from Boston. From thence we had a full view of the town, stretched out a mile and a half upon the shore in a semi-circle. We landed at Long Wharf, which we walked straight up, having a row of houses on one side, and near two hundred sail [sic] of ships on the other. I lodged at a public house; went to bed at eleven. Appee followed me, drunk, between one and two in the morning.

Sat., September 25th. I called several times at Mr. Price, the Commissary's, before I found him at home. At first he looked as not believing me to be a Clergyman (my ship-clothes not being the best credentials). But when I returned in my habit (Dr. Cutler having met him in meantime, informed him of me), he received me very cordially, and pressed me to live with him while I stayed in Boston.

Sun., September 26th. I preached in the morning at Dr. Cutler's church, in the afternoon at Mr. Price's, on the one thing needful. [Cf. No. 6.]

In the evening I first fell into company with Mr. John Chicheley, a right honest zealous advocate for the Church of England, who has, on that account, been cruelly persecuted by the Presbyterians.

Fri., October 1st. I wrote to my brother concerning my return to Georgia, which I found myself inclined to refer wholly to God.

Sat., October 2d. I rode out with Mr. Price, in his chaise, to see the country, which is wonderfully delightful. The only passage out of town is a neck of land about two hundred yards over; all the rest being encircled with the sea. The temperate air, the clear rivulets, and the beautiful hills and dales, which we everywhere met with, seemed to present the very reverse of Georgia.

Sun., October 3d. After near two months' want [lack] of it, I again enjoyed the benefit of the sacrament, which I assisted Dr. Cutler to administer. I preached on, "There the wicked cease from troubling, and there the weary are at rest": as I did again in the afternoon of Mr. Price, though I found my strength sensibly abated.

Sun., October 17th. While I was talking at Mr. Chicheley's on spiritual religion, his wife observed that I seemed to have much the same way of thinking with Mr. Law. Glad I was and surprised to hear that good man mentioned; and confessed, all I knew of religion was through him. I found she was well acquainted with this *Serious Call*; and has one of the two that are in New England. I borrowed it, and passed the evening in reading it to the family (Mr. Williams's, where I have been some days). His daughter and he seemed satisfied and affected.

Tuesday and Wednesday. I grew worse and worse; and on Thursday, October 21st, was forced to keep [to] my chamber through pain. Appee came, and laboured all he could to dissuade me from the voyage, promising himself to deliver my letters and papers, and excuse me to Mr. Oglethorpe. Mr. Price, Williams, &c., joined him: but I put an end to their importunity, by assuring them, nothing less than death should hinder my embarking.

Thur., December 2d. By four in the afternoon we came within sight of Beachy-Head; but the wind refreshing, by nine we found ourselves almost unawares over against Dover. . . . I returned thanks to God for bringing us to the haven where we would be; got my few things in readiness, and laid me down, without disquiet or impatience for two or three hours.

Sat., December 4th. Appee was so very grievous to us, that not only I, but all the passengers, resolved this should be the last day of their acquaintance. At six in the evening we came safe to London. I immediately took coach for Charles Rivington's, leaving my friend Appee, who promised to come the next day, and pay what he owed me.

My namesake was much rejoiced to see me, and gave me great cause of rejoicing by his account of our Oxford friends.

No. 5   Sermon: "The Single Eye"

This sermon and the one which follows it were probably composed by John Wesley and transcribed from his copies by Charles during the Atlantic crossing. These sermons were first published in an 1816 edition prepared by Charles's widow (*Sermons by the Late Charles Wesley*) and are reprinted here from that copy. Each of these sermons was preached by Charles in America, as his journal indicates.

"The Single Eye" is a significant example of Charles's early preaching, since it follows the standard homiletical style of the day, and establishes purity of intention as a dominant theme of the brothers' homilies, prior to their famous conversions in May 1738. Sanctification is described as an utter consecration of the whole person to God. Holiness meant wholeness for the Wesleys, and even in this early example their vision was full-orbed. The sermon was preached by Charles on March 14, 1736, during his first Sunday service among the colonists of Frederica.

The light of the body is the eye: if therefore thine eye be single, thy whole body shall be full of light. But if thine eye be evil, thy whole body shall be full of darkness. [Matt. 6:22, 23]
The good providence of God hath at length brought you to the haven where you desired to be. This is the time which you so wished to find— this is the place you have so longed to arrive at. What then ought to be your thoughts, your designs, your resolutions, now the Almighty God hath granted your heart's desire? Consider well what ought to be your conduct; now choose whether you will serve God or not: but consider that if you do serve him, you must do it with all your mind; that no man can serve two masters, for ye cannot serve God and Mammon; either you must give to God your whole heart, or none. He cannot, will not, have a divided heart; either wholly lay aside the thoughts of pleasing him, and choose another master, or let the pleasing him be your one aim in all your thoughts, all your words, and all your actions. Believe your Lord himself, you can find no middle way: "The light of the body is the eye; if therefore thine eye be single, thy whole body shall be full of light: but if thine eye be not single, but evil, thy whole body shall be full of darkness."

I am persuaded there is no one of you here present that will not earnestly attend while, in the name of that God who hath hitherto defended us, and is now present with us, I

First briefly explain these important words of our Lord, and

Secondly apply them to the present circumstances.

And first, may the God who spoke them enable me so to explain them, that the meaning may sink deep into your hearts!

"The light of the body is the eye"; that is, the intention is to the soul what the eye is to the body. As every part of the body is directed by the eye, so every power of the soul is in all its movements directed by the intention!

As every turn of the foot or hand depends upon and is governed by the eye, so on the eye of the mind depends every deliberate movement of the understanding and the affections, and consequently of whatever depends upon these, as do most of our words and actions. If therefore thine eye be single, that is, if thy intention be not divided into two ends—if in all thy thoughts, words, and works, thou hast only one view, namely, to serve and please God, thy whole body shall be full of light; this single intention will be a light in all thy paths; all darkness will vanish before it, all will be plain before thy face; thou wilt clearly see the way wherein thou shouldest go, and steadily walk therein.

But if thine eye be evil, if thy intention be not single, if thou hast a divided aim, if besides that of pleasing God thou hast a desire to please thyself, to do thy own will—if thou aimest at anything but the one thing needful, namely, a recovery of the image of God in thy soul, thy whole body shall be full of darkness: thou wilt see no light which way soever thou turnest thyself; never wilt thou be free from doubt and perplexity, never out of uncertainty and entanglement.

As thou art continually aiming at what cannot be achieved, thou wilt be continually disappointed. The thick darkness of ignorance, and guilt, and misery, will gather around thee more and more, nor wilt thou be able while encompassed with such a cloud, ever to recover the way of light and peace.

The sum is this: as long as thou hast but one end in all thy thoughts, and words, and actions, to please God, or, which is the same thing, to improve in his ways of holiness, in the love of God, and of thy neighbor, so long shalt thou clearly perceive what is conducive to it. Thy God, whom thou servest, shall so tenderly watch over thee, that light, and love, and peace, shall guide all thy ways, and shine upon all thy paths; but no sooner shalt thou divide thy heart, and aim at any other end but holiness, than the light from which thou turnest away being withdrawn, thou shalt not know whither thou goest: ignorance, sin and misery, shall overspread thee, till thou fallest into utter darkness.

Secondly, to apply these words to your present circumstances was the next thing proposed; in order to do which more effectually, I shall, by the assistance of God, give you some directions concerning a single intention, and exhort you to practice them.

I would not willingly believe that any of you need to be directed to have a single eye in your religious exercises. To aim at the favour or praise of men, or indeed any thing beside the pleasing of God, in sacrament, prayer, or any duty of the like nature, is such an affront both to God and man, that we should be very cautious of charging any one with it, even in our heart. It may be enough, therefore, barely to observe, that there is no name sufficiently expressive of the folly of those hypocrites who in any of these solemn offices have any other view than to please God and save their own souls.

But you are not, perhaps, so well aware that the same singleness of intention is full as necessary in every part of business as it is in your devotions; yet this is the very truth. Unless your single view be to please God, and to be upright before him, the most lawful business becomes unsanctified; for it is no more allowed a Christian to work, than it is to pray, with any other intention; and a mixture of impure motives does as much pollute our employments as it does our prayers.

Everything that proceeds from, and is suitable to, this intention, is holy, just and good; and every thing which does not proceed from an upright heart and single eye is so far evil and unholy.

This, therefore, is the second direction I would give—to preserve a single intention in all your business, which indeed converts it into religion, which ennobles every employment, and renders the meanest offices of life a reasonable sacrifice, acceptable to God through Jesus Christ.

Nor is a single eye less essential in our refreshments than in our occupations and devotions, as every creature of God is good, if be sanctified by the Spirit of God and by prayer.

Without this sort of prayer, at least an *intention to please* him by using it, no creature is good, nor can be used without injury to ourselves; and lest we should imagine that meats and drinks were too little and insignificant matters for the Almighty to regard, he has been graciously pleased to remove this suspicion, by giving you a third direction in express words by his apostle, "whether ye eat or drink, or whatever ye do, do all to the glory of God." [1 Cor. 10:31]

Whatever ye do:—this plainly comprises our recreations as well as refreshments; a fourth direction therefore equally important is, let the same pure intention be preserved in these likewise. It is his will that you should use exercise for your health, and delight your eyes with the works of nature and the wonders of creation, in such a measure and manner as will prepare you for business or devotion; so far, therefore, as your present state renders them necessary, to this end you are to use them, and no other.

One direction more is important before I close this head, and that is, that you, above all others, are required to keep a single eye in your conversations. Whether devotion or business be the subject, or whether you converse for social enjoyment and recreation, in whatever case, you are enjoined to aim at the glory of God. Any other motive is evil, and comes from evil: it is an idle word, or conversation, rather, as the term should be translated; and of every such idle word, our Lord plainly tells us, we shall give an account at the day of judgement.

I have now laid before you, in the plainest manner I was able, the directions wherein this single intention must be observed; nothing remains but to exhort you instantly, zealously, and diligently, to practice them.

The God of your fathers hath lately given you a most gracious testimony that he hath not forsaken you or your children. Your eyes have seen that 'his ears are not heavy that they should not hear, neither his hand shortened that it cannot save.' You have cried unto him in your trouble, and he hath delivered you out of your distress. He hath led you through the terrors of the great deep; he there made bare his mighty arm before you—at his word the stormy wind arose and lifted up the waves thereof—we reeled to and fro, and staggered like drunken men, and were at our wits' end, when he made the storm to cease so that the waves thereof were still. He hath prepared a table for you in the way wherein you went; even there, with corn and wine hath he sustained you. Some of you he hath raised from sickness, to some he hath forbidden sickness to approach; to all of you, who allowed spiritual blessings, he hath afforded them. Yea in these he hath spoken to the hearts even of some who were unmindful of his mercies; and now 'he hath brought you to the haven where ye would be.' What reward then will ye give unto the Lord for all the benefits he hath done for you? Love him with all your hearts, serve him with all your strength, forget the things which are behind—pleasures, riches, honours—in a word, whatever does not lead to God.

Behold all things about you are become new, be ye likewise new creatures. From this hour let your eye be single. Whatever ye speak, or think, or do, let God be your aim, and God alone. Let your great end be to please him, in all your business, your refreshments, your recreations, your converse, as well as in religious duties.—Let this be your one design.

"He that hath ears to hear, let him hear." Have one intention, one desire, one hope, even that the God whom ye worship may be your God, and your All, in time and in eternity!

O be not of a double mind, think of nothing else, seek nothing else—to love God and be beloved by him is enough!

Fix your eyes upon this one point, and your whole soul shall be full of light! God will continually lift up the light of his countenance upon you, his Holy Spirit shall dwell in you, and shine more and more unto the perfect day. He shall purify your hearts by faith from every earthly thought and unholy affection; he shall establish your souls with so lively a hope of his favour, as already lays hold on the prize of your high calling; he shall fill you with peace, and joy, and love—love, the brightness of his glory, the express of his person—love which never ceaseth, never faileth, but still extends its vivifying flame, still goeth on conquering and to conquer, till what was a weak, blind, wavering, sinful creature shall be filled with all the fulness of God, and worship in his presence when time shall be no more!

No. 6   Sermon: "The One Thing Needful"
(CW *Sermons*, 1816)

Charles Wesley preached this sermon twice on September 26, 1736, while he was in Boston waiting for his ship to be made seaworthy enough for the voyage back to England. The sermon was also preached in England, both before and after Charles's conversion.[20] During the Wesleyan revival it became his springboard into extemporaneous preaching.[21] "The One Thing Needful" gives further elaboration to Charles's conception of Christian Perfection, emphasizing the symmetry and unqualified character of it; both of these elements would later distinguish his conception of sanctification from that of his brother John.

One Thing Is Needful. [Luke 10:42]
  Could we imagine an intelligent being, entirely a stranger to the state of this world and its inhabitants, to take a view of their various enterprises and employments, and thence conjecture the end of their existence, he surely would conclude that these creatures were designed to be occupied with many things: while he observed not only the difference of the ends which different men were pursuing, but how vast a multitude of objects were successively pursued by almost every person, he fairly might infer that the sons of men were placed upon the earth to gratify their several inclinations either with pleasure, riches, honor, or power.
  How astonished would he be to hear their Creator declare to all without distinction—"One thing is needful!" but how much more astonished when he knew that this one thing needful for all men, their own business, the one end of their existence, was none of all those things which occupied mankind, none of all those ends they were pursuing, none of all those engagements wherein they were so deeply absorbed, which filled their hearts and employed their hands—nay, that it was an end not only distinct from, but contrary to them all; as contrary as light and darkness, heaven and hell, the kingdom of God and that of Satan!
  The only thought he could form in their favour must be, that they had a surplusage of time at their command, and therefore trifled a few hours because they were assured of thousands of years wherein to work. But how beyond measure would he be amazed when informed that these were creatures of a day; that as they yesterday arose out of the dust, so tomorrow they would return to it; that the time allotted for their great work

was but a span long, a little speck, a moment, and yet that they had no manner of assurance of not being snatched away in the midst of this moment, or indeed at the very commencement of it—when he saw all men were placed on a narrow, weak, tottering bridge, either end of which was swallowed up in eternity! that the waves and storms that passed over it were continually bearing away one after another in an hour when they expected it not; and that those who yet stood knew not but they should plunge into the great gulf the very next instant, but well knew that if they fell before they had finished the end of their existence they were lost, destroyed, undone—forever!

How would all utterance, nay, all idea[s] be lost! how would he express, how would he conceive the senselessness, the madness, of those creatures who, being in such a situation, could think of any thing, could speak of any thing else, could do any thing else besides, could find time for any other design or care, but of ensuring—the one thing needful!

It cannot, therefore, be an improper employment,

First, to observe what this one thing is; and,

Secondly, to consider a few of the numerous reasons that prove this to be the one thing needful.

We may first observe what this one thing is, in which many things are comprised; as are all the works of our callings, all that properly belong to our several stations in this world; insomuch that whoever neglects any of these so far neglects the one thing needful; and this indeed can no otherwise be pursued than by performing them in such a manner as in and by every one to advance our great work. Now this great work, this one thing needful, is the renewal of our fallen nature. In the image of God was man created, but a little lower than the angels: his nature was perfect, angelical, divine; he was a dignified image of the God of glory; he bore his stamp on every part of his soul; the brightness of his Creator shone mightily upon him. But sin has now effaced the image of God! He is no longer nearly allied to angels; alas! he is sunk lower than the very beasts of the field! His soul is not only earthly, addicted to covetousness and idolatry—sensual, a lover of pleasure more than of God; but devilish, inclined to hatred, malice, and revenge! Thus is the mighty fallen! the glory is departed from him; his lustre is swallowed up in utter darkness!

From the glorious liberty in which he was created, he is fallen into the basest bondage. That evil spirit, whose slave he is now become, holds him so fast in prison that he cannot extricate himself. He hath bound him with a thousand chains, even the heavy chains of his own vile affections; for every inordinate appetite, every unholy passion, as it is the express image of the god of this world, so it is the most galling yoke, the most grievous chain, that can bind a free-born spirit; and with these is every child of Adam, every one that is born into this world, so loaded, that he cannot lift up an eye, or raise a thought, to heaven; nay, his whole soul cleaveth to the dust! These chains of darkness under which we groan do not only hold us in on every side, but they are within us also; they enter into the inmost recesses of our soul, they pierce its very substance. Vile affections are not only so many chains, but likewise so many diseases. Our nature is distempered as well as enslaved; "the whole head is sick, and the whole heart faint." [Isa. 1:5] Our body, soul, and spirit, are infected, overspread, consumed with the most fatal moral leprosy; every one of our brutal passions and diabolical tempers, every kind of pride, sensuality, and selfishness, is one of those deadly wounds full of corruption.

To recover our first estate from which we are fallen is the one thing needful: to re-exchange the image of Satan for the image of God, bondage for freedom, sickness for health! Our one great business is to erase out of our souls the likeness of our destroyer, and to be born again, to be formed anew after the likeness of our Creator. This is our concern, to shake off this servile yoke, and regain our native liberty; to cast away every chain, every passion, that does not accord with an angelical nature. The one work we have to do is return from the gates of death, to have our diseases cured, our wounds healed, and ourselves restored to perfect soundness.

Let us in the second place consider a few of the numberless reasons which prove that this is the one thing needful, that this alone is to be kept in view, and pursued at all times and in all places; not indeed by neglecting our temporal affairs, but by making them all minister unto it: by so conducting them all, that every step therein may be a step to this higher end. Now that the recovery of the image of God, of this glorious liberty, this perfect restoration, is the one thing needful upon earth, appears first from hence, that the enjoyment of them was the end of our creation; for man was created to love God, and to this end alone, even to love the Lord his God with all his heart, and soul and mind, and strength. Love is the very image of God, it is the brightness of his glory. By love, man is not only rendered like him, but in some sense one with him. If any man love God, God loveth him, and maketh his abode with him; he dwelleth in God, and God in him; and he that is thus joined to the Lord is one spirit.

Love is perfect freedom. As there is no fear or pain, so there is no constraint in love. Whoever acts from this principle alone, he doeth whatsoever he will; all his thoughts move spontaneously, they follow the bent of his mind, and dwell on the beloved object; all his words are dictated by his heart, for out of the abundance of the heart the mouth speaketh; all his actions are the result of pure choice. Love is the breath of his soul, the full exertion of all his powers, the perfection of all its faculties; therefore since the enjoyment of these was the one end of our creation, the recovering of them is "the one thing needful."

The same truth appears, secondly from its being the end of our redemption by Jesus Christ; of all that our blessed Lord did and suffered for us; of his incarnation, his life, his death, his resurrection, his ascension into heaven, and the descent of the Holy Spirit. All these miracles of love were wrought with no other view than to restore us to health and freedom, to happiness and immortality. Thus he himself testifies of the end of his coming into this world; 'The Spirit of the Lord is upon me—he hath sent me to heal the broken-hearted, to preach deliverance to the captives'; [Luke 16:18] or, as the prophet expresses it, "to preach good tidings to the meek, to bind up the broken-hearted, to proclaim liberty to the captives, and the opening of the prison to them that are bound." [Isa. 51:1–2]

For this alone the blessed Saviour lived, that he might remove every spiritual disease from our nature; for this only he died, that he might deliver those who were all their life-time subject to bondage: and it was in pursuance of the very same design that he gave us his merciful law. The end of his command was only our health, liberty, and perfection, or in one comprehensive word, Charity; and the branches of it centre in this one point, our renewal in the love of God; either enjoining what is necessary for our recovery, or forbidding what is obstructive of it; therefore this being the one end of our redemption, as well as our creation, is the one thing needful for us upon earth.

Thirdly, it is the one end of all the dispensations of Providence. Pleasure and pain, health and sickness, riches and poverty, honour and dishonour, friends and enemies, are all bestowed by his unerring wisdom and goodness with a view to this one thing. The will of God, in allotting us our several portions of all these, is solely for our sanctification; our recovery from the vile bondage, the love of his creatures, to the free love of our Creator. All his providences, be they mild or severe, point at no other object than this; they are all designed either to wean us from what is not, or to unite us to what is, worthy of our affection. Are they pleasing? then they are intended to lift our hearts to the Parent of all good. Are they painful? then they are means of eradicating those passions that forcibly withhold us from him: so that all lead the same way, either directly or indirectly, either by gratitude, or disappointment; for to those who have ears to hear, every loss, especially of what was nearest and dearest to us, speaks as clearly as if it were an articulate voice from heaven, "Little children, keep yourselves from idols" [1 John 5:21]—every sorrow, every pain, every mortification, "Love not the world, neither the things of the world" [1 John 2:15]—every pleasure, with a small still voice, "Thou shalt love the Lord thy God with all thy heart." [Matt. 22:37, Deut. 6:5]

To the same end are all the internal dispensations of God, all the influences of his Holy Spirit, whether he gives us joy or sorrow of heart, whether he inspires us with vigour and cheerfulness, or permits us to sink into deadness of soul, into dejection and heaviness, it is the same view; namely, to restore us to health, to liberty, to holiness; these are all designed to heal those inbred diseases of our nature, self-love and the love of the world. They are all given, together with the external dispensation of our daily bread, to enable us to convert them into spiritual nourishment, and to recover his love, which is health to our souls. Therefore the renewal of our natures in this love being not only the one end of our creation and redemption, but likewise of all the providence of God over us, and all the operations of his Spirit in us, it must be as the eternal wisdom of God hath declared it, "the one thing needful."

How great reason, even in the Christian world, there is to resume the apostle's exhortation, "Awake thou that sleepest, and arise from the dead?" [Eph. 5:14—this same passage would later become the text for Charles's most famous sermon] Hath not Christ given thee light? why then sittest thou in the shadow of death? What slumber is this which oppresses thee? knowest thou not that one thing is needful? What then are these many things with which thou art encumbered? Why hath any but this great concern the least place in thy thoughts? Is the entertainment of the senses the one thing needful? or the gratifying of the imagination with uncommon, or great, or beautiful objects? Our blessed Lord speaketh not thus: he saith not that the one thing needful is to acquire wealth, or increase what thou hast already; nor yet to possess a large share of that fairest earthly fruit, learning. No; though any of these may sometimes be conducive to, not one of them is the one thing needful, which simply is to regain an angelical nature; to recover the image wherein we were formed, to be like the Most High! This alone is the one end of our abode on earth; for this alone did the Son of God pour forth his precious blood, that he might form a people to himself, "zealous of good works"; for this alone does his Holy Spirit watch over us, that we, who without this divine influence are not able to please him, may be unerringly directed to walk in his ways.

One thing we have to do, to press forward to this mark of the prize of the high calling; to emerge out of chains, diseases, death, into liberty, health, and life immortal! Let us well observe that our Lord doth not call this our *chief*, but the one thing, all others being connected with, or quite foreign to the end of life: on this let us fix our single view, our pure unmixed intention, regarding nothing, small or great, but as it has reference to this. We must use many means, but ever let us remember we have but one end; for as while our eye is single our whole body will be full of light, so, should it ever cease to be single, in that moment our whole body would be full of darkness.

Be we then continually watchful over our souls; that there be no duplicity in our intention; be it our one view in all our thoughts and words, and actions, to be partakers of the divine nature, to regain the highest measure possible of faith which works by love, that faith which unites us to God! I say, to regain the *highest measure* possible for us; for whoever will plead for any abatement of health, life, and glory? Let us then labour to be perfectly whole, to burst asunder every chain of sin and misery, to attain the fullest conquest over this body of death, the most entire renovation of our natures; knowing this, that when the Son of Man shall send forth his angels to cast the double-minded into outer darkness, then shall the single of heart receive the one thing they sought, even the salvation purchased by the Redeemer, and shine forth as the sun in the kingdom of their Father! Now to God the Father, God the Son, and God the Holy Ghost, be ascribed all honour and glory, adoration and worship, both now and for ever. Amen.

NOTES

1. Cf. *JW Works*, XIII, pp. 225–232, "Reasons Against a Separation from the Church of England."

2. This same phraseology appears in the first verse of one of Charles's unpublished hymns from the period of John's ordinations:

> And is it come to this? and has the Man
>   On whose Integrity our Church relied,
> Betray'd his trust, render'd our boastings vain,
>   And fal'n a Victim to ambitiuous Pride?

"Ms. Ordinations," No. 3, p. 3. The "boastings" refers to the Wesleys' repeated pledge never to separate from the Church of England.

3. The letter, as found in "Ms. Ordinations," has this sentence written in Byrom's shorthand, perhaps to hide Charles's somewhat cynical remark. Another copy of the letter, located in *Letters Relating to the Wesley Family*, Folio I, pp. 43–44, has the sentence written out in longhand; it is an exact transcription of the shorthand section in "Ms. Ordinations."

4. This letter was first published in *The Proceedings of the Wesley Historical Society*, 25 (June 1945), pp. 17–20, though appearing in another form, attributed to John Wesley. Frank Baker, in *Proceedings of the Wesley Historical Society*, 25 (Dec. 1946), pp. 97–104, correctly traced it to Charles Wesley's own hand.

5. Miss Anne Granville was the youngest daughter of Colonel and Mrs. Granville of Buckland. Betty Kirkham was the younger daughter of the Rev. and Mrs. Lionel Kirkham of Stanton, Gloucestershire. Her older brother was Robert Kirkham, a student at Merton College, Oxford, and member of the Holy Club. Robert was probably the initial point of contact between the Wesleys and these young ladies. There is some suggestion that he played the role of matchmaker between his sister and John Wesley, though unsuccessfully. Cf. Telford, *CW Journal*, pp. 280, 291–292.

6. The quotation is from Milton's *Paradise Lost*, I: 250–253, cited a bit imperfectly.

7. Compare *P.W.*, I, 49–51 and the 1780 *M.H.B.*, pp. 151, #CXLVIII, where John Wesley reprinted four of Charles's original six verses (3–6) in a slightly altered form.

8. Baker, *Representative Verse, op. cit.*, p. 153.

9. James Edward Oglethorpe (1696–1785) was a "soldier, statesman, philanthropist, prison reformer, founder and first governor of the colony of Georgia" (Telford, *CW Journal, ibid.*, p. 298).

10. Benjamin Ingham was a friend of the Wesleys at Oxford. He was the "moving force in three or four different groups of combinations of individuals," some of whom were styled "Methodists" and yet are not mentioned in John Wesley's Oxford diaries. Charles Wesley was Ingham's closest friend and spiritual advisor. He taught the younger student to keep a diary, gave him the rules and resolutions that shaped the Holy Club and led the small group which Ingham attended regularly. When the leaders of the Club transplanted their mission to the New World, Delamotte, a close associate of John Wesley, accompanied him to work in the Savannah area, while Ingham went to Frederica with Charles. Ingham's shorthand diary has recently been located and is now being transcribed by Richard Heitzenrater. Cf. Heitzenrater's unpublished Ph.D. dissertation, "John Wesley and the Oxford Methodists" (Duke University, 1972), pp. 32f, for a description of Ingham's role in the Oxford group.

11. *JW Journal,* I, pp. 133–136. John's journal reports both Mrs. Hawkins's contentious temper, and her desire to become a better Christian. His entry for January 12, 1736, states: "Mrs. Hawkins expressed a desire of receiving the Holy Communion. Several being apprised of it, warned me of her insincerity, and laid many crimes to her charge, of which I informed her. In the evening she replied clearly and calmly to every article of the charge, and with such an appearance of innocence as to most particulars, and of an entire change of the rest, that I could no longer doubt of her sincere desire to be not only almost but altogether a Christian. She accordingly received the Holy Communion the Sunday following and at every opportunity since. The right hand of the Lord still hath the pre-eminence, the right hand of the Lord bringeth mighty things to pass." John's shorthand diary entry for Tues., January 13, indicates that the younger brother steadfastly opposed John's resolution to admit Mrs. Hawkins to the sacrament. Certainly this opposition forms a part of the background of Charles's dispute with Hawkins, and his reference to John's convert here.

12. The Telford edition of Charles's journal incorporates a note from Dr. Hawkins, which Wesley penned into his diary in shorthand. It began, "Being by your priestly order confined, the care of the sick is no longer incumbent on me." Charles visited the physician in jail and tried in vain to convince Hawkins that he had no hand in his internment. The next day Charles's shorthand reported a further escalation of tensions as the Hawkinses and Welches engineered a jail break, in which Mrs. Hawkins twice broke water-bottles over the sentinels' heads. The longhand record resumes with the phrase "In the Evening . . ." Out of this fracas came the charges of mutiny or sedition, and the recriminations upon Charles because of the doctor's inability to treat Mrs. Lawley. Telford, *CW Journal,* pp. 35–36. Telford credits Nehemiah Curnock with the actual transcription of the shorthand.

13. Eighteenth-century medicine prescribed "bleeding," or the removal of small quantities of blood, as a virtual panacea—it would cure almost any ailment. It was thought to take the impurities out of a person's system and thereby aid recovery. Typically, it had quite the opposite effect because of the weakened state of patient.

14. These three verbs are borrowed from Cicero's (106–43 B.C.) *Second Speech Against Catiline,* though with slight variation. The original reads: *Abiit, Ecessit, Evasit, Erupit.* My thanks to Dr. Stockin for the translation and identification of this and the following Latin citations.

15. The term "Meshech" refers to a people and country in ancient Asia Minor. The Old Testament lists this name among the sons of Japheth (Gen. 10:12). In the prophecies of Ezekiel the "Meshech" became stereotypical of a barbarous and warlike society (Ezek. 32:36; 38:2, 13; 39:1); this is certainly how Wesley had come to see the inhabitants of Frederica.

16. These Latin phrases are from Juvenal's (60?–120?) *Satires,* the 10th on "The Vanity of Human Wishes." (Verses 85, 86.)

17. The shorthand transcription is from Telford, *CW Journal,* pp. 35–36. The Wesleys often recorded material of a private or sensitive nature in Byrom's shorthand to protect it from the eyes of a prying public.

18. The Latin might be translated either: "Last of all, it is by this *destiny* . . ." or "by this *fate* . . . ."

19. *Ibid.,* p. 40.

20. Jackson, *CW Journal,* I, pp. 45, 78, 132.

21. *Ibid.,* p. 132.

2 / Charles's Personal Pentecost

By December 5, 1736, Charles Wesley began discharging the responsibilities General Oglethorpe had given him upon leaving Georgia. He met with Mr. Towers and the other Trustees of the Colony, and deposited his dispatches and records into their hands. Within another month Oglethorpe arrived in England. He found Charles's record of the events in the New World a bit melodramatic, commenting that the journal was "writ with a great deal of spirit." Wesley retorted, "all I could answer for was, that it was writ with a great deal of truth."

Charles's next two years were filled with serious bouts of illness, and with his efforts to give a full report of the affairs of the colony and to raise support on behalf of the religious mission there. George Whitefield offered himself for service in Georgia, and the younger Wesley also resolved to return, "if I could be of any use as a Clergyman; but as to my Secretary's place, I begged [Oglethorpe] to tell me where, when, and how I should resign it."

Between visits with dignitaries of the colony and the church, as well as with his physicians and sickbed, these two years held happier moments. Relationships with family and friends were rekindled. Visits to Tiverton and Oxford were frequent, as were Charles's opportunities to enjoy Christian fellowship or preach, and in these happier moments some of his sense of failure in the Georgia mission seemed relieved. But his illness was unabated; it had the result of forestalling Charles's return to the New World until John Wesley's arrival in England in February of 1738.

It is in the midst of this illness that Charles first met Peter Böhler, a Moravian, and then Mr. Bray. Böhler, a pietist possessed of charisma of nearly prophetic intensity, pressed Wesley on the Reformation issue of salvation by grace through faith. Bray, a mechanic and a man of simple faith, continued the onslaught until Charles reached an experiential and theological point of transition—his "conversion". Theologically his conversion meant a reordering of his soteriology on the basis of the Moravian's doctrine of justification by faith. It signaled a transition from what Charles described as "the legal state" (which sought salvation by good endeavors) to what he termed "receiving the atonement" or "receiving Christ," and living by faith in His merits. Experientially, it meant a "comfort" or "perfect peace,'' an inward sense of God's acceptance made real to Charles, and a concomitant and continuing sense of assurance of that same acceptance. Charles's journal gives not only graphic descriptions of his own inward odyssey and insights into eighteenth-century spirituality, but also a sense of the wholistic mission that flowed out of his conversion. By May 26, not three days after his experience, Charles reported that he administered the sacrament to condemned prisoners, preached faith to ''an accidental visitant'' and won over his propensity to ''intemperance'' at table. The realization Wesley reached in May 1738, while it was hardly the instantaneous one Peter Böhler promised, was one that had far-reaching theological, social, and experiential impact on Charles, and upon the world through him.

No. 7   Journal Selections: February 18–May 26, 1738

Sat., February 18th [1738]. I rode over to Stanton-Harcourt, to see John Gambold and my sister. My brother met us. We prayed and sang together. In the evening I prayed at Mr. Sarney's, with some scholars, and a Moravian.

Wed. February 22d. . . . At five I had some close conversation with Peter Böhler, who pressed upon our scholars the necessity of combining [i.e. meeting for fellowship], and instanced in many awakened, but fallen asleep again, for want of it. He talked much of the necessity of prayer and faith.

Fri., February 24th. At six in the evening, an hour after I had taken my electuary, the tooth-ache returned more violently than ever. I smoked tobacco; which set me a vomiting, and took away my senses and pain together. At eleven I waked in extreme pain, which I thought would quickly separate soul and body. Soon after Peter Böhler came to my bedside. I asked him to pray for me. He seemed unwilling at first, but beginning very faintly, he raised his voice by degrees, and prayed for my recovery with strange confidence. Then he took me by the hand, and calmly said, "You will not die now." I thought within myself, "I cannot hold out in this pain till morning. If it abates before, I believe I may recover." He asked me, "Do you hope to be saved?" "Yes." "For what reason do you hope it?" "Because I have used my best endeavours to serve God." He shook his head, and said no more. I thought him uncharitable, saying in my heart, "What, are not my endeavours a sufficient ground of hope? Would he rob me of my endeavours? I have nothing else to trust to."

By the morning my pain was moderated. Ted Bentham, calling, then persuaded me to be blooded. I continued in great pain. In the evening he brought Dr. Manaton. On Saturday morning I was blooded again; and at night a third time.

Tues., February 28th. My dear James Hutton came post [haste] from London, and brought me Dr. Cockburn's letter and directions.[1] As soon as I was able, I sent my brother at Tiverton [Samuel] the following account:

"Dear Brother,—I borrow another's hand, as I cannot use my own. You remember Dr. South's saying ["I have been within the jaws of death, but he was not suffered to shut his mouth upon me"]. I ought never to forget it. Dr. Manaton told me, he expected to have found me dead at his second visit. This several remarkable accidents concurred to hinder. I had kept a week before the pleurisy came, and taken physic twice. At midnight it seized me so violently, that I never expected to see the morning. In the preceeding afternoon I had taken Dr. Cockburn's electuary, and an hour after was visited by so outrageous a tooth-ache, that it forced me to the abominable remedy of the pipe. This quickly made me discharge my as-tringent, and, in all probability, saved my life; binding medicines being poison in a pleuritic fever. I took my illness for the flux, and so never thought of sending for a physician. T. Bentham fetched him against my will, and was probably the instrument of saving my life a second time. Dr. M. called in Dr. Fruin. They bled me three times, and poured down droughts, oils, and apozems without end. For four days the balance was even. Then, as Spencer says, 'I over-wrestled my strong enemy.' Ever since I have been slowly gathering strength; and yesterday took my first journey to my sister's [Betty?] room, who has been with me from the beginning, and no small comfort to me.

"One consequence of my sickness you will not be sorry for,—its stop-ping my sudden return to Georgia. For the Doctor tells me, to undertake a voyage now would be certain death. Some reasons for *his* not going my brother [John] will mention to you in person. . . ."[2]

Mon., April 3d. By my brother's advice, I resolved to give up my Secre-tary's place; and to-day wrote my letter of resignation.

Wed., April 12th. I received Mr. Oglethorpe's answer to my letter of resignation; wherein he offered, if I would keep my place, to get it supplied in my absence by a deputy.

Sat., April 15th. Drs. Fruin and Manaton called, and forbad my voyage. Both as physicians and friends they advised me not to go, but stay at College, since I might, as senior Master, expect offices and preferment.

Wed., April 19th. I came up to town, to take my leave of Mr. Oglethorpe, who received me with his accustomed kindness. The next day I had the satisfaction of once more meeting that man of God, Peter Böhler.

Tues., April 25th. Soon after five, we were met in our little chapel, Mrs. Delamotte came to us. We sang, and fell into a dispute whether conversion was gradual or instantaneous. My brother was very positive for the latter, and very shockingly; mentioned some late instances of gross sinners be-lieving in a moment. I was much offended at his worse than unedifying discourse. Mrs. Delamotte left us abruptly. I stayed, and insisted, a man need not know when first he had faith. His obstinacy in favouring the contrary opinion drove me at last out of the room. Mr. Broughton was only not so much as scandalized as myself. After dinner, he and my brother returned to town. I stayed behind, and read them [the Delamottes] the Life of Mr. Halyburton: one instance, but only one, of instantaneous conversion.

Wed., April 26th. I passed the day at Mr. Piers's, in singing, and reading, and mutual encouragement. In the evening we finished Halyburton. The meltingness it occasioned in me (like those before) soon passed away as a morning cloud. Next morning I returned to London.

Fri., April 28th. No sooner was I got to James Hutton's, having removed my things thither from his father's, than the pain in my side returned, and with that my fever. Having disappointed God in his last visitation, he has now again brought me to the bed of sickness. Towards midnight I received some relief by bleeding. In morning Dr. Cockburn came to see me; and a better physician, Peter Böhler, whom God had detained in England for my good. He stood by my bedside, and prayed over me, that now at least I might see the divine intention, in this and my late illness. I immediately thought it might be that I should again consider Böhler's doctrine of faith; examine myself whether I was in the faith; and if I was not, never cease seeking and longing after it, till I attained it.

Mon., May 1st. Mr. Piers called to see me. I exhorted him to labour after that faith which he thinks I have, and I know I have not. After receiving the sacrament, I felt a small anticipation of peace, and said, "Now I have demonstration against the Moravian doctrine that a man cannot have peace without assurance of his pardon. I now have peace, yet cannot say of a surety that my sins are forgiven." The next and several times after that I received the sacrament, I had not so much as bare attention, God no longer trusting me with comfort, which I should immediately turn against himself.

For some days following I felt a faint longing for faith; and could pray for nothing else. My desires were quickened by a letter of Mr. Edmunds, seeking Christ as in an agony.

Sat., May 6th. God still kept up the little spark of desire, which he himself had enkindled in me; and I seemed determined to speak of, and wish for, nothing but faith in Christ. Yet could not this preserve me from sin; which I this day ran into with my eyes wide open: so that after ten years' vain struggling, I own and feel it absolutely unconquerable. Bearing witness to the truth before Miss Delamotte, Mr. Baldwyn, and others, I found my desires of apprehending Christ increased.

Thur., May 11th. I was just going to remove to old Mr. Hutton's,[3] when God sent Mr. Bray to me, a poor ignorant mechanic, who knows nothing but Christ; yet by knowing him, knows and discerns all things. Some time ago I had taken leave of Peter Böhler, confessed my unbelief and want of forgiveness, but declared my firm persuasion that I should receive the atonement before I died. His answer was, "Be it unto thee according to thy faith."

Mr. Bray is now to supply Böhler's place. We prayed together for faith. I was quite overpowered and melted into tears, and hereby induced to think it was God's will that I should go to his house, and not to Mr. Hutton's. He was of the same judgement. Accordingly I was carried thither in a chair.

His sister I found in earnest pursuit of Christ; his wife well inclined to conversion. I had not been here long, when Mr. Broughton called. I hoped to find him altered like myself; but alas! his time is not yet come. As to M. Turner, he gave her up; "but for you, M. Bray," said he, "I hope you are still in your senses, and not run mad after a faith which must be felt." He went on contradicting and blaspheming. I thought it my duty to withstand him, and to confess my want of faith. "God help you, poor man," he replied: "if I could think you have not faith, I am sure it would drive me to despair." I put all my hopes of ever attaining it, or eternal salvation, upon this assertion, *"I have not now the faith of the Gospel."*

As soon as he left us, Mr. Bray read me many comfortable scriptures, which greatly strengthened my desire; so that I was persuaded I should not leave his house, before I believed with my heart unto righteousness.

Fri., May 12th. I waked in the same blessed temper, hungry and thirsty after God. I began Isaiah, and seemed to see that to me were the promises made, and would be fulfilled, for that Christ loved me. I found myself more desirous, more assured I should believe. This day (and indeed my whole time) I spent in discoursing on faith, either with those that had it, or those that sought it; in reading the Scripture, and in prayer. . . .

Sat., May 13th. I waked without Christ; yet still desirous of finding him. Soon after W. Delamotte came, and read me the 68th Psalm, strangely full of comfortable promises. Toward noon I was enabled to pray with desire and hope, and to lay claim to the promises in general. The afternoon I spent with my friends, in mutual exhortation to wait patiently for the Lord in prayer and reading. At night my brother came, exceedingly heavy. I forced him (as he had often forced me) to sing a hymn to Christ, and almost thought He would come while we were singing: assured He would come quickly. *At night* I received much light and comfort from the Scriptures.

Sun., May 14th. The beginning of the day I was very heavy, weary, and unable to pray; but the desire soon returned, and I found much comfort both in prayer and in the word, my eyes being opened more and more to discern and lay hold on the promises. I longed to find Christ, that I might show him to all mankind; that I might praise, that I might love him. . . .

Tues., May 16th. I waked weary, faint, and heartless. My brother Hall coming to see me, I urged him to examine himself, whether he was in the faith. Two questions decided the matter: "Are you sure that is light?" "Yes." "Are you sure of the things unseen; of Christ being in you of a truth?" "Yes; infinitely surer." In the afternoon I seemed deeply sensible of my misery, in being without Christ.

Wed., May 17th. I experienced the power of Christ rescuing me in temptation. To-day I first saw Luther on the Galatians, which Mr. Holland had accidentally lit upon. We began, and found him nobly full of faith. My friend, in hearing him, was so affected, as to breathe out sighs and groans unutterable. I marvelled that we were so soon and so entirely removed from him that called us into the grace of Christ, unto another Gospel. Who would believe our Church had been founded on this important article of justification by faith alone? I am astonished I should ever think this a new doctrine; especially while our Articles and Homilies stand unrepealed, and the key of knowledge is not yet taken away.

From this time I endeavoured to ground as many of our friends as came in this fundamental truth, salvation by faith alone, not an idle, dead faith, but a faith which works by love, and is necessarily productive of all good works and all holiness.

I spent some hours this evening in private with Martin Luther, who has greatly blessed me, especially his conclusion of the 2d chapter. I laboured, waited, and prayed, to feel "who loved *me*, and gave himself for *me*." When nature, near exhausted, forced me to bed, I opened the book upon, "For he will finish the work, and cut it short in righteousness, because a short work will the Lord make upon the earth." After this comfortable assurance that He would come, and would not tarry, I slept in peace.

Fri., May 19th. At five this morning the pain and difficulty in breathing returned. The Surgeon was sent for; but I fell asleep before he could bleed me a second time. I was easier all day, after taking Dr. Cockburn's medicines. I had not much desire. I received the sacrament; but not Christ. At seven Mrs. Turner came, and told me, I should not rise from that bed till I believed. I believed her saying, and asked, "Has God then bestowed faith upon you?" "Yes, he has." "Why, have you peace with God?" "Yes, perfect peace." "And do you love Christ above all things?" "I do, above all things incomparably." "Then you are willing to die?" "I am; and would be glad to die this moment; for I know all my sins are blotted out; the handwriting that was against me is taken out of the way, and nailed to his cross. He has saved me by his death; he has washed me with his blood; he has hid me in his wounds. I have peace in Him and rejoice with joy unspeakable, and full of glory."

Her answers were so full to these and the most searching questions I could ask, that I had no doubt of her having received the atonement; and waited for it myself with a more assured hope. Feeling an anticipation of joy upon her account, and thanking Christ as I could, I looked for him all night with prayers and sighs and unceasing desires.

Sat., May 20th. I waked much disappointed, and continued all day in great dejection, which the sacrament did not in the least abate. Nevertheless God would not suffer me to doubt the truth of his promises. Mr. Bray, too, seemed troubled at my not yet believing, and complained of his uneasiness and want of patience. "But so it is with me," says he; "when my faith begins to fail, God gives me some sign to support it." He then opened a Testament, and read the first words that presented, Matt. 9:1:

"And he entered into a ship, and passed over, and came into his own city. And behold, they brought to him a man sick of the palsy, lying on a bed: and Jesus, seeing their faith, said unto the sick of the palsy, Son, be of good cheer; thy sins be forgiven thee. And, behold, certain of the scribes and Pharisees said within themselves, This man blasphemeth. And Jesus, knowing their thoughts, said, Wherefore think ye evil in your hearts? For whether is easier, to say, Thy sins be forgiven thee, or to say, Arise and walk? But that ye may know that the Son of man hath power on earth to forgive sins, (then saith he to the sick of the palsy), Arise, take up thy bed, and go unto thine own house. And he arose, and departed to his house. And when the multitude saw it, they marvelled, and glorified God, which had given such power unto man."

It was a long while before he could read this through, for tears of joy; and I saw herein, and firmly believed, that his faith would be available for the healing of me.

THE DAY OF PENTECOST

Sun., May 21st, 1738. I waked in hope and expectation of His coming. At nine my brother and some friends came, and sang an hymn to the Holy Ghost. My comfort and hope were hereby increased. In about half-an-hour they went: I betook myself to prayer; the substance as follows:— "O Jesus, thou hast said, 'I will come unto you'; thou has said, 'I will send the Comforter unto you'; thou hast said, 'My Father and I will come unto you, and make our abode with you.' Thou art God who canst not lie; I wholly rely upon thy most true promise: accomplish it in thy time and manner." Having said this, I was composing myself to sleep, in quietness and peace, when I heard one come in (Mrs. Musgrave, I thought, by the voice) and say, "In the name of Jesus of Nazareth, arise, and believe, and thou shalt be healed of all thy infirmities." I wondered how it should enter into her head to speak in that manner. The words struck me to the heart. I sighed, and said within myself, "O that Christ would but speak thus to me!" I lay musing and trembling: then thought, "but what if it should be Him? I will send at least to see." I rang, and, Mrs. Turner coming, I desired her to send up Mrs. Musgrave. She went down, and, returning, said, "Mrs. Musgrave had not been up here." My heart sank within me at the word, and I hoped it might be Christ indeed. However, I sent her down again to inquire, and felt in the meantime a strange palpitation of heart. I said, yet feared to say, "I believe, I believe!" She came up again and said, "It was I, a weak, sinful creature, spoke: but the words were Christ's: he commanded me to say them, and so constrained me that I could not forbear."

I sent for Mr. Bray, and asked him whether I believed. He answered, I ought not to doubt of it: it was Christ spoke to me. He knew it; and willed us to pray together: "but first," said he, "I will read what I have casually opened upon: 'Blessed is the man whose unrighteousness is forgiven, and whose sin is covered: blessed is the man to whom the Lord imputeth no sin, and in whose spirit is no guilt.'" Still I felt a violent opposition and reluctance to believe; yet still the Spirit of God strove with my own and the evil spirit, till by degrees he chased away the darkness of my unbelief. I found myself convinced, I know not how, nor when; and immediately fell to intercession. . . .

I now found myself at peace with God, and rejoiced in hope of loving Christ. My temper for the rest of the day was, mistrust of my own great, but before unknown, weakness. I saw that by faith I stood; by the continual support of faith, which kept me from falling, though of my self I am ever sinking into sin. I went to bed still sensible of my own weakness, (I humbly hope to be more and more so), yet content of Christ's protection.

Mon., May 22d. Under his protection I waked next morning, and rejoiced in reading the 107th Psalm, so nobly describing what God had done for my soul. I fell asleep again, and waked out of a dream that I was fighting with two devils; had one under my feet; the other faced me some times, but faded, and sunk, and vanished away, upon my telling him I belonged to Christ.

To-day I saw him chiefly as my King, and found him in his power: but saw little of the love of Christ crucified, or of my sins past: though more, I humbly hope, of my own weakness and his strength. I had many evil thoughts darted into my mind, but I rejected them immediately (yet not I). At noon I rose, continually fainting, nevertheless upheld. I was greatly strengthened by Isa. 43, which God directed me to. "But now thus saith the Lord that created thee, O Jacob, and he that formed thee, O Israel, Fear not: for I have redeemed thee, I have called thee by name; thou art mine. When thou passest through the waters, I will be with thee; and through the rivers, they shall not overflow thee: when thou walkest through the fire, thou shalt not be burned; neither shall the flame kindle upon thee. For I am the Lord thy God, the Holy One of Israel, thy Saviour."

My brother coming, we joined in intercession for him. In the midst of prayer, I almost believed the Holy Ghost was coming upon him. In the evening we sang and prayed again. I found myself very weak in body, but thought I ought to pray for my friends, being the only Priest among them. I kneeled down, and was immediately strengthened, both mind and body. The enemy did not lose such an opportunity of tempting me to pride: but, God be praised, my strength did I ascribe unto Him. I was often since assisted to pray readily and earnestly, without a form. Not unto me, O Lord, not unto me, but to thy name be the glory!

An old friend called to see me, under great apprehensions that I was running mad. His fears were not a little increased by my telling him the prayer of faith had healed me when sick at Oxford. "He looked to see the rays about my head," he said, and more to that purpose. I begged him, for his own sake, not to pass sentence till he had his full evidence concerning me. This he could not promise, but faintly prayed me to flee from London, and in despair of me, took his leave. . . .

Tues., May 23d. I waked under the protection of Christ, and gave myself up, soul and body, to him. At nine I began an hymn upon my conversion, but was persuaded to break off, for fear of pride. Mr. Bray coming, encouraged me to proceed in spite of Satan. I prayed Christ to stand by me, and finished the hymn. Upon my afterwards showing it to Mr. Bray, the devil threw in a fiery dart, suggesting, that it was wrong, and I had displeased God. My heart sunk within me; when, casting my eye upon a Prayer-book, I met with an answer for him. "Why boastest thou thyself, thou tyrant, that thou canst do mischief?" Upon this, I clearly discerned it was a device of the enemy to keep back glory from God. And it is most usual with him to preach humility, when speaking will endanger his kingdom, or do honour to Christ. Least of all would he have us tell what things God has done for our souls, so tenderly does he guard us from pride. But God has showed me, he can defend me from it, while speaking for him. In his name therefore, and through his strength, I will perform my vows unto the Lord, of not hiding his righteousness within my heart, if it should ever please him to plant it there.

Throughout this day he has kept up in me a constant sense of my own weakness. At night I was tempted to think the reason of my believing before others, was my sincerity. I rejected the thought with horror, and remained more than conqueror, through Him that loved me.

Wed., May 24th. . . . At eight I prayed by myself for love; with some feeling, and assurance of feeling more. Towards ten, my brother was brought in triumph by a troop of our friends, and declared, "I believe." We sang the hymn with great joy, and parted with prayer. At midnight I gave myself up to Christ; assured I was safe, sleeping or waking. Had continual experience of his power to overrule all temptation; and confessed, with joy and surprise, that he was able to do exceeding and abundantly for me, above what I can ask or think.

Thur., May 25th. I commend myself to Christ, my Prophet, Priest and King. Miss Delamotte came in a better mind. Before communicating, I left it to Christ, whether, or in what measure, he would please to manifest himself to me, in this breaking of bread. I had no particular attention to the prayers: but in the prayer of consecration I saw, by the eye of faith, or rather, had a glimpse of, Christ's broken, mangled body, as taking [sic] down from the cross. Still I could not observe the prayer, but only repeat with tears, "O love, love!" At the same time, I felt great peace and joy; and assurance of feeling more, when it is best.

Soon after I was a little cast down, by feeling some temptation, and foreseeing more; but God lifted me up by his word. "Fear not: for I have redeemed thee, I have called thee by thy name; thou art mine. When thou passest through the waters, I will be with thee; and through the rivers, they shall not overflow thee: when thou walkest through the fire, thou shalt not be burned; neither shall the flame kindle upon thee." [Isa. 43] This promise was fulfilled in me when under frequent motions of sin: I looked up to Christ, and found them beaten down continually.

Fri., May 26th. We joined this morning in supplication for the poor malefactors, while passing to execution; and in the sacrament commended their souls to Christ. The great comfort we found therein made us confidently hope some of them were received as the penitent thief at the last hour. I was much refreshed soon after by Miss Delamotte, who, by the mercy of Christ, is brought back again, and more athirst after him than ever. I dined with great liberty of spirit, being amazed to find my old enemy, intemperance, so suddenly subdued, that I have almost forgot I was ever in bondage to him. In the evening I broke through my own unwillingness, and at last preached faith in Christ to an accidental visitant.

CONVERSION HYMNS

Three hymns vie for the place of honor reserved for the designation "The Wesleys' Conversion Hymn." Charles mentioned composing "an hymn upon my conversion," on May 23, 1738, which he and John sang in celebration together the next evening at the older brother's announcement: "I believe!" The traditional ascription has gone to "Christ the friend of sinners" (Where shall my wondering soul begin?), and there is still good evidence to commend that identification to us; yet, "Free Grace" (And can it be that I should gain) and "Hymn for Whitsunday" (Granted is the Saviour's Prayer) also possess strong ties to this same event and are worthy of our consideration in examining Charles's conversion.[4] All three hymns were first published in *Hymns and Sacred Poems* (1739).

No. 8 "Christ the Friend of Sinners"

The hymn bears a title framed from one of Charles's favorite epithets for Jesus (appearing nearly 150 times in his later hymns alone!). It communicates a sense of Charles's pilgrimage from "Death and Sin" to an "Antepast [foretaste] of Heaven." His *Journal* (I, p. 94) indicates that Charles began the conversion hymn and then laid it aside for fear of pride. Bray prevailed upon him to complete the song, which Wesley did, though recording an apology regarding his humility: ". . . God showed me he could defend me from it [pride], while speaking for him. In his name therefore, and through his strength, I will perform my vows unto the Lord, of not *hiding his righteousness within my heart* [emphasis added], if it should ever please him to plant it there." The phraseology of the fifth and sixth lines of Charles's third verse reflects his journal's description of the background of the conversion hymn.[5]

The phrase "A brand pluck'd from the fire" became a standard Wesleyan soteriological epigram. Formed on the mold of Zech. 3:2, and ratified in a deliverance from an inferno of flames at the Epworth rectory, the image was allegorized into a redemption phrase utilized by both brothers.[6] The hymn, written in the first person, places the language of testimony in the singer's mouth; and like the conversion of May 1738, it moves quickly from expressing a sense of pardon or comfort to preaching faith: "Believe . . . Only believe—and yours is heaven."[7]

1   Where shall my wondering soul begin?
      How shall I all to heaven aspire?
    A slave redeem'd from death and sin,
      A brand pluck'd from eternal fire,
    How shall I equal triumphs raise,
    And sing my great Deliverer's praise?

2   O, how shall I the goodness tell,
      Father, which Thou to me hast show'd?
    That I, a child of wrath and hell,
      I should be call'd a child of God!
    Should know, should feel my sins forgiven,
    Blest with this antepast of heaven!

3   And shall I slight my Father's love,
      Or basely fear His gifts to own?
    Unmindful of His favours prove?
      Shall I, the hallow'd cross to shun,
    Refuse His righteousness t' impart,
    By hiding it within my heart?

4   No—though the ancient dragon rage,
      And call forth all his hosts to war;
    Though earth's self-righteous sons engage;
      Them, and their god, alike I dare:
    Jesus, the sinner's Friend, proclaim;
    Jesus, to sinners still the same.

5   Outcasts of men, to you I call,
      Harlots, and publicans, and thieves!
    He spreads His arms t' embrace you all;
      Sinners alone His grace receives;
    No need of Him the righteous have,
    He came the lost to seek and save.

6   Come, all ye *Magdalens* in lust,
      Ye ruffians fell in murders old;
    Repent, and live: despair and trust!
      Jesus for you to death was sold;
    Though hell protest, and earth repine,
    He died for crimes like yours—and mine.

7 Come, O my guilty brethren, come,
      Groaning beneath your load of sin!
   His bleeding heart shall make you room,
      His open side shall take you in.
   He calls you now, invites you home:
   Come, O my guilty brethren, come!

8 For you the purple current flow'd
      In pardons from His wounded side:
   Languish'd for you th' eternal God,
      For you the Prince of Glory died.
   Believe, and all your guilt's forgiven;
   Only believe—and yours is heaven.

No. 9 "Free Grace"

This hymn, which a few scholars suggest may have been the famous "conversion hymn,"[8] voices with particular poignancy the wonderment that Charles felt in God's acceptance. Once again, the hymn is framed in the first person, and seems to be born in the author's biography.[9]

1 And can it be, that I should gain
      An interest in the Saviour's blood?
   Died He for me?—who caused His pain!
      For me?—who Him to death pursued.
   Amazing love! how can it be
   That Thou, my God, shouldst die for me?

2 'Tis mystery all! th' Immortal dies!
      Who can explore His strange design?
   In vain the first-born seraph tries
      To sound the depths of Love Divine.
   'Tis mercy all! Let earth adore;
   Let angel minds inquire no more.

3 He left His Father's throne above,
      (So free, so infinite His grace!)
   Emptied Himself of all but love,
      And bled for *Adam's* helpless race:
   'Tis mercy all, immense and free!
   For, O my God! it found out me!

4 Long my imprison'd spirit lay,
      Fast bound in sin and nature's night:
   Thine eye diffused a quickening ray;
      I woke; the dungeon flamed with light;
   My chains fell off, my heart was free,
   I rose, went forth, and follow'd Thee.

5   Still the small inward voice I hear,
       That whispers all my sins forgiven;
    Still the atoning blood is near,
       That quench'd the wrath of hostile Heaven:
    I feel the life His wounds impart;
    I feel my Saviour in my heart.

6   No condemnation now I dread,
       Jesus, and all in Him, is mine:
    Alive in Him, my Living Head,
       And clothed in righteousness Divine,
    Bold I approach th' eternal throne,
    And claim the crown, through Christ, my own.

No. 10   "Hymn for Whitsunday"

This hymn was certainly associated with Charles's conversion, since his journal
records that it was sung in the presence of Mr. Ainsworth, and "at our repeating the
line of the hymn, 'now descend, and shake the earth,' he fell down as in agony."
"I found," Wesley continued, "a general delight in their singing, but little attention: yet was not disquieted." (*Journal*, I, 95.) The lines quoted by the journal are
found in verse eight of this hymn; its theme and designation as a hymn for Pentecost
are consonant with Charles's conversion. But it remains an open question as to
whether this was the hymn John and Charles Wesley sang together the next day.[10]
The mood is clearly more sedate here than in the two previous hymns, and that
might disqualify it from the ecstasy of Charles's personal Pentecost. His journal
account for the 24th of May continued: "We passed the afternoon in prayer, singing, and conference." (*Ibid.*) The following hymn was probably *one* of the songs
they sang that day.[11]

1   Granted is the Saviour's prayer,
    Sent the gracious Comforter;
    Promise of our parting Lord,
    Jesus to His heaven restored:

2   Christ; who, now gone up on high,
    Captive leads captivity;
    While His foes from Him receive
    Grace, that God with man may live.

3   God, the everlasting God,
    Makes with mortals His abode;
    Whom the heavens cannot contain,
    He vouchsafes to dwell in man.

4   Never will He thence depart,
    Inmate of an humble heart;

Carrying on His work within,
Striving till He cast out sin.

5   There He helps our feeble moans,
Deepens our imperfect groans;
Intercedes in silence there,
Sighs th' unutterable prayer.

6   Come, Divine, and peaceful Guest,
Enter our devoted breast;
Holy Ghost, our hearts inspire,
Kindle there the Gospel-fire.

7   Crown the agonizing strife,
Principle, and Lord of life;
Life Divine in us renew,
Thou the Gift and Giver too!

8   Now descend and shake the earth,
Wake us into second birth;
Now Thy quickening influence give,
Blow—and these dry bones shall live!

9   Brood Thou o'er our nature's night,
Darkness kindles into light;
Spread Thy over-shadowing wings,
Order from confusion springs.

10   Pain, and sin, and sorrow cease;
Thee we taste, and all is peace;
Joy Divine in Thee we prove,
Light of truth, and fire of love.

No. 11   "Congratulations to a Friend, Upon Believing in Christ"

This hymn (*Hymns and Sacred Poems*, 1739) was probably written by Charles for John Wesley upon the elder brother's announcement: "I believe."[12]

1   What morn on thee with sweeter ray,
    Or brighter lustre e'er hath shined?
Be blest the memorable day
    That gave thee Jesus Christ to find!
Gave thee to taste His perfect grace,
From death to life in Him to pass!

2   O, how diversified the scene,
    Since first that heart began to beat!

Evil and few thy days have been:
  In suffering, and in comfort, great,
Oft hast Thou groan'd beneath thy load,
And sunk—into the arms of God!

3 Long did all hell its powers engage,
     And fill'd thy darken'd soul with fears:
   Baffled at length the dragon's rage,
     At length the' atoning blood appears:
   Thy light is come, thy mourning's o'er,
   Look up; for thou shalt weep no more!

4 Blest be the Name that set thee free,
     The Name that sure salvation brings!
   The Sun of Righteousness on thee
     Has rose with healing in His wings.
   Away let grief and sighing flee;
   Jesus has died for thee—for thee!

5 And will He now forsake His own,
     Or lose the purchase of His blood?
   No! for He looks with pity down,
     He watches over thee for good;
   Gracious He eyes thee from above,
   And guards and feeds thee with His Love.

6 Since thou wast precious in His sight,
     How highly favour'd hast thou been!
   Upborne by faith to glory's height,
     The Saviour-God thine eyes have seen,
   Thy heart has felt its sins forgiven,
   And tastes anticipated heaven.

7 Still may His love thy fortress be,
     And make thee still His darling care,
   Settle, confirm, and stablish thee,
     On eagle's wings thy spirit bear:
   Fill thee with heaven, and ever shed
   His choicest blessings on thy head.

8 Thus may He comfort thee below,
     Thus may He all His graces give:
   Him but in part thou here canst know:
     Yet here by faith submit to live;
   Help me to fight my passage through,
   Nor seize thy heaven till I may too.

9 Or, if the sovereign wise decree
     First number thee among the blest,

(The only good I'd envy thee),
 Translating to an earlier rest;
Near in thy latest hour, may I
Instruct, and learn of thee, to die.

10 Mix'd with the choirs that hover round
  And all the adverse powers control,
Angel of peace may I be found
  To animate thy panting soul,
Point out the crown, and smooth thy way
To regions of eternal day.

11 Fired with the thought, I see thee now
  Triumphant meet the King of Fears!
Steadfast thy heart, serene thy brow;
  Divinely confident appears
Thy mounting soul, and spreads abroad,
And swells to be dissolved in God.

12 Is this the soul so late weigh'd down
  By cares and sins, by griefs and pains?
Whither are all thy terrors gone?
  Jesus for thee the victory gains;
And death, and sin, and Satan yield
To faith's unconquerable shield.

13 Blest be the God that calls thee home;
  Faithful to thee His mercies prove:
Through death's dark vale He bids thee come,
  And more than conquer in His love;
Robes thee in righteousness Divine,
And makes the crown of glory thine!

No. 12   "For the Anniversary Day of One's Conversion"

Charles continued to look back upon his conversion as a significant turning point in his life. This hymn, probably written in May of 1739, is one of his most famous compositions; it was written, as the title implies, in celebration of the day he "began to live." It was first published in its entirety in *Hymns and Sacred Poems* (1740), but John Wesley's editorial pen soon pared it to eight verses, and the reworked version began with Charles's seventh verse (*Hymns and Spiritual Songs*, 1753). With further editorial changes, it began appearing as #1 in the Methodist hymnbooks beginning with the famous *A Collection of Hymns for the Use of the People Called Methodists* of 1780. The hymn vibrates with experience and drama. Verses four, five, and six are full of the *Christus pro me* Charles learned from Luther and from Böhler. Verse ten forms a transition point between testimony and invitation, and early in verse eleven Christ's Word of forgiveness becomes a contemporaneous Word audible to the singer/reader.[13] Tradition tells of a conversation Charles Wesley had with Peter Böhler in May of 1739: discussing the importance of confessing Christ, the fiery Moravian exclaimed, "Had I a thousand tongues, I would praise Christ with them all!" Such pregnant words were not wasted on Charles Wesley; they formed the foundation of the most famous verse of this hymn (#7).[14]

1   Glory to God, and praise and love
      Be ever, ever given;
    By Saints below, and Saints above,
      The church in earth and Heaven.

2   On this glad day the glorious Sun
      Of Righteousness arose;
    On my benighted soul He shone,
      And fill'd it with repose.

3   Sudden expired the legal strife;
      'Twas then I ceased to grieve;
    My second, real, living life
      I then began to live.

4   Then with my *heart* I first believed,
      Believed with faith Divine;
    Power with the Holy Ghost received
      To call the Saviour *mine*.

5   I felt my Lord's atoning blood
      Close to *my* soul applied;
    Me, me He loved—the Son of God
      For *me*, for *me*, He died!

6   I found, and own'd His promise true,
      Ascertain'd of *my* part;
    My pardon pass'd in heaven I *knew*,
      When written on my heart.

7   O for a thousand tongues to sing
      My dear Redeemer's praise!
    The glories of my God and King,
      The triumphs of His grace.

8   My gracious Master, and my God,
      Assist me to proclaim,
    To spread through all the earth abroad
      The honors of Thy name.

9   Jesus, the name that charms our fears,
      That bids our sorrows cease;

'Tis music in the sinner's ears,
    'Tis life, and health, and peace!

10 He breaks the power of cancell'd sin,
        He sets the prisoner free;
    His blood can make the foulest clean,
        His blood avail'd for me.

11 He speaks; and, listening to His voice,
        New life the dead receive,
    The mournful, broken hearts rejoice,
        The humble poor *believe*.

12 Hear Him, ye deaf; His praise, ye dumb,
        Your loosen'd tongues employ;
    Ye blind, behold your Saviour come;
        And leap, ye lame, for joy.

13 Look unto Him, ye nations; own
        Your God, ye fallen race!
    Look, and be saved through faith alone;
        But justified by grace!

14 See all your sins on Jesus laid;
        The Lamb of God was slain,
    His soul was once an offering made
        For *every soul* of man.

15 Harlots, and publicans, and thieves
        In holy triumph join;
    Saved is the sinner that believes
        From crimes as great as mine.

16 Murderers, and all ye hellish crew,
        Ye sons of lust and pride,
    Believe the Saviour died for you;
        For me the Saviour died.

17 Awake from guilty nature's sleep,
        And Christ shall give you light,
    Cast all your sins into the deep,
        And wash the *Ethiop* white.

18 With me, your chief, you then shall *know*,
        Shall feel your sins forgiven;
    Anticipate your heaven below,
        And own that love is heaven.

No. 13   Letter to Sally
(*The Journal of Charles Wesley*, 1849)

Charles continued to look to that Pentecost Sunday in May 1738 as a pivotal point for his faith, life, and ministry. But seen from the distance of twenty-two years, continuance in the faith counted as much as its first blush. In a characteristic gesture of warmth Wesley turned from the topic of his conversion to affirm that the woman he cherished was as clear an example of God's grace to him as was that religious experience so many years before.[15]

Westminster, Whitsunday, 1760

My dearest Sally,—This I once called the anniversary of my conversion. Just twenty-two years ago I thought I received the first grain of faith. But what does that avail me, if I have not the Spirit now? "I account that the long-suffering of the Lord is salvation"; and would fain believe He has reserved me so long for good, and not for evil.

Eleven years ago He gave me another token of His love, in my beloved friend; and surely He never meant us to part on the other side of time. His design in uniting us here was, that we should continue one to all eternity.

I had not time to be particular yesterday. In the morning I rode to Paddington; passed near two hours with our most intimate friends, and loving Mr. Shirley; spent two hours more in gentle riding. At Hyde-park Gate a gentleman called after me. I stopped, and Sir Charles Hotham ran up to my horse, and saluted me with the same joy as if returned from the dead. At two I dined, with Mr. Shirley and Fletcher, at the widow Heritage's; drank tea at M. Carteret's, and prayed all of us according to God.

A French author I am reading has rebuked my unwillingness to accept obligations, and convinced me that the root thereof is pride.

Do not think because I got little rest last night, that therefore I am in pain. My breast is tolerably easy; my stomach quite so. Our friends at St. James's-place pity you exceedingly, as supposing you more uneasy at Bristol than you would be here.

I designed to have assisted at the chapel this morning; but want of sleep altered my resolution; and I lay down in church time, and slept two hours.

The Lord Jesus speak it into your inmost soul, "I am the way, the truth, and the life!"

NOTES

1. James Hutton (1715–1795) was converted at the home of his father under the preaching of John Wesley. A bookseller and printer by trade, he also formed a religious society, which met at Fetter Lane. He and the Wesleys continued to have contact through the Fetter Lane Society, but later drifted apart as Hutton became a prominent layman among the English Moravians, while the Wesleys broke with them in

the mid-1740s. Despite their differences Hutton and Charles were able to maintain their friendship. Telford, *CW Journal*, p. 288.

2. The events leading up to John Wesley's hasty departure from Georgia were not trusted to the mails. Cf. John's "Sixth Savannah Journal," Nehemiah Curnock, ed., *The Standard Journal of John Wesley, A.M.* (London: Robert Culley, n.d.), vol. I, pp. 313–414, which describes John's unhappy courtship of "Miss Sophy," and the eventual scandal he caused by repelling her from the sacrament of the Church. John fled Georgia just ahead of legal proceedings against him!

3. "Old Mr. Hutton" is the Rev. John Hutton, father of James. He lived on Great College Street, near Westminster Abbey, and almost next door to Charles's brother Samuel (while the latter served as head usher at Westminster).

4. Neil Dixon, "The Wesleys' Conversion Hymn," *Proceedings of the Wesley Historical Society,* Vol. 37, (Feb. 1967), pp. 43–47.

5. Cf. *JW Journal*, III, pp. 453–454, for his account of the fire; *ibid.*, IV, p. 90, for the image's continued relevancy as it appears in his protracted epitaph (Nov. 26, 1753): "Here lieth the body of John Wesley, a brand plucked from the burning." Jackson, *CW Journal* (II, p. 97), also carried John's premature epitaph, but with an emendation that made the metaphor clearer: "Here lieth the body of John Wesley, a brand, *not once* only, plucked out of the fire" [emphasis added]. The deliverance from the flames at Epworth, and the experience at Aldersgate were formed into a single redemptive moment through this imagery.

6. *P.W.*, I, p. 91.

7. The hymn is reprinted here from *P.W.*, I, 91–93.

8. Jackson, *Life, op. cit.*, I, p. 137; James Lightwood, *Methodist Music of the Eighteenth Century* (London: Epworth Press, 1927), p. 18.

9. The hymn is reprinted here from *P.W.*, I, pp. 105–106. It is also carried, in an altered form, in most modern Protestant hymnals.

10. Peter Grant, in "The Wesleys' Conversion Hymn," *Proceedings of the Wesley Historical Society,* 35 (Sept. 1966), pp. 161–164, argues that this was the same hymn which was later sung by the brothers on May 24. Neil Dixon, "The Wesleys' Conversion Hymn," *op. cit.*, responds to Grant's arguments and concludes that "Christ the Friend of Sinners" was actually the Wesleys' conversion hymn.

11. The hymn is reprinted here from *P.W.*, I, pp. 188–189.

12. *P.W.*, I, pp. 180–183. He comments on the context of the hymn, p. 180; cf. Henry Bett, *Hymns of Methodism, op. cit.*, p. 20.

13. *P.W.*, I, pp. 299–301.

14. John Telford, *The Methodist Hymn Book Illustrated, op. cit.*, p. 39; cf. John Julian, *A Dictionary of Hymnology, op. cit.*

15. Jackson, *CW Journal*, II, p. 239.

3 / The First Fruits
of the Methodist Revival

Charles Wesley's conversion began in him a tidal wave of spiritual energy and action. Two days after his personal Pentecost, Charles began spreading the good news about salvation by faith. In the afterglow of his own experience he spoke to a few friends, and ministered in intercessory prayer, serving most directly through spiritual conversation. As his health returned he stepped into his ministerial vocation with renewed strength and vigor. His journal for the days following the conversion finds him writing sermons, officiating at vespers, and speaking to others about spiritual formation. This personal dimension of his ministry would continue in the work of the Methodist Societies, but soon he would return to the pulpits of important churches and the university. Gradually the religious establishment closed both of those avenues of ministry, and then Charles followed his brother and George Whitefield into that innovation—open air preaching. His journal reports worsening relations with the Anglican establishment, and painful interviews with bishops of the church and leaders of the university whom Wesley held in deep regard.

Barred from the pulpits, Charles soon preached to crowds larger than the churches could hold. The exclusion, however, was a mixed blessing since it exposed the evangelist to the whims of the multitude, and the younger Wesley faced more than his fair share of mob violence. For a while public opinion turned against the Methodists, and Charles was dragged to court (on several occasions) by those who wished to silence him. But nothing seemed to slow him down, not violence, abuse or quasi-legal harassment. The frail and faith-filled little man not only evangelized most of England and Wales, he also planted Methodism in Ireland with a tenacity that caused it to remain and flourish.

The journal record from the earliest years of the revival is copious. The selections offered below are intended to highlight representative incidents, themes, and statements from the earliest years of Charles's public ministry. One cannot help but marvel at the change in the man and his impact since Wesley's first attempt at ministry in Georgia.

No. 14 Journal Selections: June 9–26, 1738

Fri., June 9th [1738]. I prayed with fervour for the family. The second lesson was blind Bartimeus. In riding to Bexley, with Mr. Piers, I spake of my experience in simplicity and confidence, and found him very ready to receive the faith. We spent the day in the same manner, Mr. Bray relating the inward workings of God upon his soul, and I the great things he had done among our friends in London. He listened eagerly to all that was said, not making the least objection, but confessing it was what he had never experienced. We walked, and sang, and prayed in the garden. He was greatly moved, and testified his full conviction, and desire of finding Christ. . . .

Sat., June 10th. In the morning lesson was that glorious description of the power of faith: "Jesus answering said unto them, Have faith in God. For verily I say unto you, That whosoever shall say unto this mountain, Be thou removed, and be thou cast into the sea; and shall not doubt in his heart, but shall believe that those things which he saith shall come to pass; he shall have whatsoever he saith. Therefore I say unto you, What things soever ye desire, when ye pray, believe that ye receive them, and ye shall have them." We pleaded this promise in behalf of our seeking friends, particularly Hetty[1] and Mr. Piers. He came with his wife. The day before our coming he had been led to read the Homily on Justification, which convinced him that in him dwelt no good thing. Now he likewise saw, that the thoughts of his heart were only evil continually, forasmuch as whatsoever is not of faith is sin.

He asked God to give him some comfort, and found it in Luke 5:23, &c.: "Whether is it easier to say, Thy sins be forgiven thee, or to say, Rise up and walk? But that ye may know that the Son of man hath power upon earth to forgive sins, (he saith unto the sick of the palsy), I say unto thee, Arise, and take up thy bed, and go unto thine own house. And immediately he rose up and before them, and took up that whereon he lay, and departed to his own house, glorifying God. And they were all amazed, and they glorified God, and were filled with fear, saying, We have seen strange things to-day."

This was the very miracle, I told him, from which God had shown his intention to heal me; and it was a sign of the like to be done by him. Mr. Bray moved for retiring to prayer. We prayed *after God*, again and again, and asked [Piers], whether he believed Christ could just now manifest himself to his soul. He answered, "Yes." We read him the promise made to the prayer of faith. Mr. Bray bade me speak the same promise to him authoritatively, and he should find Christ make it good. I had not faith to do it. He made me pray again, and then read Psalm 65. I felt every word of it for my friend, particularly, "Thou that hearest the prayer, unto thee shall all flesh come. Blessed is the man whom thou choosest and receivest unto thee: he shall dwell in thy court, and shall be satisfied with the plenteousness of thy house, even of thy holy temple. Thou shalt show us wonderful things in thy righteousness, O God of our salvation, thou that art the hope of all the ends of the earth," &c.

Seeing the great confidence of Mr. Bray, and the deep humility of Mr. Piers, I began to think the promise would be fulfilled before we left the room. My fellow-worker with God seemed full of faith and the Holy Ghost, and told him, "If you can but touch the hem of his garment, you shall be made whole." We prayed for him a third time, the Spirit greatly helping our infirmities, and then asked if he believed. He answered, "Yes": the Spirit witnessing with our spirits, that his heart was as our heart. Bray said, "I now know of a truth that Christ is in you." We were all filled with joy; returned thanks, and prayed for a blessing on his ministry; and then brought him down in triumph. Miss Betsy was greatly strengthened hereby, and bold to confess "she believed." All her speech now was, "I only hope that I shall never lose this comfort."

The day was spent in prayer and conference. Mrs. Piers was, with all ease, convinced of unbelief. After supper I discoursed on faith from the lesson. The poor servants received the word gladly.

Sun., June 11th. While Mr. Piers was preaching upon death, I found great joy in feeling myself willing, or rather, desirous, to die. After prayers we joined in intercession for Mr. and Mrs. Delamotte; then for poor Hetty: I received much comfort in reading Luther.

We took coach for church. In singing I observed Hetty join with a mixture of fear and joy. I earnestly prayed, and expected she should meet with something to confirm her in the service. Both Psalms and lessons were full of consolation.

We adjourned to Mr. Piers, and joined in prayer for a poor woman in despair, one Mrs. Searl, whom Satan had bound these many years. I saw her pass by in the morning, and was touched with a sense of her misery. After pleading his promise of being with us to the end of the world, we went down to her in the name of Jesus. I asked her, whether she thought God was love; and not anger, as Satan would persuade her. Then I preached the Gospel, which she received with all imaginable eagerness. When we had for some time continued together in prayer, she rose up another creature, strongly and explicitly [declaring] her faith in the blood of Christ, and full persuasion that she was accepted in the Beloved. Hetty then declared, that she could not but believe Christ died for her, even for her. We gave thanks for both, with much exultation and triumph.

After family prayer I expounded the lesson, and, going up to my chamber, asked the maid (Mary) how she found herself. She answered, "O, Sir, what you said was very comfortable, how that Christ was made sin for me, that I might be made the righteousness of God in Him; that is, he was put in my place, and I in his." "Do you then believe this, that Christ died for you?" "Yes, I do believe it; and I found myself so as I never did before, when you spoke the word." "But do you find within yourself, that your sins are forgiven?" "Yes, I do." These and the like answers, which she made with great simplicity, convinced me, that faith had come to her by hearing. We joined in giving glory to God; for we perceived and confessed it was his doing. It pleased him likewise to bless me with a deep and hitherto unknown dread of ascribing anything to myself.

Tues., June 13th. Mr. Piers was sent for to a dying woman. She was in despair, "having done so much evil, and so little good." He declared to her the glad tidings of salvation, that as all her good, were it ten thousand times more, could never save her, so all her evil would never hurt her,—if she could repent and believe; if she could lay hold on Christ by a living faith, and look for salvation by grace only. This was comfort indeed. She gladly quitted her own merits for Christ's; the Holy Ghost wrought faith in her heart, which she expressed in a calm, cheerful, triumphant expectation of death. Her fears and agonies were at an end. Being justified by faith, she had peace with God; and only entered farther into her rest, by dying a few hours after. The spectators were melted into tears. She calmly passed into the heavenly Canaan, and has there brought up a good report of her faithful Pastor, who, under Christ, hath saved her soul from death.

These were the first-fruits of his ministry; and I find him strengthened hereby, and more assured that the Gospel is the power of God unto salvation, to every one that believeth. . . .

Sat., June 24th. Riding to Blendon in the morning, I met William Delamotte, just come from Cambridge. He had left town well-disposed to the obedience of faith; but now I observed his countenance altered. He had been strongly prejudiced by the good folk at London. At Blendon I found Mr. Delamotte, not overcordial, yet civil; met letters from my mother, heavily complaining of my brother's forsaking her, and requiring me to accept of the first preferment that offered, on pain of disobedience. This a little disquieted me. I was not much comforted by William Delamotte; but extremely moved for him, and could not refrain from tears. His sisters joined us. I began preaching faith, and free grace. His objection was, that it was unjust of God to make sinners equal with us, who had laboured perhaps many years. We proposed singing an hymn. He saw the title, "Faith in Christ," and owned he could not bear it.

On our way to church, I again proclaimed to him the glad tidings of salvation. He was exceedingly heavy, and, by his own confession, miserable; yet could he not receive this saying, "We are justified freely by faith alone." The lesson comforted me concerning him. "Behold, I will send my messenger, and he shall prepare the way before me: and the Lord, whom ye seek, shall suddenly come to his temple, even the messenger of the covenant, whom ye delight in: behold, he shall come, saith the Lord." To all such as think it hard to lose the merit of their good works, the Scripture spake as follows: "Your words have been stout against me, saith the Lord: yet ye say, What have we spoken so much against thee? Ye have said, It is vain to serve God: and what profit is it that we have kept his ordinances, and that we have walked mournfully before the Lord of hosts?"

Mon., June 26th. I waited upon Mrs. Delamotte, expecting what happened. She fell abruptly upon my sermon, for the false doctrine therein. I answered, "I staked my all upon the truth of it." She went on, "It is hard people must have their children seduced in their absence.[2] If everyone must have your faith, what will become of all the world? Have you this assurance, Mr. Piers?" "Yes, Madam, in some degree: I thank God for it." "I am sorry to hear it." One of the company cried, "I am glad to hear it, and bless God for him, and wish all mankind had it too."

She moved for reading a sermon of Archbishop [John] Sharp's. Piers read. We excepted continually to his unscriptural doctrine. Much dispute ensued. She accused my brother with preaching an instantaneous faith. "As to that," I replied, "we cannot but speak the things which we have seen and heard. I received it in that manner; as have above thirty others in my presence." She started up, said she could not bear it, and ran out of the house. William protested against her behaviour. . . . At six I took my leave. Poor Hannah and Mary came to the door, and caught hold of my hand. Hannah cried, "Don't be discouraged, Sir: I hope we shall all continue steadfast." I could not refrain from tears. Hetty came in: I exhorted her to persevere. I took to horse. William seemed much better disposed than his mother; promised to come and see me the next day. I joined with Mr. Piers in singing, *"Shall I, for fear of feeble man, / Thy Spirit's course in me restrain?"* and in hearty prayer for Mrs. Delamotte.

No. 15   Hymn: "Boldness in the Gospel"

This hymn, first published in the Wesleys' *Hymns and Sacred Poems* (1739), vibrates with the vigor and holy boldness with which Charles approached these early months of ministry. It was translated from Johann J. Winckler's German "Sollt ich, aus Furcht vor Menschenkindern" (*Hymn Book of the Congregation at Herrnhut*, 1735, 17 verses). Tradition has credited John Wesley with this paraphrase, and it gained enough popularity to be reissued in his standard *Collection of Hymns for the Use of the People Called Methodists* (1780), with the omission of the last three verses printed below. The hymn appears frequently in Charles's journal as a prayerful petition for courage in the face of ministerial adversity.[3]

1   Shall I, for fear of feeble man,
   Thy Spirit's course in me restrain?
   Or, undismay'd, in deed and word
   Be a true witness to my Lord?

2   Awed by a mortal's frown, shall I
   Conceal the word of God Most High?

How can then before Thee shall I dare
To stand, or how Thy anger bear?

3 Shall I, to soothe th' unholy throng,
Soften Thy truths, and smooth my tongue?
To gain earth's gilded toys, or flee
The cross, endured my God, by Thee?

4 What then is he whose scorn I dread,
Whose wrath or hate makes me afraid?
A man! an heir of death! a slave
To sin! a bubble on the wave!

5 Yea, let man rage! since Thou wilt spread
Thy shadowing wings around my head;
Since in all pain Thy tender love
Will still my sweet refreshment prove.

6 Saviour of men! Thy searching eye
Does all my inmost thoughts descry:
Doth aught on earth my wishes raise:
Or the world's favour, or its praise?

7 The love of Christ does me constrain
To seek the wandering souls of men;
With cries, entreaties, tears, to save,
To snatch them from the gaping grave.

8 For this let men revile my name;
No cross I shun, I fear no shame:
All hail, reproach! and welcome, pain!
Only Thy terrors, Lord, restrain.

9 My life, my blood I here present;
I for Thy truth they may be spent,
Fulfill Thy sovereign counsel, Lord!
Thy will be done! Thy name adored!

10 Give me Thy strength, O God of power!
Then let winds blow, or thunders roar,
Thy faithful witness will I be—
'Tis fix'd! I can do all through Thee!

No. 16 Journal Selection: July 2, 1738

Sun., July 2d. Being to preach this morning for the first time [since his conversion], I received strength for the work of the ministry, in prayer and singing. The whole service at Basingshaw was wonderfully animating, especially the Gospel concerning the miraculous draught of fishes. [Luke 5:4–7] I preached salvation by faith to a deeply attentive audience: I gave the cup. Observing a woman full of reverence, I asked her if she had forgiveness of sins. She answered, with great sweetness and humility, "Yes, I know it now that I have forgiveness."

I preached again at London-Wall, without fear or weariness. As I was going into the church, a woman caught hold of my hand, and blessed me most heartily, telling me she had received forgiveness of sins while I was preaching in the morning.

In the evening we met, a troop of us, at Mr. Sims's. There was one Mrs. Harper there, who had this day in like manner received the Spirit, by the hearing of faith; but feared to confess it. We sung the hymn to Christ. At the words, *"Who for me, for me hath died,"* she burst into tears and outcries, "I believe, I believe!" and sunk down. She continued, and increased in the assurance of faith; full of peace, and joy, and love.

We sang and prayed again. I observed one of the maids run out, and following, found her full of tears, and joy, and love. I asked what ailed her. She answered, as soon as joy would let her, that "Christ died for her!" She appeared quite overpowered with his love.

No. 17   Hymn: "To the Son"

This hymn was also first published in *Hymns and Sacred Poems* (1739). It places the "for me" *(Christus pro me)* language, which Charles found so powerful in reading Luther, upon the lips of the singer of the hymn. The hymn became very popular, emerging in the 1780 hymnal unaltered.[4]

1   O Filial Deity,
          Accept my new-born cry!
    See the travail of Thy soul,
          Saviour, and be satisfied;
    Take me now, possess me whole,
          Who for me, for me hast died!

2   Of life Thou art the tree,
          My immortality!
    Feed this tender branch of Thine,
          Ceaseless influence derive,
    Thou the true, the heavenly Vine,
          Grafted into Thee I live.

3   Of life the Fountain Thou,
          I know—I feel it now!

Faint and dead no more I droop;
  Thou art in me; Thy supplies,
Every moment springing up,
  Into life eternal rise.

4   Thou the good Shepherd art,
       From Thee I ne'er shall part:
Thou my Keeper and my Guide,
       Make me still Thy tender care,
Gently lead me by Thy side,
       Sweetly in Thy bosom bear.

5   Thou art my daily bread;
       O Christ, Thou art my head:
Motion, virtue, strength to me,
       Me Thy living member flow;
Nourish'd I, and fed by Thee,
       Up to Thee in all things grow.

6   Prophet, to me reveal
       Thy Father's perfect will.
Never mortal spake like Thee,
       Human prophet like Divine;
Loud and strong their voices be,
       Small and still and inward Thine!

7   On Thee, my Priest, I call;
       Thy blood atoned for all.
Still the Lamb as slain appears;
       Still Thou stand'st before the throne,
Ever offering up thy ["my" in 1782 ed.] prayers,
       These presenting with Thy own.

8   Jesu! Thou art my King;
       From Thee my strength I bring!
Shadow'd by Thy mighty hand,
       Saviour, who shall pluck me thence?
Faith supports, by faith I stand
       Strong as Thy omnipotence.

9   O filial Deity,
       Accept my new-born cry!
See the travail of Thy soul,
       Saviour, and be satisfied;
Take me now, possess me whole,
       Who for me, for me hast died!

No. 18   Journal Selections: July 3–10, 1738

Mon., July 3d. I had some discourse with my friendly namesake, Charles Rivington. I begged him to suspend his judgement, till he heard me preach.

Tues., July 4th. I received a letter from my brother [Samuel] at Tiverton, full of heavy charges. At Mr. Spark's I found Jephtha Harris. I convinced him so far, that he owned he had been prejudiced against the truth; and had not faith. I carried him to Mr. Bray's; prayed over him, and pleaded the promises. All were much affected.

I corrected a sermon of Mr. Spark's on justification. Took coach for Bexley. On the way I was enabled to pray for my brother. I heard a good account of Mrs. Delamotte, that she was almost beat out of her own righteousness.

Honest Frank made one of our congregations this evening, and gave a comfortable account of the little flock at Blendon. I received a fuller account from Hetty; informing me that her mother was convinced of unbelief, and much ashamed of her behaviour towards me.[5]

Sun., July 9th. I preached my brother's sermon upon faith at ———, and a second time in St. Sepulchre's vestry.[6] In walking home with Mrs. Burton, I said, "Surely there must be something which you are not willing to give up, or God would have given you comfort before now." She answered only by her tears. After praying for her at Mr. Bray's, I lay down; rose; stopped her going home, and carried her with James and Mrs. Turner from the company to pray. After prayer, in which I was much assisted, I found her under a great concern, trembling, and cold; longing, yet dreading, to say "she believed." We prayed again. She then said, with much struggling, "Lord, I believe; help thou my unbelief." She repeated it several times, and gained strength by each repetition.

Mon., July 10th. At Mr. Spark's request, I went with him, Mr. Bray, and Mr. Burnham, to Newgate; and preached to ten malefactors, under sentence of death; but with a heavy heart. My old prejudices against the possibility of a death-bed repentance still hung upon me; and I could hardly hope there was mercy for those whose time was so short. But in the midst of my languid discourse, a sudden spirit of faith came upon me, and I promised them all pardon, in the name of Jesus Christ, if they would then, as at the last hour, repent, and believe the Gospel. Nay, I did believe they would accept of the proffered mercy, and could not help telling them, "I had no doubt but God would give me every soul of them."

In going to Mr. Chapman's I met Margaret Beutinman, and bade her follow, for we were several of us to join in prayer there. James Hutton, Mr. Holland, Mr. and Mrs. Sims got thither soon after us. We sang, and pleaded the promises. In the midst of prayer, Margaret received the atonement, and professed her faith without wavering; her love to Christ, and willingness to die that moment. We returned thanks for her, and I then offered to go. They pressed me to stay a little longer: I did so, and heard Mrs. Storer, a sister of Mr. Bray's, complain of the hardness of her heart. She owned she had been under the utmost uneasiness, since our last meeting at her brother's, unable to pray, or find any rest to her soul. While we were singing the hymn to the Father, she did find the rest she sighed after; was quite pierced, as she said, her heart ready to burst, and her whole nature overpowered. We went to prayers, and then opened the scripture, "I thank thee, O Father, Lord of heaven and earth, that thou hast hid these things from the wise and prudent, and hast revealed them unto babes." She then was strengthened to profess her faith, and increased in peace and joy. As we walked, she said she could not have conceived how these things could be; what the change was which we spoke of. Her faith was farther confirmed by public prayer; and she continued all the evening full of comfort, and peace that passeth all understanding.

No. 19 Hymn: "Of Thanksgiving to the Father"

This is probably the hymn mentioned in Charles's journal entry for July 10, 1738, since it comes from the same hymnal as the preceding song and fits the context and title indicated in the journal. The hymn is a celebration of thanksgiving for renewed relationship with God, through faith in Christ; the parable of the prodigal son (Luke 15:11f) supplied imagery for describing the reconciliation of the sinner and his or her heavenly father. It appeared in the 1780 hymnal, shortened by the omission of verse five, but otherwise unaltered.[7]

1   Thee, O my God and King,
        My Father, Thee I sing!
Hear well-pleased the joyous sound,
        Praise from earth and heaven receive;
Lost, I now in Christ am found,
        Dead, by faith in Christ I live.

2   Father, behold Thy son;
        In Christ I am Thy own.
Stranger long to Thee and rest,
        See the prodigal is come;
Open wide Thine arms and breast,
        Take the weary wanderer home.

3   Thine eye observed from far,
        Thy pity look'd me near;
Me Thy bowels yearn'd to see,
        Me Thy mercy ran to find,
Empty, poor, and void of Thee,
        Hungry, sick, and faint, and blind.

4   Thou on my neck didst fall,
           Thy kiss forgave me all:
      Still the gracious words I hear,
           Words that make the Saviour mine,
      "Haste, for him the robe prepare;
           His be righteousness Divine!"

5   Thee then, my God and King,
           My Father, Thee I sing!
      Hear well-pleased the joyous sound,
           Praise from earth and heaven receive;
      Lost, I now in Christ am found,
           Dead, by faith in Christ I live.

No. 20   Journal Selections: July 11–18, 1738

Tues., July 11th. I preached with earnestness to the prisoners from the second lesson. One or two of them were deeply affected. . . .

Mr. Sparks this morning asked me whether I would preach for him at St. Helen's. I agreed to supply Mr. Broughton's place, who is now at Oxford, arming our friends against the faith. The pain in my side was very violent; but I looked up to Christ, and owned his healing power. At the same time, that came into my mind, "Out of weakness were made strong." No sooner did I enter the coach than the pain left me, and I preached faith in Christ to a vast congregation, with great boldness, adding much extempore.

After sermon, Mrs. Hind, with whom Mr. Broughton lodges, sent for me; owned her agreement to the doctrine and pressed me to come and talk with Mr. Broughton, who, she could not but believe, must himself agree to it.

From her I went to Mr. Sims, and found that God had set his seal to my ministry; Mr. Dandy and Miss Brandford declaring, faith had come to them by hearing me. We rejoiced, and gave thanks from the ground of the heart.

Wed., July 12th. I preached at Newgate to the condemned felons, and visited one of them in his cell, sick of a fever; a poor black that had robbed his master. I told him of one who came down from heaven to save lost sinners, and him in particular; described the sufferings of the Son of God, his sorrows, agony and death. He listened with all the signs of eager astonishment; the tears trickled down his cheeks while he cried, "What! was it for me? Did God suffer all this for so poor a creature as me?" I left him waiting for the salvation of God.

In the evening Mr. Washington of Queen's [College] came to dispute with me. I simply testified my want [lack] of faith three months ago, and my having it now; asked whether he could lay down his life for the truth of his being in the faith; whether he allowed Christ to be as really present in the believing soul, as in the third heavens; told him he was yet in his sins, and knew nothing, and begged him to pray for direction.

Thur., July 13th. I read prayers and preached at Newgate, and administered the sacrament to our friends, with five of the felons. I was much
affected and assisted in prayer for them; and exhorted them with great
comfort and confidence.

Fri., July 14th. I received the sacrament from the Ordinary; spake strongly to the poor malefactors; and to the sick Negro in the condemned hole,
moved by his sorrow and earnest desire of Christ Jesus.

Sat., July 15th. I preached there [Newgate] again with an enlarged heart;
and rejoiced with my poor happy Black; who now *believes* the Son of God
loved him, and gave himself for him.

Sun., July 16th. Metcalf and Savage came: the latter received faith on
Friday night, in prayer, and is now filled with comfort, peace, and joy. I
took coach with Metcalf; preached the threefold state with boldness;[8] gave
the sacrament. I went thence to Mrs. Claggett's; sang, rejoiced, and gave
thanks, in behalf of both the maids, now added to the church by true
divine faith. Mr. Claggett coming in by mistake, we laid hold on and
carried him with us to Black-Friars. Very weak and faint, yet was I
strengthened to preach for above an hour. I was carried to bed full of
pain, expecting my fever; yet believing it could not return, unless it were
best.

Mon., July 17th. I rose free from pain. At Newgate I preached on death
(which they must suffer the day after to-morrow). Mr. Sparks assisted in
giving the sacrament. Another clergyman was there. Newington asked me
to go in the coach with him. At one I was with the Black in his cell; James
Hutton assisting. Two more of the malefactors came. I had great help and
power in prayer. One rose, and said, he felt his heart all on fire, so as he
never found himself before; he was all in a sweat; believed Christ died for
him. I found myself overwhelmed with the love of Christ to sinners. The
Black was quite happy. The other criminal was in an excellent temper;
believing, or on the point of it. I talked to another, concerning faith in
Christ; he was greatly moved. The Lord, I trust, will help *his* unbelief
also. . . .

Tues., July 18th. The Ordinary read prayers and preached. I administered the sacrament to the Black, and eight more; having first instructed
them in the nature of it. I spake comfortably to them afterwards.

In the cells, one told me, that whenever he offered to pray, or had a
serious thought, something came and hindered him; was with him almost
continually; and once appeared. After we had prayed for him *in faith*, he
rose amazingly comforted, full of joy and love; so that we could not doubt
his having received the atonement.

At night I was locked in with Bray in one of the cells. We wrestled in
mighty prayer. All the criminals were present; and all delightfully cheerful.
The soldier, in particular, found his comfort and joy increase every moment. Another, from the time he communicated, has been in perfect peace.
Joy was visible in all their faces. We sang,

Behold the Saviour of mankind,
  Nail'd to the shameful tree!
How vast the love that him inclined
  To bleed and die for thee! &c.

It was one of the most triumphant hours I have ever known. Yet on [entry ends here].

No. 21   Hymn: "On the Crucifixion," by Samuel Wesley Sr.

This hymn, which figured so prominently in the Methodist revival, was composed by the father of John and Charles Wesley. It was first published in their *Hymns and Sacred Poems* (1739). Enjoying sustained popularity, the hymn reappeared in John's "big" hymnbook of 1780 and has continued into the modern Methodist hymnals. It utilizes the poetic sense of drama that figures so prominently in Charles's compositions; the crucified Christ is hung before the mind's eye in order to elicit the response of faith and love in the singer or hearer. The approach of the hymn clearly follows the more traditional pattern of narrating the events to the reader (as in the work of Dr. Isaac Watts). Charles would later break with this tradition by assigning to the singer one of the roles in the biblical drama.[9]

1   Behold the Saviour of mankind,
      Nail'd to the shameful tree!
    How vast the love that Him inclined
      To bleed and die for thee!

2   Hark how He groans! while Nature shakes,
      And earth's strong pillars bend!
    The Temple's veil in sunder breaks,
      The solid marbles rend.

3   'Tis done! the precious ransom's paid;
      "Receive my soul," He cries:
    See where He bows His sacred head!
      He bows His head, and dies.

4   But soon He'll break Death's envious chain,
      And in full glory shine!
    O Lamb of God, was ever pain,
      Was ever love like Thine!

No. 22   Journal Selection: July 19, 1738

Wed., July 19th. I rose very heavy, and backward to visit them for the last time. At six I prayed and sang with them all together. The Ordinary would read prayers, and preached most miserably. Mr. Sparks and Mr. Broughton were present. I felt my heart full of tender love to the latter. He administered. All ten received. Then he prayed; and I after him.

At half-hour past nine their irons were knocked off, and their hands tied. I went in a coach with Sparks, Washington, and a friend of Newington's (N. himself not being permitted). By half-hour past ten we came to Tyburn, waited till eleven: then were brought the children appointed to die. I got upon the cart with Sparks and Broughton: the Ordinary endeavoured to follow, when the poor prisoners begged he might not come; and the mob kept him down.

I prayed first, then Sparks and Broughton. We had prayed before that our Lord would show there was a power superior to the fear of death. Newington had quite forgot his pain. They were all cheerful; full of comfort, peace, and triumph; assuredly persuaded Christ had died for them, and waited to receive them into paradise. Greenaway was impatient to be with Christ.

The Black had spied me coming out of the coach, and saluted me with his looks. As often as his eyes met mine, he smiled with the most composed, delightful countenance I ever saw. Read caught hold of my hand in a transport of joy. Newington seemed perfectly pleased. Hudson declared he was never better, or more at ease, in mind and body. None showed any natural terror of death; no fear, or crying, or tears. All expressed their desire of our following them to paradise. I never saw such calm triumph, such incredible indifference to dying. We sang several hymns; particularly,

> Behold, the Saviour of mankind,
>   Nail'd to the shameful tree! [No. 21]

and the hymn entitled, "Faith in Christ," which concludes,

> A guilty, weak, and helpless worm,[10]
>   Into thy hand I fall:
> Be thou my life, my righteousness,
>   My Jesus, and my all.

We prayed Him, in earnest faith, to receive their spirits. I could do nothing but rejoice: kissed Newington and Hudson; took leave of each in particular. Mr. Broughton bade them not be surprised when the cart should draw away.[11] They cheerfully replied, they should not; expressed some concern how we should get back to our coach. We left them going to meet their Lord, ready for the Bridegroom. When the cart drew off, not one stirred, or struggled for life, but meekly gave up their spirits. Exactly at twelve they were turned off. I spoke a few suitable words to the crowd; and returned, full of peace and confidence in our friends' happiness. That hour under the gallows was the most blessed hour of my life.

No. 23   Hymn: "For Condemned Malefactors"

This hymn, published only in Charles's *Hymns and Sacred Poems* (1749 edition), was composed in the context of situations like the one reported above. Charles continued this early pattern of visiting prisoners, and he was especially concerned for those who were soon to meet their end. "For Condemned Malefactors" is cast in the form of a prayer, spoken in first person by a condemned prisoner to the One who also died as a condemned malefactor. Verses nine through fourteen weave the Matt. 27 account into Charles's exposition of the passage from Psalm 79. His journal reports that it was Wesley's practice to "recommend to two condemned malefactors the example of the penitent thief." (Aug. 27, 1745)[12]

O let the sorrowful sighing of the prisoners come before Thee: according to the greatness of Thy power, preserve Thou those that are appointed to die. [Psalm 79:12, Book of Common Prayer version]

1   O Thou that hangest on the tree,
        Our curse and sufferings to remove,
     Pity the souls that look to Thee,
        And save us by Thy dying love.

2   Outcasts of men, to Thee we fly,
        To Thee who wilt the worst receive;
     Forgive, and make us fit to die;
        Alas! we are not fit to live.

3   We own our punishment is just,
        We suffer for our evil here,
     But in Thy sufferings, Lord, we trust,
        Thine, only Thine our souls can clear.

4   We have no outward righteousness,
        No merits, or good works to plead;
     We only can be saved by grace;
        Thy grace will here be free indeed.

5   Save us by grace through faith alone,
        A faith Thou must Thyself impart,
     A faith that *would* by works be shown,
        A faith that purifies the heart.

6   A faith that doth the mountains move,
        A faith that shows our sins forgiven,
     A faith that sweetly works by love,
        And ascertains our claim to heaven.

7   This is the faith we humbly seek,
        The faith in Thine all-cleansing blood;

That blood which doth for sinners plead
O let it speak us up to God!

8 Canst Thou reject our dying prayer,
   Or cast us out who come to Thee?
Our sins ah! wherefore didst Thou bear!
   Jesu, remember *Calvary!*

9 Number'd with the transgressors Thou,
   Between the felons crucified,
Speak to our hearts, and tell us now
   Wherefore hast Thou for sinners died!

10 For us wast Thou not lifted up?
   For us a bleeding Victim made?
That we, the abjects we, might hope,
   Thou hast for all a ransom paid.

11 O might we with our closing eyes
   Thee in Thy blood vesture see,
And cast us on Thy sacrifice:
   Jesus, My Lord, remember me!

12 Thou art into Thy Kingdom come:
   I own Thee with my parting breath,
God of all grace, reverse my doom,
   And save me from eternal death.

13 Hast Thou not wrought the sure belief
   I feel *this moment* in Thy blood?
And am not I the dying thief?
   And art not Thou my Lord, my God?

14 Thy blood to all our souls apply,
   To them, to me Thy Spirit give,
And I (let each cry out) and I
   With Thee in paradise shall live.

NOTES

1. Charles's sister Mehetabel, a favorite of Charles's. To his credit, Charles remained a close friend and confidant throughout her misfortunes. One of her letters to John Wesley (1743) suggests that these discussions with Charles in 1738 resulted in her own religious awakening.

2. William Delamotte (1717–1743) was then a student at Cambridge. His mother here charges Charles with corrupting him with this "false doctrine," justification by faith. William was converted through the efforts of Charles and Ingham, and for a time worked with the Methodists. He later joined the Moravians after the Wesleys broke with the Fetter Lane Society.

3. It is #270 in the 1780 *M.H.B.*, *P.W.*, I, pp. 177–179. For the German text see John Louis Nuelson, *John Wesley and the German Hymn* (Clavery, England: A. S. Holbrook, 1977), pp. 123–124.

4. #186, p. 189, in 1780 *M.H.B.*, *P.W.*, I, pp. 97–98.

5. Susanna Wesley (1669–1742) was living with her son, Samuel Jr., at Tiverton after the death of her husband. Initially she seems to have reacted rather strongly against John's and Charles's newly found formulation of salvation by faith. She apparently was won over to the Methodists' doctrine, and was reconciled to her youngest son.

6. This "sermon upon faith" was probably John Wesley's "Salvation by Faith," which he had preached at St. Mary's, "before the University at Oxford," four weeks prior to Charles's use of it (June 11, 1738). It was later published as Standard Sermon #1. Cf. *J. W. Works*, V, pp. 7–17.

7. 1780 *M.H.B.*, #184, p. 187; *P.W.*, I, pp. 96–97.

8. This sermon was probably based on 1 John 3:14, a text from which Charles extrapolated "three laws" (based on Rom. 7:23 and 8:2) that correspond to the "three moral states of human nature." The first state is "the law of sin," under which people rest in their sins. The second state is "the law of the mind," in which people recognize sin and sometimes oppose it, "reproved of sin, but not rescued from it"; this Charles characterized as a "state of contention" and "imperfect life." The third state he called "the law of the Spirit and life," in which the mind is so awakened by the Spirit of God that one does not commit willful sin. The third state Charles characterized as one of "health," "vigour," "a state of victory," or having Christ "formed in your hearts by faith." This sermon, written in the shorthand developed by John Byrom, has recently been discovered, and will be published in *CW Shorthand Sermons, op. cit.*

9. 1780 *M.H.B.*, #22, pp. 27–28; *P.W.*, I, pp. 117–118. The United Methodist *Book of Hymns* (1964), for example, carries this hymn as #428.

10. This hymn does not appear in the Methodist hymnals of the period.

11. Typically, the felons stood on a horse-drawn cart beneath a scaffold or tree, with nooses around their necks. When the cart was driven away, their execution by hanging resulted.

12. *P.W.*, IV, pp. 460–461.

4 / A Man in the Middle

With its rapid growth, Methodism's relations with the Anglican religious establishment became increasingly strained. In Charles's mind, Methodists were simply another religious society within the Church of England, but several of the societies in which the Wesleys participated (Shaw's and Fetter Lane) were drifting away from Anglicanism—if not becoming openly hostile to it. The Wesleys' association with the societies hurt their standing in the eyes of their fellow churchmen, as did their emphasis upon religious experience and "vehement" preaching of "justification by faith only." The fall of 1738 and summer of 1739 were full of irony for Charles; he found himself chiding his friends Shaw, Bray, and Stonehouse for not conforming to the rubrics of the Church of England, at exactly the same time as the Anglican establishment questioned Wesley's own "regularity," or ecclesiastical propriety.

To their fellow Anglicans, the Wesleys seemed irregular and "enthusiastic" (an eighteenth-century euphemism for "witless religious fanatics"). Many of Charles's hearers considered his soteriology an "innovation," a polite synonym for "heretical," so he took pains to appeal to Anglican homilies and Articles of Religion as he presented his case. Strained interviews with bishops, archbishops, and university officials would follow. Ecclesiastical officials also pointed to the irregularity of Charles's credentials, when the question arose in a debate over his authority to baptize. Charles's staunch Episcopalian polity allowed him to count lay baptism as no baptism at all, and hence he was willing to rebaptize those Dissenters who upon coming to faith through his evangelism requested it of him. The Bishop of London was of another opinion, and Charles's interviews with him are hardly a model of ecclesiastical diplomacy. Since he was not serving a parish Charles possessed no license to preach, nor did the nature of his relationship with the Bishop of London suggest that his Lordship would be willing to grant him one. These ecclesiastical irregularities soon barred him (forcibly in a few cases) from Anglican pulpits.

In light of his increased ministerial activity and continued illness, his friends forbade a return to Georgia. Charles's family hoped he would accept a "living" (benefice), but his friends knew Wesley's temperament and health were better suited for the academic life, and urged him to seek to return to Oxford as a fellow (of Christ Church). The avalanche of revival, however, solved Charles's vocational dilemma; in less than two years Methodism had moved from the parlors and back-rooms of London and Oxford out on to the vast greens of Moorfields and Kennington-Common, where more than ten thousand people stood to hear Charles Wesley preach.

No. 24 Journal Selections: August 26, 1738–July 1, 1739

Sun., August 26th [1738]. I was with Mr. Stonehouse: possessed with a strange fancy, that a man must be wholly sanctified before he can know that he is justified.[1]

Mon., August 28th. I came in the coach to Oxford; rejoiced at Mr. Fox's, with Mr. Kinchin, Hutchins, and other Christian friends.

Tues., August 29th. I preached to the poor prisoners in the Castle [prison]. Many [Methodists], with Mr. Watson, were present at the Society. All of one mind; earnestly seeking Christ. I read the Homilies, and continued instant in prayer. A woman cried out, "Where have I been so long? I have been in darkness: I never shall be delivered out of it,"—and burst into tears. Mrs. Cleminger, too, appeared in the pangs of new birth.

Thur., August 31st. I waited upon the Dean [of Christ Church College, Oxford]; but we could not quite agree in our notions of faith. He wondered we had not hit upon the Homilies sooner: treated me with great candor and friendliness.

At the Society I read my sermon, "The Scripture hath concluded all under sin," and urged upon each my usual question, "Do you deserve to be damned?" Mrs. Platt, with the utmost vehemence, cried out, "Yes; I do, I do!" I prayed, that if God saw there any contrite soul, he would fulfill his promises, of coming and making his abode with it. "If thou has sent thy Spirit to reprove any sinner of sin, in the name of Jesus Christ, I claim salvation for that sinner!" Again she broke out into strong cries, but of joy, not sorrow, being quite overpowered with the love of Christ. I asked her, if she believed in Jesus. She answered in full assurance of faith. We sang and rejoiced over her, (she still continued kneeling), joined in thanksgiving; but her voice was heard above ours.

Mr. Kinchin asked, "Have you forgiveness of sins?" "I am perfectly assured I have." "Have you the earnest of the Spirit in your heart?" "I have; I know I have: I feel it now within." Her answers to these and the like questions were expressive of the strongest confidence, to the great encouragement of all present. . . .

Fri., September 1st. I took coach for London. Between five and six reached Mrs. Claggett's. They heartily joined me in praise and prayer. Mr. Claggett was very friendly. James Hutton supped with us. I found several at Bray's. After prayer he told me, God plainly forbids my return to America, by my success here.

Sun., September 3d. I preached salvation by faith at Westminster Abbey; gave the cup. In the afternoon I preached at St. Botolph's; and expounded Rom. 2, at Sims's, to above two hundred people. . . .

Sun., September 10th. I preached faith in the morning at Sir George Wheeler's chapel, and assisted at the sacrament. In the afternoon at St. Botolph's. In the evening at Sims's I was much strengthened to pray and expound to above three hundred attentive souls. Another lost sheep was now brought home.

Wed., September 27th. In our way to Oxford, I talked closely with my fellow-traveller, Mr. Combes. He expressed his desire of faith: I was moved to sing, "Salvation by faith," then "Faith in Christ."[2] I told him, if the Spirit had convinced him of unbelief, he could of righteousness also, even before we reached Oxford. I stopped and prayed that he might believe. Immediately he told me, he was in such a blessed temper, as he never before experienced. We halted, and went to prayers. He testified the great delight he felt, saying, it was heaven, if it would but continue. While we were discoursing, the fire within him, he said, diffused itself through every part; he was brim full of joy, (yet not knowing he believed), and eager to praise God. He called upon me to join. "Was I now in heaven, I could not think of my sins; I should only think of praising God." We sang and shouted all the way to Oxford. . . .

Thur., September 28th. I called on my friend that was, John Sarney, now entirely estranged by the offense of the cross. I rode to my *constant* friend, John Gambold. Mr. Combes communicated with us: his warmth, he told me, had returned through his *professing* his faith. I left Mrs. Gambold in confident hope of soon receiving it. I preached boldly at Oxford; prayed after God, with Mr. Wells.

Sun., October 15th. I heard Hutchins at St. Lawrence's; had much comfort and meltings in prayer after the sacrament. I preached "The One Thing Needful" at Islington, and added much extempore; sang at Mr. Stonehouse's: Sims's was excessively crowded in the evening; spake with much boldness and warmth. At Bray's I found the bands meeting. Mr. Stonehouse was there, in a most childlike [i.e. humble] spirit. I was moved to pray for him earnestly, and according to God. I asked particularly that some one might *then* receive the atonement. While they were going, E—— came; complained of the pain and burden of sin, that bruised him. I took him aside with Hutchins. He received faith in immediate answer to our prayer; professed it; full of peace, and joy, and love. I expressed a strong desire to pray for Mr. Stonehouse. I prayed again with vehemence and tears. Bray was greatly affected; so were James and all the rest: yet no answer. Mr. Stonehouse said, the blessing was withheld from him to increase our importunity [i.e. persistence].

Fri., October 20th. Seeing so few present at St. Antholin's, I thought of preaching extempore: afraid: yet ventured on the promise, "Lo, I am with you always"; and spake on justification from Rom. 3, for three quarters of an hour, without hesitation. Glory be to God, who keepeth his promises for ever.

Sat., October 21st. I waited with my brother on the Bishop of London, to answer the complaints he had heard against us, that we preached an absolute assurance of salvation. Some of his words were, "If by 'assurance' you mean an inward persuasion, whereby a man is conscious in himself, after examining his life by the law of God, and weighing his own sincerity, that he is in a state of salvation, and acceptable to God; I don't see how any good Christian can be without such an assurance." "This," we answered, "is what we contend for: but we have been charged as Antinomians, for preaching justification by faith only." "Can any one preach otherwise, who agrees to our Church and the Scriptures?" "Indeed, by preaching it strongly, and not inculcating good works, many have been made Antinomians in theory, though not in practice: especially in King Charles' time." "But there is a heavy charge against us Bishops, by your bringing the Archbishop's authority for re-baptizing an adult." My brother answered, "That he had expressly declared the contrary: yet," added he, "if a person dissatisfied with lay-baptism should desire episcopal, I should think it my duty to administer it, after having acquainted the Bishop according to the canon." "Well; I am against it myself, where any one has had the Dissenters' baptism."[3]

Next my brother inquired, whether his reading in a Religious Society made it a conventicle.[4] His Lordship warily referred us to the laws; but upon our urging the question, "Are the Religious Societies conventicles?" he answered, "No; I think not: however, you can read the acts and laws as well as I: I determine nothing." We hoped his Lordship would not henceforward receive an accusation against a Presbyter [Anglican priest], but at the mouth of two or three witnesses. He said, "No; by no means. And you may have free access to me at all times." We thanked him, and took our leave.

Sun., November 12th. Mr. Piers refused me his pulpit, through fear of man; pretending tenderness to his flock. I plainly told him, if he so rejected my testimony, I would come to see him no more. I walked back to town [London] in the strength of the Lord; and expounded at Sims's. All were dissolved in tears.

Tues., November 14th. I had another conference with his Lordship [Bishop] of London. "I have used your Lordship's permission to wait upon you. A woman desires me to baptize her; not being satisfied with her baptism by a Dissenter: she says sure and unsure is not the same." He immediately took fire, and interrupted me: "I wholly disapprove of it: it is irregular." "My Lord, I did not expect your approbation. I only came, in obedience, to give you notice of my intention." "It is irregular. I never receive any such information, but from the Minister [parish priest]." "My Lord, the Rubric [rule] does not so much as require the Minister to give you notice, but any discrete person. I have the Minister's leave." "Who gave you authority to baptize?" "Your Lordship: and I shall exercise it in any part of the known world." "Are you a licensed Curate?" "I have the leave of the proper Minister." "But don't you know, no man can exercise parochial duty in London, without my leave? It is only *sub silentio.*" "But you know many do take that permission for authority; and you yourself allow it." "It is one thing to connive, and another to approve. I have power to inhibit you." "Does your Lordship exert that power? Do you now inhibit me?" "O, why will you push things to an extreme? I do not inhibit you." "Why then, my Lord, according to your own conscience, you permit or authorize me." "I have a power to punish, and to forbear punishing." "That seems to imply, that I have done something worthy of punishment. I should be glad to know, what I may answer. Does your Lordship charge me with any crime?" "No, no: I charge you with no crime." "Do you then dispense with my giving you notice of any baptizing for the future?" "I neither dispense, nor not dispense."

He railed at Lawrence on lay-baptism; blamed my brother's sermon, as inclining to Antinomianism. I charged Archbishop Tillotson with denying the faith. He allowed it, and owned they ran into one extreme, to avoid another. He concluded the conference with, "Well, Sir, you knew my judgement before, and you know it now. Good morrow to you."

I read prayers at Islington, and baptized an adult; Mr. Stonehouse, M. Sims, and M. Burton, being the witnesses.

Wed., November 22d. I set out for Oxford.

Sat., November 25th. I felt a pining desire to die; foreseeing the infinite dangers and troubles of life. At Mr. Wells's I preached *the* faith of the Gospel to him and Mr. Hoare. Charles carried me to the Castle. I read prayers, and was afterwards constrained to speak freely and fully. I was much cheered by it myself. I rode with Mr. Wells and Kinchin to Coggs, where we spent the evening in prayer and the Scriptures.

Tues., November 28th. I dined in Christ-Church Hall [his college] as one not belonging to them.

Wed., November 29th. After morning prayers, I called on Mr. Whitefield, who pressed me to accept of a College living. I read prayers, and preached at the Castle.

Sat., December 9th. I was with the Dean; who complained of my brother's obscurity in his sermon on salvation;[5] and expressly denied the assurance of faith, and earnest of the Spirit.

Thur., December 21st. At St. Antholin's the Clerk [of session] asked my name, and said, "Dr. Venn has forbidden any Methodist to preach. Do you call yourself a Methodist?" "I do not: the world may call me what they please." "Well, Sir," said he, "it is pity the people should go away without preaching. You may preach." I did so, on good works.

Tues., December 26th. George Whitefield preached. We had the sacrament this and the four following days. On Thursday my brother preached; on Friday, George Whitefield; and on Saturday, Mr. Robson. The whole week was a festival indeed; a joyful season, holy unto the Lord.

Tuesday, January 2d, 1739. I was at Mr. Stonehouse's with M. Vaughan and others. I urged him to throw away his mystics; but he adhered to them with greater obstinacy. I saw myself in him.

Fri., January 5th. My brother, Mr. Seward, Hall, Whitefield, Ingham, Kinchin, Hutchins, all set upon me; but I could not agree to settle at Oxford, without farther direction from God.

Wed., January 17th. George Whitefield gave us so promising account of Oxford, that I found myself strongly inclined to go.

Wed., February 21st. I heard that Cowley living [benefice] was disposed of; and rejoiced.[6] With my brother I waited on the Archbishop. He showed us great affection; spoke mildly of Mr. Whitefield; cautioned us to give no more umbrage than was necessary for our own defense; to forbear exceptionable phrases; to keep to the doctrines of the Church. We told him we expected persecution; would abide by the Church till her Articles and Homilies were repealed. He assured us he knew of no design in the governors of the Church to innovate; and neither should there be any innovation while he lived: avowed justification by faith only; and his joy to see us as often as we pleased.

From him we went to the Bishop of London; who denied his having condemned or even heard much of us. G. Whitefield's Journal, he said, was tainted with enthusiasm, though he was himself a pious, well-meaning youth. He warned us against Antinomianism, and dismissed us kindly. . . .

Sun., February 25th. I preached justification by faith at Bexley. In the beginning of my discourse about twenty went out of church. They were better pleased with (or at least more patient of) me in the afternoon, while I preached on the woman at our Saviour's feet. Faint and spent at Blendon, I revived by exhorting above two hundred of the poor.

Wed., February 28th. I meet the bands at J. Bray's and cautioned them against schism. I was violently opposed by one who should have seconded me. They urged me to go to Oxford: but I understood them, and begged to be excused.

Sat., March 10th. I went to Newgate with my usual reluctance; preached with freedom; and in prayer had great power, as all present seemed to confess. I expounded at Beach-lane: in prayer I asked some token, if our Gospel really is a ministration of the Spirit; and I inquired if any had received an answer. One, and another, and another testified their sense of the divine presence. We rejoiced as men that divide the spoil.

Sun., March 11th. I preached justification at St. Catherine's [London]. I baptized two women at Islington (five adults I baptized some time before), and preached with great liberty from the woman of Samaria. My friend Stonehouse was very peevish with me for a trifle [the argument at Bray's above?], and very warm. I kept my temper, but was hindered in my expounding by his disputes. . . .

Tues., April 17th. I tried in vain to check Mr. Shaw in his wild rambling talk against the Christian priesthood. At last I told him, I would oppose him to the utmost; and either he or I must quit the Society. . . .

Wed., April 18th. I met Mr. Shaw at James's [Hutton]. He insisted that there would be no priesthood; but he himself could baptize and administer the other sacrament as well as any man. [. . .] In my expounding I warned [the Society] strongly against schism; into which Shaw's notions must necessarily lead. The Society were all for my brother's immediate return.

Wed., April 25th. I began Potter on Church Government: a seasonable antidote against the growing spirit of delusion.[7] I heard G. Whitefield, very powerful, at Fetter-lane. I was with him and Howel Harris, a man after my own heart. George related the dismal effect of Shaw's doctrine at Oxford. Both Howel and he insisted on Shaw's expulsion from the Society. . . .

Fri., April 27th. I heard G. Whitefield in Islington churchyard. The numerous congregation could not have been more affected within the walls. I exhorted them at Fetter-lane to continue steadfast in the means of grace [i.e. sacraments].

Sat., April 28th. Mr. Stonehouse was much concerned that we should so misunderstand, as if he had forbid G. Whitefield's preaching in his church. To-day he preached out again. After him, Bowers got up to speak: I conjured him not; but he beat me down, and *followed his impulse*. I carried many away with me.[8] In the evening I expounded at Exall's. A woman received the atonement.

Sun., April 29th. At Islington vestry the Churchwardens forbad my preaching: demanded my local licence.[9] I said nothing but that "I heard them." Scions was very abusive; bidding me shake off the dust of my feet, &c; and said, "You have all the spirit of the devil," mentioning Mr. Whitefield, Stonehouse, and me by name.

After prayers Mr. Stonehouse made way for me to the pulpit: I offered to go up, when one Cotteril, and a Beadle, forcibly kept me back. I thought of, "The servant of the Lord must not strive"; and yielded. Mr. Streat preached. I assisted at the sacrament. I preached afterwards at our house, and prayed fervently for the opposers. I waited on Justice Elliot. He had gone with Sir John Gunson into the vestry, and severly chid [sic] the Churchwardens; who had made the Clerk read the canon, call a vestry, &c. Mr. Streat advised to ask Mr. Stonehouse to discharge me from ever preaching again.

In the afternoon Scions abused Streat himself at the vestry; abused us; owned he said, "the devil was in us all." I read prayers; Mr. Scott preached. At night I was greatly strengthened to expound, and pray for our persecutors. All were mild and peaceable among the bands. I heard that George [Whitefield] had had above ten thousand hearers.

Mon., April 30th. I preached at the Marshalsea [prison]. Mr. Stonehouse told us, he had been with the Bishop, but left him close, shut up, sour, refusing to answer but to the written case. . . .

Tues., May 1st. During the time of prayers, the Churchwardens still kept guard on the pulpit-stairs. I was not inclined to fight my way through them. Mr. Stonehouse preached a thundering sermon (unless their consciences are seared). I took notes of it. . . . [At James's Society] A poor harlot was struck down by the word. She, and all, were melted into tears, and prayers, and strong cries for her. I have good hope this brand will also be plucked out of the fire.

Wed., May 16th. . . . I attended G. Whitefield to Blackheath. He preached in the rain to many listening sinners. At Fetter-lane a dispute arose about lay-preaching. Many, particularly Bray, and Fish, were very zealous for it. Mr. Whitefield and I declared against it.

Tues., May 29th. Franklyn, a farmer, invited me to preach in his field. I did so, to about five hundred, on, "Repent, for the kingdom of heaven is at hand." I returned to the house rejoicing.[10]

Thur., May 31st. A Quaker sent me a pressing invitation to preach at Thackstead. I scrupled preaching in another's parish, till I had been refused the church. Many Quakers, and near seven hundred others, attended, while I declared in the highways, "The Scripture hath concluded all under sin."

Mon., June 4th. . . . I met Shaw, the self-ordained Priest. He was brim full of proud wrath and fierceness. His spirit suited to his principles. I could do him no good; but was kept calm and benevolent towards him; therefore he could do me no harm. I stood by G. Whitefield, while he preached on the mount in Blackheath. The cries of the wounded were heard on every side. What has Satan gained by turning him out of the churches?

Fri., June 15th. The last time I had met Mr. Stonehouse and our opposers in the vestry, he astonished by telling me, "He had consented that I should preach no more." I thought in myself, "What is man?" or "What is friendship?" and said nothing. To-day, in company with my brother and him, I mentioned, without intending it, my exclusion through his consent. He pleaded, that the Bishop of London had justified his Churchwardens in their forcible expulsion of me: but at last was quite melted down; would do anything to repair his fault; resolved no other should be excluded by him, as I had been.

Sun., June 17th. My brother preached to above ten thousand people (as was supposed) in Moorfields, and to a still larger congregation on Kennington-Common. I preached twice in the prison.

Tues., June 19th. I was at Lambeth with Mr. Piers. His Grace [The Archbishop, Potter] expressly forbad him to let any of us preach in his church: charged us with breach of the canon. I mentioned the Bishop of London's authorizing my forcible exclusion. He would not hear me; he did not dispute. He asked me what call I hold. I answered, "A dispensation of the Gospel is committed to me." "That is, to St. Paul; but I do not dispute: and will not proceed to excommunication YET." "Your Grace has taught me in your book on Church Government, that a man unjustly excommunicated is not thereby cut off from communion with Christ." "Of that I am the judge." I asked him, if Mr. Whitefield's success was not a spiritual sign, and sufficient proof of his call: recommended Gamaliel's advice.[11] He dismissed us; Piers, with kind professions; me, with all the marks of his displeasure. . . .

Sat., June 23d. Some of the persons set at liberty came, and called on me to return him thanks in their behalf. Twelve received forgiveness, it seems, last night; another in this hour. I dined at Mr. Stonehouse's. My inward conflict continued. I perceived it was the fear of man; and that, by preaching in the field next Sunday, as George Whitefield urges me, I shall break down the bridge, and become desperate. I retired, and prayed for particular direction; offering up my friends, my liberty, my life, for Christ's sake and the Gospel's. I was somewhat less burdened; yet could not be quite easy, till I gave up all.

Sun., June 24th. St. John Baptist day. The first scripture I cast my eye upon, was, "Then came the servant unto him, and said, Master, what shall we do?" I prayed with West, and went forth in the name of Jesus Christ. I found near ten thousand helpless sinners waiting for the word, in Moorfields. I invited them in my Master's words, as well as name: "Come unto me, all ye that travail, and are heavy laden, and I will give you rest." The Lord was with me, even me, his meanest [least] messenger, according to his promise. At St. Paul's, the Psalms, Lessons &c., for the day, put fresh life into me. So did the sacrament. My load was gone, and all my doubts and scruples. God shone upon my path; and I knew this was his will concerning me. At Newington, the Rector, Mr. Motte, desired me to preach. My text was, "All have sinned, and come short of the glory of God; being justified freely," &c. I walked on to the Commons, and cried to multitudes upon multitudes, "Repent ye, and believe the Gospel." The Lord was my strength, and my mouth, and my wisdom. O that all would therefore praise the Lord for his goodness!

Fri., June 29th. . . . I reached Oxford the next day.

Sat., June 30th. I waited upon the Dean, who spoke with unusual severity against field-preaching and Mr. Whitefield: explained away all inward religion, and union with God.

That the world, and their God, abhor our manner of acting I have too sensible proof. This whole week has the messenger of Satan been buffeting me with uninterrupted temptation.

Sun., July 1st. I preached my sermon on justification before the University, with great boldness. All were attentive. One could not help but weeping. At night I received power to expound; several Gownsmen [scholars] were present; some mocked.

No. 25   Sermon: On Romans 3:23–25

This sermon, preached Sunday, July 1, 1739, as the manuscript indicates, "before the University in Oxford," is one of the earliest extant examples of Charles's pulpit work. It is the most complete statement of his presentation of "justification by faith only," and comes to us in the polished form of a sermon presented to a learned, Anglican audience. The sermon, only recently discovered, has been transcribed from Charles's shorthand by Thomas Albin and Oliver Beckelegge, and is published here for the first time, with their permission. The portions lined through below show how Charles edited his homily as he composed it.

Let us pray for all mankind, for the catholick [sic] Church; especially that part of it established in these kingdoms; for our Gracious Sovereign Lord, GEORGE of Great Britain, France, and Ireland, King, Defender of the Faith; for their Royal Highnesses, Frederick, Prince of Wales, ye Princess of Wales, the Duke, the Princesses, and all the Royal Family. For his majesty's most honorable Privy Council, the Nobility, Clergy, Gentry, and Commons of this land; for all schools and nurseries of true religion and useful learning; particularly ye two Universities. And here in Oxford, for the Right Honorable Charles[Butler], Earl of Arran, our Honoured Lord and Chancellor; for the very worthy ye Vice-Chancellor;[12] for all the Doctors, both ye Proctors, all heads and governors of Colleges and Halls with their respective societies; and (as I am more especially obliged) for ye good estate of Christ Church; and therein for the Reverend the Dean, ye Rt. Reverend, and the Reverend the Canons, ye students, chaplains, commoners, and all other members of that society.

Let us bless GOD unfeignedly for all his mercy in Christ Jesus, spiritual and temporal; particularly for the liberality of our founder and benefactors, among whom was Henry VIII, the munificent founder of Christ Church. Let us commend to His fatherly compassion the afflicted, and conclude our prayers saying:[13]

Our Father which art in heaven, hallowed be Thy Name. Thy Kingdom come. Thy will be done in earth as it is in heaven. Give us this day our daily bread; and forgive us our trespasses, as we forgive them that trespass against us. And lead us not into temptation, but deliver us from evil, For thine is the kingdom, the power and the glory, for ever and ever. Amen.

Rom. 3:23, 24, 25: All have sinned and come short of the glory of God, being justified freely by His grace, through the redemption that is in Jesus Christ: whom God hath set forth to be a propitiation through faith in His blood.

In this epistle [the] Spirit of God by the mouth of His apostle, first convinces the world of sin and then of righteousness. Herein is the righteousness of God revealed from heaven against all ungodliness and unrighteousness of men who hold the truth in unrighteousness: as the heathen are first proved to do, because they lived not up to the light of nature, or that knowledge of Himself which God had showed unto them. God therefore for their unthankfulness and adultery gave them over to uncleanness, to vile affections, to a reprobate mind: he stirred the best in them to chastise the vile: unnatural[?] lust[?] to punish[?] learned[?] pride.

Next He proveth the Jews to hold the truth in unrighteousness, and declares them inexcusable and self-condemned for judging others, because they did the same things which they condemned. There were called Jews indeed, and rested in the law, and made their boast of God. But they did not keep the law they gloried in, but dishonoured God by transgressing it. They broke it in its spiritual meaning. In heart they were thieves, adulterers, sacrilegists, and were all concluded in sin by, "He is not a Jew which is one outwardly; neither is that circumcision which is outward in the flesh: but he is a Jew which is one inwardly, and [whose] circumcision is that of the heart; in the spirit not the letter, whose praise is not of men but of God."

To convince them that they were in no wise better by nature than the heathen, he shows from Scripture that there is no one righteous, no, not one; and then observes, "Now we know that what things soever the law saith, it saith to them that are under the law; that every mouth may be stopped, and all the world become guilty before God."

Therefore by the deeds of the law shall no flesh be justified in His sight. The consequence is inevitable. Because all men without exception are breakers of the law, therefore by his obedience to the law shall no man living be justified with God. For by the law (the moral law) is the knowledge of sin (only, but no deliverance from it), but now (that all men are condemned and proved to have no sufficient righteousness of their own) the righteousness of God without the law (that is as contradistinguished from legal righteousness from our own moral obedience) is manifested, being witnessed by the law and the prophets; even the righteousness of God (not of men) which is by faith of Jesus Christ (which by faith as the instrument of receiving it) is (imputed) unto all, and (bestowed or put) upon all them that believe: for there is no (natural) difference, for (as it follows in the words of my text) all have sinned, and come short of the glory of God: being justified freely by His grace through the redemption that is in Jesus Christ; whom God hath set forth to be a propitiation through faith in His blood.

In discoursing upon each word I shall first show that all have sinned and come short of the glory of God. Secondly, that we are justified freely by His grace through the redemption that is in Jesus Christ. Thirdly, I shall show what that faith is through which we receive the atonement *applied to our soul in particular:* and fourthly, I shall conclude with a particular application.[14]

I am first to show that all have sinned and come short of the glory of God, 'usterountai tas doxes tou theou are deprived of the glory of God, the glorious image of Him that created them. This is the cause of all actual transgressions sin, our having lost the moral perfection of the divine nature. First then I shall show that we have sinned originally and then actually.

God created man in His own image, after His likeness. He made him perfect, but a little lower than the angels, one in heart and mind[?] with Himself! a real partaker of the divine nature. But man soon fell from that original dignity. He sinned by eating of the forbidden fruit, and in the day that he ate he spiritually died. The life of his soul, consisting in its union with God (like as the natural life consists in the union of soul and body), his spiritual life, I say, was extinguished. The glory immediately departed from him, and he knew that he was naked: in the view of[?] God, stripped of the divine image: a motley mixture of beast and devil.

In the moment that he was thus alienated from the life of God, his understanding was darkened through ignorance that was then in him. Then also, he first felt the torment of self-will, and hell of pride. His heart was turned within him, from good to evil, from the Creator to the creature: his very soul clave to the dust, and all his affection became earthly, sensual, devilish.

In him we see the type and father of us all. We all inherit from him a miserable, corrupt and sinful nature. We are a race of fallen spirits. We are all by nature children of wrath, ignorant of good, and haters of God. For the natural man (that is, man without exception while in a state of nature), receiveth not the things of the Spirit of God: for they are foolishness unto him, neither can he know them because they are spiritually discerned. The carnal mind is enmity against God; for it is not[?] [subject] to the law of God, neither indeed can be. All the powers of men are totally depraved. The whole head is sick, and the whole heart faint. From the sole of the foot even unto the head there is no soundness in him, but wounds and bruises and putrefying sores: his understanding is darkened, his will perverse, his affections set on earthly things. Pride and concupiscence make up his wretched composition; and if you take away that spark of God which was restored to him at his redemption, there remains in him nothing but pure beast and devil.

Such are we all through original sin, or "that fault and corruption of the nature of every man, whereby man is very far gone from original righteousness and is of his own nature inclined to evil, so that the flesh lusteth always contrary to the Spirit."[15] That this infection is, and remains, both in the unregenerate and regenerate, our own church teaches us agreeable to the Scripture and experience: and those happy men *thus together* who deny this corruption, are themselves the strongest proof of it. How else were it possible for one pretending to reason, to imagine such a creature as man could in his present state come out of the hands of a pure and wise and mighty God. As the workman, such must be the workmanship. A powerful, perfect, happy being could make nothing weak, imperfect or miserable. Man therefore must have undergone a change since his first creation. Of his very thinking upon his sensible damnation in those astonishing contrarieties he finds within himself.[16]

He finds two opposite principles, inclining him to good and evil, which nothing can account for but the scriptural doctrine of a [fallen race?].

But I now speak to those who acknowledge all Scripture to be given by inspiration of God: and while we receive His testimony we must own that we are literally born in sin, and consequently children of wrath and heirs of hell. We are naturally engendered of the offspring of Adam. A corrupt tree can bring forth only corrupt fruit; and such as is the fountain, such must be the stream. Whence every man must say with David, "Behold, I was shapen in wickedness, and in sin did my mother conceive me"; or with Eliphaz, "What is man that he should be clean, and he that is born of a woman that he should be righteous?" (How then can man be justified with God, or how can he be clean that is born of woman?) Alas, in him dwelleth no good thing; but sin dwelleth in him; his inward parts are very wickedness; his heart is deceitful above all things, and desperately wicked; nay, every motion of the thoughts of his heart is only evil continually.

How truly does our church teach us that this infusion of nature in every person born into the world deserveth God's wrath and damnation; for saith not the Scripture so? By ones [sic] man's disobedience many are made sinners; by the offense of one, judgement is come upon all men to condemnation. In Adam all died. Sin by him entered into the world, and death by sin, and so death passed upon all men for that all have sinned in him. Death reigns by one, even spiritual, temporal, and eternal death. In the midst of life we are in spiritual death: a foolish[?] boasting [exercise?] brings on our torment; and that consigns us to the death that never dies, the fire that never shall be quenched.

Such is the portion of our natural inheritance. We are all involved in the g[uilt?] of ours, which like the ancient flood has overspread the face of the earth, and swept all before it into a miserable eternity. The Scripture hath concluded all under sin: and that not only original, but also actual. This the great apostle shows at large in the words preceding my text, where speaking of Jews and Gentiles he asks, "Are we better than they (are we in ourselves better than the most profligate sinners?). No, in no wise." For he has before proved both Jews and Gentiles that they are all under sin. As it is written, "There is none righteous, no, not one. They are all gone out of the way, they are together become unprofitable, there is none that doeth good, no, not one. Now we know that what things soever the law saith, it saith to them that are under the law, that every mouth may be stopped and all the world become guilty before God. There is no difference. All have sinned and come short of the glory of God." There is not a just man upon earth, said the preacher, that doeth good and sinneth not: and we have therefore the greatest reason, every one of us, to say with the man after God's own heart. "Enter not into judgment with thy servant, Oh Lord, for in Thy sight shall no man living be justified. If thou, Lord, wilt be extreme to mark what is done amiss, who may abide it?"

From these and many other Scriptures, it is evident that if we say we have no sin, we deceive ourselves and the truth is not in us; if we say we have not actually sinned, we make God a liar and His word is not in us. We have offended and in many things do still offend all.

This will appear still plainer to us, if we consider the nature and extent of that law in the transgressing of which sin consists. Indeed while we look upon it as did the carnal Jews, as do the generality of Christians, to be merely an outward fence of restraint, we may flatter ourselves that we keep the law, because we abstain from the outward act of sin. But this is the least part of the law. It does indeed condemn every one of gross sin, and he that so committeth sin is of the devil; but it no wise condemns every idle word and every unholy thought. He breaks the law who breaks it outwardly and in the letter; but not he only. The law is spiritual, that is, it has a meaning infinitely broader, higher and deeper than we can at first sight perceive, or indeed than we can ever perceive till God hath opened our eyes by that Spirit which He hath promised to send that He may reprove the world of sin. Without His operation it is impossible to discern the full sense and spirituality of the law, though our Lord Himself came down from heaven to discover it. Of this we need no stronger proof than those Christians, as they are called, who read His sermon on the Mount, and yet continue utterly ignorant of what spiritual righteousness means.

Throughout that excellent discourse, our Lord sets Himself to rescue the law from those softening, polluting, gross interpretations the Scribes and Pharisees had put upon it, who had purged it of all its spiritual meaning and truth that whosoever observed it outwardly fulfilled it effectually. In opposition to this our divine teacher explains that law which He only could fulfill. He begins with discussing those holy tempers without which all outward obedience is formal and pharisaical. For all our pretensions to righteousness are vain till we taste that poverty of spirit, to which alone belongs the kingdom of heaven; till we not only see but feel our misery, and go mourning all the day long, refusing to be conformed by any created good, and looking for the Holy Ghost the Comforter. To this must be added a meekness which no injuries can overcome, no affronts or indignities can exasperate; a hunger and thirst after divine righteousness as much stronger than the natural appetite, as spiritual food is better than bodily; a purity of heart which sees God and only God in everything. Merciful we must likewise be as our Father which is in heaven is merciful; and lastly peacemakers, like unto Him when He was in Christ reconciling the world to himself. After all, the world, or they that will not be reconciled to Him, must set to their seal that we belong to Christ, by reviling and persecuting[?] and saying all manner of evil against us falsely for His sake, while we rejoice and are exceeding glad, in nothing terrified by our adversaries, which is to them an evident token of perdition, but to us of salvation, and that of God.

Such are the tempers requisite of every Christian as obedient[?] unto salvation[?]. Herein must our righteousness exceed the righteousness of the Scribes and Pharisees, or we shall in no wise enter into the kingdom of heaven. God is a Spirit, and they that worship Him must worship Him in spirit and in truth. He requires the heart; a spiritual not a mere literal obedience, the power of godliness not the bare form. Wherefore if we allow Him to be a true interpreter of the law, we must acknowledge ourselves to be transgressors of it. Two instances in the sixth chapter: commandments [in] which our Lord Himself assures us that not only he that sheddeth man's blood transgresses it, but that whosoever is angry with his brother without a cause, whosoever expresses that anger in an opprobrious name or slighting word is guilty of murder.

The seventh commandment He explains in like manner, extending to the first wandering of the desire: so that a single thought, a secret motion of the heart makes a man in the sight of God a murderer or an adulterer. And here He may justly say to every one of us, Thou art the man! Thou art a murderer, thou art an adulterer! For which of us can say he never felt any thought of causeless anger against his brother? He that hath ever felt the least degree of hatred against another whether [valid or not?], he stands convicted of murder: for he that hateth his brother is a murderer.

With respect to the adulterer, likewise we may make our Lord's commandment, He that is without sin amongst you, let him first cast a stone at her. But suppose our hearts could acquit us of having ever known one impure thought throughout our lives, are we hereby justified of this charge? No, in no wise. The apostle informs us of a spiritual adultery. Ye adulterers and adulteresses, said he, know ye not that the whole conversation of our life is one continued act habit of rebellion, treachery, and unfaithfulness to that one husband to whom ye were espoused in baptism . . . unless you have indeed renounced that world which ye then so solemnly promised and vowed to renounce. If you have now any share in its pursuits after riches, honour and pleasures, any conformity to its affections, any hope of keeping faith[?] with it, that is whosoever who are not led by the Spirit of God in love, then do you live in an habit of secret adultery, then are you friends to the world and enemies to God.

To those among us who are thus of the world, that is who either love or are loved by it, it may hence appear that they have not so much as the Pharisee's plea. "I thank God that I am not as other men are, extortioners, unjust, adulterers!" But suppose we had[?]; does righteousness stand in negatives only? Does it not require good to be done as well as evil to be left undone? Yes doubtless, we may answer, and go on with our boasting Pharisee, "I fast twice a week, I give tithes of all that I possess," or to put it in other words, ["]I use[17] all the means of grace, I do much good." It is well: he is no fulfiller of the law that does not; but neither is he that does, unless all these actions proceed from a heart entirely devoted to God; unless they are fruits of that perfect love required by the first and great commandment, "Thou shalt love the Lord thy God with all thy heart and mind and strength." Who among us is there that can say, This have I done: I have so loved God; with my entire affection, with the utmost extent of my understanding, with all and every degree of all my powers and feelings[?], with the whole capacity and possibility[?] of my soul. Who of all the sons of Adam could ever say it? Else we must confess, with man this is impossible: their very mouth is stopped indeed, and all the world become guilty before God.

As evil doers[?] are we concluded under sin by almost every part of the gospel. "Pray without ceasing; in everything give thanks; rejoice evermore; whether ye eat or drink or whatsoever ye do, do all to the glory of God." But these Scriptures, some one will say, are not to be taken literally. I ask that person, who told you so? The world, the flesh and the devil did, I grant you; but not Christ: and their authority will never bear you out in your contempt of this: no, not though you could confront Him (which God forbid you ever should) with ten thousand of his own [almighty Scriptures?]. Yea, let God be true, and every man a liar. He hath assured us the law is spiritual, and the commandment holy and just and good. He hath likewise shown us a way whereby the righteousness of the law may be [ful]filled in us without our bringing it down to the practice of modern Christians. If we will hearken unto Him more than unto man, we cannot be acquitted[?], the law does in the rigour require perfection, or universal unsinning[?] obedience, to which we must therefore come up, or own ourselves transgressors. For whosoever shall keep the whole law, and yet offend in one point, he is guilty of all: and cursed is every one that continueth not in all things which are written in the book of the law to do them.

Nor is the doing them outwardly the doing them at all. God requireth truth in the inward parts: and he that is in Christ is a new creature in the strictest sense; old things are passed away in him and all things are become new. He has a new heart, a right spirit created in him, and has undergone an entire change. He is as different from what he was as light from darkness, life from death, the kingdom of God from that of Satan. But except a man be thus born again, he cannot see the kingdom of God; he cannot so much as discern there is any such thing as that kingdom of God within him, which is righteousness and peace and joy in the Holy Ghost. But till he knows this expressly, he knows nothing yet as he ought to know. So far is he from not offending in any, that he offends in every point of the law; so far is he from keeping the whole, that he does not fulfill the least part of it. Nor can he fulfill it in any, nor can he help breaking it in every particular, till he is renewed in the image of his maker, and so born of God as not to commit sin; till Christ, the end of the law for righteousness unto everyone that believeth, be of God made unto him wisdom and righteousness and sanctification and redemption.

This brings me to my second head, "We are justified freely by His grace through the redemption that is in Jesus Christ." A most important truth, as that on which alone depends the salvation of all men; but which no child of Adam can receive till he is truly convinced of sin; till he receives the sentence of death in himself, that he may not trust in himself; till, in a word, he owns and feels that all his desert is hell.

Before a man is thus deeply sensible of his misery, all attempts to remove it must prove vain and unfruitful. Before he can take any step towards his divine Physician, he must know and confess and groan under his disease. He must acknowledge it is by him incurable, and in just despair go out of himself for a remedy. "Come unto Me, says the God of our health, all ye that labour and are heavy laden and I will give you rest." He calls none but the weary and heavy laden because He knows no one else will come. Such only do I invite in His name; such as are not startled or offended at being told they deserve not one, but ten thousand hells, even as many as their own infinite sins and transgressions.

Every sinner deserves to be damned, every man is a sinner, therefore every man deserves to be damned. Which of the promises can be denied without denying the Scriptures? "The wages of sin are death; the wrath of God is revealed against all unrighteousness of men, and there is no one righteous, no, not one." The Scriptures hath concluded all under sin. To convince the world of this, is the first office of the Holy Spirit; and when a man is truly convinced of sin, then and not till then, may he be convinced of righteousness also; even the righteousness of God which is by faith of Jesus Christ unto all and upon all them that believe; for there is no difference; for all have sinned and come short of the glory of God, being justified freely by His grace, through the redemption that is in Jesus Christ.

I shall deliver this offending[?] doctrine of justification by faith only, in the words of our own excellent Church as they are plainly set forth in the homilies.[18]

"Because all men be sinners and offenders against God and breakers of His law and commandments, therefore can no man by his own acts, works or deeds, seem they ever so good, be justified or made righteous before God; but every man of necessity is constrained to seek for another righteousness or justification to be received at God's own hand, that is to say, the forgiveness of his sins and trespasses. And this justification or righteousness which we so receive is of God's mercy and Christ's merits embraced by faith, is taken, accepted and allowed of God for our perfect and full justification."

For the more full understanding hereof, it is our duty ever to remember the great mercy of God, how that all the world being wrapped in sin by breaking of the law, God sent His only Son our Saviour Christ into this world to fulfill the law for us, and by the shedding of His most precious blood, to make a sacrifice and satisfaction or amends to His Father for our sins, and assuage His wrath and indignation conceived against us for the same.

This is that justification which St. Paul speaketh of when he said, "No man can be justified by the works of the law, but freely by faith in Christ

Jesus." And again, we believe in Christ that we be justified freely by the faith of Christ and not by the works of the law, because no man shall be justified by the works of the law.

God in the mystery of our redemption hath so tempered His mercy and justice together, that He would neither by His justice condemn us without mercy, nor by His mercy deliver us clearly without justice or payment of a just ransom. And whereas it lay not in us to pay it, He provided a ransom for us which was the most precious body and blood of His most dear and best beloved Son Jesus Christ; who besides this ransom fulfilled the law for us perfectly; and so the justice of God and His mercy did embrace together and fulfilled the mystery of our redemption.

Of this justice and mercy knit together speaketh St. Paul [in] Rom. 3. All have sinned and come short of the glory of God, being justified freely by His grace, through the redemption that is in Jesus Christ. And chapter ten, Christ is the end of the law for righteousness to every one that believeth. And chapter eight, for what the law could not do in that it was weak through the flesh, God, sending His own Son in the likeness of sinful flesh, and for sin, condemned sin in the flesh, that the righteousness of the law might be fulfilled in us, who walk not after the flesh but after Spirit.

In these places the apostle touches three things which must go together in our justification. Upon God's part, His great mercy and grace; upon Christ's part, justice, that is the satisfaction of God's justice, or the price of our redemption by the offering of His body and shedding of His blood with fulfilling of the law perfectly and thoroughly; and upon our part, true and lively faith in the merits of Jesus Christ, which yet is not ours but by God's working in us.

St. Paul declareth here nothing upon the behalf of man concerning his justification, but only a true and lively faith, which nevertheless is the gift of God. And yet this faith doth not shut out repentance, hope, love, and the fear of God in every believer that is justified, but it shutteth them out from the office of justifying. So that although they be all present in him that is justified, yet they justify not all together.

Neither doth faith shut out our own good works necessarily to be done afterwards of duty towards God, but it excludeth them so that we may not do them with this intent, to be made just by doing them. For all good works that we can do be imperfect, and therefore not able to deserve our justification: but our justification doth come freely by the mercy of God; and that of so great and free mercy, that whereas all the world was not able of themselves to pay any part towards their ransom, it pleased our heavenly Father of His infinite mercy, without any our deserving, to prepare for us the most precious jewels of Christ's body and blood, whereby our ransom might be fully paid, the law fulfilled, and His justice satisfied. So that Christ is now the righteousness of all them that do believe in Him.[19]

That no man can be justified by his own good works, that no man fulfilleth the law according to the strict rigour of the law St. Paul proveth in his epistle to the Galatians, saying thus: "If there had been any law given which could have given life, verily righteousness should have been by the law." And again he saith, "If righteousness came by the law, then Christ is dead in vain." And again, "You that are justified by the law are fallen from grace." And to the Ephesians, "By grace ye are saved through faith, and that not of yourselves; it is the gift of God; not of works, lest any man should boast." And to be short, the sum of all Paul's disputation is this: that if righteousness come by works, then it cometh not by grace; and if it come of grace, then it cometh not of works. And to this end tend all the prophets as St. Peter saith, "To Him give all the prophets witness, that through His name whosoever believeth in Him shall receive remission of sins."

This faith holy Scripture teacheth us is the strong rock and foundation of the Christian religion. This doctrine all ancient authors of Christ's Church do approve. This doctrine advanceth and setteth forth the true glory of Christ, and beateth down the vainglory of man; this doctrine whosoever denieth is not to be accounted for a Christian man, nor for a setter-forth of Christ's glory, but for an adversary to Christ and His gospel, and for a setter-forth of man's vainglory.

Justification is not the office of man but of God, for man cannot make himself righteous by his own works, neither in whole nor in part: for that were the greatest arrogancy and presumption of man that Antichrist could set up against God, to affirm that a man might by his own works take away and purge his own sins, and so justify himself. But justification is the office of God only, and is not a thing which we render unto Him, but which we receive of Him, by His own free mercy and by the only merit of His most dearly beloved Son, our only Redeemer, Saviour and Justifier, Jesus Christ.

This is the doctrine of Scripture and our own Church concerning justification which she thus sums up in her Articles: "We are accounted righteous before God, only for the merit of our Lord Jesus Christ through faith, and not for our own works or deservings. Wherefore, that we are justified by faith only, is a most wholesome doctrine, and one very full of comfort, as more largely is expressed in the Homily of Justification."[20]

Of works done before justification, her judgment is this: "Works done before the grace of Christ, and inspiration of His Spirit, are not pleasing to God, forasmuch as they spring not of faith in Jesus Christ, neither do they make men meet [i.e. "suitable"] to receive grace, or, as the school authors [medieval scholastics] say, to deserve the grace of congruity: yea rather, because they are not done as God hath willed and commanded them to be done, we doubt not but they have the nature of sin."[21]

Neither can those good works which are the fruits of faith, and follow after justification, put away sins and endure the severity of God's judgments.[22] It costs more to redeem a soul; more than all good works of all men, so that man must let that alone forever. That we must leave to God. It is God that justifieth. It is the blood of Christ that cleanses from all sin.

It is the Lord God that taketh away the sin of the world. And he that doth not acknowledge this, and doth not utterly renounce his own righteousness as filthy rags, and seeks to be justified freely by grace through faith, that man is in his sins and in his blood to this hour. Unless he relies, not on anything he is or does, but on the death of Christ alone, as the one sufficient sacrifice, oblation and satisfaction for the sins of the whole world, unless in the matter[?] of justification he puts himself upon a level with [the] vilest sinners, looking like them to receive a free pardon from the mere mercy of God in Christ Jesus, unless he can submit to be justified as ungodly, he never can be justified at all. For he is of those who justify themselves; of those who, following after the law of righteousness, have not attained to the law of righteousness, because they sought it not by faith, but as it were by works of the law[?]. While gross but self-condemned and believing sinners, who followed not after righteousness, attain to righteousness, even the righteousness which is of faith. They are accepted while the self-righteous one is cast out: verily, verily, Christ saith unto him, the publicans and harlots go into the kingdom of God before you!

The sum of all is this: They that be whole need not a physician, but they that be sick. Christ came not to call the righteous but sinners to repentance. He is the friend and Saviour of sinners; not indeed of those who continue in sin, but of those who feel the weight of it, and groan to Him for deliverance. Whosoever is saved by Him, is saved as a sinner. His mouth is first stopped, he becomes guilty before God, and submits to be justified freely by His grace through the redemption that is in Jesus Christ. He counts all things but loss that he may win Christ, and be found in Him, not having his own righteousness which is of the law, but that which is through the faith of Christ, the redemption which is of God by faith.

Whosoever is justified is justified by a simple act of faith in Christ Jesus, without any reference to works past, present or to come. Indeed till a sinner does exert[?] this act of faith he is in a state of condemnation. He that believeth on Him is not condemned, but he that believeth not is condemned already, because he hath not believed on the name of the only begotten Son of God. He that believeth on the Son hath everlasting life, but he that believeth not the Son shall not see life, but the wrath of God abideth on him. Verily, verily, Christ saith unto you, he that heareth my word and believeth on Him that sent Me hath everlasting life, and shall not come unto condemnation, but is passed from death unto life. In the moment wherein a self-despairing sinner looks up with faith to Christ Jesus, in that selfsame moment the power of the Lord is present to heal him; his sins are forgiven, his person[?] is accepted, his faith hath made him whole. He was a sinner, but he is washed, but he is justified in the name of the Lord Jesus, and by the Spirit of our God.

What the faith is, through which we thus receive the atonement and apply Christ and all His merits to our soul in particular, was the third thing

I proposed discoursing upon. Our Church describes it thus: The true, lively and converting faith, the sure and substantial faith which saveth sinners, is not only a common belief of the Articles of our creed, but it is also a true trust and confidence of the mercy of God through our Lord Jesus Christ, and a steadfast hope of all good things to be received at God's hand. It is not in the mouth and outward person only, but liveth and stirreth inwardly in the heart. It is the sure conviction of the benefits which we trust to receive of God, a certifying and sure looking for Him. It is no dead, vain or unfruitful thing, but a thing of perfect virtue, of wonderful operation or working and strength, bringing forth all good motions and good works.[23]

The faith which justifies is not purely an assent to things credible as credible[?]; it is not that speculative, notional, eerie shadow which floats in the heads of some learned men; it is not a lifeless, cold, historical faith, common to devils and nominal Christians; it is not learnt of books or men; it is not a human thing, but a divine energy. We believe according to the working of the mighty power of God. By grace ye are. The faith by which we are saved is not of ourselves; it is the gift of God; not of works lest any man boast. We can as well reach heaven with our h[ands?], as believe by any act or power or strength of our own. For effecting faith There is required a stroke of omnipotence. It can only be wrought in the soul by Him who made it. We believe according to the working of the mighty power of God. God who commanded the light to shine out of darkness, must shine in our hearts to give the knowledge of the glory of God in the face of Jesus Christ. Faith does not stand in the wisdom of men but in the power of God. No man can call Jesus the Lord but by the Holy Ghost.

When Peter made that confession of faith, Thou art the Son of the Living God, Jesus answered and said unto him, Blessed art thou, Simon Peter, for flesh and blood hath not revealed it unto thee, but My Father which is in heaven. So our Lord Himself assures us no man can come unto the Son except the Father draw him. No man cometh to the Father, but by the Son. They only believe, to whom it is given to know the mind of Christ. Eye hath not seen, nor ear heard, neither have entered into the hearts of men, the things which God hath prepared for them that love him. But God hath revealed them unto us by His Spirit, for the Spirit searcheth all things, yea, the deep things of God. For what man knoweth the things of a man but the spirit of man which is in him? Even so the things of God knoweth no man but the Spirit of God, for they are foolishness unto him; neither can he know them because they are spiritually discerned. God hath hid these things from the wise and prudent, and revealed them unto babes. No man knoweth the Son but the Father, neither knoweth any man the Father save the Son, and he to whomsoever the Son will reveal Him.

These and numberless other Scriptures demonstrate the impossibility of believing till God hath given us the Spirit of revelation. We can never know the things of God till He hath revealed them by His Spirit, till we have received the Son of God that we should know the things which are freely given us of God. For this cause Jesus is called the author of our Faith: and we are said to receive the Spirit by the hearing of faith, because we receive in one and the same moment, power to believe and the Holy Ghost, who is therefore called the Spirit of faith. And a true faith we cannot have till God gives unto us the Holy Ghost purifying our hearts by faith.

We need no further testimony to prove that faith is wrought by Him from whom every good and perfect gift cometh. God is plainly the cause of faith: what are its effects? They are spiritually these: peace, love, joy, victory over the world, the flesh and the devil, fellowship with God, the indwelling of His Spirit, present salvation and everlasting life.

Being justified by faith we have peace with God (attested by that inward peace which passes all understanding): and not only so, but we also have joy in God through our Lord Jesus Christ by whom we have now received the atonement. In whom we have redemption through His blood, the forgiveness of sins. Whom having not seen we love; in whom, though now we see Him not, yet believing, we rejoice with joy unspeakable and full of glory, receiving the end of our faith, even the salvation of our souls. Receiving it now in part, for by grace ye are saved through faith, and he that believeth hath everlasting life.

Faith works by love. The love of God is shed abroad in all believers' hearts by the Holy Ghost which is given unto them. This love they show by keeping His commandments; which no one except believers can keep. But they are delivered not only from the guilt but also from the power of sin. The law of the spirit of life which is in Christ Jesus hath made them free from the law of sin and death. Sin shall not have dominion over them, for they are not under the law but under grace. They were the servants of sin, but they have obeyed from the heart that form of doctrine which was delivered to them. Being then made free from sin, they become the servants of righteousness. Jesus is their Jesus by having for He hath saved them from their sins. He that believeth is born of God; and whosoever is born of God doth not commit sin, for His seed remaineth in him, and he cannot sin because he is born of God.

Whatsoever is born of God overcometh the world also. And this is the victory that overcometh the world, even our faith. Who is he that overcometh the world but he that believeth that Jesus is the Son of God? [1 John 5:4, 5] Nor can the prince of this world stand before him. He takes unto him the shield of faith, and thereby quenches all the fiery darts of the devil. He resists him steadfastly in the faith, and the devil flees from him. The spirit of this world continually oppresses the spirit of holiness[?], and he is more than conqueror through Christ that loveth him and dwelleth in his heart by faith.

This is the greatest and most glorious privilege of the true believer. "Whosoever shall confess that Jesus is the Son of God, God dwelleth in him and he in God:" [1 John 4:15] and hereby knoweth he that God abideth

in him, by the Spirit which He hath given him. He that believeth hath the
witness in him, even the Son of God bearing witness with his spirit that he
is a child of God. Christ is formed in his heart by faith. He is one with
Christ and Christ with him. He is a real partaker of the divine nature. Truly
his fellowship is with the Father and the Son. The Father and the Son are
come unto him and make their abode with him, and his very body is the
temple of the Holy Ghost.

Such are the privileges of all true believers. But alas where shall we find
them? How are the faithful distinguished from among the children of men?
When the Son of man cometh shall He find faith upon earth? We have lost
the very notion of it, and denied it its first and peculiar office, namely
judging us before God. A preacher of justification by faith only is now
looked upon as a setter-forth of new doctrines, and his audience are ready to
cry out, Thou bringest strange things to our ears. It is therefore wholly
seasonable that I should therefore apply myself (as I proposed in the fourth
part) first to them who deny this doctrine, and secondly to you who receive
it.

And firstly, as to those that deny this doctrine, and ignorantly call it
new, and pronounce the preachers of it schismatics. Would they look into
their Bibles they would find it as old as Christianity; as old as the fall of
man and his redemption in Christ Jesus, who was the lamb slain from the
foundation of the world to take away the sins of the world. But they do
therefore err because they know not the Scriptures, neither the power of
faith. They find no such mighty efficacy in their own [hearsay?] faith, and
so cannot conceive how faith only should justify. That their faith cannot we
readily grant; for if it could, the devils having the very same would be
justified too. But what must they do then in order to their justification?
Why they will take in good works to their cause (outwardly good I mean)
and the business is done. The works of a heathen, and the faith of a devil,
will, in their judgment, make a man a complete Christian, and fully justify
him in the sight of God.

Thus mighty are those men in the Scriptures; and as deeply skilled are
they in the doctrines of our own Church. Tell me, you that are of the
church, do ye not hear the Church? I know ye do; and to you I therefore
appeal. Judge you, which are the schismatics, we who maintain or they
who deny justification by faith only? Indeed they are worse than
schismatics who deny; for if they have ever subscribed to our Articles, they
are perjured schismatics. God forbid that I, or any of my brethren, should
preach another gospel; for we have so declared upon oath our belief of
justification by faith only, and for us to hold another doctrine would be
w[idely?] felt inexcusable perjury.

One infamous evasion I know there is, but hope we all have it in equal
abhorrence, namely that every man may subscribe the Articles in his own
sense. Suppose it granted that the seventeenth Article ["Of Predestination
and Election"] is purposely so worded as to take in persons of differing

sentiments, what is this to those Articles where the sense is plain, precise and distinct?[24] As it is in that of justification; for the full understanding of which the church refers us to her homilies and thereby ties us down to the one sense therein delivered. Nor is it in the power of words more fully and plainly to express any truth, than she has there expressed that everlasting truth, "We are justified by faith only without works."

What then my brethren, can we think of those who swear to those Articles in a sense altogether repugnant to the true intended one? Who declare upon oath their belief that we are justified by faith only: that is, say they in their hearts, not by faith only, but by a papistic jumble of faith and works. What horrid mockery is this of God and man! Can charity itself suppose that their mental reservations acquits them of perjury? Or does it not rather wholly aggravate it? I shall not say any more of this wicked subterfuge, than that it was taught by our modern Arius:[25] that hereby he subscribed[?] our Articles though he denied the Lord that bought him; as might his elder brother have done, or another heretic old or new.

Let not those therefore who deny this doctrine any longer call themselves of the Church of England. They may be of the Church of Rome, but cannot be of ours, who allow works any share in justification with God. Papists indeed they are, though they may not know it, for they lay the wood, hay, stubble of their own works, not as the superstructure, but as the very foundation, of their acceptance with God. Pharisees are they, for they justify themselves; perjured are they likewise, as many of them as have sworn to the truth of what they disbelieved. In short, they may call themselves anything but Church of England men and Christians; for such we can never allow them to be; since to repeat the words of our own Church: "Whosoever denieth this doctrine, is not to be counted for a Christian man, nor for a setter-forth of Christ's gospel, but for a setter-forth of man's vainglory, an adversary of Christ and His gospel."

This is our Church's censure of all that bring any other doctrine than justification by faith only; she call them antichrists who presume to say they can by their own works justify themselves and profess them such.[26] But alas! how are these antichrists multiplied upon earth! Our pulpits speak a quite different language from our Articles and homilies: the writings of our most celebrated divines [i.e. theologians] are full of justification by faith *and* works. The religion of Christ is utterly denied, exploded, and blasphemed. It were needless to name all these Judases Christians (if I may so call them who our Church denies to be any Christian at all), but as God shall give me strength; I mean to name them, and that upon the housetop, and to warn the people of God to beware of false prophets.

This is not justifying faith, says one of them, to lay hold on the righteousness and merits of Christ for the pardon of our sins, that is to trust and confide only in that as the meritorious cause of our pardon.[27] He goes on (this angel of the church of God) to do the devil's work, pulling down that Church of which he is a pillar, and labouring to overturn what she calls the strong root and foundation of the Christian religion, justification by faith only. I tremble to think (and so should all his admirers) of that terrible sentence pronounced by the great apostle, "Though we or an angel from heaven preach any other gospel unto you than that which we have preached unto you, let him be accursed." [Gal. 1:8] To preach justification by faith and works is, if we may believe an inspired apostle, to preach another gospel; and he repeats the doom of all such preachers, "As we said before, so say I now again, if any man preach any other gospel unto you than that ye have received, let him be accursed." [Gal. 1:9]

So speaks the great asserter[?] of justification by faith only, who as a wise master builder, laid this sure ~~lays this only~~ foundation of all good works and holiness, and ~~assures tells~~ assures us, other foundation can no man lay than that is laid, which is Christ Jesus. On this very doctrine our church was founded and flourished for 100 years. But alas, was the father of the Reformation [i.e. Luther], to rise again and visit us, how would he take up the apostle's words, "I marvel that ye are so soon removed from Him that called you into the grace of Christ unto another gospel! I am afraid of you, lest I have bestowed upon you labour in vain. Christ is become of none effect unto you, whosoever of you are justified by the law, ye are fallen from grace. Ye did run well; who ~~hath~~ did hinder you, that ye should not obey the truth. This persuasion cometh not of him that called you. A little leaven leaveneth the whole lump." [Gal. 3:1f]

Would to God, my brethren, the following words were applicable to us all, "I have confidence in you through the Lord that ye will be none otherwise minded!" [Gal. 5:10] Would to God that everyone who hath not made shipwreck of the faith would avow and preach and publish it upon the housetop. Suffer ye the word of exhortation from the least and meanest of your brethren. O consider, I beseech you, by the mercies of God, whether this be not the cause of all our vice and infidelity, our not holding the head[?] (I speak of the generality), our not laying the foundation, or not adhering to our own principles.

We may debate our apostasy from the time of the Grand Rebellion: unto which many were drawn who maintained justification by faith only. For no better a reason than this we renounced the doctrine (though it still confronts us in our Articles and Homilies) ~~and ran headstrong unto works, popery, and deism[?]. But woe unto the men who first dared preach justification by faith and works; who laid this stumbling block in our way. Good hath it been for them had they never been born. Or if as soon as born, they had a millstone tied about their necks, and been cast into the depth of the sea! But let not us deny the truth because some hold it in unrighteousness.~~ But woe unto the men by whom the offense came. It had been better for them that a millstone had been hanged about their neck and they cast into the sea. Woe unto them who stumbled at this rock of offense, and first dared to teach justification by faith and works. Good it had been for those men had they never been born. But let not us, my brethren, increase the unhappy number.

Let us not deny the truth because some hold it in unrighteousness, professing to know God, while in works they denied Him. Oh what an advantage did Satan then get over us! By filling the mouths of his children with faith in Christ; saving faith, justifying faith, he hath driven and kept it out of the hearts of almost all this nation.

But be not ye ignorant of his devices. This place was always a bulwark against those inroads[?], a rampart against vice and infidelity. Ye are the salt of the earth. But if the salt hath lost its savour, wherewith shall it be seasoned? Ye are the eyes of this people: but if the light which is in you be darkness, how great is that darkness! Here is the fountain: and if that be pure, the river of the flood thereof shall make glad the city of our God. Oh that our glorious title might but ever be that of the true Church of England men! Oh let not the enemies of our Church any longer triumph in our having fallen from the d[octrine of?] r[edemption?]. Let it not be said concerning (her) our desolate mother, there is none to guide her, of all the sons which she hath brought up. Never ourselves but Christ Jesus the Lord: the Lord our righteousness: Christ made unto us of God wisdom, righteousness, sanctification, and redemption. Righteousness first, then immediately sanctification. First let us insist that we are justified freely, that is forgiven and accepted for Christ's sake, not our own; justified in our sins and our blood; justified as ungodly by faith only without works. And then upon this sure foundation let us build the gold, silver, precious stones of good works, and inward holiness. Oh let us not corrupt the gospel of Christ by allowing the least share in our justification with God. Corrupt it, said I? Rather let us not overthrow it. For by not acknowledging Christ to be the sole ground of our acceptance, we tread under foot the Son of God, and count the blood of the covenant, wherewith we were sanctified, an unholy thing, and do despite to the Son of God.

God hath much against us because we have left our first love, even that pure love which is wrought by faith. Let us remember therefore from whence we are fallen, and repent and do the first works, or alas, He will come unto us quickly, and will remove our candlestick out of his place, except we repent. Year after year hath He come to his barren fig tree seeking fruit and finding none. Brethren, even now the word is gone forth, cut it down, why cumbereth it the earth ground? Brethren, even now He is coming to take away the Kingdom of God from us, and to give it to another nation bringing forth the fruits thereof. Oh, who will stand before Him in the great day to turn away His righteous indignation lest He should destroy us? Who will stand, rise up, with me against the wicked, who will take Who will become protecting angels to a guilty land? Who will rise up with me God against the wicked, who will take His my part against the evil doers.

M B F [My brethren in faith?] upon you I call that ye come to the help of the Lord, against the self-righteous. Would Ye masters[?] in Israel, lead the way. Be determined not to know or preach anything save Jesus Christ and Him crucified. Preach the gospel in simplicity. Insist on justification by faith only, even by faith in the blood of Jesus, that only name given under heaven whereby we may be saved. Alas I call here[?] to record against you this day! As many of you as bring another doctrine, I call the ~~whole~~ Church of God in all ages, the noble army of martyrs, especially those of our own nation who have sealed this truth with their blood, these and the whole church militant and triumphant I call to testify against you that ye have erred from the faith and trampled upon the everlasting gospel. Brethren, I am now free from the blood of every man; look ye to that! I have declared the truth, I have borne my testimony, I have delivered my own soul!

[End of sermon: the following benediction written in with a different pen.]

Now to God the Father, who first loved us and made us accepted in the Beloved; to God the Son who loves us and washed us from our sins in His own blood, to God the Holy Ghost who sheddeth abroad the love of God in our hearts, be all praise and all glory in time and in eternity!

No. 26   Journal Selections: July 2–22, 1739

Mon., July 2d. Mr. Gambold came. He had been with the Vice-Chancellor, and well received. I visited the Vice-Chancellor, at his own desire: gave him a full account of the Methodists; which he approved: but objected the irregularity of our doing good in other men's parishes; charged Mr. Whitefield with insincerity, and breach of promise; appealed to the Dean, and appointed a second meeting there. All were against my sermon, as liable to be misunderstood.

Tues., July 3d. . . . At night I had another conference with the Dean; who cited Mr. Whitefield to judgement. I said, "Mr. Dean, he shall be ready to answer your citation." He used his utmost address to bring me off from preaching abroad [out of doors], from expounding in houses, from singing psalms: denied justification by faith only, and all vital religion: promised me, however, to read [William] Law and Pascal.[28]

Sun., July 8th. Near ten thousand, by computation, gave diligent heed to the word preached in Moorfields [London]: "Thou shall call his name Jesus; for he shall save his people from their sins." Number seemed greatly affected. Walking over an open field to Kennington-Common, I was met by a man, who threatened me for a trespass.[29] I preached "Christ our wisdom, righteousness, sanctification, and redemption," to double my morning congregation: and the Lord Almighty bowed their hearts before him.

Sun., July 22d. I never knew till now the strength of temptation, and energy of sin. Who, that conferred with flesh and blood, would covet great success? I live in a continual storm. My soul is alway in my hand. The enemy thrust sore at me, that I may fall; and a worse enemy than the devil is in my own heart. *Miror aliquem praedictorem salvari!* [Latin: "I marvel that such a perverted fellow is saved!"] I received, I humbly hope, a fresh pardon in the sacrament at St. Paul's. I would have preached at the Fleet; but the Warden forbad. I preached at the Marshalsea.

No. 27   Letter to George Whitefield

In the following letter, written on August 10, 1739, Charles Wesley described the "labours and conflicts" which he felt under the increase of the revival.[30]

Dear George,—I forgot to mention the most material occurrence at Plaistow; namely, that a Clergyman was there convinced of sin. He stood under me, and appeared, throughout my discourse, under the strongest perturbation of mind. In our return we were much delighted with an old spiritual Quaker, who is clear in justification by faith only. At Marylebone a footman was convinced of more than sin; and now waits with confidence for all the power of faith. Friend Keen seems to have experience, and is right in the foundation.

I cannot preach out on the week-days for the expense of coach, nor accept of dear Mr. Seward's offer; to which I should be less backward, would he take my advice. But while he is so lavish of his Lord's goods, I cannot counsel that this ruin should in any degree *seem* to be under my hand.

I am continually tempted to leave off preaching, and hide myself like J. Hutchins. I should then be freer from temptation, and at leisure to attend my own improvement. God continues to work *by* me, but not *in* me, that I can perceive. Do not reckon upon me, my brother, in the work God is doing: for I cannot expect he should long employ one who is ever longing and murmuring to be discharged. I rejoice in your success, and pray for its increase a thousand fold.

NOTES

1. The Rev. George Stonehouse (1714–1793) was rector of St. Mary's Church, Islington, from 1736 to 1740. He was a close associate of the Wesleys in the early years of the revival. By 1740, however, he had identified himself more directly with the English Moravians and in that year he resigned his vicarage to retire to Woodstock to live a life of "stillness." Cf. Chapter 7, "The Stillness Controversy."

2. It does not seem possible to identify these hymns on the basis of Charles's description here. The Methodist hymnbooks of the period do not carry songs named by the titles "Salvation by Faith" and "Faith in Christ." If these phrases are taken to be descriptions, and not exact titles, they could easily refer to almost any of Charles's hymns. "The Just Shall Live by Faith," from *Hymns and Sacred Poems* (1740) and "Salvation by Grace" from the same collection seem to be likely identifications. Cf. *P.W.*, I, p. 332; II, p. 77.

3. "Dissenters" refers to those English Protestants who did not subscribe to the Anglican doctrines and practices established by the Elizabethan Settlement of 1559. In a broader sense the term also describes those Protestants who did not identify themselves with the Church of England, e.g. Congregationalists, Presbyterians, Quakers, and Baptists.

4. In the early church any religious meeting could aptly be called a "conventicle," but the term took on more specific connotations after 1664 when the English Parliament (under the reign of Charles II) passed the "Conventicle Act." The legislation banned religious meetings of five or more persons, outside the bounds of the public worship conducted by the Church of England. The clear intention of the act was the repression of the Puritans and other religious nonconformists. Bringing the charge against the Methodist societies suggests that they were perceived as separating themselves from the Church of England, or undermining her unity.

5. This "sermon of salvation," to which the dean of the college objected, was probably John Wesley's "Salvation by Faith." He preached it before the university on June 11, 1738. The Wesleys would later preach three additional homilies of similar tone at that location. John delivered "The Almost Christian" on July 25, 1741; Charles's "Awake, Thou That Sleepest" was heard on April 4, 1742, and John's "Scriptural Christianity" on August 24, 1744. Cf. *J.W. Works*, V, pp. 7–52. Charles's sermon is reprinted below.

6. With this position filled, Charles would be under less pressure (and temptation) to accept a living and withdraw from the frantic pace of the Methodist revival. He "rejoiced," no doubt, because he understood this development as a sort of "direction from God" he had anticipated in the January 5, 1739, journal entry.

7. The Rev. John Potter (1674–1747) was archbishop of Canterbury from 1737 till his death. Prior to coming to that see, Potter had been bishop of Oxford and had at that time ordained several of the Oxford Methodists, including Charles Wesley (deacon), John Wesley, Benjamin Ingham, and James Hervey. Charles showed some acumen by studying Potter's published position prior to his interview with the archbishop. Potter's *Discourse of Church Government* (1707) showed his high church sympathies and became one of the standard treatments of ecclesiology in that day. John Wesley had also studied the bishop's book while in Georgia (*JW Journal*, I, p. 270, Sept. 6, 1736). Potter seems to have been well disposed toward the Methodists, despite his apparent opposition to Charles's baptisms and preaching at Mr. Pier's church.

John Wesley sought Potter's advice (March 1735) when his elder brother Samuel had used John's ordinations vows to try to force him to follow their father at Epworth, instead of going to Georgia as a missionary. Potter responded to John's plight in writing:

> "Dear Sir:—It doth not seem to me that at your ordination you engaged yourself to undertake the cure of any parish, provided you can as a clergyman better serve God and His Church in your present or some other situation." [*J.W. Letters*, I, p. 182.]

John Telford recorded Charles Wesley's recollection that the archbishop told Wesley that the Methodists "might leaven the whole" if they remained attached to the Church of England. Charles's response was that he "feared their Lordships cared for none of these things. Still I should hope if God raised up but one Primitive ["authentic"] Bishop and commanded the porter to open the door" [to the Kingdom of God] (*ibid.*, VIII, p. 267). Despite his reservations about the Wesleys, the bishop's sentiments toward them were positive: "These gentlemen are irregular; but they have done good; and I pray God to bless them" (Telford, *CW Journal*, p. 301).

8. That is to say, Charles walked out as the layman Bowers stood up to preach, and many other people followed Wesley's example.

9. "License" refers to official approval for Charles to preach in this Episcopal jurisdiction. It would have to have been granted by the bishop of London. The "churchwardens" are the lay leaders of an Anglican parish. Their office includes the encouragement of the parishioners in the practice of "true religion," preservation of the unity of the church, and care of the church's physical property.

10. This occasion marks the beginning of Charles's open-air evangelism.

11. "Gamaliel's Advice" is from Acts 5:38–39: "And now I say unto you. Refrain from these men, and let them alone; if this counsel or this work be of men, it will come to nought: But if it be of God, ye cannot overthrow it; lest haply ye be found even to fight against God" (KJV).

12. Theophils Leigh, D.D., was Master of Balliol College and vice-chancellor from 1738 to 1740.

13. Charles's prayer for the university was written in longhand, the Lord's Prayer in shorthand.

14. The right-hand margin of Charles's manuscript carries the Roman numerials I, II, III, IV, indicating the outline points of his sermon.

15. Anglican Article IX, "Of Original or Birth-Sin," is quoted with minor omissions.

16. This sentence is incomplete in the original manuscript.

17. In the manuscript the letter "h" appears above the word "use" suggesting, perhaps, the reading of "habitually use."

18. This paragraph is cited, almost verbatim, from the Anglican homily (number three, book one) "Of Salvation." The next eight paragraphs of Charles's sermon closely follow the text of that standard homily.

19. The next three paragraphs are extracted from the second part of the Homily "Of Salvation."

20. Anglican Article XI, "Of the Justification of Man," is quoted with only minor omissions.

21. Anglican Article XIII, "Of Works Before Justification," is woven into Charles's text.

22. Here Charles paraphrases Article XII and merges it into his sentence. The article "Of Good Works" reads, "Albeit that Good Works, which are the fruits of Faith, and follow after Justification, cannot put away our sins, and endure the severity of God's judgment; yet are they pleasing and acceptable to God in Christ, and do spring out necessarily of a true and lively Faith; insomuch that by them a lively Faith may be as evidently known as a tree discerned by the fruit."

23. Extracted from the Anglican standard homily "Of Faith."

24. Both Augustinian (or "Reformed") and Arminian ("Laudian") interpretations of Predestination and Election existed side-by-side in the Church of England, under the formulation of Article XVII.

25. Albin and Beckerlegge (in *CW Shorthand Sermons, op. cit.*) suggest that the "modern Arius" Charles referred to was Dr. Samuel Clark (1675–1757). A controversy over subscribing to the Anglican articles raged in the Church of England during the latter part of the seventeenth and early part of the eighteenth century. The introduction to Samuel Clark's *The Scripture Doctrine of the Trinity* (1712) fueled the fires of controversy since it seemed to make the individual's "reasonable" conscience the final authority in judging whether the church's creedal formulation of the doctrine of the Trinity was in harmony with Scripture. The fray was joined by a host of combatants including Dr. Waterland, who published *The Case of Arian Subscription Considered* in 1721. The title may suggest Charles's identification of Clark as the "modern Arius." Wesley's disparaging remarks about Tillotson (below) may have been occasioned by Clark's use of the archbishop's works to defend his own position.

26. The phrase beginning "who presume . . . ." is an insertion written on the back of the page facing the text to the left.

27. In the margin Charles wrote: "173 sermon on justifying faith, page 460, 3rd, volume, Tillotson."

28. William Law (1686–1761), mystic and non-juror, whose books *Practical Treatise on Christian Perfection* (1726) and *A Serious Call* (1728) were particularly influential for the Wesleys. They occasionally visited Law at his home at Putney, esteeming him as their "oracle" or spiritual adviser. They eventually broke with him over the issue of justification by faith. Blaise Pascal (1623–1662) was a French mathematician and Roman Catholic writer on religious matters. His christocentric Christianity, emphasis upon conversion and religious experience, made his works attractive to both Wesleys. *Pensées* (1670) was his most famous contribution to religious literature.

29. This was only the beginning of the civil suits that would be threatened, and a few actually brought against Charles Wesley. The receipt for Charles's fine has survived. He was charged £10 in damages and an additional £9.16s. 8d. in taxes and court costs. At the bottom of the receipt Wesley scrawled, "I paid them for things I never took," and on the back of the paper he continued, "To be re-judged in that [eschatological] day."

30. Jackson, *CW Journal*, I, pp. 158–159.

5 / He Offers Christ to All

Excluded from the Anglican churches, Charles took his evangelistic work directly to the unchurched masses. Preaching in the open air, he addressed multitudes of people and was simultaneously exposed to the hostility of his opposition. Occasionally the local clerics were among the instigators. Wesley's ability to win silence, if not to win the opposition over to his point of view, allowed him to make the best of these confrontations. His travels increased, and wherever he went he evangelized the masses, established Methodist societies, and visited already existing classes.

No. 28   Letter to John Wesley
(The Journal of Charles Wesley, 1849)

Bengeworth and Evesham, August 20, 1739

Dear Brother,—We left the brethren at Oxford much edified, and two gownsmen, beside C. Graves, thoroughly awakened. On Saturday afternoon God brought us hither. Mr. Seward being from home, there was no admittance for us, his wife being an opposer, and having refused to see G. Whitefield before me. At seven Mr. Seward found us at our inn, and carried us home. I expounded at eight in the school-room, which contains two hundred; and held out the promises from John 16: "I will send the Comforter," &c.

On Sunday morning I preached from George Whitefield's pulpit, the wall, "Repent ye, and believe the Gospel." The notice being short, we had only a few hundreds, but such as those described in the morning lesson, "These were more noble than those of Thessalonica, in that they received the word with all readiness of mind." In the evening I showed to near two thousand their Saviour in the good Samaritan. [Cf. No. 29] Many, I am persuaded, found themselves ready for the oil and wine. Once more God strengthened me at nine to open the new covenant at the school-house, which was crowded with deeply attentive sinners.

No. 29   Hymn: "The Good Samaritan"

The parable of the Good Samaritan was one of Charles Wesley's favorite sermon texts; unfortunately, this sermon has not survived. His hymn of the same title, based on Luke 10:30, develops the same allegorical imagery suggested in Charles's letter above. In the hymn and sermon the parable is allegorized into a paradigm of redemption. It is recast as a poetic drama in which the singer becomes the traveler injured by "the mortal wound of sin." The priest and the Levite become the blind guides of a new age who pass the spokesman by. Christ, the Good Samaritan, has compassion upon our plight and pours in "the wine and oil of grace" to cure the singer's sin-sickness. The hymn was first published in *Hymns and Sacred Poems* (1742). A shortened form was reissued in John's 1780, standard *A Collection of Hymns for the Use of the People Called Methodists*.[2]

1   Woe is me! what tongue can tell
        My sad afflicted state?
     Who my anguish can reveal,
        Or all my woe relate?
     Fallen among thieves I am,
   And they have robb'd me of my God,
     Turn'd my glory into shame,
        And left me in my blood.

2   God was once my glorious dress,
        And I like Him did shine;
     Satan of His righteousness
        Hath spoil'd this soul of mine;
     By the mortal wound of sin,
   'Twixt God and me the parting made:
     Dead in *Adam*, dead within,
        My soul is wholly dead.

3   I have lost the life Divine,
        And when this outward breath
     To the Giver I resign,
        Must die the second death.
     Naked, helpless, stript of God,
   And at the latest gasp I lie:
     Who beholds me in my blood,
        And saves me ere I die?

4   Lo! the priest comes down in vain,
        And sees my sad distress,
     Sees the state of fallen man,
        But cannot give me ease:
     Patriarchs and prophets old

Observe my wretched, desperate case;
    Me expiring they behold,
      But leave me as I was.

5   Lo! the *Levite* me espies,
    And stops to view my grief,
    Looks on me, and bids me rise,
      But offers no relief.
All my wounds he open tears,
    And searches them, alas! in vain;
    Fill'd with anguish, griefs, and fears,
      He leaves me in my pain.

6   O Thou Good *Samaritan*
    In Thee is all my hope;
    Only Thou canst succour man,
      And raise the fallen up.
Hearken to my dying cry,
    My wounds compassionately see,
    Me a sinner pass not by,
      Who gasp for help to Thee.

7   Still Thou journey'st where I am,
    And still Thy bowels move;
    Pity is with Thee the same,
      And all Thy heart is love.
Stoop to a poor sinner, stoop,
    And let Thy healing grace abound;
    Heal my bruises, and bind up
      My spirit's every wound.

8   Saviour of my soul, draw nigh,
    In mercy haste to me;
    At the point of death I lie,
      And cannot come to Thee.
Now Thy kind relief afford,
    The wine and oil of grace pour in;
    Good Physician, speak the word,
      And heal my soul of sin.

9   Pity to my dying cries
    Hath drawn Thee from above,
    Hovering over me with eyes
      Of tenderness and love:
Now, e'en now I see Thy face,
    The balm of *Gilead* I receive;

Thou hast saved me by Thy grace,
And bade the sinner live.

10   Surely now the bitterness
          Of second death is past:
       O my Life, my Righteousness,
          On Thee my soul is cast.
       Thou hast brought me to Thine inn,
       And I am of Thy promise sure;
          Thou shalt cleanse me from all sin,
          And all my sickness cure.

11   Perfect then the work begun,
          And make the sinner whole;
       All Thy will on me be done,
          My body, spirit, soul.
       Still preserve me safe from harms,
       And kindly for Thy patient care;
          Take me, Jesu, to Thine arms,
          And keep me ever there.

No. 30   Journal Selections: August 21–25, 1739

Tues., August 21st [1739]. I besought my hearers to be reconciled to God. I found Miss P. had been greatly strengthened by last night's expounding, and could scarce forbear crying out, "She was Lazarus; and if they would come to Christ, he would raise them, as he had her." All night she continued singing in her heart; and discovered more and more of that genuine mark of his disciples, love.

I was prevailed upon to stay over this day. God soon showed us *his* design in it. Our singing in the garden drew two sincere women to us, who sought Christ sorrowing. After reading the promises in Isaiah, we prayed, and they received them accomplished in themselves. We were upon a mount, which reminded us of Tabor, through the joy wherewith our Master filled us. How shall I be thankful enough for his bringing me hither! While we were singing, a poor drunken servant of Mr. Seward's was struck. His master had last night given him warning; but now he seems effectually called. We spent the afternoon most delightfully in Isaiah. At seven the Society met. I could hardly speak through my cold; but it was suspended, while I showed the natural man his picture in blind Bartimaeus. Many were ready to cry after Jesus for mercy. The three that had lately received their sight were much strengthened. Miss P. declared her cure before two hundred witnesses; many of them gay young gentlewomen. They received her testimony, flocked round about her, and pressed her on all sides to come to see them. By this open confession, she purchased to herself great boldness in the faith.

Wed., August 22d. This morning the work upon poor Robin appeared to be God's work. The words that made the first impression were,

"Tis mercy all, immense and free,
  For, O my God, it found out me!" [Cf. No. 9 above.]

He now seems full of sorrow, and joy, and astonishment, and love. The world, too, set to their seal that he belongs to Christ.

Here I cannot but observe the narrow spirit of those that hold particular redemption. I have had not disputes with them, yet they have me in abomination. Mrs. Seward is irreconcilably angry with me; "for he offers Christ to all." Her maids are of the same spirit; and their Baptist teacher insists that I ought to have my gown stripped over my ears. . . .

Sat., August 25th. I showed them in the street, that to them and to their children was the promise made. Some are, I trust, on the point of receiving it. . . .

At Gloucester I received an invitation from F. Drummond. I dined with her and several of the friends, particularly Josiah Martin, a spiritual man, as far as I can discern. My heart was enlarged, and knit to them in love. I went to the field at five. An old intimate acquaintance (Mrs. Kirkham)[4] stood in my way, and challenged me, "What, Mr. Wesley, is it you I see? Is it possible that you who can preach at Christ-church, St. Mary's and &c., should come hither after a mob?" I cut her short with, "The work which my Master giveth me, must I not do it?" and went to my mob, or (to put it in the Pharisee's phrase) this people which is accursed. Thousands heard me gladly, while I told them their privilege of the Holy Ghost, the Comforter, and exhorted them to come for him to Christ as poor lost sinners. I continued my discourse till night.

No. 31 Letter [addressee uncertain]
(*The Journal of Charles Wesley,* 1849)

Gloucester, August 25th [1739].

Before I went forth into the streets and highways, I sent, after my custom, to borrow the church. The Minister (one of the better disposed) sent back a civil message, that he would be glad to drink a glass of wine with me, but durst not lend me his pulpit for fifty guineas.

Mr. Whitefield durst lend me his field, which did just as well. For near an hour and a half God gave me voice and strength to exhort about two thousand sinners to repent and believe the Gospel. My voice and strength failed together; neither do I want them when my work is done. Being invited to Painswick, I waited upon the Lord, and renewed my strength.

We found near one thousand gathered in the street. I have but one subject, on which I discoursed from 2 Cor. 5:19: "God was in Christ, reconciling the world unto himself." I besought them earnestly to be reconciled, and the rebels seemed inclinable to lay down their arms. A young Presbyterian teacher clave to us. I received fresh strength to expound the good Samaritan, at a public-house, which was full above stairs and below.

No. 32   Letter[5] [addressee uncertain]
(*The Journal of Charles Wesley,* 1849)

Runwick, August 26th [1739?].
   The Minister here lent me his pulpit. I stood at the window, (which was taken down,) and turned to the larger congregation of above two thousand, in the church-yard. They appeared greedy to hear, while I testified, "God so loved the world that he gave his only-begotten Son," &c. These are, I think, more noble than those at Evesham.
   After sermon, a woman came to me, who had received faith in hearing Mr. Whitefield. She was terrified at having lost her comfort. I explained to her that wilderness-state into which the believer is *generally* led by the Spirit to be tempted, as soon as he is baptized by the Holy Ghost. This confirmed her in a patient looking for His return whom her soul loveth.
   We dined at Mr. Ellis's of Ebly. I met our brother Ellis, who has the blessing of believing parents; two sisters awakened; one only brother continues an abandoned prodigal. In the afternoon I preached again to a Kennington congregation. The church was full as it could crowd. Thousands stood in the church-yard. It was the most beautiful sight I ever beheld. The people filled the gradually-rising area, which was shut up on three sides by a vast perpendicular hill. On the top and bottom of this hill was a circular row of trees. In this amphitheatre they stood, deeply attentive, while I called upon them in Christ's words, "Come unto me, all that are weary." [No. 33] The tears of many testified that they were ready to enter into that rest. God enabled me to lift up my voice like a trumpet; so that all distinctly heard me. I concluded with singing an invitation to sinners. . . .

No. 33   Hymn: On Matt. 9:20: "Come unto Me ye that labour and are heavy laden and I will give you rest."

Charles's sermon on Jesus' call to the weary and heavy-laden has not survived but one of his popular hymns based on this passage shows how he approached that comfortable text. This hymn was first published in *Hymns and Sacred Poems* (1742), and saw service again in John's 1780 "big hymnbook," in a shortened form. Inward rest ("comfort") was one of Charles's standard themes, elaborated here in the context of his conception of Christian Perfection. While the hymn was published jointly by the Wesleys, the phrasing (''dear'' in verse 7) indicates it was not written by John.[6]

1   O that my load of sin were gone!
        O that I could at last submit
    At Jesus' feet to lay it down,
        To lay my soul at Jesus' feet!

2   When shall mine eyes behold the Lamb,
        The God of my salvation see?
    Weary, O Lord, Thou know'st I am;
        Yet still I cannot come to Thee.

3   Mark the hard travail of my soul,
        With pity view my labouring breast;
    O give me faith to make me whole,
        And speak my misery into rest.

4   Rest for my soul I long to find;
        Saviour of all, if mine Thou art,
    Give me Thy Meek and lowly mind,
        And stamp Thine image on my heart.

5   Break off the yoke of inbred sin,
        And fully set my spirit free;
    I cannot rest, till pure within,
        Till I am wholly lost in Thee.

6   Fain would I learn of Thee, my God,
        Thy light and easy burden prove,
    The cross all stain'd with hallow'd blood,
        The labour of Thy dying love;

7   This moment would I take it up,
        And after my dear Master bear,
    With Thee ascend to *Calvary's* top,
        And bow my head and suffer there.

8   I would: but Thou must give the power,
        My heart from every sin release;
    Bring near, bring near the joyful hour,
        And fill me with Thy perfect peace.

9   Come, Lord, the drooping sinner cheer,
        Nor let Thy chariot-wheels delay;
    Appear in my poor heart, appear;
        My God, my Saviour, come away.

10   One deep unto another cries,
        My misery, Lord, implores Thy grace:
     When wilt Thou hear, and bow the skies?
        When shall I see my Jesu' face?

11   The hireling longeth for his hire—
        But only punishment is mine;
     My merits are eternal fire—
        But heaven and happiness are Thine.

12   Give me Thy life; for Thou my death
        Hast swallow'd up in victory,
     Quicken'd me with Thy latest breath,
        And died that I might live to Thee.

13   This, only this, is all my hope,
        And doth my sinking soul sustain;
     Thy faithful mercies hold me up,
        My Saviour did not die in vain.

14   Answer Thy death's design in me;
        The guilt and power of sin remove,
     Redeem from all iniquity,
        Renew, and perfect me in love.

No. 34   Journal Selections: September 2–4, 1739

   Sun., September 2d [1739]. There was supposed to be above four thousand at the Bowling-green. My subject was, "To you and to your children
is the promise made." Many experienced the great power of truth. I received the sacrament at St. Nicholas; dined at M.N.'s full of faith and love.
I prayed by Mr. Coulston, desirous to be with Christ.
   I preached at Rose-green, to near five thousand souls, upon "God so
loved the world." They heard me patiently; and some gladly. I was quite
spent by the time I got to Weaver's-hall. The scoffers gave me new life. For
two hours I preached the law; and then was fresh for the love-feast. We
could not part before eleven.
   Mon., September 3d. I had some discourse with a gentleman, who had
been offended at the cryings out.[7] My sermon upon the Holy Ghost had
been blessed to his conviction, and stripped him of his outside Christianity. I found Weaver's-hall as full as it could hold; and proceeded in
Isaiah. I dined with the gentleman above mentioned, and spoke fully and
strongly of the things of the kingdom. Then read him my own case. He laid
down his arms, confessed he knew nothing yet as he ought to know; and is
now looking for that faith which is the gift of God.
   I preached at the brick-yard, to upwards of five thousand, from 1 Cor.

6:9. I marvelled at their taking it so patiently, when I showed them they were all adulterers, thieves, idolaters, &c. Then expounded John 1 in Gloucester-lane, with demonstration of the Spirit. I spent a delightful hour in prayer with a band; and were all melted into a sense of our deep poverty.

Tues., September 4th. . . . At four I preached over against the school in Kingswood, to some thousands (colliers chiefly), and held out the promises from Isaiah 35: "The wilderness and the solitary places shall be glad for them; and the desert shall rejoice, and blossom as the rose." [No. 35, etc.] I triumphed in God's mercy to these outcasts, (for he hath called them a people who were not a people), and in the accomplishment of that scripture, "Then the eyes of the blind shall be opened, and the ears of the deaf shall be unstopped; then shall the lame man leap as a hart, and the tongue of the dumb will sing; for in the wilderness shall water break out, and streams in the desert." O how gladly do the poor receive the Gospel! We hardly knew how to part. . . .

As was typical of Charles's hymns, the message was tailored to suit the singer. In the first hymn for the colliers, verse seven describes the transformation these hard-working and hard-living miners have undergone. First published in *Hymns and Sacred Poems* (1740), the hymn was also carried in the 1780 standard hymnbook as #195.[8] The second hymn was of a later vintage; dating (probably) from the mid-1740s, it was first published in Charles's *Hymns and Sacred Poems* (1749 edition). "My brethren beloved, Your Calling ye see" was reprinted in the 1780 standard hymnal with the second verse omitted.[9] In each case Wesley emphasizes that the grace of Christ liberates these "outcasts of men" from their sin, guilt, and lowly station and makes them "His own."

No. 35   Hymn: "For the Kingswood Colliers"

1   Glory to God, whose sovereign grace
    Hath animated senseless stones,
Call'd us to stand before His face,
    And raised us into *Abraham's* sons.

2   The people that in darkness lay,
    In sin and error's deadly shade,
Have seen a glorious Gospel day,
    In Jesu's lovely face display'd.

3   Thou only, Lord, the work hast done,
    And bared Thine arm in all our sight;
Hast made the reprobates Thy own,
    And claim'd the outcasts as Thy right.

4 Thy single arm, Almighty Lord,
      To us the great salvation brought;
   Thy Word, Thy all-creating Word,
      That spake at first the world from nought.

5 For this the saints lift up their voice,
      And ceaseless praise to Thee is given;
   For this the hosts above rejoice:
      We raise the happiness of heaven.

6 For this, no longer sons of night,
      To Thee our thanks and hearts we give;
   To Thee who call'd us into light,
      To Thee we die, to Thee we live.

7 Suffice that for the season past
      Hell's horrid language fill'd our tongues,
   We all Thy words behind us cast,
      And loudly sang the drunkard's songs.

8 But, O the power of grace Divine!
      In hymns we now our voices raise,
   Loudly in strange hosannas join,
      And blasphemies are turn'd to praise!

   Praise God, from whom all blessings flow;
   Praise Him, all creatures here below;
   Praise Him above, ye heavenly host;
   Praise Father, Son, and Holy Ghost.

No. 36   Hymn: "For the Kingswood Colliers" (another)

1 My brethren beloved, Your calling ye see:
   In Jesus approved, No goodness have we:
   No riches or merit, No wisdom or might,
   But all things inherit Through Jesus' right.

2 Our God would not have One reprobate die:
   Who all men would have Hath no man pass'd by:
   His boundless compassion On sinners doth call;
   He offers salvation Through mercy to all.

3 Yet not many wise His summons obey;
   And great ones despise So vulgar a way;
   And strong ones will never Their helplessness own,
   Or stoop to find favour Through mercy alone.

4 And therefore our God The outcasts hath chose,
   His righteousness show'd To heathen like us:
   When wise ones rejected His offers of grace,
   His goodness elected The foolish and base.

5 To baffle the wise, and noble, and strong,
   He bade us arise, An impotent throng:
   Poor ignorant wretches We gladly embrace
   A Prophet that teaches Salvation by grace.

6 The things that were not His mercy bids live;
   His mercy unbought We freely receive,
   His gracious compassion We thankfully prove,
   And all our salvation Ascribe to His love.

No. 37 Journal Selections: September 7–30, 1739

Fri., September 7th. At Weaver's-hall I expounded Isa. 3, where the Prophet alike condemns notorious profligates, worldly-minded men, and well dressed ladies. . . .

The house and yards of S. England were crowded as usual. The scripture from which I discoursed was John 1. God was with my mouth. I preached and prayed believing. I was led to ask [for] a sign of God's universal love. He always answers that prayer. A poor ignorant man stood up, as God's witness, that in Christ he had redemption through his blood, the forgiveness of sins; that he knew and felt it by such a love to every human soul, as he was irresistible. We all confessed that God was with him of a truth. Our prayers were answered on M. Ayres likewise; which she testified before us all.

Sat. September 8th. . . . At the bowling-green, I prayed God to direct me what to preach upon, and opened on Ezekiel's vision of the dry bones: "So I prophesied as I was commanded: and as I prophesied, there was a noise, and, behold, a shaking!" The breath of God attended his word. A man sunk down under it. A woman screamed for mercy, so as to drown my voice. Never did I see the like power among us. Coming home, I met M. Skinner, who told me she had found Christ at the expounding last Monday, and went home full of melting joy and love.

At the room I preached from Rom. 4. God set to his seal. A woman testified she had then received the witness of the Spirit; was sure her sins were forgiven; full of love and joy in the Holy Ghost; knew Christ was hers, and could even, as she said, fly away to heaven. Another declared she had never been able to apply the promises till last night, but then received the power; knew Christ died for her; said, she had laboured many years to justify herself, and warned us earnestly not to do as she had done; not to mingle our own works with the blood of Christ.

Sun., September 9th. At the bowling-green I preached on, "When he is come, he shall convince the world of sin, and of righteousness," &c. The green was quite full. I never spoke more searchingly. I would have passed on to the second office of the Spirit, convincing of righteousness, but was again and again brought back, and constrained to dwell upon the law. As often as I returned, some Pharisees quitted the field; feeling the sharpness of the two-edged sword.

Two thousand at Rose-green stood patient in the rain, while I explained how the Spirit convinces of righteousness and of judgment. After the sermon, a poor collier afforded me matter of rejoicing (his wife received the atonement some days before). He had been with me before; owned he was the wickedest fellow alive a month ago; but now finds no rest in his flesh by reason of his sin. Observing him much dejected yesterday at the thanksgiving, I asked him if he was sick. "No, no," he answered; "my sickness is of my soul." Here he informed me he had come home with such a weight upon him, that he was ready to sink. It continued all night; but joy and deliverance came in the morning. He was lightened of his load, and now declared that he believed in Jesus. The room was excessively crowded. I spoke to their hearts from Rom. 5. Two who had been scoffing, desired our prayers for them. For between two and three hours God strengthened me for his work.

Wed., September 26th. I received much light and strength to expound Isa. 30. A woman sank down in deep distress. Several who wait for faith were affected greatly. From one to three, more came than I was able to talk with; all seeking what many have found. In particular, Anne Sparrin was filled with joy in believing, while we were at prayers last Monday. So was Mrs. Williams, in going home from church. Susanna Trapman likewise sees *her* interest in the blood of Jesus. Elizabeth Parsons, whom the evil spirit has often torn, is sensible now, that he is cast out. It is observable of the two last, that they have never been baptized. I now require no farther proof that one may be an *inward* Christian without baptism. They are both desirous of it; and who can forbid water?

Abraham Staples informs me that on Saturday was three weeks, while I was preaching, "Lazarus, come forth," he was called out of his natural state, and raised to the life of faith. "I felt," said he, "that my sins were forgiven, by a peace and warmth within me, which have continued ever since." "Then you know," said I, "that the Spirit of God is a Spirit of burning?" "Yes," he answered, "and a Spirit of shaking too; for he turns me upside down. I am full of joy and life, and could be always a-praying; should be glad to die this moment. What knowledge I have, I have given me of God; for I am no scholar; I can neither write nor read."

Sarah Pearce declares, she received the first comfort in hearing Rom. 5 explained. She was then justified; but did not draw nigh in full assurance of faith, till last night. Every word I spoke came with power. She had the witness of her own spirit or conscience, that all the marks I mentioned were in her; and the Spirit of God came in doubt. Some of her words were, "I was once extremely enlarged toward them, and all mankind, in an inexpressible manner. I do not depend upon a start of comfort; but find it increase ever since it began. I perceive a great change in myself; and expect a greater. I feel a divine attraction in my soul. I was once so afraid of death, that I durst not sleep; but now I do not fear it at all. I desire nothing on earth. I dread nothing but sin. God suffers me to be strongly tempted; but I know, when he gives faith he will try it."

See here the true assurance of faith! How consistent an humble, not doubting, a filial, not servile, fear of offending! I desire not *such* an assurance as blots out those scriptures, "Be not high-minded, but fear"; "Work out your salvation with fear and trembling," &c. God keep me in continual fear, lest, by any means, when I have preached to others, I myself should be a cast-away.

At the Mills I preached upon, "As Moses lifted up the serpent in the wilderness, even so," &c. I spoke plainly to the womenbands of their unadvisableness, want of love, and bearing one another's burdens. We found an immediate effect in the enlargement of our hearts. Some were convinced that they had thought too highly of themselves; and that their first love, like their first joy, was only a foretaste of that temper which continually rules in a new heart.

Fri., September 28th. Christianity flourishes under the cross. None who follow after Christ want [lack] that badge of discipleship. Wives and children are beaten, and turned out of doors; and the persecutors are the complainers. It is always the lamb that troubles the water. Every Sunday damnation is denounced against all that hear us Papists, us Jesuits, us seducers, us bringers in of the Pretender. The Clergy murmur aloud at the number of communicants, and threaten to repel them; yet will not the world bear that we should talk of persecution. No; for the world is Christian now, and the offense of the cross ceased. Alas! what would they farther [sic]? Some lose their bread, some their habitations; one suffers stripes, another confinement; and yet we must not call this persecution. Doubtless they will find some other name for it, when they do God service by killing us.

To-day Mary Hanney was with me. While she continued a drunkard, a swearer, and company-keeper, it was very well; she and her father agreed entirely. But from the time of her turning to God, he has used her most inhumanly. Yesterday he beat her, and drove her out of doors, following her with imprecations and threatenings to murder her, if ever she returned. When she was cast out, Jesus found her, and said unto her by his Spirit, "Be of good cheer, thy sins are forgiven thee." She continued all the night in joy unspeakable, and can now with confidence call God her Father. . . .

Sat., September 29th. I breakfasted with six or eight awakened sinners, who are hourly waiting for the consolation of Israel. I prayed by a dying woman, and cut off her confidence in the flesh. As sure as I ask the question, "Why do you hope to be saved?" I receive the woeful answer, "Because I have done no harm," or "Because I have used my endeavours." This comes of our telling the people, "God, upon your sincere endeavours, will accept you." There were several present, whom I stripped of their filthy rags [i.e. self-righteousness] and sent naked to Christ. . . .

At the bowling-green I explained the first words that presented: "Now faith is the substance of things hoped for, the evidence of things not seen." Afterwards I enforced obedience to the powers that be, from Rom. 13; and showed the scandalous inconsistency of your high-Churchmen, who disclaim resistance, and yet practice it; continually speaking evil of dignitaries, nay, of the ruler of the people, as well as of those who are put in authority under him. Fewer than I expected were offended at me.

Sun., September 30th. I found my usual congregation at Hanham; and showed them their Saviour, from Isa. 53. Many tears of love or desire were shed. At the Hall I expounded "the woman taken in adultery." Some, convicted by their own conscience, went out.

No. 38   Sermon: Charles's Exposition of John 8

Charles preached from the eighth chapter of John's Gospel at least three times in 1739: February 20 at Mr. Stonehouse's, April 15 at Islington, and September 30 in Bristol. The homiletical style is the sort of line-by-line exposition that seems to have characterized much of Wesley's evangelistic work. Charles moved easily from the Pharisees of the biblical narrative to the pharisaical attitudes of eighteenth-century England. The sermon preaches the gospel of acceptance, and subtly attacks self-justification in favor of repentance and justification by faith.

The style of this sermon makes an obvious departure from the more formal (Anglican style) homilies Charles preached at Oxford. It is a free-flowing treatment that he aptly describes as an "exposition." The following sermon was only recently discovered among Charles's manuscripts and transcribed from the shorthand of Dr. John Byrom by Thomas Albin and Oliver Beckerlegge.[10]

I.N.I.[11]

John 8:1 &c. Jesus went unto the Mount of Olives; and early in the morning He came again into the Temple, and all the people came unto Him; and He sat down and taught them. And the Scribes and Pharisees brought unto Him a woman taken in adultery; and when they had set her in the midst, they say unto Him, Master, this woman was taken in adultery, in the very act. Now Moses in the law commanded us, that such should be stoned; but what sayest thou? This they said, tempting Him, that they might have to accuse Him. But Jesus stooped down, and with His finger wrote on the ground as though He heard them not. So when they continued asking Him, He lift[ed] up Himself and said unto them, He that is without sin among you, let him first cast a stone at her. And again He stooped down and wrote on the ground. And they which heard it, being convicted by their own conscience, went out one by one, beginning at the eldest, even unto the last. And Jesus was left alone, and the woman standing in the midst. When Jesus had lift[ed] up Himself, and saw none but the woman, he said to her, Woman, where are those thine accusers? Hath no man condemned thee? She said, No man, Lord. And Jesus said unto her, Neither do I condemn thee; go, and sin no more.

Jesus went unto the Mount of Olives; and early in the morning He came again into the Temple. The life of Christ is the life of Christians; who, if they are Christians indeed, walk as He also walked, spending their time in works of piety and charity, on the Mount or with the multitude. From prayer they return with their Lord to doing good, from doing good they retire to prayer. Each fits for other; retirement for action, and action for retirement.

And early in the morning He came again into the Temple leaving us an example that we should tread in His steps. A Christian therefore as such, is early at his devotions; else he has nothing of Christ but the name.

He came again into the Temple, and all the people came unto Him. It is into the temple we must come, if we would find Christ. At the hours of prayer, it is here only we must look for Him. Whosoever wholly[?] neglects to seek Him here shall find Him nowhere else. Many indeed come to this place without coming to this place. Many miss finding Him here because they come Scribes and Pharisees; and they who would forbear assembling themselves together are no followers of Christ; they are quite out of His way; they cannot find, for they will not seek Him.

All the people came unto Him. All the publicans and sinners drew nigh unto Him to hear Him, saith St. Luke (15:1), but have any of the rulers believed on Him? No! They were too wise and too holy. But this people which is accursed, harlots and publicans, run after Him, the poor have the gospel preached to them.

He sat down and taught them for they only had ears to hear: they were not whole, but such as had need of a physician: they were not righteous but sinners, and utterly lost without Him: therefore they were the very persons he came to call to repentance; they were the very persons He came to seek and to save, and accordingly these outcasts of men were almost His only followers.

He taught them for they knew themselves ignorant: He healed them, for they felt themselves sick: He pardoned them, for they confessed themselves sinners; He saved them, for they owned they deserved to be damned.

The Scribes and Pharisees brought unto Him a woman taken in adultery. What a triumph is here for Scribes and Pharisees! A woman taken in adultery! What a glorious occasion of setting forth their own virtues; their spotless chastity, their zeal for justice, their abhorrence of sinners! On this unholy[?] occasion they can touch sinners without being defiled, when they are dragging them to execution; and they are never so happy as in this employment; they never shone so bright as by this comparison!

They brought unto Him, the friend of publicans and sinners! As they truly called Him, though He was so in a sense more glorious than their malice meant it. Seeking to gratify their revenge no less than their pride, *they brought unto Him a woman taken in adultery*. And why the woman rather; since the man's offense was equal if not greater? Perhaps they hope for more likely matter to accuse Christ in the case of the woman than of the man, as supposing His merciful disposition might more probably incline Him to compassion against her wickedness, and so illegally to acquit her.

And when they had set her in the midst. Shame must make way for punishment. She had escaped too cheaply had they suffered her to die without first insulting and triumphing over her. Therefore they drag her out to light, and place her in the face of the congregation. See then this miserable adulteress! How she stands confounded in the midst of that gazing and disdainful multitude! How she hides her head, and with trembling silence expects and anticipates the dreadful sentence.

Not so the Scribes and Pharisees. They stand forth to accuse her. With boldness and confidence *they say unto Him, Master, this woman was taken in adultery, in the very act.* How plausibly do they begin! With what reverence do they accost Him! With what veneration to His person, and deference to His judgment! What holy, honest and conscientious men are these! Such strict lovers of justice! Such devout followers of Christ! So we should be apt to think of them; but He who made and knows their hearts tells us this is but done to tempt Him. Whence we may justly infer that the highest outward profession of righteousness, the greatest seeming esteem of it, is perfectly consistent with all filthiness of spirit, and may proceed from the corrupt heart of a wholly false, hypocritical Pharisee.

But what say these holy executioners? *Master, this woman was taken in adultery, in the very act.* This is made an aggravation of her guilt. *"She was taken!"* And with a Pharisee this is all in all. It is not the guilt, but its discovery, makes the sinner. ~~Sin concealed is with them no sin at all, with them the~~ [I?]. It is not the sin but the scandal they are afraid of. Sin concealed is with them no sin at all; but when detected it is most abominable. If they can hide their vices from men they think themselves as good as innocent; while only God and their own conscience knows it, they are safe enough. But alas, what shall it avail them to lurk awhile under the mask of innocence! When the secrets of all hearts shall so soon be revealed, and God shall bring to light the hidden things of darkness. In that day they shall find their conscience more than a thousand witnesses, and God more than a thousand consciences.

Till then they may happily pose for saints, and hide their sin under a seeming abhorrence of sin, and drown their own guilt in a clamorous cry for justice upon others. So [did] their holy predecessors in the history before us. They accuse and loudly call for ~~justice~~ punishment against a notorious offender. *Now Moses in the law commanded us, that such should be stoned, but what sayest thou?* What a suspicious, subtle, ensnaring question! Here, they think, He cannot escape, but which way soever He answer, must give them the occasion they sought for. *For this they said, tempting him, that they might have to accuse him.* Like their father the devil, the tempter, the accuser! and who therefore tempts that he may accuse; like his genuine[?] children of this generation, who come after the preacher, laying wait for Him, and seeking to catch something out of His mouth that they may accuse Him. Poor miserable men, who know not who exploits you, ye consider not who sends you, or that you are the apostles of Satan. He inspires your thoughts, he speaks your words, he sets you to work, and he will pay you for your wages. ~~But to return~~

Now Moses in the law commanded us, that such should be stoned, but what sayest thou? They know Christ's inclination to mercy and compassion. Their self-righteous souls had been often grieved at seeing Him eat with known sinners. They had murmured at Him receiving them, His dismissing one, justifying another, inviting and speaking kindly to all. Hence they hope His pity might draw Him to acquit her, whom the law condemned; and they would not have desired a better advantage than that He should contradict their received lawgiver. "We are Moses' disciples; we know God spoke to Moses" and had our Lord spoken otherwise, they would have had ᵕ accuse Him. It is still the aim of those that are enemies to the truth to set Christ and Moses at variance; particularly as to the use of the law. "You make void the law through faith," say they, "that is, through your doctrine of justification by faith only." ~~But~~ We answer with St. Paul, "Yea, we establish the law. Christ and Moses are two inseparable friends; each speaks for each. One confirms the other. They are subordinate[?] not opposite. Moses as the servant, Christ the Son: Moses as the schoolmaster; Christ to supply Moses. "By Him all that believe are justified from all things from which they could not be justified by the law." ~~If~~ Moses brings us to Christ; Christ brings us to glory. Faith does not ~~overthrow~~ destroy good works, unless the cause ~~overthrows~~ destroys the effect. Faith alone is necessary unto justification, works to[12] evidence our justification as consequences not conditions, as fruits not causes.

As vainly therefore do our Pharisees labour to make Christ contradict Moses, as ~~work~~ their predecessors of old whom we are now considering. These reasoned thus—"Either he must clear the guilty, or condemn her. If he acquits her, where is His justice; if He condemns her, where is His mercy?["] Let them exhort a legal sentence, and they thereby blast the honour of his clemency[?]. Let Him consent to the law, and He loses His reputation with the people, and His enemies will immediately cry, "See here your friend of sinners! who condemns them without mercy; who inflicts the cruelest punishment; who stones them that are brought unto Him!" Howsoever He answers, they gain their point; He cannot escape; but they will have to accuse Him either of injustice or unmercifulness.

Such is the cunning folly of vain men that would hope to beguile wisdom itself!

But Jesus stooped down, and with His finger wrote on the ground as though He heard them not. Silence and neglect is their first answer; and in many cases we shall find it the best.

As though He heard them not. His ear is not heavy that it cannot hear our calls for mercy; His ear is ever open to the sinner's cry, but when devils and Pharisees cry out for justice, He becomes as a deaf man and one that heareth not. How often have our sins demanded justice against us, and He would not hear? So rich is He in goodness and forbearance and long-suffering, so slow to anger and averse from punishing! which He therefore calls His strange work and comes to it, as it were, with the utmost reluctance. Nay, He pauses in the very act of punishing; He lays aside the lifted bolt; His justice lingers and relents and yields: He drops the lifted bolt and says "How shall I give thee up, O Ephraim!"

The more unwilling He seems to give an answer, the more eager they are to exhort one from Him. And in this case we are to follow our Lord's example, when our Pharisees insist and urge us to answer, we must at last reply plainly and fully. We are even under a necessity of uncasing[?] them, of tearing off the mask and exposing them to the people. *So when they continued asking Him, He lift up Himself and said unto them, He that is without sin, let him first cast a stone at her.* He lifted Himself up, as if His action had said, I was willing to let you escape, I was loath to shame you, since you will needs have it, and by your vehemence force my justice, I must tell you there is no one of you, but is as faulty as she whom you accuse. There is no difference; only your sin is secret, and hers notorious. You have more need to make your own peace with God by a humble repentance, than to urge severity against her. Death is justly due to such horrid offenses, but what then would become of you? She deserves to die; but not by your unclean hands. Your hearts know you are not honest enough to accuse.

He that is without sin among you, let him first cast a stone at her. How wise an answer; how worthy of Him that spoke it! Here both His justice and His mercy are preserved. He takes neither part of our dilemma, not condemning either Moses or the sinner. In this punishment the witnesses were first to lay their hands upon the guilty; well therefore doth our Lord check these accusers with the conscience of their so foul incompetency. He takes off these bloody hands by turning their eyes upon themselves. Innocence is justly required in the accuser. She is worthy to be stoned, but by whom? Who shall first cast the stones at her? Not Scribes and Pharisees. Ill would it become hands as guilty as her own. With what face, with what heart could they stone their own sin in another person!

These Scribes and Pharisees, we know, were noted for holiness. They went beyond even our good sort of people, and in all outward appearances were most exemplary saints; but God's ~~justice is not as man's justice~~ His thoughts are not as our thoughts. These are they that justify themselves before men but God knoweth their hearts ~~and searcheth them out to~~ for that which is highly esteemed among men is abominable with Him. He searcheth them out to perfection. In vain do they hope to escape that all seeing eye which can find fully in the angels. The heavens are not clean in His sight; how much less they that dwell in houses of clay, now least of all the self-justifying Pharisees! Such as be unrighteous shall not stand in His sight; and now they find it. Now indeed His eyes are as a flame of fire; and out of His mouth goeth a sharp two-edged sword, and His countenance is as the sun shineth in His strength. No wonder therefore that Pharisees cannot behold Him, but are thunderstruck, astonished, confounded! The accusers are cast down, the high looks are fallen; Pharisees themselves are silent, and no longer outrageous against notorious sinners.

Perhaps these secret sins, with which our Lord now stops their clamorous mouths, had been long since forgot. They thought no more of them, and said, Hath not God forgotten? But all these things are noted in His book, and are now brought to remembrance by their Judge. "These things hast thou done, and I held my peace, and thou thoughtest wickedly that I am even such a one as thyself. But I will reprove thee, and set before thee the things which thou hast done." So will God speak to every lurking sinner, but if we would that He should not remember our sins, we should never forget them ourselves. Let them be ever before us that He may not set them in the light of His countenance; and for the time to come let us see ourselves [as] seen by Him, and we shall not dare to offend.

And again He stooped down and wrote on the ground, to give them an opportunity of escaping unobserved. He seems to disregard them, but we all know how His medicine worked. Accordingly, we do not see them stand out in their innocence. No! Their hearts misgive them, and they feared if they had stood out, He would have utterly shamed them, by displaying all their old sins, and turning their pretended saintliness inside out. This was a discovery they were not fond of; especially before the people, who began to find them out, and to beware of Scribes, Pharisees, and hypocrites. They see the rod held over them (had just now), they felt the smart, and willingly spared our Lord any further explanation; going out by d[?] one by one, that they might not seem driven away.

And they which heard it, being convicted by their own consciences, went out one by one, beginning at the eldest, even unto the last. Oh irresistible truth! Oh wonderful power of conscience! Man can no more stand out against that, than that can stand against God. When the Almighty, whose substance[?] it is, sets it on work, it has, as it were, the force of omnipotence. When that says, we are guilty, there is no denying. In vain does the world acquit us while our hearts are consumed by the worm that never dies. No wicked man need seek out of himself a judge, accuser, witness, tormenter.

And they which heard it, being convicted by their own consciences, went out.
How boldly did these hypocrites set upon Christ! With what insolent triumph, what diabolical subtlety, what foulness of self-righteousness! Now
they are thunderstruck, and drop away confounded. No sooner do they
hear of their own sins from the mouth of Christ, but they are gone. He had
given them a convincing proof that He was God, and as such had power to
forgive sins upon earth. They ought therefore to have humbly confessed
their sins unto Him, and earnestly prayed that Him to forgive them their
sins, and to cleanse them of all unrighteousness. But you will not easily
bring a Pharisee to that, to own himself a sinner, and deserving to be
damned. No, instead of that, he turns his back upon his Saviour and
hastens away.

A Pharisee cares not how little he hears, either of the power of God, or
the multitude of his sins. When he does hear a searching truth, which he
cannot deny and will not receive, he has nothing else for it but to flee as
fast as he can. This, as it is a certain token of guilt, so it is an infallible mark
of a Pharisee, your turning your back upon the ambassadors of Christ and
by despising them, despising Him that sent them: your going out of
Church, as your predecessors out of the Temple, and thereby counting and
proclaiming yourselves unworthy of eternal life. By this speechless action
you cry out, like Paul in the council, "I am a Pharisee, and the son of a
Pharisee." You make the application of what is spoken to yourselves, as
plainly as if you answered with an audible voice, "I am the man! My
conscience is my accuser! I cannot cast the first stone. I myself am a secret
adulterer, an hypocritical fornicator; and come not to the light because
I love the darkness, and cannot bear the light because my deeds are
evil."

My brethren, I wait to see which of you goes out now. If your conscience
will not let you stay, I would even favour your escape, and not see you—
was it not, that by seeing you I might recommend you to the prayers of the
congregation. Indeed you need them Whosoever among you has as many
among you as have ever dared to go out of church, for you are in the very
qualm of bitterness, in the bond of iniquity, and now you know you cannot
fly from conviction, I think it my duty to tell you so.

You that go out of Church, and yet call yourselves Christians, to you I
speak, and set before you the things which you have done. You are they
that cannot endure sound doctrine. Well do you Pharisees reject the counsel of God against yourselves, even His counsel to save lost sinners, to
justify them truly when they own they deserve to be damned. But you
spurn away from you so cheap salvation; you will not accept of Jesus
Christ upon His own so easy terms; you will not have this man reign over
you. When I speak as the oracles of God, and tell you the truth as it is in
Jesus, it is a small thing, think you, not to receive my testimony. Nay, but
in not receiving it, in not embracing these offers of salvation by grace, you
have trodden under foot the Son of God, and counted the blood of the

covenant an unholy thing, and done despite unto the Spirit of grace. Ye stiffnecked and uncircumcised in heart and ears, ye do always resist the Holy Ghost. Though you are cut to the heart and gnash upon me with your teeth, yet must I warn you of your wickedness, else you shall die in your iniquity, but your blood will God require at my hand. Wherefore in His name who hath set me a watchman unto the house of Israel, I warn you of the dreadful consequences of your having so denied the Lord that bought you; for which, unless you truly repent, you shall surely die in your iniquity. But I have delivered my own soul. Hear ye this and tremble, you who have turned your back upon a Saviour! For to you am I sent to cry aloud and spare not, to lift up my voice like a trumpet, and show you your transgressions and your sins. How shall you escape who have neglected so great salvation! Why, hitherto you have never thought about it. . . .[13] If I come amongst you preaching the gospel; if it be the gospel, and you have rejected it, and I shake off the dust of my feet again, "Verily, Verily," Christ saith unto you, "it shall be more tolerable for Sodom and Gomorrah in the day of judgement than for you."

Unhappy foolish men! What doth it profit you to flee from Him? If you could run away from God it were something; but while ye move in Him what do ye? Where go ye? You may run from His mercy; you cannot from His justice. Nay, you must run upon His justice by fleeing from His mercy.

Repent therefore of this your wickedness, and pray God if perhaps it may be forgiven you. Humble yourselves under the mighty hand of God; bow your stiff necks, ye rebellious worms; ye potentates of the earth strive no longer with your Maker. Justify God in His saying; clear Him who ye have judged, and confess you do deserve to be damned. Till you do confess it, you still continue are in a state of damnation still, as surely as God is true. And the man that dares tell you otherwise, to say peace, peace, where there is no peace, he shall bear his burden, whosoever he be. I myself shall rise up in judgment against that man: and I put my all hopes[14] of finding mercy in that day upon the truth of what I know of this report, that whosoever does not confess from his heart believe he deserves to be damned, is in a state of damnation to this very hour!

Return we now to the history. *And Jesus was left alone, and the woman standing in the midst.* Jesus was left alone by the Scribes and Pharisees, but the people and the mournful adulteress remained. She still stands in the midst being fastened down by her own guilt, but not daring hope of mercy. Oh how well was this sinner to be left there! Could she be in a safer refuge, where should she have rather fled? Happy, happy are we, if when convinced of sin we can set ourselves before our that judge, who is our surety, our advocate, our redeemer, our ransom, our peace!

Some hope she doubtless had from her accusers being gone; but a much stronger fear of the punishment she deserved. Divided she is, but not equally between hope and fear, and now while she trembles in expectation of a sentence, she hears *Woman, where are those thine accusers?* We do not

hear Him railing on her, or reviling her; He doth not say, Thou vile creature, thou execrable adulteress, thou shameless strumpet, but *Woman,
where are those thine accusers?* Those who but now so importunately demanded justice against thee, who hauled thee so triumphantly to execution? Has the Ethiopian changed his skin, or the Pharisee forgot his impla-
cable hatred against open sinners? Whence it is that their cries for blood are
suspended and they suffer the prey to be taken out of their teeth? What
unnatural compassion is this which makes them drop their charge and
leave a gross sinner any hope of mercy? Is it out of pity that they leave thee
unpunished? Or is it not rather guilt which has driven them away, and
withheld their foul hands from inflicting a punishment they themselves
deserve?

Hath no one condemned thee?, or cast the first stone at thee? Is there then
none among [them] without sin? Is there none righteous, no not one, even
among the self-justifying Scribes and Pharisees? He seems, as it were, to
triumph over sin far more abominable than hers.

She said, No man, Lord. And what, though every man had condemned, if
God acquitted her? *And Jesus said unto her, neither do I condemn thee, go, and
sin no more.* A ~~sound~~ gracious word! A comfortable sound in the ears of a
despairing sinner! *Neither do I condemn thee,* I judge no man. For God sent
not His Son into the world to condemn the world, but that the world
through Him should be saved. "As I live, saith the Lord, I have no pleasure in the death of the wicked." Man's miserable justice often times has;
but God is love, and mercy rejoices against judgment.

It is thus in the case before us. The Pharisees thought He could not save
so great a sinner; He therefore shows them He can. But these things were
written for our instruction; for our sakes principally he lets her go free, to
convince us our sins cannot be too great for His mercy, and to show us the
temper which fits us for our pardon.

When a notorious sinner is hauled to justice, and by men not even
suffered to live, let him by the Holy Ghost call Jesus Lord, and he shall
know that the arm of the Lord is not shortened, but that Christ is able to
save to the uttermost all that come unto God by Him. Oh that the greatest
sinner now out of hell were present, that I might show unto him the way of
salvation, and make him a free offer of it in the blood of Jesus! "This is a
faithful saying and worthy of all men to be received, that Christ Jesus came
into the world to save sinners; of whom I am chief." This let him see and
feel. Let him place himself like the miserable adulteress in the presence of
his judge, not daring so much as to lift up his eyes, but with confusion of
face, and horror of heart confess that all his desert is hell. Let him be as
fully convinced that he deserves damnation, as the woman that she deserved a temporal punishment. Let him stand before his judge trembling
and self-condemned; let him become guilty before God, having his mouth
stopped, and before his eyes the sentence of eternal death. Let ~~him be this~~
the greatest sinner upon earth be thus humbled, thus convinced, and to

him, even to him, do I glory in giving encouragement. To him do I publish the glad tidings of a Saviour. And he may have a strong consolation, who flies for refuge to lay hold upon the hope which I set before him: Jesus Christ, the same yesterday, today, and forever! Christ Jesus, the same physician of them that that [sic] are sick, the same quickener of them that are dead in trespasses and sins, the same justifier of the ungodly, the same friend of publicans and sinners, the same Lamb of God that taketh away the sin of the world. Believe this, Oh thou chief of sinners; believe he suffered once for all, the just for the unjust; He tasted death for every man; He loved thee and gave Himself for thee. Then shalt thou feel the power of this Scripture: "Hath no man condemned thee?"—Let any, let every man upon earth, let all the devils in hell condemn thee too, and thou canst believe ~~in him~~ in Jesus, he Himself shall say, *I do not condemn thee, ~~will Jesus say,~~ go, and sin no more.*

He that believeth on the ~~Jesus Christ~~ Son of God shall never come into condemnation, but may boldly make the apostle's challenge, who shall lay anything to the charge of God's elect? It is God that justifieth; who is he that condemneth? It is Christ that died; yea rather, that is risen again; who is even at the right hand of God; who also maketh intercession for us! How great or many soever his sins have been, it matters not. Although we think he was the first born son of the devil, he had seven devils, his name was legion,—but he is washed, but he is sanctified, but he is justified in the name of the Lord Jesus, and by the Spirit of our God.

I know the offense this gives to Pharisees. Here therefore will I join issue with you self-righteous ones, and show you what manner of spirit ye are of. This woman is my touchstone, and shall discover your counterfeit virtue. What says your holiness to an adulteress, a notorious, open sinner? Is pity the first emotion you feel at the sight of her, and do your eyes gush out with water, because she hath not kept God's law? Do you see your-selves in her? Do you immediately look within and say, "I am as this adulteress! By nature I am in no wise better than she. There is no difference but that which grace hath made." Are you ready to encourage the first divine spark of grace in her, the compassion on her while she is yet a great way off? And can you run unto her, while she is beginning to come to herself and say, I will arise and go to my Father? Can you put yourself upon a level with her, and take her unto your bosom and call her sister the moment she looks up to the brazen serpent?[15]

Are you thus affected towards her, thus full of pity, sorrow and love, and duly humbled under a sense of your own like sinfulness? Or do you not find the contrary tempers? Are you not out of patience at the sight or mention of her? Does not the Pharisee rise within you in resentment and disdain and ~~hatred~~ abhorrence and vindictiveness? Are you not like the troubled sea when it cannot rest, whose waters cast up mire and dirt? Have you put away from you all bitterness and wrath and anger and evil speak-ing? Or do you exercise all these tempers upon her? Dare you bring against her what Michael durst not the devil, a railing accusation? Do you not find a disdain and loathing of her person; and can you understand that distinction of hating the sin, but loving the sinner? Deal plainly with yourself and examine whether you do not think stoning too good for her, and are you not for tearing the creature to pieces? I need not multiply these questions. If you do feel a fierceness and bitterness against sinners, a scornful disdain, an unrelenting hate, a forwardness to accuse, a readiness to condemn, a joy and triumph in their punishment, however you may cloak this spirit under the mask of zeal for justice, it is the Pharisee, it is the devil in you. It is as contrary to the mind which was in Jesus, as loth to darkness to light, hell to heaven, you to Christians.

Fury is not in me, saith God. The Lord is full of mercy and compassion, long-suffering, and of great kindness, and repenteth Him of the evil. God is love; love in Himself, love towards a world of sinners. He wept over the bloody city, He lamented and mourned for Scribes and Pharisees, He prayed for His very murderers. He was brought as a lamb to the slaughter, and as a sheep before his shearers is dumb, so he opened not His mouth. When He was reviled, He reviled not again; when He suffered, He threatened not, but committed Himself to Him that judgeth righteously. And can you call yourselves followers of the meek and lowly Jesus? You that allow no mercy, no place for repentance to known sinners, but deliver them over to Satan in the fullness of your own self-righteousness? You who brought out nothing but threatenings against them, and think you are called, like Samuel, to hew them to pieces in the presence of the Lord?[16] Nay, you even pride yourselves in this temper, and would have your outrageousness pass for virtue. Your very vices must be countenanced, and you yourselves [are] thought to be the children of God for that very thing which proves you children of the devil. Saints you are indeed. But it is of his and the world's making. For had not the god of this world blinded your eyes, were you not given up to a strange delusion, you could not so believe a lie, or as much as dream there is anything of [a] Christian in you.

Bring forth the meanest object of your scorn, the filthiest prostitute that walks the streets, and he that is without sin among you, let him first cast a stone at her. Tell the searcher of hearts, in whose presence ye are, that you never had any lustful thought in your lives; and then, and not till then, let your hands be upon her. If you are convicted by your own consciences of but one impure thought which you ever entertained, then consider who checked that thought, and restrained you from running into her excess of lewdness. Give God the glory, and confess that you are a sinner, that you are as this harlot; whose wickedness, like yours, began with a single thought. Who maketh thee to differ from another? from a notorious sinner, from an abandoned harlot? If you think you make yourself differ from her, then are you as much worse than this harlot as filthiness of spirit flesh is worse than filthiness [of flesh] (of spirit),[17] or a devil worse than a beast.

But the most notorious offenders sinners go unpunished? Should any sincere person ask the question I would answer, no in no wise; but you are not to revenge yourselves; neither is anyone to punish, but the ruler whom God hath ordained; he beareth not the sword in vain for he is the minister of God to execute wrath upon him that doth evil. And let him follow the example of a judge of our own, who never pronounced sentence without tears. As to you my brethren, let me earnestly warn you against that abominable abhorrence, that sinful bitterness against sinners, in which some men's righteousness altogether consists; against that spirit which rails[?] on the children of unbelief. Let me at the same time recommend to you the deepest compassion, the utmost gentleness, the tenderest love, towards known sinners; towards even the worst of sinners, the Pharisees. It is my duty to ~~bring forth~~ warn you of these serpents, this generation of vipers, that you may beware of the Scribes' and Pharisees' hypocrisy. With my Lord I must rebuke them sharply that you, and if possible they, may be sound in the faith. But you and I must ~~bless and~~ love and pray for them, and bless them. I hope, my dear brethren, you can ~~heartily~~ truly say with me, I do not despise others, no, not even Pharisees. I am as other men; I am as this publican; nay, I was as this Pharisee; nor can I therefore cast the first stone at him. For I have swelled with proud wrath against sinners greater, as I supposed, because more scandalous than myself. Though I am a sinful man myself, though I am altogether born in sin, I have said to the gross sinner, Depart from me, stand by thyself! But God has opened my closed[?] eyes; but God has stopped my mouth, and from a Pharisee changed me into a publican.[18]

GOD BE MERCIFUL TO ME A SINNER!

No. 39   Journal Selections: October 11, 1739–July 15, 1740

Thur., October 11th. [1739]. I expounded the prodigal son among our colliers. Many a one, if not most of them, is ready to say, "I will rise, and go to my Father." At six I began John 1, at the widow Jones's. It was the first time of my preaching by night in the open air. The yard contained about four hundred. The house was likewise full. Great power was in the midst. Satan blasphemed without, but durst not venture his children too near the Gospel, when I offered Christ Jesus to them. The enemy hurried them away; and all we could do was to pray for them.

Sat., October 13th. I waited with my brother upon a Minister, about baptizing some of his parish. He complained heavily of the multitude of our communicants, and produced the canon against strangers [communing]. He could not admit that as a reason for their coming to his church, that they had no sacrament at their own. I offered my assistance to lessen his *trouble;* but he declined it. "There were a hundred of new communicants," he told us, "last Sunday; and I am credibly informed, some of them came out of spite of me." We bless God for this cause of offense, and pray it may never be removed.

Sun., October 14th. I took horse for Bradford, the Minister having offered me his pulpit. But yesterday his heart failed; he feared his church would be pulled down; he feared the Bishop would be displeased. I went to the church, and thence to the Common, where I preached forgiveness of sins to many serious hearers. In the evening I returned to Bristol.

Fri., October 19th. . . . I read part of Mr. Law on Regeneration to our Society. How promising the beginning! how lame the conclusion! *Sensi hominem!* [Latin: I perceived the man!] Christianity, he rightly tells us, is a recovery of the divine image; and a Christian is a fallen spirit restored, and reinstated in paradise; a living mirror of Father, Son, and Holy Ghost. After this, he supposes it possible for him to be insensible of such a change; to be happy and holy, translated into Eden, renewed in the likeness of God, one with the Father, Son and Holy Ghost, and yet not know it. Nay, we are not to expect, or bid others expect, any such consciousness, if we listen to one who too plainly demonstrates, by this wretched inconsistency, that his knowledge of the new birth is mostly in theory. . . .

Sat., October 27th. I preached at the green, on the strong man armed [Matt. 12:29] and disturbed him [Satan] in his place.

I pressed the use of means [of grace], as means, from Isa. 59, which is full of promises to those that walk in the ordinances with a sincere heart. I took occasion to show the degeneracy of our modern Pharisees. Their predecessors fasted twice a week; but these maintain their character for holiness at a cheaper rate. In reverence to the Church, some keep their public day on Friday. None of them regard it, though enjoined, as a fast. As to prayer and sacrament, their neglect is equally notorious. And yet these men cry out, "The Church, the Church!" when they will not hear the Church themselves; but despise her authority, trample upon her orders, teach contrary to her Articles and Homilies, and break her Canons, every man of them, who *of late* pretend to press their observance.

Wed., June 4th [1740]. I preached at Mary[le]bone, on "What must I do to be saved?" The opposers had threatened me hard; but all they now could do was to curse and swear. I only *invited* them to Christ. But I am more and more persuaded, that the law has its use, and Moses must bring us to Christ. The promises to the unawakened are pearls before swine. First the hammer must break the rocks; then we *may* preach Christ the crucified.

Mon., June 30th. I spent a week at Oxford to little purpose but that of obedience to man for the Lord's sake. In the Hall I read my two lectures on Psalm 130, preaching repentance towards God and faith in Jesus Christ. But learned Gallio cared for none of those things. . . .

Sat., July 12th. I passed the afternoon with [the colliers]. They grow in grace, and in the knowledge of our Lord Jesus Christ. We cannot be among them, and not perceive the divine presence.

Sun., July 13th. I gave the sacrament to above seventy of them, different from those who received the last time. I preached at Rose green on the fall of man (Gen. 3). I dare not depart from the work, while God so strengthens me therein. We walked over the waste to the school [Kingswood], singing and rejoicing. It was their love-feast. Two hundred were assembled in the Spirit of Jesus. Never have I seen and *felt* such a congregation of faithful souls. I question whether Hernhuth [*sic*] can now afford the like.[19]

Tues., July 15th. To the colliers I described, what many of them have experienced, religion, a participation in the divine nature. At Bristol I pressed the example of the primitive Christians (Acts 2) and tasted something of their spirit.

No. 40   Hymn: "Primitive Christianity"

This long poem was first published at the end of John Wesley's *An Earnest Appeal to Men of Reason and Religion,* in 1743. Like John's tract, Charles's poem had an apologetic thrust; examining the piety of the early church, Wesley asks, *"Where shall I wander now to find / The successors they left behind?"* While attacking sectarianism, and affirming his loyalty to the established church, Charles leaves no doubt that (in his mind at least) the Methodists represented what was best in the apostolic church. The hymn is a sort of poetic parallel to John Wesley's "The Character of a Methodist."[20] In each case, the writer described the movement as an attempt to recapture the essential doctrines and piety of the Christian faith. The hymn, despite its length, was carried in the standard 1780 hymnal; it is a quintessential statement of how the Wesleys understood Methodism. The second chapter of 1 Peter (KJV) figures prominently in the structure and phraseology of the hymn.[21]

Part I

1   Happy the souls that first believed,
    To Jesus and each other cleaved;
    Join'd by the unction from above,
    In mystic fellowship of love.

2   Meek, simple followers of the Lamb,
    They lived, and spake, and thought the same!
    Brake the commemorative bread,
    And drank the Spirit of their Head.

3   On God they cast their every care,
    Wrestling with God in mighty prayer
    They claim'd the grace through Jesus given,
    By prayer they shut, and open'd heaven.

4   To Jesus they perform'd their vow,
    A little church in every house;
    They joyfully conspired to raise
    Their ceaseless sacrifice of praise.

5   Propriety was there unknown,
    None call'd what he possess'd his own;
    Where all the common blessing share
    No selfish happiness was there.

6   With grace abundantly endued,
    A pure, believing multitude,
    They all were of one heart and soul,
    And only love inspired the whole.

7   O what an age of golden days!
    O what a choice, peculiar [elect] race!
    Wash'd in the Lamb's all-cleansing blood,
    Anointed kings and priests to God!

8   Where shall I wander now to find
    The successors they left behind?
    The faithful, whom I seek in vain,
    Are minish'd from the sons of men.

9   Ye different sects, who all declare,
    "Lo, here is Christ!" or, "Christ is there!"
    Your stronger proof Divinely give,
    And show me where the Christians live.

10 Your claim, alas! ye cannot prove;
    Ye want [lack] the genuine mark of love:
    Thou only, Lord, Thine own canst show,
    For sure Thou hast a church below.

11 The gates of hell cannot prevail;
    The church on earth can never fail:
    Ah! join me to Thy secret ones!
    Ah! gather all Thy living stones!

12 Scatter'd o'er all the earth they lie,
    Till Thou collect them with Thine eye;
    Draw by the music of Thy name,
    And charm into a beauteous frame.

13 For this the pleading Spirit groans,
    And cries in all Thy banish'd ones;
    Greatest of gifts, Thy love impart,
    And make us of one mind and heart.

14 Join every soul that looks to Thee,
    In bonds of perfect charity;
    Now, Lord, the glorious fullness give,
    And *all in all* for ever live!

Part II

1 Jesus, from whom all blessings flow,
   Great builder of Thy church below;
   If now, Thy Spirit moves my breast,
   Hear, and fulfill Thine own request!

2 The few that truly call Thee Lord,
   And wait Thy sanctifying word,
   And Thee their utmost Saviour own;
   Unite and perfect them in one.

3 Gather them in on every side,
   And in Thy tabernacle hide;
   Give them a resting-place to find,
   A covert from the storm, and wind.

4 O find them out some calm recess,
   Some unfrequent wilderness!
   Thou, Lord, the secret place prepare,
   And hide, and feed *the Woman* there.

5 Thither collect Thy little flock,
   Under the shadow of their Rock!
   The holy seed, the royal race,
   The standing monuments of Thy grace.

6 O let them all Thy mind express,
   Stand forth Thy chosen witnesses;
   Thy power unto salvation show,
   And perfect holiness below.

7 The fullness of Thy grace receive,
   And simply to Thy glory live;
   Strongly reflect the light Divine,
   And in a land of darkness shine.

8 In them let all mankind behold
   How Christians lived in days of old;
   Mighty their envious foes to move,
   A proverb of reproach—and love.

9 O make them of one soul and heart,
   The all-conforming mind impart;
   Spirit of peace and unity,
   The sinless mind that was in Thee.

10 Call them into Thy wondrous light,
   Worthy to walk with Thee in white!

Make up Thy jewels, Lord, and show
The glorious, spotless church below!

11   From every sinful wrinkle free,
     Redeem'd from all iniquity,
     The fellowship of saints make known,
     And, O my God, might I be one!

12   O might my lot be cast with these;
     The least of Jesu's witnesses:
     O that my Lord would count me meet [suitable]
     To wash His dear disciples' feet!

13   This only thing do I require:
     Thou know'st 'tis all my heart's desire,
     Freely what I receive to give,
     The servant of Thy church to live:

14   After my lowly Lord to go,
     And wait upon Thy saints below;
     Enjoy the grace to angels given,
     And serve the royal heirs of heaven.

15   Lord, if I now Thy drawings feel,
     And ask according to Thy will,
     Confirm the prayer, the seal impart,
     And speak the answer to my heart.

16   Tell me, or Thou shalt never go,
     "Thy prayer is heard, it shall be so;"
     The word hath pass'd Thy lips, and I
     Shall with Thy people live and die.

No. 41   Journal Selections: July 16–August 6, 1740

Wed., July 16th. I was convincing the natural man of sin, when a poor sinner cried out vehemently, "What do you mean by looking at *me*, and directing yourself to *me*, and telling *me* I shall be damned?" I did then address myself to him; but he hurried away with the utmost precipitation.

At the time of intercession [in prayer], the Spirit greatly helped our infirmities. We began with particulars, but at last were enlarged in prayer for all mankind.

I dissuaded one who was strongly tempted to leave the fellowship. The devil knows what he does: *Divide et impera* [Latin: Divide and rule] will carry the world before him.

While I was meeting the bands, my mouth was opened to rebuke, reprove, exhort, in words not my own. All trembled before the presence of

God. I was forced to cut off a rotten member; but I felt such love and pity at the time, as humbled me into the dust. It was as if one criminal was made to execute another. We betook ourselves to fervent prayer for him, and the Society. The Spirit was poured out; and we returned to the Lord in weeping, and mourning, and praying.

Thur., July 17th. I admitted near thirty new members into the Society.

Sun., July 20th. Our poor colliers being repelled from the Lord's table, by most of the Bristol Ministers, I exhorted them, notwithstanding, to continue daily with one accord in the temple; where the wickedest administrator [of the sacrament] can neither spoil the prayers, nor poison the sacrament. *These* poor sinners *have* ears to hear.

Sun., July 27th. I heard a miserable sermon at Temple church, recommending religion as the most likely way to raise a fortune. After it, proclamation was made, "that all should depart who were not of the parish." While the shepherd was driving away the lambs, I stayed, suspecting nothing, till the Clerk [of session] came to me, and said "Mr. Beacher bids you to go away, for he will not give you the sacrament." I went to the vestry-door, and mildly asked Mr. Beacher to admit me. He asked, "Áre you of this parish?" I answered, "Sir, you *see* I am a Clergyman." Dropping his first pretense, he charged me with rebellion in expounding the Scriptures without authority; and said in express word, "I repel you from the sacrament." I replied, "I cite you to answer this before Jesus Christ at the day of judgment." This enraged him above measure. He called out, *"Here, take away this man!"* The constables were ordered to attend, I suppose lest the furious colliers should take the sacrament by force: but I saved them the trouble of taking away this man, and quietly retired.

I preached the Gospel in Kingswood with double power, from Isa. 40: "Comfort ye, comfort ye, my people, saith your God." . . . At Rose-green, though my bodily strength was gone, I was carried out beyond myself in speaking of God's free grace to sinners.

Tues., August 5th. I talked sharply to Jenny Dechamps, a girl of twelve years old; who now confessed that her fits and cryings out (above thirty of them) were all feigned, that Mr. Wesley might take notice of her.

Wed., August 6th. In great heaviness I spoke to the women-bands, as taking my farewell: sang the hymn which begins:

> While sickness shakes the house of clay,
> And, sapp'd by pain's continued course,
> My nature hastens to decay,
> And waits the fever's friendly force. [No. 42]

After speaking a few faint words to the brethren, I was immediately taken with a shivering; and then the fever came.

The next morning I was bled, and carried by M[rs.] Hooper to her house. There I looked into the Bible, and met with, "The Lord will strengthen him upon the bed of languishing, thou wilt make all his bed in his sickness."

My pain and disease increased for ten days; so that there was no hope for my life: but then Jesus touched my hand, and rebuked the fever, and it left me. I had no apprehension of death myself. It was reported I was dead, and published in the papers: but God had not finished (O that he had effectually begun!) his work in me: therefore he held my soul in life; and made all things work together for my recovery.

Dr. Middleton, an utter stranger to me, God raised up, and sent to my assistance. He refused taking any fees, and told the apothecary he would pay for my physic, if I could not. He attended me constantly, as the divine blessing did his prescriptions; so that in less than a fortnight the danger was over.

For the next fortnight I recovered slowly, but had little use of my legs, and none of my head. . . . When I was just able to stand, my brother came from London. We rode out most days in Mr. Wane's or an hired chariot, comparing our dangers, temptations, and deliverances.

I found myself, after this visitation, more desirous and able to pray; more afraid of sin, more earnestly longing for deliverance, and the fullness of Christian salvation [i.e. death and perfection].

No. 42   Hymn: "Written in Sickness"

The hymn, linked to the illness Charles reported above, was published in the 1740 edition of *Hymns and Sacred Poems*. It is characteristic of Charles's occasional ambivalence about this life, since the present form of existence meant sin and separation from God, whereas crossing the threshold into afterlife purified and brought perfection and complete unity with God in Christ. This hymn saw rather limited publication, due undoubtedly in part to Charles's doctrine of perfection in the instant of death and John's antipathy for it.[22]

1   While sickness shakes the house of clay,
       And, sapp'd by pain's continued course,
    My nature hastens to decay,
       And waits the fever's friendly force.

2   Whither should my glad soul aspire,
       But heavenward to my Saviour's breast?
    Wafted on wings of warm desire,
       To gain her everlasting rest.

3   O, when shall I no longer call
       This earthly tabernacle mine?
    When shall the shatter'd mansion fall,
       And rise rebuilt by hands Divine?

4   Burden'd beneath this fleshly load,
      Earnestly here for ease I groan,
    Athirst for Thee the living God,
      And ever struggling to be gone.

5   Where Thou, and only Thou art loved,
      Far from the world's insidious art,
    Beyond the range of fiends removed,
      And safe from my deceitful heart;

6   There let me rest, and sin no more:
      Come quickly, Lord, and end the strife,
    Hasten my last, my mortal hour,
      Swallow me up in endless life.

7   Ah! let it not my Lord displease,
      That eager thus for death I sue,
    Toward the high prize impatient press,
      And snatch the crown to conquest due.

8   Master, Thy greatness wants not me:
      O, how should I Thy cause defend!
    Captain, release, and set me free;
      Here let my useless warfare end.

9   'Tis not the pain I seek to shun,
      The destined cross, and purging fire;
    Sin do I fear, and sin alone,
      Thee, only Thee do I desire.

10 For Thee, within myself, for Thee
      I groan, and for th' adoption wait,
    When death shall set my spirit free,
      And make my liberty complete.

11 No longer, then, my Lord, defer,
      From earth and sin to take me home;
    Now let my eyes behold Thee near;
      Come quickly, O my Saviour, come.

No. 43 Journal Selections: September 7–28, 1740

Sun., September 7th. As soon as my bodily weakness would permit, I returned to my old hours of retirement; but with fear, and earnest prayer that I might not rest in my own works or endeavours.

Mr. Cary's Curate informed us, that Mr. Cary had ordered him to repel my brother and me from the sacrament.

Mon., September 15th. I passed two or three days at Mr. Author's, in Kingswood, and, by the blessing of God, recovered the use of my understanding, which was so clouded that I could neither read nor think.

Fri., September 26th. I was greatly assisted in the evening to preach the Christian Perfection, that is, utter dominion over sin; constant peace, and love, and joy in the Holy Ghost; the full assurance of faith, righteousness, and true holiness. I see more and more into the height of our privileges, and that God will give them to me.

Sun., September 28th. At the sacrament I received power to believe sin shall not have dominion over me. I reached many hearts in expounding blind Bartimaeus. [No. 44]

Our love-feast was such as deserved the name. We all rejoiced in hope of the glory of God.

No. 44   Hymn: "Waiting for Redemption No. 3"

This hymn, one of four by this same title in *Hymns and Sacred Poems* (1749 edition), is a fine example of Charles's treatment of gospel pericopes. In this case several biblical characters are assembled as examples of those who, upon seeking healing by Jesus, were reconciled to God; for Charles their situation was a metaphor for sin, and healing mirrored redemption. Blind Bartimaeus emerges in verse five, and the treatment there suggests how Charles preached freedom from sin from that biblical passage. Worthy of note is the way in which Wesley applies the term "redemption" here; it is clearly a synonym for sanctification, as the singer longs to be "purged from all sin" and "perfectly made whole."[23]

1   Jesu, Thy word for ever lives,
    A new accomplishment receives
       In sinners lost like me;
    Thy word doth all my soul express,
    In every picture of distress
       I read my misery.

2   Written for me the gospel page,
    The word of God from age to age
       Steadfast remains, and sure:
    Thou show'st my wants; but help them too,
    Thy miracles of healing show,
       And let me read my cure.

3   Thy servant, Lord, in torment is,
    The palsy, sin, is my disease,

My better half is dead:
O cause me Thy free grace to feel,
And by Thy love my numbness heal,
    Thy quickening Spirit shed.

4   I am not worthy, Lord, that Thou
    To such an abject worm shouldst bow,
        Or enter my poor soul:
    But only speak the gracious word,
    And I shall be at once restored,
        And perfectly made whole.

5   A begging *Bartim[a]eus* I,
    Naked, and blind, for mercy cry,
        If mercy is for me,
    Jesus, Thou Son of David hear,
    Stand still, and call, and draw me near,
        And bid the sinner see.

6   A leper at Thy feet I fall;
    And still for mercy, mercy call,
        Till I am purged from sin;
    With pity see my desperate case,
    And O! put forth Thy hand of grace,
        And touch my nature clean.

7   Borne by the prayer of faith I lie,
    And long to meet Thy pitying eye,
        And feebly gasp to heaven;
    O make in me Thy power appear,
    And answer, "Son, be of good cheer,
        Thy sins are all forgiven."

8   O Son of Man, Thy power make known,
    Thy all with me may gladly own
        Thou canst on earth forgive,
    Bid me take up my bed, and go,
    Cause me to walk with Thee below,
        And then to heaven receive.

No. 45   Journal Selection: September 29, 1740

Mon., September 29th. God was wonderfully with our assembly, and opened my eyes to see the promise of holiness, or perfection, not in some, but in almost every scripture. [No. 46]

No. 46   Hymn: "Pleading the Promise of Sanctification"

This hymn, first published in *Hymns and Sacred Poems* (1742) and reprinted in *A Collection of Hymns for the Use of the People Called Methodists* (1780), was based on the text of Ezek. 36:23. It is a good example of the way in which Charles found the "promise of holiness . . . in almost every scripture." The hymn takes on the language of prayer, while the singer "pleads the promise" for inner purity as the early Methodists did in their societies. The allusion to "Canaan" (verse 14), as above, typified the entrance into the "rest" of reconciliation, and the inheritance of full salvation. Eleven of Charles's original twenty-eight verses were formed into two separate hymns in the standard collection of 1780.[24]

1   God of all power, and truth, and grace,
    Which shall from age to age endure,
  Whose word, when heaven and earth shall pass,
    Remains, and stands forever sure:

2   Calmly to Thee my soul looks up,
    And waits Thy promises to prove,
  The object of my steadfast hope,
    The seal of Thine eternal love.

3   That I Thy mercy may proclaim,
    That all mankind Thy truth may see,
  Hallow Thy great and glorious name,
    And perfect holiness in me.

4   Chose from the world if now I stand
    Adorn'd in righteousness Divine,
  If brought into the promised land
    I justly call the Saviour mine,—

5   Perform the work Thou hast begun,
    My inmost soul to Thee convert,
  Love me, for ever love Thine own,
    And sprinkle with Thy blood my heart.

6   Thy sanctifying Spirit pour,
    To quench my thirst and wash me clean;
  Now, Father, let the gracious shower
    Descend, and make me pure from sin.

7   Purge me from every sinful blot,
    My idols all be cast aside;
  Cleanse me from every evil thought,
    From all the filth of self and pride.

8   Give me a new perfect heart,
    From doubt, and fear, and sorrow free;

The mind which was in Christ impart,
  And let my spirit cleave to Thee.

9 O take this heart of stone away,
    (Thy sway it doth not, cannot own),
  In me no longer let it stay;
    O take away this heart of stone.

10 The hatred of the carnal mind
    Out of my flesh at once remove;
  Give me a tender heart, resign'd,
    And pure, and full of faith and love.

11 Within me Thy good Spirit place,
    Spirit of health, and love, and power;
  Plant in me Thy victorious grace,
    And sin shall never enter more.

12 Cause me to walk in Christ my Way;
    And I Thy statutes shall fulfill,
  In every point Thy law obey,
    And perfectly perform Thy will.

13 Hast Thou not said, who canst not lie,
    That I Thy law shall keep and do?
  Lord, I believe, though men deny;
    They all are false, but Thou are true.

14 O that I now, from sin released,
    Thy word might to the utmost prove!
  Enter into the promised rest,
    The *Canaan* of Thy perfect love.

15 There let me ever, ever dwell;
    Be Thou my God, and I will be
  Thy servant: O set to Thy seal;
    Give me eternal life in Thee.

16 From all remaining filth within
    Let me in Thee salvation have;
  From actual and from inbred sin
    My ransom'd soul persist to save.

17 Wash out my deep original stain—
    Tell me no more it cannot be,
  Demons or men! The Lamb was slain,
    His blood was all pour'd out for me.

18 Sprinkle it, Jesu, on my heart!
    One drop of Thine all-cleansing blood

Shall make my sinfulness depart,
   And fill me with the life of God.

19 Father, supply my every need;
     Sustain the life Thyself hast given:
  Call for the never-failing Bread,
     The manna that comes down from heaven.

20 The gracious fruits of righteousness,
     Thy blessings' unexhausted store,
  In me abundantly increase,
     Nor let me ever hunger more.

21 Let me no more, in deep complaint,
     My leanness, O my leanness! cry;
  Alone consumed with pining want,
     Of all my Father's children, I!

22 The painful thirst, the fond desire,
     The joyous presence shall remove,
  While my full soul doth still require
     Thy whole eternity of love.

23 Holy, and true, and righteous Lord,
     I wait to prove Thy perfect will;
  Be mindful of Thy gracious word,
     And stamp me with Thy Spirit's seal.

24 Thy faithful mercies let me find,
     In which Thou causest me to trust;
  Give me the meek and lowly mind,
     And lay my spirit in the dust.

25 Show me how foul my heart hath been,
     When all renew'd by grace I am;
  When Thou hast emptied me of sin,
     Show me the fullness of my shame.

26 Open my faith's interior eye;
     Display Thy glory from above,
  And all I am shall sink and die,
     Lost in astonishment and love.

27 Confound, o'erpower me with Thy grace;
     I would be by myself abhorr'd.
  (All might, all majesty, all praise,
     All glory be to Christ my Lord!)

28 Now let me gain perfection's height;
     Now let me into nothing fall,

Be less than nothing in Thy sight,
And feel that Christ is all in all.

No. 47   Journal Selections: April 25–July 16, 1741

Sat., April 25th [1741]. The word at night was refreshing to our souls. Our thanksgiving-notes multiply more and more. One wrote thus:— "There was not a word came out of your mouth last night, but I could apply it to my own soul, and witness it the doctrine of Christ. I know that Christ is a whole Saviour. I know the blood of Christ has washed away all my sins. I am sure the Lord will make me perfect in love before I go hence, and am no more seen.

"O for a thousand tongues to sing
My dear Redeemer's praise!" &c. [No. 12]

Sun., May 3d. At Kingswood, as soon as I named my text, "It is finished!" the love of Christ crucified so constrained me, that I burst into tears, and felt strong sympathy with Him in His sufferings. In like manner the whole congregation looked upon Him who they pierced, and mourned. . . .

Sat., July 11th. I preached at Bristol, then among the colliers, a third time at Bath, a fourth at Sawford, and yet again in the Wood. Let God have the glory. Preaching five times a day, when he calls me to it, no more wearies the flesh than preaching once.

Satan took it ill to be attacked in his head-quarters, that Sodom of our land, Bath. While I was explaining the trembling jailer's question ["Sirs, what must I do to be saved?" Acts. 16:30], he [Satan] raged horribly in his children. They went out, and came back again, as if each man's name were Legion [Mark 5:9]. My power increased with the opposition. The sincere were melted into tears and strong desires of salvation.

Sun., July 12th. I preached from Titus 2:11 &c. The power and seal of God is never wanting while I declare the *two great truths* of the everlasting Gospel, universal redemption and Christian Perfection.

At Kingswood I received Jane Sheep into the fold by baptism, which she felt in that moment to be for the remission of sins.

Thur., July 16th. I discoursed on Lazarus raised. I dined at Lanissan [Wales], and preached to the Society and a few others, chiefly predesti-narians. Without touching the dispute, I simply declared the scriptural marks of election; whereby some, I believe, were cut off from their vain confidence [i.e. in election]. The sincere ones clave to me. Who can resist the power of love? A loving messenger of a loving God might drive re-probation out of Wales, without once naming it.

In the evening, at Cardiff, Mr. Wells and Hodges shamed me by pa-tiently sitting by to hear *me* preach. My subject was "Wrestling Jacob."

[No. 48] Some whole sinners were offended at the sick and wounded, who cried out for a physician [Matt. 9:12], but such offenses must needs come.

No. 48   Hymn: "Wrestling Jacob"

Although Charles's sermon on this text is not extant, one of his most famous hymns (also formed on the Jacob narrative) survives to suggest how the younger Wesley might have expounded that Gen. 32 account. In Charles Wesley's hands the account of Jacob wrestling with the angel became a description of the Christian's struggle for Perfect Love. John Wesley announced his brother's death and concluded his obituary in the minutes of the 1788 Methodist Conference by pointing to this very hymn: ". . . Dr. Watts did not scruple to say, that 'that single poem, *Wrestling Jacob*, was worth all the verses he himself had written.'" This hymn was first published in *Hymns and Sacred Poems* (1742) and later appeared in the standard 1780 hymnal.[25]

1   Come, O Thou Traveller unknown,
        Whom still I hold, but cannot see,
    My company before is gone,
        And I am left with Thee;
    With Thee all night I mean to stay,
    And wrestle till the break of day.

2   I need not tell Thee who I am,
        My misery or sin declare,
    Thyself hast call'd me by my name,
        Look on Thy hands, and read it there;
    But who, I ask Thee, who art Thou?
    Tell me Thy name, and tell me now.

3   In vain Thou strugglest to get free,
        I never will unloose my hold;
    Art thou the Man that died for me?
        The secret of Thy love unfold;
    Wrestling I will not let Thee go
        Till I Thy name, Thy nature know.

4   Wilt Thou not yet to me reveal
        Thy new, unutterable name?
    Tell me, I still beseech Thee, tell;
        To know it now resolved I am;
    Wrestling I will not let Thee go
    Till I Thy name, Thy nature know.

5   'Tis all in vain to hold Thy tongue,
        Or touch the hollow of my thigh;

Though every sinew be unstrung,
　　Out of my arms Thou shalt not fly;
Wrestling I will not let Thee go
Till I Thy name, Thy nature know.

6　What though my shrinking flesh complain,
　　And murmur to contend so long,
I rise superior to my pain,
　　When I am weak then I am strong;
And when my all of strength shall fail,
I shall with the God-man prevail.

7　My strength is gone, my nature dies,
　　I sink beneath Thy weighty hand,
Faint to revive, and fall to rise;
　　I fall, and yet by faith I stand,
I stand, and will not let Thee go,
Till I Thy name, Thy nature know.

8　Yield to me now; for I am weak,
　　But confident in self-despair:
Speak to my heart, in blessings speak,
　　Be conquer'd by my instant prayer;
Speak, or Thou never hence shalt move,
And tell me if Thy name is Love.

9　'Tis Love! 'tis Love! Thou diedst for me;
　　I hear Thy whisper in my heart:
The morning breaks, the shadows flee:
　　Pure UNIVERSAL LOVE Thou art;
To me, to all Thy bowels move;[a]
Thy nature, and Thy name is Love.

10　My prayer hath power with God; the grace
　　Unspeakable I now receive,
Through faith I see Thee face to face;
　　I see Thee face to face, and live:
In ʾain I have not wept and strove;
Thy nature and Thy name is Love.

11　I know Thee, Saviour, who Thou art,
　　Jesus, the feeble sinner's Friend;
Nor wilt Thou with the night depart,
　　But stay, and love me to the end;
Thy mercies never shall remove;
Thy nature, and Thy name is Love.

---

[a]"bowels" of love, as in Song of Solomon 5:4 (KJV).

12   The Sun of Righteousness on me
        Hath rose with healing in His wings;
     Wither'd my nature's strength, from Thee
        My soul its life and succour brings;
     My help is all laid up above;
     Thy nature, and Thy name is Love.

13   Contended now upon my thigh
        I halt, till life's short journey end;
     All helplessness, all weakness, I
        On Thee alone for strength depend,
     Nor have I power from Thee to move;
     Thy nature, and Thy name is Love.

14   Lame as I am, I take the prey,
        Hell, earth, and sin with ease o'ercome;
     I leap for joy, pursue my way,
        And as a bounding hart fly home,
     Through all eternity to prove,
     Thy nature, and Thy name is Love.

No. 49   Journal Selections: July 17–August 25, 1741

Fri., July 17th. . . . Mr. Carne [a local clergyman] stood up all the prayers and sermon-time. . . . I never read prayers with more inward feeling. Like strength was given me to explain the "good Samaritan" for two hours. . . . I could not help smiling at Mr. Carne, who had come, as he said, on the purpose to judge me; and his judgment was, "Sir, you have got very good lungs: but you will make the people melancholy. I saw them crying throughout the church." Then he turned on Mr. Jones [another minister], and told him he would make himself ridiculous all over the country by encouraging such a fellow [as Wesley]. I was afraid of despising him, and therefore passed on, and left them together. Mr. Jones almost overcame his evil with good, but could not prevail upon him [Carne] to come under the same roof with me. . . .

Tues., August 25th. . . . For three hours we sang, and rejoiced, and gave thanks; then rode to Porthkerry, where I read prayers, and discoursed near two hours on the pool of Bethesda. [No. 50] The whole congregation were in tears.

I returned to the castle, and met some hundreds of the poor neighbors in our chapel, the dining-room. I exhorted them to build up one another, from Mal. 2:16–18: "Then they that feared the Lord spake often one to another," &c. At ten we parted. We kept on rejoicing till one in the morning.

No. 50   Hymn: "The Pool of Bethesda" (based on John 5:2ff)

Once again one of Charles's most frequently preached sermons survives as an echo
in his hymn from the same period. His allegorical treatment of the Johannine
narrative takes the imagery of sickness and healing as the central themes; these
become metaphors of sin and full salvation in Wesley's application. This approach
is certainly consonant with the agenda of the Methodist evangelist. The "thirty
years" mentioned in verse six is not necessarily an autobiographical statement,
since that figure emerges in the biblical passage (John 5:5). The hymn was first
published in *Hymns and Sacred Poems* (1742) and reappeared in a shortened form
in 1780.[26]

1   Jesu, take my sins away,
            And make me know Thy name;
       Thou art now as yesterday,
            And evermore the same:
       Thou my true *Bethesda* be;
       I know within Thy arms is room,
            All the world may unto Thee,
                Their House of Mercy, come.

2   See the porches open wide!
            Thy mercy all may prove,
       All the world is justified
            By universal love.
       Halt and wither'd when they lie,
       And sick, and impotent, and blind,
            Sinners may in Thee espy
                The Saviour of mankind.

3   See me lying at the pool,
            And waiting for thy grace;
       O come down into my soul,
            Disclose Thy angel-face!
       If to me Thy bowels move,
       If now Thou dost my sickness feel,
            Let the Spirit of Thy love
                Thy helpless sinner heal.

4   Sick of anger, pride, and lust,
            And unbelief I am;
       Yet in Thee for health I trust,
            In Jesu's sovereign name.

Were I taken into Thee,
Could I but step into the pool,
   I from every malady
     Should be made whole.

5   Persons Thou dost not respect;
      Whoe'er for mercy call
Thou in no wise wilt reject,
     Thy mercy is for all;
Thou wouldst freely all restore,
(Would all the gracious season find,)
    Fill with goodness, love, and power,
     And with an healthful mind.

6   Mercy then there is for me
     (Away my doubts and fears!)
Plagued with an infirmity
    For more than thirty years;
Jesu, cast a pitying eye;
Thou long hast known my desperate case,
    Poor and helpless here I lie,
     And wait the healing grace.

7   Long hath Thy good Spirit strove
     With my distemper'd soul,
But I still refused Thy love
    And would not be made whole:
Hardly now at last I yield,
I yield with all my sins to part;
    Let my soul be fully heal'd,
     And thoroughly cleansed my heart.

8   Sin is now my sore disease;
     But though I would be free,
When the water troubled is
    There is no help for me:
Others find a cure, not I;
In Thee they wash away their sin;
    I, alas! have no man nigh,
     To put my weakness in.

9   Pain and sickness, at Thy word,
     And sin and sorrow flies;
Speak to me, Almighty Lord,
    And bid my spirit rise;
Bid me take my burden up,

The bed on which Thyself didst lie,
   When on *Calvary's* steep top
     My Jesus deign'd to die.

10   Bid me bear the hallow'd cross
      Which Thou has borne before,
    Walk in all Thy righteous laws,
      And go and sin no more,
   Lest the heaviest curse of all,
The vile apostate's curse, I prove;
   To the hottest hell they fall
     Who fall from pardoning love.

11   But Thou canst preserve from sin,
      And stablish me with grace,
    Keep my helpless soul within
      Thy arms through all my days:
   Jesu, on Thee alone
For preserving grace depend;
   Love me freely, love Thine own,
     And love me to the end.

No. 51   Journal Selections: August 26–27, 1741

Wed., August 26th. I prayed by a dying woman, who waits for redemption from *all* iniquity *here;* otherwise, she knows she will not see God. About noon I applied, at John Deer's Society, "But ye are washed, but ye are sanctified," &c. Never have I spoken more closely to those who rest in the first gift [justification]. Some, who seemed to be pillars, begin to find themselves shaken reeds. . . .

Thur., August 27th. Great power was among us, while I spake on the walls of Jericho falling down; [No. 52] but much greater at prison, where I recommended to two condemned malefactors the example of the penitent thief. [No. 23] Both burst into tears. The congregation sympathized, and joined in fervent prayer, that our Lord would remember them, now he is come into his kingdom.

I went to a revel at Lavane, and dissuaded them from their *innocent* diversions [No. 53] in St. Peter's words: "For the time past of our life may suffice us to have wrought the will of the Gentiles, when we walked in lasciviousness, lusts, excess of wine, revellings, banquetings, and abominable idolatries." An old dancer of threescore fell down under the stroke of the hammer. She could never be convinced before that there was any harm in those innocent pleasures. O that her fellows might likewise confess, "She that liveth in pleasures is dead while she liveth."

I prayed by a poor persecutor, who had found mercy at the last hour; then expounded Ezekiel's vision of dry bones. A poor drunkard spoke the whole time, but without interrupting me or the congregation; for the hand of the Lord was over us.

No. 52   Hymn: "The Taking of Jericho" (based on Josh. 6)

Wesley's rendition turned the biblical passage into a soteriological narrative. Jericho is that stronghold "within," "the strength of inbred sin." A new captain, or Joshua, leads the assault against the citadel of unregenerate human will. His victory signifies a characteristic Wesleyan theme: freedom from the guilt and power of sin. Interestingly enough, "Joshua" and "Jesus" stem from the same etymological roots, and this linguistic connection formed the basis of Charles Wesley's exposition of the passage.[27] The hymn was published only in Charles's *Hymns and Sacred Poems* (1749 edition).[28]

1   Arise, ye men of war,
          Prevent the morning ray,
       Prepare, your Captain cries, prepare,
          Your Captain leads the way:
          He calls you forth to fight,
          Where yonder ramparts rise,
       Ramparts of a stupendous height,
          Ramparts that touch the skies.

2   Who dares approach those towers?
          Who can those walls o'erturn?
       The city braves all human powers,
          And laughs a siege to scorn.
          Who shall the city take,
          The *Jericho* within?
       Not all the powers of earth can shake,
          The strength of inbred sin.

3   Impregnable it stands,
          Strong, and wall'd up to heaven;
       But God into our *Joshua's* hands
          The citadel hath given;
          The fortress and its kind,
          And all its valiant men,
       Our Captain to the ground shall bring,
          And on their ruins reign.

4   All power He hath to quell,
          And conquer and o'erthrow,

All power in heaven, and earth, and hell,
   To root out every foe;
   Through Him divinely bold
   Let all His soldiers fight,
Now of your Captain's strength take hold,
   And conquer in His might.

5   Ye people all pass on;
   Ye men of war surround
The city by your Captain won;
   Attend the trumpet's sound:
   The priests whom He hath chose
   Pass on before the Lord,
And each a ram's-horn trumpet blows,
   The trumpet of the word.

6   The holy ark they bear,
   The covenant of His grace,
And tidings of great joy declare
   To all the fallen race:
   They make His mercies known,
   His promises they show:
Go in the track your guides have shown,
   To certain conquest go.

7   In sight of God proceed,
   Follow the ark Divine,
In all the ways and statutes tread,
   Which He hath pleased t' enjoin:
   Pray always, fast and pray,
   And watch to do His will;
All His commands with joy obey,
   All righteousness fulfill.

8   With patience persevere,
   Still in His ways be found,
Still to the city walls draw near,
   And day by day surround;
   Continue in His word,
   On all His means attend,
Bearing the burden of the Lord,
   And hoping to the end.

9   Arise, your strength renew,
   Your glorious toil repeat,
Follow the ark, your Lord pursue,
   And for His promise wait;

In deepest silence go;
Your *Joshua* cries, Be still,
Assured His truth and power to know,
And prove His perfect will.

10   Tried to the uttermost
His faithful words shall be,
Who in the strength of Jesus trust
Shall gain the victory:
But wait for your reward,
And give your clamours o'er,
Tarry the leisure of your Lord,
Nor every murmur more.

11   The solemn day draws nigh,
When sin shall have its doom,
Faith sees it with an eagle's eye,
And cries, The day is come;
The seventh morn I see,
And hasten to be blest,
Enjoy an instant victory,
An antedated rest.

12   The walls are compass'd round,
The circuit is the last:
The ark stands still: the trumpets sound
A long continued blast:
The people turn their eyes
On the devoted walls;
And shout, the mighty *Joshua* cries,
And lo! the city falls!

13   Its proud aspiring brow
Lies level with the ground;
It lies, and not one stone is now
Upon another found.
The walls are flat, the deep
Foundations are o'erthrown;
The lofty fortress is an heap,
And sin is trodden down.

14   The strength of sin is lost,
And *Babylon* the great
Is fallen, fallen to the dust,
Has found its final fate.
Partakers of our hope,
We seize what God hath given,

And trampling down all sin go up,
   And straight ascend to heaven.

15   But shall not sin remain,
        And in its ruins live?
No, Lord; we trust, and not in vain,
     Thy fullness to receive:
     Thy strength and saving grace
     Thou shalt for us employ,
The being of all sin erase,
     And utterly destroy.

16   Actual and inbred sin
        Shall feel Thy two-edged sword:
The city is, with all therein,
     Devoted to the Lord:
     Thy word cannot be broke,
     Thou wilt Thine arm display,
Thou wilt with one continual stroke
     Our sin for ever slay.

17   Woman, and man, and beast,
        And ox, and ass, and sheep,
All, all at once shall be oppressed
     By death's eternal sleep;
     Never to rise again,
     Both young and old shall fall;
Not one shall 'scape, not one remain,
     But die, and perish all.

18   The human beast and fiend
        Thou, Lord, shall take away,
And make the old transgression end,
     And all its relics slay;
     The proud and carnal will,
     The selfish vain desire,
Thou all our sins at once shalt kill,
     And burn them all with fire.

No. 53 Hymn: "Innocent Diversions"

Methodist "Watchnight Services" began as a creative alternative to the "innocent diversions" of the alehouses.[29] The Watchnights were times of prayer, praise, and preaching, held on Saturday nights to encourage the Methodists to put their time to a better use than in their former days. Charles's *Hymns and Sacred Poems* (1749 edition) held nineteen "Hymns for the Watchnight." The hymn below, #17 in the collection, carries an apology for the Watchnight (verses 1, 5) and a polemic against the "Innocent Diversions" that fill the lives of "the slaves of excess." Charles's sentiments here are consonant with those voiced by his brother John in his famous sermon "On Redeeming the Time."[30]

1   Come let us anew
     Our pleasures pursue:
     For *Christian* delight
The day is too short; let us borrow the night.
     Sanctified joy
     Each moment employ,
     To Jesus's praise,
And spend, and be spent in the triumph of grace.

2   The slaves of excess,
     Their sense to please
     Whole nights can bestow,
And on in a circle of riot they go:
     Poor prodigal, they
     The night into day
     By revelings turn,
And all the restraints of sobriety scorn.

3   The drunkards proclaim
     At midnight their shame,
     Their sacrifice bring,
And loud to the praise of *their* master they sing.
     The hellish desires
     Which Satan inspires,
     In sonnets they breathe,
And shouting descend to the mansions of death.

4   The civiller crowd,
     In theatres proud,
     Acknowledge his power,
And Satan in nightly assemblies adore:
     To the masque and the ball
     They fly at his call;
     Or in pleasures excel,
And chant in a grove to the harpers of hell.

5   And shall we not sing
     Our Master and King

---

[a]Ranelagh's Gardens, VauxHall, &c.

While other men are at rest,
With Jesus admitted at midnight to feast?
   Here only we may
   With innocence stay,
   Th' enjoyment improve,
And abide at the banquet of Jesus's love.

6   In Him is bestow'd
    The spiritual food,
    The manna Divine,
And Jesus's love is far better than wine:
   With joy we receive
   The blessing, and give
   By day and by night
All thanks to the Source of our endless delight.

7   Our concert of praise
    To Jesus we raise,
    And all the night long
Continue the new evangelical song:
   We dance to the fame
   Of Jesus's name,
   The joy it imparts
Is heaven begun in our musical hearts.

8   Thus, thus we bestow
    Our moments below,
    And singing remove,
With all the redeem'd to the *Sion* above:
   There, there shall we stand
   With our harps in our hand,
   Interrupted no more,
And eternally sing, and rejoice, and adore.

No. 54 Journal Selection: August 28, 1741

Fri., August 28th. I preached again in Porthkerry Church. Many cried after Jesus, with the woman of Canaan. [No. 55] It was a time of great refreshing. I returned in the coach with Mr. and Mrs. Jones, and a little girl of eight years old, who has not outlived the simple life, or that breath of God, which is the first enmity to the seed of the subtle serpent. . . . I spent the evening in conference with those who desired to be of the Society, which was now begun in the name of Jesus Christ the Saviour of all men. I sang and prayed with them till ten; with the family till midnight.

No. 55   Hymn: "The Woman of Canaan"

The following hymn, based on the Matt. 15:22–28 account, demonstrates Charles's
treatment of that pericope. The singer of the hymn becomes the Canaanite woman,
her unworthiness becomes our own, as does the report of her acceptance by Christ
by grace through faith. Wesley's treatment of the Gospel narrative is formed around
what he considered to be its salient theme, salvation by free grace, and he constructed his own narrative in a way that emphasized and communicated that center.
This hymn, first appearing in *Hymns and Sacred Poems* (1742), was very popular
(as was Charles's sermon on the same passage). It was reissued in the standard
Collection of 1780, though in a shortened form.[31]

1   Lord, regard my earnest cry,
           A potsherd of the earth;
       A poor guilty worm am I,
           A *Canaanite* by birth;
       Save me from this tyranny,
   From all the power of Satan save;
       Mercy, mercy upon me,
           Thou Son of *David*, have.

2   Still Thou answerest not a word
           To my repeated prayer;
       Hear Thine own disciples, Lord,
           Who in my sorrows share;
       O Let them prevail with Thee
   To grant the blessing which I crave:
       Mercy, mercy upon me,
           Thou Son of *David*, have.

3   Send, O send me now away
           By granting my request;
       Still I follow Thee, and pray,
           And will not let Thee rest;
       Ever crying after Thee,
   Till Thou my helplessness relieve:
       Mercy, mercy upon me,
           Thou Son of *David*, have.

4   To the sheep of *Israel's* fold
           Thou in Thy flesh wast sent,
       But the Gentiles now behold
           In Thee their Covenant:
       See me then, with pity see,
       A sinner whom Thou camest to save;

Mercy, mercy upon me,
　Thou Son of *David*, have.

5　Still to Thee, my God, I come,
　　And mercy I implore;
　Thee (but how shall I presume),
　　Thee, trembling I adore,
　Dare not stand before Thy face,
But lowly at Thy feet I fall;
　Help me, Jesu; show Thy grace,
　　Thy grace is free for all.

6　Still I cannot part with Thee,
　　I will not let Thee go;
　Mercy, mercy unto me,
　　O Son of *David*, show;
　Vilest of the sinful race,
On Thee importunate I call;
　Help me, Jesu; show Thy grace,
　　Thy grace is free for all.

7　Nothing am I in Thy sight,
　　Nothing have I to plead;
　Unto dogs it is not right
　　To cast the children's bread;
　Yet the dogs the crumbs may eat,
That from their master's table fall;
　Let the fragments be my meat,
　　Thy grace is free for all.

8　Give me, Lord, the victory,
　　My heart's desire fulfill;
　Let it now be done to me
　　According to my will;
　Give me living bread to eat,
And say, in answer to my call,
　"*Canaanite*, thy faith is great,
　　My grace is free for all."

9　If Thy grace for all is free,
　　Thy call *now* let *me* hear,
　Show this token upon me,
　　And bring salvation near;
　Now the gracious word repeat,
The word of healing to my soul,
　"*Canaanite*, thy faith is great,
　　Thy faith hath made thee whole."

No. 56   Sermon: "Awake, Thou That Sleepest"

This sermon, Charles's most famous, was preached "Before the University of Oxford," Sunday, April 4, 1742.[32] It follows a homiletical style similar to that of the earlier Oxford sermon (No. 25). Charles's journal record of the occasion of this preaching is missing; though, in view of the reception he last received among "the gownsmen," it is very likely that "Awake, Thou That Sleepest" closed the university's churches to Charles in the same way that "Scriptural Christianity" brought an end to John Wesley's preaching there.[33] At any rate, it is clear that "Awake" is the last sermon Charles preached at the university proper, though he continued to work in the town and among the students.

Charles's contrast of "waking" and "sleeping," so central to the thrust of this sermon, was formed on the pattern of the Eph. 5:14 text. The identification also had roots in his own biography, since these same words had been used by Peter Böhler to describe Wesley's "natural state" and consequent conversion.[34] The sermon is a veritable patchwork of biblical phrases and allusions that treat the doctrines of sin and salvation with Charles's characteristic directness.

Awake, thou that sleepest, and arise from the dead and Christ shall give thee light. [Eph. 5:14]

In discoursing on these words, I shall, with the help of God,

First, Describe the sleepers, to whom they are spoken;

Secondly, Enforce the exhortation, "Awake, thou that sleepest, and arise from the dead"; and

Thirdly, Explain the promise made to such as do awake and arise: "Christ shall give thee light."

I. 1. And, First, as to the sleepers here spoken to. By sleep is signified the natural state of man; that deep sleep of the soul, into which the sin of Adam hath cast all who spring from his loins; that supineness, indolence, and stupidity, that insensibility of his real condition, wherein every man comes into the world, and continues till the voice of God awakes him.

2. Now, "they that sleep, sleep in the night." The state of nature is a state of utter darkness; a state wherein "darkness covers the earth, and gross darkness the people." The poor unawakened sinner, how much knowledge soever he may have as to other things, has no knowledge of himself: in this respect "he knoweth nothing yet as he ought to know." He knows not that he is a fallen spirit, whose only business in the present world is, to recover from his fall, to regain that image of God wherein he was created. He sees *no necessity* for the *one thing needful*, even that inward universal change, that "birth from above," figured out by baptism, which is the beginning of that total renovation, that sanctification of spirit, soul, and body, "without which no man shall see the Lord."

3. Full of all diseases as he is, he fancies himself in perfect health. Fast bound in misery and iron, he dreams that he is at liberty. He says, "Peace! Peace!" while the devil, as "a strong man armed," is in full possession of

his soul. He sleeps on still, and takes his rest, though hell is moved from beneath to meet him; though the pit, from whence there is no return, hath opened its mouth to swallow him up. A fire is kindled around him, yet he knoweth it not; yea, it burns him, yet he lays it not to heart.

4. By one who sleeps, we are, therefore, to understand (and would to God we might all understand it!) a sinner satisfied in his sins; contented to remain in his fallen state, to live and die without the image of God; one who is ignorant both of his disease, and of the only remedy for it; one who never was warned, or never regarded the warning voice of God, "to flee from the wrath to come"; one that never saw he was in danger of hellfire, or cried out in the earnestness of his soul, "What must I do to be saved?"

5. If this sleeper be not outwardly vicious, his sleep is usually the deepest of all: Whether he be of the Laodicean spirit, "neither cold nor hot," but a quiet, rational, inoffensive, good-natured professor [i.e. one who makes a profession of faith] of the religion of his fathers; or whether he be zealous and orthodox, and, "after the most straitest sect of our religion," live "a Pharisee"; that is, according to the scriptural account, one that justifies himself; one that labours to establish his own righteousness, as the ground of his acceptance with God.

6. This is he, who, "having a form of godliness, denies the power thereof"; yea, and probably reviles it, wheresoever it is found, as mere extravagance and delusion. Meanwhile, the wretched self-deceiver thanks God that he is "not as other men are; adulterers, unjust, extortioners." No, he doeth no wrong to any man. He "fasts twice a week," uses all the means of grace, is constant at church and sacrament; yea, and "gives tithes of all that he has"; does all the good that he can: "Touching the righteousness of the law," he is "blameless." He wants [lacks] nothing of godliness, but the power; nothing of religion, but the spirit; nothing of Christianity, but the truth and the life.

7. But know ye not, that, however highly esteemed among men such a Christian as this may be, he is an abomination in the sight of God, and an heir of every woe which the Son of God, yesterday, to-day, and for ever, denounces against "Scribes and Pharisees, hypocrites"? He hath "made clean the outside of the cup and the platter," but within is full of all filthiness. "An evil disease cleaveth still unto him, so that his inward parts are very wickedness." Our Lord fitly compares him to a "painted sepulchre," which "appears beautiful without"; but, nevertheless, is "full of dead men's bones, and of all sinews and flesh are come upon them, and the skin covers them above: But there is no breath in them, no Spirit of the living God." And, "if any man have not the Spirit of Christ, he is none of his." "Ye are Christ's, if so be that the Spirit of Christ dwell in you." But, if not, God knoweth that ye abide in death, even until now.

8. This is another character of the sleeper here spoken to. He abides in death, though he knows it not. He is dead unto God, "dead in trespasses and sins." For, "to be carnally minded is death." Even as it is written, "By

one man sin entered into the world, and death by sin; and so death passed upon all men," not only temporal death, but likewise spiritual and eternal. "In that day that thou eatest," said God to Adam, "thou shalt surely die": Not bodily (unless as he then became mortal), but spiritually: Thou shalt lose the life of thy soul; thou shalt die to God; shalt be separated from him, thy essential life and happiness.

9. Thus first was dissolved the vital union of our soul with God; insomuch that "in the midst of" natural "life, we are" now in spiritual "death." And herein we remain till the Second Adam becomes a quickening Spirit to us, till he raises the dead, the dead in sin, in pleasure, riches, or honours. But before any dead soul can live, he "hears" (hearkens to) "the voice of the Son of God": He is made sensible of his lost estate, and receives the sentence of death in himself. He knows himself to be "dead while he liveth"; dead to God, and all the things of God; having no more power to perform the actions of a living Christian, than a dead body to perform the functions of a living man.

10. And most certain it is, that one dead in sin has not "sense exercised to discern spiritual good and evil." "Having eyes, he sees not; he hath ears, and hears not." He doth not "taste and see that the Lord is gracious." He "hath not seen God at any time," nor "heard his voice," nor "handled the word of life." In vain is the name of Jesus "like ointment poured forth, and all his garments smell of myrrh, aloes, and cassia." The soul that sleepeth in death, hath no perception of any objects of this kind. His heart is "past feeling," and understandeth none of these things.

11. And hence, having no spiritual sense, no inlets of spiritual knowledge, the natural man receiveth not the things of the Spirit of God; nay, he is so far from receiving them, that whatsoever is spiritually discerned is mere foolishness unto him. He is not content with being utterly ignorant of spiritual things, but he denies the very existence of them. And spiritual sensation itself is to him the foolishness of folly. "How," saith he, "can these things be? How can a man *know* that he is alive to God?" Even as you know that your body is now alive. Faith is the life of the soul; and if ye have this life abiding in you, ye want no marks to evidence it *to yourself* but 'elegchos pneumatos* [Greek: spirit of conviction], that divine consciousness, that *witness of* God, which is more and greater than ten thousand human witnesses.

12. If he doth not now bear witness with thy spirit, that thou art a child of God, O that he might convince thee, thou poor unawakened sinner, by his demonstration and power, that thou are a child of the devil! O that, as I prophesy, there might now be "a noise and a shaking"; and may "the bones come together, bone to his bone!" Then, "come from the four winds, O Breath! and breathe on these slain, that they may live." And do not ye harden your hearts, and resist the Holy Ghost, who even now is come to convince you of sin, "because you believe not on the name of the only begotten Son of God."

II. 1. Wherefore, "awake, thou that sleepest, and arise from the dead." God calleth thee now by my mouth; and bids thee know thyself, thou fallen spirit, thy true state and only concern below. "What meanest thou, O sleeper? Arise! Call upon thy God, if so be thy God will think upon thee, that thou perish not." A mighty tempest is stirred up round about thee, and thou art sinking into the depths of perdition, the gulf of God's judgments. If thou wouldst escape them, cast thyself into them. "Judge thyself, and thou shalt not be judged of the Lord."

2. Awake, awake! Stand up this moment, lest thou "drink at the Lord's hand the cup of his fury." Stir up thyself to lay hold on the Lord, the Lord Thy Righteousness, mighty to save! "Shake thyself from the dust." At least, let the earthquake of God's threatenings shake thee. Awake, and cry out with the trembling jailer, "What must I do to be saved?" And never rest till thou believest on the Lord Jesus, with a faith which is his gift, by the operation of his Spirit.

3. If I speak to any one of you, more than to another, it is to thee who thinkest thyself unconcerned in this exhortation. "I have a message from God unto thee." In his name, I warn thee, "to flee from the wrath to come." Thou unholy soul, see thy picture in condemned Peter, lying in the dark dungeon, between the soldiers, bound with two chains, the keepers before the door keeping the prison. The night is far spent, the morning is at hand, when thou art to be brought forth to execution. And in these dreadful circumstances, thou art fast asleep; thou art fast asleep in the devil's arms, on the brink of the pit, in the jaws of everlasting destruction!

4. O may the Angel of the Lord come upon thee, and the light shine into thy prison! And mayest thou feel the stroke of an Almighty Hand, raising thee, with, "Arise up quickly, gird thyself, and bind on thy sandals, cast thy garments about thee, and follow me."

5. Awake, thou everlasting spirit, out of thy dream of worldly happiness! Did not God create thee for himself? Then thou canst not rest till thou restest in him. Return, thou wanderer! Fly back to thy ark. This is not thy home. Think not of building tabernacles here. Thou art but a stranger, a sojourner upon earth; a creature of a day, but just launching out into an unchangeable state. Make haste. Eternity is at hand. Eternity depends on this moment; an eternity of happiness or an eternity of misery!

6. In what state is thy soul? Was God, while I am yet speaking, to require it of thee, art thou ready to meet death, and judgment? Canst thou stand in his sight, who is of "purer eyes than to behold iniquity?" Art thou "meet to be partaker of the inheritance of the saints in light?" Hast thou "fought a good fight, and kept the faith?" Hast thou secured the one thing needful? Hast thou recovered the image of God, even righteousness and true holiness? Hast thou put off the old man, and put on the new? Art thou clothed upon with Christ?

7. Hast thou oil in thy lamp? grace in thy heart? Dost thou "love the Lord thy God with all thy heart, and with all thy mind, and with all thy soul,

and with all thy strength?" Is that mind in thee which was also in Christ Jesus? Art thou a Christian indeed; that is, a new creature? Are old things passed away, and all things become new?

8. Art thou a "partaker of the divine nature"? Knowest thou not, that "Christ is in thee, except thou be reprobate"? Knowest thou, that God "dwelleth in thee, and thou in God, by his Spirit, which he hath given thee"? Knowest thou not that "thy body is a temple of the Holy Ghost, which thou hast of God"? Hast thou "received the Holy Ghost"? Or, dost thou start at the question, not knowing "whether there be any Holy Ghost"?

9. If it offends thee, be thou assured, that thou neither art a Christian, nor desirest to be one. Nay, thy very prayer is turned into sin; and thou hast solemnly mocked God this very day, by praying for the inspiration of his Holy Spirit, when thou didst not believe there was any such thing to be received.

10. Yet, on the authority of God's word, and our own Church, I must repeat the question, "Hast thou received the Holy Ghost?" If thou hast not, thou art not yet a Christian. For a Christian is a man that is "anointed with the Holy Ghost and with power." Thou art not yet made a partaker of pure religion and undefiled. Dost thou know what religion is? that it is a participation of the divine nature; the life of God in the soul of man; Christ formed in the heart; "Christ in thee, the hope of glory?" happiness and holiness; heaven begun upon earth? "a kingdom of God within thee; not meat and drink," no outward thing; "but righteousness, and peace, and joy in the Holy Ghost?" an everlasting kingdom brought into thy soul; a "peace of God, that passeth all understanding"; a "joy unspeakable, and full of glory"?

11. Knowest thou, that, "in Jesus Christ, neither circumcision availeth anything, nor uncircumcision; but faith that worketh by love"; but a new creation? Seest thou the necessity of that inward change, that spiritual birth, that life from the dead, that holiness? And art thou thoroughly convinced, that without it no man shall see the Lord? Art thou labouring after it? "giving all diligence to make thy calling and election sure?" "working out thy salvation with fear and trembling?" "agonizing to enter in at the strait gate?" Art thou in earnest about thy soul? And canst thou tell the Searcher of hearts, "Thou, O God, art the thing that I long for! Lord, thou knowest all things! Thou knowest that I *would* love thee!"?

12. Thou hopest to be saved; but what reason hast thou to give of the hope that is in thee? Is it because thou hast done no harm? or, because thou hast done much good? or, because thou art not like other men; but wise, or learned, or honest, and morally good; esteemed of men, and of a fair reputation? Alas! all this will never bring thee to God. It is in his account lighter than vanity. Dost thou know Jesus Christ, whom he hath sent? Hath he taught thee, that "by grace we are saved through faith; and not of ourselves: It is the gift of God: Not of works, lest any man should boast?"

Hast thou received the faithful saying, as the whole foundation of thy hope, "that Jesus Christ came into the world to save sinners"? Hast thou learned what that meaneth, "I came not to call the righteous, but sinners to repentance. I am not sent, but unto the lost sheep"? Art thou (he that heareth, let him understand!) lost, dead, *damned already?* Dost thou feel thy wants? Art thou "poor in spirit"? mourning for God, and refusing to be comforted? Is the prodigal "come to himself," and well content to be therefore thought "beside himself," by those who are still feeding upon the husks which he hath left? Art thou willing to live godly in Christ Jesus? And dost thou therefore suffer persecution? Do men say all manner of evil against thee falsely, for the Son of Man's sake?

13. O that in all these questions ye may hear the voice that wakes the dead; and feel the hammer of the word, which breaketh the rocks in pieces! "If ye will hear his voice to-day, while it is called to-day, harden not your hearts." Now, "awake, thou that sleepest" in spiritual death, that thou sleep not in death eternal! Feel thy lost estate, and "arise from the dead." Leave thine old companions in sin and death. Follow thou Jesus, and let the dead bury their dead. "Save thyself from this untoward generation." "Come out from among them, and be thou separate, and touch not the unclean thing, and the Lord shall receive thee." "Christ shall give thee light."

III. 1. This promise, I come, lastly, to explain. And how encouraging a consideration is this, that whosoever thou art, who obeyest his call, thou canst not seek his face in vain! If thou even now "awakest, and ariseth from the dead," he hath bound himself to "give thee light." "The Lord shall give thee grace and glory"; the light of his grace here, and the light of his glory when thou receivest the crown that fadeth not away. "Thy light shall break forth as the morning, and thy darkness be as the noon-day." "God, who commandeth the light to shine out of darkness, shall shine in thy heart; to give the knowledge of the glory of God in the face of Jesus Christ." "On them that fear the Lord shall the Sun of Righteousness arise with healing in his wings." And in that day it shall be said unto thee, "Arise, shine; for thy light is come, and the glory of the Lord is risen upon thee." For Christ shall reveal himself in thee: And he is the true Light.

2. God is light, and will give himself to every awakened sinner that waiteth for him: And thou shalt then be a temple of the living God, and Christ shall "dwell in thy heart by faith": And, "being rooted and grounded in love, thou shalt be able to comprehend with all saints, what is the breadth, and length, and depth, and height of that love of Christ which passeth knowledge."

3. Ye see your calling, brethren. We are called to be "an habitation of God through his Spirit"; and through his Spirit dwelling in us, to be saints here, and partakers of the inheritance of the saints in light. So exceeding great are the promises which are given unto us, actually given unto us who

believe! For by faith "we receive, not the spirit of the world, but the Spirit which is of God"—the sum of all the promises—"that we may know the things that are freely given to us of God."

4. The Spirit of Christ is that great gift of God, which, at sundry times, and in divers manners, he hath promised to man, and hath fully bestowed since the time that Christ was glorified. Those promises, before made to the fathers, he hath thus fulfilled: "I will put my Spirit within you, and cause you to walk in my statutes." [Ezek. 36:27] "I will pour water upon him that is thirsty, and floods upon the dry ground: I will pour my Spirit upon thy seed, and my blessing upon thine offspring." [Isaiah xliv.3]

5. Ye may all be living witnesses of these things; of remission of sins, and the gift of the Holy Ghost. "If thou canst believe, all things are possible to him that believeth." "Who among you is there that feareth the Lord"; and yet walketh on "in darkness, and hath no light?" I ask thee, in the name of Jesus, believest thou that his arm is not shortened at all? that he is still mighty to save? that he is the same yesterday, to-day, and for ever? that he hath now power on earth to forgive sins? "Son, be of good cheer; thy sins are forgiven." God, for Christ's sake, hath forgiven thee. Receive this, "not as the word of man; but as it is indeed the word of God"; and thou art justified freely through faith. Thou shalt be sanctified also through faith which is in Jesus, and shalt set to thy seal, even thine, that "God hath given unto us eternal life, and this life is in his Son."

6. Men and brethren, let me freely speak unto you; and suffer ye the word of exhortation, even from one least esteemed in the Church. Your conscience beareth you witness in the Holy Ghost, that these things are so, if so be ye have tasted that the Lord is gracious. "This is eternal life, to know the only true God, and Jesus Christ whom he hath sent." This experimental knowledge, and this alone, is true Christianity. He is a Christian who hath received the Spirit of Christ. He is not a Christian who hath not received him. Neither is it possible to have received him, and not know it. "For, at that day" (when he cometh, saith our Lord), "ye shall know that I am in my Father, and you in me, and I in you." This is that "Spirit of Truth, whom the world cannot receive, because it seeth him not, neither knoweth him: But ye know him; for he dwelleth with you, and shall be in you" (John 14:17).

7. The world cannot receive him, but utterly reject[s] the Promise of the Father, contradicting and blaspheming. But every spirit which confesseth not this is not of God. Yea, "this is that spirit of Antichrist, whereof ye have heard that it should come into the world; and even now it is in the world." He is Antichrist whosoever denies the inspiration of the Holy Ghost, or that the indwelling Spirit of God is the common privilege of all believers, the blessing of the gospel, the unspeakable gift, the universal promise, the criterion of a real Christian.

8. It nothing helps them to say, "We do not deny the *assistance* of God's Spirit; but only this *inspiration*, this *receiving of the Holy Ghost*, and being

sensible of it. It is only this *feeling of the Spirit*, this being *moved* by the Spirit, or *filled* with it, which we deny to have any place in sound religion." But, in *only denying this*, you deny the whole Scriptures; the whole truth, and promise, and testimony of God.

9. Our own excellent Church knows nothing of this devilish distinction; but speaks plainly of "feeling the Spirit of Christ" [*Article* XVII]; and of being "moved by the Holy Ghost" [*Office of Consecrating Priests*], and knowing and "feeling there is no other name than that of Jesus" [*Visitation of the Sick*], whereby we can receive life and salvation. She teaches us all to pray for the "inspiration of the Holy Spirit" [*Collect Before Holy Communion*]; yea, that we may be "filled with the Holy Ghost" [*Order of Confirmation*]. Nay, every Presbyter of hers professes to receive the Holy Ghost by the imposition of hands. Therefore, to deny any of these is, in effect, to renounce the Church of England, as well as the whole Christian Revelation.

10. But "the wisdom of God" was always "foolishness with men." No marvel, then, that the great mystery of the gospel should be now also "hid from the wise and prudent," as well as in the days of old; that it should be almost universally denied, ridiculed, and exploded, as mere frenzy; and that all who dare avow it still are branded with the names of madmen and enthusiasts! This is "that falling away" which was to come; that general apostasy, of all orders and degrees of men, which we even now find to have overspread the earth. "Run to and fro in the streets of Jerusalem, and see if ye can find a man," a man that loveth the Lord his God with all his heart, and serveth him with all his strength. How does our own land mourn (that we look no farther) under the overflowings of ungodliness! What villa[i]nies of every kind are committed day by day; yea, too often with impunity, by those who sin with a high hand, and glory in their shame! Who can reckon up the oaths, curses, profaneness, blasphemies; the lying, slandering, evil-speaking; the sabbath-breaking, gluttony, drunkenness, revenge; the whoredoms, adulteries, and various uncleanness; the frauds, injustice, oppression, extortion, which overspread our land as a flood?

11. And even among those who have kept themselves pure from these grosser abominations, how much anger and pride, how much sloth and idleness, how much softness and effeminacy, how much luxury and self-indulgence, how much covetousness and ambition, how much thirst of praise, how much love of the world, how much fear of man, is to be found! Meanwhile, how little of true religion! For, where is he that loveth either God or his neighbor, as he hath given us commandment? On the one hand, are those who have not so much as the form of godliness; on the other, are those who have the form only: There stands *open*, there the *painted*, sepulchre. So that in very deed, whosoever were earnestly to behold any public gathering together of the people (I fear those in our churches are not to be excepted), might easily perceive, "that the one part were Sadducees, and the other Pharisees"; the one having almost as little

concern about religion, as if there were "no resurrection, neither angel nor spirit"; and the other, making it a mere lifeless form, a dull round of external performances, without either true faith, or the love of God, or joy in the Holy Ghost!

12. Would to God I could except *us* of this place! "Brethren, my heart's desire, and prayer to God, for you is, that ye may be saved" from this overflowing of ungodliness; and that here may its proud waves be stayed! But is it so indeed? God knoweth, yea, and our own consciences, it is not. Ye have not kept yourselves pure. Corrupt are we also and abominable; and few are there that understand any more; few that worship God in spirit and in truth. We, too, are "a generation that set not our hearts aright, and whose spirit cleaveth not steadfastly unto God": He hath appointed us indeed to be "the salt of the earth; but if the salt hath lost its savour, it is thenceforth good for nothing, but to be cast out and to be trodden under-foot of men."

13. And "shall I not visit for these things, saith the Lord? Shall not my soul be avenged on such a nation as this?" Yea, we know not how soon he may say to the sword, "Sword, go through this land!" He hath given us long space to repent. He lets us alone this year also: But he warns and awakens us by thunder. His judgments are abroad in the earth; and we have all reason to expect the heaviest of all, even that he "should come unto us quickly, and remove our candlestick out of its place, except we repent and do the first works"; unless we return to the principles of the Reformation, the truth and simplicity of the gospel. Perhaps we are now resisting the last effort of divine grace to save us. Perhaps we have well nigh "filled up the measure of our iniquities," by rejecting the counsel of God against ourselves, and casting out his messengers.

14. O God, "in the midst of wrath, remember mercy!" Be glorified in our reformation, not in our destruction! Let us "hear the rod, and him that appointed it"! Now, that thy "judgments are abroad in the earth," let the inhabitants of the world "learn righteousness"!

15. My brethren, it is high time for us to awake out of sleep; before this the "great trumpet of the Lord be blown," and our land become a field of blood. O may we speedily see the things that make for our peace, before they are hid from our eyes! "Turn thou us, O good Lord, and let thine anger cease from us. O Lord, look down from heaven, behold and visit this vine"; and cause us to know "the time of our visitation." "Help us, O God of our salvation, for the glory of Thy name! O deliver us, and be merciful to our sins, for Thy name's sake! And so we will not go back from Thee. O let us live, and we shall call upon Thy name. Turn us, again, O Lord God of Hosts! Show the light of Thy countenance, and we shall be whole.

"Now unto Him that is able to do exceeding abundantly above all that we can ask or think, according to the power that worketh in us, unto Him be glory in the Church, by Christ Jesus, throughout all ages, world without end.—Amen!"

No. 57 Hymn: "On the True Use of Musick"

Methodist tradition connects the hymn by this title with Charles Wesley's confrontation with a crowd of drunken sailors. The rabble interrupted Charles's preaching by half singing, half shouting one of the dance hall ditties of the period that immortalized the scandalous deeds of one "Nancy Dawson." With typical wit Wesley allowed that he liked their melody (which must have been similar to the tune of "Here we go round the mulberry bush") but not their lewd lyrics.[35]

Like Elijah of old, Wesley devised a contest for the gods of music. He challenged the sailors to return later in the day, promising to have a song they could all sing together; expecting to make more sport of the Methodist, they agreed to come, only to be won to the faith by Charles's apology for the proper use of music.

The two Wesleyan hymns by this title are especially significant, since they are the only direct statements Charles made regarding his rationale for writing his 9,000 hymns. The hymn below probably originated in his famous confrontation with the mob. It is preserved in manuscript form in "Ms. Occasional" and was published in Charles's *Hymns and Sacred Poems* (1749 edition). The capitalization and spelling of the manuscript hymn are preserved below.[36]

1   Listed into the Cause of Sin,
        Why should a Good be Evil?
    Musick, alas! too long has been
        Prest to obey the Devil:
    Drunken, or lewd, or light the Lay
        Flow'd to the Soul's Undoing,
    Widen'd, and strew'd with Flowers the Way
        Down to Eternal Ruin.

2   Who on the Part of GOD will rise,
        Innocent Sound recover,
    Fly on the Prey, and take the Prize,
        Plunder the Carnal Lover,
    Strip him of every moving Strain,
        Every melting Measure,
    Musick in Virtue's Cause retain,
        Rescue the Holy Pleasure?

3   Come let us try if JESU[S]'s Love
        Will not as well inspire us:
    This is the Theme of Those above,
        This upon Earth shall fire us.
    Say, if your Hearts are tun'd to sing,
        Is there a Subject greater?
    Harmony all its Strains may bring,
        JESUS's Name is sweeter.

4 JESUS the Soul of Musick is;
    His is the Noblest Passion:
JESUS's Name is Joy and Peace,
    Happiness and Salvation:
JESUS's Name the Dead can raise,
    Shew us our Sins forgiven,
Fill us with all the Life of Grace,
    Carry us up to Heaven.

5 Who hath a Right like Us to sing,
    Us whom his Mercy raises?
Merry our Hearts, for CHRIST is King,
    Cheerful are all our Faces:
Who of his Love doth once partake
    He evermore rejoices:
Melody in our Hearts we make,
    Echoing to our Voices.

6 He that a sprinkled Conscience hath,
    He that in GOD is merry,
Let him sing Psalms, the Spirit saith,
    Joyful, and never weary,
Offer the Sacrifice of Praise,
    Hearty, and never ceasing
Spiritual Songs and Anthems raise,
    Honour, and Thanks and Blessing.

7 Then let us in his Praises join,
    Triumph in his Salvation,
Glory ascribe to Grace Divine,
    Worship, and Adoration:
Heaven already is begun,
    Open'd in Each Believer;
Only believe, and still sing on,
    Heaven is Ours forever.

REDEMPTION HYMNS

Charles's hymns had their foundation and focus in this work as an evangelist. One of his later hymnals bore a title that made this connection explicit, *Hymns for those that Seek, and those that Have, Redemption in the Blood of Jesus Christ* (1747). Those "Redemption Hymns" communicate, as well as any in the Wesleyan corpus, the concerns of the Methodist Revival. A selection of them is given below to illustrate how Charles's pastoral role was manifested as clearly in song as in sermon. In addition to the hymns from the 1747 collection, an important hymn from *Hymns and Sacred Poems* (1749 edition) is presented as a poignant example of Charles's call for a Christian "charity," or selfless love, which manifests itself as certainly in action as in aspiration.

No. 58   Redemption Hymn: I

1   Jesus, My Lord, attend
        Thy fallen creature's cry,
   And show Thyself the sinner's Friend,
        And set me up on high:
        From hell's oppressive power,
        From earth and sin release,
   And to Thy Father's grace restore,
        And to Thy perfect peace.

2   For this, alas! I mourn
        In helpless unbelief,
   But Thou my wretched heart canst turn,
        And heal my sin and grief,
        Salvation in Thy name
        To dying souls is given,
   And all may, through Thy merit, claim
        A right to life and heaven.

3   Thy blood and righteousness
        I make my only plea,
   My present and eternal peace
        Are both derived from Thee:
        Rivers of life Divine
        From Thee their Fountain flow,
   All[,] all who know that love of Thine
        The joy of angels know.

4   O then impute, impart
        To me Thy righteousness,
   And let me taste how good Thou art,
        How full of truth and grace:
        That Thou canst here forgive
        I long to testify,
   And justified by faith to live,
        And in that faith to die.

No. 59   Redemption Hymn: II[38]

1   O How sweet it is to languish
        For our God,
        Till His blood
     Eases all our anguish!
     Blest we are in expectation
        Of the bliss,
        Power and peace,
     Pardon and salvation.

2   We shall soon enjoy the favour
        (Now the hope
        Lifts us up)
     Of our loving Saviour.
     Confident, for God hath spoken,
        Till the grace
        We embrace,
     Hold we fast the token.

3   Though the world will not believe it,
        Sure the word
        Of our Lord,
     All that ask receive it.
     We shall live the life of heaven,
        While below
        We shall know
     Here our sins forgiven.

4   Though they call our hope delusion,
        Jesus here
        Shall appear,
     To our sin's confusion.
     All the virtues of His passion
        We shall share,
        And declare,
     In the creation.

5   Jesus shall impute His merit
        Unto all
        Those that call
     For His promised Spirit;
     Pour into our hearts the pardon,
        Make us bud,
        By His blood,
     As a water'd garden.

6   O the soul-transporting pleasure
        Which we feel,
        Waiting still
    For the heavenly treasure!
    O the joy of expectation!
        Happy we
        Soon shall see
    All the Lord's salvation.

No. 60   Redemption Hymn: IV, "The Invitation"[39]

1   Weary souls, who wander wide
        From the central point of bliss,
    Turn to Jesus crucified,
        Fly to those dear wounds of His,
    Sink into the purple flood,
    Rise into the life of God!

2   Find in Christ the way of peace,
        Peace unspeakable, unknown:
    By His pain He gives you ease,
        Life by His expiring groan;
    Rise exalted by His fall,
    Find in Christ your all in all.

3   O believe the record true,
        God to you His Son hath given,
    Ye may now be happy too,
        Live on earth the life of heaven;
    Live the life of heaven above,
    All the life of glorious love.

4   This is the universal bliss,
        Bliss for every soul design'd,
    God's original promise this,
        God's greatest gift to all mankind:
    Blest in Christ this moment be,
    Blest to all eternity!

No. 61   Redemption Hymn: IX[40]

1   Love Divine, all loves excelling,
        Joy of heaven, to earth come down,
    Fix in us Thy humble dwelling,
        All Thy faithful mercies crown:

Jesu, Thou art all compassion,
   Pure, unbounded love Thou art,
Visit us with Thy salvation,
   Enter every trembling heart.

2 Breathe, O breathe Thy loving Spirit,
     Into every troubled breast,
  Let us all in Thee inherit,
     Let us find that second rest:
  Take away our *power* of sinning,
     Alpha and Omega be,
  End of faith as its Beginning,
     Set our hearts at liberty.

3 Come, almighty to deliver,
     Let us all Thy life receive;
  Suddenly return, and never,
     Never more Thy temples leave.
  Thee we would be always blessing,
     Serve Thee as Thy hosts above,
  Pray, and praise Thee without ceasing,
     Glory in Thy perfect love.

4 Finish then Thy new creation,
     Pure, and spotless let us be,
  Let us see Thy great salvation,
     Perfectly restored in Thee:
  Changed from glory into glory,
     Till in heaven we take our place,
  Till we cast our crowns before Thee,
     Lost in wonder, love and praise!

No. 62 Redemption Hymn: XVII, "For a Minister of Christ"[41]

1 Jesus, my strength and righteousness,
     My Saviour, and my King,
  Triumphantly Thy name I bless,
     Thy conquering name I sing.
  Thou, Lord, hast magnified Thy name,
     Thou hast maintain'd Thy cause,
  And I enjoy the glorious shame,
     The scandal of Thy cross.

2 Thou gavest me to speak thy word
     In the appointed hour,
  I have proclaim'd my dying Lord,

And felt Thy Spirit's power:
Superior to my foes I stood,
 Above their smile or frown,
On all the strangers to Thy blood
 With pitying love look'd down.

3 O let me have Thy presence still,
  Set as flint my face,
To show the counsel of Thy will,
  Which save a world by grace.
O let me never blush to own
  The glorious gospel word,
Which saves a world through faith alone,
  Faith in a bleeding Lord!

4 This is the saving power of God:
  Whoe'er this word receive,
Feel all th' effects of Jesu's blood,
  And *sensibly* believe:
Saved from the guilt and power of sin
  By instantaneous grace,
They trust to have Thy *life brought in*,
  And *always* see Thy face.

5 The pure in heart Thy face shall see
  Before they hence remove,
Redeem'd from all iniquity,
  And perfected in love.
This is the great salvation! This
  The prize at which we aim,
The end of faith, the hidden bliss,
  The new, mysterious name.

6 The name inscribed in the white stone,
  The unbeginning Word,
The mystery so long unknown,
  The secret of the Lord.
The living bread sent down from heaven,
  The saints' and angels' food,
Th' immortal seed, the little leaven,
  The effluence of God!

7 The tree of life, that blooms and grows
  In th' midst of paradise,
The pure and living stream, that flows
  Back to its native skies:
The Spirit's law, the covenant seal,
  Th' eternal righteousness,

The glorious joy unspeakable,
   Th' unutterable peace!

8 The treasure in the gospel-field,
      The wisdom from above,
   Hid from the wise, to babes reveal'd,
      The precious pearl of love;
   The mystic power of godliness,
      The end of death and sin,
   The antepast of heavenly bliss,
      The kingdom fix'd within.

9 The Morning Star, that glittering bright,
      Shine to the perfect day,
   The Sun of Righteousness—the Light,
      The Life, the Truth, the Way:
   The image of the living God,
      His nature, and His mind,
   Himself He hath on us bestow'd,
      And all in Christ we find.

No. 63   Redemption Hymn: L, "The Great Supper"

This hymn, located in manuscript form in "Ms. Cheshunt," was published in
Redemption Hymns (1747) and reprinted in a shortened form in John Wesley's
Collection of 1780. The hymn is printed in its manuscript form, with permission of
the Cheshunt College Foundation. The manuscript version differs from the published hymn in a few minor instances.[42]

1 Come, sinners, to the Gospel Feast,
   Let every soul be Jesus' Guest,
   You need not one be left behind.
   For GOD hath bidden All Mankind.

2 Sent by my Lord, on You I call,
   The Invitation is to All,
   Come all the World; Come, Sinner, Thou,
   All Things in Christ are ready now.

3 Jesus to you His Fullness brings,
   A feast of Marrow and fat things:
   All, all in Christ is freely given,
   Pardon, and Happiness[a] and Heaven.

---

[a] 1747 ed., "holiness"

4   Do not begin to make excuse,
    Ah! do not you His grace refuse;
    Your worldly Cares and Pleasures leave,
    And take what Jesus hath to give.

5   Your Grounds forsake, your Oxen quit,
    Your every Earthly thought forget,
    Seek not the Comforts of this Life,
    Nor lose your Saviour for a Wife.

6   "Have me excus'd," Why will ye say?
    Why will ye for Damnation pray?
    Have you excus'd—from Joy and Peace!
    Have you excus'd—from Happiness!

7   Excus'd from coming to a Feast!
    Excus'd from being Jesus' Guest!
    From knowing *now* your Sins forgiven,
    From tasting *here* the Joys of Heaven!

8   Excus'd, alas! why should you be
    From Health, and Life, and Liberty,
    From entering into Glorious Rest,
    From leaning on your Saviour's Breast!

9   Yet must I, Lord, to Thee complain,
    The World hath made Thine Offers vain;
    Too Busy, or too Happy they,
    They will not, Lord, Thy Call obey.

10 Go then, my angry Master said,
    Since these on all My Mercies tread,
    Invite the Rich and Great no more,
    But preach My Gospel to the Poor.

11 Confer not thou with Flesh and Blood,
    Go quickly forth, invite the Crowd,
    Search every Lane, and every Street,
    And bring in all the Souls you meet.

12 Come then, ye Souls by sin opprest,
    Ye restless Wanderers after Rest,
    Ye Poor, and Maim'd, and Halt, and Blind,
    In Christ a hearty Welcome find.

13 Sinners my Gracious Lord receives,
    Harlots, and Publicans, and Thieves;
    Drunkards, and all ye Hellish Crew,
    I have a Message now to you.

14   Come, and partake the Gospel Feast,
Be saved from Sin, in Jesus rest:
O taste the Goodness of our God,
And eat His Flesh, and drink His Blood.

15   'Tis done; my All-redeeming Lord,
I have gone forth, and preach'd Thy Word,
The Sinners to Thy Feast are come,
And yet, O Jesus,[b] here is room.

16   Go then, my Lord again enjoin'd,
And other wandering Sinners find;
Go to the Hedges and Highways,
And offer All My Pardoning Grace.

17   The worst unto My Supper press,
Monsters of daring Wickedness,
Tell them My Grace for All is free,
They cannot be too Lost[c] for Me.

18   Tell them, their Sins are all forgiven,
Tell every Creature under Heaven
I died to save them from all Sin,
And force the Rebels[d] to come in.

19   Ye vagrant Souls, on You I call,
(O that my Voice could reach you all!)
Ye all are freely Justified,
Ye all may live, for God[e] hath died.

20   My Message as from God receive,
Ye all may come to Christ, and live:
O let His love your Hearts constrain,
Nor suffer Him to die in vain.

21   His Love is mighty to compel,
His Conquering Love consent to feel;
Yield to His Love's resistless power,
And fight against your God no more!

22   See Him set forth before your Eyes,
Behold the Bleeding Sacrifice!
His offer'd Love make haste t' embrace,
And freely now be sav'd by grace.

---

[b]1747 ed., "Saviour"
[c]1747 ed., "bad"
[d]1747 ed., "vagrants"
[e]1747 ed., "Christ"

23 Ye who believe His record true
    Shall sup with Him, and He with you;
    Come to the Feast; be saved from sin,
    For Jesus waits to take you in.

24 This is the time, no more delay,
    This is the acceptable day,
    Come in, this moment, at His call,
    And live for Him who died for All.

No. 64   Hymn: "Invitation to Sinners"
(*Hymns and Sacred Poems*, 1749)[43]

1   All ye that pass by,
            To Jesus draw nigh,
    To you is it nothing that Jesus should die?
            Your Ransom and Peace,
            Your Surety He is,
    Come, see if there ever was sorrow like His.

2   For what you have done
            His blood must atone:
    The Father had punish'd for you His dear Son.
            The Lord in the day
            Of His anger lay
    Your sins on the Lamb; and He bore them away.

3   He answer'd for all,
            O come at His call,
    And low at His cross with astonishment fall.
            But lift up your eyes
            At Jesus' cries:
    Impassive He suffers, immortal He dies.

4   He dies to atone
            For sins not His own;
    Your debt He hath paid, and your work He hath done.
            Ye all may receive
            The peace He did leave,
    Who made intercession "My Father forgive!"

5   For you, and for me[,]
            He pray'd on the tree,
    The prayer is accepted, the sinner is free.
            The sinner am I,
            Who on Jesus rely,
    And come for the pardon God cannot deny.

6   My pardon I claim,
        For a sinner I am,
A sinner believing in Jesus' name.
        He purchased the grace,
        Which I now embrace:
O Father, Thou know'st He hath died in my place.

7   His death is my plea,
        My Advocate see,
And hear the blood speak that hath answer'd for me.
        Acquitted I was,
        When He bled on the cross,
And by losing His life He hath carried my cause.

No. 65   Hymn: "Before Any Work of Charity [i.e. "Love"]: In the Work"[44]

(*Hymns and Sacred Poems*, 1749)

1   I come, O God, to do Thy will,
        With Jesus in my view,
    A servant of His servants still,
        My Pattern I pursue.

2   My loving labour I repeat,
        Obedient to His word,
    And wash His dear disciples' feet,
        And wait upon my Lord.

3   I have my Saviour always near,
        On Him I now attend,
    I see Him in His members here,
        My Brother, and my Friend.

4   Shivering beneath those rags He stands,
        Again exposed, and bare,
    And stretches out His helpless hands,
        And asks my tender care.

5   And shall I not relief afford,
        Put off my costly dress,
    Tear it away to clothe my Lord,
        Who hides my sinfulness!

6   Drink to a thirsty Christ I give,
        An hungry Christ I feed,
    The stranger to my house receive,
        Who here shall lay his head.

7 Sick and in prison will I find,
   And all his sorrows cheer,
Or bring him forth, and doubly kind
   Relieve, and tend him here.

8 In sickness will I make his bed,
   The cordial draught prepare,
My hands shall hold his fainting head,
   And all his burden bear.

9 Surely I now my Saviour see,
   In this poor worm conceal'd,
Wounded He asks relief of me,
   Who all my wounds hath heal'd.

10 My needy Jesus I descry,
    And in this object meet,
Sick, and in pain I see Him lie,
    And gasping at my feet.

11 Paleness His dying face o'erspreads,
    His griefs I more than see,
My heart at Jesu's suffering bleeds
    With softest sympathy.

12 I fill my Lord's afflictions up,
    His welcome burden bear,
And gladly drink His bitter cup,
    And all His sorrows share.

13 Yes, Lord, with joy, and grief, and love
    I now behold Thy face,
My God descended from above
    To suffer in my place.

14 Thy visage marr'd with tears and blood,
    Mine eyes of faith survey,
As when on yonder cross my God
    A bleeding Victim lay.

15 Torn with the whips, and nails, and spear
    Thy sacred body was;
O might it now to all appear
    As hanging on the cross!

16 O that to Thee the world might bow,
    And know Thy saving name,
And see, and serve, as I do now,
    And love the bleeding Lamb!

NOTES

1. Jackson, *CW Journal*, I, pp. 160–161.

2. *M.H.B.*, #108, pp. 111–112, utilizes verses 2, 3, 4, 5, of Charles's original hymn. Cf. *P.W.*, II, pp. 156–158.

3. Jackson, *CW Journal*, I, pp. 162–164.

4. Mrs. Kirkham was the wife of Rev. Lionel Kirkham, Rector of Stanton in Gloucestershire, and had been a friend to him since Wesley's Oxford days.

5. Jackson, *CW Journal*, I, p. 165.

6. *M.H.B.*, #377, p. 371, applies verses 1, 4, 5, 6, 8, 9 of Charles's original poem. Cf. *P.W.*, II, pp. 144–146. In his own writings John Wesley indicated that he studiously avoided using the word "dear" to refer to the Deity (*JW Works*, VII, p. 294).

7. The Methodist revival brought with it strong emotions: guilt and freedom from it, "mourning" and "joy unspeakable." Occasionally, the plainer people of Charles's congregations gave voice to their hearts, apparently to the offense of more "proper" folk.

8. *M.H.B.*, pp. 198–199; *P.W.*, I, pp. 287–288.

9. *M.H.B.*, #204, p. 206; *P.W.*, V, pp. 390–391.

10. Cf. Thomas Albin, "Charles Wesley's Earliest Evangelical Sermons," *Methodist History*, Vol. 21, No. 1 (Oct. 1982), pp. 60–63. The manuscript is housed in the Methodist Archives and Research Centre, The John Rylands University Library of Manchester, Manchester, England. It was transcribed and printed here with the kind permission of the Methodist Church Archives and History Committee and Mr. Albin.

11. The abbreviation stands for "In the Name of Jesus."

12. The manuscript carries a scribal error at this point: "ot," in the original.

13. A rhetorical pause indicated in the text.

14. The writer seemed to be torn between two options in phraseology: wanting to say either "my hopes" or "all of my hopes." Instead of either, however, he wrote, "my all hopes."

15. Charles's metaphor is based on John 3:14: "As Moses lifted up the serpent in the wilderness, even so must the Son of Man be lifted up: . . ." This bronze serpent became an important Christological image for Wesley.

16. Cf. I Sam. 15:33.

17. The phrase "of the Spirit" is written twice in the manuscript, and then lined through. The context here suggests that Charles intended the reading offered in brackets.

18. The allusion is drawn from Luke 18:9–15, where Jesus' parable contrasts a self-righteous Pharisee and a publican convinced of his own unworthiness before God. The latter person prayed, "God be merciful to me a sinner," and ". . . went down to his house justified rather than the other: for everyone that exalteth himself shall be abased; and he that humbleth himself shall be exalted."

19. Hernhutt was a Moravian community established by Count von Zinzendorf in Saxony, Germany. John Wesley and Benjamin Ingham visited Hernhutt (June 15–Sept. 16, 1738), and returned with mixed reports of the piety and fellowship of the community. Cf. *JW Works*, II, pp. 3–63.

20. Cf. *JW Works*, VIII, pp. 339–347.

21. *M.H.B.*, #16, pp. 20–21, carried this hymn in two parts of eleven verses each. Only one verse, number seven, was omitted. cf. *P.W.* V, pp. 479–84.

22. *P.W.*, I, pp. 242–244.

23. *P.W.* IV, pp. 378–380.

24. *M.H.B.*, #380 and #381, pp. 374–375. #380 utilizes verses 1, 3, 9, 19, 20, 21, and 22 of Charles's original; #381 is fashioned from verses 23, 26, 27, 28. Cf. *P.W.*, II, pp. 319–323.

25. *M.H.B.*, #136, pp. 138–140; verses 5–7 of the original were omitted, cf. *P.W.*, II, pp. 173–176. Cf. *JW Works*, XIII, p. 514, for his evaluation of Charles's "Wrestling Jacob."

26. *M.H.B.*, #160, pp. 162–164, is formed out of verses 1, 3, 5, 6, 7, 9, and 10 of the original; cf. *P.W.*, II, pp. 153–155.

27. The *YS*'s family of Hebrew words is the etymological root of both names. In the early Old Testament, "Joshua" is a synonym for "Hoshea" or "salvation" (Num. 13:8, 16). In later Jewish literature (Hebrew and Aramaic) the name became "Jeshua" as in 1 Chron. 24:11 and 1 Esd. 5:8, 24. It came into New Testament Greek as "Jesous," which has been rendered "Jesus." Matt. 1:21 explained the name with the soteriological significance that Wesley used as an ideological bridge to connect the Old and New Testaments.

28. *P.W.*, V, pp. 44–48.

29. Baker, *Representative Verse, op. cit.*, p. 114.

30. *P.W.*, V, pp. 282–284; cf. *JW Works*, VII, pp. 67–75.

31. *M.H.B.*, #158, pp. 160–161, applies verses 1, 4, 5, 7, 8, and 9 of the original. Compare *P.W.*, II, pp. 150–152.

32. Charles's sermon has been published in *JW Works*, V, pp. 25–36.

33. Cf. *JW Works*, V, pp. 36–52, for John's sermon, "Scriptural Christianity." Compare *JW Journal*, III, pp. 147–148, and Jackson, *CW Journal*, I, pp. 380–381, for the university's reaction to John's preaching.

34. Jackson, *CW Journal*, I, p. 82.

35. Luke Wiseman, *Charles Wesley, Evangelist and Poet* (New York: Abingdon, 1932), pp. 91–92; Baker, *Representative Verse, op. cit.*, p. 117.

36. Ms. Occasional, pp. 74–76, located at the Methodist Archives and Research Center, John Rylands University Library of Manchester, Manchester, England. Printed here by permission of the Methodist Church Archives and History Committee, England.

37. *P.W.*, IV, pp. 207–208.

38. *Ibid.*, pp. 208–210.

39. *Ibid.*, pp. 212–213.

40. *Ibid.*, pp. 219–220; John Wesley omitted v. 2 in 1780 hymnbook (No. 374) probably because of his objection to the line: "Take away our *power* of sinning."

41. *Ibid.*, pp. 232–234.

42. *M.H.B.*, #2, pp. 1ff, made up of verses 1, 2, 12, 14, 19–22, and 24 of the original. The hymn is printed here from "Ms. Cheshunt," pp. 40–43. The manuscript is held by the Cheshunt College Foundation, Westminster College, Cambridge, England. It is printed with the kind permission of Dr. S. H. Mayor and the Cheshunt Foundation.

43. *P.W.*, IV, pp. 371–372; in *Hymns and Sacred Poems*, 1749, it is No. 42.

44. *Ibid.*, V, pp. 19–21; in *Hymns and Sacred Poems*, 1749, it is No. 125.

6 / Out of the Den of the Lion

The revival shook eighteenth-century society through the radical changes it brought in the lives of men and women. Its conception of Christian discipleship challenged both the mores of the age and the *modus operandi* of the religious establishment. The superstitions of the ignorant, instability of the political situation, rabid anti-Catholicism, and growing anticlericalism fueled popular opposition to the Wesleys. Charles saw this opposition as the natural reaction of a fallen world confronted with the gospel of Christ; according to him, "it is always the Lamb who troubles the waters." Divisions caused within families combined with bigotry of class, politics, and religion to create a volatile evangelistic climate. By the early 1740s mob violence became a fact of life for Charles Wesley and the Methodists. Deprived of civil rights and due process of law, persecution became a badge of discipleship among them. Adhering to the beatitudes and the doctrine of nonresistance ("turn the other cheek"), Charles and his followers suffered physical peril and loss of property at the hands of "the rabble." Yet the constancy of their Christianity and the tenacity of their faith gradually won the respect of their oppressors, and not a few of "the enemies" eventually joined Methodist societies.

No. 66   Journal Selections: March 16–17, 1740

Sun., March 16th [1740]. I preached the law and Gospel last night, from Isa. 40, with much freedom and power: appointed the usual place for preaching. Mr. Henry [Seward] came to dissuade me; said, "Four Constables are ordered to apprehend you, if you come near my brother's wall: so come at your peril."

I walked toward the place. An officer from the Mayor met and desired me to come to him. I said I would first wait upon the Lord, and then upon him, whom I reverenced for his office's sake. I went on, Mr. Henry met me with threats and revilings. I began singing,

> Shall I, for fear of feeble man,
>   Thy Spirit's course in me restrain? [No. 15]

He ran about raving like a madman, and quickly got some men for his purpose; who laid hold on me. I asked by what authority? Where was their warrant? Let them show that, I would save them the trouble of using violence. They said they had none, but I should not preach there; and hurried me away amid the cries of the people. Truly their tongues were set on fire of hell. Henry cried, "Take him away, and duck him." I broke out into singing with T[homas] Maxfield, and let them carry me whither they would. At the bridge in the lane they left me. There I stood, out of the liberty of the Corporation, and gave out,

> Angel of God, whate'er betide,
> Thy summons I obey! [No. 67]

Some hundreds they could not frighten from hearing me, on, "If God be for us, who can be against us?" Never did I feel so much what I spoke. The word did not return empty; as the tears on all sides testified.

Then I waited upon Mr. Mayor: the poor sincere ones followed me trembling. He was a little warm [i.e. angry] at my not coming before. I gave him reason, and added, that I knew no law of God or man which I had transgressed; if there was any such, desired no favour. He said he should not have denied me leave to preach, even in his own yard; but Mr. Henry Seward and the 'Pothecary had assured him, it would quite cast his brother down again. I said it would rather restore him; for our Gospel was life from the dead.

A lawyer began declaiming against my making the poor gentleman mad. I granted, "You fools must count his life madness." Here a Clergyman spoke much,—and nothing. As near as I could pick out his meaning, he grumbled at Mr. Whitefield's speaking against the Clergy in his [published] Journal. I told him, if he himself was a carnal, worldly-minded Clergyman, I might do what he would call railing,—warn God's people to beware of false Prophets. I did not say, because I did not know him, that he was one of those shepherds that fed themselves, not the flock; of those dumb dogs that could not bark; of those greedy dogs that could never have enough: if he was, I was sorry for him, and must leave that sentence of Chrysostom with him, "Hell is paved with the skulls of Christian Priests."

He charged me with making a division in Mr. Seward's family. I asked, "Are you a preacher of the Gospel, and do not know the effect it has among men? 'There shall be five in one house, two against three, and three against two.' " He laughed, and cried to his companion, "Did not I tell you he would bring that?" I urged the necessity of persecution, if one of a family was first awakened. "Awakened!" said he, "I don't know what you mean by that." "I mean, your speaking truth, when you tell God the remembrance of your sins is grievous to you, the burden intolerable." I turned from him, and asked the Mayor, whether he approved the treatment I had met with. He said, "By no means"; and if I complained, he would bind the men over to answer it at the sessions. I told him I did not complain, neither would I prosecute them, as they well knew. I assured him, I had waited upon him, not out of interest, for I wanted nothing of him; not out of fear, for I had done no wrong, and wanted no human support; but out of true respect, and to show him I believed the powers that be are ordained of God.

In church the Minister I had talked with, Mr. Pr., seemed utterly confounded at the Second Lesson, John 3. That saying in the Epistle, likewise, was sadly inconsistent with some of his: "But as then he that was born after the flesh persecuted him that was born after the Spirit, even so it is now." In his pulpit (Nicodemus's stronghold), he strained hard to draw a parallel between the Pharisees and Methodists. I suppose because we preach self-justification. In the evening I preached without interruption, "The blind receive their sight," &c. Our Lord was present. None stirred for the rain. The school-house was crowded at seven. I spoke convincingly, to some scoffers in particular, who could not long stand it.

> "Sing ye to our God above
>   Praise eternal as his love!"

We have seen wonderful things to-day.

No. 67   Hymn: "At Setting Out to Preach the Gospel"[1]
(*Hymns and Sacred Poems*, 1740)

1   Angel of God, whate'er betide,
        Thy summons I obey,
    Jesus, I take Thee for my Guide,
        And walk in Thee my Way.

2   Secure from danger and from dread.
        Nor earth nor hell shall move,
    Since over me Thy hand hath spread
        The banner of Thy love.

3   To leave my Captain I disdain,
        Behind I will not stay,
    Though shame, and loss, and bonds, and pain,
        And death obstruct the way.

4   Me to Thy suffering Self conform,
        And arm me with Thy power;
    Then burst the cloud, descend the storm,
        And come the fiery hour.

5   Then shall I bear Thy utmost will,
        When first the strength is given:—

Come, foolish world, my body kill,
And drive my soul to heaven!

No. 68   Journal Selections: March 17, 1740–May 26, 1743

Mon., March 17th. My yesterday's treatment provoked many to love. They receive me the more gladly into their houses, because Mr. Seward's is shut against me. . . .

Mr. Henry Seward, mad with passion at my stay, spreads the news of it everywhere, and much increases my audience. To-night I proceeded in the beatitudes. When I came to the last, "Blessed are they which are persecuted," our enemies, not knowing the Scriptures, fulfilled them. A troop poured in from a neighboring alehouse, and set their champion, a schoolmaster, upon a bench over against me. For near an hour he spoke for his master, and I for mine; but my voice prevailed. Sometimes we prayed, sometimes sang and gave thanks. The Lord our God was with us, and the shout of the King was amongst us. In the midst of the tumult, reproach, and blasphemy, I enjoyed a sweet calm within, even while I preached the Gospel with most contention. These slighter conflicts must fit me for greater.

Tues., March 18th. Last night's disturbance, we now hear, was contrived at the alehouse by the 'Squire and Rector. . . .

Sat., May 21st [1743]. . . . I walked with many of the brethren to Walsal, singing. We were received with the old complaint, "Behold, they that turn the world upside down are come here also." I walked through the town amidst the noisy greetings of our enemies, and stood on the steps of the market-house. An host of men was laid against us. The floods lifted up their voice, and raged horribly. I opened the book on the first presented words, Acts. 20:24: "But none of these things move me; neither count I my life dear unto myself, so that I have received of the Lord Jesus, to testify the Gospel of the grace of God."

The street was full of Ephesian beasts (the principal man setting them on), who roared, and shouted, and threw stones incessantly. Many struck, without hurting, me. I besought them in calm love to be reconciled to God in Christ. While I was departing, a stream of ruffians was suffered to bear me from the steps. I rose, and, having given the blessing, was beat down again. So the third time, when we had returned thanks to the God of our salvation. I then, from the steps, bade them depart in peace, and walked quietly back through the thickest rioters. They reviled us, but had no commission to touch an hair on our heads.

Wed., May 25th. In the afternoon I came to the flock in Sheffield, who are as sheep in the midst of wolves; the Ministers having so stirred up the people, that they are ready to tear them in pieces. Most of them have passed through the fire of *stillness*, which came to try them, as soon as they tasted the grace of the Lord.

At six I went to the Society-house, next door to our brother Bennet's. Hell from beneath was moved to oppose us. As soon as I was in the desk with David Taylor, the flood began to lift up their voice. An officer (Ensign Garden) contradicted and blasphemed. I took no notice of him, and sung on. The stones flew thick, hitting the desk and people. To save them and the house, I gave notice I should preach out [of doors], and look the enemy in the face.

The whole army of the aliens followed me. The Captain laid hold on me, and began reviling. I gave him for answer, "A Word in season; or, Advice to a Soldier";[2] then prayed, particularly for His Majesty King George, and then preached the Gospel with much contention. The stones often struck me in the face. After sermon I prayed for sinners, as servants of their master, the devil; upon which the Captain ran at me with great fury, threatening revenge for my abusing, as he called it, "the King his master." He forced his way through the brethren, drew his sword, and presented it to my breast. My breast was immediately steeled. I threw it open, and, fixing mine eye on his, smiled in his face, and calmly said, "I fear God, and honour the King." His countenance fell in a moment, he fetched a deep sigh, put up his sword, and quietly left the place.

To one of the company, who afterwards informed me, he had said, "You shall see, if I do but hold my sword to his breast, he will faint away." So perhaps I should, had I had only his principles to trust to; but if at that time I was not afraid, no thanks to my natural courage.

We returned to our brother Bennet's, and gave ourselves unto prayer. The rioters followed, and exceeded in their outrage all I have seen before. Those of Moorfields, Cardiff, and Walsal were lambs [compared] to these. As there is no King in Israel, (no Magistrate, I mean, in Sheffield), every man does as seems good in his own eyes. Satan now put it into their heads to pull down the Society-house, and they set to their work, while we were praying and praising God. It was a glorious time with us. Every word of exhortation sunk deep, every prayer was sealed, and many found the Spirit of glory resting on them.

One sent for the Constable, who came up, and desired me to leave the town, "since I was the occasion of all this disturbance." I thanked him for his advice, withal assuring him "I should not go a moment sooner for this uproar; was sorry for *their* sakes that they had no law or justice among them: as for myself, I had my protection, and knew my business, as I supposed he did his." In proof whereof, he went from us, and encouraged the mob.

They pressed hard to break the door. I would have gone out to them, but the brethren would not suffer me. They laboured all night for their master, and by morning had pulled down one end of the house. I could compare them to nothing but the men of Sodom, or those coming out of the tombs exceeding fierce. Their outcries often waked me in the night; yet I believe I got more sleep than any of my neighbors.

Thurs., May 26th. At five I expounded [on] the pool of Bethesda; and stayed, conversing with the Society, till eight. I breakfasted with several of the brethren from Yorkshire, Derbyshire, Lancashire, and Cheshire. I met a daughter of affliction, who had long mourned in Sion. God gave me immediate faith for her, which I made proof of in prayer; and in that instant she received *the comfort*. It being agreed that I should preach in the heart of the town, I went forth, nothing doubting. We heard our enemies shouting from afar. I stood up in the midst of them, and read the first words that offered. "If God be for us, who can be against us? He that spareth not his own Son," &c. God made bare his arm in the sight of the Heathen, and so restrained the fierceness of men, so that not one lifted up hand or voice against us.

I took David Taylor, and walked through the open street to our brother Bennet's, with the multitude at my heels. We passed by the spot where the [Society] house stood: they had not left one stone upon another. Nevertheless, the foundation standeth sure, as I told one of them, and our house not made with hands, eternal in the heavens. The mob attended me to my lodgings with great civility; but as soon as I entered the house, they renewed their threatenings to pull it down. The windows were smashed in an instant; and my poor host so frightened, that he was ready to give up his shield [of faith].

He had been for a warrant to Mr. Buck, a Justice of Peace, in Rotherham; who refused him, unless he would promise to forsake this way.

The house was now on the point of being taken by storm. I was writing within, when the cry of my poor friend and his family, I thought, called me out to those sons of Belial. In the midst of the rabble I found a friend of Edward's, with the Riot Act. At their desire, I took and read it, and made a suitable exhortation. One of the sturdiest rebels our Constable seized, and carried away captive into the house. I marvelled at the patience of his companions; but the Lord overawed them. What was done with the prisoners, I know not; for in five minutes I was fast asleep in the room they had dismantled. I feared no cold, but dropped asleep with that word, "Scatter thou the people that delight in war." I afterwards heard that, within the hour, they had all quitted the place.

No. 69 Hymn: "After Deliverance from Death
by the Fall of an House"
(*Hymns and Sacred Poems*, 1749)

The first and second printings of this hymn carried the original title, but John emended the third edition to read "After Deliverance from Death by the Fall of an Horse." While either reading is possible (cf. entry for May 30th, 1743, No. 70

below), the phraseology and timing of the hymn links it to precisely this period
when the mobs literally tore houses down to get at Charles Wesley. In his hymn
Charles's thanksgiving for the Divine deliverance merges with his expectation of
the Lord's eschatological visitation and the ensuing vindication of the righteous
ones who now are undergoing oppression. Wesley's eschatological imagery was
strongly influenced by the phraseology of Revelation (6:14; 20:13) and 2 Peter
(3:10–13) in the KJV.[3]

1   Glory and thanks to God we give!
        Our sacred hairs are number'd all,
    Not one, we find, without His leave,
        Not one unto the ground can fall.

2   How blest whom Jesus calls His own,
        How quiet, and secure from harms!
    The adversary cast us down,
        The Saviour caught us in His arms.

3   'Twas Jesus check'd his straighten'd chain,
        And curb'd the malice of our foe,
    Allow'd to touch our flesh with pain,
        No farther could the murderer go.

4   'Twas Jesus raised our bodies up,
        And stronger by our fall we stand!
    Our life is hid with Christ our Hope,
        Hid in the hollow of His hand.

5   We rest in His protection here;
        But languish for the final day,
    When Christ shall in the clouds appear,
        And heaven and earth shall pass away.

6   The great archangel's trump shall sound,
        (While twice ten thousand thunders roar),
    Tear up the graves, and cleave to the ground,
        And make the greedy sea restore.

7   The greedy sea shall yield her dead,
        The earth no more her slain conceal,
    Sinners shall lift their guilty head,
        And shrink to see a yawning hell.

8   But we who now our Lord confess,
        And faithful to the end endure,
    Shall stand in Jesus' righteousness,
        Stand as the Rock of Ages sure.

9   We, while the stars from heaven shall fall,
        And mountains are on mountains hurl'd,

Shall stand unmoved amidst them all,
And smile to see a burning world.

10 See the celestial bodies roll
In spires of smoke beneath our feet!
They shrivel as a parchment scroll!
Th' elements melt with fervent heat!

11 The earth and all the works therein
Dissolves by raging flames destroy'd,
While we survey the awful scene,
And mount above the fiery void.

12 By faith we now transcend the skies,
And on that ruin'd world look down,
By love above all height we rise,
And share the everlasting throne.

No. 70 Journal Selections: May 27–October 25, 1743

Fri., May 27th. At five I took leave of the Society in those comfortable words, "Confirming the souls," &c. I had the extraordinary blessing I expected. Our hearts were knit together, and greatly comforted. We rejoiced in hope of the glorious appearing of the great God, who had now delivered us out of the mouth of the lions.

David Taylor informed me, that the people of Thorpe, through which we should pass, were exceeding mad against us. So we found them, as we approached the place, and were turning down the lane to Barley-hall. The ambush rose, and assaulted us with stones, eggs, and dirt. My horse flew from side to side, till he forced his way through them. David Taylor they wounded in the forehead, which bled much: his hat he lost in the fray. I returned, and asked what was the reason a Clergyman should not pass without such treatment. At first the rioters scattered; but their Captain, rallying, answered with horrible imprecations, and stones that would have killed both man and beast, had they not been turned aside by an hand unseen. My horse took fright, and hurried away with me down a steep hill, till we came to a lane, which I turned up, and took a circuit to find our brother Johnson's. The enemy spied me from afar, and followed, shouting. Blessed be God, I got no hurt, but only eggs and dirt. My clothes indeed abhorred me, and my arm pained me a little by a blow I received at Sheffield. David Taylor had got just before me to Barley-hall, with the sisters, whom God had hid in the hollow of his hand.

I met many sincere souls assembled to hear the word of God. Never have I known a greater power of love. All were drowned in tears; yet very happy. The scripture I met was, "Blessed be the Lord God of Israel; for he hath visited and redeemed his people." We rejoiced in the God of our salvation, who hath compassed us about with songs of deliverance. . . .

Mon., May 30th. Near Ripley my horse threw, and fell upon me. My companion thought I had broke my neck; but my leg only was bruised, my hand sprained, and my head stunned; which spoiled my making hymns, or thinking at all, till the next day; when the Lord brought us safe to Newcastle.

Fri., July 22d. I rode in the rain to Morva, a settlement of tinners; to whom I could preach nothing but Gospel.

I had just named my text at St. Ives, "Comfort ye, comfort ye my people, saith your God," when an army of rebels broke in upon us, like those at Sheffield or Wednesbury. They began in a most outrageous manner, threatening to murder the people, if they did not go out that moment. They broke the sconces, dashed the windows in pieces, tore away the shutters, benches, poor-box, and all but the stone walls. I stood silently looking on; but mine eyes were unto the Lord. They swore bitterly I should not preach there again; which I disproved, by immediately telling them Christ died for them all. Several times they lifted up their hands and clubs to strike me; but a stronger arm restrained them. They beat and dragged the women about, particularly one of great age, and trampled on them without mercy. The longer they stayed, and the more they raged, the more power I found from above. I bade the people stand still and see the salvation of God; resolving to continue with them, and see the end. In about an hour the word came, "Hitherto shalt thou come, and no farther." The ruffians fell to quarreling among themselves, broke the Town-Clerk's (their captain's) head, and drove one another out of the room.

Having kept the field, we gave thanks for the victory; and in prayer the Spirit of glory rested upon us. Going home, we met the Mayor, with another Justice, and went back to show him the havoc which the gentlemen and their mob had made. He commended our people as the most quiet, inoffensive subjects, encouraged us to sue for justice, said he was no more secure from such lawless violence than we, wished us success, and left us rejoicing in our strong Helper.

Sat., July 23d. I cannot find one of this people who fears those that can kill the body only. It was next to a miracle, that no more mischief was done last night. The gentlemen had resolved to destroy all within doors. They came upon us like roaring lions, headed by the Mayor's son. He struck out the candles with his cane, and began courageously beating the women. I laid my hand upon him, and said, "Sir, you appear like a gentleman: I desire you would show it, by restraining these of the baser sort. Let them strike the men, or me, if they please, but not hurt the poor helpless women and children." He was turned into a friend immediately, and laboured the whole time to quiet his associates. Some, not of the Society, were likewise provoked to stand up for us, and put themselves between: others held the ruffians, and made use of an arm of flesh. Some of our bitterest enemies were brought over by the meekness of the sufferers, and malice of the persecutors. They had sworn to drive us all out, and then take possession of our house; but their commission did not go so far. One was overheard saying to his companions, as they were going off, "I think the desk is insured: we could not touch it, or come near it."

I proved the devil a liar, by preaching in the room at five. The words I first met were Isa. 54: "For thou shalt break forth on the right hand and on the left. Fear not; for thou shalt not be ashamed: neither be thou confounded; for thou shalt not be put to shame. Behold, I have created the smith, and the waster to destroy. No weapon that is formed against thee shall prosper," &c.

I preached at Gwennap to near two thousand hungry souls, who devoured the word of reconciliation. Half my audience were tinners from about Redruth, which, I hear, is *taken*. God has given us their hearts. If any man speak against us, say they, he deserves to be stoned. Again I expounded in the room at St. Ives, and advised the Society to possess their souls in patience, not threatenings, or even mentioning the late uproar, but suffering all things for the sake of Jesus Christ.

Mon., July 25th. The Mayor told us, that the Ministers were the principal authors of all this evil, by continually representing us in their sermons as Popish emissaries, and urging the enraged multitude to take all manner of ways to stop us. Their whole preaching is cursings and lies; yet they modestly say, my fellow-labourer and I are the cause of all the disturbance. It is always the lamb that troubles the water.

Yesterday we were stoned as Popish incendiaries; to-day, it is our turn to have favour with the people.

Tues., July 26th. I showed my brethren their calling from Matt. 10:22: "Ye shall be hated of all men for my name's sake: but he that endureth to the end, the same shall be saved."

At the Pool one stopped and demanded my letters of orders.[4] I marveled at Mr. Churchwarden's ignorance, gave him my Oxford sermon, and rode on. He followed me with another gentleman, and vowed I should not preach in *his parish*. When I began he shouted, and hallooed, and put his hat to my mouth. We went to another place: he followed us like Shimei.[5] I told him, I should surely deliver my message, unless his master was stronger than mine. After much contention I walked away, with near two thousand people, most part tinners, the next parish, as my wise Churchwarden supposed. He followed us another mile, and a warm walk he had of it; but left us on the borders of the neighboring parish. However, to take my leave of it, I preached on what he called *his*. In spite of Satan, the poor had the Gospel preached to them, and heard it joyfully. Great was their zeal and affection toward me. I marvel not that Satan should fight for his kingdom: it begins to shake in this place.

All was quiet at St. Ives, the Mayor having declared his resolution to swear twenty new Constables, and suppress the rioters by force of arms. Their drum he has sent [for] and seized. All the time I was preaching, he stood at a little distance, to awe the rebels. He has set the whole town against him, by not giving us up to their fury: but he plainly told Mr. Hoblin, the fire-and-faggot Minister, that he would not be perjured, to gratify any man's malice.[6] Us he informed, that he had often heard Mr. Hoblin say, "They ought to drive us away by blows, not arguments."

Thur., July 28th. . . . I began explaining the beatitudes at St. Ives. None interrupted. I do not despair but some of our persecutors themselves may yet, before we depart, receive that *damnable Popish doctrine,* as Mr. Hoblin calls it, of justification by faith only.

Fri., July 29th. I rode to Morva, and invited the whole nation of tinners to Christ. I took the names of several who were desirous of joining in a Society. The adversaries have laboured with all their might to hinder this good work: but we doubt not our seeing a glorious church in this place.

We rode four miles farther, to Zunning, and took up our lodging at an hospitable farmer's.

I walked with our brother Shepherd to the Land's-end, and sang, on the extremest point of the rocks,

> Come, Divine Immanuel, come,
> Take possession of thy home;
> Now thy mercy's wings expand,
> Stretch throughout the happy land.
>
> Carry on thy victory,
> Spread thy rule from sea to sea;
> Re-convert the ransom'd race;
> Save us, save us, Lord, by grace.
>
> Take the purchase of thy blood,
> Bring us to a pardoning God;
> Give us eyes to see our day,
> Hearts the glorious truth t' obey.
>
> Ears to hear the Gospel sound,
> "Grace doth more than sin abound";
> God appeared, and man forgiven,
> Peace on earth, and joy in heaven.
>
> O that every soul might be
> Suddenly subdued to thee!
> O that all in thee might know
> Everlasting life below!
>
> Now thy mercy's wings expand,
> Stretch throughout the happy land,
> Take possession of thy home,
> Come, Divine Immanuel, come.[7]

I rode back to St. Just, and went from the evening service to a plain by the town, *made* for field-preaching. I stood on a green bank, and cried, "All we like sheep have gone astray; we have turned every one to his own way," &c. About two thousand, mostly tinners, attended, no one offering to stir, or move an hand or tongue. The fields are white unto harvest: Lord, send forth labourers! . . .

Tues., October 25th. I was much encouraged by the faith and patience of our brethren from Wednesbury [No. 71]; who gave me some of the particulars of the late persecution. My brother, they told me, had been dragged about for three hours by the mob of three towns. [. . .] The instrument of his deliverance at last was the ringleader of the mob, the greatest profligate in the country. He carried him through the river upon his shoulders. A sister they threw into it. Another's arm they broke. No farther hurt was done our people; but many of our enemies were sadly wounded.

The minister of Darlston sent my brother word, he would join with him in any measures to punish the rioters; that the meek behaviour of our people, and their constancy in suffering, convinced him the counsel was of God; and he wished all his parish Methodists.

They pressed me to come and preach to them in the midst of the town. This was the sign agreed on betwixt my brother and me: if they asked me, I was to go. Accordingly, we set out in the dark, and came to Francis Ward's, whence my brother had been carried last Thursday night. I found the brethren assembled, standing fast in one mind and spirit, in nothing terrified by their adversaries. The word given me for them was, "Watch ye, stand fast in the faith, quit yourselves like men, be strong." Jesus was in the midst, and covered us with a covering of his Spirit. Never was I before in so primitive an assembly. We sang praises lustily, and with a good courage; and could all set to our seal to the truth of our Lord's saying, "Blessed are they that are persecuted for righteousness' sake." . . .

I took several new members into the Society; and, among them, the young man whose arm was broke, and (upon trial) Munchin, the late captain of the mob. He has been constantly under the word since he rescued my brother. I asked him what he thought of him. "Think of him!" said he: "That he is a man of God; and God was on his side, when so mony of us could not kill one mon." [sic]

No. 71   Hymn: "For the Brethren at Wednesbury"[8]
(Hymns and Sacred Poems, 1749)

1   Dear dying Lamb, for whom alone
    We suffer pain, and shame, and loss,
  Hear Thine afflicted people groan,
    Crush'd by the burden of Thy cross,
  And bear our fainting spirits up,
  And bless the bitter, sacred cup.

2 Drunkards, and slaves of lewd excess,
   Bad, lawless men, Thou knowest, we lived:
The world and we were then at peace,
   No devil his own servants grieved,
Evil we did, but suffer'd none:
The world will always love its own.

3 But now we would Thy word obey,
   And strive t' escape the wrath Divine,
Exposed to all, an helpless prey,
   Bruised by our enemies, and Thine,
As sheep 'midst ravaging wolves we lie,
And daily grieve, and daily die.

4 Smitten, we turn the other cheek,
   Our ease, and name, and goods forego;
Help, or redress no longer seek
   In any child of man below;
The powers Thou didst for us ordain,
For us they bear the sword in vain.

5 But wilt Thou not at last appear,
   Into Thine hand the matter take?
We look for no protection here,
   But Thee our only refuge make,
To Thee, O righteous Judge, appeal,
And wait Thine acceptable will.

6 Thou wilt not shut Thy bowels up,
   Or justice to th' oppress'd deny;
Thy mercy's ears Thou canst not stop
   Against the mournful prisoners' cry,
Who ever make our humble moan,
And look for help to Thee alone.

7 Then help us meekly to sustain
   The cross of man's oppressive power,
To slight the shame, endure the pain,
   And calmly wait the welcome hour,
That brings the fiery chariot down,
And whirls us to our heavenly crown.

No. 72   Hymn: "The Trial of Faith"[9]
Christ also suffered, leaving us an example.

Charles's *Hymns and Sacred Poems* (1749 edition) appeared with numerous "Hymns for the Persecuted." They are coterminous with the persecutions reported in his journal entries of the mid-1740s and are consonant with the sentiments voiced there.

1 Come, O my soul, the call obey,
      Take up the burden of thy Lord!
  His practice is thy living way,
      Thy guide His pure unerring word,
  The lovely perfect pattern read,
  And haste in all His steps to tread.

2 What did my Lord from sinners bear?
      His patience is the rule for me:
  Walking in Him I cannot err:
      And lo! the Man of Griefs I see,
  Whose life one scene of sufferings was,
  Quite from the manger to the cross.

3 Here then my calling I discern
      ('Tis written in affliction's book),
  My first, and latest lesson learn,
      For nothing here but sufferings look,
  I bow me to the will Divine,
  To suffer *with* my Lord be mine.

4 To suffer as my Lord I come:
      How did the Lamb His wrongs endure?
  Clamorous, and warm? or meek, and dumb?
      Did He by force His life secure?
  His injured innocence defend;
  Or bear His burden to the end?

5 Did He evade the pain, and shame,
      Impatient of unjust disgrace?
  Did He throw off the imputed blame?
      Did He from spitting hide His face?
  Did He to man for succour fly;
  Or offer up Himself, and die?

6 When nature sunk beneath her load,
      Would He the dreadful cup decline?
  Prostrate, and bruised, and sweating blood,
      "Father, Thy will be done, not Mine,"
  He speaks, and meets His enemies,
  And gives them power Himself to seize.

7 The word, which struck them to the ground,
      Could it not strike them into hell?
  Whom all the hosts of heaven surround,
      He will not force by force repel.

"Put up," He cries, thy needless "sword,"
Nor stain the meekness of thy Lord.

8   He chides His rash disciple's zeal,
       Accepts not man's nor angel's aid:
    Vouchsafes His wounded foe to heal:
       The hands, that had His murderers made,
    He stretches out; He lets them bind
    The hands that could unmake mankind.

9   Doth He in deed or word gainsay,
       Or ask or struggle to be freed?
    They lead the speechless Lamb away;
       To scorn, and pain, and death they lead
    The speechless Lamb; resign'd unto
    The utmost earth and hell could do.

10 O that I might like Him *withstand*,
       Like Him mine innocence *clear*,
    Like Him *resist* the ruffian band,
       Like Him *refuse* the cross to bear,
    Like Him the persecutor *fly*;
    Like Him submit to live, and die?

No. 73   Journal Selections: February 3–5, 1744

Fri., February 3. I preached and prayed with the Society, and beat down the fiery, self-avenging spirit of resistance [to the violence], which was rising in some, to disgrace, if not destroy the work of God.

I preached, unmolested, within sight of Dudley. Many Shimeis *called* after me, and that was all. I waited on the friendly Captain Dudley, who has stood in the gap at Tipton-green, and kept off persecution, while it raged all around. I returned in peace through the enemy's country.

On Tuesday next, they have given it out, that they will come with all the rabble of the country, and pull down the houses, and destroy the goods of our poor brethren. One would think there was no King in Israel. There is certainly no Magistrate, who will put them to shame in anything. Mr. Constable offered to make oath of their lives being in danger; but the Justice refused it, saying, he could do nothing. Others of our complaining brethren met with the same redress, being driven away with revilings. The Magistrates do not themselves tear off their clothes, and beat them [the Methodists]; they only stand by, and see others do it. One of them told Mr. Jones, it was the best thing the mob ever did, so to treat the Methodists; and he would himself give £5 to drive them out of the country. Another, when our brother Ward begged his protection, himself delivered him up to the mercy of the mob (who half murdered him before), threw his hat round his head, and cried, "Huzza, boys! Well done! Stand up for the Church!"

No wonder that the mob, so encouraged, should say and believe that there is no law for Methodists. Accordingly, like outlaws they treat them, breaking their houses, and taking away their goods at pleasure; extorting money from those that have it, and cruelly beating those that have not.

The poor people from Darlston are the greatest sufferers. The rioters lately summoned them, by proclamation of the crier, to come to such a public house, and set to their hand that they would never hear the Methodist Preachers, or they should have their houses pulled down. About a hundred they compelled by blows. Notwithstanding which, both then and at other times, they have broken into their houses, robbing and destroying. And still if they hear any of them singing or reading the Scripture, they force them with all impunity. They watch their houses, that none may go to Wednesbury; and scarce a man or woman but has been knocked down in attempting it.

Their enemies are the basest of the people, who will not work themselves, but live, more to their inclination, on the labours of others. I wonder the gentlemen who set them on, are so shortsighted as not to see that the little all of our poor colliers will soon be devoured; and then these sons of rapine will turn upon their foolish masters, who have raised a devil they cannot lay.

Sat., February 4th. I discoursed from Isa. 54:17: "No weapon that is formed against thee shall prosper." This promise shall be fulfilled in our day. I spoke with those of our brethren who have this world's goods, and found them entirely resigned to the will of God. All thoughts of resistance are over, blessed be the Lord; and the chief of them said to me, "Naked came I into the world, and I can but go naked out of it." They are resolved by the grace of God to follow my advice, and suffer all things. Only I would have had them go round again to the Justices, and make information of their danger. Mr. Constable said, he had just been with one of them, who redressed him with the bitter reproaches; that the rest are of the same mind, and cannot plead ignorance of the intended riot, because the rioters have had the boldness to set up papers in the towns, particularly Walsal, inviting all *the country to rise with them, and destroy the Methodists.*

At noon I returned to Birmingham, having continued two days in the lions' den, unhurt.

Sun., February 5th. I preached in the Bull-ring, close to the church, where they rang the bells, threw dirt and stones all the time. None struck me, till I had finished my discourse. Then I got several blows from the mob that followed me, till we took shelter at a sister's. I received much strength and comfort with the sacrament.

I preached again in Wednesbury, to a large congregation, many of whom come to hear the word at peril of their lives. I encouraged them from Isa. 51: "Awake, awake, put on strength, O arm of the Lord," &c. Here, and in

252

CHARLES WESLEY

the Society, our Captain, we found, doth not send us a warfare at our own charge.

No. 74   Hymn: "Written After a Deliverance"[10]
(*Hymns and Sacred Poems*, 1749)

1   Jesus, Thy saving name I bless,
Deliver'd out of my distress,
   Thy faithfulness I prove;
I magnify Thy mercy's power:
My refuge in the trying hour
   Was Thy almighty love.

2   Snatch'd from the rage of cruel men,
Brought up out of the lions' den,
   And through the burning flame:
Jesus, Thine outstretch'd hand I see,
Might, wisdom, strength ascribe to Thee,
   And bless Thy saving name.

3   Hereby Thou favourest me, I know,
Because Thou wouldst not let the foe
   My hunted soul destroy:
Better than life Thy favour is,
'Tis pure delight, and perfect bliss,
   And everlasting joy.

4   Saved by a miracle of grace,
Lord, I with thankful heart embrace
   The token of Thy love:
This, this the comfortable sign,
That I the firstborn church shall join,
   And bless Thy name above.

No. 75   Hymns for the Persecuted: Hymn 1[11]
(*Hymns and Sacred Poems*, 1749)

1   Jesu, the growing work is Thine,
   And who shall hinder its success?
In vain the alien armies join,
   Thy glorious gospel to suppress,
And vow, with Satan's aid, t' o'erthrow
The work Thy grace revives below.

2   The wary world, and *Julian* wise,[12]
    Wise with the wisdom from beneath,
Awhile its *milder* malice tries,
    And lets these mad enthusiasts *breathe,*
Breathe to infect their purest air,
And spread the plague of virtue there.

3   Wondering the calm despisers stand,
    And dream that *they* the respite give:
Restrain'd by Thine o'erruling hand,
    They kindly suffer us to live,
Live, to defy their master's frown,
And turn his kingdom upside down.

4   Still the old Dragon bites his chain,
    Not yet commission'd from on high;
Rage the fierce *Pharisees* in vain,
    Away with them, the Zealots cry;
And hoary *Caiaphas* exclaims,
And *Bonner* dooms us to the flames.[13]

5   But our great God, who reigns on high,
    Shall laugh their haughty rage to scorn,
Scatter their evil with His eye,
    Or to His praise their fierceness turn;
While all their efforts to remove
His church, shall stablish her in love.

6   Yes, Lord, Thy promise-word is true,
    Our sacred hairs are number'd all;
Though earth, and hell our lives pursue,
    Without Thy leave we cannot fall:
And if Thou slack the murderer's chain,
We suffer but with Thee to reign.

7   Our sufferings shall advance Thy cause,
    And blunt the persecutor's sword,
Dispread the victory of Thy cross,
    And glorify our conquering Lord;
Evil shall work for *Sion's* good:
Its seed is still the martyr's blood.

No. 76   Journal Selection: March 14, 1744

Wed., March 14th. Setting out for J. B.'s Societies, one told me, there
was a Constable with a warrant, in which my name was mentioned. I sent

for him, and he showed it [to] me. It was "to summon witnesses to some treasonable words said to be spoken by one Westley." The poor man trembled; said he had no business with me, and was right glad to get it out of his hands. He was afterwards of my audience and wept, as did most. I was then taking horse, but found such bar or burden crossing me, that I could not stay, lest the enemies should say I durst not stand trial. I knew not how to determine [what to do] but by a lot. We prayed; and the lot come for my stay.

It was much upon my mind that I should be called to bear my testimony, and vindicate the loyalty of God's people. By the order of Providence, several Justices are now at Wakefield. A woman stands to it, that she heard me talk treason; but there is an overruling Providence. I found it hard not to pre-mediate or think of to-morrow. . . .

No. 77   Hymn: "Written in Going to Wakefield to Answer a Charge of Treason"
(*Hymns and Sacred Poems*, 1749)[14]

1   Jesu, in this hour be near,
    On Thy servant's side appear,
    Call'd Thine honour to maintain,
    Help a feeble child of man.

2   Thou who at Thy creature's bar
    Didst Thy Deity declare,
    Now my mouth and wisdom be,
    Witness for Thyself in me.

3   Gladly before rulers brought,
    Free from trouble as from thought,
    Let me Thee in them revere,
    Own Thine awful minister.

4   All of mine be cast aside,
    Anger, fear, and guile, and pride,
    Only give me from above
    Simple faith, and humble love.

5   Set my face, and fix my heart,
    Now the promised power impart,
    Meek, submissive, and resign'd
    Arm me with Thy constant mind.

6   Let me trample on the foe,
    Conquering, and to conquer go,
    Till above *his* world I rise,
    Judge th' accuser in the skies.

No. 78   Journal Selection: March 15, 1744

Thurs., March 15th. . . . I rode to Wakefield, and at eleven waited upon Justice Burton at his inn, and two other Justices, Sir Rowland Wynn, and the Rev. Mr. Zouch. I told him, I had seen a warrant of his, to summon witnesses to some treasonable words, "said to be spoken by one Westley"; that I had put off my journey to London to wait upon him, and answer whatever should be laid to my charge.

He answered, he had nothing to say against me, and I might depart. I replied, that was not sufficient, without clearing my character, and that of many innocent people, whom their enemies were pleased to call Methodists. "Vindicate them!" said my brother Clergymen: "that you will find a very hard task." I answered, "As hard as you may think it, I will engage to prove that they all, to a man, are true members of the Church of England, and loyal subjects of His Majesty King George." I then desired they would administer to me the oaths, and added, "If it was not too much trouble, I could wish, gentlemen, you would send for every Methodist in England, and give them the same opportunity you do me, of declaring their loyalty upon oath."

Justice Burton said, he was informed that we constantly prayed for the Pretender in all our Societies, or *nocturnal meetings*, as Mr. Zouch called them. I answered, "The very reverse is true. We constantly pray for His Majesty King George by name. These are such hymns as we sing in our Societies, a sermon I preached before the University, another my brother preached there, his Appeals, and a few more treatises, containing our principles and practice." Here I gave him our books, and was bold to say, "I am as true a Church-of-England man, and as loyal a subject as any man in the kingdom." "That is impossible," they cried all; but as it was not my business to dispute, and as I could not answer till the witnesses appeared, I withdrew without farther reply.

While I waited at a neighbouring house, one of the brethren brought me the Constable of Birstal, whose heart God hath touched. He told me, he had summoned the principal witness, Mary Castle, on whose information the warrant was granted, and who was setting out on horseback, when the news came to Birstal that I was not gone forward to London, as they expected, but round to Wakefield. Hearing this, she turned back, and declared to him, that she did not hear the treasonable words herself; but another woman told her so. Three more witnesses, who were to swear my words, retracted likewise, and knew nothing of the matter: the fifth, good Mr. Woods, the alehouse keeper, is forthcoming, it seems, in the afternoon.

Now I plainly see the consequence of my not appearing here to look my enemies in the face. Had I gone on my journey, here would have been witnesses enough, and oaths enough, to stir up a persecution against the Methodists. I took the witnesses' names,—Mary Castle, W. Walker, Lionel

Knowles, Arthur Furth, Joseph Woods; and a copy of the warrant, as
follows:—

> West-riding of Yorkshire.—To the Constable of Birstal, in the said Riding,
> or Deputy.
> These are, in His Majesty's name, to require and command you to summon
> Mary Castle of Birstal aforesaid, and all such persons as you are informed can
> give any information against one Westley, or any other of the Methodist
> speakers, for speaking any treasonable words or exhortations, as praying for
> the banished, or for the Pretender, &c. to appear before me, and other His
> Majesty's Justices of the Peace for the said Riding, at the White Hart in
> Wakefield, on the 15th March instant, by ten of the clock in the forenoon, to
> be examined, and to declare the truth of what they, and each of them, know,
> touching the premises; and that you likewise make a return hereof before us
> on the same day. Fail not. Given under my hand the 10th of March, 1744.
>
> E. Burton

Between two and three honest Mr. Woods came, and started back at the
sight of me, as if he had trod upon a serpent. One of our brothers took hold
on him, and told me he trembled every joint of him. The Justice's Clerk had
bid the Constable to bring him to him as soon as ever he came; but notwithstanding all the Clerk's instructions, Woods frankly confessed, now he was
come, he had nothing to say; and would not have come at all, had they not
forced him.

I waited at the door, where the Justices were examining the disaffected,
till seven. I took public notice of Mr. Oherhausen, the Moravian Teacher;
but not of Mr. Kendrick. When all their business was over, and I had been
insulted at their door from eleven in the morning till seven at night, I was
sent for, and asked, "What would Mr. Wesley desire?" Wesley. "I desire
nothing, but to know what is alleged against me?" Justice Burton said,
"What hope of truth is from him? he is another of them." Then addressing
to me, "Here are two of your brethren; one so silly, it is a shame he should
ever set up for a teacher; and the other has told us a thousand lies and
equivocations upon oath. He has not wit enough, for he would make a
complete Jesuit." I looked round, and said, "I see none of my brethren
here, but this gentleman," pointing to the Reverend Justice, who looked as
if he did not thank me for claiming him. Burton. "Why do you not know
this man?" (showing me Kendrick.) Wesley. "Yes, Sir, very well; for two
years ago I expelled him from our Society in London, for setting up for a
Preacher." To this poor Kendrick assented; which put a stop to farther
reflections on the Methodists.

Justice Burton then said I might depart, for they had nothing against me.
Wesley. "Sir, that is not sufficient: I cannot depart till my character is fully
cleared. It is no trifling matter. Even my life is concerned in the charge."
Burton. "I did not summon you to appear." Wesley. "I was the person
meant by 'one Westley,' and supposed words were the occasion of your

order, which I read, signed with your name." Burton. "I will not deny my order. I did send to summon the witnesses." Wesley. "Yes; and I took down their names from the Constable's paper. The principal witness, Mary Castle, was setting out, but, hearing I was here, she turned back, and declared to the Constable she only heard another say I spoke treason. Three more of the witnesses recanted for the same reason: and Mr. Woods, who is here, says he has nothing to say, and should not have come neither [sic], had he not been forced by the Minister. Had I not been here, he would have had enough to say; and ye would have had witnesses and oaths enough; but I suppose my coming has prevented theirs." One of the Justices added, "I suppose so too."

They all seemed satisfied, and would have had me so too; but I insisted on their hearing Mr. Woods. Burton. "Do you desire he may be called as an evidence for you?" Wesley. "I desire he may be heard as an evidence against me, if he has aught to lay to my charge." Then Mr. Zouch asked Woods what he had to say, what were the words I spoke. Woods was as backward to speak as they to hear him, but was at last compelled to say, "I have nothing to say against the gentleman; I only heard him pray that the Lord would call home his banished." Zouch. "But were there no words before or after, which pointed to these troublesome times?" Woods. "No, none at all." Wesley. "It was on February 12th, before the earliest news of the invasion. But if folly and malice may be interpreters, any words which any of you gentlemen speak may be construed into treason." Zouch. "It is very true." Wesley. "Now, gentlemen, give me leave to explain my own words. I had no thoughts of praying for the Pretender, but for those that confess themselves strangers and pilgrims upon earth, who seek a country, knowing this is not their place. The Scriptures, you, Sir, know," (to the Clergyman) "speak of us as captive exiles, who are absent from the Lord while in the body. We are not at home till we are in heaven." Zouch. "I thought you would so explain the words; and it is a fair interpretation." I asked if they were all satisfied. They said they were, and cleared me as fully as I desired.

I then asked them again to administer to me the oaths. Mr. Zouch looked on my sermon; asked who ordained me (the Archbishop and Bishop of London the same week), and said, with the rest, it was quite unnecessary, since I was a Clergyman, and Student of Christ-church, and had preached before the University, and taken the oaths before. Yet I motioned it again, till they acknowledged in explicit terms "my loyalty unquestionable." I then presented Sir Rowland and Mr. Zouch with the Appeal, and took my leave.

Half [an] hour after we set out for Birstal, and a joyful journey we had. Our Brethren met us on the road, and we gathered together on the hill, and sang praises lustily, with a good courage. Their enemies were rising at Birstal, full of the Wednesbury devil on presumption of my not finding justice at Wakefield: wherein they were more confirmed by my delay. They had begun pulling down John Nelson's house, when our singing damped and put them to flight. Now I see, if I had not gone to confront my enemies, or had been evil intreated at Wakefield, it might have occasioned a general persecution here, which the Lord hath now crushed in the birth. No weapon that is formed against us in judgment we shall condemn.

No. 79   Hymn: "Afterwards"
(*Hymns and Sacred Poems*, 1749)[15]

1   Who that trusted in the Lord
    Was ever put to shame?
Live, by heaven and earth adored,
    Thou all-victorious Lamb:
Thou hast magnified Thy power,
    Thou in my defense hast stood,
Kept my soul in danger's hour,
    And arm'd with Thy blood.

2   Satan's slaves against me rose,
    And sought my life to slay;
Thou hast baffled all my foes,
    And spoil'd them of their prey;
Thou hast cast the' accuser down,
    Hast maintain'd Thy servant's right,
Made mine innocence known,
    And clear as noonday light.

3   Evil to my charge they laid,
    And crimes I never knew;
But my Lord the snare display'd,
    And dragg'd the fiend to view;
Glared his bold malicious lie!
    Satan, show thine art again,
Hunt the precious life, and try,
    To take my soul in vain.

4   Thou, my great redeeming God,
    My Jesus still art near,
Kept by Thee, nor secret fraud,
    Nor open force I fear;
Safe amidst the snares of death,
    Guarded by the King of kings,
Glad to live, and die beneath
    The shadow of Thy wings.

No. 80   Journal Selection: July 4, 1746

Fri., July 4th. At Wendron an huge multitude listened to the invitation, "Ho, every one that thirsteth, come ye to the waters." I explained to the infant Society the design of their meeting.

NOTES

1. *P.W.*, I, p. 294.

2. *A Word in Season: Or, Advice to a Soldier*, first published in 1744, was a Wesleyan evangelistic tract directed toward those in military occupations. Since soldiers live closely with the prospect of war, the themes of death and judgment emerged prominently in John's treatise; though it turns toward ethics as well as evangelism. Cf. *JW Works*, XI, pp. 198–202.

3. *P.W.*, V, pp. 381–382.

4. "Orders" here refers to Charles's ministerial credentials.

5. "Shimei," son of Gera, was a Benjaminite who plagued King David's journey through the hill country of Judah with stones and curses; cf. 2 Sam. 16:5–13; 19:16–19. This allusion is a fine example of the way Charles identified and interpreted his life situations in the light of the biblical narratives.

6. "Fire-and-faggot minister" is an English equivalent for the revivalist "fire-and-brimstone" preacher. "Faggot" refers to a bundle of twigs, bound together to burn hotter in the hearth.

7. The hymn was later titled "Written At Land's End," and published in *Hymns and Sacred Poems*, 1749. The original is given here in its entirety. Cf. *P.W.*, V, pp. 133–134.

8. *P.W.*, V, pp. 251–253.

9. *Ibid.*, pp. 141–143.

10. The hymn was published in Charles's *Hymns and Sacred Poems*, 1749, #CXCII; cf. *P.W.*, V, p. 108.

11. Published in Charles's *Hymns and Sacred Poems*, 1749, #LXXVI; cf. *P.W.*, V, pp. 250–251.

12. The "Julian" here probably refers to Julian, emperor of Rome during 361–363. The church remembered him as "Julian the Apostate," since he did not follow the Christianity of his predecessor Constantine. An adherent to the ancient philosophies, Julian did not directly persecute the Christians through physical martyrdom; rather, he suppressed them by mockery and his liberal patronage of non-Christian teaching.

13. A myriad of interesting allusions appear in this verse. The chained "Dragon" is the eschatological destroyer from Rev. 20:1–4. The "Pharisees" is Charles's favorite metaphor for externally religious people. "Caiaphas" was the high priest who engineered the arrest and trial of Jesus (John 18). "Bonner" is Edmund Bonner (1500?–1569), a conservative Henrican bishop who opposed the growing Protestant character of the English Reformation. He was finally deprived of his see in London (1549) and imprisoned for his failure to affirm the religious reforms made under Protestant Edward VI. When Catholic Queen Mary I ascended to the English throne (1553–1558) Bonner was restored to his place of prominence. Fox's *Acts and Monuments* (1563)—more popularly known as *The Book of Martyrs*— styles the bishop "Bloody Bonner," and lays upon him the responsibility for the Protestant martyrdoms of the Marian counterreformation; a period in which nearly one thousand persons were consigned to the flames. More recent research (cf. Gina Alexander, "Bonner and the Marian Persecutions," *History*, vol. 60, 1975, pp. 374f) suggests he *was* a villain (perhaps) but not quite the monster Fox had painted him.

14. *P.W.*, V, pp. 382–383.

15. *Ibid.*, pp. 383–384.

7 / The Stillness Controversy

Charles Wesley's hymns and sermons were tools of evangelism and Christian nurture. As early Methodism was shaken by controversies his hymns also took on a polemical tone and became his ablest instruments in defending the movement. His polemical interests ranged from the issue of theodicy in *Hymns Occasioned by the Earthquakes* (1750)[1] to a matter near and dear to Charles's heart in "An Apology for the Enemies of Music."[2]

His hymns often assumed a posture that was prophetically critical toward eighteenth-century Christianity. The enlightenment's christologies drew charges of "Arians," "Socinians," and "vain philosophies" in Charles's hymns. The deists were poetically transformed into modern day Sadducees for their uneasiness about supernaturalism, while the orthodox Anglicans became "Pharisees" for their pride, arrogance, and hostility toward the Methodists.[3] His *Short Hymns on Select Passages of Scripture,* especially those based on the Gospel of Luke, decried the materialism of his age. His hymn "The Man of Fashion" was a biting criticism of the trendy gentry and their aristocratic arrogance. In a similar way religious hypocrisy, which Charles described as a "mask of piety," was often singled out for special criticism.

Four major theological controversies emerged in the Methodism of Wesley's day; two, "stillness" and "predestination," ran their course during the earliest years of the revival. Two other disputes erupted two decades later, concerning Christian perfection and Methodism's relationship with the Church of England. Although these controversies threatened to diffuse the Wesleyan revival by schism, weathering the storms of controversy clarified Methodism's social, sacramental, and Arminian theology.

Each of these four controversies endangered elements of Methodism that Charles Wesley believed to be essential, each elicited hymns of protest and ringing rebuke, and each was decisively formative for the direction Methodist doctrine would ultimately take.

From their early days in the Epworth manse, through the Holy Club at Oxford and on to the first formative years of their ministry, the Wesley brothers practiced a highly disciplined and energetic piety. William Law (who, John Wesley admitted, "was an oracle to him once") and their other contemporaries emphasized inwardness and feeling over external aids to piety like Scripture, tradition, Sacrament, and deeds of Christian love. This "mystical" posture was reinforced by the growing Moravian influence in the Fetter Lane Society, where both Wesleys and other Methodists fellowshipped with John Molther, the Moravian missionary, and others. Charles styled them "the still brethren" because of their practice of waiting in stillness for the leading of the Spirit of God. He argued that they emphasized "the inner light" over the written Word, and hence tried the Word by their spirits rather than their spirits by the Word of God. Their religion had become a matter of personal impressions rather than response to the revelation of God in active obedience. Wesley disliked their elevation of the "inner" over the outward dimension of the faith, and lamented the fact that Word, Sacrament, and Christian service were falling into disuse. Further, these opponents were "holy solitaries" so bent on introspection and self-improvement that they turned away from the needs of the neighbor and the fellowship of Christians.

The stillness controversy of the 1740s was an affront to Charles Wesley's theological symmetry, which held the inner and outer dimensions of the faith together. It was a scandal to his sacramental theology and directly contradicted to the pattern of "social holiness" that both brothers had established in the "preface" to *Hymns and Sacred Poems*, 1739 edition. The mystical epistemology also led to serious practical abuses, such as denying the people the comfort of Scripture, prayer, and Sacrament, which Charles Wesley opposed in dialogue and preaching, in poem and song.

No. 81   "Preface" to *Hymns and Sacred Poems,* 1739[4]

This preface, probably penned by John Wesley, aptly characterizes the Wesleys' dissatisfaction with the "mystic divines." It is clearly a joint statement ("we had once [held in] veneration") that epitomizes the center of the Wesleyan gospel. Charles mined much of his poetic polemic against the Moravians from this preface.

1. Some verses, it may be observed, in the following Collection, were wrote [sic] upon the scheme of the Mystic divines. And these, 'tis owned, we had once in great veneration, as the best explainers of the Gospel of Christ. But we are now convinced that we therein greatly erred: not knowing the Scriptures, neither the power of God. And because this is an error which many serious minds are sooner or later exposed to, and which indeed most easily besets those who seek the Lord Jesus in sincerity; we believe ourselves indispensably obliged in the presence of God, and angels, and men, to declare wherein we apprehend those writers not to teach the truth as it is in Jesus.

2. And first, we apprehend them to lay another foundation. They are careful indeed to pull down our own works, and to prove, that by the

deeds of the law shall no flesh be justified. But why is this? Only, to establish our own righteousness in the place of our own works. They speak largely and well against expecting to be accepted of God for our virtuous actions; and then teach, that we are to be accepted for our virtuous habits or tempers. Still the ground of our acceptance is placed in ourselves. . . . Neither our own inward nor outward righteousness is the ground of our justification. Holiness of heart, as well as of life, is not the cause, but the effect of it. The sole cause of our acceptance with God (or, that for the sake of which, on the account of which, we are accepted) is the righteousness and death of Christ, who fulfilled God's law, and died in our stead. And even the condition of it is not (as they suppose) our holiness either of heart or life: but our faith alone; faith contradistinguished from holiness as well as from good works. Other foundation therefore can no man lay, without being an adversary to Christ and His Gospel, than faith alone, though necessarily producing both, yet not including either good works or holiness.

3. But supposing them to have laid the foundation right, the manner of building thereon which they advise is quite opposite to that prescribed by Christ. He commands to *build up one another.* They advise, "To the desert, to the desert, and God will build you up." Numberless are the commendations that occur in all their writings, not of retirement intermixed with conversation, but of an entire seclusion from men (perhaps for months and years), in order to purify the soul. Whereas, according to the judgment of our Lord, and the writings of His apostles, it is only when we are knit together, that we have nourishment from Him, and increase with the increase of God. Neither is there any time when the weakest member can say to the strongest, or the strongest to the weakest, "I have no need of thee." . . . [Eph. 4:15, 16]

4. So widely distant is the manner of building up souls in Christ taught by St. Paul, from that taught by the Mystics! Nor do they differ as to the foundation, or the manner of building thereon, more than they do with regard to the superstructure. For the religion these authors would edify us in is solitary religion. If thou wilt be perfect, say they, "trouble not thyself about outward works. It is better to work virtues in the will. He hath attained the true resignation, who hath estranged himself from all outward works, that God may work inwardly in him, without any turning to outward things. . . ."

5. Directly opposite to this is the Gospel of Christ. Solitary religion is not to be found there. "Holy solitaries" is a phrase no more consistent with the Gospel than holy adulterers. The Gospel of Christ knows of no religion, but social; no holiness, but social holiness. Faith working by love is the length and breadth and depth and height of Christian perfection. This commandment have we from Christ, that he who loves God, loves his neighbor also; and that we manifest our love by doing good unto all men, especially to them that are of the household of faith. And, in truth,

whosoever loveth his brethren not in word only, but as Christ loved him, cannot be zealous of good works. He feels in his soul a burning, restless desire of spending and being spent for them. My Father, will he say, worketh hitherto, and I work: and, at all possible opportunities, he is, like his Master, going about doing good.

6. This then is the way: walk ye in it, whosoever ye are that have believed in His name. Ye know, other foundation can no man lay, than that which is laid, even Jesus Christ. Ye feel that by grace ye are saved through faith; saved from sin, by Christ formed in your hearts, and from fear, by His Spirit bearing witness with your spirit, that ye are the sons of God. Ye are taught of God, not to forsake the assembling of yourselves together, as the manner of some is; but to instruct, admonish, exhort, reprove, comfort, confirm, and every way build up one another. Ye have an unction from the Holy One, that teacheth you to renounce any other or higher perfection, than faith working by love, faith zealous of good works, faith as it hath opportunity doing good unto all men. As ye have therefore received Jesus Christ the Lord, so walk ye in Him: rooted and built up in Him, and stablished in the faith, and abounding therein more and more. . . .

No. 82   Journal Selections: August 10, 1739–April 22, 1740

Fri., August 10th [1739]. . . . To-day I carried J. Bray to Mr. Law, who resolved all his feelings and experiences into fits or natural affections, and advised him to take no notice of his comforts, which he had better be without than with. He blamed Mr. Whitefield's Journals, and way of proceeding; said, he had had great hopes, that the Methodists would have been better dispersed by little and little into livings, and have leavened the whole lump. I told him my experience. "Then am I," said he, "far below you (if you are right), not worthy to bear your shoes." He agreed to our notion of faith, but would have it, that all men held it: was fully against laymen's expounding, as the very worst thing, both for themselves and others. I told him, he was my schoolmaster to bring me to Christ; but the reason why I did not come sooner to Him, was my seeking to be sanctified before I was justified. . . .[5]

Thur., April 3d [1740]. . . . I talked with poor perverted Mr. Simpson. The still ones have carried their point. He said some were prejudiced against the Moravian brethren; and particularly against Molther: but that he had received great benefit from them. I asked whether he was *still in* the means of grace, or *out* of them. "Means of grace!" he answered; "there are none. Neither is there any good to be got by those you call such, or any obligation upon us to use them. Sometimes I go to church and Sacrament for example['s] sake: but it is a thing of mere indifference. Most of us have cast them off. You must not speak a word in recommendation of them: that is setting people upon working [out their salvation]."

What shall we say to these things? I then *said* little, but thought, "Ah, my brother! you have set the wolf to keep the sheep."

Good-Friday, April 4th. . . . After preaching, James Hutton came to fetch me to Molther, at J. Bray's. I chose rather to fast than eat; and to pray in God's house, than dispute in another's. I called with Maxfield on Molther in the afternoon. He did not much open himself; only talked in general against running after ordinances. We parted as we met, without either prayer or singing. The time for these poor exercises is past. Brother Maxfield was scandalized at their trifling; which is perfectly consistent with stillness; though Christian exhortation is not. . . .

Sat., April 5th. I spent an hour with Charles Delamotte. The Philistines have been upon him, and prevailed. He has given up the ordinances, as to their being matter of duty. Only his practice lies a little behind his faith. He uses them still.

He would not have me plead for them. "They are mere outward things. Our brethren have left them off. It would only cause divisions to bring them up again. Let them drop, and speak of the weightier matters of the law." I told him, I would hear them of their own mouth, who talked against the ordinances; first have my full evidence, and then speak and not spare. . . .

A separation I foresee unavoidable. All means have been taken to wean our friends of their esteem for us. God never used us, say they, as instruments to convert one soul. Indeed, I have just received a noble testimony of W.[illiam] Seward's to the contrary. But he and George Whitefield are reprobated for unbelievers. In a letter now received, George writes, "Remember what Luther says, 'Rather let heaven and earth come together, than one tittle of truth perish.'" . . .

Easter-day, April 6th. At the Foundery I strongly preached Christ, and the power of his resurrection, from Phi. 3:9, 10. My intention was, not to mention one word of the controverted points, till I had spoke [sic] with each of the seducers. But God ordered it better; and led me, I know not how, *in ipsam aciem et certamen* [Latin: into the very line of battle and struggle]. My mouth was opened to ask, "Who hath bewitched you, that you should let go your Saviour? that you should cast away your shield and your confidence, and deny you ever knew him?" More to this purpose I said; and then followed a burst of general sorrow. The whole congregation was in tears. I called them back to their Saviour, even *theirs*, in words which were not mine; pressed obedience to the divine ordinances; and prayed my Lord to stay his hand, and not set to his seal, unless I spake as the oracles of God. . . . I dined at Hiland's, halting between two. Bell, Simpson, and the others, when the bell rung [sic] for church, said, "It is good for us to be here." "Well, then," said I, "I will go myself, and leave you to your antichristian liberty." Upon this they started up and bore me company.

One of them told a poor man in my hearing, "That comfort you received at the sacrament was given you by the devil." I should less blasphemously have called it, the drawing of the Father, or preventing grace. . . .

I asked Bray whether he denied the ordinances to be commands. He answered indirectly, "I grant them to be great privileges." (Edmunds confessed more honestly, that he had cast them off.) Whether he had not denied George Whitefield to have faith? This question he answered by begging to be excused [from replying to] it. He denounced grievous woes against the women, for suffering Maxfield to be present, contrary to order. That order, they said, had been impressed upon them when no Minister was present; and they were threatened to be turned out, unless they consented to it. I put my brother Bray in mind of his respect for the Prophetess Lavington, to show he was not infallible.

We plainly saw his stillness ruffled; he showed it by threatening to renounce all care of the bands, till they refused Maxfield admittance. I told him I did not see what good he had done them since our leaving London: asked if he could charge me with preaching me another gospel: preferred Molther to myself, yet I declared I would not give place to him by subjection, no, not for an hour; but whosoever cast off the ordinances, I would cast off him, although he was my own brother. We concluded our conference with thanksgiving.

Below, J.[ohn] Bray asked me whether I should come to my band on Monday. I answered, "No." He modestly replied, "Then you shall be expelled."

Wed., April 9th. . . . This was to prepare us for Fetter-lane, whither I carried brother Maxfield. I was in a mild, open, loving frame. The brethren could not contain long, Hutton began with objecting to Maxfield's presence at the women's lovefeast. I spoke as reconciling as I could (but strong cannot bear with the weak); desired their prayers, that what I knew not, the Lord would show me.

James [Hutton] welcomed Maxfield by telling him, "If ever you speak to any of the women as you used to do at Bristol, you must not come here." Maxfield was the only *still* person among us. The old man [i.e. anger] rose in me; but my Lord kept me within bounds.

Simpson took upon himself next to reprove me for mentioning myself in preaching, and showing such vehemence, which was all animal [i.e. wild, or demonic] spirits. I took him up short, that I should not ask him, or any of the brethren, how an ambassador of Christ should speak. [. . .] After much thwarting, I told them they did not deserve a true Minister of Christ. James began giving me good words; but Simpson spoiled all again, by accusing me with "preaching up the ordinances." I got home, weary, wounded, and bruised, and faint, through the contradiction of sinners; *poor* sinners, as they call themselves, these heady, violent, fierce contenders for stillness. I could not bear the thought of meeting them again.

I finished Isaiah 1 at the Foundery, which led me to speak explicitly on the ordinances. God gave me great power, or, as our brethren will have it, animal spirits, sealing my words upon many hearts. . . .

Fri., April 11th. The still brethren confront me with my brother's authority, pretending that he consented not to speak of the ordinances, that is, in effect to give them up, but leave it to one's choice, whether they would use them or not. That necessity is laid upon us to walk in them, that "Do this in remembrance of me" has the nature of a command they absolutely deny. From "Woe unto having offended or stumbled one of these little ones," was no proof that he did not believe in Jesus, but a dreadful proof that the offender had better never have been born. Poor Simpson was present, but could not stand it. He withdrew dejected; I hope, shaken: for a mighty power accompanied the word. . . .

Mr. Simpson called, and laid down his two postulatums, that, 1. The ordinances are not commands. 2. It is impossible to doubt after justification. I maintained the contradictory; plainly told him, they were fighting against God, robbing Him of His glory, offending His little ones, and were under a strong delusion. . . .

Sun., April 13th. I spoke strong words of waiting for Christ *in* the use of means. In vain do our brethren dissuade. They have set the house on fire, and now say they will be quiet if I will. [. . .] I received the sacrament at St. Paul's. The last time I communicated there, was in company with our whole Society. Who hath bewitched them, that they should not obey their Saviour? A Moravian, by declaring some months ago, he had long sought Christ in the ordinances in vain; but on his leaving them off, immediately found him. [Their sinful] Nature caught the word; and our brethren cast off all the means at once. . . .

Tues., April 22d. I met Molther at M.[r] Ibison's. He expressly denies that grace, or the Spirit, is transmitted through the means, particularly through the sacrament. This, he insists, is no command; is for believers only, that is, for such that *are* sanctified, have Christ fully formed in their hearts. Faith, he teaches, is inconsistent with any following doubt, or selfish thought. Forgiveness, and the witness of the Spirit, the indwelling, the seal, are *always* given *together*. Faith, in *this* sense, is a pre-requisite of baptism. That is, the candidate must have received the Holy Ghost, must have Christ living in him, must be justified, and sanctified, must be born of God,—*in order* to—his being born of God. . . .

At Crouch's Society many were wounded. I left among them the hymn entitled, "The Means of Grace," which I have printed as an antidote to stillness. [No. 83.]

I found my brother at the Foundery, and praised God for his seasonable return. Mr. Simpson, &c., had sent for him, to stop my "preaching up the ordinances."

I attended my brother to Fetter-lane. The first hour passed in dumb show, as usual; the next in trifles not worth naming. John Bray, who seems to be a pillar, if not the main one, expelled one brother, and reproved me for not attending my band. We parted as we met, with little of singing, less of prayer, and nothing of love. However, they carried their point, which was to divert my brother from speaking.

No. 83   Hymn: "The Means of Grace"
(*Hymns and Sacred Poems*, 1739, 1740)

In this hymn, which seems to strike an autobiographical chord, Wesley steered a mediating course between the extreme of trusting the means of grace as a basis of one's acceptance before God, and the opposite extreme of avoiding them altogether. It marks an interesting juxtaposition between Charles, as "the [former] legal man" bent on working out his own salvation, and the Moravians who avoided all externals as hindrances to robust faith. In an artful *coup de grâce* Charles expounded his own sacramental theology using his opponents' stillness phraseology. The effective presence of Christ in the Eucharist ("the virtue of His blood") caused the participant to experience that genuine "stillness" that comes from an awareness of having entered the presence of God ("Be still and know that I am God"). Wesley's sacramental theology replaced the Moravian "stillness" with the awesome stillness born in a Divine-human encounter. The "means" are pressed as avenues for meeting God, rather than barriers to that redemptive encounter. The last line of the hymn drew the editorial attention of John Wesley, who reacted against the implication that Christ would drive the seeking sinner from His presence.[6] Charles's phraseology was probably connected to his doctrine of complete resignation to the will of God.

1   Long have I seem'd to serve Thee, Lord,
    With unavailing pain;
  Fasted, and pray'd and read Thy word,
    And heard it preach'd, in vain.

2   Oft did I with th' assembly join,
    And near Thine altar drew;
  A form of godliness was mine,
    The power I never knew.

3   To please Thee thus (at last I see)
    In vain I hoped and strove:
  For what are outward things to Thee,
    Unless they spring from love?

4   I see the perfect law requires
    Truth in the inward parts,
  Our full consent, our whole desires,
    Our undivided hearts.

5   But I of *means* have made my boast,
    Of *means* an idol made;

The spirit in the letter lost,
    The substance in the shade.

6 I rested in the outward law,
    Nor knew its deep design;
  The length and breadth I never saw,
    The height of love Divine.

7 Where am I now, or what my hope?
    What can my weakness do?
  JESU, to Thee my soul looks up,
    'Tis Thou must make it new.

8 Thine is the work, and Thine alone—
    But shall I idly stand?
  Shall I the written Rule disown,
    And slight my God's command?

9 Wildly shall I from Thine turn back,
    A better path to find;
  Thy holy ordinance forsake,
    And cast Thy words behind?

10 Forbid it, gracious Lord, that I
    Should ever learn Thee so!
  No—let *me* with Thy word comply,
    If I thy love would know.

11 Suffice for me, that Thou, my Lord,
    Hast bid me fast and pray:
  Thy will be done, Thy name adored;
    'Tis only mine t' obey.

12 Thou bidd'st me search the Sacred Leaves,
    And taste the hallow'd Bread:
  The kind commands my soul receives,
    And longs on Thee to feed.

13 Still for Thy loving kindness, Lord,
    I in Thy temple wait;
  I look to find Thee in Thy word,
    Or at Thy table meet.

14 Here, *in Thine own appointed ways,*
    I wait to learn Thy will:
  Silent I stand before Thy face,
    And hear Thee say, "Be still!"

15 "Be still—and know that I am God!"
    'Tis all I live to know;

To feel the virtue of Thy blood,
  And spread its praise below.

16 I wait my vigour to renew,
     Thine image to retrieve,
   The veil of outward thing pass through,
     And gasp in Thee to live.

17 I work, and own the labour vain;
     And *thus* from works I cease:
   I strive, and see my fruitless pain,
     Till God create my peace.

18 Fruitless, till Thou Thyself impart,
     Must all my efforts prove:
   They cannot change a sinful heart,
     They cannot purchase love.

19 I do the thing Thy laws enjoin,
     And *then* the strife give o'er:
   To Thee I *then* the whole resign:
     I *trust* in means no more.

20 I trust in Him who stands between
     The Father's wrath and me:
   JESU! Thou great eternal Mean,
     I look for all from Thee.

21 Thy mercy pleads, Thy truth requires,
     Thy promise call Thee down!
   Not for the sake of my desires—
     But, O! regard Thine own!

22 I seek no motive out of Thee:
     Thine own desires fulfill;
   If now Thy bowels yearn on me,
     On me perform Thy will.

23 Doom, if Thou canst, to endless pains,
     And drive me from Thy face:
   But if Thy stronger love constrains,
     Let me be *saved by grace*.

No. 84   Journal Selections: April 24–June 24, 1740

Thur., April 24. My brother spoke after my own heart. His text, "Thou
fool, that which thou sowest is not quickened, except it die." Simpson and

other disputers heard him describe that wilderness-state.[7] They will not now say that my brother and I preach different Gospels.

To the Society he demonstrated the ordinances to be both means of grace and commands of God. His power rested on us. None opened their mouth against the truth. We trust the little flock, who were following their new leaders into ruin, will now, through grace, come back again.

Fri., April 25th. . . . I sent a friend at Bristol the following account:— "My brother came most critically. The snare, we trust, will now be broken and many simple souls delivered. Many here [London] insist that a part of their Christian calling is liberty *from* obeying, not liberty *to* obey. The unjustified, say they, are *to be still;* that is, not to search the Scriptures, not to pray, not to communicate, not to do good, to endeavour, not to desire: for it is impossible to use means without trusting in them. Their practice is agreeable to their principles. Lazy and proud themselves, bitter and censorious toward others, they trample upon the ordinances, and despise the commands of Christ. I see no middle point wherein we can meet."

Tues., May 13th. . . . I met the men Leaders at Bray's, and was surprised to find about twenty of the still brethren there; and more, to hear they constantly meet on Thursday and Sunday, while I am preaching at the Foundery. The reason is obvious.

I bore my testimony for the ordinances and weak faith. Asked whether they did not hold, 1. That the means of grace are neither commands nor means; 2. That forgiveness is never given but together with the abiding witness of the Spirit? James Hutton would not have them give me any answer. I said, if they durst not avow their principles, I should take their silence for confession, and warn God's people against them.

Tues., May 20th. . . . I went with Maxfield to Bray's, as a fool to the correction of stocks. I laboured for peace: but only the Almighty can root out those cursed tares of pride, contempt, and self-sufficiency, with which our Moravianized brethren are overrun.

Thur., May 29th. I expounded Isa. 58, a chapter most contradictory to the doctrine of our [still] brethren. I dined at friend Keen's, a Quaker and a Christian; and read George Whitefield's account of God's dealings with him.[8] The love and esteem he expresses for me filled me with confusion, and brought back my fear, lest, after having preached to others, I should be myself cast-away. . . .

Fri., May 30th. I had yet another conference, but could not convince our dear brother Simpson. He cannot allow there are more than four Christians in London, which are Molther, M. Eusters, Wheeler's maid, and Bell. Of the last he roundly affirms, that he is holier than Moses, the meekest of men; than Abraham, the friend of God; than David, the man after God's own heart; than Elijah and Enoch, who walked with God, and were translated. As to our father Abraham, he denies him to have had any right faith at all.

Mon., June 9th. I dined at Mr. Wild's, in Islington, and rejoiced over a few *unperverted* souls. The shepherd, alas, is smitten, and the sheep are scattered; but not all. God has left himself a very small remnant.

Wed., June 11th. I was constrained to bear my testimony for the last time at [Delamotte's in] Blendon. . . . I rode on softly to Eltham, cast out by my dearest friends. I pray God it may not be laid to theirs, or their seducers', charge! . . .

I returned to be exercised by our *still* brethren's contradiction. My brother proposed new-modelling the bands, and setting by themselves those few who were still for the ordinances. Great clamour was raised by this proposal. The noisy *still*-ones well knew that they had carried their point, by wearying out the sincere ones, scattered among them, one or two in a band of disputers, who had harassed and sawn them asunder; so that a remnant is scarcely left. They grudged us even this remnant, which would soon be all their own, unless immediately rescued out of their hand. Benjamin Ingham seconded us; and obtained that the name should be called over, and as many as were aggrieved put into new bands.

We gathered up our wreck,—*raros nantes in gurgite vasto* [Latin: swimmers appear here and there in the vast eddy][9] for nine out of ten are swallowed up in the dead sea of stillness. Oh, why was not this done six months ago? How fatal was our delay and false moderation! "Let them alone, and they will soon be weary, and come to themselves of course," said one,—*unus qui nobis cunctando resitituet rem!* [Latin: One man restored the state to us by delaying!][10] I tremble at the consequence. Will they submit themselves to every ordinance of man, who refuse subjection to the ordinances of God? I told them plainly I SHOULD ONLY CONTINUE WITH THEM SO LONG AS THEY CONTINUED IN THE CHURCH OF ENGLAND. My every word was grievous to them. I am a thorn in their sides, and they cannot bear me.

They *modestly* denied that we had any by hearsay proof of their denying the ordinances. I asked them all and every one, particularly Bray, Bell, &c., whether they would now acknowledge them to be commands or duties; whether they sinned in omitting them; whether they did not leave it to every man's fancy to use them or not; whether they did not exclude all from the Lord's table, excepting those who *they* called believers. These questions I put too close to be evaded; . . . Honest Bell and some others insisted upon their antichristian liberty. The rest put by their stillness, and delivered me over to Satan for a blasphemer, a very Saul (for to him they compare me), out of blind zeal persecuting the church of Christ.

Thur., June 19th. . . . By noon we came to Oxford. I called M. Ford, and found her shut up. She besought me *not to speak* in the Society, not to make disturbances and divisions, &c. I told her, I spoke no other words than I had from the beginning; whence then her unusual apprehensions? Mr. Simpson's presence accounted for it. Wherever he comes, his first business is to supplant us, which he does by insinuating himself, under the appearance of our friend.

To the Society I described the stillness of the first Christians (Acts 2:42) who continued *in* the Apostles' doctrine, and *in* fellowship, and *in* breaking of bread, and *in* prayers.

Tues., June 24th. I preached Christ, the way, the truth, and the life, to one thousand little children at Kingswood. At the room I proceeded in St. John. Some were present who fancy themselves elect, and therefore sink back into their old habits. Without meddling in the dispute, I rebuked them sharply, and yet in much love. I read my Journal to the bands, as an antidote to stillness.

No. 85   Hymn: "The Love Feast"
(*Hymns and Sacred Poems*, 1739, 1740)

This is a portion of a long hymn (five parts, four verses in each part) that stems from the stillness controversy. It opposes the separatist tendencies and depreciation of the "ordinances" prevalent among the "Moravianized Methodists."[11]

Part III

1   Let us join ('tis God commands),
    Let us join our hearts and hands;
    Help to gain our calling's hope,
    Build we each the other up.

    God His blessing shall dispense,
    God shall crown His ordinance,
    Meet in His appointed ways,
    Nourish us with social grace.

2   Let us as brethren love,
    Faithfully His gifts improve,
    Carry on the earnest strife,
    Walk in holiness of life.

    Still forget the things behind,
    Follow Christ in heart and mind,
    Toward the mark unwearied press,
    Seize the crown of righteousness.

3   Plead we thus for faith *alone*,
    Faith which by our works is shown;
    God it is who justifies,
    Only faith the grace *applies*,—

    Active faith that lives within,
    Conquers hell, and death, and sin,

Hallows whom it first made whole,
Forms the Saviour in the soul.

4 Let us for this faith contend,
   Sure salvation is its end;
   Heaven already is begun,
   Everlasting life is won:

   Only let us persevere
   Till we see our Lord appear,
   Never from the Rock remove,
   Saved by faith which works by love.

No. 86 Hymn: "The Bloody Issue Cured"
(*Hymns and Sacred Poems*, 1749)

This hymn was appended to the fourth installment of Charles's published journal, which suggests it was composed between 1740 and 1744; it was written during the Moravian controversy and then republished in *Hymns and Sacred Poems*, 1749 edition. In this treatment Wesley described the Lord's Supper using an analogy based on the pericope of the woman with a hemorrhage (Matt. 9:20–23). Just as Jesus healed the woman through the instrument of her touching the hem of His garment, so also He heals our sin and separation through His sacramental ordinance. A magical view of the Eucharist is eschewed in favor of Charles's christocentric approach, based on the effective presence of Christ in the sacramental event. Verse eight criticizes "the thoughtless throng" who will not use the means whereby the contemporary Christian might follow the pattern of the woman, using the means of grace to touch Christ.

1 How shall a sinner come to God?
   A fountain of polluted blood
      For years my plague hath been;
   From *Adam* the infection came,
   My nature is with his the same,
      The same with his my sin.

2 In me the stubborn evil reigns,
   The poison spreads throughout my veins;
      A loathsome sore disease
   Makes all my soul and life unclean,
   My every word, work, thought is sin,
      And desperate wickedness.

3 Long have I lived in grief and pain,
   And suffer'd many things in vain,
      And all physicians tried;

Nor men nor means my soul can heal,
The plague is still incurable,
  The fountain is undried.

4 No help can I from these receive,
Nor men nor means can e'er relieve,
  Or give my spirit ease;
Still worse and worse my case I find;
Here then I cast them all behind,
  From all my works I cease.

5 I use, but *trust* in means no more,
Give my self-saving labours o'er,
  Th' unequal task forbear;
My strength is spent, my strife is past,
Hardly I give up all at last,
  And yield to self-despair.

6 I find brought in a better hope,
Succour there is for me laid up,
  For every helpless soul;
Salvation is in Jesu's name,
Could I but touch His garment's hem,
  Even I should be made whole.

7 His body doth the cure dispense,
His garment is the ordinance
  In which He deigns t' appear;
The word, the prayer, the broken bread,
Virtue from Him doth here proceed,
  And I shall find Him here.

8 I follow'd with the thoughtless throng,
And press'd, and crowded Him too long,
  And weigh'd Him down with sin;
But *Him* I did not hope to *touch*,
I never used the means as *such*,
  Or look'd to be made clean.

9 The spirit of an healthful mind
I waited not in them to find,
  The Bread that comes from heaven;
Beyond my form I did not go,
The power of godliness to know,
  And feel my sins forgiven.

10 But now I seek to touch my Lord,
To hear His whisper in the word,
  To feel His Spirit blow;

To catch the love of which I read,
To taste Him in the mystic bread,
    And all His sweetness know.

11 'Tis here, in hope my God to find,
With humble awe I come behind,
    And wait His grace to prove;
Before His face I dare not stand,
But faith puts forth a trembling hand,
    To apprehend His love.

12 Surely His healing power is nigh;
I touch Him now! by faith ev'n I,
    My Lord, lay hold on Thee:
Thy power is present now to heal,
I feel, through all my soul I feel
    That Jesus died for me.

13 Issues from Thee a purer flood,
The poison'd fountain of my blood
    Is a moment dried;
The sovereign antidote takes place,
And I am freely saved by grace,
    And I am justified.

14 I glory in redemption found:
Jesus, my Lord, and God, look round,
    The conscious sinner see;
'Tis I have touch'd Thy clothes, and own
The miracle Thy grace hath done,
    On such a worm as me.

15 Behold me prostrate at Thy feet,
And hear me thankfully repeat
    The mercies of my God!
I felt from Thee the medicine flow,
I tell Thee all the truth, and show
    The virtue of Thy blood.

16 With lowly reverential fear
I testify, that Thou art near
    To all who seek Thy love;
Saviour of all I Thee proclaim;
The world may know Thy healing name,
    And all its wonders prove.

17 Speak then once more, and tell my soul,
Sinner, thy faith hath made thee whole,
    Thy plague of sin is o'er;

Be perfected in holiness,
Depart in everlasting peace,
    Depart, and sin no more.

The Wesleys' *Hymns on the Lord's Supper*, of 1745, should also be read against the backdrop of the stillness controversy and its concomitant impact upon Methodism's eucharistic theology. The 166 eucharistic hymns, published along with an extract from Dr. Brevint's "The Christian Sacrament and Sacrifice" as their introduction, stand as a monument to the Wesleys' belief that sound theology is the best apologetic response. Hymn #LXXXVI (No. 98 below) is as direct a polemic against the Moravianized Methodists as appears in the collection. The brothers published the hymnal jointly, perhaps to squelch rumors of their own division over sacramentology, and to rule out the possibility of opponents attempting to use one Wesley's authority against the other. The title page carries both their names, and beneath them the identification "Presbyters of the Church of England," as if to remind the reader of Methodism's connection with the established church and her sacraments in the face of an opposition party that hoped to sever both connections.[12]

No. 87 Eucharistic Hymn: II

1 In this expressive bread I see
   The wheat by man cut down for me,
       And beat, and bruised, and ground:
   The heavy plagues, and pains, and blows,
   Which Jesus suffer'd from His foes,
       Are in this emblem found.

2 The bread dried up and burnt with fire
   Presents the Father's vengeful ire,
       Which my Redeemer bore:
   Into His bones the fire He sent,
   Till all the flaming darts were spent,
       And Justice ask'd no more.

3 Why hast Thou, Lord, forsook Thine own?
   Alas! what evil hath He done,
       The spotless Lamb of God?
   Cut off, not for Himself, but me,
   He bears my sins on yonder tree,
       And pays my debt in blood.

4 Seized by the rage of sinful man
   I see Him bound, and bruised, and slain;
       'Tis done, the Martyr dies!
   His life to ransom ours is given,

And lo! the fiercest fire of heaven
Consumes the Sacrifice.

No. 88   Eucharistic Hymn: VIII

1   Come, to the supper, come,
        Sinners, there still is room;
    Every soul may be His guest,
        Jesus gives the general word;
    Share the monumental feast,
        Eat the supper of your Lord.

2   In this authentic sign
        Behold the stamp Divine:
    Christ revives His sufferings here,
        Still exposes them to view;
    See the Crucified appear,
        Now believe He died for you.

No. 89   Eucharistic Hymn: XXVIII
Sec. II. "As it is a Sign and Means of Grace"

1   Author of our salvation, Thee
        With lowly thankful hearts we praise,
    Author of this great mystery,
        Figure and means of saving grace.

2   The sacred, true, effectual sign,
        Thy body and Thy blood it shows;
    The glorious instrument Divine
        Thy mercy and Thy strength bestows.

3   We see the blood that seals our peace,
        Thy pardoning mercy we receive:
    The bread doth visibly express
        The strength through which our spirits live.

4   Our spirits drink a fresh supply,
        And eat the bread so freely given,
    Till borne on eagle's wings we fly,
        And banquet with our Lord in heaven.

No. 90   Eucharistic Hymn: XXIX

1   O Thou who this mysterious bread
        Didst in *Emmaus* break,

Return, herewith our souls to feed,
And to Thy followers speak.

2 Unseal the volume of Thy grace,
Apply the gospel word,
Open our eyes to see Thy face,
Our hearts to know the Lord.

3 Of Thee we commune still, and mourn
Till Thou the veil remove;
Talk with us, and our hearts shall burn
With flames of fervent love.

4 Enkindle now the heavenly zeal,
And make Thy mercy known,
And give our pardon'd souls to feel
That God and love are one.

No. 91   Eucharistic Hymn: XXXIII

1 Jesu, dear, redeeming Lord,
Magnify Thy dying word;
In Thy ordinance appear,
Come, and meet Thy followers here.

2 In the rite Thou has enjoin'd
Let us now our Saviour find,
Drink Thy blood for sinners shed,
Taste Thee in the broken bread.

3 Thou our faithful hearts prepare,
Thou Thy pardoning grace declare;
Thou that hast for sinners died,
Show Thyself the Crucified.

4 All the power of sin remove,
Fill us with Thy perfect love,
Stamp us with the stamp Divine,
Seal our souls for ever Thine.

No. 92   Eucharistic Hymn: XLVII

1 Jesu, Thy weakest servants bless,
Give what these hallow'd signs express,
And, what Thou givest, secure;
Pardon into my soul convey,
Strength in Thy pardoning love to stay,
And to the end endure.

2 Raise, and enable me to stand,
Save out of the destroyer's hand
This helpless soul of mine;
Vouchsafe me then Thy strengthening grace,
And with the arms of love embrace,
And keep me ever Thine.

No. 93   Eucharistic Hymn: LIII

1 O God of truth and love,
Let us Thy mercy prove;
Bless Thine ordinance Divine,
Let it now effectual be,
Answer all its great design,
All its gracious ends in me.

2 O might the sacred word
Set forth our dying Lord,
Point us to Thy sufferings past,
Present grace and strength impart,
Give our ravish'd souls a taste,
Pledge of glory in our heart.

3 Come in Thy Spirit down,
Thine institution crown;
Lamb of God, as slain appear,
Life of all believers Thou,
Let us now perceive Thee near,
Come, Thou Hope of glory, now.

No. 94   Eucharistic Hymn: LIV

1 Why did my dying Lord ordain
This dear memorial of His love?
Might we not all by faith obtain,
By faith the mountain sin remove,
Enjoy the sense of sins forgiven,
And holiness, the taste of heaven?

2 It seem'd to my Redemer good
That faith should *here* His coming wait,
Should here receive immortal food,
Grow up in Him Divinely great,
And, fill'd with holy violence, seize
The glorious crown of righteousness.

3 Saviour, Thou didst the mystery give,
    That I Thy nature might partake;
Thou bidd'st me outward signs receive,
    One with Thyself my soul to make;
My body, soul, and spirit to join
Inseparably one with Thine.

4 The prayer, the fast, the word conveys,
    When mix'd with faith, Thy life to me;
In all the channels of Thy grace
    I still have fellowship with Thee:
But chiefly here my soul is fed
With fullness of immortal bread.

5 Communion closer far I feel,
    And deeper drink th' atoning blood;
The joy is more unspeakable,
    And yields me larger draughts of God,
The nature faints beneath the power,
And faith fill'd up can hold no more.

No. 95   Eucharistic Hymn: LVII

1 O the depth of love Divine,
    Th' unfathomable grace!
Who shall say how bread and wine
    God into man conveys!
How the bread His flesh imparts,
    How the wine transmits His blood,
Fills His faithful people's hearts
    With all the life of God!

2 Let the wisest mortal show
    How we the grace receive,
Feeble elements bestow
    A power not theirs to give.
Who explains the wondrous way,
    How through these the virtue came?
These the virtue did convey,
    Yet still remain the same.

3 How can heavenly spirits rise,
    By earthly matter fed,
Drink herewith Divine supplies,
    And eat immortal bread?
Ask the Father's Wisdom *how*;
    Him that did the means ordain!

Angels round our altars bow
  To search it out in vain.

4 Sure and real is the grace,
     The manner be unknown;
   Only meet us in Thy ways,
     And perfect us in one.
   Let us taste the heavenly powers;
     Lord, we ask for nothing more:
   Thine to bless, 'tis only ours
     To wonder and adore.

No. 96   Eucharistic Hymn: LXVI

1 Jesu, my Lord and God, bestow
   All which Thy sacrament doth show,
     And make the real sign
   A sure effectual means of grace,
   Then sanctify my heart, and bless,
     And make it all like Thine.

2 Great is Thy faithfulness and love,
   Thine ordinance can never prove
     Of none effect, and vain;
   Only do Thou my heart prepare
   To find Thy real presence there,
     And all Thy fullness gain.

No. 97   Eucharistic Hymn: LXXII

1 Come, Holy Ghost, Thine influence shed,
     And realize the sign;
   Thy life infuse into the bread,
     Thy power into the wine.

2 Effectual let the tokens prove,
     And made, by heavenly art,
   Fit channels to convey Thy love,
     To every faithful heart.

No. 98   Eucharistic Hymn: LXXXVI

1   And shall I let Him go?
           If now I do not *feel*
   The streams of living water flow,
           Shall I forsake the well?

2   Because He hides His face,
        Shall I no longer stay,
But leave the channels of His grace,
        And cast the means away?

3   Get thee behind me, fiend,
        On others try thy skill,
Here let thy hellish whispers end,
        To thee I say, *Be still!*

4   Jesus hath spoke the word,
        His will my reason is;
Do this in memory of thy Lord,
        Jesus hath said, *Do this!*

5   He bids me eat the bread,
        He bids me drink the wine;
No other motive, Lord, I need,
        No other word than Thine.

6   I cheerfully comply
        With what my Lord doth say;
Let others ask a reason why,
        My glory is t' obey.

7   His will is good and just:
        Shall I His will withstand?
If Jesus bids me lick the dust,
        I bow at His command.

8   Because He saith, *Do this,*
        This I will always do;
Till Jesus come in glorious bliss,
        I *thus* His death will *show.*

No. 99   Eucharistic Hymn: CXXIII

1   O Thou whose offering on the tree
        The legal offerings all foreshow'd,
Borrow'd their whole effects from Thee,
        And drew their virtue from Thy blood:
The blood of goats and bullocks slain
        Could never for one sin atone:
To purge the guilty offerer's stain
        Thine was the work, and *Thine* alone.

2   Vain in themselves their duties were,
        Their services could never please,

Till join'd with Thine, and made to share
   The merits of Thy righteousness;
Forward they cast a faithful look
   On Thy approaching sacrifice,
And thence their pleasing savour took,
   And rose accepted in the skies.

3 Those feeble types and shadows old
   Are all in Thee, the Truth, fulfill'd,
And through this sacrament we hold
   The substance in our hearts reveal'd;
By faith we see Thy sufferings past
   In this mysterious rite brought back,
And on Thy grand oblation cast
   Its saving benefit partake.

4 Memorial of Thy sacrifice,
   This Eucharistic mystery
The full atoning grace supplies,
   And sanctifies our gifts in Thee:
Our persons and performance please,
   While God in Thee looks down from heaven,
Our acceptable service sees,
   And whispers all our sins forgiven.

No. 100   Eucharistic Hymn: CXLII

1   Come we that record
        The death of our Lord,
        The death let us bear,
By faithful remembrance His sacrifice share.

2   Shall we let our God groan
        And suffer alone?
        Or to *Calvary* fly,
And nobly resolve with our Master to die?

3   His servants shall be
        With Him on the tree,
        Where Jesus was slain
His crucified servants shall always remain.

4   By the cross we abide
        Where Jesus hath died,
        To all we are dead;
The members can never outlive their own Head.

5   Poor penitents, we
         Expect not to see
         His glory above,
Till first we have drank of the cup of His love;

6   Till first we partake
         The cross for His sake,
         And thankfully own
The cup of His love and His sorrow are one.

7   Conform'd to His death
         If we suffer beneath,
         With Him we shall know
The power of His first resurrection below.

8   If His death we receive,
         His life we shall live;
         If His cross we sustain,
His joy and His crown we in heaven shall gain.

No. 101   Eucharistic Hymn: CXLV

1   Father, into Thy hands alone
       I have my all restored,
    My all, Thy property I own,
       The steward of the Lord.

2   Hereafter none can take away
       My life, or goods, or fame;
    Ready at Thy demand to lay
       Them down I always am.

3   Confiding in Thy only love
       Through Him who died for me,
    I wait Thy faithfulness to prove,
       And give back all to Thee.

4   Take when Thou wilt into Thy hands,
       And as Thou wilt require;
    Resume by the *Sabean* bands,
       Or devouring fire.

5   Determined all Thy will t' obey,
       Thy blessings I restore;
    Give, Lord, or take Thy gifts away,
       I praise Thee evermore.

NOTES

1. These hymns were published in two *Hymns Occasioned by the Earthquakes* (1750). There are a total of thirty "Hymns for Earthquakes" in the two collections. Cf. *P.W.* VI, pp. 73–96.

2. *P.W.* VIII, p. 444.

3. Cf. *P.W.* XII, p. 402, #2916.

4. For the full text of this "Preface," cf. *P.W.* I, pp. ix–xxiii.

5. The reversal of the order of salvation, placing sanctification prior to justification, indicates that Charles linked William Law with the "mystical divines" who laid the foundation of their faith in themselves.

6. John Wesley's open letter to Mr. Church, "The Principles of a Methodist Father Explained" (*JW Works,* VIII, pp. 435–436). Church objected to the connection drawn between "grace" and "pain" in verse 20 of the hymn, charging "stoic insensibility." John replied by completing the verses Church cited, and setting the hymn in the larger context, an encounter with God. cf. *P.W.* I, pp. 233–236.

7. "The Wilderness State" was a Wesleyan allusion drawn from the Exodus narrative of wilderness wanderings, and it became a soteriological allegory for the progress of a pilgrim in faith. Having been delivered by faith, the pilgrims have not yet fully entered into their perfect rest and are "tempted and tormented." John Wesley's sermon by the same title (*JW Works,* VI, pp. 77–91) offered an apt explanation:

> . . . After God had wrought a great deliverance for Israel, by bringing them out of the house of bondage, they did not immediately enter into the land which he had promised to their fathers; but "wandered out of the way in the wilderness," and were variously tempted and distressed. In like manner, after God has delivered them that fear him from the bondage of sin and Satan; after they are "justified by his grace, through the redemption that is in Jesus," yet not many of them immediately enter into "the rest which remaineth for the people of God." The greater part of them wander, more or less, out of the good way into which he had brought them. They come, as it were, into a "waste and howling desert," where they are variously tempted and tormented. And this, some, in allusion to the case of the Israelites, have termed, "a wilderness state" [pp. 77–78].

8. Thomas Keen, whom Wesley described as "a mild and candid Quaker," was converted under Charles Wesley's preaching on August 7, 1739. The following year Keen penned this letter to encourage his "father" in the faith while he was in the throes of the "stillness" controversy.

> May 15th, 1740. My Friend,—I hear there are divisions among you; for some say, "I am of Wesley"; and others, "I am of Molther." But I say, "I am of Christ; and what He bids me to do, I will do, and not trust in any man." Here some will say, "What Christ bids you do, is, to believe, and *be still*"; but does He bid me to do nothing else? He bids me so "let my light shine before men, that they may glorify my Father which is in heaven." He likewise says, "The Scribes and Pharisees sit in Moses's chair: all, therefore, whatsoever they bid you observe, that observe and do." But how can I know what they bid me do, except I go to hear them? Again, Christ bids me observe all things which He commands the Apostles; and with such He will be to the end of the world: but if I do not observe and do his commands, He will not be with me. He bids me "do this in remembrance of" Him. Now, if any man can prove this is not a command, I will obey it no longer. But whosoever "breaketh one of these least commandments, and teacheth men so, shall be called least in the kingdom of heaven."
>
> As to *stillness,* our Saviour saith, "The kingdom of heaven suffereth violence, and the violent take it by force"; and "Strive to enter in at the strait gate." And St. Paul saith, "Work out your own salvation with fear and trembling"; and "God is a rewarder of them that diligently seek Him." Now, these scriptures imply somewhat more than barely sitting still. Some deny that there are any means of grace; but I will be thankful for them, since it was in them I first heard you preach faith in Christ; and, had I not been there, I must have been without faith to this day. One

told me, when you preached, you had nature in your face. So will every one who speaks with zeal; but no matter for that, if he has but grace in his heart.

My friend, there are many teachers, but few fathers. But you are my father, who begat me by the Gospel; and, I trust, many more. May the Lord lead you into all truth! So prays your friend. [Cf. Thomas Jackson, *Life of Charles Wesley, op. cit.*, I, p. 221.]

9. This journal entry describes "the new-ordering" of the Methodist societies, and a formal separation with the Moravians. Charles quotes from Vergil's *Aeneid*, I, verse 118, to describe the plight of the Methodist swimmers in the dead sea of "stillness." I am grateful to my colleague Dr. Gordon Stockin for identification of this verse and the one that follows in note 10.

10. This saying is from the early Latin poet, Quintus Ennius, who wrote the *Annales*. The line above is from book 12, describing how Quintus Fabius Maximus Cunctator saved Rome during the second war with Carthage by delaying the invaders in the narrow mountain passes, and thereby depleting the Cathaginian troops before they reached Rome. As the title suggests, the Romans remembered Quintus Fabius as the "Cunctator," or "delayer." In this case Charles remembers with regret someone (probably John Wesley) having used this saying to justify delay in dealing with the Moravianized Methodists.

11. Cf. *P.W.*, I, pp. 350–356, for the full text of this hymn.

12. Cf. *P.W.* III, pp. 181–342, for a reprint of this hymnal.

8 / The Predestination Controversy

The second major theological dispute to arise in early Methodism that elicited Wesleyan hymns and shaped Methodist doctrine had its locus in the emergence of a so-called predestinarian party. There are hints of predestinarian sentiments among the Methodists from the very beginning of the movement, as George Whitefield, one of the great preachers of the revival, took a Reformed posture from the outset. By November of 1740 the two soteriological perspectives threatened to divide Methodism. The Wesleys' Kingswood school in Bristol became a center of predestinarian theology as John Cennick, a closet Calvinist, emerged as leader of the predestinarian party by December 6, 1740.

While the Wesleys had been advocates of Arminian soteriology from their Oxford days, Charles's opposition to the emergence of predestinarian theology within Methodism had practical concerns attached to it. The emergence of a second "party" foreshadowed further dispute and possible division in the fledgling movement at the same time the "stillness" controversy was raging in London. But beyond his obvious concern for unity was what Charles termed the "narrow spirit" of the predestinarians. This phrase was a sort of theological pun, since their conception of the scope of atonement extended it only to the "elect," and was hence narrower than Charles's doctrine of the unlimited efficacy of Christ's death. For Charles, this same "narrowness" manifested itself in the dimensions of their Christian concern; he seemed to connect the doctrine of the limited atonement with elitism or spiritual arrogance among the self-styled elect. Contrariwise, for those uncertain in their faith the narrow gospel amounted to an attack on their assurance or comfort. Hence Charles's journal records several counseling sessions with those who had been "grievously tormented with the spirit of reprobation." Antinomianism was another danger Charles saw in the predestinarian party, and his journal chronicles instances in which the naive or simple-minded turned unconditional election into a license that guaranteed redemption despite one's moral or practical abuses. Charles's most characteristic weapons in the fray were his hymns and homilies, though he occasionally relied on his Oxford rhetorical training to debate an opponent into submission.

The controversy continued through the 1740s, but was particularly heated in the

287

opening years of the decade. The Wesleys and Whitefield eventually separated, only to be reunited near the end of their lives. The hymnal entitled *Hymns on God's Everlasting Love* (1741) grew out of this debate and still smolders with some of the heat it generated. By the end of the decade the intensity of the dispute had waned, and in his later years Charles preached his Arminian doctrines constructively and without the polemical pointedness of the earlier years; hence, he wrote, "I warn them against that sweet doctrine, 'once in grace, always in grace,' but not in a controversial way. . . ."[1]

The predestinarian controversy was formative for Methodism in setting Arminian parameters on the *dimensions* of God's grace while still coming "to the very edge of Calvinism" when considering the Divine initiative in redemption.[2] Even more significant, in opposition to what he termed "the horrible decree" of reprobation, Charles generated hymns that emphasized free grace, unbounded love, and the walk of careful discipleship (conditional election). Hence, several of those emphases that would come to characterize Wesleyan theology were consolidated and sharpened through the predestinarian controversy.

No. 102   Journal Selections: September 22, 1738– December 6, 1740

Fri., September 22d [1738]. At Bray's I expounded Eph. 1. A dispute arising about absolute predestination, I entered my protest against that doctrine.

Fri., June 22d [1739]. The sower of tares is beginning to trouble us with disputes about predestination. My brother was wonderfully owned at Wapping last week, while asserting the contrary truth. To-night I asked in prayer, that if God would have all men to be saved, he would show some token for good upon us. Three were justified in immediate answer to that prayer. We prayed again; several fell down under the power of God, present to witness his universal love.

Sat., September 22d [1739]. . . . In the afternoon I spoke a word of caution to one who seems strong in the faith, and begins to be lifted up; the sure effect of her growing acquaintance with some of Calvin's followers.

In the bowling-green I showed the nature and life of faith from Gal. 2:20; and then justification by faith alone, at the Hall. Two Clergymen were present. I proved from Scripture, and our own Church, that all were Papists, Pharisees, Antichrists, and accursed, who brought any other doctrine. Some of my hearers were forced to turn their backs.

Tues., July 29th [1740]. One, pestered with the Predestinarians, desired me to expound Rom. 9. I did, through Christ strengthening me, in an extraordinary manner. The poor creature Wildboar contradicted and blasphemed, and even *called for damnation upon his own soul, if Christ died for all, and if God was willing that all men should be saved.* The power of the Lord was present so much the more. Many believed in their heart, and made confession with their mouth, of Jesus Christ the Saviour of all men. I have not known a more triumphant night since I knew Bristol.

Tues., October 28th. . . . I was led in the evening to preach universal redemption from those words, "The Lord is not willing that any should perish, but that all should come to repentance." The Spirit mightily confirmed that irresistible truth.

Sun., November 30th. . . . I expounded the lesson at Kingswood. It was Hebrews 6.[3] I prayed Christ our Teacher to enlighten the people and me; and began my discourse with fear and trembling. The Spirit gave me utterance. I calmly warned them against apostasy, and spake with great tenderness and caution. But who can stand before envy and bigotry? The strong ones were offended. The poison of Calvin has drunk up their spirit of love. Anne Ayling and Anne Davis could not refrain from railing. John Cennick never offered to stop them. Alas! we have set the wolf to keep the sheep! God gave me great moderation toward him, who, for many months, has been undermining our doctrine and authority.

Tues., December 2d. I had a conference in Kingswood with Mr. Cennick and his friends, but could come to no agreement, though I offered entirely to drop the controversy if he would.

Sat., December 6th. I wrote my brother a full account of the predestinarian party, their practices and designs, particularly "to have a church within themselves, and to give themselves the sacrament in bread and water."

No. 103:   Letter to John Cennick (December 1740[?])[4]
(Jackson's *Life of Charles Wesley*, 1841)

My Dearest Brother, John Cennick,—In much love and tenderness I speak. You came to Kingswood upon my brother's sending for you. You served under him in the Gospel as a son. I need not say how well he loved you. You used the authority he gave you to overthrow his doctrine. You everywhere contradicted it. Whether true or false, is not the question: but you ought first to have fairly told him, "I preach contrary to you. Are you willing notwithstanding, that I should continue in your house gainsaying you? If you are not, I have no place in these regions. You have a right to this open dealing. I now give you fair warning. Shall I stay here opposing you, or shall I depart?"

My brother, have you dealt thus honestly and openly with him? No; but you have stolen away the people's heart from him. And when some of them basely treated their best friend, God only excepted, how patiently did you take it! When did you ever vindicate us, as we have you? Why did you not plainly tell them?—"You are eternally indebted to these men. Think not that I will stay among you, to head a party against my dearest friend—and brother, as he suffers me to call him, having humbled himself for my

sake, and give me (no Bishop, Priest, or Deacon) the right hand of fellowship. If I hear that one word more is spoken against him, I will leave
you that moment, and never see your face more."

This had been just and honest and not more than we have deserved at
your hands. I say we; for God is my witness how condescendingly loving I
have been toward you. Yet did you so forget yourself, as both openly and
privately to contradict my doctrine; while, in the mean time, I was a deaf
man that heard not, neither answered a word, either in private or public.

Ah, my brother! I am distressed for you. I would—but you will not
receive my saying. Therefore I can only commit you to Him who commanded us to forgive one another, even as God, for Christ's sake, hath
forgiven us.

Charles Wesley's journal is silent on the first four months of spring 1741. It is clear
from his remarks above, and from his brother's journal entries of that period,[5] that
the predestination controversy would cause the same sort of schism in Bristol that
"stillness" had caused in the London Society. By February 2, 1741, the Wesleys'
uneasy truce with George Whitefield had ended after one of the Calvinistic evangelist's letters against them was published. John Wesley traveled to Kingswood to
meet with the predestinarian party. John Cennick, Thomas Bissicks, and Ann
Ayling emerged as leaders of the opposition; and Wesley was particularly incensed
about their "speaking against me behind my back," and that they "had formed
themselves into a separate society." They replied that he and Charles preached false
doctrine, "that there is righteousness in man." John Wesley quipped that there is
righteousness in a person "after the righteousness of Christ is imputed to him by
faith." He accused John Cennick of being the source of the half-truth and produced
a letter that Cennick had written to Whitefield. It incriminated the schoolmaster of
Kingswood as an opponent of the Wesleys' doctrine, and as one who sought to
supplant their leadership in the Society; the letter also hints at the impact of Charles
Wesley's preaching at Kingswood in late 1740.[6]

On Tuesday, February 24, John met the bands in Bristol, and in that session he
pruned "disorderly walkers" from the membership list. Over forty people separated from the Society. Saturday of the same week (February 28) John Wesley
assembled the bands again, this time reading a "paper" that censured the principal
leaders of the predestinarian party. The elder Wesley's document laid out his
complaints against Cennick, Bissicks, and Ayling, pledging their expulsion from
the Society if they did not "confess their fault" and do what was within their power
to repair the schism.[7]

On Saturday, March 7, 1741, John Wesley repeated his charges against the
predestinarians. They responded by laying the cause of separation wholly upon the
doctrinal issue: "It is our holding election that is the true cause of your separating
with us" (Bissicks's statement). Wesley replied that several predestinarians func-
tioned in the Methodist societies, and he "never put any one out . . . because of
that opinion." Bissicks said that the party was willing to remain in the Society if

Cennick was retained in his former position at Kingswood; Wesley made Cennick's continuance contingent upon confession and repentance of his misdeeds, but Cennick refused. Hence, John recorded, "I rejoined, It seems, then, that nothing remains but for each [person] to choose which society he pleases." After a short time of prayer, Cennick and fifty-two others walked out of the Society, leaving about ninety people continuing in connection with the Wesleys.

No. 104 Journal Selections: April 12–July 16, 1741

Sun., April 12 [1741]. At Kingswood, while I was repeating B. H.'s dying testimony, the Spirit came down "as a mighty rushing wind." Just then the predestinarians came in from hearing Cennick. In battles of shaking did He fight with them. We were all aflame with love.

I gave the sacrament to the bands of Kingswood, not of Bristol, in obedience, as I told them, to the Church of England, which requires a weekly sacrament at every Cathedral. But as they had it not there, and on this particular Sunday were refused it at Temple-Church (I myself, with many of them, having been repelled), I therefore administered it to them in our school; and, had we wanted an house, would justify doing it in the midst of the Wood. I strongly urged the duty of their receiving it as often as they could be admitted at the churches.

I had prayed God to show me some token if this was his will concerning us: and, indeed, my prayer was answered; for such a sacrament was I never present before. We received the sure pledge of our Saviour's dying love, and were most of us filled with all peace and joy in believing.

I preached a fourth time at Bristol: read the bands my Journal of what was lately passed in London [i.e. the stillness controversy]. It occasioned a grief which, mixed with pity, violated not their joy. I gave them all the treatise on Predestination.[8]

Mon., April 13th. While I was in great love, warning the bands, the Spirit of power came down, the fountain was set open, my mouth and heart enlarged, and I spoke such words as I cannot repeat. Many sunk under the love of Christ crucified, and were constrained to break out, "Christ died for all." Some confessed, with tears of joy, they were going to leave us, but could now die for the truth of this doctrine.

Thur., April 16th. One of our old men in the Wood complained to me, that the separatists had got from him the treatise against Predestination, and burnt it. In like manner they *answer* all they can lay hands on; but they do nothing, unless they could burn one more book,—the Bible.

Wed., April 22d. I sharply reproved three or four inflexible Pharisees; then prayed the Lord to give me words of consolation, and immediately I was filled with power, which broke out as a mighty torrent. All our hearts caught fire as in a moment, and such tears and strong cryings followed, as quite drowned my voice. I sat still while the prayer of the humble pierced the clouds, and entered into the ears of the Lord of sabbath. All present received an answer of peace; and, from his love in their hearts, testified that Christ died for all.

Tues., May 19th. I am more and more confirmed in the truth by its miserably opposers. I talked lately with Mr. H——, and urged him with this dilemma: "For what did God make this reprobate? to be damned, or to be saved?" He durst not say God made even Judas to be damned, and would not say God made him to be saved. I desired to know for what third end he could make him; but all the answer I could get was, "It is not a fair question."

Next I asked, "Whether he that believeth not shall not be damned, because he believeth not?" "Yes," he answered; and I replied, "Because he believeth not what?" Here he hesitated, and I was forced to help him out with the Apostle's answer, "That they all might be damned who believed not the truth." "What truth," I asked again, "but the truth of the Gospel of *their* salvation? If it is not the Gospel of *their* salvation, and yet they are bound to believe it, then they are bound to believe a lie, under pain of damnation; and the Apostle should have said, 'That they all might be damned who believed not *a lie.*'" This drove him to assert, that no man was damned for *actual* unbelief, but only for what he called *original*; that is, for not believing before he was born. "But where," said I, "is the justice of this?" He answered, not over-hastily, "I confess there is a mystery in reprobation." Or, to put it in Beza's words, which I then read to him, "We believe, though it is incomprehensible, that it is just to damn such as do not deserve it."

Farther I asked him, "Why does God command all men everywhere to repent? Why does he call, and offer his grace to, reprobates? Why does his Spirit strive with every child of man for *some* time, though not always?" I could get no answer, and so read him one of his friend Calvin's: "God speaketh to them, that they may be the deafer; He gives light to them, that they may be the blinder; He offers instruction to them, that they may be the more ignorant; and uses the remedy, that they may *not* be healed." [Calvin, *Institutes*, I. iii. c. 24]

Never did I meet with a more pitiful advocate of a more pitiful cause. And yet I believe he could say as much for reprobation as another. I told him *his* predestination had got a millstone about its neck, and would infallibly be drowned, if he did not part it from reprobation.

At Kingswood I preached on those much-perverted words, "I pray not for the world, but for them which thou hast given me;" that is, His apostles. He does not take in believers of future ages till verse 20. Then in verse 21 he prays for the unbelieving world; "that," to use Mr. Baxter's words on the place, "by *their* concord, the *world* may be won to Christianity." [*Paraphrase on the New Testament*; see again on verse 23: "That this lustre of their excellency and concord may convince the world that thou hast sent me."] So far is our Lord from not praying for the world *at all* that in this very chapter he prays once for his first disciples, once for believers in after-ages, and *twice* for the *world* that lieth in wickedness, that the world may *believe*— that the world may *know.*

He who prays for all men himself, and commands us to pray for all men, was with us, and showed us, with the demonstration of his Spirit, that he is not willing any should perish, but that all should come to the knowledge of the truth, and be saved.

Mon., June 8th. A woman spoke to me of her husband. He was under strong convictions, while he attended the word; but the first time he heard the *other Gospel,* came home *elect,* and, in proof of it, *beat his wife.* His seriousness was at an end. His work was done. God doth not behold iniquity in Jacob; therefore the iniquity and cruelty towards her abound. He uses her worse than a Turk (his predestinarian brother), and tells her, if he killed her he could not be damned. . . .

Sun., June 28th. A day much to be remembered. I preached in Bristol on repentance; at Kendalshire on temptation, with more life. My strength increased with my work; so that in the afternoon I was filled with power; and again at Baptist-mills.

Last night Howel Harris [a Welsh Methodist preacher] told me he would come to our Society. I bade him come in God's name. We were singing:

"Thee triumphantly we praise, . . ." [No. 105]

when W. Hooper, by my order, brought him. I prayed according to God; gave out a hymn which we might all join in. The hand of Lord was upon me. I asked Howel whether he had a mind to speak, and sat by for half an hour, while he gave an account of his conversion by *irresistible grace,* mixing with his experience the impossibility of falling, God's unchangeableness, &c. I could not but observe the ungenerousness of my friend; and after hearing him long and patiently, was moved to rise up, and ask in the name of Jesus, "Ye that are spiritual, doth the Spirit which is in you suffer me still to keep silence, and let my brother go on? Can I do it without bringing the blood of these souls upon me?" A woman first cried out (Mrs. Rawlins, I think), "The wounds of Jesus answer, 'No.'" Then many others repeated, "No, no, no"; and a whole cloud of witnesses arose, declaring "Christ died for all!"

I asked again, "Would you have my brother Harris proceed, or would you not? If you would hear him, I will be silent all night." Again they forbade me in strong words; upon which I gave out,

"Break forth into joy,
  Your Comforter sing," &c. [No. 48]

They did break forth as the voice of many waters, or mighty thunderings. O what a burst of joy was there in the midst of us! The God and Saviour of all men magnified his universal love.

Howel Harris would have entered into dispute, but was stopped. "Then," said he, "you thrust me out." "No," said I, "we do not: you are welcome to stay as long as you please. We acknowledge you a child of God." Yet again he began, "If you do not believe irresistible grace"; and I cut off the sentences of reprobation which I foresaw coming, with,

> "Praise God, from whom pure blessings flow,
> Whose bowels yearn *on all* below;
> Who would not have one sinner lost;
> Praise Father, Son, and Holy Ghost."[9]

Here Mr. Labbe pulled him away, and carried him from us. We betook ourselves to prayer, in which the Spirit wonderfully helped our infirmities. Great was the company, both of mourners and rejoicers. We perceived God had taken the matter into his own hand, and we arose to maintain his own cause. My mouth, and all their hearts were opened. I spake as I never spake before, and all agreed in one testimony. . . . I acknowledged the grace given our dear brother Harris, and excused his estrangement from me through the wickedness of his counselors. I spake, I know not what, words of exhortation and instruction.

The Spirit of their Father spake in many; and this I have found since, that just when I began to stop Howel, several felt in themselves that the time was come; and, if I had deferred it, would themselves have rebuked the madness of the Prophet.

Thur., July 16th. I discoursed on Lazarus raised. I dined at Lanissan [Wales], and preached to the Society and a few others, chiefly pre-destinarians. Without touching the dispute, I simply declared the scriptural marks of election; whereby some, I believe, were cut off from their vain confidence. The sincere ones clave to me. Who can resist the power of love? A loving messenger of a loving God might drive reprobation out of Wales, without even naming it. . . .

No. 105 Hymn: "Gloria Patri"
(*Hymns on God's Everlasting Love*, 1741)

1 Father of mankind, whose love
    In Christ for all is free,
Thou hast sent Him from above
    To bring us all to Thee;
Thou hast every heart inclined
    Christ the Saviour to embrace,
All those heavenly drawings find,
    All *may* be saved by grace.

2 Christ, the true and living Light,
    Thou shinest into all,

Lightest every son of night
   That fell in *Adam's* fall:
Bear we witness unto Thee,
   Thou Thy light to all dost give,
That the world through it *might* see
   Their Saviour, and believe.

3 Holy Ghost, all-quickening Fire,
    Thou givest each his day,
  Dost one spark of life inspire
    In every castaway;
  Not to aggravate his sin,
    Not his sorer doom to seal,
  But that he *might* let Thee in
    And all Thy fullness feel.

4 Father, Son and Holy Ghost,
    All glory be to Thee;
  The whole world of sinners lost
    To save Thou dost agree:
  Thee triumphantly we praise,
    Vie with all Thy hosts above,
  Shout Thine universal grace,
    Thine everlasting love.

In a letter he wrote in late 1741, George Whitefield complained to John Wesley, "Dear Brother Charles is more and more rash. He has lately printed some very bad hymns."[10] These "very bad," "rash" hymns were Charles's *Hymns on God's Everlasting Love*, which he wrote to dispute predestination and its theological corollaries. "Everlasting love" was juxtaposed against the Calvinist "horrible decree" of reprobation and the "narrow gospel" of limited atonement.

    As the predestinarian controversy swept through Methodism, dividing the Society at Bristol and separating the Wesleys from Whitefield, Selina Countess of Huntingdon, and most of the societies in Wales, Charles published two series of hymns that set forth the leading elements of his Arminian gospel in a constructive fashion, and also criticized the views of his predestinarian opponents. The first hymnal was published by Felix Farley in 1741; the complete title was very descriptive of its contents: *Hymns on God's Everlasting Love, To Which is Added the 'Cry of a Reprobate,' and 'The Horrible Decree.'* The second collection was entitled *Hymns on God's Everlasting Love (Second Series)*, and was published in London by William Strahan in late 1741 or early 1742.

    The thrust of both collections was firmly established in their first hymn, which made the phrase "everlasting love" a Wesleyan synonym for a gospel of unlimited atonement and prevenient grace. The hymn of seventeen verses affirms the limitless dimensions of Christ's saving death over twenty-three times! Charles's conception of the unlimited atonement had two important corollaries. The first was conditional election. Hence, the distinction between the saved and lost lay not with the Lamb, "His pity no exception makes" (verse 7); rather, as he wrote, "All the hindrance is in me." The second vital theme was Charles's conception of "free grace," the universal offer of the Gospel; the hymn by that title, and the other hymns of these two collections, resound with the word "all"; it offers an alternative to the Calvinist doctrines of particular election and limited atonement. The balance point between "everlasting love" and "free grace" is found in the evangelist's insistence that since grace is "undistinguished" the distinction between the saved and the lost rests squarely upon the response of the person who has been prepared by "preventing grace."

No. 106   Hymns on God's Everlasting Love, First Series: I

1   Father, whose *everlasting love*
       Thy only Son for sinners gave,
     Whose grace to *all* did *freely* move,
       And sent Him down a *world* to save:

2   Help us Thy mercy to extol,
       Immense, unfathom'd, unconfined;
     To praise the Lamb who *died for all,*
       The *general Saviour of mankind.*

3   Thy *undistinguishing regard*
       Was cast on *Adam's* fallen race;
     For all Thou hast in Christ prepared
       Sufficient, sovereign, saving grace.

4   Jesus hath said, we *all* shall hope,
       Preventing grace for all is free:
     "And I, if I be lifted up,
       I will *draw all men* unto Me."

5   What soul those drawings never knew?
       With whom hath not Thy Spirit strove?
     We all *must* own that God is true,
       We all *may* feel that God is love.

6   O *all ye ends of earth,* behold
       The bleeding, all-atoning Lamb!
     Look unto Him for sinners sold,
       Look and be *saved* through Jesu's name.

7   Behold the Lamb of God, who takes
       The sins of all the world away!

His pity no exception makes;
    But all that *will* receive Him, *may.*

8 *A world* He suffer'd to redeem;
    For *all* He hath th' atonement made:
  For those that *will not come* to Him
    The ransom of His life was paid.

9 Their Lord, unto *His own* He came;
    His own were who *received Him not,*
  Denied and trampled on His name
    And blood, by which themselves were bought.

10 Who under foot their Saviour trod,
    Exposed *afresh,* and *crucified,*
  Who trampled on the Son of God,—
    For them, for them, their Saviour died.

11 For those who at the judgement day
    On Him they pierced shall *look* with pain;
  The Lamb for every *castaway,*
    For *every soul of man* was slain.

12 Why then, Thou universal Love,
    Should any of Thy grace despair?
  To all, to all, Thy bowels move,
    But straiten'd in our own we are.

13 'Tis *we,* the wretched abjects *we,*
    Our blasphemies on Thee translate;
  We think that fury is in Thee,
    Horribly think, that God is hate.

14 'Thou hast compell'd the lost to die,
    Hast *reprobated* from Thy face;
  Hast others saved, but them pass'd by,
    Or mock'd with only *damning grace.* *

15 How long, Thou jealous God! how long
    Shall impious worms Thy word disprove,
  Thy justice stain, Thy mercy wrong,
    Deny Thy faithfulness and love?

16 Still shall the hellish doctrine stand,
    And Thee for its dire author claim?
  No: let it sink at Thy command
    Down to the pit from whence it came.

---

* "Damning grace" is more commonly called "common grace."

17   Arise, O God, maintain Thy cause!
       The fullness of the *Gentiles* call:
       Lift up the standard of Thy cross,
          And *all* shall own Thou diedst for all.

No. 107   Hymns on God's Everlasting Love, First Series: V

1   To the meek and gentle Lamb
          I pour out my complaint;
      Will not hide from Thee my shame,
          But tell Thee what I want:
      I am full of sin and pride;
          I am all unclean, unclean;
      Till Thy Spirit here abide,
          I cannot cease from sin.

2   Clearly do I see the way,
          My foot is on the path;
      Now, this instant, *now* I may
          Draw near by simple faith:
      Thou art not a distant God,
          Thou art still to sinners near;
      Every moment, if I would,
          My heart might feel Thee near.

3   Free as air Thy mercy streams,
          Thy universal grace
      Shine with undistinguish'd beams
          On all the fallen race:
      All from Thee a power receive
          To reject, or hear, Thy call;
      All *may* choose to die, or live;
          Thy grace is free for all.

4   All the hindrance is in me:
          Thou ready art to save;
      But I will not come to Thee,
          That I Thy life may have.
      Stubborn and rebellious still,
          From Thy arms of love I fly:
      Yes, I will be lost; I will,
          In spite of mercy, die.

5   Holy, meek, and gentle Lamb,
          With me what canst Thou do?

Though Thou leav'st me as I am,
  I own Thee good and true.
Thou wouldst have me life embrace,
  Thou for me and all wast slain,
Thou hast offer'd me Thy grace;
  'Twas I that made it vain.

6 O that I might yield at last,
     By dying love subdued!
   Lord, on Thee my soul is cast,
     The purchase of Thy blood:
   If Thou wilt the sinner have,
     Thou canst work to will in me;
   When, and as Thou pleasest, save;
     I leave it all to Thee.

No. 108 Hymns on God's Everlasting Love, First Series: X, "Jesus Christ, the Saviour of All Men"

In this exposition of unlimited atonement and God's universal love, Wesley picked
up one of the Calvinist catch-phrases ("passed by"), originally used as a euphemism for those who are not elected to salvation, and turned it into a polemic on that
same doctrine.[11]

1 See, sinners in the gospel glass,
     The Friend and Saviour of mankind!
   Not one of all th' apostate race
     But may in Him salvation find:
   His thoughts, and words, and actions prove—
   His life and death—that God is love.

2 Behold the Lamb of God, who bears
     The sins of all the world away!
   A servant's form He meekly wears,
     He sojourns in a house of clay;
   His glory is no longer seen,
   But God with God is man with men.

3 See where the God incarnate stands,
     And calls His wandering creatures home!
   He all day long spreads out His hands,—
     "Come, weary souls, to Jesus come!
   Ye all may hide you in My breast;
   Believe, and I will give you rest.

4   "Ah! do not of My goodness doubt,
        My saving grace for all is free;
    I will in nowise cast him out
        Who comes, a sinner, unto Me;
    I can to none Myself deny;
    Why, sinners, *will ye* perish, why?

5   (The mournful cause let Jesus tell)
        "They *will not* come to Me, and live:
    I did not force them to rebel,
        Or call when I had nought to give,
    Invite them to believe a lie,
    Or any soul of man *pass by*."

6   Sinners, believe the gospel word;
        Jesus is come, your souls to save!
    Jesus is come, your common Lord!
        Pardon ye all in Him may have;
    May now be saved, whoever will;
    This Man receiveth sinners still.

7   See where the lame, the halt, the blind,
        The deaf, the dumb, the sick, the poor,
    Flock to the Friend of human kind,
        And freely all accept their cure;
    To whom doth He His help deny?
    To whom in His days of flesh *pass by*?

8   Did not His word the fiends expel,
        The lepers cleanse, and raise the dead?
    Did He not all their sickness heal,
        And satisfy their every need?
    Did He reject His helpless clay,
    Or send them sorrowful away?

9   Nay, but His bowels yearn'd to see
        The people hungry, scatter'd, faint;
    Nay, but He utter'd over thee
        Jerusalem, a true complaint;
    Jerusalem, who shedd'st His blood,
    That, with His tears, for thee hath flow'd.

10 How oft for thy hard-heartedness
        Did Jesus in his Spirit groan!
    The things belonging to thy peace,
        Hadst thou, O bloody city, known,
    Thee, turning in thy gracious day,
    He never would have cast away.

11 He wept, because thou *wouldst* not see
        The grace which sure salvation brings:
    How oft would He have gather'd thee,
        And cherish'd underneath His wings;
    But thou *wouldst not*—unhappy thou!
    And justly art thou harden'd now.

12 Would Jesus have the sinner die?
        Why hangs He then on yonder tree?
    What means that strange expiring cry
        (Sinners, He prays for you and me),
    "Forgive them, Father, O forgive,
    They know not that by me they live!"

13 He prays for those that shed His blood:
        And who from Jesu's blood is pure?
    Who hath not crucified his God?
        Whose sins did not His death procure?
    If all have sinn'd through *Adam's* fall,
    Our Second *Adam* died for all.

14 *Adam* descended from above
        Our loss of *Eden* to retrieve,
    Great God of universal love,
        If all the world in Thee *may* live,
    In us a quickening Spirit be,
    And witness, Thou hast died for me.

15 Extend to me the cleansing tide
        Which freely flow'd for all mankind,
    Open the fountain of Thy side,
        In Thee may I redemption find,
    Give *me* redemption in Thy blood;
    For me and all mankind it flow'd.

16 Dear, loving, all-atoning Lamb,
        Thee by Thy painful agony,
    Thy bloody sweat, Thy grief and shame,
        Thy cross and passion on the tree,
    Thy precious death, and life, I pray—
    Take all, take all my sins away!

17 O let me kiss Thy bleeding feet,
        And bathe, and wash them with my tears;
    The story of Thy love repeat
        In every drooping sinner's ears,
    That all may hear the quickening sound:
    If I, even I, have mercy found!

18   O let Thy love my heart constrain,
         Thy love for every sinner free,
      That every fallen soul of man
         May taste grace that found out me;
      That all mankind, with me, may prove
      Thy sovereign, everlasting love.

No. 109   Hymns on God's Everlasting Love, First Series: XIV, "God's Sovereign, Everlasting Love"

Particularly interesting in this hymn is Wesley's remaking of the Calvinist "sovereign" (i.e. irresistible) grace into "sovereign, everlasting love." The development serves as an important example of the Wesleyan conception of prevenient grace, which "hath lured, call'd and drawn me from above." This alluring kindness sets Charles's soteriology in the context of human inability and the Divine initiative, and yet since God's grace can also be spurned, "sovereign love" lays the full fault of reprobation at the sinner's own feet.

1   O all-redeeming Lord,
            Thy kindness I record:
         Me Thy kindness hath allured,
            Call'd, and drawn me from above;
         Sweetly am I thus assured
            Of Thy everlasting love.

2   But is Thy grace less free
            For others than for me?
         Lord, I have not learn'd Thee so;
            Good to every man Thou art,
         Free as air Thy mercies flow;
            So I feel it in my heart.

3   Thee every soul may find
            Loving to all mankind;
         All have once Thy drawings proved,
            Every soul may say, with me,
         Me the Friend of sinners loved,
            Loved from all eternity.

4   Before His name I knew
            Me to Himself He drew,
         My unconscious heart inclined
            To pursue some good unknown;
         Happiness I long'd to find,
            Happiness is God alone.

5   God is the thing I sought,
         But then I knew it not:
Who shall show me any good?
      (With the many still I cried)
Rest was only in Thy blood,
         Who for me, for all, hast died.

6   The world's Desire and Hope
         For this was lifted up;
Lord, Thou didst hereby engage
      To draw all men unto Thee,
All in every place and age:
         Grace for all mankind is free!

7   The Spirit of Thy love
         With every soul hath strove;
Every fallen soul of man
      May recover from his fall,
See the Lamb for sinners slain,
         Feel that He hath died for all.

8   Thou dost not mock our race
         With insufficient grace;
Thou hast reprobated none,
      Thou from *Pharaoh's* blood art free;
Thou didst once for all atone—
         Judas, Esau, Cain, and me.

No. 110 Hymns on God's Everlasting Love, First Series: XVII, "The Horrible Decree"

In this poetic polemic Charles carries on a dialogue with the Calvinists, placing their lines on the lips of "sinners" and then responding directly to his characterization of his opponents' theology. The "horrible decree" refers to God's decree which elects some to eternal salvation and condemns others to damnation.

1   Ah! gentle, gracious Dove;
       And art Thou grieved in me,
That sinners should restrain Thy love,
      And say, "It is not free:
It is not free for *all*;
      The *most* Thou *passest by*,
And mockest with a fruitless call
       Whom Thou hast doom'd to die."

2   They think Thee *not sincere*
         In giving each his day:
     "Thou only draw'st the sinner near,
         To cast him quite away;
         To aggravate his sin,
             His sure damnation seal,
     Thou show'st him heaven, and say'st, Go in,—
         And thrusts him into hell."

3   O HORRIBLE DECREE,
         Worthy of whence it came!
     Forgive their hellish blasphemy
         Who charge it on the Lamb,
         Whose pity Him inclined
             To leave His throne above,
     The Friend and Saviour of mankind,
         The God of grace and love.

4   O gracious, loving Lord,
         I feel Thy bowels yearn;
     For those who slight the gospel word
         I share in Thy concern:
         How art Thou grieved to be
             By ransom'd worms withstood!
     How dost Thou bleed afresh, to see
         Them trample on Thy blood!

5   To limit Thee they dare,
         Blaspheme Thee to Thy face,
     Deny their fellow worms a share
         In Thy redeeming grace;
         All for their own they take,
             Thy righteousness engross,
     Of none effect to *most* they make
         The merits of Thy cross.

6   Sinners, abhor the fiend:
         His *other* gospel hear—
     "The God of truth did not intend
         The thing His words declare;
         He offers grace to all,
             Which most cannot embrace,
     Mock'd with an ineffectual call
         And insufficient grace."

7   *"The righteous God consign'd*
         Them over to their doom,

And sent the Saviour of mankind
*   To damn them from the womb:*
To damn for falling short
*   Of what they could not do,*
For not believing the report
*   Of that which was not true."*

8   "*The God of love* pass'd by
        The most of those that fell,
Ordain'd poor reprobates to die,
    And forced them into hell."
        "*He did not do the deed*
        (Some have more mildly raved),
He did not damn *them—but decreed*
        They should never be saved."

9   "*He did not them bereave*
        Of life, or stop their breath;
His grace He only would not give,
        And starved their souls to death."
        Satanic sophistry!
        But still, all-gracious God,
They charge the sinner's death on Thee,
        Who bought'st him with Thy blood.

10   They think with shrieks and cries
        To please the Lord of Hosts,
And offer Thee, in sacrifice,
        Millions of slaughter'd ghosts;
        With new-born babies they fill
        The dire infernal shade,
For such (they say) *was Thy great will*
        Before the world was made.

11   How long, O God, how long
        Shall Satan's rage proceed!
Wilt Thou not soon avenge the wrong,
        And crush the serpent's head?
        Surely Thou shalt at last
        Bruise him beneath our feet;
The devil and his doctrine cast
        Into the burning pit.

12   Arise, O God, arise;
        Thy glorious truth maintain;
Hold forth the bloody Sacrifice,
        For every sinner slain!

> Defend Thy mercy's cause,
> Lift up the standard of Thy cross,
> Draw all men unto Thee.

13   O vindicate Thy grace,
> Which every soul may prove;
> Us in Thy arms of love embrace,
> Of everlasting love.
> Give the pure gospel word,
> Thy preachers multiply;
> Let all confess their common Lord,
> And dare for Him to die.

14   My life I here present,
> My heart's last drop of blood:
> O let it all be freely spent
> In proof that Thou art good;
> Art good to all that breathe,
> Who all may pardon have;
> Thou willest not the sinner's death,
> But all the world *wouldst* save.

15   O take me at my word;
> But arm me with Thy power,
> Then call me forth to suffer, Lord,
> To meet the fiery hour:
> In death will I proclaim
> That all *may* hear Thy call,
> And clap my hands amidst the flame,
> And shout,—HE DIED FOR ALL.

No. 111   Hymns on God's Everlasting Love, Second Series: XVI, "Free Grace"

This hymn is the most complete extant treatment of Charles's theology of grace. He presents his entire soteriology as being a function of "free grace," and hence undercuts the charges of a Pelagian anthropology, or works as contributing to one's salvation. It was first published subjoined to John Wesley's sermon of this same title, and then reappeared in the hymnal of 1741.[12]

1   Come, let us join our friends above,
> The God of our salvation praise,
> The God of everlasting love,
> The God of universal grace.

2   'Tis not by works that we have done,
> 'Twas grace alone His heart inclined,

'Twas grace that gave His only Son
   To taste of death for all mankind.

3 For every man He tasted death;
   And hence we in His sight appear,
 Not lifting up our eyes beneath,
   But publishing His mercy here.

4 This is the ground of all our hope,
   The fountain this of all our good,
 Jesus for all was lifted up,
   And shed for all His precious blood.

5 His blood, for all a ransom given,
   Has wash'd away the general sin;
 He closed His eyes to open heaven,
   And all, who will, may enter in.

6 He worketh once to will in all,
   Or mercy we could ne'er embrace;
 He calls with an effectual call,
   And bids us all receive His grace.

7 Thou drawest all men unto Thee,
   Grace doth to every soul appear;
 Preventing grace for all is free,
   And brings to all salvation near.

8 Had not Thy grace salvation brought,
   Thyself we never could desire;
 Thy grace suggests our first good thought,
   Thy only grace doth all inspire.

9 By nature only free to ill,
   We never had one motion known
 Of good, hadst Thou not given the will,
   And wrought it by Thy grace alone.

10 'Twas grace, when we in sin were dead,
   Us from the death of sin did raise;
 Grace only hath the difference made;
   Whate'er we are, we are by grace.

11 When on Thy love we turn'd our back,
   Thou wouldst not shut Thy mercy's door,
 The forfeiture Thou wouldst not take,
   Thy grace did still our souls restore.

12 When twice ten thousand times we fell,
   Thou gav'st us still a longer space,

Didst freely our backslidings heal,
  And show'dst Thy more abundant grace.

13 'Twas grace from hell that brought us up;
      Lo! to Thy sovereign grace we bow,
    Through sovereign grace we still have hope,
      Thy sovereign grace supports us now.

14 Grace only doth from sin restrain,
      From which our nature cannot cease;
    By grace we still Thy grace retain,
      And wait to feel Thy perfect peace.

15 Kept by the mercy of our God,
      Through faith, to full salvation's hour,
    Jesu, we spread Thy name abroad,
      And glorify Thy gracious power.

16 The constant miracle we own
      By which we every moment live,
    To grace, to Thy free grace alone,
      The whole of our salvation give.

17 Strongly upheld by Thy right hand,
      Thy all-redeeming love we praise;
    The monuments of Thy grace we stand,
      Thy free, Thine universal grace.

18 By grace we draw our every breath;
      By grace we live, and move and are;
    By grace we 'scape the second death;
      By grace we now Thy grace declare.

19 From the first feeble thought of good
      To when the perfect grace is given,
    'Tis all of grace; by grace renew'd,
      From hell we pass through earth to heaven.

20 We need no reprobates to prove
      That grace, free grace, is truly free;
    Who cannot see that God is love,
      Open your eyes and look on me.

21 On us, whom Jesus hath call'd forth
      To' assert that all His grace may have,
    To vindicate His passion's wroth
      Enough ten thousand worlds to save.

22 He made it possible for all
      His gift of righteousness t' embrace;

We all may answer to His call,
  May all be freely saved by grace.

23 He promised all mankind to draw;
  We feel Him draw us from above,
  And preach with Him the gracious law,
  And publish the DECREE OF LOVE.

24 Behold the all-atoning Lamb;
  Come, sinners, at the gospel call;
  Look, and be saved through Jesu's name;
  We witness He hath died for all.

25 We join with all our friends above,
  The God of our salvation praise,
  The God of everlasting love,
  The God of universal grace.

NOTES

1. Jackson, *CW Journal,* II, p. 118.

2. The minutes from the Methodist Conference in Bristol, August 2, 1745, indicate that those assembled considered the movement's theology in contrast to Calvinism and Antinomianism:

> Q. 22. Does not the truth of the gospel lie very near both to Calvinism and Antinomianism?
> A. Indeed it does; as it were, within a hair's breadth: So that it is altogether foolish and sinful, because we do not quite agree with either one or the other, to run from them as far ever as we can.
> Q. 23. Wherein may we come to the very edge of Calvinism?
> A. (1) In ascribing all good to the free grace of God. (2) In denying all natural free-will, and all power antecedent to grace. And, (3) In excluding all merit from man; even for what he has or does by the grace of God.
> Q. 24. Wherein may we come to the edge of Antinomianism?
> A. (1) In exalting the merits and love of Christ. (2) In rejoicing evermore. (*JW Works,* VIII, pp. 284–285)

3. Heb. 6:4–6 would have been easily expounded in a manner that opposed the Calvinistic conception of eternal security in one's salvation: "For it is impossible for those who tasted of the heavenly gift, and were made partakers of the Holy Ghost, And have tasted the good word of God, and the powers of the world to come, If they shall fall away, to renew them again unto repentance; seeing they crucify to themselves the Son of God afresh, and put *him* to an open shame." (KJV)

4. The letter is printed only in Jackson's *Life of Charles Wesley, op. cit.,* I, pp. 250–251.

5. *JW Works,* II, pp. 426–434.

6. Cennick's letter to George Whitefield (*JW Works,* I, p. 300):

> "My Dear Brother,   Jan. 17, 1741
> "That you might come quickly, I have written a second time. I sit solitary, like Eli, waiting what will become of the ark. And while I wait, and fear the carrying of it away among my people, my trouble increases daily. How glorious did the Gospel seem once to flourish in Kingswood!—I spake of the everlasting love of Christ with sweet power. But now brother Charles [Wesley] is suffered to open his mouth against this truth, while the frighted sheep gaze and fly, as if no shepherd was among them. It is just as though Satan was now making war with the saints in a

more than common way. O pray for the distressed lambs yet left in this place, that they faint not! Surely they would, if preaching would do it: For they have nothing whereon to rest (who now attend on the sermons), but their own faithfulness.

"With Universal Redemption, brother Charles pleases the world: Brother John follows him in every thing. I believe no Atheist can more preach against Predestination than they: And all who believe Election are counted enemies to God, and called so.

"Fly, dear brother. I am as alone: I am in the midst of the plague. If God give thee leave, make haste."

7. John Wesley's "Paper" against the Predestinarians has also been preserved in his journal (*JW Works*, I, p. 301):

By many witnesses, it appears that several members of the band society at Kingswood have made it their common practice to scoff at the preaching of Mr. John and Charles Wesley; that they have censured and spoken evil of them behind their backs, at the very time they professed love and esteem to their faces; that they have studiously endeavoured to prejudice other members of that society against them; and, in order thereto, have belied and slandered them in divers instances.

Therefore, not for their opinions, nor for any of them (whether they be right or wrong), but for the causes above-mentioned, viz. for their scoffing at the Word and ministers of God, for their tale-bearing, back biting, and evil speaking, for their dissembling, lying and slandering:

I, John Wesley, by the consent and approbation of the band-societies in Kingswood, do declare the persons above-mentioned to be no longer members thereof. Neither will they be so accounted, until they openly confess their fault, and thereby do what in them lies to remove the scandal they have given.

8. There are several possible identifications for this "tract on predestination." John Wesley printed several small treatises on the topic, all of which had appeared by the end of 1741: his sermon on *Free Grace* (1739), *Serious Considerations Concerning the Doctrines of Election and Reprobation* (1740), *Absolute Predestination* (1741), *A Dialogue Between a Predestinarian and His Friend* (1741), and *The Scripture Doctrine Concerning Predestination, Election, and Reprobation* (1741).

9. This short hymn is #V, from *Hymns on God's Everlasting Love, First Series* (1741). It is given here in its entirety.

10. *JW Letters*, I, p. 352. cf. *P.W.* III, pp. 3–106.

11. Compare the phraseology of this hymn with John T. McNeill, ed., *Calvin: Institutes of the Christian Religion* (Philadelphia: Westminster Press, 1960), III, 22:1, p. 932.

12. Charles's hymn "Free Grace" was first published as a supplement to one of John Wesley's sermons by the same title. John's published sermons, fourth series, offers #CXXVIII under the title. Its inscription indicated that the sermon was "Preached in Bristol, in the year 1740"; it comes to us out of the midst of the predestinarian debate. The sermon is based on Rom. 8:32: "He that spared not his own Son, but delivered him up for us, how shall he not with him also freely give us all things?" (KJV) The sermon capitalizes on the latter portion of the passage to emphasize the connection between God's free grace and his everlasting love: in each case "love" is an operative synonym for "grace," and it is extended to "all." Cf. *P.W.* III, pp. 93–96.

9 / Domestic Life

COURTSHIP AND MARRIAGE

Quite unlike his older brother John, Charles Wesley was happily married, a devoted husband and doting father. Although his published journal is relatively silent about his private life, his hymns and correspondence intersect to form a revealing picture of the younger Wesley. Courtship and marriage were complicated matters in proper eighteenth-century England. In Charles's case, affairs of the heart were further complicated by the public character of his work, by his tenuous financial situation, and by a covenant Charles and John Wesley had made not to marry without the other's approval.

The relationship between Charles and Sarah Gwynne started out innocently enough, but gradually escalated to the point where his journal no longer called her "Miss Gwynne," or "Miss Sally"; she was becoming his "dearest friend," an appellation he reserved for his wife life long. Their relationship was formed through his visits to the Gwynne household in Garth, in the mountains of Wales. Mr. Gwynne occasionally traveled with Charles in Wales. Soon Sally also went on these excursions, but always under the watchful eye of her father. The couple had been acquainted for eighteen months when they began to make plans to marry, an event that the custom of the day made more like a corporate merger than a romantic union. Not wholly impressed with the means of a Methodist preacher, Mrs. Gwynne demanded that Charles demonstrate his ability to raise one hundred pounds *per annum* before her consent for the marriage could be given. Sarah, an attractive and talented woman some eighteen years Wesley's junior, would be amply provided for before her family could bear to see her leave their bountiful home.

Charles's letters to Sally are full of piety and propriety, but there is real warmth underneath. And although the haggling with his brother and his future in-laws must have robbed the wedding of a bit of its luster we have no hint of it from Charles. His fatherly friend, Vincent Perronet, pastor at Shoreham, saved the day by convincing the Gwynnes that Charles was a man of substance, if not property and wealth. The match was a happy one, but it was also rooted in an understanding that he would continue his evangelistic travels and vegetarian diet.

In the early years of marriage Charles traveled relentlessly. Sally occasionally accompanied him on the trek from Bristol to her native Wales and back, or went with him to London. As children came, Sally traveled less; and Charles's letters to her, while remaining bravely upbeat, were also full of concern for her and their children. Charles's health and family responsibilities eventually kept him first in Bristol and then more completely in London (1771). He continued to make forays into the countryside, but the latter years of his ministerial work were devoted more to the care of the urban Methodist societies and the composition of hymns.

No. 112   Journal Selections: August 28, 1747–April 19, 1748

Fri., August 28th [1747: Wales]. . . . At nine I preached in the street, repentance and faith. The people behaved with great decency. Mr. Gwynne came to see me at Mr. Phillips's, with two of his family.

My soul seemed pleased to take acquaintance with them. We rode to Maesmynis church. I preached, and Mr. Williams after me in Welsh. At four I expounded the good Samaritan in the street; and He was present, binding up our wounds. I preached a fourth time at Garth, on, "Comfort ye, comfort ye my people." The whole family received us as messengers of God; and is such we are, they received Him that sent us.

Thur., March 24th [1748]. I resolved to push for Garth, finding my strength would never hold out for three more days' of riding. At five I set out in hard rain, which continued all day. We went through perils of waters. . . . I had no more rest than the night before.

Fri., March 25th. I took horse again at five, the rain attending us still. At eight I was comforted by the sight of Mr. Phillips, at Llanidloes. The weather grew more severe. The violent wind drove the hard rain full in our faces. I rode till I could ride no more; walked the last hour; and by five dropped down at Garth. All ran to nurse me. I got a little refreshment, and at seven made a feeble attempt to preach. They quickly put me to bed. I had a terrible night, worse than ever.

Sat., March 26th, and the five following days, I was exercised with strong pain, notwithstanding all the means used to remove it. My short intervals were filled up with conference, prayer, and singing.

Sun., April 3d. Through the divine blessing on the tender care of my friends, I recovered so much strength that I read prayers, and gave the sacrament to the family.

Tues., April 5th. She drove me to Builth. I took horse at three. Mr. Gwynne and Miss Sally accompanied me the first hour. Then I rode on alone, weary, but supported. . . .

Tues., April 19th. I had communicated my embryo intentions to my brother while in Ireland, which he neither opposed, nor much encouraged. It was then a distant first thought, not likely ever to come to a proposal; as I had not given the least hint, either to Miss Gwynne or the family. To-day I rode over to Shoreham, and told Mr. Perronet all my heart. I have always had a fear, but no *thought,* of marrying, for many years past, even from my first preaching of the Gospel. But within this twelvemonth that though had forced itself in, "How know I, whether it be best for me to marry, or no?" Certainly better now than later: and if not now, what security that I shall not then? It should be now, or not at all.

Mr. Perronet encouraged me to pray, and wait for a providential opening. I expressed the various searching of my heart in many hymns on the important occasion.

Charles's hymns of this occasion are preserved in a slim manuscript collection, which Frank Baker has called "Ms. Deliberate." The volume is introduced with a brief note that connects the hymns with Charles's journal entry of April 19, 1748. The hymns are filled with Charles's inner turmoil over whether or not he ought to take Sally as his wife. A short preface, signed by "S. Wesley Jr., Charles's daughter," offered the context of the manuscript hymns:

> These hymns were written by the Rev'd Charles Wesley during his intention òf marrying Miss Gwynne, afterwards his beloved wife. The piety and submission of his mind in the beginning of the attachment is deeply manifested, and their children have reason humbly to hope a blessing at last sick [?] rest upon each of them, while Father so depreciated taking one step without the Divine Guidance.
>
> Many outward obstacles were removed during the attachment, and one sign which He requested was granted against all appearance; the consent and full approval of Mrs. Gwynne (the Mother) who at first was reluctant. Without this approbation they each consider'd that Providence opposed their union.

No. 113   "Ms. Deliberate": Hymn II[1]

1   Heavenly Counsellor Divine,
        Waiting for thy will I stand:
    Both mine Eyes, Thou knowst are Thine,
        Reach me out an Helping Hand:
    Thou my faithful Pilot be,
        While these threatening Billows roar
    Guide thro' Life's tempestuous Sea,
        Land me on the Happy Shore.

2   In this howling Wilderness,
        Lo! I trust on Thee alone,
    Thee in all my ways confess,
        Sole Disposer of Thine own:
    Sure to err without thy Sight,
        Sure to contradict thy Will,
    Guide my wandering Footsteps right,
        Bring me to thy holy Hill.

3   Will Thou Lord, Thine own forsake,
        Stop thine ears against my cry,
    Let me Fatally mistake
        Who on Thee for Light rely?
    Canst Thou while for Help I pray,
        While my Soul on Thee I cast,
    Turn the Blind out of the way,
        Leave me to Myself at Last?

4   Surely, Lord, the Fear is vain;
        Thou art merciful and True,
    Thou shalt make thy Counsel plain,
        Thou shalt teach me what to do,
    On my Heart the Answer seal,
        Signify thy Love's Decree
    Shew me all thy Blessed Will—
        When, & how I leave to Thee.

No. 114   "Ms. Deliberate": Hymn IV[2]

1   Christ, my life, my only treasure
        Thou alone
        Mould Thine own
    After thy goodpleasure.

2   Thou, who paidst my Price ~~shalt have~~ direct me,
        Thine I am
        Holy Lamb,
    Save, and always save me.

3   Order Thou my *my whole Condition*,
        Chuse my state
        Fix my Fate,
    By thy wise Decision.

4   From all Earthly Expectation
        Set me free
        Seize for Thee
    All my strength of Passion.

5   Into absolute subjection
        Be it brought
        Every thought,
    Every fond Affection.

6   That which most my Soul requires
        For thy sake
        Hold it back
    Purge my Best Desires.

7   Keep from me thy loveliest Creature,
        Till I prove
        Jesus' Love
    Infinitely sweeter;

8   Till with purest Passion panting
        Cries my Heart
        "Where Thou art
    "Nothing more is wanting."

9   Blest with thine Abiding Spirit,
        Fully blest
        Now I rest,
    All in Thee inherit.

10 Heaven is now with Jesus given;
        Christ in me,
        Thou shalt be
    Mine Eternal Heaven.

No. 115   "Ms. Deliberate": Hymn XI[3]

1   Thou, righteous God, whose Plague I bear,
        Whose plague I from my Youth have borne,
    Shut up in Temporal Despair,
        Ordain'd to suffer, & to mourn;

2   If now I had forgot to grieve,
        As every Penal Storm were o'er,
    Forgive, the Senseless Wretch forgive,
        And all my Chastisement restore.

3   Asham'd of having hop'd for Rest,
        Or ask'd for Comfort here below,
    Lo! I revoke the rash Request,
        And sink again in desp'rate Woe.

4   Submissive to the Stroke again
        I bow my faint devoted Head,
    Till Thou discharge the latest Pain,
        And write me free among the Dead.

5   Ah! what have I to do with Peace,
        Or Converse sweet, or Social Love?
    From Man, & all his Help, I cease,
        From Earth, & all her Goods remove:

6   Waking out of my Dream of Hope
        I see the fond Delusion end,

And give the whole Creation up,
    And live and die—without a Friend.

Q[uery]?

No. 116   Letter to Sally

Published here for the first time, with permission of the Methodist Church Archives
and History Committee, England.[4]

April 30, 1748

When the Poor and Needy seek water and there is none and their
Tongue faileth for thirst, I the Lord will help them. I the God of Jesus will
not forsake them. This Promise is continually fulfilled upon you, and every
seeking comfortless soul. But I hope the Consolation of Israel is now with
you, and you do not doubt the Faithful Mercies of God. Surely He hath a
Favour for you and has given you many Tokens of his Love. Expect far
more, and greater, even the accomplishment of all his propitious[?] Promises in you. *After* you have suffered awhile, the God of all grace shall make
you perfect. In patience hope[?] of your Soul—and you shall at last be filled
with all the Fullness of God.

You will not forget that you are a letter in my debt. On Monday [night
might?] I propose setting out to visit my Brother. Please direct as usual. My
strength is returned, so that I am almost ready for another Voyage.[5] O
when shall I reach the great Haven of Charity! How many knots would be
cut by my sudden escape out of Life! I look forward, and my coward Soul
faints at the Prospect.—But I have neither time nor Inclination to burthen
[sic] you with my complaints. The hymns, when I can get an Hour to
transcribe them, will shew [sic] my wretched Heart.

Farewell, Farewell in
both worlds thro[ugh] Christ Jesus!

No. 117   Journal Selections: June 16–August 11, 1748

Thur., June 16th. I visited the brethren in Cardiff [Wales], Lanmase,
Cowbridge, &c., and exhorted them to strengthen the things that remain.

Mon., June 20th. I returned with Kitty Jones to Bristol. Mr. Gwynne and
Miss Sally were got there a little before me; till,

Sat., June 25th. I carried them to see my Christian friends, my principal
ones especially at Kingswood.

Tues., June 28th. Quite spent with examining the classes, I was much
revived in singing with Miss Burdock and Sally.

Sat., July 2d. I lodged my fellow-travellers in the Foundery.

Fri., July 22d. At five I took horse with Mr. Gwynne, Sally, and M. Boult. We reached Cirencester before two. I preached in a yard from, "The redeemed of the Lord shall return, and come with songs," &c. . . .

Sun., July 24th. I rose from my boards at four. I carried Sally to Kingswood. . . .

Mon., August 1st. We set out for Garth; lodged at Abergavenny.

Tues., August 2d. In the afternoon Mrs. Gwynne received us with a cordial welcome.

Mon., August 8th. Mr. Gwynne, with Miss Sally and Betsy, accompanied me as far as Llanidloes. I preached with great enlargement. The poor people received the word with tears of joy. I parted with tears from my dearest friends, and rode on with Mr. Phillips to Machynlleth.

Thur., August 11th. I passed the day in my Prophet's chamber, or closet among the rocks. Only in the evening I walked up the mountain, and wandered in a wilderness of rocks with my inseparable friends.

No. 118   Letter to Sally

Charles's letter is full of longing for Perfect Love, a desire which he hoped Sally shared with him. While this concern is consonant with Wesley's piety, there are a few hints of more than one sort of "love" at work in this letter. The closing allusions to the church as "the Bride" of Christ and the eschatological consummation of love in "the Marriage Supper of the Lamb" might also be read with a double meaning. The letter is published here for the first time, by permission of the Methodist Church Archives and History Committee, England.[6]

H.[oly] H.[ead], August 12 [1748].

I write this from the prophet's chamber where I am still detained a willing prisoner to converse with my best beloved [unclear] Friend. I ask you, is your heart cheerful? And answer for you, that it surely is or mine would be in greater heaviness. Who is it that so strangely bears our burthens [sic]? The Creator of all the ends of the earth. He who fainteth not, neither is weary. He who loved us and gave Himself for us.

I am enabled to pray for you in every prayer that you may have the abiding witness of his love, that nothing may ever damp your Desires or slacken your Pursuit of that supreme good; that all sufficient Happiness which is in Jesus. O settle [unclear] it in your Heart that in Him all Fullness dwells, and that one Touch, One Word, one Look from Him can fill you with present Heaven. Both you and I have still a baptism to be baptized with; and how should we be straitened till it is accomplished! This, this is the One Thing Needful—not a Friend, not Health—not Life itself, but— the pure perfect Love of Christ Jesus.—O give me Love or else I die!—O give me Love, and *let* me die! I am weary of my want of Love—weary to Death; and would fain throw off this Body; that I may Love Him who so loved me.

If you do indeed love me for His sake (and I can as soon doubt my being alive) O wrestle with that Friend of Sinners [Christ] in my behalf, and let Him not go till He bless me with the Taste[?] of his Love! How shall I feed his Lambs unless I love Him? How shall I give up all, even those Friends who are dearer to me than my own Soul? How shall I suffer for One I do not love? O eternal Spirit of Love come down into my Heart and into my Friend's [Sally] Heart, and knit us together in the Bond of Perfectness[?]. Lead us by the waters of Comfort, swallow up our will in Thine. Make ready the Bride, and then call us up to the Marriage Supper of the Lamb!

No. 119   Journal Selections: November 4, 1748–
September 7, 1749

Fri., November 4th. I imparted my design [to marry] to Mrs. Vigor, who advised me with all kindness and freedom of a Christian friend.

Fri., November 11th. My brother and I having promised each other (as soon as he came from Georgia), that we would neither of us marry, or take any step towards it, without the other's knowledge and consent, to-day I fairly and fully communicated every thought of my heart. He had proposed three persons to me, S.[arah] P.[errin?], M.[iss] W.[ells?], and S.[ally] G.[wynne]; and entirely approved of my choice of the last. We consulted together about every particular, and were of one heart and mind in all things.

Fri., December 2d. By nine I found them at Garth, singing, and was most affectionately received by all, especially Mrs. Gwynne.

I advised with Sally how to proceed. Her judgment was, that I should write to her mother. . . .

Sun., December 4th. I rode with Sally and Betsy to Maesmynis. Our Lord administered strong consolation to our souls by the word and sacrament. At Builth, also, we were all melted into tears. I preached at Garth with the same blessing. I took farther counsel with Sally, quite above all guile or reserve. I was afraid of making the proposal. The door of prayer was always open.

Mon., December 5th. I spake with Miss Becky [Gwynne, Sally's sister], who heartily engaged in the cause, and at night communicated it to her mother, whose answer was, "she would rather give her child to Mr. Wesley than to any man in England." She afterwards spoke to me with great friendliness above all suspicion of underhand dealing (the appearance of which I was most afraid of); said, she had no manner of objection but "want of fortune." I propose £100 a year. She answered, her daughter could expect no more.

Thur., December 8th. I was a little tried by the brutishness of my friend Philips, who got my advocate, M——n, over to his side. But their buffetings did me no great harm.

Mr. Gwynne leaving the whole to his wife, I talked the matter fully over, and left it wholly with her to determine. She behaved in the most obliging manner, and *promised her consent*, if I could answer for £100 a year.

Sat., December 10th. Mr. Philips called [on] me, whom I mildly put by. I preached the next day, with great utterance and emotion. I talked once more with Mrs. Gwynne, entirely open and friendly. She promised to tell me if any new objection arose, and confessed, "I had acted like a gentleman in all things."

Mon., December 12th. I took a cheerful leave, and set out with Harry and Mr. Philips, somewhat milder. His only concern now was for the people. Them, also, I told him, my brother and I had taken into the account, and I had taken no one step without my brother's express advice and direction. . . .

Sat., December 17th. . . . By four I found my brother at the Foundery [London], and rejoiced his heart with the account of my prosperous journey.

He had advised me to make the experiment directly, by going to Garth, and talking with Mrs. Gwynne. Her negative (or his or Sally's) I should have received as an absolute prohibition from God. But hitherto it seems as if the way was opened by particular Providence.

Mon., December 19th. So my wise and worthy friend at Shoreham [Rev. Vincent Perronet] thought, when I communicated to him the late transactions. As to my own judgment, I set it entirely out of the question, being afraid of nothing so much as of trusting my own heart.

Wed., December 21st. I talked with Mr. Blackwell,[7] who very freely and kindly promised to assist in the subscription of £100 a year. I thought it better to be obliged for a maintenance to ten or a dozen friends, than to five hundred or five thousand of the people.

Fri., December 30th. I met Mr. Blackwell with my brother, who proposes £100 a year be paid me out of the [sale of] the books.

Tues., January 3d, 1749. My brother wrote as follows to Mrs. Gwynne. I enclosed it in my own, and sent both letters, after offering them up to the divine proposal. . . .

Fri., January 13th. I read, undisturbed, a letter from Mrs. Gwynne, dissatisfied with my brother's proposal. I visited Mr. Perronet the next day. He has indeed acted the part of a father: another proof whereof this letter of his to Mrs. Gwynne:—

Shoreham, January 14th, 1749.

Madam,—As the trouble of this proceeds from the most sincere friendship, I have reason to believe you will easily excuse it.

Give me leave then, Madam, to say, that if you and worthy Mr. Gwynne are of opinion that the match proposed by the Rev. Mr. Charles Wesley be of God, neither of you will suffer any objections, drawn from this world, to break it off. Alas, Madam! what is all this world, and the glories of it? How little does the world appear to that mind, whose affections are set on things above! This state is what I trust you are seriously seeking after. I am sure it is a state worth every Christian's seeking after, and what every Christian must seek after, if ever he hopes to get to heaven.

I have a daughter now designed for a pious gentleman, whose fortune is not half that of our friend's; and yet I would not exchange him for a Star and Garter. I only mention this that I might not appear to offer an opinion which I would not follow myself.

However, I have been hitherto speaking as if Mr. Wesley's circumstances really wanted an apology: but this is not the case. The very writings of these two gentlemen are, *even at this time, a very valuable estate*; and when it shall please God to open the minds of people more, and prejudice if worn off, it will be still much more valuable. I have seen what an able bookseller has valued a great part of their works at, which is £2,500: but I will venture to say, *that this is not half their value*. They are works which will last and sell while any sense of true religion and learning remain among us. However, as they are not of the same nature with an estate in land, they cannot be either sold or pledged without the most manifest loss and inconvenience.

I shall trouble you, Madam, no farther, than only to add, that from the time I had the pleasure of seeing Miss Gwynne at my house, I have often had her upon my mind. I then perceived so much grace and good sense in that young lady, that, when this affair was first mentioned to me, I could not help rejoicing at what promised so much happiness to the church of God.

May that God, in whose hands are the hearts of the children of men, direct all of you in such manner as may tend to the promoting His honour, and the kingdom of His dear Son. I am, with great respect to worthy Mr. Gwynne, yourself, and good family, Madam,

Your very sincere and affectionate friend and servant,

Vincent Perronet.

Mon., January 23d. I received letters from Garth, consenting to our proposals.

Fri., February 17th. Our wanderings through the bogs, &c., ended at eight in the evening. Sally met me, before I entered the house, with news that her brother was come, and very vehement against the match: yet he received us with great courtesy.

Sat., February 18th. Mrs. Gwynne was extremely open and affectionate; has fought my battles with her own relations, particularly her son, who has behaved very violently towards her. Miss Becky told him, he might think it is a great honour done him by our proposal. Mrs. Gwynne, my brother, and I, had a conference. He repeated his proposals, and agreed to make them good; being entirely reconciled to the settlement, for which Mr. Gwynne and Mr. Perronet were to be the Trustees.

Sun., February 19th. I returned to Garth from the sacrament at Maesmynis. Mr. H. Gwynne was very obliging. I drove his father to church, where we heard a good sermon. I had a conference with my brother and Sally. She promised to let me continue my vegetable diet and travelling.

Mon., February 20th. Mr. H[enry] Gwynne was now as affable as the rest; said he had nothing to object, and behaved as if his heart was entirely turned towards us.

Tues., February 21st. My brother and Charles Perronet left us. I stayed a week longer, preaching twice a day.

Sun., February 26th. Mrs. Gwynne assured me, she should not change; talked freely of our marriage, and would have got me to promise not to go again to Ireland. But Sally would not let me, saying, she should be glad herself to visit the many gracious souls in that country.

Mon., February 27th. I commended them once more to God, and took horse with Harry. . . .

Fri., March 3d. I met George Whitefield, and made him quite happy by acquainting him with my design [to marry].

Mon., March 6th. I mentioned it to the select band, desiring their prayers, not their advice.

Wed., March 29th. Having, by the help of Mr. Llyod and his Lawyers, settled everything to Mrs. Gwynne's wish, I set out at three, with Charles Perronet, for Bristol, in my way to Wales. [. . .]

Sat., April 1st. Just as we were setting out for Wales, my brother appeared full of scruples, and refused to go to Garth [for the wedding]. I kept my temper, and promised, "if he could not be satisfied there, to desist." I saw all was still in God's hands, and committed myself to Him.

Sun., April 2d. . . . I had wrote [sic] our friends notice, that I should be at Cardiff to-morrow, and on Tuesday or Wednesday at Garth. But I found my brother had appointed to preach in several places till Friday; which I did not take kindly.

Mon., April 3d. He seemed quite averse to signing his own agreement: yet at five we set out with a heavy heart. . . .

Fri., April 7th. I rose at four, and got an hour for prayer and the Scripture. That word in particular came with power to my heart, "Thus saith the Lord, If my covenant be not with day and night, and if I have not appointed the ordinances of earth and heaven; then I will cast away my seed of Jacob, and David my servant,—for I will cause their captivity to return, and will have mercy upon them."

I came to Garth by nine; found them at breakfast; almost equally welcome to all. We talked over matters with Mrs. Gwynne; and all my brother's fear were scattered. We read over the settlement. Mrs. Gwynne proposed a bond, till it could be signed. My brother signed the bond; Miss Becky and Miss Musgrave witnessed it.

We crowded as much prayer as we could into the day.

Sat., April 8th.

> Sweet day! so cool, so calm, so bright,
> The bridal day of the earth and sky.

Not a cloud was to be seen from morning till night. I rose at four; spent three hours and a half in prayer, or singing with my brother, with Sally, with Beck. At eight I led MY SALLY to church. Her father, sisters, Laddy Rudd, Grace Bowen, Betty Williams, and I think, Billy Tucker, and Mr. James were all the persons present. At the church-door I thought of the prophecy of a jealous friend, "that if we were even at the church-door to be married, she was sure, by revelation, that we could get no farther." We both smiled at the remembrance. We got farther. Mr. Gwynne gave her to me (under God): my brother joined our hands. It was a most solemn season of love! Never had I more of the divine presence at the sacrament.

My brother gave out the following hymn:—

Come, thou everlasting Lord,
By our trembling hearts adored;
Come, thou heaven-descended Guest,
Bidden to the marriage-feast!

Sweetly in the midst appear,
With thy chosen followers here;
Grant us the peculiar grace,
Show to all thy glorious face.

Now the veil of sin withdraw,
Fill our souls with sacred awe,—
Awe that dare not speak or move,
Reverence of humble love.

Love that doth its Lord descry,
Ever intimately nigh,
Hears whom it exalts to see,
Feels the present Deity.

Let on us thy Spirit rest,
Dwell in each devoted breast;
Thou with thy disciples sit,
Thou thy works of grace repeat.

Now the ancient wonder show,
Manifest thy power below;
All our thoughts exalt, refine,
Turn the water into wine.

Stop the hurrying spirit's haste,
Change the soul's ignoble taste;
Nature into grace improve,
Earthly into heavenly love.

Raise our hearts to things on high,
To our Bridegroom in the sky;
Heaven our hope and highest aim,
Mystic marriage of the Lamb.

O might each obtain a share
Of the pure enjoyments there;
Now, in rapturous surprise,
Drink the wine of paradise;

Own, amidst the rich repast,
Thou hast given the best at last;
Wine that cheers the host above,
The best wine of perfect love![8]

He then prayed over us in strong faith. We walked back to the house, and joined again in prayer. Prayer and thanksgiving was our whole employment. We were cheerful without mirth, serious without sadness. A stranger, that intermeddleth not with our joy, said, "It looked more like a funeral than a wedding." My brother seemed the happiest person among us.

Mon., April 10th. At four my brother took his leave of us. I passed the day in prayer, chiefly with my dearest friend. . . .

Thur., April 20th. I took my leave of Garth in those words of our Lord, "Be thou faithful unto death, and I will give thee a crown of life."

Fri., April 21st. I took horse with Sally, Betsy, and my father. We slept at Abergavenny.

Sat., April 22d. I cheerfully left my partner for the Master's work, and rode on with Harry to Bristol. We made so much haste, that I left all my strength behind me. . . .

Fri., April 28th. Some letters from Garth brought life with them. I prayed and wept over the beloved writers. . . .

Sat., May 27th. I hired a small house, near my worthy friend Vigor's [in Bristol], such an one as suited a stranger and pilgrim upon earth.

Fri., June 2d. I took horse at two, and got to Hereford by one. At half-hour past three my beloved Sally, with Mrs. Gwynne and her sister Peggy, found me at the Falcon. We sang, rejoiced, and gave thanks till Mr. and Mrs. Hervey came. After dinner we drank tea at their house, and went to see the cathedral. I wanted work; there was no door opened.

Fri., June 9th. I rode with Sally to Leominster, and expounded Isa. 55 in the market-place. The Minister was there again: all serious, some visibly affected. Dr. Young['s poetry][9] entertained us till we got to Coleford, late at night. It was a fair-time. With difficulty we got a [sic] private lodgings.

Sat., June 24th. We waited upon Dr. Middleton, who received us very cordially.[10] All look upon Sally with my eyes.

Fri., September 1st. By eleven we saluted our friend Vigor. I saw my house, and consecrated it by prayer and thanksgiving. I spent an hour at the preaching-room in intercession. I began the hour of retirement with joint prayer. Alone, I was in some measure sensible of the divine presence. I opened the book on those words, "While they spake, Jesus stood in the midst of them, and said, Peace be unto you." At six our first guests, Mrs. Vigor and her sisters, passed an useful hour with us. I preached on the first words I met, Rom. 12:1: "I beseech you therefore, brethren, by the mercies of God, that ye present your bodies as a living sacrifice," &c. The power and blessing of God was with us. Half-hour past nine I slept comfortably in my own house, yet not my own.

Mon., September 4th. I rose with my partner at four. . . . We sang this hymn in my family:—

> God of faithful Abraham, hear
>   His feeble son and thine,
> In thy glorious power appear,
>   And bless my just design:
> Lo! I come to serve thy will,
>   All thy blessed will to prove;
> Fired with patriarchal zeal,
>   And pure primeval love.
>
> Me and mine I fain would give
>   A sacrifice to Thee,
> By the ancient model live,
>   The true simplicity;
> Walk as in my Maker's sight,
>   Free from worldly guile and care,
> Praise my innocent delight,
>   And all my business prayer.
> Whom to me thy goodness lends
>   Till life's last gasp is o'er,
> Servants, relatives, and friends,
>   I promise to restore;
> All shall on thy side appear,
>   All shall in thy service join,
> Principled with godly fear,
>   And worshippers divine.
>
> Them, as much as lies in me,
>   I will through grace persuade,
> Seize, and turn their souls to Thee
>   For whom their souls were made;
> Bring them to th' atoning blood
>   (Blood that speaks a world forgiven),
> Make them serious, wise, and good,
>   And train them up for heaven.

Thur., September 7th. As often as I minister the word, our Lord ministers his grace through it. He blessed me also in private, as well as family, prayer, and conference with my Christian friends; in a word, whatsoever I do prospers.

DECEMBER 1753

The recent recovery of a manuscript fragment of Charles's journal, written in the shorthand of Dr. Byrom, fills in one of the major gaps in the published record of Wesley's work. Even more significant, however, is the way in which this manuscript fragment illuminates a six-day span in the life of Charles Wesley. In the fragment we capture a glimpse of the Methodist minister deeply immersed in Christian service, and the veil of silence and understatement has been pushed aside. We become privy to thoughts and details about his life that Charles sought to keep from the public eye. This personal side of the writer is quite significant for us, since it helps us see the maker of the hymns as both pastor and husband, beset by soul-straining responsibilities of both flock and family.

I am grateful to Mr. and Mrs. Douglas Lister, Leigh-on-Sea, England, for their assistance in making this transcription; to the Methodist Church Archives and History Committee, England, for permission to publish the piece originally; and to Mr. Charles Cole and the United Methodist Publishing House for permission to reprint portions of an article I wrote for the *Quarterly Review*.[11]

In the selection below, published and unpublished journal material has been woven together; the shorthand material will appear in italics. Selections of Charles's correspondence are also interspersed with the journal material and several hymns that seem to have been written during this period are appended to the journal record.

His journal entry for November 29, 1753, locates Charles at Bath, attending to the needs of the Methodist societies in that area. The same day he received news that his brother, John Wesley, was near death: "At two, as Mr. Hutchinson and I were setting out, we were met by a letter from Mr. Briggs, informing me, that I must make haste if I would see my brother alive."

John Hutchinson was a person under Charles's pastoral care. Wesley calls him his "patient"; he was in the throes of a mental or emotional disorder. Hence, Charles took Hutchinson with him on the forced march back to London, because he was afraid to leave the man alone in his disturbed state of mind. When Charles finally arrived at his brother's side, John had already composed his epitaph.

On December 4, 1753, Charles's second day in London while John was still battling his "consumption," letters arrived from Charles's home in Bristol. His wife, Sally, had been stricken with smallpox, and his son showed signs of contracting the disease as well.

The passage which follows traces Charles's return trip to Bristol. Once again he took John Hutchinson with him. Charles hoped to arrive at his destination prior to the death of loved ones; and, again, he traveled carrying the heavy burden of a ministry which he and his brother usually shared.

No. 120   Journal Selection: December 1, 1753

Sat., December 1st [1753]. My companion was strengthened to set out again before seven. Soon after four we were brought safe to M. Boult's [London]. She had no expectation of us, and was therefore quite unprepared. I had no other place to lodge my poor friend than the noisy Foundery. He had not more sleep than I expected.

No. 121   Letter to Sally[12]

The Foundery [London], December 1st [1753?] My dearest Sally,—God has conducted us hither through an easy, prosperous journey. My companion is better for it, not worse. But, first, you expect news of my brother. He is at Lewisham, considerably better, yet still in imminent danger, being far gone, and very suddenly, in a consumption. I cannot acquit my friends of unpardonable negligence, since not one of them sent me word of his condition, but left me to hear it by chance. I hasten to him to-morrow morning, when I have stationed my patient at Mrs. Boult's. To-night he lodges in the green room; I in S. Aspernal's.

Send this immediately to S. Jones, and bid her see it, that Wick be not neglected on Monday night. I passed my word that I or John Jones should preach there. Frank Walker, or whoever supplies our place, must inform them, that we hasten to see my brother before he dies.

Our tenderest love to dear Bell, S. Vigor, T. Hamilton, John James, &c. If my brother recovers, his life will be given to our prayers. Pray always, and faint not. Farewell.

No. 122   Journal Selections: December 2–3, 1753

Sun., December 2nd. The first news I heard last night, in Moorfields, was, that my brother was something better. I rode at nine to Lewisham; found him with my sister and Mrs. Blackwell and Mrs. Dewal. I fell on his neck, and wept. All present were alike affected. Last Wednesday he changed for the better, while the people were praying for him at the Foundery. He has rested well ever since: his cough is abated, and his strength increased. Yet it is most probable he will not recover, being far gone in a galloping consumption, just as my elder brother was at his age.

I followed him to his chamber, with my sister, and prayed with strong desire, and a good hope of his recovery. All last Tuesday they expected his death every hour. He expected the same, and wrote his own epitaph. . . . He made it his request to his wife and me, to forget all that is past; which I very readily agreed to, and once more offered her my service, in great sincerity. Neither will I suspect hers, but hope she will *DO* as she *SAYS*.

I have been generally blamed for my absence in this time of danger. Several asked, "Does Mr. Charles know of his brother's illness?" and were answered, "Yes, yes; many have informed him." All my correspondents agreed in their accounts that my brother was much better; of which his ministering in the chapel last Sunday left me no doubt. Then they might have apprized me of his danger; but none thought of me till Tuesday, when they looked for his death every hour. He had ordered letters to be wrote by Charles Perronet to the Preachers, to meet on the 21st instant; but not a word was sent to me. Now I hear, several letters were wrote [sic] to me on Tuesday night; but I have left them unreceived at Bristol.

I attended my brother while he rode out for the air, and was surprised to see him hold out for three quarters of an hour, and even gallop back the whole way.

In the afternoon I met the Leaders [of the Society], and spoke them comfort; then called on my patient, John Hutchinson, whose journey has done him more good than harm.

My text at the Foundery was 1 John 5:14, 15: . . . Whether the congregation received benefit, I know not, being myself confused and overwhelmed with trouble and sorrow. . . .

Mon., December 3d. I was at a loss for a subject at five, when I opened the Revelation, and, with fear and trembling, began to expound it. Our Lord was with us of a truth, and comforted our hearts with the blessed hope of his coming to reign before his ancients gloriously. Martin Luther, in a time of trouble, used to say, "Let us sing the forty-sixth Psalm." I would rather say, "Let us read the Revelation of Jesus Christ." What is any private or public loss, or calamity; what are all the advantages Satan ever gained or shall gain, over particular men or churches; when all things, good and evil, Christ's power and Antichrist's, conspire to hasten the grand event, to fulfill the mystery of God, and make all the kingdoms of the earth become the kingdoms of Christ?

I asked each of the select band whether they could pray in faith for my brother's life. . . . I called on loving, faithful D. P. and then visited my patient [Hutchinson] at Mr. L.[loyd]'s. With him I stayed till near one, the time I had appointed for prayer at the Foundery. . . . From intercession I waited on my sister to Dr. Forthergill; who is much pleased with his patient [John Wesley]'s present case, and greatly approves of his hastening to the Hotwells at Bristol. To-morrow afternoon he promises to visit him at Lewisham. The rest of the day I passed with John Hutchinson.

No. 123   Letter to Sally[13]

London, December 3d [1753].

Dearest Sally,—I hope you have recovered [from] your fright. My brother may live if he hastens to Bristol. Prayer is made daily by the church to

God for him; yet no one, that I can find, has received his petition. Whether he comes or not, I am stationed here till after Christmas.

We performed our journey most successfully: without one quarrel. One we narrowly escaped, through my returning to the watch [prayer]. The first night he passed (rather than slept) at the noisy Foundery. Last night Mr. Lloyd hardly prevailed on him to spend in Devonshire-square, where he would be heartily welcome while he stays in town; but cannot be persuaded to accept of our friend's offer. Whether he will have patience to wait here for my return to Bristol, or send up for Bell, and go to die at Leeds, a little time will show.

My brother entreated me, yesterday, and his wife, to forget all that is past on both sides. I *sincerely* told him I would, for his as well as Christ's sake. My sister said the same.

Mr. Blackwell assures me Mr. L[loyd's] security is unquestionable. What say you to Mr. Ianson's immediately settling the affair [their marital agreement]? Write by the first post to me at the Foundery. Mrs. B.[oult] and D.[ewal] send you a loving heart. They have but one, you know, between them.

Salute M[rs.] Vigor in my name, and T. H.[Hamilton], and J. James, and Sarah Jones, and all friends. Dudy Perronet salutes you in great love, as does Mr. Lloyd. I am going to consult Dr. Fothergill; shall see Betsy, the first friend I see *purposely*.

Next Friday we spend in prayer for my brother, meeting at five, seven, ten, and one. Join all who love him for his work's sake.

My love to George [Whitefield?], if with you. What news from Wales? Pray always, and faint not. . . . I have no time for idleness. All of my brother's business lies on me. . . . Who is your Chaplain? When none is near, you should read prayers yourself, as my mother, and many besides have done.

Be much in private prayer. What the Lord will do with me I know not; but am fully persuaded I shall not long survive my brother. . . . Farewell.

No. 124   Journal Selections: December 4–11, 1753

Tues., December 4th. I proceed in the Revelation, and found the blessing promised to those who read or hear the words of that book [Rev. 1:3]. . . . I told the Society on Sunday night, that I neither could nor would stand in my brother's place (if God took him to Himself); for I had neither the body, nor mind, nor talents, nor grace for it.

This morning I got the long-wished-for opportunity of talking fully to him of all which has passed since his marriage;[14] and the result of our conference was perfect harmony.

Mrs. Dewal and Blackwell observed, what a fair opportunity my wife might have had for inoculating [for smallpox] with her sister. I answered, that I left everyone to his own conscience; but for my part, I looked upon it as taking the matter out of God's hands; and I should choose, if it depended on me, to trust her entirely to Him.

Before five I returned to the Foundery, and found two letters from Lady Huntingdon; the first informing me they apprehended my wife has taken ill of the small-pox, as soon as I left her; the second, that it was come out, and the confluent kind.

She had been frightened (after my departure) with one's abruptly telling her, my brother was dead, and sickened immediately. I immediately consulted Mr. L[loyd], who advised me to fly where my heart directed. "But what can I do with Mr. Hutchinson?" "Take him with you by all means." I went and made him the offer, [here the published record breaks off and the shorthand begins] *but took care to tell him before hand that I should not leave my wife till she was out of danger, that therefore he could not be at my house. He flew into a most outrageous passion, calling it turning him out of my house, as in vain I laboured to set him right, Mrs. Phillips and Felt[?] assisting me. My mind and body were quite spent with travel. I left him at the height of his madness, met Mr. Lloyd, who encouraged me to hasten to Bristol whether he [Hutchinson] would [ac]company me or no.* I preached on "Let not your hearts be troubled—In my Father's house are many mansions," etc. I met good old Mr. P——, informed him of my journey. *Strove once more to reason with the whirlwind* [Hutchinson] *but increased my own burden thereby without lessening his. Lay down to rest with J.[ohn] J.[ones], a man of a better spirit who knows to weep with them that weep.*

Wed., December 5th. At Five [I] found John Hutchinson, after a restless night, as the troubled sea. *He had given a loose to his own passions, and spent the night in thinking what bitter things he would say to me. All the devil could put into his heart to torment himself, or me, he uttered. Lady Huntingdon was the chief mark of his malice, "that vile, wicked woman," as he called her, that nasty baggage, that hypocritical goat, etc., etc. In vain I offered to receive him into my house if we found my wife out of danger, or whenever she should be out of danger; that in the meanwhile he might lodge at Captain James' who had invited him or Mrs. Vigor's [house] or my own room in the Horsefair or Mrs. Wilson's next door to me. He was proof to all our entreaties.*

> Nec magis . . . tractabilis audit
> Quam si dura vilia aut . . . est marspatia cautes.[15]

I told him the chaise would be at the door by 6, when he must determine whether to go or stay. He suffered me to go without him, and I sent for John Jones to [ac]company me. Just as we were setting out John Hutchinson came, thrust out by Mrs. Felt. My flesh shrank at taking him in, a miserable comforter to me in my lowest distress; yet I durst not leave him in such a condition, a sure prey to Satan. The lightest consequence of his stay in London (where he grows worse every day) is bodily death. I therefore tried again to pacify him; but he was for quitting the chaise before we got through the city, and returning in a coach to his uncle's, there he said he would send for all his worldly friends[?], go to the Fleece [a pub?] *and give a loose to his heart's desires. I thought of poor Ignatius chained to his ten leopards.*[16] *I had all ten in one. At Hounslow we got a fresh chaise and I ever[?] persuaded him to go forward. At Salter[?] he rested a while and rode thence to Reading. There we had another desperate quarrel and he was again on the point of returning; yet was he over ruled[?] to drive on to Newbury, and instead of comforting me all the way* [he] *insulted my sorrow and spoke against my wife. I was so hindered and distracted by him that I could pray very little. As soon as I was released I took a walk by myself and poured out my heart in prayer, or my burden had been too heavy for me to bear. He was affrighted at my absence, and set upon the people of the inn to hunt after me. In under an hour I returned and he offered to go another stage to Marlborough. On the way he acknowledged his fault and promised amendment. But at Marlborough he relapsed again, and fell upon me for my weakness etc. I ordered a bed to myself in another chamber. He followed me in a transport of rage, laid hold of me and began dragging me back to his room. I did not follow readily; which made him roar as if possessed, and drew all the family to us. Had I put forth my strength he could not have prevailed but I was afraid to hurt him, and therefore let him drag me through a long gallery to his chamber. Then he locked me in. The servants without were frightened, fearing murder, and broke open the door. He made me sit down and I allowed him an hour to cool, then he fell on his knees and begged my pardon for the violence he had offered me and for so exposing himself and me. I said all that I could to soothe him and then betook me to rest in* [the] *other room.*

Thurs., December 6th. He had been sorely tempted in the night to cut his throat. When I came in he fell down again and asked my pardon, promising nevermore to grieve me. We set We set out at 7,[17] *but before we came to Bath his temper began to break out again, and before we reached Bristol, was as violent as ever. I resolved in myself nevermore to trust myself shut up with him; having passed 2 days as in hell.* and came to Bristol by 4. I found my dearest friend on a restless bed of pain, loaded with the worst kind of the disease. Mrs. Vigor and Jones were ministering to her day and night. S. Burges, a most tender, skillful Christian woman, was her nurse. Dr. Middleton had been a father to her. Good Lady Huntingdon attends her constantly twice a day, having deferred her journey to her son on this account. She had expressed a longing desire to see me, just before I came, and rejoiced for the consolation. I saw her alive; but O how changed! The whole head faint, and the whole heart sick from the crown of the head to the [18] soles of her feet there is no soundness. Yet, under her sorest burthen [sic], she blessed God, that she had not been inoculated; receiving the disease as immediately sent from Him. I found the door of prayer wide open, and entirely acquiesced in the divine will. I would not have it otherwise. God chuse [sic] for me and mine, in time and and eternity! *My poor friend* [Hutchinson] *vilely awaited as a messenger of Satan to buffet me. Mrs. Vigor offered him a bed at her house, but he flew out into the street, I followed and laid hold of him. He would needs go and proceed for himself. I reasoned with him but in vain. I told him there was but one bed in my house for me. He said I might lie out and leave it to him. I showed him the need of*

*my never stirring from my wife till out of danger, and the great hurt he would do
her if he could lodge in the house. His coughing would disturb and kill her. He
answered what was my wife more than another, that I made such a do with her, that
she had more care than his sister would have, who was far better than her in fortune,
and a deal of such stuff; that it was the greatest cruelty in me thus to turn him out of
my house desolate after I had brought him from all his friends, not to let him lodge
there one night till he could look about him. He desired me to leave him, which I
absolutely refused to dreading the consequences. He said he would go to Colter. It
was now dark. I went with him, and by the way told him our friends' fears that his
sister was infected by the smallpox. Once or twice he softened but immediately
relapsed again into his strange madness. I comforted myself that it was my last trial
with him, and having delivered him to his sister, dropped down. The strength of
nature could carry me no further. Mrs. Galitan was there and ran to Lady Huntingdon for a cordial.*[19] *I recovered myself in about an hour, then Lady Huntingdon
took me home in her coach. She joined with us in prayer for my afflicted partner,
whom we found as I left her. I hastened to the Room and stopped the people just as
they [were] scattering. The men told me, I rejoiced their hearts by "My brother
lives." [I] gave a short account of him, joined in fervent prayer, both for him and my
wife; and the Lord greatly comforted us!*

Sat., Dec. 7th. All this day she grew worse and worse, yet still the most threatening symptoms were kept off. We met at 7 and joined in mighty prayer for my brother
and her. At 10 we had powerful prayer. My very soul was drawn out and the souls
of all present. At one we wrestled again and could not doubt but our Lord heard us!

Sat., Dec. 8th. We expect the child [Charles's son, John Wesley Jr.] to be
taken every hour. I should be thankful if God spare him till his mother be out of
danger. She draws nearer and nearer to the crisis. God has satisfied me in "dreadful
past the observation darker every hour," yet after all this prayer ought I doubt?

Sun., Dec. 9th. 11th day [of his wife's illness]. I ministered the sacrament at
Kingswood and prayed with great feeling for my brother and her. She is now
brought very low indeed, being often ready to faint and die under her burden. For
about an hour in the afternoon I watched her while the glimmering lamp of life
seemed every moment ready to go out. She got a little rest in the night. I preached
on "let not your heart be troubled."

Mon. Dec. 10th. The 12th day. All day the pox began to turn in her face which is
now a good deal sunk, and her feet began to swell and burn and be sore. She is not
quite so low as she was, yet at times her fainting fits return, and she still lies
struggling as in the toils of death. Who knoweth what another day and night will
bring forth?

Tues., Dec. 11th. The 13th day. I was called between 3 and 4. She lay fainting as
before. In a momentous pause the important die of life and death spun doubtfully ere
it fell and turned up life! I prayed for her, and she revived. She has had a better
night than we expected, and if she gets over another night we shall hope the worst is
past.

6 [o'clock]. She had a fit of coughing and feared being choked, but recovered,
drank, and fell asleep, till 11. She waked now and then to drink, and lay quiet and

composed after it. Lady Huntingdon called and was . . . [here the manuscript breaks off]

Sally Wesley survived the smallpox, although her comely features were so marred by it that the difference in her and Charles's ages melted away. Charles's journal is missing for the closing days of 1753, but his correspondence locates him back in London. His infant son contracted the disease, and a letter from his sister-in-law, Rebecca Gwynne, reached him with the news. Charles, it seems, was unable to reach Bristol prior to Jacky's death. The pathos of this period of his life was preserved only in Charles's hymns, several of which reflect the ordeal. A few of the selections seemed to be linked to Sally's illness; somewhat thinly disguised by Charles's habit of calling her "his friend," they also enjoyed circulation in one of Wesley's later hymnals.

Several of the hymns are connected to the sickness and death of young John Wesley Jr., a child of eighteen months. The Wesley family found themselves forced to deal with the anguish of infant death and unanswered prayer. Charles's thoughts seemed drawn to the narrative of Abraham and Isaac, a father asked to give his long-awaited son back to God (Gen. 22). "Resignation" became a key word in his many hymns on the child's death; it spoke both of their struggle to accept the young child's death and their determined resolution to return him to God's care.

No. 125   Hymn: "Oblation of a Sick Friend"
(*Hymns for a Family*, 1767)

1   God of love, with pity see,
    Succour our infirmity;
    Father, let Thy will be done;
    Thine we say, but mean our own.

2   Can we of ourselves resign
    The most precious loan Divine?
    With Thy loveliest creature part?
    Lord, Thou seest our bleeding heart.

3   Whom Thyself hast planted there,
    From our bleeding heart to tear,
    This most sensibly we feel,
    This we own impossible.

4   Dearest of Thy gifts below,
    Nature cannot let her go;
    Nature, till by grace subdued,
    Will not give her back to God.

5   But we *would* receive the power
    Every blessing to restore,

Would to Thy design bow,
Would be meekly willing now.

6 If Thou *wilt* Thine own revoke,
Now inflict the sudden stroke,
Take our eyes' and hearts' desire,
Let her in Thine arms expire.

7 Stripp'd of all, we trust in Thee,
As our day our strength shall be;
Jesus, Lord, we come to prove
All the virtue of Thy love.

8 When the creature-streams are dry,
Thou Thyself our wants supply;
Thou of life the Fountain art,
Rise eternal in our heart.

No. 126 Hymn: "For a Child in the Small-Pox"
(*Hymns for a Family*, 1767)

1 Father, by the tender name
     Thou for man vouchsaf'st to bear,
We Thy needful succour claim,
     We implore Thy pitying care,
For our stricken child distress'd:
     Wilt Thou not our load remove,
Calm the tumult in our breast,
     Manifest Thy saving love?

2 Love inflicts the plague severe,
     Love the dire distemper sends:
Let Thy heavenly messenger
     Answer all Thy gracious ends:
Give us power to watch and pray
     Trembling at the threaten'd loss:
Tear our hearts from earth away,
     Nail them to Thy bleeding cross.

3 Fain we would obedient prove,
     Here on rugged *Calvary*
Render back the son we love,
     Yield our only son to Thee:
While he on the altar lies,
     We to Thy decree submit,
Offer up our sacrifice,
     Weep in silence at Thy feet.

4   Human tears may freely flow
       Authorised by tears Divine,
    Till Thine awful will we know,
       Comprehend Thy whole design:
    Jesus wept! and so may we:
       Jesus, suffering all Thy will,
    Felt the soft infirmity;
       Feels His Creature's sorrow still.

5   Father of our patient Lord,
       Strengthen us with Him to grieve,
    Prostrate to receive Thy word,
       All Thy counsel to receive:
    Though we would the cup decline,
       Govern'd by Thy will alone,
    Ours we struggle to resign:
       Thine, and only Thine, be done.

6   Life and death are in Thine hand:
       In Thine hand our child we see
    Waiting Thy benign command,
       Less beloved by us than Thee:
    Need we then his life request?
       Jesus understands our fears,
    Reads a mother's panting breast,
       Knows the meaning of her tears.

7   Jesus blends them with His own,
       Mindful of His suffering days:
    Father, hear Thy pleading Son,
       Son of Man for us He prays:
    What for us He asks, bestow:
       Ours He makes His own request:
    Send us life or death; we know,
       Life, or death from Thee is best.

No. 127   Hymn: "On the Death of a Child"
(*Funeral Hymns*, second series, 1759)

This was a very long hymn in its original form, consisting of fifty-one sorrowful
verses. The first of eight original parts is printed here.

Part I

1   Dead! dead! the child I loved so well!
       Transported to the world above!

I need no more my heart conceal:
   I never dared indulge my love:
But may I not indulge my grief,
And seek in tears a sad relief?

2 Mine earthly happiness is fled,
    His mother's joy, his father's hope:
O had I died in *Isaac's* stead!
    He *should* have lived, my age's prop,
He should have closed his father's eyes,
And follow'd me to paradise.

3 But hath not Heaven, who first bestow'd,
   A right to take His gifts away?
I bow me to the sovereign God,
    Who snatch'd him from the evil day!
Yet nature *will* repeat her moan,
And fondly cry, "My son, my son!"

4 Turn from him, turn, officious thought!
    Officious thought presents again
The thousand little acts he wrought,
    Which wound my heart with soothing pain:
His looks, his winning gestures rise,
His waving hands, and laughing eyes!

5 Those waving hands no more shall move,
    Those laughing eyes shall smile no more:
He cannot now engage our love
    With sweet insinuating power,
Our weak unguarded hearts ensnare,
And rival his Creator here.

6 From us, as we from him, secure,
    Caught to his heavenly Father's breast,
He waits, till we the bliss ensure,
    From all these stormy sorrows rest,
And see him with our angel stand,
To waft, and welcome us to land.

The Wesleys struggled through the ordeal of December 1753, and they came to consider it a time when their faith was tried in "the refiner's fire" and proven true. Charles's journal puts him back on the road by July 8, 1754, yet his and Sally's lives were markedly changed by the child's death. Sally folded a lock of his golden hair into a sheet of paper and labeled it: "My dear Jacky Wesley's hair: who died of the small-pox, on Monday, Jan. 7th, 1753–4, aged a year, four months, and seventeen days. I shall go to him; but he never shall return to me." When Sally's friend and nurse, Grace Bowen, died on January 7, 1755, it jogged Charles's heart and mind back to a year earlier as he penned a note and poem to Sally from Brecon. The hymn quoted for Grace Bowen (below) was published in his *Funeral Hymns* of 1746. The new hymn begun for the anniversary of Jacky's death was never published.

No. 128   Letter to Sally[20]

January 7th, 1754–5, Brecon, three o'clock.

'Tis finish'd, 'tis done!
  The spirit is fled,
The prisoner is gone,
  The Christian is dead!
The Christian is living,—

and we shall live also, when we have shook off this body of death, and overtaken our happy, happy friend [Grace Bowen] in paradise.

I rode hard to see her before her flight; but it is my loss, not hers, that the chariot carried her up last Thursday. I only write in utmost haste, to assure my best-beloved friend that I am perfectly well, and all our friends here. More in my next. Salute our friends in both squares.

Farewell in Christ.

Hail the *sad* memorable day,
  On which my Isaac's soul took wing!
With us he *would* no longer stay;
  But, soaring where archangels sing,
Join'd the congratulating choir,
And swell'd their highest raptures higher.

His soul, attuned to heavenly praise,
  Its strong celestial bias show'd;
And, fluttering to regain its place,
  He broke the cage, and reach'd his God:
He pitch'd in yon bright realms above,
Where all is harmony and love, &c.

Imperfect.

A MISCELLANY OF DOMESTIC HYMNS AND LETTERS

Charles Wesley's correspondence lacked the high-flying theology that characterized many of his brother's epistles. Charles's letters typically communicated "his history" to Sally and the children, listed his successes and failures, and reported his lamentable health. Greetings were sent and received from their many friends, and pangs of loneliness and poverty were whispered between the lines.

HIS BEST-BELOVED FRIEND

The following selections were probably written soon after the Wesleys' wedding, since they do not mention their children. They show Charles trying to adjust to being separated from his new bride. He seems (especially in letter No. 130) to be feeling some guilt over being away from home so often. He urges her to pursue her own intellectual and spiritual development in his absence.

No. 129   Letter to Sally[21]

Moorfields, April 10th, Easter-day.

My prayer for my dearest partner and myself is, that we may know Him, and the power of his resurrection.

The Lord (we found this morning) is risen indeed! At the table we received the Spirit of prayer for my dear desolate mother, the Church of England. O pray for the peace of Jerusalem! they shall prosper that love her.

One [person] desired to return thanks for the seal of forgiveness received under my word on Thursday night.

Do not neglect your short-hand; do not neglect your music; but, above all, do not neglect your prayers.

My love to S. Gwynne, and our other friends. Poor disconsolate Mr. Belson greets you, and J. Boult sends her *duty*.

My heart is with you. I want you every day and hour. I should be with you always, or not at all; for no one can supply your place. Adieu.

No. 130   Letter to Sally[22]

Tuesday Night

Dear Sally,—On Wednesday morning I shall probably, *most* probably, see you; but I dare not set my heart upon it, lest my eagerness should cause a disappointment.

Yesterday I passed at St. Anne's, where we wanted nothing but you. Mr. Bridgen set out with me at three in the morning. We dodged most of the showers; but the thunder and lightning kept us in awe all day. At six we drank tea, in [sic] our return, with Sally Hardwick, when I dropped asleep, caught a cold that stiffened my whole frame. By ten I reached my lodgings.

I rose this morning at five, and washed away my complaints in a bath, near the Foundery, which I make use of almost every day.

Never was I more satisfied with your absence, than during this scorching weather; but I almost envy you in your cool hall at Ludlow. All yesterday was storm and tempest. The thunder almost deafened us. My eyes still ache with the lightning.

I have just been reading the letters, and praying for you. We had a blessed opportunity. Remember me at five [their agreed-upon hour of prayer]. I am weary of my own unprofitableness, and ashamed that I have been of so little use to my dearest Sally. It is well that you have one Friend who *may* be depended on. To Him I constantly command you. Our sister Lambert sends her love.

Farewell.

Charles's *Hymns and Sacred Poems* (1749) carried fifty-five hymns "For Christian Friends." These hymns were composed during the time of his courtship (and before), and while they were suitable for any friendship, not a few of them seem to have "Sally," his "best of friends," in mind. The hymns vibrate with piety and personal warmth, demonstrating Wesley to have been—as John Gambol said of him—"a man made for friendship."

No. 131   Hymns for Christian Friends: 12

1   See, O Lord, Thy servant see,
        And graciously approve
    My other self, and next to Thee
        The object of my love:
    The love, wherewith my heart runs o'er,
        I dare to Thee present,
    Thine all-indulging grace adore,
        And bless Thine instrument.

2   My gifts and comforts all, I know,
        From Thee alone descend;
    Thou only couldst on me bestow
        So true, and kind a friend.
    Cast in one mould by art Divine
        Our blended souls agree,
    And pair'd above our spirits join
        In sacred harmony.

3   As sent, to bless me, from above
        Thy creature I receive,

To turn my utmost strength of love
    On Him for whom I live;
To raise, and help my weakness on,
    Th' angelic power is given,
He comes in human form sent down,
    And guards my soul to heaven.

4 Thankful from Thy bless'd hands I take
    Th' inestimable loan,
And stand prepared to give him back,
    To render Thee Thine own:
I dare not to Thy creature cleave,
    Thy creature, Lord, recall,
Thy glory still to Thee I give,
    That Thou art all in all.

No. 132 Hymns for Christian Friends: 16

1 Author of the peace unknown,
    Lover of my friend and me,
Who of twain hast made us one,
    One preserve us still in Thee,
All our heighten'd blessings bless,
Crown our hopes with full success.

2 Centre of our hopes Thou art,
    End of our enlarged desires:
Stamp Thine image on our heart,
    Fill us now with holy fires,
Cemented by love Divine,
Seal our souls for ever Thine.

3 All our works in Thee be wrought,
    Level'd at one common aim,
Every word, and every thought
    Purge in the refining flame,
Lead us through the paths of peace
On to perfect holiness.

4 Let us both together rise,
    To Thy glorious life restored,
Here regain our paradise,
    Here prepare to meet our Lord.
Here enjoy the earnest given,
Travel hand in hand to heaven.

SALLY'S BIRTHDAY

No. 133   Letter to Sally[23]

Hatfield, October 12th–23d, 1756.

Blessed be the day on which my dearest Sally was born! It has been continual sunshine; the fairest, calmest, brightest day, since I left you in Bristol. Such may all your succeeding ones be; at least may you enjoy that "perpetual sunshine of the spotless mind." The Lord lift up the light of his countenance upon you while you are reading this, and put gladness in your heart! May you taste the powers of the world to come, and be partaker of the Holy Ghost!

No. 134   Hymn: "On the Birthday of a Friend"
(*Hymns for the Use of Families and on Various Occasions*, 1767)

1   Come away to the skies
         My beloved arise,
    And rejoice on the day thou was born,
         On the festival day
         Come exalting away,
    To thy heavenly country return.

2   We have laid up our love
         And treasure above,
    Though our bodies continue below;
         The redeem'd of the Lord
         We remember His word,
    And with singing to *Sion* we go.

3   With singing we praise
         The original grace
    By our heavenly Father bestow'd,
         Our being receive
         From His bounty, and live
    To the honour and glory of God.

4   For Thy glory we are,
         Created to share
    Both the nature and kingdom Divine:
         Created again,
         That our souls may remain
    In time and eternity Thine.

5   With thanks we approve
         The design of Thy love
    Which hath join'd us, in Jesus' name,

So united in heart,
That we never can part,
Till we meet at the feast of the Lamb.

6   There, there at His feet
We shall suddenly meet,
And be parted in body no more,
We shall sing to our lyres
With the heavenly choirs,
And our Saviour in glory adore.

7   Hallelujah we sing
To our Father and King,
And His rapturous praises repeat;
To the Lamb that was slain
Hallelujah again
Sing all heaven, and fall at His feet.

8   In assurance of hope
We to Jesus look up,
Till His banner unfurl'd in the air
From our graves we shall see,
And cry out IT IS HE,
And fly up to acknowledge Him there!

HUSBAND AND FATHER

Charles was a loving father in an age that expected fathers to be stern and mothers to be tender. His inquiries about his children and hymns for children reveal the joy he felt as a father. His frequent absences weighed heavy upon Charles. He was gone from his family for as much as two months at a time, forced to measure their growth by unreliable post, and the arrival of their teeth. The growth of his family and declining health gradually curtailed Charles's travels.

The death of five of his children in infancy tinged the Wesleys' early years of marriage and letters with sadness. Sally was heartbroken with these tragedies, and Charles's letters tried to console her despite his own misery. These deaths, coupled with Charles's own frail health, led to a preoccupation with death in his later hymns and letters; but in accordance with his piety, faith was victorious in the face of the final enemy.

No. 135   Letter to Sally[24]

The Foundery, September 21st.
My dearest of friends,—you will learn obedience by the things you suffer. Jacky's loss, and Patty's [two of their children], and Grace Bowen's,

&c, are to prepare you for mine. Me you will outlive many years, I am persuaded, in spite of the warning, as you call it, or the idle trick of the enemy, as I think it. Had it been from a good spirit, I know, after my last prayer, it would have been repeated. But make all the use of it you can, and let it stir you up to more constant prayer. Why do you leave Mrs. Gaussen out of your "kind remembrance"? You have no friend loves you better. Poor Betsy should come, whether to Bath or Bristol, as soon as able; and doubtless they will lose no time in sending her. . . .

The Lord is wonderfully with us. His word is a two-edged sword. I preach every morning to a crowded audience. Last night the divine presence overwhelmed us, while I met the Leaders: our flesh did indeed keep *silence* before Him. In family prayer, a poor girl (Mrs. W.[esley]'s servant) cried out in the pangs of the new birth. We wrestled for her in prayer: I look for the answer of peace every hour. You can hardly believe how quiet and comfortably we live in this house.

I hope Mrs. W. keeps her distance. If malice is stronger in her than pride, she will pay you a mischievous visit. Poor Mr. Lefevre breakfasted with me this morning, and lamented that he cannot love her. Blessed be God, I can, and desire to love her more. What is her debt of one hundred pence to ours of one hundred thousand talents? [Matt. 18:23f]

My work calls me. The Lord bless my beloved Sally with a praying, loving heart!

No. 136   Letter to Sally[25]

Barnstaple, September 10th.

My dearest partner,—I am got into a conjurer's circle, or enchanted castle, and can find no way out. The stronger my niece grows, the more conversible, and harder to be left. I have been deeply engaged in my brother's [Samuel Wesley Jr.] manuscript poems; but want time to copy them. However, one I send you as a sample:

On the Death of His Child

Adieu, my Nutty, dearly bought!
I envy thee, but pity not;
Happy the port betime to gain,
Secure from shame, and guilt, and pain.
No lover false thy touch beguiled,
No wicked and unthankful child
Tortured with grief thy riper years,
Or crush'd with woes thy hoary hairs.
O blest, beyond misfortune blest,
And safe in never-ending rest!
Let me, if not for thee, my dear,

Drop for myself a secret tear:
For me, my best of life-time knows
Decreasing friends, and growing foes;
To those whom most I wish'd to please,
The cause of pining and disease;
Alive, in storms and tempests toss'd;
And dead—perhaps for ever lost.
If doom'd to feel eternal pain,
Never to meet with thee again,
Though midst the pangs of stinging thought,
And bodings of despair, if aught
Could make me pleased with life to be,
'Tis, that I being gave to thee.

You will see how exactly this suits me, if you only put *Patty* instead of *Nutty*. I cannot but believe it will not be long before I overtake my brother [in death]. Therefore was I constrained to come hither at this time, as a debt I owed him. I shall last as long as I can, that you may be assured of, seeing it is my duty to God and you.

For my sake you must be equally careful. Woe be to you, if I find you fallen away! If you starve yourself, you starve my child, unborn. Charles I am under no concern for. . . .

This day three weeks I hope to pass with my dearest Sally, Becky, and Betsy, to *say* nothing of Charley, as I *think* nothing of him. Yet if he has got a tooth, tell me so in a line to Tiverton. . . . You will be glad to hear I have quite recovered my first day's ride, and am now doubly careful not to *run* into the same inconvenience. My few remaining days I would willingly spend in peace and retirement, and

Walk thoughtful on the silent, solemn shore
Of that vast ocean I must sail so soon.

My Sally will help me forward. O let us be diligent to be found in Him in peace, without spot, and blameless. Adieu.

No. 137 Hymn: "For Little Children"
(*Hymns for Children*, 1763)

1   Lover of little children, Thee,
       O Jesus, we adore;
    Our kind and loving Saviour be,
       Both now and evermore.

2   O take us up into Thine arms,
       And we are truly bless'd;
    Thy new-born babes are safe from harms,
       While harbour'd in Thy breast.

3   There let us ever, ever sleep,
        Strangers to guilt and care;
    Free from the world of evil, keep
        Our tender spirits there.

4   Still, as we grow in years, in grace
        And wisdom let us grow;
    But never leave Thy dear embrace,
        But never evil know.

5   Strong let us in Thy grace abide,
        But ignorant of ill;
    In malice, subtlety, and pride
        Let us be children still.

6   Lover of little children, Thee,
        O Jesus, we adore;
    Our kind and loving Saviour be
        Both now and evermore.

No. 138   Letter to Sally[26]

London, August 21st, 1766.
My dear Sally,—What news of Sammy's invisible tormentors? All flesh is grass, you see in him. When his teeth break out, he may recover his strength and looks, and be the finest child in Bristol, till more teeth pull him down.

Last night my brother came. This morning we spent two blessed hours with G.[eorge] Whitefield. The threefold cord, we trust, will never more be broken. On Tuesday next my brother is to preach in Lady Huntingdon's chapel at Bath. That and all her chapels (not to say, as I might, herself also) are now put into the hands of us three.

It is agreed that I stay here till Monday three weeks. Then (that is, September 15th) I hope to take coach with Miss Darby, and embrace you all on the 16th. . . .

My brother and sister [John Wesley and wife] will call on you, I presume, next Wednesday. She continues quite placid and tame. You can be courteous without trusting her. . . .

No news by last post from Bristol. I shall want £20 added to buy £1,000 stock, and have but £20 towards it; but God will provide. Ask Mr. James if you or he can make more of your money. Ask Mr. Stokes (if accessible) the same question. My blessing to the dear children. I long to see them, and their mother also. In Jacky's cries with his teeth, I often hear Sammy's. The Lord Jesus hear, and preserve, and bless you all!

No. 139   Hymn: "For a Child Cutting His Teeth"
(Hymns for a Family, 1767)

1   Suffering for another's sin,
      Why should innocence complain?
    Sin by *Adam* enter'd in,
      Sin engendering grief and pain;
    Sin entail'd on all our race,
      Forces harmless babes to cry,
    Born to sorrow and distress,
      Born to feel, lament, and die.

2   Tortured in his tender frame,
      Struggling with convulsive throes,
    Doth he not aloud proclaim
      Guilt the cause of all our woes?
    Guilt, whose sad effects appear,
      Guilt original we own,
    See it in that starting tear,
      Hear it in that heaving groan!

3   Man's intemperate offense
      In its punishment we read;
    Speechless, by his aching sense
      Guilty doth our infant plead;
    Instruments of sin and pain,
      Signs of guilt and misery
    Eve's incontinence explain,
      Point us to the tasted tree.

4   There the bitter root we find,
      Fatal source of nature's ill,
    Ill which all our fallen kind
      With this young apostate feel:
    But what we can ne'er remove
      Jesus came to sanctify,
    Second *Adam* from above,
      Born for us to live and die.

5   Help, the woman's heavenly Seed,
      Thou that didst our sorrows take,
    Turn aside the death decreed,
      Save him for Thy nature's sake!
    Pitying Son of man and God,
      Still Thy creature's pains endure;
    Quench the fever with Thy blood,
      Bless him with a perfect cure.

6   Thine it is to bless and heal,
      Thine to rescue and repair:
    On our child the answer seal,
      Thou who didst suggest the prayer:
    Send salvation to this house;
      Then, to double health restored,
    I and mine will pay our vows,
      I and mine will serve the Lord.

No. 140   Letter to Sally[27]

Lovel's-court, Tuesday night [1768]

Father, not as I will but as thou wilt. Thy will be done on earth, as it is in heaven! Let my dearest companion in trouble offer up this prayer with as much of her heart as she can: and God, who knoweth whereof we are made, and considereth that we are but dust, will, for Christ's sake, accept our weakest, most imperfect, desire of resignation. I know, the surest way to preserve our children, is to trust them with Him who loves them infinitely better than we can do. I received your trying news this morning [regarding the death of John James Wesley, aged seven months]; walked directly with my sympathizing friend F.[letcher?] to take a place. All full, but the Bath coach for to-morrow. I shall come thereby somewhat later to my beloved Sally, and Charley, and his sister. But the Lord is with you already; the Lord is with you always. This has been a solemn day. You must not deny my love to my sweet boy, if I am enabled to resign him for his heavenly Father to dispose of. I cannot doubt His wisdom or goodness. He will infallibly do what is best, not only for our children, but for us, in time and eternity. Be comforted by this assurance. Many mourn with, and pray for, you and your little ones. I shall tread on the heels of my letter, if the Lord prosper my journey. He comes with me. Let us continually expect Him, the great Physician of soul and body. Peace be with you! May the Lord Jesus himself speak it into your heart, "My peace I give unto you!"

No. 141   Hymn: "A Mother's Act of Resignation
on the Death of a Child"
(*Hymns for a Family*, 1767)

1   Peace, my heart, be calm, be still,
    Subject to my Father's will!
    God in Jesus reconciled
    Calls for *His* beloved child,
    Who on me Himself bestow'd
    Claims the purchase of His blood.

2   Child of prayer, by grace Divine
    Him I willingly resign,

Through his last convulsive throes
Born into the true repose,
Born into the world above,
Glorious world of light and love!

3 Through the purple fountain brought,
To his Saviour's bosom caught,
Him in the pure mantle clad,
In the milk-white robe array'd,
Follower of the Lamb I see;
See the joy prepared for me.

4 Lord, for this alone I stay;
Fit me for eternal day;
Then Thou wilt receive Thy bride
To the souls beatified,
Then with all Thy saints I meet,
Then my rapture is complete.

No. 142   Letter to Sally[28]

London, July 7th.

My dearest friend,—Can you cast all your care upon Him who careth for you and your little ones? If I could not trust Him with you, I should be much uneasy. Is Sally sickened yet? I should not be very sorry, or very anxious, if she was. She cannot have the distemper at a better time. . . .

Saturday night.

No letter from Sally concerning herself and children! You want, it seems, to try my patience. I will be even with you, and try your courage, by informing you (but the information comes by Charles Perronet) that the people of Canterbury are in the utmost confusion, the men all up in arms, the women all screaming, through a sudden alarm and panic that the French are seen off Dover. It is a false alarm, that is certain, or it would have been here before any private letter. I think I must steal away to you to be quiet [calm]; for Mr. Ireland and Dr. Middleton have *insured* you and Bristol.

Get a friend to write when you cannot, or I shall have no rest in my spirit. The Lord bless you with his peace! Adieu.

No. 143   Hymn: "A Hymn for Love"
(*Hymns for a Family*, 1767)

1 Ask if a mother's heart is kind,
    To her own suckling child;
Then ask, Is God to love inclined,
    Or my Redeemer mild?

2   A mother may perhaps neglect,
      And her own son forget,
    But Jesus never will reject
      A sinner at His feet.

3   Ask, if the sun doth once mistake
      His true celestial road;
    Then ask, if Jesus can forsake
      The purchase of His blood?

4   The sun at last shall lose his way,
      And into darkness fall;
    But Jesus at that endless day
      Shall be our All in all.

No. 144   Letter to Sally[29]

Monday night.

My dear Sally's letter is this moment delivered. Blessed be God who holds your soul in life! Send out your daughter as soon as you safely can; and let not Charles lose a day for riding. Nanny will be best out. Samuel, I think, will escape his bout. My love to children and friends. Encourage Charles in writing, riding and music. As to the last, he needs no spur, but attention only. His first letter will be an answer to mine.

God has met us with a blessing here. Yesterday my subject at Spitalfields was, "Let us therefore come boldly to the throne of grace, that we may obtain mercy," &c. The chapel was crowded. The spirit of love rested on us. . . .

Suffer me to boast a little. Never did the people seem to love me better, or I them. They are brethren who dwell together in unity. I was feasted all Sunday long. B. Evans, my host, and his wife do their utmost to make my lodging agreeable. It is a most delightful place, in the air, clean as a Friend's house. Beck is in love with it. Poor Mrs. Footit begged me with tears to sleep at her house, when at their end of the town. S. Heritage, and Hannah, and S. Macdonald, Kemp, and five hundred more, inquire and salute you in increasing love. Nancy White remembers you in her dying prayers.

Farewell in Christ.

No. 145   Letter to Sally[30]

London, January 5th.

My dear Sally's letter, this moment received, has awakened all my love and concern for our dearest boy. But I hope you will have the comfort, while reading this, to see him as well as you wish. If not (and the Lord is pleased to try us farther), let us remember we are not our own; neither are our children. The most likely way to keep them is, to give them up in the spirit of daily sacrifice. I know not what God will do with them; only I know He will do what is best, whether that be to take them early or late to paradise.

Every illness he has will be, in your apprehension, the small-pox. I do not think he will have it till he has all his teeth. If your uneasiness for him continues, you must pity and wean his sister. . . .

On Monday my brother returns, and puts an end to our holidays. I am going to print my Hymns for Children. . . .

I depend on constant intelligence concerning Charley, till *you* think him out of danger. Poor Lady Robert is quite miserable, lest her children should live to be wicked. From this fear I am at present delivered; being assured, if I will give God leave to resume my children in their infancy, He will either so resume them, or bring them up for Himself.

No. 146   Hymn: "A Father's Prayer for His Son"
(*Hymns for a Family*, 1767)

1   God of my thoughtless infancy,
      My giddy youth, and riper age,
   Pierced with Thy love, I worship Thee,
      My God, my Guide through every stage;
   From countless sins, and griefs, and snares
      Preserved, Thy guardian hand I own,
   And borne and saved to hoary hairs,
      Ask the same mercy for my son.

2   Not yet the commandment slain,
      O may he uncorrupted live,
   His simple innocence retain
      And dread an unknown God to grieve:
   Restrain'd, prevented by Thy love,
      Give him the evil to refuse,
   And feel Thy drawings from above,
      And good, and life, and virtue choose.

3   When near the slippery paths of vice
      With heedless steps he runs secure,
   Preserve the favourite of the skies,
      And keep his life and conscience pure:
   Shorten his time for childish play,
      From youthful lusts and passions screen,
   Nor leave him in the wilds to stray
      Of pleasure, vanity, and sin.

4 Soon may the all-inspiring Dove
    With brooding wings his soul o'erspread:
  The hidden principle of love,
    The pure, incorruptible seed,
  Hasten into his heart to sow;
    And when the word of power takes place,
  Let every blossom knit and grow,
    And ripen into perfect grace.

FOR YOUNG MEN AND WOMEN

As his children grew Charles's letters began to inquire more directly about their spiritual and intellectual development. Soon Charles Jr. and Sally Jr. occasionally accompanied their father on his ministerial journeys. Several interesting letters from Charles to his children have survived. His topics run the gamut from a pastor's concern for their religious seriousness to a father's impatience with Sally's fledgling attempts at walking in "fashionable" heels. He has fatherly advice for Charles about marriage, and is inquisitive about Sally's "friend" Mr. John Russel—when will they meet? He brings parental pressure to bear on the boys' attention to their music, as well as upon Sally's diligence with her poetry and devotional readings.

Charles's correspondence to his sons and daughter show both his pride in them, and a perplexity at his inability to inculcate his own values in them. They showed little of their father's interest in Methodism. Both sons moved into musical vocations. Charles Jr. became an unsuccessful secular musician and had none of the spiritual fervor of his namesake. Samuel Jr., a talented organist, hoped to become a church musician, but the spartan tastes of Methodism provided no place or stimulation for his genius. Through his love of liturgy, cathedral music, and perhaps also a woman, the youngest son of the first Methodist became a Roman Catholic. Charles Sr. seemed to be hastened to his grave with that development. Sam's uncle John tried to reconcile Sam to Methodism, because Catholicism held fewer attractions than bigamy, but without success. The second son perpetuated his father's talents by producing one of the musical luminaries of the next generation, Samuel Sebastian Wesley, albeit through an "irregular" union. Of Charles Wesley's three surviving children only Sally Wesley found her intellectual and religious heritage in a way that would have pleased her father; but it is unclear whether she ever found in Methodism the same sense of fulfillment he did.

No. 147 Letter to Sally[31]

Bristol, September 7th.
Sunday, September 6th, I rode with my brother in his chaise to Kingswood, and had a feast indeed with our beloved colliers.

Sam will have many more escapes. Great will be his trials; but the Lord will deliver him out of all. Sally must buy experience and heedfulness by a few more falls. I have received a very good letter from her.

I did not think to tell you, yet I will (not to frighten you, but to increase yor thankfulness), that last week, as I was quietly walking my horse, he fell down, all four, with me, and on me, as I thought, till I rose covered with dust, but not at all hurt. Miss Morgan was with me. I left her at the Fishponds, and walked contented home. N.B. I shall never more ride that beast.

My brother is set out for the country Societies. My brother says Sally [Charles's daughter] was much awakened, while she met some of her equals here. Pity we could not find her suitable companions in London. Among the serious she would be serious, and more.

Sam wants more pains to be taken with him. If I should not live to help him, it will lie all upon you. Make him a living Christian, and he will never wish to be a dead Papist.

My dear Charles [his son],—Send me a letter in the enclosed frank, and a punctual account of your proceedings, readings, composings, &c. Your aunt Waller will help you to some thin paper, in which you, and your brother and mother, may write at once.

What do you understand by that scripture phrase, "God gave him favour in the sight of—such an one?" Does it not teach you to refer *all* good to God? He raises us up our friends, and expects our thankful acknowledgement of it. Such is Lady Gatehouse, Mr. Barrington, and others. And if God be for us, who can be against us? "Acquaint thyself now with Him, and be at peace"; that is, know God, and be happy.

You must give my very kindest love to all and every one of our family at Tarriers. Look out for a fair opportunity of visiting his Lordship. Perhaps you may get a scholar [music student] by it. Sam also should go, in gratitude as well as interest, and oblige my Lord to the best of his power.

On this day [a] month I hope to set out with my brother for London. Your mother tells me Sam is very seriously inclined [eg. toward religion]. You and your sister must increase my satisfaction on his account. My father I have heard say, "God had shown him he should have all his nineteen children about him in heaven." I have the same blessed hope for my eight.

His blessing be upon you all!

No. 148   Letter to His Son, Charles Jr.[32]

Bristol, August 30th, 1782.

Dear Charles,—If any man would learn to pray (the proverb says), let him go to sea. I say, If any man would learn to pray, let him think about marrying; for if he thinks aright, he will expect the blessing and success from God alone; and ask it in frequent and earnest prayer. Hitherto, my dear Charles, your thoughts of marriage have not made you more serious, but more light, more unadvisable, more distracted. This has slackened my desire to see you settled before I leave you. You do not yet take the way to be happy in a married state: you do not sufficiently take God into your council.

No one step or action in life has so much influence on eternity as marriage. It is an heaven or an hell (they say) in this world; much more so in the next. The angel in Watts's ode,—

> Mark, said he, that happy pair!
> Marriage helps religion there;
>   Where kindred souls their God pursue,
>   They break with double vigour through
> The dull, incumbent air.

In order to your social happiness, make God your friend. Be earnest to serve and please Him. You began well, by rising at six. Your plea of the necessity sometimes of sitting up late will not serve you. Never sit up late, but when you cannot help it; and resolve to get an habit of rising. I must own I have no heart or hope, till you recover your rising.

We expected to hear from you all before now. I defer writing to Mr. Barham, till you tell me you have sent the instrument to Mr. Grinfield, at Ely-house, No. 9. What account can you give of your scholars? of your Deptford excursion? of your friend at court or the Doctor? of Mrs. Mitz, and of Miss Carr? the last, not least, in love. Your mother joins in love to them and you, not forgetting sister Hall, and my brother-poet.

Saturday, August 31st.
I called this morning on Wasbro. He has lost both his brothers. But "the hand of the diligent maketh rich." Yesterday he taught twenty-nine scholars. He has fitted up a room for you, whenever you are disposed to come and teach him harmony gratis. His son he promises you on your own terms. David Williams sends you his daughter only.

Sunday morning, September 1st.
Yours came last night. I am going to preach at Temple church. To save your honour, you should never promise to play at any church, till you know the organ. I should be of your party, if in town, when you entertain his Lordship. . . .

You have now had a taste of a churchwarden's feast. What have you lost by not have been at an hundred such feasts? The world live to eat: we eat to live. The more experience you gain, the more clearly you will be convinced, that the way of the world, in more things, is just the reverse of what is right, and wise, and good.

My respects to the Doctor [Shepherd of Windsor]. God have you in his keeping!

Your affectionate father, C.W.

No. 149 Hymn: "The Young Man's Hymn"
(*Hymns for a Family*, 1767)

1 How shall a young unstable man
    To evil prone like me,
His actions and his heart maintain
    From all pollution free?
Thee, Lord, that I may not forsake,
    Or every turn aside,
Thy precepts for my rule I take,
    Thy Spirit for my guide.

2 Govern'd by the engrafted word,
    And principled with grace,
I shall not yield to sin abhorr'd,
    Or give to passion place:
From youthful lusts I still shall flee,
    From all the paths of vice,
My omnipresent Saviour see,
    And walk before Thine eyes.

3 Saviour, to me Thy Spirit give,
    That through His power I may
Thy word effectually believe,
    And faithfully obey;
From every great transgression pure,
    For all Thy will prepared,
Thy servant to the end endure,
    And gain the full reward.

No. 150 Letter to His Daughter, Sally Jr.[33]

Mary[le]bone, October 11th, 1777.

My dear Sally,—I greatly miss you here, yet comfort myself with the thought that you are happy in your friends at Guildford. For their sake, as well as yours, I am content to want [i.e. "miss"] you a little longer; but hope nothing will hinder our meeting on Friday next.

I think you may avail yourself of my small knowledge of books and poetry. I am not yet too old to assist you a little in your reading, and perhaps improve your taste in versifying. You need not dread my severity. I have a laudable partiality for my own children. Witness your brothers, whom I do not love a jot better than you; only be you as ready to show me your verses as they their music.

The evening I have set aside for reading with you and them. We should begin with history. A plan or order of study is absolutely necessary. Without that, the more you read, the more you are confused, and never rise above [being] a smatterer in learning.

Take care you do not devour all Mr. Russel's library. If you do, you will never be able to digest it. Your mother joins in love to Charles and you, and all your hospitable friends. When shall we see Mr. John Russel?

I am almost confined with a swelled face. It will probably subside before your return. Direct a few lines for me at the Foundery, whence my horse is brought every morning. If Charles does not make more haste, Sam will overtake him in Latin. Till twelve I dedicate to all three. Wishing you the true knowledge and true happiness, I remain,

My dear Sally's father and friend, C. Wesley.

No. 151   Letter to His Daughter, Sally Jr.[34]

Both my dear Sally's letters I have received, and rejoice that you have so soon recovered your fall. If it was occasioned by the narrow fashionable heels, I think it will be a warning to you, and reduce you to reason. Providence saved you from a like accident at Guildford. Beware a third time!

That you gained by the despised Methodists, if nothing more,—the knowledge of what true religion consists in; namely, in happiness and holiness; in peace and love; in the favour and image of God restored; in paradise regained; in a birth from above, a kingdom within you; a participation of the divine nature. The principal means or instrument of this is faith; which faith is the gift of God, given to every one that asks.

The two grand hindrances of prayer, and consequently of faith, are self-love and pride: therefore our Lord so strongly enjoins us self-denial and humility.

"If any man will come after me, let him deny himself, and take up his cross daily, and follow me." And, "How CAN ye believe who RECEIVE HONOUR one of another, and seek not the honour which cometh from God ONLY?" Here, you see, pride is an insurmountable obstacle to believing. Yet the desire of praise is inseparable from our fallen nature. All we can do, till faith come, is not to seek it; not to indulge our own will; not to neglect the means of attaining faith and forgiveness, especially prayer, and the Scriptures.

My brother thinks you was [sic] in some measure awakened while you met in a band. Great good may be got by Christian fellowship, or (if ye are unequally yoked) great evil. I left you entirely to yourself here, being always afraid you would meet some stumbling-block in the Society, which might give you an (unjust) prejudice against religion itself.

You will be glad to communicate any good news you hear of Miny Dyer. I should be so sorry to lose her.

We have many friends while we do not need them. Not that I question the sincerity of any of our London friends, or am insensible of their late civilities to you. Your hosts at Wimbledon are truly obliging. Mr. Bankes must give me leave to canvass Dr. Lloyd at my return, and try if he cannot get employment for him. I am too selfish to wish him banished to Wales. We must detain him among us, to do him good; and first to teach him a habit of sleeping and rising *early*. I have made a convert here of Miss Chapman's boarder, Miss Morgan, who goes to bed at ten, and rises at six. This good beginning has led her into a regular improvement of all her time. She accompanies me in my daily rides; she follows the plan of study which I have given her; she has got a good part of Prior's [poem] Solomon by heart. I am now teaching her short-hand; as she is as willing to receive help and instruction as I am to give it.

Why am I not as useful to my own daughter? You have a thirst after knowledge, and a capacity for it. Your want of resolution to rise, and study regularly, had discouraged me. Carry but these two points, and, behold, I am entirely at your service. Whether your brothers go on or stand still, I would go on constantly in assisting you. I would read something with you every day, and do what good I can for the little time I shall be with you.

Your ["]Ode on Peace["] I have corrected, at least, if not amended. You must begin immediately to be regular, to be diligent, to be tightly. Thomas à Kempis, I think, you would now relish, and [William] Law's *Serious Call*. Your first hour, remember, is always sacred.

Follow Miss Morgan's example. Be as glad of my help as if I was not your father. If I live another year, I can communicate to you sufficient knowledge to go on without me. It might be of great use to you, if I read the [Edward Young's] *Night Thoughts* with you, and pointed out the passages best worth your getting by heart. You may take your turn of riding with me (a dress might be procured), and then we should have many a learned conference.

Was I to finish my course at this time and place, my dear Sally would be sorry she has made no more use of me. Ye might certainly more avail yourselves of my knowledge and dear-bought experience. I could, at least, save your abundance of needless trouble and pains, merely by directing you what to read, and what to pass over. Meantime, commit to your memory the following lines:—

> Voracious Learning, often over-fed
> Digests not into sense its motley meal.
> This forager on others' wisdom leaves

His native farm, his reason, quite untill'd.
With mix'd manure he surfeits the rank soil,
Dung'd, but not dress'd, and rich to beggary;
A pomp untameable of weeds prevails:
Her servant's wealth encumber'd Wisdom mourns.

I am writing this at Mr. Lediard's, who salutes you (and his wife likewise) with great, not mere, civility. Every day I have endless inquiries after you.

You will make yourself, I doubt not, as agreeable as you can to our hospitable friends. Tell them my heart is often with them. Perhaps I may give it your host under my own hand. Dying men, they say, are prophets. I seem to foresee his future usefulness. May his latter end be better than his beginning! his last works more than first! You may read, if you please, to him and his partner, the description of religion in the beginning of this. I would not that you or they should rest short of it. Wishing you all which Christ would have you be, I remain,

My beloved Sally's faithful friend and father,
Charles Wesley.

No. 152   Hymn: "The Maiden's Hymn"
(*Hymns for a Family*, 1767)

1   Holy Child of heavenly birth
    God made man, and born on earth,
    Virgin's Son, impart to me
    Thy unsullied purity.

2   In my pilgrimage below
    Only Thee I pant to know,
    Every creature I resign,
    Thine, both soul and body, Thine.

3   Fairer than the sons of men,
    Over me Thy sway maintain:
    Perfect loveliness Thou art,
    Take my undivided heart.

4   All my heart to Thee I give,
    All Thy holiness receive,
    Live to make my Saviour known,
    Live to please my God alone:

5   Free from low, distracting care,
    For the happy day prepare,
    For the joys that never die,
    For my Bridegroom in the sky.

6   Here betroth'd to Thee in love,
    I shall see my Lord above,
    Lean on my Redeemer's breast,
    In Thy arms for ever rest.

NOTES

1. "Ms. Deliberate" pp. 3–4. The manuscript is a part of the Lambplough Collection, now located in the Methodist Archives and Research Centre, The John Rylands University Library of Manchester, Manchester, England. This hymn and others from "Ms. Deliberate" are published with permission of the Methodist Church Archives and History Committee, England.

2. *Ibid.*, pp. 5–6.

3. *Ibid.*, p. 23.

4. Manuscript letter, housed at the Methodist Archives and Research Centre, The John Rylands University Library of Manchester, Manchester, England. Located in *Charles Wesley Folio IV*, p. 84.

5. Charles had recently returned from a mission to Ireland, and contemplated a return trip.

6. Manuscript letter, housed at the Methodist Archives and Research Centre, The John Rylands University Library of Manchester, Manchester, England. Located in *Charles Wesley Folio, IV*, p. 85.

7. Ebenezer Blackwell, a resident of Lewisham and a London banker, was a friend of Charles and the Methodists. His advice was often solicited on financial matters, and he was also a frequent contributor to Methodist causes. Several of Charles's letters to him have survived (Jackson, *CW Journal*, II, pp. 170–178), and Wesley's affection for Ebenezer and his wife was preserved in lengthy hymns he composed for their funerals (*P.W.*, VI, pp. 323f, 352f).

8. This hymn was later published as "A Wedding Song," #163, in Charles Wesley, *Hymns for the Use of the Families and on Various Occasions* (Bristol, 1767).

9. Edward Young (1683–1776), a popular poet of the mid-eighteenth century, remembered for his work *Night Thoughts*. Young was one of Charles's favorite contemporary poets, as his journal entry for July 30, 1754, indicated: "I began once more transcribing Dr. Young's 'Night Thoughts'. No writings but the inspired are more useful to me." Echoes of Young's verses can be detected in several of Wesley's own poems.

10. A resident of Bristol, Middleton was both a close friend and family physician to the Charles Wesleys. He first appears in Charles's journal on August 6, 1740, during one of Wesley's severe illnesses: "Dr. Middleton, an utter stranger to me, God raised up, and sent to my assistance. He refused taking my fees, and told the Apothecary he would pay for my physic, if I could not. He attended me constantly, as the divine blessing did his prescriptions; so that in less than a fortnight the danger was over." Charles wrote a moving hymn for physicians that was probably framed with Middleton in mind. Middleton died on December 16, 1760, and was memorialized in one of Wesley's unpublished funeral hymns (cf. *P.W.*, V, p. 391 and VI, pp. 300–306).

11. John R. Tyson, with Douglas Lister, "Charles Wesley Pastor: A Glimpse Inside His Shorthand Journal," *Quarterly Review*, Vol. 4, No. 1 (Spring 1984), pp. 9–22.

12. Jackson, *CW Journal*, II, pp. 191–192.

13. *Ibid.*, p. 193.

14. John and Charles had a serious dispute in 1749, the infamous Grace Murray affair. John had violated his own rule by arranging to marry Grace without consulting or conferring with his brother. Grace had been converted under Charles's ministry, and then served as matron of the Methodist Orphan House in Newcastle. She nursed John Wesley to health during one of his visits to that city. He saw in her a suitable companion and began movements toward matrimony, but talk about town was that Grace was

two-timing the two Johns. Betrothed to one John Bennet, a Methodist preacher, she turned her attentions toward the other John. Confronted with the news barely a month before the wedding, Charles exploded into action. Hoping, it is supposed, to put an end to the scandal he rode to Newcastle to get the story directly from the pair. John was not in town, but finding Grace, Charles reunited her with Bennet, performing the marriage himself. The Wesley brothers had a showdown at Leeds. John was heartbroken, and felt betrayed by both Bennet and his brother. Charles's blood was still boiling; he showed no sensitivity to John's wounds. Sharp words were exchanged, and not even a mutual friend like George Whitefield could easily undo the damage.

John reacted to his hurt by marrying Mrs. Vazeille, the widow of a banker. She appears in Charles's journal in the summer of 1749, tersely described as "a woman of a sorrowful spirit." Frustrated in his first attempt at matrimony, John would not risk further interference. On February 2, 1751, Charles reported: "My brother, returned from Oxford, sent for me, and told me, *he was resolved to marry!* I was thunderstruck, and could only answer, he had given me the first blow, and his marriage would come like the *coup de grace*. Trusty Ned Perronet followed, and told me, the person was Mrs. Vazeille! one of whom I have never had the least suspicion. I refused his company to the chapel, and retired to mourn with my faithful Sally."

It is small wonder that there was a degree of tension between Charles and his sister-in-law! Tradition has, further, remembered her as a virago; headstrong and hot-tempered (like Charles!) and suspicious of John's every move. While the brothers and their wives tried to maintain civil relations between them, the mixture was explosive at best. Here, standing at what all thought might be John's deathbed, all three had ample instances worth forgiving and forgetting (December 3). As John recovered he and Charles were able to talk amiably about the events of the last four years, and to a large degree put their differences behind them.

15. This passage is taken from Vergil's *Aeneid*, VI, pp. 470–471. Filling in the omissions in the quotations the translation reads: "But by no tears is he moved, nor does he yield hearing any words," and "She is moved no more in countenance by his speech begun than if she stood in flint or Marpesian rock." The passage describes Aeneas's indifference to Dido's pleading; Marpesus was a mountain on the island of Paros, famous for very hard marble. I am grateful to my colleague F. Gordon Stockin for this identification and translation.

16. Sometime between A.D. 98 and 117, Ignatius, Bishop of Antioch, was taken to Rome to face wild beasts in the arena. On his way to his death the bishop addressed letters to many of the churches he passed, hoping to encourage and edify them. The following passage from his *Letter to Rome* forms the background of Charles's metaphor: "Even now as a prisoner, I am learning to forgo my own wishes. All the way from Syria to Rome I am fighting with wild beasts, by land and sea, night and day, chained as I am to ten leopards (I mean to a detachment of soldiers), who only get worse the better you treat them. But by their injustices I am becoming a better disciple, though not for that reason am I acquitted." (Cyril C. Richardson, ed., *Early Christian Fathers* [New York: Macmillian, 1978], p. 104.)

17. The repetition of the phrase "We set" indicates that Charles wrote it first in shorthand and then in longhand. The repetition was not accidental. His intention was to make this section of the journal somewhat intelligible to the reader who could not follow the shorthand. Hence even the general reader would know "Thurs., Dec. 6, We set out at 7 . . . And came to Bristol by 4," but he used the shorthand to hide his resolution never to travel with John Hutchinson from the general public.

18. Here the original manuscript breaks off in mid-phrase, but the editor of the published journal filled in the rest of the sentence from the biblical quotation (Isa. 1:5,6).

19. In eighteenth-century parlance a "cordial" refers to any medicine, food, or beverage that invigorates the heart and stimulates the circulation; most typically it is a "comforting or exhilarating drink." This usage is attested in Jonathon Swift's *Gulliver's Travels* (1727), II, pp. viii, 168: "Observing I was ready to faint, [he] gave me a cordial to comfort me." Cf. James Murray, ed., *A New English Dictionary on Historical Principles* [hereafter OED] (Oxford: Clarendon Press, 1983), Vol. II, pt. 2, p. 987.

20. Jackson, *CW Journal*, II, pp. 197–198. Cf. *P.W.*, VI, p. 196.
21. *Ibid.*, II, pp. 181–182.
22. *Ibid.*, p. 182.
23. *Ibid.*, p. 200.
24. *Ibid.*, pp. 217–218.
25. *Ibid.*, pp. 224–225.
26. *Ibid.*, pp. 247–248.
27. *Ibid.*, p. 250.
28. *Ibid.*, pp. 255–256.
29. *Ibid.*, pp. 256–257.
30. *Ibid.*, pp. 257–258.
31. *Ibid.*, pp. 271–272.
32. *Ibid.*, pp. 272–274.
33. *Ibid.*, p. 276.
34. *Ibid.*, pp. 276–279.

10 / Christian Perfection and Its Pretenders

Charles Wesley deemed Christian Perfection one of "the two great truths of the everlasting Gospel" (the other being "universal redemption").[1] It was the soteriological axis of his theology, a point around which a constellation of redemption themes revolved. Sanctification, as articulated in even his earliest preaching [No. 6], was the "one thing needful"—a renovation of the whole person in the image of God and mind of Christ. But the doctrine, despite its vital position in Wesleyan soteriology, was difficult to articulate. It demanded both theological balance and personal humility from its adherents in order to avoid extravagant claims and abuses of Wesley's sanctification language and vision.

The Wesleyan doctrine of Christian Perfection became the focal point for several theological controversies among the early Methodists. It even appeared to set John and Charles against each other at precisely the time when the movement was threatened by still another serious schism in the London Society.

The series of debates focused on three interrelated issues; first, was sanctification to be understood as an instantaneous or gradual work? Second, was it to be expected at any time in this life or only at the threshold of death? And, finally, was the Wesleyan conception of "perfection" to be qualified in order to allow for "mistakes" and hence spoken of as a volitional renovation—"Perfect Love"; or was this "perfection" of an unqualified sort, nothing less than the restoration of the *imago Dei* or formation of the "mind of Christ" within? In each case it seemed that John Wesley preferred the former alternatives, while his brother Charles was more apt to opt for the latter.

THE ARTICLE OF DEATH

The first Methodist dispute over sanctification came in the mid-1740s, and had to do with the timing of Christian Perfection. The Wesleys emphasized a synthesis of instantaneous and pilgrimage language when talking about salvation from all sin, urging Christian Perfection both as a possibility in this life and as an on-going, lifelong quest. As the brothers began articulating their respective views it seemed that John Wesley was more likely to characterize Christian Perfection as a Perfect Love that caused inner conformity with the will of God, and hence thought of it as an instantaneous gift that brought purity of intentions ("The Single Eye" [No. 5]) with an infusion of God's love. This sort of perfection was liable to improve and grow, but was to be expected at any time.

Charles more typically thought of Christian Perfection as the restitution of the *imago Dei* and the concomitant removal of original sin. He therefore tended to expect an unqualified sort of perfection that was to be realized on the threshold between life and death. The respective views of the two brothers were further complicated, in the early years at least, by John Wesley's editorial control over the content of the Methodist hymnals, and therefore over the content of Charles's hymns. While there was always a strong basic agreement between the Wesleys on the doctrine of Christian Perfection, it is also clear that each brother had his own characteristic emphases; one that emerged quite early was Charles's expectation that perfection occurred at the threshold of death.

No. 153   Journal Selections: May 1–14, 1741

Fri., May 1st [1741]. I visited a sister dying in the Lord; and then two others, one mourning after, then rejoicing in, God her Saviour. I found sister Hooper sick of love. Her body too, sunk under it. . . .

Mon., May 4th. I passed an hour in weeping with some that wept; then rejoiced over our sister Hooper. The more the outward man decayeth, the inner is renewed. For one whole night she had wrestled with the powers of darkness. This is that evil day, that fiery trial. But having done all, she stood unshaken. From henceforth she was kept in perfect peace, and that wicked one touched her not. . . .

I saw my dear friend again, in great bodily weakness, but strong in the Lord, and in the power of his might. "The Spirit," said she, "bears witness every moment with my spirit, that I am a child of God." I spoke to her Physician, who said he had little hope of her recovery; "only," added he, "she has no dread upon her spirits, which is generally the worst symptom. Most people die for fear of dying: but I never met with such people as yours. They are none of them afraid of death; but calm, and patient, and resigned to the last." He said to her, "Madam, be not cast down." She answered smiling, "Sir, I shall never be cast down."

At Downing I explained good old Simeon's confession: "Lord, now lettest thou thy servant depart in peace," &c. Our sister Hooper was present in spirit. I hastened back and asked, "How are you now?" Her answer was, "Full, full of love."

Wed., May 6th. I found our sister Hooper just at the haven. She expressed, while able to speak, her fullness of confidence and love; her desire to be with Christ. . . .

At my next visit, I saw her in her latest conflict. The angel of death was come, and but a few moments between her and a blessed eternity. We poured out our souls to God for her, her children and ourselves, the Church and Ministers, and all mankind. I had some perception of her joy. My soul was tenderly affected for her sufferings, yet the joy swallowed up the sorrow. How much more then did *her* consolations abound! The servants of Christ suffer nothing. I asked her whether she was not in great pain. "Yes," she answered, "but in greater joy. I would not be without either." But do you not prefer life to death?" She replied, "All is alike to me; let Christ choose; I have no will of my own." This is that holiness, or absolute resignation, or Christian Perfection! . . .

A few moments before she had breathed her last, I found such a complication of grief, joy, love, envy, as quite overpowered me. I fell upon the bed, and in that instant her spirit ascended to God. I felt our souls knit together by the violent struggle of mine to follow her.

When I saw the breathless temple of the Holy Ghost, my heart was still, and a calm resignation took place. We knelt down, and gave God thanks from the ground of our heart. We then had recourse to the book of comfort, and found it written. "He was a burning and a shining light: and ye were willing for a season to rejoice in his light." The next word was for us: "Let us labour therefore to enter into that rest." Even so, come Lord Jesus, and give us an inheritance among all them that are sanctified!

Thur., May 14th. I visited our sister Lillington, whom her Saviour had brought to a bed of sickness, before she knew he was *her* Saviour. She told me, two nights ago she saw herself as it were drooping into hell, when suddenly a ray of light was darted into her soul, and filled her with all peace and joy in believing. All fear of hell, death, and sin fled away in that same moment.

Fri., May 15th. I saw our sister Lillington again; still without fear, desiring nothing but to be with Christ. "I never felt," said she, "such love before: I love every soul; I am all love,—and so is God. He is loving unto every man: He would have all men to be saved."

Sat., May 16th. I visited another of our sisters, who was triumphing over death. I asked her, "Do you know Christ died for you?" "Yes," she answered joyfully, "for me, and for the whole world. He has begun, and he will finish, his work in my soul." "But will he save you," I said, "from *all* sin?" She replied, "I know he will. There shall no sin remain in me."

No. 154 Hymn: "A Funeral Hymn for Mrs. Hooper"
(*Hymns and Sacred Poems*, 1742)

1   Come, to the house of mourning come,
    The house of serious, solemn joy;
  Let us, till all are taken home,
    Our lives in songs of praise employ.

2   Accomplish'd is our sister's strife,
        Her happier soul is gone before,
    Her struggle for eternal life,
        Her glorious agony is o'er.

3   The captive exile is released,
        Is with her Lord in paradise,
    Of perfect paradise possest,
        And waiting for the heavenly prize.

4   In her no spot of sin remain'd,
        To shake her confidence in God;
    The victory here she more than gain'd,
        Triumphant through her Saviour's blood.

5   She now the fight of faith hath fought,
        Finish'd and won the Christian race;
    She found on earth the Lord she sought,
        And now beholds Him face to face.

6   She died in sure and steadfast hope,
        By Jesus wholly sanctified;
    Her perfect spirit she gave up,
        And sunk into His arms, and died.

7   Thus may we all our parting breath
        Into the Saviour's hands resign:
    O Jesu, let me die her death,
        And let her latter end be mine!

Christian Perfection was a perennial topic of discussion at the earliest Methodist annual conferences. The minutes of those conferences show how the doctrine developed among them. In each case questions for consideration were posed and answers were suggested until consensus was reached; the answers recorded in the minutes then reflected a distillation of that working session. While these "Minutes" were clearly consensus statements of Methodist theology, Charles Wesley was present and active in each of these sessions, and certainly his views are reflected in these deliberations.

The conferences of 1744 considered the nature of sanctification, defining it as being "renewed in the image of God, in righteousness and true holiness." The relationship between justification and sanctification was explored the next year at the Methodist conference held in Bristol, and there the troublesome question of the timing of entire sanctification emerged. It was concluded that all Christians must possess this gift, in "the very article of death," since without holiness a person "cannot see the Lord." In 1747, at the third Methodist conference, the "article of death" continued to be a matter of debate. Whether Charles Wesley was one of those at the conference who "differed from us" on the timing of sanctification is not clear. It is clear from his hymns of the period that he had come to affirm with increasing emphasis that the reality of entire sanctification or Christian Perfection was known chiefly at the threshold of death.[2]

John Wesley's tract *Christian Perfection* noted that the conference ended with unanimity: "Nor do I remember that in any one of these conferences [1744, 1745, 1747] we had one dissenting voice; but whatever doubts any one had when we met, they were all removed before we parted."[3] Yet, the polemical purpose of John's tract, written in the heat of the debates of the mid-1760s, was to emphasize a history of the Methodists' unanimity in their conception of Christian Perfection. In point of fact, John's record is hardly an accurate analysis of Charles's changing conception of the doctrine.

In 1746 the Wesleys published a hymnal entitled *Hymns of Petition and Thanksgiving for the Promise of the Father*. Since manuscripts of these hymns have not survived, it is impossible to cut the knot of "the vex'd problem of joint authorship." The hymnal was subtitled *Hymns for Whit-Sunday,* or Pentecost. The day was the anniversary of Charles's conversion; it held deep religious and theological significance for him and he certainly had a hand in these hymns.

Interestingly enough, the texts for these thirty-two *Hymns for Pentecost* are drawn from the Gospel according to St. John; not a single one springs from the book of Acts! In fact almost all of the texts are from the so-called Upper-Room Discourses of John 13–16. Herein the theological import of these hymns is found; they explain Christian Perfection in the nexus of the Johannine description of the role of the Holy Spirit, as One who makes the ascended Christ present in the lives of His disciples. Thus, the coming of the Comforter is "the Promise of the Father," and that coming effects full salvation since the Spirit both applies the "blood" of Christ (or "grace") and forms the "mind of Christ," or Perfect Love, within the Christian. These hymns, although relatively unknown, evidence an extremely important step in the Wesleys' conception of Christian Perfection since they connect Christology and pneumatology in the larger context of their theology of redemption.

No. 155   Hymns for Pentecost: I

1   Father of everlasting grace,
     Thy goodness and Thy truth we praise,
        Thy goodness and Thy truth we prove:
     Thou hast in honour of Thy Son
     THE GIFT unspeakable sent down,
        The Spirit of life, and power, and love:

2   Thou has THE PROPHECY fulfill'd,
     The grand original compact seal'd,
        For which Thy word and oath were join'd:
     THE PROMISE to our fallen head,
     To every child of *Adam* made,
        Is now pour'd out on all mankind.

3 The purchased Comforter *is* given,
  For Jesus is return'd to heaven,
    To claim, and then THE GRACE impart:
  Our day of Pentecost is come,
  And God vouchsafes to fix His home
    In every poor expecting heart.

4 Father, on Thee whoever call,
  Confess Thy promise is for all,
    While every one that asks receives,
  Receives the Gift, and Giver too,
  And witnesses that Thou art true,
    And in Thy Spirit walks, and lives.

5 Not to a single age confined,
  For every soul of man design'd,
    O God, we now that Spirit claim:
  To us the Holy Ghost impart,
  Breathe Him into our panting heart,
    Thou hear'st us ask in Jesu's name.

6 Send us the Spirit of Thy Son,
  To make the depths of Godhead known,
    To make us share the life Divine;
  Send Him the sprinkled blood t' apply,
  Send Him, our souls to sanctify,
    And show, and seal us ever Thine.

7 So shall we pray, and never cease,
  So shall we thankfully confess
    Thy wisdom, truth, and power, and love;
  With joy unspeakable adore,
  And bless, and praise Thee evermore,
    And serve Thee like Thy hosts above:

8 Till added to that heavenly choir,
  We raise our sons of triumph higher,
    And praise Thee in a bolder strain,
  Out-soar the first-born seraph's flight,
  And sing with all our friends in light
    Thine everlasting love to man.

No. 156   Hymns for Pentecost: XII
John 14:25, 26, 27

1 Jesus, we on the word depend
    Spoken by Thee while present here,

The Father in My name shall send
   The Holy Ghost, the Comforter.

2 That promise made to *Adam's* race,
    Now, Lord, in us, even us fulfill,
  And give the Spirit of Thy grace,
    To teach us all Thy perfect will.

3 That heavenly Teacher of mankind,
    That Guide infallible impart,
  To bring Thy sayings to our mind,
    And write them on our faithful heart.

4 He only can the words apply
    Through which we endless life possess,
  And deal to each *his* legacy,
    His Lord's unutterable peace.

5 That peace of God, that peace of Thine
    O might He now to us bring in,
  And fill our souls with power Divine,
    And make an end of fear and sin;

6 The length and breadth of love reveal,
    The height and depth of Deity,
  And all the sons of glory seal,
    And change, and make us all like Thee.

No. 157 Hymns for Pentecost: XIV
John 15:26, 27

1 Jesus, our exalted Head,
    Regard Thy people's prayer,
  Send us in Thy body's stead
    Th' abiding Comforter,
  From Thy dazzling throne above,
    From Thy Father's glorious seat
  Send the Spirit of truth and love,
    Th' eternal PARACLETE.

2 Issuing forth from Him and Thee
    O let THE BLESSING flow,
  Pour the streaming Deity
    On all Thy church below;
  Him to testify Thy grace,
    Him to teach how good Thou art,
  Him to vouch Thy Godhead, place
    In every faithful heart.

3 God of God, and Light of light,
      Thee let Him now reveal,
   Justify us by Thy right,
      And stamp us with Thy seal;
   Fill our souls with joy and peace,
      Wisdom, grace, and utterance give,
   Constitute Thy witnesses,
      And in Thy members live.

4 By the HOLY GHOST we wait
      To say Thou art the Lord,
   Saved, and to our first estate
      In perfect love restored;
   Then we shall in every breath
      Testify the power we prove,
   Publish Thee in life and death
      The God of truth and love.

In 1749 Charles published his two volumes of *Hymns and Sacred Poems*. The hymnal was hastily constructed from earlier manuscripts, with many of the hymns being drawn from the mid-1740s; some may have been even older. It was probably Charles's first solo production, and the contents of the 1749 edition escaped John's editorial eye; hence the older brother voiced his disclaimer, "As I did not see these before they were published, there were some things in them which I did not approve of."[4] Charles's unaltered hymns carried numerous examples of their author's hope for an entire sanctification that became a reality as one laid down life in death. His theology of suffering also emerged in these same hymns as he began to weave costly discipleship and the purifying effects of suffering into his sanctification themes.

No. 158   Hymn: "For One in a Declining State of Health"
(*Hymns and Sacred Poems*, 1749)

1 God of my life, for Thee I pine,
   For Thee I cheerfully decline,
      And hasten to decay,
   Summon'd to take my place above,
   I hear the call, "Arise, My love,
      My fair one, come away!"

2 Obedient to the voice of God,
   I soon shall quit this earthly clod,
      Shall lay my body down;
   Th' immortal principle aspires,
   And swells my soul with strong desires
      To grasp the starry crown.

3 The more the outward man decays,
   The inner feels Thy strengthening grace,
       And knows that Thou art mine:
   Partaker of my glorious hope,
   I here shall after Thee wake up,
       Shall in Thine image shine.

4 Thou wilt not leave Thy work undone,
   But finish what Thou hast begun,
       Before I hence remove;
   I shall be, Master, as Thou art,
   Holy, and meek, and pure in heart,
       And perfected in love.

5 Thou wilt cut short Thy work of grace,
   And perfect in a babe of Thy praise,
       And strength for me ordain:
   Thy blood shall make me thoroughly clean,
   And not one spot of inbred sin
       Shall in my flesh remain.

6 Dear Lamb, if Thou for me couldst die,
   Thy love shall wholly sanctify,
       Thy love shall seal me Thine;
   Thou wilt from me no more depart,
   My all in life and death Thou art,
       Thou art for ever mine.

No. 159   Hymn: "The Trial of Faith"
(*Hymns and Sacred Poems*, 1749)

1 Saviour of all, what hast Thou done,
       What hast Thou suffer'd on the tree?
   Why didst Thou groan Thy mortal groan,
       Obedient unto death for me?
   The mystery of Thy passion show,
   The end of all Thy griefs below.

2 Thy soul for sin an offering made
       Hath clear'd this guilty soul of mine;
   Thou hast for me a ransom paid,
       To change my human to Divine,
   To cleanse from all iniquity,
   And make the sinner all like Thee.

3 Pardon, and grace, and heaven buy,
       My bleeding Sacrifice expired:

But didst Thou not my pattern die,
  That by Thy glorious Spirit fired,
Faithful I might to death endure,
And make the crown by suffering sure?

4   Thou didst the meek example leave,
      That I might in Thy footsteps tread;
    Might like the Man of sorrows grieve,
      And groan, and bow with Thee my head;
    Thy dying in my body bear,
    And all Thy state of passion share.

5   Thy every perfect servant, Lord,
      Shall as his patient Master be,
    To all Thine inward life restored,
      And outwardly conform'd to Thee,
    Out of Thy grave the saint shall rise,
    And grasp through death the glorious prize.

6   This is the straight, and royal way,
      That leads us to the courts above;
    Here let me ever stay,
      Till on the wings of perfect love
    I take my last triumphant flight
    From *Calvary's* to *Sion's* height.

Charles's emphasis on entire sanctification taking place in the moments before death became even more pronounced in the hymns of his declining years. His repeated illnesses and personal tragedies may have played a role in this augmented emphasis on the "article of death," but it is also clear that he had maintained this point of view long before the publication of his *Short Hymns on Select Passages of Scripture*, in 1762. Thousands of those "Short Hymns" have survived in manuscript (and many remain unpublished). The careful eye can detect the editorial pen of John Wesley in those manuscripts as he prepared his brother's hymns for publication after Charles's death. Several of John's editorial reactions are preserved in the hymns below.

No. 160   Short Hymn on Josh. 6:20
When the people heard the sound of the trumpet, &c.

In Charles's poetic commentary the Israelites' seven marches around Jericho's walls became a metaphor for the long quest for entire sanctification. His closing line suggests that the goal is attained only in death—"the latest turn." John disagreed with the parameters Charles's hymn set for Christian Perfection. Where Charles prolonged perfection till the end of one's labors, John demanded that one might expect it in this life and at any time, "When God Pleases!"

<blockquote>

1   Then let us urge our way,
          And work, and suffer on,
  Nor dream, the first, or second, day
          Will throw the bulwarks down:
          We on the sacred morn
          Our sevenfold toil repeat,
    Expecting that the latest turn
          Our labour shall complete.[a]

2   Then, then we shall obtain
          The victory one and all,
  The number of perfection gain,
          And see the city fall,
          Partakers of our hope
          Our callings' glorious prize,
  To finish'd holiness go up,
          And then go on to paradise.

</blockquote>

No. 161   Short Hymn on Matt. 20:22
Ye know not what ye ask.

1   Advancement in Thy Kingdom here
     Who'er impatiently desire,
  They know not, Lord, the pangs severe,
     The trials which they *first* require:
  They all *must* first Thy sufferings share,
     Ambitious of their calling's prize,
  And every day Thy burdens bear,
     And thus to late perfection rise.

2   Nature would fain evade, or flee
     That sad necessity of pain;
  But who refuse to die with Thee,
     With Thee shall never, never reign:
  The sorrow doth the joy ensure,
     The crown for conquerors prepared;
  And all who to the end endure,
     Shall grasp through death the full reward.

---

[a][When God Pleases!]

No. 162 Hymn: "Preparation for Death"

Charles's hymns entitled *Preparation for Death*, a few of which were published in 1772, represent the final stage of development in his connection between Christian Perfection and death. Charles's declining years were full of illness and pain, and death weighed heavily upon his mind. The most poignant example of this period is found in a piece that Charles left in manuscript. In this hymn, Charles's longing for sanctification blends with his desire for death; the anticipated result of that double desire is perfection or the restitution of the *imago Dei*. The hymn is published here for the first time, by permission of the Methodist Church Archives and History Committee, England.

1 Thou to whom all hearts are known,
    Attend the cry of mine
Hear in me thy Spirit's groan
    For purity divine;
Languishing for my remove [death],
    I wait thine image to retrieve;
Fill me, Jesus, with Thy love,
    And to thyself receive.

2 Destitute of holiness,
    I am not like my Lord,
Am not ready to possess
    The saints' immense reward;
No; my God I cannot see,
    Unless, before I hence ~~remove~~ depart,
Thou implant thyself in me
    And make me pure in heart.

3 Partner of thy nature then,
    And in thine image found,
Saviour, call me up to reign
    With life immortal crown'd,
With thy glorious presence blest
    In speechless ecstasies to gaze,
Folded in thy arms to rest,
    And breathe eternal praise.[5]

PERFECTION "SET TOO HIGH"

Perhaps the heart of the difficulty of the Wesleyan doctrine of Christian Perfection was to be found in the collision of John's qualified (volitional) definition of sin and penchant for pressing the instantaneous blessing, and Charles's unqualified conception of perfection as restitution of the *imago Dei*. One of the clearest instances of John's volitional conception of sin appeared in his sermon entitled, "The Great Privilege of those that are born of God," based on 1 John 3:9. The "Privilege" John preached was "sinlessness," which was synonymous with "being born of God," and his entire construct hinged upon his definition of "sin":

> By sin I here understand outward sin, according to the plain common acceptation [*sic*] of the word; an actual voluntary transgression of the law; of the revealed, written law of God; of any commandment of God, acknowledged to be such at the time it is transgressed. But 'whosoever is born of God,' while he abideth in faith and love, and the spirit of prayer and thanksgiving, not only doth not, but cannot thus commit sin.[6]

While John's conception of sin as a "voluntary transgression of the law" has both traditional support and ethical cogency, it is clearly a qualified conception allowing for "mistakes" and sins of ignorance ("sin improperly so-called") but not ill-will. Charles's more characteristic concern was an absolute renovation, the removal of the very roots of one's "bosom sin," and the restitution of the *imago Dei* within. John's qualified conception of sin may have made him more optimistic about the instantaneous reception of "the blessing" at any point of life; whereas Charles's more stringent standard seemed to push him more and more toward the gradual conception of sanctification, which looked for its reception in "the article of death." Thus it seemed that by the end of the 1750s the brothers were moving in different directions in their respective doctrines of Christian Perfection.

The disputed doctrine was pushed into the forefront in the early 1760s by schism in the London Methodist Society. Thomas Maxfield and George Bell, two of the Wesleys' lay preachers, became the chief actors in the controversy. Charles's unqualified doctrine of renovation and John's instantaneous blessing formed a volatile combination in the hands of fanatics like Maxfield and Bell; they soon formed a small cadre of followers who walked about London "as perfect as the angels are perfect." Their extravagant claims and experiential elitism quickly divided the Methodist Society, and soon gained a broader attention. The dispute was a public relations fiasco, occurring at just the time when Methodism had begun to clear itself of charges of "enthusiasm" and "fanaticism." The London controversy, as John Wesley wrote, "made the very name of Perfection stink in the nostrils even of those who loved and honored it before."[7] The dispute also seemed to galvanize his own convictions about the nature and timing of Christian Perfection.

Charles's *Hymns and Sacred Poems,* 1749 edition, shows him at the mid-point of the development of his doctrine of sanctification. In it he pressed the unqualified conception of Christian Perfection, and yet insisted that it was attainable in this life. Hence, Charles typically created a juxtaposition between the infinite possibilities of God's grace and the apparent impossibility of living without sin in this world. He hoped for perfection "here," and criticized those who would set parameters on God's unlimited grace—thereby cutting off the possibility of perfection because of their self-will. This tension, which depicted Christian Perfection as an impossible possibility, continued to play an important role in his later hymns.

No. 163 Hymn: "Waiting for Full Redemption"
(*Hymns and Sacred Poems*, 1749)

As many who received Him, to them he gave power to become the sons of God, even to them that believe on His name. [John 1:12]

1 Jesus, in Thine all-saving name
    We steadfastly believe,
And lo! the promised power we claim,
    Which Thou art bound to give:
Power to become the sons of God,
    An all-sufficient power,
We look to have on us bestow'd
    A power to sin no more.

2 We yield to be redeem'd from sin,
    The life Divine to live,
Open our hearts to take Thee in,
    And all Thy grace receive.
Thee we receive as God and man,
    Both in One Person join'd,
To finish the redeeming plan,
    To rescue all mankind.

3 On both Thy natures we rely,
    Neither can save alone;
The God could not for sinners die,
    The man could not atone.
The merit of a suffering God
    Hath bought our perfect peace,
It stamp'd the value on that blood
    Which sign'd our soul's release.

4 Thy precious blood hath wash'd away
    The universal sin;
And every child of *Adam* may
    Have all Thy life brought in.
Thy office is to teach, and bless,
    T' atone, and sanctify;
Ready the Spirit of Thy grace
    The merits to apply.

5   To Thee, O Christ, the praise we give,
        Thy threefold function sing,
    The Lord's Anointed One receive,
        Our Prophet, Priest, and King.
    Thou, only Thou, our wisdom art,
        Our strength and righteousness;
    Sprinkle, inform, and rule our heart,
        Victorious Prince of Peace.

6   Foolish, we come to learn of Thee,
        Guilty, to be forgiven;
    Poor, sinful worms to be made free
        From sin, and fit for heaven.
    Teach us the perfect will of God,
        For us, and in us pray;
    Wash us in Thine all-cleansing blood;
        Thy kingly power display.

7   Kingly power in us exert,
        Our rebel heart subdue;
    More than subdue our rebel heart,
        Thine utmost virtue show.
    Show us Thy sanctifying grace,
        And take our sin away;
    Its being utterly erase,
        All, all its relics slay.

8   Jesu, we in Thy name believe,
        Which fiends and men deny,
    To them we dare not credit give
        Who give our God the lie.
    Jesus, the power of Jesu' name
        Our sinless souls shall feel;
    Lord, we believe Thee still the same,
        An utmost Saviour still.

9   Thou wilt to us Thy name impart,
        Thou bear'st it not in vain:
    What Thou art call'd Thou surely art,
        Saviour of sinful man.
    Into Thy name, Thy nature, we
        Assuredly believe,
    Jesus from sin, Thee, only Thee
        Our Jesus we receive.

10 Our Jesus Thou from future woe,
        From present wrath Divine,

Shalt save us from our sins below,
   And make our souls like Thine.
Jesus from all the power of sin,
   From all the being too,
Thy grace shall make us thoroughly clean,
   And perfectly renew.

11 Jesus from pride, from wrath, from lust,
     Our inward Jesus be,
From every evil thought we trust
     To be redeem'd by Thee.
When Thou dost in our flesh appear,
     We shall the promise prove,
Saved into all perfection *here*,
     Renew'd in sinless love.

12 Come, O Thou Prophet, Priest, and King,
     Thou Son of God, and man,
Into our souls Thy fullness bring,
     Instruct, atone, and reign.
Holy, and pure, as just, and wise,
     We would be in Thy right,
Less than Thine all cannot suffice,
     We grasp the infinite.

13 Our Jesus Thee, entire, and whole
     With willing heart we take;
Fill ours, and every faithful soul
     For Thy own mercy's sake;
We wait to know Thine utmost name,
     Thy nature's heavenly powers,
One undivided Christ we claim,
     And all Thou art is ours.

No. 164 Hymn: "Waiting for Full Redemption"
(*Hymns and Sacred Poems*, 1749)

1 And shall we then abide in sin,
     Nor hope on earth to be set free?
Hath Jesus bled to wash us clean
     To save from all iniquity,
And can He not His blood apply,
And cleanse, and save us—till we die?

2 Alas! if their report be true,
     Who teach that sin must still *remain*,

If sin we scarcely can subdue,
  But never *full* redemption gain,
Where is Thy power, almighty Lord?
Where is Thine everlasting word?

3 Where is the glorious church below,
     From every spot and wrinkle free?
   The trees that to perfection grow,
     The saints that blameless walk with Thee,
   Adorn'd in linen white and clean,
   The born of God that cannot sin?

4 Where are in Christ the creatures new,
     The monuments of Thy saving power,
   The witness that God is true,
     The pillars that go out no more,
   Th' election of peculiar grace,
   The chosen priests, the royal race?

5 Where are the spirits to Jesus join'd
     Freed from the law of death and sin?
   The Saviour's pure and spotless mind?
     The endless righteousness brought in?
   The heavenly man, the heart renew'd,
   The living portraiture of God?

6 The Spirit of power, and health, and love,
     The Pledge, the Witness, and the Seal,
   Th' unerring unction from above,
     The glorious gift unspeakable,
   The hidden life, the wide-spread leaven,
   The law fulfill'd in earth and heaven!

7 Can the good God His grace deny?
     Th' Almighty God want power to save?
   Th' Omniscient err? the Faithful lie?
     All, all Thy attributes we have;
   Thy wisdom, power, and goodness join
   To save us, with an oath Divine.

8 Lord, we believe, and rest secure,
     Thine utmost promises to prove,
   To rise restored, and thoroughly pure,
     In all thine image of Thy love,
   Fill'd with the glorious life unknown,
   For ever sanctified in one.

Charles's polemical replies to the sanctification controversy appeared in *Short Hymns on Select Passages of Scripture*, published in 1762. The title of the hymnal was characteristically descriptive; the hymns were short, generally no longer than two verses, and more often comprised only one stanza. While we have no clear picture of the life situation behind the hymns, they seem to reflect Charles's poetical-devotional study of the Scriptures, and occasionally touch various issues that affected Wesley's life during the early 1760s. Charles continued to write "Short Hymns" throughout the 1760s, but an additional volume never appeared in print. If we are to judge by John Wesley's disapproval of a few of these poems, it seems he did not have the opportunity to edit the 1762 volumes prior to their publication. His attitude toward the manuscript "Short Hymns" was such that very few of the literally thousands of them ever made their way into print after Charles's death.

The *Short Hymns* published in 1762 appeared with a preface that set the volume squarely in the context of the sanctification controversy; in fact, Charles may have rushed the volumes into print in order to try to stem the tide of fanatical doctrines of perfection among the Methodists. He seemed to find himself on the horns of a pastoral dilemma; on the one hand he wanted to attack those arrogant, angelic perfectionists who had provided so much ammunition for Methodism's detractors, yet on the other hand he sought to give a solid and positive statement of the doctrine to aid the ardent inquirer. Thus, Charles's preface asks: "Who can check the self-confident, without discouraging the self-diffident?" The preface began and ended with its author ascribing all glory to God, and the opening and closing lines also offer a forlorn reminder of the impact that Charles's continuing ill-health had upon his work.

The volume continued several of Charles's standard themes, such as Christian Perfection as an impossible possibility, but he made a decided move away from the instantaneous reception of "the blessing." "Gradual" was one of his favorite descriptions for perfection, and imagery of growth and maturation became his standard sanctification metaphors. He continued to press the unqualified conception of Christian Perfection, which John Wesley found to be a mark "set too high." And Charles also shot a few stinging stanzas at the pretenders to perfection, criticizing their lack of humility by wryly suggesting that the very claim of perfection invites the sort of religious pride that proves one has not the blessing; hence, following Jesus' parable he concludes that sanctification must be hid in the field of one's life rather than being pridefully flaunted.

No. 165 "Preface" to *Short Hymns on Select Passages of Scripture*, 1762

God, having graciously laid His hand upon my body, and disabled me for the principal work of the ministry, has thereby given me an unexpected occasion of writing the following hymns. Many of the thoughts are borrowed from Mr. Henry's Comment, Dr. Gell on the Pentateuch, and Bengelius on the New Testament.

Several of the hymns are intended to prove, and several to guard, the doctrine of Christian Perfection. I durst not publish one without the other.

In the latter sort I use some severity; not against particular persons, but against Enthusiasts and Antinomians, who, by not living up their profession, *give abundant occasion to them that seek it, and cause the truth to be evil spoke of.*

Such there have been, in every age, in every revival or religion. But this does in no wise justify the men who put darkness for light, and light for darkness; who call the wisdom of God foolishness, and all real religion Enthusiasm.

When the wheat springs up, the tares also appear, and both grow together until the harvest: yet is there an essential difference between them. This occasions a difference in my expressions; and as great a seeming contradiction, as when I *declare with St. Paul, a man is justified by faith, and not by works,* and with St. James, *A man is justified by works, and not by faith only.*

My desire is, rightly to divide the word of Truth: but *who is sufficient for these things?* Who can check the self-confident, without discouraging the self-diffident? I trust God, that none of the latter will take to themselves what belongs to the former only.

Reader, if God ministers grace to thy soul through any of these hymns, give Him the glory, and offer up a prayer for the weak instrument, that, whenever I finish my course, I may depart in peace, having seen in Jesus Christ His great salvation.

No. 166   John Wesley's Letter to Dorothy Furly

John Wesley felt the force of Charles's *Short Hymns* not only in the younger Wesley's attacks upon the "self-confident" perfectionists, but also in connection with Charles's insistence upon the unqualified ideal. John's displeasure with some of these hymns is reflected in his editorial comments on them. John's letter to Mrs. Dorothy Furly, written the same year that Charles's collection of *Short Hymns* appeared, registered John's complaints about Charles's conception of Christian Perfection and the *Short Hymns*.[8]

St. Ives, September 15, 1762.
My Dear Sister,—Whereunto you have attained hold fast. But expect that greater things are at hand; although our friend talks as if you were not to expect them till the article of death.

Certainly sanctification (in the proper sense) is "an instantaneous deliverance from all sin," and includes "an instantaneous power then given to cleave to God." Yet this sanctification (at least in the lower degrees) does not include a power never to think an useless thought nor ever speak a useless word. I myself believe that such a perfection is inconsistent with living in a corruptible body; for this makes it impossible "always to think right." While we breathe we shall more or less mistake. If, therefore, Christian Perfection implies this, we must not expect it till after death.

I want you to be all love. This is the Perfection I believe and teach. And this perfection is consistent with a thousand nervous disorders, which that high-strained perfection is not. Indeed, my judgment is that (in this case particularly) to overdo is to undo, and that to set perfection too high (so high as no man that we ever heard or read of attained) is the most effectual (because unsuspected) way of driving it out of the world.

Take care you are not hurt by anything in the *Short Hymns* contrary to the doctrines you have long received. Peace be with your spirit! I am, Your affectionate brother.

No. 167   John Wesley's Letter to Charles

In a second letter from late 1762, John Wesley reported the schism that was brewing in the London Society. His account names Thomas Maxfield, trusted associate of both brothers, as the source of the disturbance.[9]

London, December 23, 1762

Dear Brother, . . . I believe several in London [Society] have imagined themselves saved from sin "upon the word of others": And these are easily known. For that work does not stand. Such imaginations soon vanish away. Some of these, and two or three others, are still wild. But the matter does not stick here. I could play with these, if Thomas Maxfield were right. He is *mali caput et fons* [Latin: the head and fountain of the evil]; so inimitably wrong-headed, and so absolutely unconvincible; and yet (what is exceedingly strange) God continues to bless his labours. My kind love to Sally. I shall soon try your patience with a long letter. Adieu!

No. 168   Short Hymn on Matt. 5:48
   Be ye perfect . . .

1   Would'st Thou require what cannot be?
    The thing impossible to me
        Is possible with God:
    I trust Thy truth to make me just,
    Th' omnipotence of love I trust,
        The virtue of Thy blood.

2   Perfection is my calling's prize,
    To which on duty's scale I rise;
        And when my toils are pass'd,
    And when I have the battle won,
    Thou in Thy precious Self alone,
        Shalt give the prize at last.

No. 169   Short Hymn on Gen. 2:1
Thus the heavens and the earth were finished.

Who madest thus the earth and skies,
 A world, a six days' work of Thine,
Thou bidd'st the new creation rise,
 Nobler effect of grace Divine!
We might spring up at Thy command,
 For glory in an instant meet;
But by Thy will at last we stand,
 In gradual holiness complete.

No. 170   Short Hymn on Prov. 4:18
The path of the just is as the shining light.

Shall we mistake the morning-ray
Of grace for the full blaze of day?
Or humbly walk in Jesu' s sight.
Glad to receive the *gradual* light[a]
More of His grace and more to know,
In faith and in experience grow,
Till all the life of Christ we prove,
And *lose ourselves* in perfect love!

No. 171   Short Hymn on Matt. 7:20
By their fruits ye shall know them.

1 Must we not then with patience wait
 False to distinguish from sincere?
Or can we on another's state
 Pronounce, *before* the fruits appear?
Can we the witnesses receive
 Who of their own perfection boast,
The fairest words as fruit receive?
 The fairest words are leaves at most.

2 How shall we then the spirits prove?
 Their actions with their words compare.
And wait—till humblest meekest love
 Their perfect nothingness declare;
But if the smallest spark of pride,
 Or selfishness, break out at last,
Set the false-witnesses aside;
 Yet hold the truth for ever fast.

---

[a]At this point John Wesley penned in: "And the sudden."

No. 172 Short Hymn on Isa. 28:16
He that believeth shall not make haste.

1 Happy the men who Jesus know,
   Who humbly walk with God below,
      His secret voice attend;
   From all tumultuous passion free,
   Their Guide invisible they see,
      And commune with their Friend.

2 O that I thus on Christ reclined,
   His quiet, meek, and even mind
      Might with Himself possess:
   I want the faith which works by hope,
   Which calmly to its Lord looks up,
      And waits for perfect peace.

3 Jesus, on me the power bestow
   To work, or rest, stand still, or go,
      As Thy design I see:
   Redeem'd from nature's hurrying strife,
   I would not take one step in life
      Without a beck from Thee.

4 No longer rash to act, or speak,
   To think or judge, I only seek
      To know Thine utmost will;
   I set my God a time no more[a]
   The kingdom when Thou wilt restore,
      And all Thy love reveal.

Unfortunately, Charles's journal for this period of time is not extant; but his brother's diary indicated that the long expected division of the London Society occurred in January 1763.

No. 173 A Selection from John Wesley's Journal[10]
London, January 23, 1763

. . . I was sitting with many of our Brethren, Mrs. Coventry [. . .] came in, threw down her [class] ticket, with those of her husband, daughters, and servants, and said they would hear two doctrines [of perfection] no longer.

---

[a]Charles's intention in this line seems to be to counter those who insist on instantaneous perfection; at the point of the asterisk John Wesley penned in: "I do, if I put Him off." He was, apparently, trying to balance Charles's progressive tendencies with the insistence upon a punctiliar event.

They had often said before Mr. M[axfield] preached perfection, but Mr.
W[esley] pulled it down. So I did, that perfection of Benjamin Harris,
G[eorge] Bell and all who abetted them. So the breach is made!

No. 174   "Ms. Scripture Hymns": Hymn 188

Set in the context of the dispute of Christian Perfection and the fracture of the
London Society, it is difficult to consider the "veteran" and "youngling" of
Charles's first hymn below (from late 1762 or early 1763) as being mere poetical
devices! They may well be caricatures of Wesley and Maxfield. The second hymn,
from the same manuscript, attacks the pride and lack of practical piety evidenced in
the strident perfectionists.[11]

He will not speak a gracious word
    The aged follower of his Lord,
Ready for Jesus' sake to die,
    Declares "the chief of sinners I!"
But now we hear a youngling say
    "Pardon'd and perfect'd in a day,
The instantaneous witness see,
    The chief of saints adore in me!"

No. 175   "Ms. Scripture Hymns": Hymn 215

1   Before He purges my sin away,
        And makes me truly free
    Is it a little thing to say,
        "I have no sin in me,"
    Is it no sin to take my ease
        As wholly sanctified,
    And slightly heal the sore disease,
        The loathsome plague of pride?

2   Perfection if I boldly claim
        My own fond heart believes
    Myself (while full of sin I am)
        Howe'er I boastingly profess
    My spotless purity
        Or real faith and solid grace,
    There is no truth in me.

3   No true humility and love,
        No true repentance,

No just or holy tempers prove,
  But all I am is a lie:
And if doubly proud,
  Myself I still miscall
I stand a witness false for God,
  Till into hell I fall.

May of 1763 found Charles Wesley in London supplying the Methodist pulpits and meeting the societies. A letter to his wife, Sally, indicates both that Maxfield's people had separated from the Wesleys' and that Charles was still optimistic about a reunion of the two groups. His preaching among the London Methodists seems to have emphasized deep humility, "resignation," or "poverty of spirit" as the focal point of perfection.

No. 176   Letter to Sally[12]

Litchfield-street, Sunday [May 27, 1763?]
My dear friend will be glad to hear we have had a feast of fat things ["plenty"] this morning. I am just come from preaching holiness for an hour, and administering to a multitude of communicants. . . .

It is observable what some will tell me, that on Thursday night, after my preaching poverty of spirit, such a spirit of humility fell upon the bands at their meeting, as had not been known for months or years past. Every mouth was stopped. They lay low in the dust before the Friend of Sinners, ashamed and confounded at His presence. One of Mr. Maxfield's Society, after hearing me, cried out, "This poverty of spirit will destroy all *our* perfection."

It is surprising, the readiness of the witnesses to receive my sayings. I do not despair of their all coming right at last.

Charles's work in London did not entirely meet with John's approval; it seems that certain points of the younger brother's doctrine of Christian Perfection (his unqualified conception perhaps) were similar to Maxfield's "enthusiastic" variety. Hence, John's letters to Charles in May and June of 1764 came with a bit of recrimination. Charles's latest hymns coupled with the way Maxfield talked and acted made the schism almost unavoidable. Once again the matter of "setting Perfection too high" came to the forefront, and now it seemed that the brothers were feuding. Charles's hymns from the immediate period were quite critical of the enthusiastic variety of perfection, and in that sense were supportive of his brother's position.

No. 177   John Wesley's Letter to Charles[13]

Haddington, May 25, 1764

Dear brother, Is there any reason why you and I should have no further intercourse [communication] with each other? I know of none; although possibly there are persons in the world, who would not be sorry for it. I hope you find peace in unity in the south [London], as we do in the north: only the seceders and Mr. Sandeman's friends are ready to eat us up. And no wonder; for these as well as Deists, and Socinians [Unitarians], I oppose *ex professo* [professedly]. But how do Thomas Maxfield and his friends go on? Quietly, or *gladiatorio animo?* [Latin: in the spirit and temper of prize-fighters] . . .

The frightful stories wrote from London made all our Preachers in the north afraid even to mutter about perfection, and of course, the people on all sides were grown good Calvinists in that point. It is what I foresaw from the beginning; that the devil would strive by Thomas Maxfield and company to drive perfection out of the kingdom.

O let you and I hold fast where unto we have attained; and let our yea be yea and our nay be nay! I feel the want of some about me that are all faith and love. No man was more profitable to me than George Bell, while he was simple of heart. O for heat and light united! My love to Sally. Adieu!

No. 178   John Wesley's Letter to Charles[14]

Stockton, July 9, 1764

Dear brother,—. . . How apt you are to take the colour of your company! When you and I [talked] together, you *seemed* at least to be of the same mind with me, and now you are all off the hooks again!—unless you only talk because you are in an humour of contradiction; and if so, I may as well blow against the wind as talk with you. I was not mad, though Thomas Maxfield was. *I* did not talk nonsense on the head [topic: Christian Perfection] as he did. I did not *act* contrary to all moral honesty. When your hymns on one hand were added to his talking and acting on the other, what was likely to be the consequence? . . .

One word more, concerning setting perfection too high. *That perfection which I believe, I can boldly preach, because I think I see five hundred witnesses of it. Of that perfection* which you preach, you do not even see any witnesses at all. Why, then you must have far more courage than me, or you could not persist in preaching it. I wonder you do not in this article fall in plumb with Mr. Whitefield. For do not you as well as he ask, "Where are the perfect ones?" I verily believe there are none upon earth, none dwelling in the body. I cordially assent to his opinion that there is *no such perfection* as *you* describe—at least, I never met an instance of it; and I doubt I never shall. Therefore, I still think to set perfection *so high* is effectually to renounce it. . . .

You are a long time getting to London. Therefore I hope you will do much good there. Yes, says William, "Mr. Charles will stop their *prating in the bands* at London, as he has done at Bristol." I believe not. I believe you will rather encourage them to speak humbly and modestly the words of truth and soberness. Great good has flowed and will flow herefrom. Let your "knowledge direct not quench the fire." That has been done too much already. I hope you will now *raise*, not *depress* their hopes. "They consider us," says honest George [Whitefield], "as setting suns. And yet it may please God we should outlive many of them." The proposal is good. But I fear our Council is little like the Senate of Capua. Come, try. Name me four senators, and I will name four more. Find such as you can, till you can find such as you would. Don't expect men "without spot or blemish." I could name six if need were, and yet not one angel; but *hoio nun Brotoi eisi* [Greek: such are mortals now].

My wife continues in an amazing [good] temper. Miracles are not ceased. Not one jarring string. O let us live now! My love to Sally.

No. 179   "Ms. John": Hymn on John 16:11[15]
Of judgement, because the prince
of this world is judged.

1   Again, Thou Spirit of burning come,
        Thy last great office to fulfill,
    To show the hellish tyrant's doom,
        The hellish tyrant's doom to seal,
    To drive him from thy sacred shrine,
    And fill our souls with life Divine.

2   Of judgement now the world convince,
        The end of Jesus coming show,
    To sentence their usurping prince,
        Him and his works destroy below.
    To finish and abolish sin
    And bring the heavenly nature in.

3   Who gauls [sic] the nations with his yoke,
        And bruises with an iron rod,
    And smites with a continual stroke,
        The world's fiercer ruler and its god,
    Wilt Thou not, Lord, from earth expel,
    And chase the fiend to his own hell.

4   Yes, Thou shalt soon pronounce his doom,
        Who rules in wrath the realms below,
    That wicked one rival consume, [our nature?]
        Avenge the nations of their foe,

In bright, vindictive lightning shine
And slay with the Breath Divine.

5   Then the whole earth again shall rest,
        And see its paradise restor'd
     Then every soul in Jesus blest
        Shall bear the Image of its Lord,
     In finish'd holiness renew'd,
     Immeasurably fill'd with God.

6   Spirit of sanctifying grace,
        Hasten that happy Gospel-day,
     Come, and restore the fallen race,
        Purge all our faith and blood away,
     Our inmost souls redeem, repair,
     And fix thy seat of judgment there.

7   Judgment to execute is thine,
        To kill and save is thine alone;
     Exert that energy Divine,
        Set up thine everlasting throne,
     The inward kingdom from above,
     The boundless power of perfect love.

8   O wou[l]dst Thou bring the final scene,
        Accomplish thy redeeming plan,
     Thy great millennial reign begin,
        That every ransom'd child of man
     That every soul may bow the knee,
     And rise to reign with God in Thee!

No. 180   "Ms. Matthew": Hymn on Matt. 9:19[16]
. . . for I am not come to call the righteous, but sinners to repentance.

1   We run before the race divine,
     If while their hearts are unrenew'd
            Hard tasks we rigorously enjoin,
        And yokes impose on converts rude;
            To men of an unconquer'd will
     Who doctrines from emotions explain
            Old bottles with new wine we fill,
     With truths they cannot contain.

2   While warm with undiscerning zeal;
     We urge the novices on too fast,
            To scale at once the holiest hill,
        As his first labour were his last;

He swells as so holy sanctified,
As perfect in a moment's space,
    He bursts with self important-pride
And loses all his real grace.

3   Eager that all should forward press,
Should see the summit with his eyes,
    Impatient for his own success
BE PERFECT NOW, the preacher cries!
    The work of grace so well begun
He ruins by his headlong haste,
    The wheat is choak'd with tares oer'run,
And Satan lays the vineyard waste.

4   Our only wisdom is to trace
The path whereby the Spirit leads,
    The usual course of saving grace
Which step by step in souls proceeds,
    Instructs them more and more to grow,
A people for their Father born;
    Till all his mind at last they know,
And ripe for God, to God return.

5   In us, most wise, most gracious Lord,
The Spirit of thy conduct give,
    That duely ministering the word,
Sinners we mar, like thee, receive,
    May never man thy work begun
Abuse one drop of grace sincere,
    But gently lead thy followers on
Till perfect all in heaven appear.

No. 181   "Ms. Matthew": Hymn on Matt. 13:31
         The kingdom of heaven is like to a grain
         of mustard seed, . . .

1 The Kingdom rises from a grain
    Into a tree by fast degrees,
Our hasty nature to restrain,
    To check our manifold forwardness
Which reaches for the when and now,
Which urges man BE PERFECT NOW.

2 Our darkest ignorance of pride
    Our unbelief, O Lord, remove,
Which sets thine oracle aside
    Thy words and actions to improve
And demand at ONCE the hallowing leaven,
And preach a shorter way to heaven.

3 O may I never teach my Lord,
     Wise above what is written be!
We by the method of Thy Word
     Bring us to full maturity,
Save us, when thou hast purged my guilt,
But save sure when and as thou will.

No. 182 John Wesley's Letter to Charles

The following letter, reflecting John's growing concern over Christian Perfection, may carry a tacit peace offering, with John suggesting that if Charles could find time to preach the instantaneous reception too then John could press the gradual work.[17]

                                        Whitehaven, June 27, 1766
Dear brother, I think you and I have abundantly too little intercourse [communication] with each other. Are we not old acquaintance? Have we not know each other for half a century? and are we not jointly engaged in such a work as probably no two other men upon earth are? Why then do we keep at such a distance? It is a mere device of Satan. But surely we ought not, at this time of day, be ignorant of his devices. Let us therefore make the full use of the little time that remains. We, at least, should think aloud, and use to the uttermost the light and grace on each bestowed. We should help each other.

        Of little life that best to make,
          And manage wisely the last stake.

    I hope you are with Billy Evans. If there is an Israelite [faithful person] indeed, I think he is one. O insist everywhere on full redemption, receivable now by faith alone! consequently to be looked for now. You are made, as it were, for this very thing. Just here you are in your element. In connection I beat you; but in strong, short, pointed sentences, you beat me. Go on, in your own way, what God has peculiarly called you to. Press the instantaneous blessing; then I shall have more time for my peculiar calling, enforcing the gradual work.
    We must have a thorough reform of the Preachers. I wish you could come to Leeds [for the Methodist Conference], with John Jones, in the machine [carriage]. It comes in two days: and after staying two days you might return. I would willingly bear your expenses up and down. I believe it would help, not hurt your health. My love to Sally.

No. 183 Short Hymn on Job 9:20
Though I were perfect, yet would I not know, . . .

Through all the precious promises
I find fulfill'd in Jesu's love,

If perfect I myself profess,
My own profession I disprove:
The purest saint that lives below
Doth his own sanctity disclaim,
The wisest owns, I nothing know,
The holiest cries, I nothing am!

No. 184   "Ms. Matthew": Hymn on Matt. 13:44
. . . the kingdom of heaven is like unto treasure
hid in a field; . . .

1 He did not proclaim to all that passed by
How happy I am HOW sanctified I
But finding a measure of heavenly power
Conceal'd the rich treasure and laboured for more.

2 The gift who receives and hastens to tell
He calls on thieves His treasure to steal;
Who plainly refuses our treasures to hide
His riches he loses thro' folly and pride.

3 The grace I have found O Jesus with Thee,
I hide in the ground for no man to see;
The grace I confide in the treasure thou art,
Who love to reside in a penitent heart.

4 Of pardon possesst my God I adore
Yet can I not rest impatient for more;
A greater salvation I languish to prove,
A deeper foundation a solider love.

5 The grace to insure the treasure concealed,
A mendicant poor I purchase the field,
Sell all to obtain it and seek it I find,
And ask till I gain it, in Jesus his mind.

No. 185   "Ms. Luke": Hymn on Luke 2:40
And the [Christ] child grew, and waxed strong. . . .

Jesus the Child by growing shows
That still He in His members grows,
His body here savours increase,
In faith and love and holiness.
No instantaneous starts we find,
But more and more of Jesus' mind
Till our full stature we attain,
And rise into a perfect man.

No. 186   "Ms. Luke": Hymn on Luke 16:15
. . . Ye are they which justify yourselves before men; . . .

1   Ye pillars in your own esteem,
        Vain is the praise which man bestows;
    Just, to yourselves and man ye seem,
        But all your hearts th' Omniscient knows;
    Men, foolish men the state approve
        Of saints entirely sanctified,
    Admiring that as Perfect Love,
        Which God abhors as perfect pride.

2   Thou Pharisee who blind and proud
        Dost righteous before men appear
    What art thou in the sight of God?
        A rotten painted sepulchre!
    Thine inward wickedness he sees,
        And will to all mankind reveal,
    Thy filthy rags of righteousness,
        Thy help not to heaven but hell.

No. 187   Short Hymn on Heb. 6:1
Let us go unto perfection.
(*Short Hymns on Select Passages of Scripture* (1762))

    "Go on? but how? from step to step?
    No; let *us* to perfection *leap!*"
    'Tis thus our hasty nature cries,
    Leap o'er the cross, to snatch the prize,
    Like *Jonah's* gourd, displays its bower,
    And blooms, and withers, in an hour.

No. 188   Short Hymn on Heb. 6:1

    Which of the *old* apostles taught
    Perfection in an instant caught,
    Show'd *our* compendious manner how,
    "Believe, and ye are perfect *now*;
    This moment wake, and seize the prize;
    Reeds, into sudden pillars rise";
    Believe delusion's ranting sons,
    And all the work is done at once!

John's letters of January and February 1767 indicate that he and Charles were at theological loggerheads over Christian Perfection and that their disagreement was becoming public knowledge. John's letter of January 27 was a masterpiece of theological bridge building; on each of the crucial issues ("thing, manner, time") he began on the grounds closest to Charles's position and then expanded his argument closer toward what was—characteristically—his own point of view. If Charles wrote responses to these letters they are not extant, but perhaps John Wesley already had his answer—in Charles's published and unpublished hymns.

No. 189   John Wesley's Letter to Charles[18]

London, January 27, 1767

Dear brother,—Some thoughts occurred to my mind this morning which I believe it may be useful to set down; the rather because it may be a means of our understanding each other clearly; that we may agree as far as ever we can and then let all the world know it.

I was thinking on Christian Perfection, with regard to the thing, the manner, and the time.

1. By perfection I mean the humble, gentle, patient love of God and man ruling all the tempers, words, and action, the whole heart, and the whole life. I do not include an impossibility of falling from it, either in part or in whole. Therefore I retract several expressions in our hymns which partly express, partly imply, such an impossibility. And I do not contend for the term sinless, though I do not object against it.

Do we agree or differ here? If we differ, wherein?

2. As to the manner. I believe this perfection is always wrought in the soul by faith, by a simple act of faith, consequently in an instant. But I believe in a gradual work both preceding and following that instant.

Do we agree or differ here?

3. As to the time, I believe this instant generally is the instant of death, the moment before the soul leaves the body. But I believe it may be ten, twenty, or forty years before death.

Do we agree or differ here?

I believe it is usually many years after justification, but that it *may be* within five years or five months after it. I know no conclusive argument to the contrary. Do you? If it *must be* many years after justification, I would be glad to know how many. *Pretium quotus arrogat annus?* [Latin: What year must claim the reward? from Horace, *Epistles*, II.i.35] And how many days or months or even years can you allow to be between perfection and death? How far from justification *must* it be? And how near death?

If it be possible, let you and I come to a good understanding, both for our own sakes and for the sake of the people.

No. 190   John Wesley's Letter to Charles[19]

London, February 12, 1767

Dear brother, . . . You are not yet [nor I probably] aware of pickthanks [those who curry favors]. Such were those who told you I did not pray for you by name in public; and they are liars into the bargain, unless they are deaf. The voice of one who truly loves God surely is—

> " 'Tis worse than death my God to love,
>   And not my God alone."

Such an one is certainly "as much athirst for sanctification as he was once for justification" [quoting a lost letter from Charles]. You remember, this used to be one of your constant questions. It is not now; therefore you are altered in your sentiments: And unless we come to an explanation, we shall inevitably contradict each other. But this ought not be in anywise, if it can possibly be avoided.

I still think, to disbelieve all the professors [of Christian Perfection] amounts to a denial of the thing. For if there be no living witnesses of what we have preached for twenty years, I cannot, dare not, preach it any longer. The whole comes to one point: Is there, or is there not, any instantaneous sanctification between justification and death? I say, Yes. You (often seem to) say No. What arguments brought you to think so? Perhaps they may convince me, too.

Nay; there is one question more, if you allow me there is such a thing; Can one who has attained it fall? Formerly I thought not; but you (with Thomas Walsh and John Jones) convinced me of my mistake. . . . Adieu!

Several of Charles's later hymns mention the change of emphasis that emerged in John's letter of January 27. They also connect sanctification with resignation of spirit (or self-will), which became an important theme in Charles's later work. His unpublished hymns on the Gospel of John indicate that Charles continued to hold to an unqualified, gradual conception of Christian Perfection, and that the Johannine Spirit-Christ nexus remained a vital sanctification theme for him.

No. 191   "Ms. John": Hymn on John 16:14–15
He shall glorify Me: for He shall receive of mine. . . .

1   Spirit of truth[,] descend,
        And with thy church abide,
    Our guardian to the end,
        Our sure, unerring guide,
    Us into the whole, counsel lead,
        Of God reveal'd below,
    And teach us all the truth we need,
        To life eternal know.

2 Whate'er Thou hear'st above,
    To us with power impart,
And shed abroad the love
    Of Jesus in our heart:
One with the Father and the Son
    Thy record is the same;
O make in us the godhead known
    Thro' faith in Jesus' name.

3 To all our souls apply
    The doctrine of our Lord,
Our conscience certify,
    And witness with the Word,
Thy realizing light display
    And show us things to come,
The after-state the final day,
    And man's eternal doom.

4 The Judge of quick and dead,
    The God of truth and love,
Who doth for sinners plead
    Our Advocate above;
Exalted by his Father there
    Thou dost exalt below,
And all his graces on earth declare,
    And all his glory show.

5 Sent in his name Thou art,
    His work to carry on,
His godhead to assert,
    And make his mercy known:
Thou searchest the deep things of God,
    Thou knowst the Saviour's mind,
And tak'st of his atoning blood,
    To sprinkle all mankind.

6 Now then of his receive,
    And show us the grace,
And all his fullness give,
    To all the ransom'd race;
Whate'er he did for sinners buy
    With his expiring groan
By faith in us reveal, apply
    And make it all our own.

7 Descending from above,
    Into our souls convey,
His comfort, joy, and love,

Which none can take away,
His merit, and his righteousness,
    Which makes an end of sin;
Apply to every heart his peace,
    And bring his kingdom in.

8 Thy plenitude of God
        That doth in Jesus dwell,
    On us thro' Him bestow'd
        To us secure and seal:
    Now let us taste our Master's bliss,
        The glorious, heavenly powers,
    For all the Father hath is His,
        And all He hath is ours.

No. 192 "Ms. John": Hymn on John 16:20, 21, 22
. . . ye shall weep and lament . . . but your sorrow shall be turned to joy

1 Jesus, dear departed Lord,
    True and gracious is thy word;
    We in part have found it true;
    All thy faithful mercies show.

2 Thou art to thy Father gone,
    Thou hast left us here alone,
    Left us a long fast to keep,
    Left us for Thy loss to weep.

3 Laugh the world, secure and glad,
    They rejoice but *we* are sad,
    We[,] alas, lament and grieve,
    Comfortless, till Thou relieve.

4 As a woman in her throes
    Sinks o'erwhelm'd with fears, and woes,
    Sinks our soul thro' grief and pain,
    Struggling to be born again.

5 As she soon forgot to mourn,
    Glad that a man-child is born,
    Let us, lighten'd of our load,
    Find deliverance in our God.

6 Jesus, visit us again,
    Look us out of grief and pain,
    Kindly comfort us that mourn,
    Into joy our sorrow turn.

7   Thy own joy to us impart,
    Root it deeply in our heart,
    Joy which none can take away
    Joy which shall for ever stay.

8   All the kingdom from above,
    All the happiness of love,
    Be it to thy mourners given,
    Pardon, holiness, and heaven.

NOTES

1. *CW Journal*, I, p. 286.
2. Selections from *JW Works*, VIII, pp. 279, 285, 293–298.

At the Foundery, Tuesday, June 26th, 1744

WAS CONSIDERED THE DOCTRINE OF SANCTIFICATION

With regard to which, the questions asked, and the substance of the answers given, were as follows:—

Q. 1. What is it to be sanctified?

A. To be renewed in the image of God, in righteousness and true holiness.

Q. 2. Is faith the condition, or the instrument, of sanctification?

A. It is both the condition and instrument of it. When we begin to believe, then sanctification begins. And as faith increases, holiness increases, till we are created new.

Q. 3. What is implied in being a perfect Christian?

A. The loving the Lord our God with all our heart, and with all our mind, and soul, and strength. (Deut. 6:5, 30:6; Ezek. 36:25–29).

Q. 4. Does this imply that all inward sin is taken away?

A. Without doubt; or how could we said to be saved "from all our uncleannesses" (verse 29)?

Q. 5. Can we know one who is thus saved? What is reasonable proof of it?

A. We cannot, without the miraculous discernment of spirits, be infallibly certain of those who are thus saved. But we apprehend, these would be the best proofs which the nature of the thing admits: (1) If we had sufficient evidence of their unblameable behaviour preceding. (2) If they gave a distinct account of the time and manner wherein they were saved from sin, and of the circumstances thereof, with such sound speech as could not be reproved. And (3) If, upon a strict inquiry afterwards from time to time, it appeared that all their tempers, and words, and actions, were holy and unreprovable.

Q. 6. How should we treat those who think they have attained this?

A. Exhort them to forget the things that are behind, and to watch and pray always, that God may search the ground of their hearts.

At the New-Room, Bristol, Friday August 2nd., 1745

ABOUT TEN, WE BEGAN TO SPEAK OF SANCTIFICATION:

WITH REGARD TO WHICH, IT WAS INQUIRED:—

Q. 1. When does inward sanctification begin?

A. In the moment we are justified. The seed of every virtue is then sown in the soul. From that time the believer gradually dies to sin, and grows in grace. Yet sin remains in him; yea, the seed of all sin, till he is sanctified throughout in spirit, soul, and body.

Q. 2. What will become of a Heathen, a Papist, a Church of England man, if he dies without being thus sanctified?

A. He cannot see the Lord. But none who seeks it sincerely shall or can die without it; though possibly he may not attain it, till the very article of death.

Q. 3. Is it ordinarily given till a little before death?

A. It is not, to those that expect it no sooner, nor consequently ask for it, at least, not in faith.

Q. 4. But ought we expect it sooner?

A. Why not? For although we grant, (1) That the generality of believers whom we have hitherto known were not so sanctified till near death; (2) That few of those to whom St. Paul wrote his Epistles were so at the time he wrote; (3) Nor he himself at the time of writing his former Epistles; Yet this does not prove that we may not to-day.

At the New-Room, Bristol, Tuesday, June 16th, 1747

It is clear from the Minutes of 1747 that by the third conference the "article of death" had become a lively issue among the Methodists. It is not clear whether Charles Wesley was among those who disputed over the "article of death"; it is clear from his hymns, however, that he held that point of view. In his *Christian Perfection,* John Wesley recalled that the conference ended on a note of unanimity, but one can wonder whether his remarks captured Charles's point of view in this matter:

Wednesday, June 17th, 1747

Q. 1. How much is allowed by our brethren who differ from us, with regard to entire sanctification?

A. They grant (1) That every one must be entirely sanctified in the article of death; (2) That till then a believer daily grows in grace, come nearer and nearer to perfection; (3) That we ought to be continually pressing after it, and to exhort all others so to do.

Q. What do we allow them?

A. We grant, (1) That many of those who have died in the faith, yea, the greater part of those we have known, were not perfected in love till a little before their death; (2) That the term sanctified is continually applied by St. Paul to all that were justified; (3) That by this term alone, he rarely, if ever, means "saved from all sin"; (4) That, consequently it is not proper to use the term in that sense, without adding the word "*wholly, entirely,*" or the like; (5) That the inspired writers almost continually speak of or to those who were justified, but very rarely to those who were wholly sanctified; (6) That, consequently, it behoves us to speak almost continually of the state of justification; but more rarely, "at least in full and explicit terms, concerning entire sanctification."

Q. What then is the point where we divide?

A. It is this: Should we expect to be saved from all sin before the article of death?

Q. Is there any clear Scripture promise of this,—that God will save us from *all* sin?

A. There is: "He shall redeem Israel from *all* his sins." (Psalm 130:8) This is more likely expressed in the prophecy of Ezekiel: "Then will I sprinkle clean water upon you, and ye shall be clean; from all your idols, will I cleanse you. I will also save you from all filthiness and all your uncleanness." (Ezek. 36:25, 29) No promise can be more clear. . . .

Q. But does any assertion answerable to this occur in the New Testament?

A. There does, and that laid down in the plainest terms. So 1 John 3:8, "For this purpose the Son of God was manifested, that he might destroy the works of the devil"; the works of the devil, without any limitation or restriction; but all sin is the work of the devil. Parallel to which is the assertion of St. Paul: "Christ loved the Church, and gave himself for it, that he might present it to himself a glorious Church, not having spot or wrinkle, or any such thing, but that it might be holy and without blemish." (Eph. 5:25–27)

Q. Does the New Testament afford any farther ground for expecting to be saved from all sin?

A. Undoubtedly it does; both in those prayers and commands, which are equivalent to the strongest assertions.

Q. What prayers to you mean?

A. Prayers for entire sanctification; which, were there no such thing, would be mere mockery of God. Such in particular are, (1) "Deliver us from evil."[. . .] Now, when this is done, when we are delivered from all evil, there can be no sin remaining. (2) "Neither pray I for these alone, but for them also who shall believe on me through their word; that all may be one; as thou Father, art in me and I in thee, that they also may be one in us; I in them, and thou in me, that they may be made perfect in one." (John 17:20–23). (3) "I bow my knees to unto God and Father of our Lord Jesus Christ, that he would grant you, that ye . . . may be filled with all the fullness of God." (Eph. 3:14, &c). (4) "The very God of peace sanctify you wholly. And I pray God, your whole spirit, soul, and body, may be preserved blameless unto the coming of our Lord Jesus Christ." (1 Thes. 5:23)

Q. What command is there to the same effect?

A. (1) "Be ye perfect, as your Father who is in heaven is perfect." (Matt. 5:48). (2) "Thou shall love the Lord thy God with all thy heart, and with all thy soul, and with all thy mind." (Matt. 22:37) But if the love of God fill all the heart, there can be no sin therein.

Q. But how does it appear that this is to be done before the article of death?

A. (1) From the very nature of a command, which is not given to the dead but to the living. Therefore, "Thou shalt love God with all thy heart" cannot mean, Thou shalt do this when thou diest; but, while thou livest.

(2) From express texts of Scripture: (i) "The grace of God, that bringeth salvation, hath appeared to all men; teaching us that, having renounced ungodliness and worldly lusts, we should live soberly, righteously, and godly in this present world; looking for the glorious appearing of our Lord Jesus Christ, who gave himself for us, that he might redeem us from all iniquity, and purify unto himself a peculiar people, zealous of good works." (Titus 2:11–14) (ii) "He hath raised up an horn of salvation for us, to perform the mercy promised our fathers; the oath which he swore to our father Abraham, that he would grant unto us, that we, being delivered out of the hands of our enemies, should serve him without fear, in holiness and righteousness before him, all the days of our life." (Luke 1:69 &c). . . .

3. *JW Works*, XI, p. 391.

4. *Ibid.*

5. "Ms. Preparation for Death" pp. 33–34. Located in the Methodist Archives and Research Centre, The John Rylands University Library of Manchester, Manchester, England. Published here by permission of the Methodist Church Archives and History Committee, England.

6. *JW Works*, V, pp. 227–228.

7. *JW Letters*, V, p. 38. This letter published in Telford's edition of John Wesley's letters is printed by permission of Epworth Press.

8. *JW Works*, XII, p. 207.

9. *Ibid.*, XII, p. 124.

10. *JW Works*, III, p. 126.

11. "Ms. Scripture Hymns" # 188 and #215. The manuscript is located in the Methodist Archives and Research Centre, The John Rylands University Library of Manchester, Manchester, England. These hymns are printed by permission of the Methodist Church Archives and History Committee, England.

12. Jackson, *CW Journal*, II, p. 266.

13. *JW Works*, XII, p. 126.

14. *JW Letters*, V, p. 19. This letter from the Standard Edition of *The Letters of John Wesley*, edited by John Telford, is printed by permission of Epworth Press.

15. "Ms. John" pp. 335–336. Located in the Methodist Archives and Research Centre, The John Rylands University Library of Manchester, Manchester, England. Printed here by permission of the Methodist Church Archives and History Committee, England. The hymn was written about August 30, 1764.

16. The manuscript, which dates from *ca.* 1764–1766, is located in the Methodist Archives and Research Centre, The John Rylands University Library of Manchester, Manchester, England. Printed here by permission of the Methodist Church Archives and History Committee, England.

17. *JW Works*, XII, pp. 130–131.

18. *JW Letters*, V, pp. 38–39. This letter is used with the permission of Epworth Press.

19. *JW Works*, XII, p. 132.

11 / The Old Ship

Charles's undying loyalty to the Church of England was one of his theological constants. While his churchmanship was tempered with a dose of Wesleyan pragmatism, allegiance to the established church was for Charles an ideal from which there could be no willful deviation. He came by his staunch churchmanship quite naturally. The two Samuels (father and older brother) both possessed intense loyalty to the Mother Church, and both men were models for Charles in his formative years.

Charles's churchmanship persisted through several controversial periods. Initially it was an issue between the Wesleys and the "Moravianized Methodists" who favored separation and disparaged Anglican sacramentology. Charles, while sharing some of their mystical tendencies, was far more committed to the church's sacraments, liturgy, and *Book of Common Prayer*. The question of churchmanship lurked in the background of the "stillness" controversy of the 1740s, and found expression in Wesley's responses to that dispute. The most characteristic element of his Anglicanism was frequent communion: Methodism remained attached to the Church of England through its eucharistic umbilical cord. As the politics of the time wedded Anglican churchmanship with loyalty to the crown, the Methodists quickly became suspect on both grounds. No small part of the mob violence against the Wesleys was traceable to anti-Catholic sentiments and English nationalism; and both of these matters became the focus of Methodist apologetics in the 1740s.

As Methodism outgrew the dual ministrations of John and Charles Wesley, the movement was forced to employ more and more lay preachers in order to carry on the day-to-day work of the societies and preaching posts. Soon the lay preachers clamored for ordination so that they could keep step with expansion, and avail the societies of the comfort of the sacraments as Methodists were increasingly being barred from the established churches. This development marked the beginning of Charles's struggle against Methodist ordinations, which in his mind—at least—signified separation from the established church. The controversy reached its pinnacle in 1784 when John Wesley's ordination of two "Elders" (priests) and Dr. Coke for episcopal oversight in America signaled the separation Charles had long dreaded. The hymns and letters ran fast and furious in those closing years, but the brothers did reach a reconciliation. Yet their burial in separate plots, Charles's Anglican and John's Methodist, remains a monumental reminder of their willingness to agree to disagree on this and other matters of "opinion."

No. 193   Journal Selections: June 11, 1740–July 25, 1743

Wed. June, 11th [1740]. . . . I told them plainly I SHOULD CONTINUE WITH THEM ONLY SO LONG AS THEY CONTINUE IN THE CHURCH OF ENGLAND. My every word was grievous to them. I am a thorn in their sides, and they cannot bear me.

Sun., July 3d. [1743]. Mr. Hall, poor Moravianized Mr. Hall, met us at the Chapel. I did him honour before the people. I expounded the Gospel as usual; and strongly avowed my inviolable attachment to the Church of England. Mr. Meriton and Graves assisted me at the sacrament. . . .

Mon., July 25th [1743]. The Mayor [Gwennap] told us, that the Ministers were the principal authors of all this evil, by continually representing us in their sermons as Popish emissaries, and urging the enraged multitude to take all manner of ways to stop us. Their whole preaching is cursing and lies: yet they modestly say, my fellow-labourer and I are the cause of all the disturbance. It is always the lamb that troubles the water. Yesterday we were stoned as Popish incendiaries; to-day it is our turn to have the favour of the people.

In 1743 the Wesleys published their second (and expanded) edition of *Collection of Psalms and Hymns*. The poetical comments on the Psalms were strongly nationalistic, and particularly supportive of the Church of England. They were, further, critical of those factions that "spoil the Apostolic tree" and hence reflect ripples of the schism with the "still brethren." Several of the hymns in that collection can be traced directly to Charles's pen through his manuscript collections. Two of these are given below.

No. 194   Hymn: Psalm 80 Adapted to the Church of England ("Ms. Clark")

This hymn survives in two manuscripts; the earlier "Ms. Clark" is written and edited in Charles's own hand. Several verses are lined through and replaced. Apparently undecided about the phraseology in verse 25, Charles carried an alternative reading below the line; the published version carried the second reading. Verses four, five, and eighteen were not carried in the published edition.[1]

1   Shepherd of Souls, the Great, the Good,
      Who lead'st ~~Joseph~~ Israel like a sheep,

Present to guard, and give them Food,
  And kindly in thy Bosom keep;

2   Hear thy afflicted People's Prayer,
      Arise out of thy holy Place,
    Stir up thy Strength, thine Arm make bare,
      And magnify thy Saving Grace vindicate thy chosen Race.

3   Haste to our Help, Thou GOD of Love,
      Supreme Almighty King of Kings,
    Descend all-glorious from above,
      Come flying on the Cherubs['] Wings.

4   Turn us again, Thou GOD of Might,
      The Brightness of thy Face display,
    So shall we walk with Thee in Light
      As Children of the Perfect Day.

5   We all shall be thro' Faith made whole,
      If Thou the Healing Grace impart,
    Thy Love shall hallow every Soul,
      And take up every sinless Heart.

6   O Lord of Hosts, O GOD of Grace,
      How long shall thy fierce anger burn
    Against Thine own peculiar Race
      Who ever pray Thee to return!

7   Thou giv'st us plenteous Draughts of Tears,
      With Tears Thou dost thy People feed,
    We sorrow till thy Face appears,
      Affliction is our Daily Bread.

8   A Strife we are to All around,
      By vile intestine Vipers torn,
    Our bitter Hous[e]hold foes abound,
      And laugh our Fallen Church to scorn.

9   Turn us again, O God, and shew
      The Brightness of thy lovely Face,
    So shall we all be Saints below,
      And wholly sav'd, and perfected in Grace.

10   Surely, O Lord, we once were Thine,
       (Thou hast for Us thy Wonders wrought)
     A generous and right noble Vine,
       When newly out of *Egypt* brought.

11   Thou didst the Heathen Stock expel,
       And chase them from their quiet Home,

Druids, and all the Brood of Hell,
    And monks of Antichristian *Rome.*

12 Planted by Thine Almighty Hand,
      Watered with Blood the Vine took Root,
    And spread thro' all the happy Land,
      And fill'd the Earth with golden Fruit.

13 The Hills were cover'd with her Shade,
      Her Branching arms extended wide
    Their fair luxuriant Honours spread,
      And flourish'd as the Cedar's Pride.

14 Her Boughs she stretched from Sea to Sea,
      And reach'd to frozen *Scotia's* shore
    (They once rever'd the Hierarchy,
      And bless'd the Mitre's Sacred Power).

15 Why then hast Thou abhor'd Thine own,
      And cast thy pleasant Plant away;
    Broke down her Hedge, her Fence o'erthrown,
      And left her to the Beasts of Prey?

16 All that go by pluck off her Grapes,
      Our *Sion* of her Children spoil,
    And Error in ten thousand Shapes
      Would every gracious Soul beguile.

17 The Boar out of the *German* Wood[a]
      Tears up her Roots with baleful Power,
    The Lion roaring for his Food,
      And all the Forest-Beasts devour.

18 Deists, and Sectaries agree,
      And *Calvin* and *Socinus* join
    To spoil the Apostolic Tree
      And Root and Branch destroy the Vine.

19 Turn Thee again, O Lord our God,
      Look down with Pity from above;
    O lay aside thy vengeful Rod
      And visit us with pardoning Love.

20 The Vineyard with Thine own Right Hand
      Hath planted in these Nations see,
    The Branch that rose at thy Command
      And yielded gracious Fruit to Thee.

---

[a]Moravians.

21   Tis now cut down and burnt with Fire:
         Arm of the Lord, awake, awake,
     Visit thy Foes in righteous Ire,
         Vengeance on all thy Haters take.

22   Look on them with thy flaming Eyes,
         The sin-consuming Virtue dart;
     And bid our Fallen Church arise,
         And make us after thy own Heart.

23   To us our Nursing-Fathers raise,
         Thy Grace be on the Great bestow'd,
     And let the King show forth thy Praise,
         And rise to build the House of GOD.

24   Thou hast ordain'd the Powers that be:
         Strengthen thy Delegate below;
     He bears the Rule deriv'd from Thee,
         O let him All thine Image shew.

25   Support him with the guardian Hand,
         Let all thy mind be seen in Him,
             Thy Royal Grace
     King of a re-converted Land,
         In goodness as in Power supreme.

26   So will we not from Thee go back,
         If Thou our ruin'd Church restore,
     No, never more will we forsake,
         No, never will we grieve thee more.

27   Revive, O GOD of Power, revive
         Thy Work in our degenerate Days,
     O let us by thy Mercy live,
         And all our Lives shall speak thy Praise.

28   Turn us again, O Lord, and shew
         The Brightness of thy lovely Face,
     So shall we all be Saints below,
         And sav'd, and perfected in Grace.

No. 195   Hymn: "Psalm 137 Paraphrased"[2]
("Cheshunt College Ms.")

1   Fast by the *Babylonish* tide,
         (The tide our Sorrows made o'erflow),
     We dropp'd our weary Limbs, and cried
         In deep distress at *Sion's* woe;

Her we bewail'd in speechless groans
In bondage with her Captive Sons.

2   Our Harps no longer vocal now,
        We cast aside untuned, unstrung,
    Forgot them pendent on the Bough:
        Let meaner Sorrows find a tongue,
    Silent we sat, and scorn'd relief,
    In all the majesty of grief.

3   In vain our haughty lords required
        A song of *Sion's* sacred strain:—
    "Sing us a song your God inspired."
        How shall our Souls exult in Pain?
    How shall the mournful Exiles sing
    While Bondslaves of a foreign King?

4   *Jerusalem*, dear hallow'd Name!
        Thee if I ever less desire,
    If less distrest for thee I am,
        Let my Right Hand forget its Lyre,
    All its harmonious Strains forgot
    When heedless of a Mother's Woe.

5   O *England's* desolate Church, if Thee,
        Tho' desolate, I remember not,
    Let me, when lost to Piety,
        Be lost myself and clean forgot.
    Cleave to the Roof of my speechless Tongue,
    When *Sion* is not all my song!

6   Let Life, itself with Language fail,
        For Thee when I forbear to mourn;
    Nay, but I will for ever wail,
        Till GOD thy captive state shall turn;
    Let this my every Breath employ,
    To grieve for thee be all my Joy!

7   O for the weeping Prophet's strains,
        The sacred Sympathy of Woe!
    I live to gather Thy Remains,
        For Thee my Tears and Blood should flow,
    My Heart amidst Thy Ruins lies,
    And only in Thy Rise I rise.

8   Remember, Lord, the Cruel Pride,
        Of *Edom* in our Evil Day,
    "Down with it to the Ground," they cried,
        "Let none the tottering Ruin stay,

Let none the sinking Church restore,
But let it fall to rise no more."

9   Surely our GOD shall Vengeance take
     On those that gloried in our Faith,
   He a full End of Sin shall make,
     Of all that held our Souls in Thrall;
   O *Babylon*, Thy Day shall come:
   Prepare to meet Thy final Doom.

10   Happy, the Man that see in Thee
     The mystic *Babylon* within;
   And fill'd with Holy Cruelty
     Disdains to spare that smallest Sin,
   And sternly takes Thy little Ones,
   And dashes all against the Stones.

11   Thou in thy Turn shalt be brought low,
     Thy Kingdom shall not always last
   The Lord thy Kingdom shall ov'rthrow,
     And lay the mighty waster waste,
   Destroy thy Being with Thy Power,
   And Pride and self shall be no more.

No. 196   Journal Selections: February 20–March 10, 1744

Mon., February 20th [1744]. I heard, without any surprise, the news of the French invasion; which only quickened us in our prayers, especially for His Majesty, King George.

In the evening I expounded what the Spirit saith to the church of Ephesus, and received extraordinary power to warn them of the sword that is coming, and to wrestle with God in prayer for the King.

John Wesley's journal entry for Mon., March 5, 1744, reported: "I was much pressed to write an address to the King." His open letter had the intention of affirming the Methodists' "most dutiful regards to [his] sacred Majesty," in the face of the political turmoil of the times. After giving the full text of the tract, John concluded: "upon farther consideration it was judged best to lay it aside." This "farther consideration" was engendered by a hotly worded letter from brother Charles; the subtitle, "The Humble Address of the Societies in England and Wales, in derision called Methodists," and the second paragraph of the tract were probably what set Charles off.[3] He reported his reaction to John's "Address" in his journal entry for the very next day.

Tues., March 6th. I wrote to my brother: "My objection to your address in the name of the Methodists is, that it would constitute us a sect; at least it would seem *to allow* that we are a body distinct from the national Church; whereas we are only a sound part of that Church. Guard against this; and in the name of the Lord address to-morrow."

Sat., March 10th. . . . I took John Healey's account of their treatment at Nottingham. The Mayor set for Thomas Westal. John went with him. Thomas desired time to read the oath, which they offered him; upon which Mr. Mayor threatened to send him to prison. While he was making his mittimus, John Healey asked, "Does not the law allow a man three hours to consider of it?" This checked their haste; and they permitted him to hear first what he should swear to. He said, it was all well and good, and what he had often heard Mr. Wesleys say, that King George was our rightful King, and no other; and he would take this oath with all his heart.

They had first asked John Healey if he would take the oaths. He answered, "I will take them now; but I would not before I heard Mr. Wesley; for I was a Jacobite till they convinced me of the truth, and of His Majesty's right." "See the old Jesuit," cries one of the venerable Aldermen, "he has all his paces, I warrant you!" Another, on Thomas Westal's holding his hand to his eyes, cried, "See, see! he is confessing his sins!" They treated them like Faithful and Christian at Vanity-fair,[a] only they did not burn them yet, or even put them in the cage. They demanded their horses for the King's service, and would not believe them that they had none, till they sent and searched.

Not finding any cause to punish, they were forced to dismiss them; but soon after the Mayor sent for Thomas Westal, and commanded him to depart the town. He answered, he should obey his orders, and accordingly came to Epworth. Here he told me he had found out who the Pretender was, for Mr. Gurney told him, many years ago there was one King James, who was turned out, and one King William taken in his place, and that then the Parliament made a law that no Papist should ever be King, by which law King James's son, whom he had now discovered to be the Pretender, was justly kept out.

Given the difficulties of the spring of 1744, it is not surprising that Methodism's relationship with the Church of England was one of the topics of conversation when the Wesleys met in conference with their preachers at the Foundery, on June 25–27 of that year. The minutes of Wednesday, June 27, treated the question directly:

---

[a]The allusion is drawn from Bunyan's *Pilgrim's Progress*. Faithful and Christian, the protagonists, find themselves at a fair established by Beelzebub in the town of Vanity for the sale of honours, pleasures, titles, lusts, and delights of all sorts. Since Christian and Faithful refuse to buy the vanities of the fair they are arrested, subjected to a mock trial, and endure all manner of persecution because they want only "to buy the Truth."

"What is the Church of England?" The Methodists' replies marked out a loyal Anglican ecclesiology, and eventually broached the question of separation. "Do we separate from the Church?" A. "We conceive not: We hold communion therewith for conscience' sake, by constantly attending both the word preached and the sacraments duly administered there in." While they considered the possibility that Methodism would "be scattered into sects and parties" or "form themselves into a distinct sect" after the Wesleys' death, the early Methodists were "persuaded [that] the body of our hearers will even after our death remain in the Church, unless they be thrust out." Yet either within or without the established church the Methodists would leaven the whole Church.[4]

In the 1750s Methodism's connection with the Church of England and its sacraments remained a point of controversy. Although the basic themes continued from the 1740s, the context and characters changed; Charles Wesley no longer contended with "the Moravianized Methodists" or "still brethren," as in the succeeding decades the Methodist lay preachers became the focus of his attention. He came to see them as undermining the movement's connection with the established church.

The roots of the problem lay in the Wesleys' Anglican sacramentology. They believed that the Eucharist was a "means of grace," and hence was vital for Christian life and nurture. Since they affirmed, with the church, that a valid sacrament was administered by an ordained minister of the Church of England, the Wesleys sent members of the Methodist Societies to their local parish churches for the Lord's Supper; John and Charles often officiated (or assisted) at those services themselves. Hence, Charles happily remembers occasions when he led a parade of Methodists into Anglican churches—sometimes swelling the congregation to the point of making it difficult to serve the sacrament.

As the Methodists began to be refused the sacrament in local churches they came to depend more and more upon ordained Anglicans, like the Wesleys, who served in the Methodist connection. With the growth of the movement lay preachers were pressed into service to lessen some of the burden the clergymen faced on lengthening circuits. But the success of the revival left the Wesleys with a sacramental dilemma; it seemed as though the Methodists were going to be forced to choose between the Anglican sacramentology, with infrequent communion as a consequence, or lay administration, with more frequent communion as a result. As was typical of him, John Wesley would later find a route around the roadblock of lay administration and seek to maintain a high view of the sacraments *and* constant communion. Equally characteristic of Charles was his refusal to accept John's innovation and his growing concern that the pride and ambitions of the Methodist lay preachers would eventually cause a schism with the Church of England.

No. 197   Hymn: "For a Lay Preacher"
(*Hymns and Sacred Poems*, 1749)

Charles's *Hymns and Sacred Poems* (1749) carried a dozen hymns "For a Preacher of the Gospel", three of which were specifically addressed to lay preachers. The first of those hymns, "For a Lay Preacher," esteems the lay preacher as an able spokesperson of God's love, and yet emphasizes a functional distinction between the lay and ordained ministries.

1 I thank Thee, Lord of earth and heaven,
     That Thou to me, e'en me, hast given
        The knowledge of Thy grace,
     (Which flesh and blood could ne'er reveal),
     And call'd a babe Thy love to tell,
        And stammer out Thy praise.

2 None of the *sacred* order I,
     Yet dare I not the grace deny
        Thou hast on me bestow'd,
     Constrain'd to *speak* in Jesu's name,
     And show poor souls th' atoning Lamb,
        And point them to His blood.

3 I now believe, and therefore speak,
     And found myself, go forth to seek
        The sheep that wander still;
     For these I toil, for these I care,
     And faithfully to all declare
        The peace which all may feel.

4 My God supply Thy servant's need,
     If Thou hast sent me forth indeed
        To make Thy goodness known;
     Thy Son in sinners' hearts reveal,
     By gracious signs my mission seal,
        And prove the word Thine own.

5 O for Thy only Jesu's sake,
     Into those arms of mercy take
        Thy meanest messenger,
     And ever in Thy keeping have,
     And grant me, Lord, at last to save
        Myself with all that hear.

No. 198 Journal Selection: August 4, 1754

Sun., August 4th [1754]. . . . I communicated at the cathedral [St. Paul's, London]. An elderly Clergyman pointed me at the table to where the Ministers were. The number of communicants begins to increase: a sign we do not make a separation, as a zealous advocate for the Church charged me in going home. I set him right, and he was in a good measure appeased.

Poor James [Hutton] has given them cause for suspicion. He too came to the cathedral at first, as my opponent told me, and pretended to bring others, till he had got so much hold of them as to take them all from it, and turn them Dissenters. How has he increased our difficulties! But the power and blessing of God can set all right. . . .

1755 was a pivotal year in Methodism's connection with the Church of England. Several of the lay preachers, including the Perronets, Joseph Cownley, and Thomas Walsh, argued for the authority to administer the Lord's Supper to those under their care, and had in fact begun to practice it. A conference was called at Leeds, May 6, to discuss the thorny issue. Over sixty-three Methodist preachers arrived to debate the "question of conservation." The number of participants certainly indicates the importance of the issue at hand. Unfortunately, Charles Wesley's journal for this crucial period is not extant, but it is possible to piece the picture together through a combination of other sources.

No. 199   Selections from John Wesley's Journal, April 28–May 6, 1755[5]

Mon., 28 [April, 1755]. I preached at Keighley, on Tuesday at Bradford, which is now as quiet as Birstall. Such a change has God wrought in the hearts of the people since John Nelson was in the dungeon here. My brother [Charles] met me at Birstall in the afternoon.

Wed., 30. We began reading together *A Gentleman's Reasons for his Dissent from the Church of England* [by Micaiah Towgood]. It is an elaborate and lively tract, and contains the strength of the cause; but it did not yield us one proof that it is lawful for us (much less our duty) to separate from it.

Thur., May 1.—I finished the *Gentleman's Reasons* (who is a dissenting minister at Exeter). In how different a spirit does this man write from honest Richard Baxter! The one dipping as it were his pen in tears, the other in vinegar and gall. Surely one page of that loving, serious Christian weighs more than volumes of this bitter, sarcastic jester.

Tues., 6.—Our Conference began at Leeds. The point on which we desired all the preachers to speak their minds at large was, "Whether we ought to separate from the Church?" Whatever was advanced on one side or the other was seriously and calmly considered; and on the third day we were all fully agreed in that general conclusion—that (whether it was *lawful* or not) it was no ways *expedient*.

At the end of that same week in May, Charles penned a letter home to Sally. It gives a brief report of the proceedings of Leeds, suggests that he and John had come to an agreement about the present plight of Methodism, and offers a few interesting asides about the younger brother's strained relationship with his sister-in-law (John's wife), whom he sarcastically calls "my good angel and sister." Charles and Mrs. John Wesley both had explosive personalities and the combination of the two of them was especially volatile.

No. 200 Letter to Sally[6]

Rotherham, Friday afternoon [May 9 or 16, 1755?].

I snatch a few moments before the congregation comes to salute my dearest Sally in the love that never faileth. Last Saturday afternoon, after my brother and I had settled everything in the four preceding days, on my way to Wakefield, I met my good angel and sister. I have done her honour before the people, and behaved (though I say it) very much like a gentleman; only that I took a French leave this morning, that is, left Leeds without telling either her or her husband.

I trust my Sally is more than patient of my absence. You should rejoice that my Lord continues to use me. May his presence make you infinite amends! . . .

I left the brethren in Conference. Yet I do not repent my trouble [in going]. You will be content to wait a little for particulars. All agreed not to separate [from the Church of England]. So the wound is healed—slightly. Yet some good news I may bring you from Leeds, if we live a month longer.

I want to hear that your sisters are both with you. If not, it is your own fault, or theirs. Three weeks I am fast at London; then we may meet, all four of us, in Charles-street, if the Lord permits. . . . Farewell.

No. 201 Epistle to John Wesley, May 25, 1755
("Ms. Epistle")

Early in May, just after the Leeds Conference, Charles dashed off a lengthy open letter to his brother John. The poetic epistle reviews the present state of the church and intends to force John into a more direct statement of his solidarity with the Church of England. Charles depicts himself as a man in the middle, "By Bigots [staunch Anglicans] branded for a Schismatick, / By real Schismaticks disown'd, decry'd . . . ." The title of the tract is significant: *An Epistle to the Reverend Mr. John Wesley, by Charles Wesley, Presbyter of the Church of England;* the younger brother wrote as an Anglican concerned about the direction Methodism was taking. Charles wasted no time putting the letter into circulation. The printer's bill (William Strahan) is extant and indicates that Charles received 3,000 copies of the *Epistle* on May 28, 1755, and ordered 1,000 more on the same day. The impact of the *Epistle* is certainly to be measured in the peeved tone of John's two letters of June 1755.

My first and last unalienable Friend,
A Brother's Thoughts with due Regard attend
A *Brother*, still *as thy own Soul belov'd*,
Who speak to learn, and write to be reprov'd:
Far from the ~~envious~~ factious undiscerning Crowd,
Distrest I fly to Thee, and *think aloud;*
I tell Thee, wise and faithful as Thou art,
The Fears and Sorrows of a burthen'd Heart,
The Workings of (a blind or heav'nly?) Zeal,
And all my Fondness for *The Church* I tell,
The Church whose Cause I serve, whose Faith approve,
Whose Altars reverence, and whose Name I love.

But does she still exist in more than Sound?
The Church—alas, where is she to be found?
Not in the Men, however *dignified*,
Who *would* her Creeds repeal, her Laws deride,
Her Prayers expunge, her Articles disown,
And thrust the Filial Godhead from his Throne.
Vainest of all their antichristian Plea,
Who cry *The Temple of the Lord are We!*
"We have the Church, nor will we quit our hold—"
Their hold of what? the Altar? or the Gold?
The Altar Theirs, who will not light the Fire,
Who spurn the Labour, but accept the Hire,
Who not for Souls, but their own Bodies care,
And leave to Underlings the Task of Pray'r?
As justly might our christen'd Heathens claim,
Thieves, Drunkards, Whoremongers, the sacred Name;
Or Rabble-rout succeed in their Endeavour
With *High Church and Sacheverell for ever!*
As *Arians* be for Orthodox allow'd,
For Saints the Sensual, Covetous, and Proud,
And Satan's Synagogue for the true Church of GOD.

Then let the zealous *Orthodox* appear,
And challenge the contested Character:
Those, who renounce the whole Dissenting Tribe,
Creeds, Articles, and Liturgy subscribe;
Their Parish-Church who never once have mist,
At Schism rail, and hate a *Methodist;*
The Company of faithful Souls' are These,
Who strive to 'stablish their own Righteousness,
But count the Faith Divine a Madman's Dream?
Howe'er they to Themselves may Pillars seem,
Of Christ, and of his Church they make no Part:
They never knew the Saviour in their Heart.

But Those who in their Heart have Jesus known,
Believers, justified by Faith alone,
Shall we not Them *the faithful People* own?
In whom the Power of Godliness is seen,
Must we not grant the Methodists *The Men?*
No: tho' we granted them from Schism free,
From wild enthuslastic Heresy,
From ev'ry wilful Crime, and moral Blot,
Yet still the Methodists *The Church* are not:
A single Faculty is not the Soul,
A Limb the Body, or a Part the Whole.

Whom then, when ev'ry vain Pretender's cast,
With Truth may we account The Church at last?
"All who have felt, deliver'd from above,
"The *holy* Faith that works by humble Love,
"All that in pure religious Worship join,
"Led by the Spirit, and the Word divine,
"Duly the Christian Mysteries partake,
"And bow to Governors for Conscience sake:"
In These *the Church of England* I descry,
And vow with *these alone* to live and die.

Yet while I warmly for her Faith contend,
Shall I her Blots and Blemishes defend?
Inventions *added* in a fatal Hour,
Human Appendages of Pomp and Power,
Whatever shines in *outward* Grandeur great,
I give it up—*a Creature of the State!*
Wide of the Church, as Hell from Heav'n is wide,
The Blaze of Riches, and the Glare of Pride,
The vain Desire to be entitled *Lord,*
The worldly Kingdom, and the princely Sword.

But should the bold usurping Spirit dare
Still higher climb, and sit in *Moses'* chair,
Power o'er my Faith and Conscience to maintain,
Shall I submit, and suffer it to reign?
Call it *the Church,* and Darkness put for Light,
Falsehood with Truth confound, and Wrong with Right?
No: I dispute the Evil's haughty Claim,
The Spirit of the World be still its Name,
Whatever call'd by Man 'tis purely Evil,
'Tis Babel, Antichrist, and Pope, and Devil!

Nor would I e'er disgrace the Church's Cause
By penal Edicts, and compulsive Laws;
(Should wicked Powers, as formerly, prevail

T'exclude her choicest Children from her Pale)
Or force my Brethren in her Forms to join,
As every Rite and Rubric were divine,
As all her Orders on the Mount were given,
And copied from the *Hierarchy* of Heaven.
Let Others for the Shape and Colour fight
Of Garments short or long, or black or white;
Or fairly match'd, in furious Battle join
For and against the Sponsors and the Sign;
Copes, Hoods, and Surplices *the Church* miscall,
And fiercely run their Heads against *the Wall;*
Far different Care is mine; o'er Earth to see
Diffus'd her true essential Piety,
To see her lift again her languid Head,
Her lovely Face from ev'ry Wrinkle freed,
Clad in the simple, pure, primeval Dress,
And beauteous with internal Holiness,
Wash'd by the Spirit and the Word from Sin,
Fair without Spot, and glorious all within.

   Alas! how distant now, how desolate,
Our fallen Zion, in her captive State!
Deserted by her Friends, and laugh'd to Scorn,
By inbred Foes, and bosom Vipers torn.
With Grief I mark their rancours Despight,
With Horror hear the clam'rous *Edomite;*
"Down with her to the Ground, who fiercely cries,
"No more to lift her Head, no more to rise!
"Down with her to the Pit, to Tophet doom
"A Church emerging From the Dregs of *Rome!*
"Can any Good come out of Popery?["]
Ye moderate Dissenters—come, and see!

   See us, when from the Papal Fire we came,
Ye frozen Sects, and warm you at the Flame,
Where for the Truth our Host of Martyrs stood,
And clapp'd their Hands, and seal'd it with their Blood!
Behold *Elijah's* fiery Steeds appear,
Discern the Chariot of *our* Israel near!
That flaming Car, for whom doth it come down?
The Spouse of Christ?—Or whore of Babylon?
For Martyrs, by the Scarlet Whore pursu'd
Thro' Racks and Fires, into the Arms of GOD.
These are the Church of Christ, by Torture driv'n
To Thrones triumphant with their Friends in Heav'n;
The Church of Christ (let all the Nations own),
The Church of Christ *and England*—is But One!

Yet vainly of our Ancestors we boast,
We who their Faith and Purity have lost,
Degenerate Branches from a noble Seed,
Corrupt, apostatiz'd, and doubly dead:
Will GOD in such a Church his Work revive!
It cannot be that these dry Bones should live.

But who to teach Almighty Grace shall dare
How far to suffer, and how long to spare?
Shall Man's bold Hand our Candlestick remove,
Or cut us off from our Redeemer's Love?
Shall Man presume to say, "There is no Hope:
"God *must* forsake, for *We* have giv'n her up:
"To save a Church so near the Gates of Hell,
"This is a thing—with GOD impossible!"

And yet this thing impossible *is* done,
The Lord *hath* made his Power and Mercy known,
Strangely reviv'd our long-extinguished Hope,
And brought out of their Graves his People up.
Soon as we prophesied in Jesus' Name,
The Noise, the Shaking, and the Spirit came!
The Bones spontaneous to each other cleav'd,
The Dead in Sin his powerful Word receiv'd,
And felt the quickening Breath of GOD, and liv'd.
Dead Souls to all the Life of Faith restor'd,
(The House of Israel now) confess the Lord,
His People and his Church, out of their Graves
They rise, and testify that Jesus saves,
That Jesus gives the multiplied Increase,
While One becomes a thousand Witnesses.

Nor can it seem to Souls already freed
Incredible, that GOD should wake the dead,
Should farther still exert his saving Power,
And call, and quicken twice ten thousand more,
Till our whole Church a mighty Host becomes,
And owns the Lord, the Opener of their Tombs.

Servant of GOD, my Yokefellow and Friend,
If GOD by *us* to the *dry Bones* could send,
By *us* out of their Graves his People raise,
By *us* display the Wonders of his Grace,
Why should we doubt his Zeal to carry on
By abler Instruments the Work begun,
To build our Temple that in Ruins lay,
And re-convert a Nation in a Day,
To bring our Sion forth, like Gold refin'd,

With all his Saints in closest union join'd
A Friend, a Nursing-mother to Mankind?

Surely the Time is come, for GOD to rise,
And turn upon our Church his glorious Eyes,
To shew her all the Riches of his Grace,
And make her throughout all the Earth a Praise:
For O! his Servants think upon her Stones,
And in their Hearts his pleading Spirit groans;
It pitieth them to see her in the Dust,
Her Lamp extinguish'd, and her Gospel lost:
Lost—till the Lord, the great Restorer came,
Extinguish'd—till his Breath reviv'd the Flame;
His Arm descending lifted up the Sign,
His Light appearing bad her *rise and shine*.
Bad her glad Children bless the heavenly Ray,
And shout the Prospect of a Gospel-day.

Meanest and least of all her Sons, may I
Unite with theirs by Faith and Sympathy!
Meanest, and least—yet can I never rest,
Or quench the Flame enkindled in my Breast:
Whether a Spark of Nature's fond Desire,
That warms my Heart, and sets my Soul on fire,
Or a pure Ray from your bright Throne above,
That melts my yearning Bowels into Love;
Even as Life, it still remains the same,
My fervent Zeal for our Jerusalem;
Stronger than Death, and permanent as true,
And purer Love, it *seems*, than Nature ever know.

For her, whom her Apostate Sons despise,
I offer up my Life in Sacrifice,
My Life in cherishing a Parent spend,
Fond of my Charge, and faithful to the End:
Not by the Bonds of sordid Interest ti'd,
Not gain'd by Wealth or Honours to her Side,
But by a *double Birth* her Servant born:
Vile for her sake, expos'd to general Scorn,
Thrust out as from her Pale, I gladly roam,
Banish'd myself, to bring her Wanderers home.
While the lost sheep of Israel's House I seek,

By Bigots branded for a Schismatick,
By real Schismaticks disown'd, decry'd,
As a blind Bigot on the Church's Side:
Yet well-content, so I my Love may shew,
My friendly Love, to be esteem'd her Foe,

Foe to her Order, Governors, and Rules:
The Song of Drunkards, and the Sport of Fools;
Or, what my Soul doth as Hell-fire reject,
A Pope—*A Count*—and Leader of a Sect.

Partner of my Reproach, who justly claim
The larger Portion of the glorious Shame,
My Pattern in the Work and Cause divine,
Say is thy Heart as *bigotted* as mine?
Wilt Thou with me in the Old Church remain,
And share her Weal or Woe, her Loss or Gain.
Spend in her Service thy Last Drop of Blood,
And die—to build the Temple of our GOD?

Thy Answer is in more than Words exprest,
I read it thro' the Window in thy Breast:
In every Action of thy Life I see
Thy faithful Love, and filial Piety.
To save a sinking Church, Thou doest not spare
Thyself, but lavish all thy Life for Her:
For Sion sake Thou wilt not hold thy Peace,
That she may grow, impatient to decrease,
To rush into thy Grave, that she may rise,
And mount with all her Children to the Skies.

What then remains for us on Earth to do,
But labour on with Jesus in our View,
Who bids us kindly for his Patients care,
Calls us the Burthen of his Church to bear,
To feed his Flock, and nothing seek beside,
And nothing know, but Jesus crucify'd.

When first sent forth to minister the Word,
Say, did we preach ourselves, or Christ the Lord?
Was it our Aim Disciples to collect,
To raise a Party, or to found a Sect?
No; but to spread the Power of Jesus' Name,
Repair the Walls of our Jerusalem,
Revive the Piety of ancient Days,
And fill the Earth with our Redeemer's Praise.

Still let us steadily pursue our End,
And only for the Faith divine contend,
Superior to the Charms of Power and Fame,
Persist thro' Life, invariably the same:
And if indulg'd our Heart's Desire to see,
Jerusalem in full Prosperity,
To pristine Faith, and Purity restor'd;
How shall we bless our good redeeming Lord,

Gladly into ~~our~~ his Hands our Children give,
Securely in their Mother's Bosom leave,
With ~~Confidence~~ calm Delight accept our late Release,
Resign our Charge to GOD, and then depart in Peace!

No. 202 John Wesley's Letter to Charles[8]

Charles, as we gather from John's replies to his correspondence, was not completely satisfied with the results of the conference at Leeds. The letter of June 20
hints that Charles was pressing his brother to declare himself directly on the issue of
separation.

London, June 20, 1755.
Dear brother,—Do not you understand that they all promised by Thomas
Walsh not to administer [the sacrament] even among themselves? I think
that an huge point given up—perhaps more than they could give up with a
clear conscience. They "showed an excellent spirit" in this very thing.
Likewise when I (not to say you) spoke once, and again spoke, *satis pro
imperio* [Terence, *Phormio,* I, iv.19: "With authority enough."] When I reflected on their answer, I admired *their* spirit and was ashamed of my own.

The practical conclusion was "Not to separate from the Church." Did we
not all agree in this? Surely either you or I must have been asleep, or we
could not differ so widely in a matter of fact!

Here is Charles Perronet raving "because his friends have given up *all,*"
and Charles Wesley "because they have given up *nothing*"; and I in midst,
staring and wondering both at one and the other.

I do not want to do anything more, unless I could bring them over to my
opinion; and I am not in haste for that.

I have no time to write anything more till I have finished the *Notes* [*on the
New Testament,* 1754]. Nor am I in haste. I stand open to the light.

Let it be worded any way. I will give [you] ten pounds between this and
Christmas;—this I think I can do, though I am just now saddled with Sulky
Hare, to pay for her board as well as learning her trade. Why do not you
send for the boy to Bristol? I do not object. . . .

Cyprian is a terrible witness of the sense of the then Church. For he
speaks it not as his own private sense, but as incontestable, allowed rule.
And by *Antistes* ["Bishop" or "overseer"] there I really believe he means
the minister of a parish.[9] That pinches me; nevertheless I think with you till
I see more light, though I should be hard set to defend myself against a
skillful adversary. When I am convinced it is my duty, I will follow
Cyprian's advice. The same say you, and no more. I do not fluctuate yet.
But I can't answer the arguments on that side of the question. Jos. Cownley
says, "For such and such reasons I dare not hear a drunkard preach or read
prayers." I answer, "I dare." But I can't answer his reasons. . . . Adieu!

Charles's poetic *Epistle* achieved its intended effect; his brother John wrote a tract entitled *Reasons Against a Separation from the Church of England*, which appeared in 1758. John's *Reasons* were published at the end of a 250-page volume called *A Preservative Against Unsettled Notions in Religion*. That book, because of its size and expense, did not receive the wide circulation Charles envisioned for the *Reasons*, so he reissued it as a separate tract in 1760 along with seven of his hymns for the lay preachers. Charles's journal indicates that he continued to oppose Methodism's drift away from the established church. Several Methodist preachers, including Skelton and Edwards, had turned their societies into distinct, dissenting churches; hence intercession for and exhortation about this issue became a more pronounced matter in 1756. Cut loose from their Anglican moorings Wesley's "children" (the Methodists) fell prey to "seducers" like the Baptists, Moravians, and Dissenters.

No. 203   Journal Selections: October 7–30, 1756

Thur., October 7th [1756]. After a most tempestuous night, I preached to a few, whom the hurricane could not keep from the word.

I had more talk with ———, who frankly confessed, "If any of our Societies should desire him to take charge of them, as a distinct body, he should not refuse them." I told him plainly, that the ground of all such designs was pride: but my words were spoken into the air. . . . Soon after, our dearest brother Grimshaw found us, and brought a blessing with him. I preached from Luke 21: "Take heed to yourselves," &c.; and farther enforced our Lord's warning on the Society. I strongly exhorted them to continue steadfast in fellowship with each other, and the whole Church of England. Our hearts were comforted and knit together.

Sun., October 10th. From Isa. 64:5, "In those is continuance, and we shall be saved," I earnestly pressed the duties of constant communicating, of hearing, reading, practicing the word, of fasting, of private, family, and public prayer. The Society I advised to continue in fellowship, and never more give place to the sower of tares, the divider of the brethren. I spoke of the breach; told them how to behave toward Mr. Skelton, and the rest who have rose up to draw away disciples after them; and insisted on that apostolical precept, "Let all your things be done in charity." I did not mention the author of the late division, being convinced he left us for bread. . . .

Mon., October 11th. After preaching at five to this solid people [at Rothwell], I returned to Leeds, and spent an hour with the Leaders. They informed me that my late exhortations have stopped some who were on the point of going over to Mr. Edward's Society, and brought others back to the Church-ordinances. A woman in particular, after hearing me on Sunday morning, went to church, which she had long forsaken, and received a manifestation of Jesus Christ in the prayers. I earnestly pressed them to recommend to their brethren, both by advice and example, the neglected duties of family and private prayer; and to watch over the flock with all diligence. . . .

Tues., October 12th. I took my leave of Leeds in prayer at William Shent's. Some having ascribed the division to him, I examined that matter to the bottom, having talked largely with all parties, especially Miss Norton, and Mr. Edwards himself. Upon the whole, I am convinced that the ground of all was Miss Norton's hatred to William Shent. This induced her to draw away Mr. Edwards from us. He could not resist the temptation of a certain provision for his family. Interest blinded his eyes, so that the means to his end seemed right and honest to him, though base and treacherous to us. As for William Shent, I do not find he did more than every upright man would have done on the occasion. He watched to counteract them who were daily seducing our children. He gave early notice to my brother of their design, and thereby drew all resentment upon himself; as every honest Preacher will *qui cum ingeniis conflictatur ejusmodi* [Latin: As every honest preacher will who wrestles with characters of that kind].[10] Since the separation (Mr. Edwards's friend informed me) he has behaved with such mildness and discretion, as has kept the rest of the flock together, when violence or harsh treatment might have scattered them all. . . . I took a friendly leave of Miss Norton, who assured me some of our ablest Preachers were entirely in Mr. Edwards's interest. *Nec nihil, nec omnia* [Latin: Neither nothing nor everything]. . . .

Mon., October 18th. [Mr. Grimshaw] accompanied me to Heptonstal; where I preached at ten on Isa. 54:5: "In those is continuance, and we shall be saved." I was very faint when I began: the more plainly did it appear that the power was not of man, but of God. I warned them of the wiles of the devil, whereby he would draw them away from the Church, and the other means of grace. I spake as the oracles of God, and God gave testimony, bowing the hearts of all present, except a few bigoted Baptists. [. . .] I knew not then, that several Baptists were present, a carnal cavilling, contentious sect, always watching to steal away our children, and make them as dead as themselves. Mr. Allen informed me that they have carried off no less than fifty out of one Society, and that several Baptist meetings are wholly made out of old Methodists. I talked largely with Mr. Grimshaw, how to remedy the evil. We agreed, 1. That nothing can save the Methodists from falling a prey to every seducer but close walking with God, in all the commandments and ordinances, especially the word and prayer, private, family, and public; 2. That the Preachers should be allowed more time in every place, to visit from house to house, after Mr. Baxter's manner; 3. That a small treatise be written, to ground and preserve them against seducers, and lodged in every family. . . .

Thur., October 21st. I finished my discourse to our Lord's disciples. I parted with my right hand, my brother and bosom-friend, Grimshaw. . . . Our Society in Manchester was upward of two hundred; but their itching ears have reduced them to half the number. To these I showed the melancholy state of the members of the Established Church, who are the most unprincipled and ignorant of all that are called Protestants; and therefore exposed to every seducer who thinks it worth his while to turn them Dissenters, Moravians, or Papists. I told them, "Of all the members of the Church of England the poor Methodists are most exposed, because serious, and therefore worth stealing; and of all the Methodists those of Manchester were in greatest danger, because the most unsettled and unadvisable." I challenged them to show me one Methodist who had ever prospered by turning Dissenter. I asked, what would become of them when my brother should die; whether they would not then be scattered, and broken into twenty sects, old and new. To prevent this, I advised them, 1. To get grace, or the love and power of God, which alone could keep and stablish their hearts; 2. To continue in all the means of obtaining this, especially the word, and prayer of all kinds; to the Scriptures daily; to go constantly to church and sacrament.

I make more allowance for this poor shattered Society because they have been sadly neglected, if not abused, by our Preachers. The Leaders [of the bands] desired me not to let ——— come among them again; for he did them more harm than good, by talking in his *witty way* against the Church and Clergy. As for poor ———, he *could* not advise them to go to church, for he never went himself; but some informed me, that he advised them *not* to go. When we set the wolf to keep the sheep, no wonder that the sheep are scattered.

Our brother Johnson tells me, since he sent the people back to church, two have received forgiveness in the prayers there; and two more in the sermon of a Church Minister. There are now three sound Preachers in these parts. If they continue steadfast, they may undo the great evil which the unsound Preachers have done, and confirm our children in their calling.

I cannot leave them in so unsettled a condition; and therefore intend, with God's leave, to spend another week among them. I talked with the Leaders, and earnestly pressed them to set an example to the flock, by walking in all the commandments and ordinances.

I wrote my thoughts to my brother [John Wesley] as follows:—

"Mr. Walker's letter deserves to be seriously considered.[11] One only thing [*sic*] occurs to me now, which might prevent in great measure the mischiefs which will probably ensue after our death; and that is, *greater, much greater deliberation and care in admitting Preachers.* Consider seriously, if we have not been too easy and too hasty in this matter. Let us pray God to show us, if this has not been the principal cause, why so many of our Preachers have lamentably miscarried. Ought any new Preacher to be received before we know that he is grounded, not only in the doctrines we teach, but in the discipline also, and particularly in the communion of the Church of England? Ought we not to try what he can answer a Baptist, a

Quaker, a Papist, as well as a Predestinarian or Moravian? If we do not insist on that *storgá* [Greek: "love" or "natural affection"] for our desolate mother [the Church of England] as a prerequisite, yet should we not be well assured that the candidate is no enemy to the Church?

"Is it not our duty to stop J. C. and such like, from railing and laughing at the Church? Should we not now, at least, shut the stable-door? The short remains of my life are devoted to this very thing, to follow our sons (as C. P. told me we should [follow] you) with buckets of water, to quench the flame of strife and division, which they have or may kindle."

Mon., October 25th. . . . [In Manchester] I rejoiced to hear of the great good Mr. Whitefield has done in the Societies. He preached as universally as my brother. He warned them everywhere against apostasy; and strongly insisted on the necessity of holiness *after* justification, illustrating it with this comparison: "What good would the King's pardon do a poor malefactor dying of a fever? So, not withstanding you have received forgiveness, unless the disease of your nature be healed by holiness, ye can never be saved." He beat down the separating spirit, highly commended the prayers and services of our Church, charged our people to meet their bands and classes constantly, and never to leave the Methodists, or God would leave them. In a word: he did his utmost to strengthen our hands, and deserves the thanks of all the churches, for his abundant labour of love.

I consulted the Leaders what could be done for this unstable people. Richard Barlow and the rest ascribed their fickleness to their neglect of the means, particularly going to church; "and when we advise them to do it, they would answer us, The Preachers do not advise us to go, neither do they go themselves." Nay, some spoke against it, even those we most confided in. My brother and I must wink very hard not to see the hearts of such men.

Thur., October 28th. . . . I was constrained to write the following letters:—

TO MR. GRIMSHAW.

Manchester, October 29th [1756].

I could not leave this poor shattered Society so soon as I proposed. They have not had fair play from our treacherous sons in the Gospel; but have been scattered by them as sheep upon the mountains. I have once more persuaded them to go to church and sacrament, and stay to carry them thither the next Lord's day.

Nothing but grace can keep our children, after our departure, from running into a thousand sects, a thousand errors. Grace, exercised, kept up, and increased in the use of all means, especially family and public prayer, and sacrament, will keep them steady. Let us labour, while we continue here, to ground and build them up in the Scriptures, and all the ordinances. Teach them to handle well the sword of the Spirit, and the shield of faith. Should I live to see you again, I trust you will assure me, there is not a member of all your Societies but reads the Scripture daily, uses private prayer, joins in family and public worship, and communicates constantly. "In those is continuance, and we shall be saved."

TO MY BELOVED BRETHREN AT LEEDS, &C.

[October 29, 1756?]

Grace and peace be multiplied! I thank God, on your behalf, for the grace which is given unto you, by which ye stand fast in one mind and in one spirit. My Master, I am persuaded, sent me unto you at this time to confirm your souls in the present truth, in your calling, in the old paths of Gospel-ordinances. O that ye may be a pattern to the flock for your unanimity and love! O that ye may continue steadfast in the word, and in fellowship, and in breaking of bread, and in prayers (private, family and public), till we all meet around the great white throne!

I knew beforehand that the Sanballats and Tobiahs would be grieved when they heard there was a man come to seek the welfare of the Church of England [Neh. 2:10]. I expected they would pervert my words, as if I should say, *"The Church could save you."* So, indeed, you and they thought till I and my brethren taught you better, and sent you *in and through* the means to Jesus Christ. But let not their slanders move you. Continue in the old ship. Jesus hath a favour for our Church; and is wonderfully visiting and reviving his work in her. It shall be shortly said, "Rejoice ye with Jerusalem, and be glad with her, all ye that love her: rejoice her joy with her, all ye that mourn for her." (Isa. 64:10 &c.)

Blessed by God, ye see your calling. Let nothing hinder your going constantly to church and sacrament. Read the Scriptures daily in your families, let there be a church in every house. The word is able to build you up; and if ye watch and pray always, ye shall be counted worthy to stand before the Son of Man.

Watch ye, therefore, and stand fast in the faith, quit yourselves like men, be strong: let all your things be done in love. I rejoice in hope of presenting you all in that day. Look up, for your eternal redemption draweth near.

[Thur., October 28th.] As the people leave work at twelve, we pitched upon that hour for our intercession. Many flocked to the house of mourning; and again the Lord was in the midst of us, making soft our hearts, and helping our infirmity to pray. We never want [lack] faith in praying for King George, and the Church of England.

I recovered another straggler; as I do every day. The enemy has had a particular grudge to this Society. His first messenger to them was a *still sister,* who abounded in visions and revelations. She came to them as in the name of the Lord, and forbade them to pray, sing, or *go to church.* . . . Her extravagance at last opened their eyes, and delivered them from the snare of mysticism. Then the Quakers, the predestinarians, the dippers, desired to have them to sift them like wheat. They were afterwards thrust sore at by Mr. Bennet, Williams, Wheatley, Cudworth, Whitford, Ball. It is a miracle that two of them are left together; yet I am persuaded, the third part will be brought through the fire.

I examined more of the Society. Most of them have known the grace of
our Lord Jesus Christ: several received it at church; one in the Litany,
another in the Lord's Prayer. With that word, "Thy Kingdom come,"
Christ came into his heart. To many he has been made known in the
breaking of bread.

Sun. October 31st. . . . I breakfasted with a wanderer, and brought him
back to his brethren. We were all at the old church; heard a good sermon
from Mr. Clayton on constant prayer; and joined to commemorate our
dying Lord. Mr. M——, the senior Chaplain, sent for me up to the table, to
administer first to me, with the other Clergy. I know not when I have
received a greater blessing. The addition of fourscore communicants made
them consecrate [the elements] twice or thrice. A few of our Dissenting
brethren communicated with us, and confessed to me afterwards, that the
Lord met them at his table. It was a passover much to be remembered. We
renewed our solemn covenant with God, and received fresh strength to
run the race set before us. . . .

From the new church I walked to our crowded room; and once more
preached up the ordinances. Now the long-delayed blessing came: the skies
as it were poured down righteousness. The words I spoke were not my
own; therefore they made their way into many hearts.

I received double power to exhort the Society (now upwards of one
hundred and fifty members), and *believed for them* that they will henceforth
walk in all the commandments and ordinances of the Lord blameless.

In 1758 Charles published a slim volume entitled *Hymns of Intercession for All
Mankind*. It reflected the political turmoil in England and within Methodism. The
forty hymns were intercessory prayers for the various religious and political entities
on the contemporary scene. The title was drawn from I Tim. 2:1: "I exhort therefore, that first of all, supplications, prayers, intercessions and giving of thanks, be
made for all men."

No. 204   Hymns of Intercession: IV,
"For the Church of England"

1   Till then preserve the faithful seed,
      The remnant left in *Britain's* land,
   The desolate Church, whose cause we plead,
      In whose defense we firmly stand,
   Her breaches mourn, her burdens bear
   In all the agony of prayer.

2   Jesus, her ruinous walls rebuild,
      And let them with Thy praise resound;
   With peace her palaces be fill'd,
      Plenty be in her temples found,

Plenty of unbought milk and wine,
Fullness of living Bread Divine.

3 Her slumbering guides and watchmen rouse,
       And on her rising ramparts place;
   Give them a voice to shake Thy house,
       The rocks to break, the dead to raise,
   To bring them up from nature's grave,
   And the whole house of *Israel* save.

4 For this Thou hear'st Thy Spirit groan,
       O that Thou wouldst Thy power display,
   Divide the heavens, and come down,
       Convert our nation in a day,
   And spread our faith through earth abroad,
   And fill the universe with God!

Charles's reprint of John Wesley's *Reasons Against a Separation from the Church
of England* appeared in 1760 along with seven hymns for the lay preachers intended
"to cut off all jealousy and Suspicion from our Friends, or Hope from our Enemies
of our having any Design of ever Separating from the Church."

No. 205 Hymns for Lay Preachers: II

1 Forth in Thy Strength, O Lord, we go,
       Forth in Thy steps and loving mind,
   To pay the gospel-debt we owe
       (The word of grace for all mankind),
   To sow th' incorruptible seed,
   And find the lost, and wake the dead.

2 The wandering sheep of *England's* fold
       Demand our first and tenderest care,
   Who under sin and Satan sold
       Usurp the *Christian* character,
   The Christian character profane,
   And take Thy *church's* name in vain,

3 Or shameless advocates of hell,
       Their crimes they *Sodom*-like confess;
   Or varnish'd with a specious zeal,
       An empty form of godliness,
   The power they impiously blaspheme,
   And call our hope a madman's dream.

4 Haters of God, yet still they cry,
       "The temple of the Lord are we!

"The church, the church!"—who dare defy
   Thy self-existent Deity,
Proudly oppose Thy righteous reign,
And crucify their God again.

5 'Gainst these by Thee sent forth to fight,
    A suffering war we calmly wage,
With patience meet their fierce despite,
    With love repay their furious rage,
Reviled, we bless; defamed, intreat;
And spurn'd, we kiss the spurner's feet.

6 Arm'd with Thine all-sufficient grace,
    Thy meek unconquerable mind,
Our foes we cordially embrace
    (The filth and refuse of mankind),
We gladly all resign our breath,
To save one precious soul from death.

No. 206 Hymns for Lay Preachers: VI

1 Great Guardian of *Britannia's* land,
    To Thee we here present our blood,
Set forth the last, a desperate band
    Devoted for our country's good,
Our brethren dear, our flesh and bone,
We live, and die, for them alone.

2 *Our brethren;* though they still disclaim,
    And us despitefully intreat,
With scornful rage cast out our name,
    Trample as dirt beneath their feet,
Out of their synagogues expel,
And doom us to the hottest hell.

3 If Thou preserve our souls in peace,
    Our brethren shall afflict in vain:
Most patient, when they most oppress,
    We all their cruel wrongs sustain,
And strengthen by Thy meekening power,
The more they hate, we love the more.

4 No, never shall their rage prevail,
    Or force us th' dry bones to leave:
The more they push us from the pale,
    The closer we to *Sion* cleave,
And daily in the temple found,
Delight to kiss the sacred ground.

5   If some defile the hallow'd place,
       The truth, and us with slanders load,
   Or fiercely from their altars chase,
       And rob us of the children's food,
   We will not quit Thy house and word,
   Or loathe the offerings of the Lord.

6   Should those who sit in *Moses'* seat
       Conspire Thy little flock to harm,
   Judge in their courts, and scourge, and beat,
       And bruise us with the ruler's arm,
   Matter of joy our shame we make,
   And bear it, Saviour, for Thy sake.

7   Or should they stir the people up
       Our goods to spoil, our limbs to tear,
   Sustain'd by that immortal hope,
       Their lawless violence we bear;
   Or laid in bonds our voices raise,
   And shake the dungeon with Thy praise.

8   A gazing-stock to fiends and men,
       When arm'd with Thine all-patient power,
   As sheep appointed to be slain,
       We wait the last, the fiery hour,
   And ne'er from *England's* Church will move,
   Till torn away—to that above.

Charles Wesley's *Short Hymns on Select Passages* (1762) continued his criticism of those Methodist lay preachers who clamored for sacramental prerogatives. Those hymns found the "upstart priests" smitten with "the loathsome leprosy of pride." Several of Charles's more polemical poems drew the attention of John's editorial pen and were expunged from later editions of the *Short Hymns*.

No. 207   Short Hymn on Num. 16:10
And seek ye the priesthood also?

   Raised from the people's lowest lees,[a]
   Guard, Lord, Thy preaching witnesses,
   Nor let their pride the honour claim
   Of sealing covenants in Thy name:
   Rather than suffer them to dare
   Usurp the priestly character,
   Save from the arrogant offense,
   And snatch them uncorrupted hence.

---

[a]J.W. "Query?"

No. 208   Short Hymn on 2 Sam. 6:7
God smote Uzzah.

1   Behold your due to *Uzzah* dead
         For touching an external sign,
    You that the priestly right invade,
         And minister in things Divine!
    Will ignorance your bodies save?
    Inquire of *Uzzah* in his grave.

2   "But lo! unless our hands sustain,
         The tottering ark will strike the ground!"
    God cannot need the help of man:
         A thousand ways with God are found
    His church in danger to defend,
    And bear her up, till time shall end.

3   UNAUTHORIZED by right Divine
         Dost thou not on the word lay hold,
    Who claim'st the *promises* for thine
         With ignorance profanely bold,
    But dost not with the terms comply?
    Forbear to touch the ark—or die?

No. 209   Short Hymn on 2 Chron. 26:18
It appertaineth not unto thee, Uzzah, . . .

1   "But now (the warm Enthusiast cries)
         The office to myself I take,
    Offering the Christian sacrifice,
         Myself a lawful priest I make,
    To me the honour appertains;
    No need of man, when God ordains.

2   "Though kings may not so far presume,
         'Tis no presumption in a clown:
    And lo, without a call from *Rome*,
         My flail, or hammer I lay down!
    And if my order's name ye seek,
    Come see a new *Melchizedek!*"

No. 210   Short Hymn on 2 Chron. 26:21
Uzzah was a leper unto the day of his death.

Ye upstart priests, your sentence know,
    The marks you can no longer hide,

Your daring deeds too plainly show
   The loathsome leprosy of pride;
And if ye still your crime deny,
Who lepers live, shall lepers die.

"Ms. Miscellaneous Hymns" carries a hymn "Written after the Conference in Aug. 1780, The Last Which the Writer Was Present At." Charles attended the annual conference reluctantly, since he did not expect to be able to stem the separatist tide of those lay preachers who sought ordination. In fact, ordination and the theoretical separation that it implied to Charles were forestalled in August; but the subtitle of the hymn suggests Wesley's resolve not to attend the succeeding conferences, and the text reflects a sense of the futility of his struggle.

No. 211 Hymn: "Written After the Conference in Aug. 1780"

1 Why should I longer, Lord, contend,
   My last, important moments spend
     In buffeting the air?
   In warning those who will not see,
   But rest in blind security,
     And rush into the snare?

2 Prophet of ills why should I live,
   Or by my sad forebodings grieve
     Whom I can serve no more?
   I only can their loss bewail
   Till life's exhausted sorrows fail,
     And the last pang is o'er.

3 Here then I quietly resign
   Into those gracious hands Divine,
     Whom I received from Thee,
   My brethren and companions dear,
   And finish with a parting tear
     My useless ministry.

4 Detach'd from every creature now,
   I humbly at Thy footstool bow,
     Accepting my release;
   If Thou the promised grace bestow,
   Salvation to Thy servant show
     And bid me die in peace.

Charles Wesley's next major hymnological contribution to his holding action against Methodism's separatist tendencies came in his "Manuscript Ordinations."

The collection, which was never published, can be tentatively dated through a letter to John Wesley (written August 12, 1784), which is carried in the back of the manuscript (p. 21). John's reply and several other letters from Charles are also appended to the hymns.

The tone of the collection is set by a quotation from William Chillingworth's *Religion of Protestants* (1638) p. 272: "That a Pretense of Reformation will acquit no man from Schism, we grant very willingly, and therefore say that It concerns every man who separates from any Church-Communion *even as his Salvation is worth* to look most carefully to it, that cause of his separation be just and necessary." The occasion generating these materials was John Wesley's ordination of Richard Whatcoat and Thomas Vasey as "Elders" (priests) and Dr. Coke as "Superintendent" (Bishop) for the Methodists in North America.

No. 212   "Ms. Ordination Hymns": I, Epigram[12]

W[esley] himself and friends betrays
  By his own good sense forsook,
While suddenly his hands he lays
  On the hot head of C——:

Yet *we* at least should spare the weak,
  His weak Co-equals *We*,
Nor blame an hoary Schismatic,
  A Saint of Eighty-three!

No. 213   "Ms. Ordination Hymns": III, Occidit, occidit![13] ["It Happened! It Happened!"]

1   And is it come to this? and has the Man
      On whose Integrity our Church relied,
    Betray'd his trust, render'd our boastings vain,
      And fal'n a Victim to ambitious Pride?

2   Whose zeal so long her Hierarchy maintain'd,
      Her humble Presbyter, her duteous Son[14]
    Call'd an High Priest, & by Himself Ordain'd,
      He glorifies himself, & mounts[a] a Throne.

3   Ah! where are all his Promises and Vows
      To spend, & to be spent for Sion's Good,
    To gather the lost sheep of Israel's house,
      The Outcasts bought by his Redeemer's blood?

---

[a]The manuscript offers "claims" (a throne) as an alternate reading penned in below the line.

4 Who won for God the wandering Souls of men,
    Subjecting multitudes to Christ's command,
He shuts his eyes, & scatters them again,
    And spreads a thou[san]d Sects throughout the land.

5 The great Restorer of Religion pure
    Ah! why should he a meaner style affect
His friends, his principle in death abjure
    ~~Founder~~ Head of Kirks, & Leader of a Sect?

6 His Charge, departing to the Wolf he leaves
    (For Who so fit to keep the Flock as He?)
And to that fawning Beast unwary gives
    "His power, & seat, & ~~much~~ great authority."

7 What e'er of weak, or human in his Plan,
    Wood, stubble, hay ~~heap'd~~ built on the Solid Base,
(His own by-laws, his own inventions vain)
    He leaves his ~~headlong~~ furious Successor to raze.

8 Secure he now the sacred Pale o'erleaps
    (Tau[gh]t by audacious C—— to slight the guilt)
And with that Besom of destruction sweeps
    The Babylon w[hi]ch his own hands had built.

9 How is the Mighty fallen from his height,
    His weapons scatter'd, & his buckler lost!
Ah! tell it not in Gath, nor cause delight
    And triumph in the proud Philistine Host.

10 Publish it not in Askelon, to make
    The world exult in his disastrous End!
Rather let every soul my Grief partake,
    And ah! my Father,[b] cry, & ah my Friend!

11 The pious Mantle o'er his Dotage spread,
    With silent tears his shameful Fall deplore,
And let him sink, forgot, among the dead
    And mention his unhappy name no more.

No. 214   "Ms. Ordination Hymns": V, Epigram[15]

1 So easily are Bishops made
    By man's, or woman's whim?
W—— his hands on C—— hath laid,
    But who laid hands on Him?

---

[b]"Brother" penned between the lines underneath "Father," as an alternate reading.

2   Hands on himself he laid, and *took*
         An Apostolic Chair:
     And then ordain'd his Creature C——
         His Heir and Successor.

3   Episcopalians, now no more
         With Presbyterians fight,
     But give your needless Contest o'er,
         "Whose Ordination's right?"

4   It matters not, if Both are One,
         Or different in degrees,
     For Lo! ye see in Prelate contain'd in John
         The whole Presbytery!

Charles's disappointment over his brother's ordinations was keen, but his anger soon subsided. Piety and pity combined to produce the following poem (which Frank Baker has aptly titled "True Yokefellows"). Where the preceding hymns were polemics directed toward John Wesley, the following hymn takes on the character of an intercessory prayer for him and the plight of the Methodists. Dating from roughly the same period as the preceding poems, i.e. mid-1785, it is the only extant example of the hymns of reconciliation from "Ms. Brothers."[16]

No. 215   "Ms. Brothers": Hymn IX

1   Happy the days, when Charles and John
       By nature and by grace were One[,]
       The same in office as in name,
       Their judgments and their will the same:
       True Yokefellows, they join'd to draw
       The galling burthen of the Law,
       And urg'd with unremitting strife
       Each other on, to work for life;
       Cheerful beneath the Legal Load,
       Joyful to do imperfect good,
       And all the Lord's command t'obey,
       Before they knew in Christ The Way.

2   In infancy their hopes and fears,
       In youth, and in their riper years,
       Their hearts were to each other known
       Attun'd in perfect Unison.
       No private End, no selfish art
       Did then the faithful Brothers part,
       No flatterer the Friends divide,

Who each from each cou[l]d nothing hide,
Neither injoy'd a good alone,
Or call'd what he possess'd his own,
Their good supreme with humble zeal
To know, and do the Master's will.

3   To both at once their Lord reveal'd
His counsel from the Wise conceal'd[,]
His will to chuse the weak and base
And save a much lov'd world by grace.
To the highways and hedges sent
They both with one Commission went,
Zealous immortal souls to win,
And force the Vagrants to come in.
He bad[e] them first for England care,
And to her Church the trueth declare
To love his own Jerusalem,
To spend, and to be spent for Them,
Outcasts of men, a thoughtless ~~Crowd~~ Herd,
Who sinning on with conscience sear'd,
Rush'd down the steep, by Satan driven,
As far from God, as hell from heaven.

4   Jesus, who sent them out by pairs,
Prosper'd his gospel-messengers,
HE their united labours bless'd,
Their flock abundantly increas'd,
Increas'd their word-begotten Sons,
And preachers rais'd from stocks & stones.

5   But rais'd out of the people's lees,
Raw, inexperienc'd Novices,
They soon their low Estate forgot,
And of themselves too highly thought,
While the ambitious Fiend stole in,
And poisoning them with his own sin,
Used as his Agents to inspire
With lofty thoughts their flatter'd Sire.

6   They urg'd the Elder Presbyter
Himself a Bishop to declare,
And then to answer their demands,
By laying on his hasty hands;
The mighty Babel to erect,
And found a new Dissenting Sect,
His Mother-Church to rend, disclaim,
And brand the Party with his Name.
But for a length of years he stood,

By a whole Army unsubdued,
By friendship kept, refus'd to yield,
And all their fiery Darts repel'd,
And check'd the Madness for a space
Of Corah's bold, rebellious race,[a]
Who heard, like Eli's sons unmov'd,
His words, too tenderly reprov'd,
"In vain you tempt me to do ill
"For separate I never will
"Will never with my Brother break,
"Will never die a Schismatick!"

7   O had he died *before* that day,
When W—— did himself betray
Did boldly on himself confer
The Apostolic Character!
O that we both had took our flight
Together to the realms of light,
Together yielded up our breath,
In life united, and in death!
Leaving an honest Name behind,
We then assur'd that Rest to find
Had past the valley undismay'd,
Nor fear'd to meet a Father's shade [ghost],
A Cloud of Witnesses inroll'd
In heaven, the sheep of England's fold,
A noble host of Martyrs too
Who faithful unto death, and true,
Spent their last breath for Sion's good,
And strove resisting unto blood.

8   God of unbounded power and grace,
Whose pleasure is to save and bless,
At whose omnipotent Decree
Things most impossible shall be,
Who only, cancelling our sin,
Canst make it as it ne'er had been;
Thine energy of love exert
And change thy favour'd Servant's heart,
Thy own prevailing Plea we plead
In ignorance he did the Deed,
The Deed which endless mischiefs fraught,
Alas, he did he knew not what.
Pity the Blind who went astray

---

[a]Corah was one of the leaders of a rebellion against Moses' authority (cf. Num. 16:1).

And turn'd the Lame out of the way;
Whom still Thou dost vouchsafe to own—
Undo the evil he hath done,
Incline him humbly to revoke
The fatal Step his haste hath took,
And his true heart again shall be
Turn'd back to England's Church and Thee.

9   Stir up thy faithful people, Lord,
To urge their suit with one accord,
And rescue thro' the Strength of prayer,
Their Father, Guide, and Minister,
His prayers for us have reach'd thy throne,
And brought us many a blessing down:
Thy blessings all on Him be shed;
With glory crown his reverend head
Found in the way of righteousness
There let him stay, and die in peace:
Let all the children of his prayers,
Seals of his Ministerial cares,
To Him by his Redeemer given,
Compose his Crown of joy in Heaven!

Charles's correspondence from this period reveals the same mixture of anger and disappointment found in the hymns above. Although he was certain that ordination meant separation, Charles would not permit the ecclesiastical issue to separate him from his brother. Finally, they agreed to disagree. Charles placed most of the blame upon Dr. Coke and the lay preachers, and continued to do all he could to keep the Methodists from "jumping ship."

No. 216   Letter to John Wesley[17]

Bristol, August 14th, 1785

Dear Brother,—I have been reading over again & again your *Reasons Against a Separation*, (printed in 1758, and in your Works) and entreat you, in the name of God, and for Christ's sake, to read them again yourself, with previous prayer, and stop, and proceed no farther, till you receive an answer to your inquiry, "Lord, what wouldest *Thou* have me to do?" [Here follow his *Reasons against a Separation from the Church of England*.]

Every word of your eleven pages deserves the deepest consideration: not to mention my testimony and hymns. Only the seventh I could wish you to read,—a prophecy which I pray God may never come to pass.

Near 30 years, since then, you have stood against the importunate solicitations of your Preachers, who have scarcely at last prevailed. I was your natural ally, and your faithful friend; and while you continued faithful to yourself, *we two* could chase a thousand. If they had not divided *us* they could never have overcome *you*.

But when once you began ordaining in [i.e. for] America, I knew (and you knew), that your Preachers here would never rest till you ordained them. You told me "they would separate by and by." The Doctor [Coke] tells me the same. His Methodist episcopal Church in Baltimore was *intended* to beget a Methodist episcopal Church here. You know he comes, armed with your authority, to make us all Dissenters. One of your sons assured me, that not a Preacher in London would refuse Orders from the Doctor. It is evident that all seek their own and prefer their own interest to your Honor, which not one of these scruples to sacrifice to his own ambition.

Alas! what trouble are you preparing for yourself, as well as for me, and for your oldest, truest, best friends! Before you have quite broken down the bridge, *stop, and consider*! If your sons have no regard for you, have some regard for yourself. *Go to your grave in peace:* at least, suffer me to go first, before this ruin is under your hand. So much, I think, you owe to my Father, to my Brother, and to me, as to stay [your hand] till I am taken from the evil. I am on the brink of the grave. Do not push me in, or embitter my last moments. Let us not leave an indelible blot on our memory; but let us leave behind us the name and character of *honest men*.

This letter is a debt to our Parents, and to our Brother, as well as to you, and to

Your faithful friend.

No. 217 John Wesley's Reply to Charles's Letter

This letter was John's reply to Charles's emphatic letter; since John's epistle also carried an apologetic note it was published in his Arminian Magazine, but without disclosing the recipient's identity. The verse of poetry quoted in the letter is from Charles's "Elegy on the Death of Mr. Jones."[18]

Plymouth, August 19th, 1785
Dear Brother,—I will tell you my thoughts with all simplicity, and wait for better information. If you agree with me, well: if not, we can, as Mr. Whitefield used to say, agree to disagree.

For these forty years I have been in doubt concerning that question, What obedience is due to

"Heathen Priests, and mitred infidels?"

I have from time to time proposed my doubts to the most pious and sensible Clergymen I know. But they gave me no satisfaction. Rather they seemed to be puzzled as well as me.

Obedience I always paid to the Bishops, in obedience to the Laws of the Land. But I cannot see that I am under any obligation to obey them farther than those laws require.

It is in obedience in these Laws that I have never exercised in England the power which I believe God has given me. I firmly believe I am a scriptural *Episkopos* [Bishop, or Overseer], as much as any man in England, or in Europe: for the uninterrupted succession I know to be a fable, which no man ever did or can prove. But this does nowise interfere with my remaining in the Church of England, from which I have no more desire to separate than I had fifty years ago. I still attend all the Ordinances of the Church, at all opportunities; and I constantly and earnestly advise all that are connected with me so to do. When Mr. Smyth pressed us to separate from the Church, he meant, "Go to church no more." And this was what I meant twenty-seven years ago, when I persuaded our brethren not to separate from the Church.

But here another question occurs, "What is the Church of England?" It is not all the people of England. Papists and Dissenters are no part thereof. It is not all the people of England, except Papists and Dissenters. Then we should have a glorious Church indeed! No: according to our twentieth Article, a particular church is "a congregation of faithful people" (*coetus credentium* are the words of our Latin edition), "among whom the Word of God is preached, and the sacraments duly administered." Here is a true logical definition, containing both the essence and the properties of a church. What then, according to this definition, is the Church of England? Does it mean all the believers in England (except the Papists and Dissenters), who have the word of God and the sacraments duly administered among them? I fear this does not come up to your idea of the Church of England. Well, what more do you include in the phrase? "Why, all the believers that adhere to the doctrine and discipline established by the Convocation under Queen Elizabeth." Nay, that discipline is well-nigh vanished away; and the doctrine both you and I adhere to.

All those reasons against a separation from the Church in this sense, I subscribe to still. What then are you frightened at? I no more separate from it now than I did in the year 1758. I submit still (though sometimes with a doubting Conscience) to "mitred infidels." I do indeed vary from them in some Points of Doctrine, and in some points of Discipline (by Preaching abroad, for instance, by praying extempore, and by forming societies); but not a hair's breadth further than I believe meet, right, and my bounded duty. I walk still by the same rule I have done for forty years. I do nothing rashly. It is not likely I should. The high-day of my blood is over. If you will go on hand in hand with me, do. But do not hinder me, if you will not help. Perhaps if you had kept close to me, I might have done better. However, with or without your help, I creep on: and as I have been hitherto, so I trust I shall always be,

Your affectionate friend and brother.

A phrase that occurs above needs explication. I do not mean I never will ordain any *while I am in England,* but not to use the power they receive while they are in England [i.e. the emergency which justifies the ordinations is only in North America, not in England, where ordained ministers are plentiful].

No. 218   Letter to John Wesley[19]

Mary[le]bone, September 8th, 1785
Dear Brother,—I will tell you my thoughts with the same simplicity. There is no danger of our quarrelling; for the Second Blow makes the quarrel; and you are the last man on earth whom I would wish to quarrel with. That juvenile line of mine,

> Heathenish Priests, and mitred infidels,

I disown, renounce, and with shame recant. I never knew of more than one "mitred infidel," and for him I took Mr. Law's word.

I do not understand what "obedience to the Bishops" you dread. They have let us alone, and left us to act just as we pleased, for these fifty years. At present some of them are quite friendly to us, particularly toward you. The churches are all open to you; and never could there be less pretense for a separation.

That you are a scriptural *Episkopos,* or Overseer, I do not dispute. And so is every Minister who has the Cure of souls. Neither *need we* dispute whether the uninterrupted succession be fabulous, as you believe, or real, as I believe; or whether Lord King be right or wrong.

Your definition of the Church of England is the same in prose with mine in verse. By the way, read over my *Epistle,* to oblige me, and tell me you have read it, and likewise your own *Reasons.*

You write, "All those reasons against a separation from the Church, I subscribe to still. What then are you frightened at? I no more separate from it than I did in the year 1758. I submit still to its Bishops. I do indeed vary from them in some points of discipline (by preaching abroad, for instance, praying extempore, and by forming societies);" [might you not add, *and by ordaining*?] "I walk still by the same Rule I have done for between forty and fifty years. I do *nothing rashly.*"

If I *cou[l]d* prove your actual separation, I *wou[l]d* not; neither wish to see it proved by any other. But do you not allow that the Doctor [Coke] has separated? Do you not know and approve of his avowed Design and Resolution to get all the Methodists of the three kingdoms into a distinct, *compact body,* a *new Episcopal* Church of his own? Have you seen his ordination sermon? Is the high-day of *his* blood over? Does *he* do nothing rashly? Have you not made yourself the author of all his actions? I need not remind you, *qui facet per alium facet per se.* [Latin: He who acts through another, does it through himself.]

I must not leave unanswered your surprising question, "What then are you frightened at?" At the Doctor's rashness, and your supporting him in his ambitious pursuits; at an approaching schism, as causeless and unprovoked as the American rebellion;—at your own eternal disgrace, and all those frightful evils which your *Reasons* describe.

"If you will go on hand in hand with me, do." I do go (or rather creep) on, in the old way in which we set out together, and trust to continue in it till I finish my course.

"Perhaps if you had kept closer to me, I might have done better." When you took that fatal step in Bristol, I kept as close to you as close could be; for I was all the time at your elbow. You might certainly have done better, if you had taken me into your council.

I thank you for your Intention to remain my friend. Herein my heart is as your heart. Whom God has joined, let not man put asunder. We have taken each other for better or worse, till death do us—part? no: but unite eternally. Therefore in the love which never faileth, I am

Your affectionate friend and brother.

No. 219   John Wesley's Reply to Charles's Letter[20]

September 13, 1785

Dear Brother,—I see no use of you and me disputing altogether; for neither of us is likely to convince the other. You say, I separate from the Church. I say, I do not. Then let it stand.

Your verse is a sad truth. I see fifty times more of England than you do; and I find few exceptions to it.

I believe Dr. Coke is as free from ambition as from covetousness. He has done nothing rashly, that I know. But he has spoke rashly, which he retracted the moment I spoke to him of it. To publish his present thoughts, what he before retracted, was not fair play. He is now such a right hand to me as Thomas Walsh was. If you will not or cannot help me yourself, do not hinder those that can and will. I must and will save as many souls as I can while I live, without being careful about what may *possibly be* when I die.

I pray do not confound the intellects of the people in London. You may thereby a little weaken my hands, but you will greatly weaken your own.

No. 220   Reply to John's Letter[21]

London, September 19th, 1785

Dear Brother,—I did not say, you separate from the Church; but I did say, "If I could prove it, I would not."

That "sad truth" is not a new truth. You saw it when you expressed in your *Reasons* such tenderness of love for the unconverted Clergy.

Of your second Thomas Walsh we had better talk than write.

How "confound their intellects"? how "weaken your hands"? I know nothing which I do to prevent the *possible* separation, but pray. God forbid I should sin against Him by ceasing to pray for the Church of England, and for you, while my breath remains in me! I am, Your affectionate brother.

No. 221   Letter to Michael Callendor[22]

Nov. 25, 1786

My dear Brother, I agree with you; Except that the Lord had left himself a small remnant we should have been as Sodom long ago. The Meth[odist]s are a part, & but a part of that Remnant: & they have prospered because they love our Jerusalem. If they ever lose their love for her, they will come to nothing. But the work of God will not fail with Them. Very many of the Clergy are awakened & converted. The evidence of the Spirit is still with the lord of the harvest: & with us His Promise for our Church, that the gates of hell shall not prevail against her.

The Preachers in general are resolved upon a Separation; and have con-quer'd at last their old [John Wesley] Father. He told me—They will turn Dissenters by and by. By his Ordaining Dr. C. &c. for America, and the Rev'd Pawson &c. for Scotland, he has given the staff out of his hand. And if they can have patience to wait for his death, they will immediately after ordain one another, & break into 20 Sects and Parties. The old Members are unanimous & will continue in the Old Ship.

For 50 years I have never lost sight of this fatal Event; and chiefly to prevent it, I have remained with the Method[ist]s to this day. Near 20 years ago I persuaded my B.[rother] to print his *Reasons Against a Separation;* which was unanswerable, even by himself. Therefore, he protests in words against a Separation while he *does* everything to promote and effect it.

His new friends labour inexhausti[b]ly to part us, but in vain. What God joined man cannot put asunder. Death itself cannot separate us. I should not write so freely, if I did not believe you love him as well as I do. He is next in my heart to God and the C[hurch] of E[ngland].

His Sons at the late Conference *generously* consented that he should live out his days in the Church: but they wait impatiently for his dropping—& then They—(who but They!) will claim the Character which our judicious Dr. has given them. Of the ablest body of Clergy in Christendom!

You and I shall be taken from the Evil. The horrible Confusion at their Dispersion. Let us trust our Lord to carry on as his own work; He needs none of us: but we need him to finish his work in our souls: and then receive us to Himself.

NOTES

1. "Ms. Clark," pp. 80–84, *ca.* 1743–1744. The manuscript is located in the Methodist Archives and Research Centre, The John Rylands University Library of Manchester, Manchester, England. The hymn is published here by permission of the Methodist Church Archives and History Committee, England.

2. "Ms. Cheshunt," pp. 101–103, *ca.* 1743–1744. This manuscript is located in the holdings of the Cheshunt College Foundation, Westminster College, Cambridge, England. The hymn is printed here by the kind permission of Dr. S. H. Mayor and the Cheshunt College Foundation.

3. John Wesley's Address, *JW Works,* I, pp. 456–457.

To THE KING'S MOST EXCELLENT MAJESTY;
The Humble Address of the Societies in England and Wales,
in derision called Methodists:

Most Gracious Sovereign,

So inconsiderable as we are, "a people scattered and peeled, and trodden under foot, from the beginning hitherto," we should in no wise have presumed, even on this great occasion, to open our lips to your Majesty, had we not been induced, indeed constrained, so to do, by two considerations: The One, that in spite of all our remonstrances on that head, we are continually represented as a peculiar sect of men, separating ourselves from the Established Church: The Other, that we are still traduced as inclined to Popery, and consequently disaffected to your Majesty.

Upon these considerations we think it incumbent upon us, if we must stand as a distinct body from our brethren, to tender for ourselves our most dutiful regards to your sacred Majesty; and to declare, in the presence of Him we serve, the King of kings, and Lord of lords, that we are a part (however mean [i.e. "small"]) of that Protestant Church, established in these kingdoms: That we unite together for this, and no other end,—to promote, so far as we may be capable, justice, mercy, and truth; the glory of God, and peace and good-will among men: That we detest and abhor the fundamental doctrines of the Church of Rome, and are steadily attached to your Majesty's royal person and illustrious house.

We cannot, indeed, say or do either more or less than we apprehend consistent with the written word of God; but we are ready to obey your Majesty to the uttermost, in all things which we conceive to be agreeable thereto. And we earnestly exhort all with whom we converse, as they fear God, to honour the King. We, of the Clergy in particular, put all men in mind to revere the higher powers, as of God; and continually declare, "Ye must needs be subject, not only for wrath, but also for conscience' sake."

Silver and gold (most of us must own) we have none: But such as we have we humbly beg your Majesty to accept; together with our hearts and prayers. May He who hath bought us with his blood, the Prince of all the kings of the earth, fight against all the enemies of your Majesty, with the two-edged sword that cometh out of his mouth! And when he called your Majesty from this throne, full of years and victories, may it be with that voice, "Come, receive the kingdom prepared for thee, from the beginning of the world!"

These are the continual prayers of your Majesty's dutiful and loyal servants,

JOHN WESLEY, &c.

But upon farther consideration it was judged best to lay it aside.

4. *JW Works,* VIII, pp. 279–281, recorded the "Minutes" from the 1744 Conference, as the Methodists considered their relationship with the Mother Church:

WEDNESDAY, June 27th [1744]
WE BEGAN TO CONSIDER POINTS OF DISCIPLINE

With regard to which, the questions asked, and the substance of the answers given, were as follows:—

Q. 1. What is the Church of England?

A. According to the Twentieth Article, the visible Church of England is the congregation of English believers, in which the pure word of God is preached, and the sacraments duly administered.

(But the word "Church" is sometimes taken, in a looser sense, for "a congregation professing to believe." So it is taken in the Twenty-sixth Article; and the first, second, and third chapters of Revelation.)

Q. 2. Who is a member of the Church of England?

A. A believer, hearing the pure word of God preached, and partaking of the sacraments duly administered, in that Church.

Q. 3. What is it to be zealous for the Church?

A. To be earnestly desirous of its welfare and increase: Of its welfare, by the confirmation of its present members, in faith, hearing, and communicating; of its increase, by the addition of new members.

Q. 4. How are we to defend the doctrine of the Church?

A. Both by our preaching and living.

Q. 5. How should we behave at a false or railing sermons?

A. If it only contain personal reflections, we may quietly suffer it: If it blaspheme the work and Spirit of God, it may be better to go out of the Church. In either case, if opportunity serve, it would be well to speak or write to the Minister.

Q. 6. How far is it our duty to obey the Bishops?

A. In all things indifferent. And on this ground of obeying them, we should observe the Canons, so far as we can with a safe conscience.

Q. 7. Do we separate from the Church?

A. We conceive not: We hold communion therewith for conscience' sake, by constantly attending both the word preached, and the sacraments administered therein.

Q. 8. What then do they mean, who say, "You separate from the Church"?

A. We cannot certainly tell. Perhaps they have no determinate meaning; unless, by the Church they mean themselves; that is, that part of the Clergy who accuse us of preaching false doctrine. And it is sure we do herein separate from them, by maintaining that which they deny.

Q. 9. But do you not weaken the Church?

A. Do not they who ask this, by *the Church*, mean themselves? We do not purposely weaken any man's hands. But accidentally we may, thus far: They who come to know the truth by us, will esteem such as deny it less that they did before.

But the Church, in the proper sense, the congregation of English believers, we do not weaken at all.

Q. 10. Do you not entail a schism on the Church? That is, is it not probable that your hearers, after your death, will be scattered into all sects and parties; or that they will form themselves into a distinct sect?

A. (1) We are persuaded the body of our hearers will even after our death remain in the Church, unless they be thrust out.

(2) We believe notwithstanding either that they will be thrust out, or that they will leaven the whole Church.

(3) We do, and will do, all we can to prevent those consequences which are supposed likely to happen after our death.

(4) But we cannot with a good conscience neglect the present opportunity of saving souls while we live, for fear of consequences which may possibly or probably happen after we are dead.

5. *JW Works*, II, pp. 328–329.

6. Jackson, *CW Journal*, II, p. 202.

7. "Ms. Epistles," pp. 89–107, *ca.* 1755. Located in the Methodist Archives and Research Centre, The John Rylands University Library of Manchester, Manchester, England. Printed here by permission of the Methodist Church Archives and History Committee.

8. *JW Works*, XII, pp. 116–118. Cf. letter of June 28, 1755.

9. The term "Antistes" is cited from Cyprian's statement *Populus a scelerato antiste separare se debet* [Latin: A people is obligated to separate itself from a wicked overseer]. "Overseer" had become an ecclesiastical term for bishop or presbyter, and hence the Wesley brothers are debating the appropriate understanding of Cyprian's injunction about separation.

The patristic phrase also emerged in the Wesleys' debate over the propriety of field preaching (cf. *JW Letters*, I, 323), where John concluded, "But what if a bishop forbids this? I do not say, as St. Cyprian, *Populus a scelerato antiste separare se debet.*" Charles's unpublished letter to Mr. Durbin (cf. "Ms. Ordinations," pp. 34–35), October 15, 1785, reports that John Wesley used Cyprian's phrase to describe his attitude toward Methodism's impending separation from the Church of England because of John's ordinations. Charles wrote:

> I have been urging [John] with the infallible certainty of a Separation as he has given the staff [of leadership] out of his hands, and his Elders will surely ordain the other Preachers, after his death, if not before it. His answer was as usual, that he did not concern himself with what wou[l]d happen after his death. I replied—"But I do: & shall therefore do all in my power to save the poor Methodists from the sin of Schism.['] He quoted the saying of Cyprian: *Populus a scelerato antiste separare debet.* I asked him if the Clergy were wickeder now than 40 years ago when he wrote his "Reasons Against a Separation." . . .

10. The citation is from Terrence's *Andria*. My thanks to Dr. Gordon Stockin for this identification and translation.

11. On September 24, 1755, John Wesley wrote the first of four letters to Rev. Samuel Walker, Vicar of Truro, on the topic of separation from the Church of England. John wrote to solicit Walker's sentiments on several issues facing the Methodists; most specifically what might be lawful grounds for separation, and whether an Anglican presbyter can appoint other ministers. On the latter point, it seems John was already considering ordinations among the Methodists. Walker wrote against separation and ordination, and urged Wesley to also write Thomas Adam, rector at Wintringham, near Barton-on-Humber. Once again the issues of lawful separation and appointment of ministers were the central issues of Wesley's letter. On the former matter John intimated: "We will not *go out* [of the Church]: if we are *thrust out*, well." He solicited Adam's opinion on the matter of Methodist appointment of ministers.

12. "Ms. Ordinations," p. 1, *ca.* 1784. The manuscript is located in the Methodist Archives and Research Centre, The John Rylands University Library of Manchester, Manchester, England. The hymn and other material from "Ms. Ordinations" is printed here by permission of the Methodist Church Archives and History Committee, England.

13. *Ibid.*, p. 3. The hymn announces that the ordinations and the separation they symbolized had occurred.

14. At this point the manuscript carries a note: "His usual signature was E.A.P.J." It refers to the brothers' custom of signing their documents *Ecclesiae Anglicanae Presbyter*—"Presbyter of the Church of England." The "J" of the designation probably stands for *Juratus,* "sworn," since both brothers used the designation as a pledge of their devotion to the Anglican community. Cf. Baker, *Representative Verse, op. cit.*, p. 368.

15. *Ibid.*, p. 135, numbered from the rear of the manuscript book.

16. "Ms. Brothers." This hymn is the only one extant in the entire manuscript, numerous others having been cut from the binding. The manuscript was located at the Methodist Archives and Research Centre, The John Rylands University Library of Manchester, but is currently irretrievable. The hymn, "True Yokefellows," is reprinted here from Frank Baker's *Representative Verse, op. cit.*, pp. 371–374, by permission of the Methodist Publishing House, Epworth Press.

17. "Ms. Ordinations," pp. 21–22. These letters are published here for the first time, by permission of the Methodist Church Archives and History Committee, England.

18. *Ibid.*, pp. 24–25.

19. *Ibid.*, pp. 27–28.
20. Jackson, *Life of Charles Wesley, op. cit.*, II, p. 398.
21. *Ibid.*
22. "Ms. Ordinations," pp. 36–37.

12 / Expositor of Scripture

As Charles explained in his laconic preface to the 1762 *Short Hymns on Select Passages of Scripture,* "God, having graciously laid His hand upon my body, and disabled me for the principal work of the ministry, has thereby given me an unexpected occasion of writing the following hymns." The recurrent illnesses of the last thirty years of his life, along with family obligations (which his brother never knew) turned Charles's primary attention from pulpit to poems.

Well over one half of his 9,000 hymns were written during those last thirty years; they were short, poetic renditions of scriptural passages. Over 5,000 of these "Short Hymns" have survived in the published edition or in manuscript form. While a few were recast for the Methodist hymnbook of 1780, the vast majority were never sung. Yet these unknown and largely unpublished poems are especially significant since they reveal the mature ideas of Charles Wesley, and in a form that was untouched by John Wesley's editorial pen. They are windows into his devotional study of the Bible, and they provide the key to the biblical hermeneutic so artfully worked out in earlier sermons.

Charles Wesley's hymns and sacred poems are mosaics of biblical phrases and allusions. They are constructed with the care and intention of a man who was both a gifted classicist and a Methodist evangelist. His poetic hermeneutic was characterized by a persistent christological focus, framed in Luther's *Christus pro me* and the Pentecost conversion of thirty years earlier. It utilized typology and allegory (along with other devices) to set the gospel message of faith and comfort in the life experience of the singer or reader.

Charles had a traditional conception of the nature of the Bible, and yet his penchant for turning biblical texts into poetic dramas recreated those same passages in startling ways. In his hymns the biblical past and the eighteenth-century present blended in a sort of eucharistic timelessness that set Christ before the reader or singer and made the Gospel past into a contemporary experience.

The hymns possess both spontaneity and emotion, but those feelings were tools in the hands of a master craftsman. Wesley was not merely a sentimentalist; his sentiment, while genuine, was an instrument of his poetic diction. Hence, we do him a disservice if we think "emotionalism" when we read of the vital role "experience" played in his hymns and theology. The fusion of doctrine and experience was the foundation of his poetic method. It created a lived theology; hence, his brother John aptly described the 1780 *Collection of Hymns for the Use of the People Called Methodists* as a "little body of experimental and practical divinity."

Perhaps even more than his brother John, Charles was *homo unius libri,* "a man of one book." Not only was the Bible the foundation of his religious epistemology (upon which tradition, reason, and experience were evaluated), but it so seasoned his own diction that in hymn and prose one can scarcely discern the difference between Wesley's words and the Bible's. His hymns and sermons were veritable patchworks of biblical words and phrases, sewn together to form his own pattern. Charles was also a talented exegete. His study and application of the Bible were not limited to the renditions of the Authorized Version of his day (King James Version), the Book of Common Prayer, or the recent commentaries (though he utilized all of these). His dexterity in Greek made him John Wesley's editor for the *New Testament Notes.*[1] Charles's poetic rendition of the "kenosis" passage in Phil. 2:7 broke through the timidity of the translators of the Authorized Version to prefigure more modern readings.[2]

He was also a scholar of the classical and Christian traditions, and a host of ancient writers (both patristic and pagan) are echoed in his verses. His love for the Anglican tradition is seen in his numerous psalms that prefer the prayer book version over that of King James's Bible. The younger Wesley also read and applied the leading biblical scholars of his day, however antiquarian they may seem to us.[3]

Charles's hymnological precursor, Isaac Watts, was a pioneer in the art of paraphrasing the Scriptures. Watts's ideal was to follow the biblical text as closely as possible and restate its message in the best (Miltonesque) poetic diction he could muster. Charles Wesley "paraphrased" (if that is even the appropriate term to use) by weaving biblical and extrabiblical words, phrases, and images together to form a new interpretive fabric. Using typology, allegory, dialogue, and other devices, Wesley shaped biblical passages into christological dramas that communicated the essence and experience of the Gospel to the singers of his day. Hence, unlike John Milton, or allegorists of an earlier age, Charles Wesley never narrated the allegorized account to the reader. We are not spectators of the events; rather, in Charles's hymns we become actors in the narrative. We are the wounded traveler, or Jacob wrestling for "the Blessing"; blind Bartimaeus's affliction becomes our own, and we are the woman taken in adultery—guilty, yet no longer accused. Where the Puritan narrates the account, the Methodist makes the singer or reader participate in the biblical drama. Where Milton used allegory to communicate ideals or principles, Wesley used the same device to recreate the biblical event afresh in the reader's imagination. He took an old poetic tool and reshaped it to meet the needs of a new age. Yet, unlike later Romantic poets, Charles did not create an idyllic or alternative history in a flight from this world; he sought to transfigure history by drawing the contemporary situation into experiential dialogue with the biblical past.

The selection of hymns below is divided into two sections. The first group reveals

Charles's conception of Scripture. The second section is a sampler of his christo-centric typologies, allegories, and soteriological dramas that communicate the experience and practical piety through the passages under consideration.

ON SCRIPTURE

Charles's favorite description for the Bible was "the oracles," a designation that emphasized the revelatory impact he felt in the Scriptures. The Scriptures were his "rule of faith"—doctrine, creed, and religious experience were all evaluated by the biblical standard. Wesley had an unambiguous confidence in the accuracy of the biblical record. His doctrine of Scripture had its basis in the connection between the Word and Spirit of God. For Charles, the Bible was the enlivened Word because of the work of the Holy Spirit, hence the Spirit—more often than the Bible—was said to be infallible in the revelatory event. The Word-Spirit nexus also explained the role of the Scriptures and Charles's approach to them, since both the written word and Holy Spirit point to Christ, the Word made flesh. Hence the Bible was a passageway to Christ and a channel through which the Gospel realities were mediated into the contemporary scene. Charles's comment on the narrative in Matt. 9:20–21 expressed well his appreciation for the Scriptures ("I blush and tremble to draw near"), and his willingness to use the Bible as "a garment" with which to "touch my Lord."

No. 222   Short Hymn on Isa. 8:20
To the Law and to the testimony.
(*Poetical Works*, IX, 380)

1   Doctrines, experiences to try,
    We to the sacred standard fly,
    Assured the Spirit of Our Lord
    Can never contradict His word:
    Whate'er His Spirit speaks in me,
    Must with the written word agree;
    If not—I cast it all aside,
    As Satan's voice, or nature's pride.

2   The test of truth and righteousness,
    O God, Thy records we confess,
    And who Thine oracles gainsay
    Have miss'd the right celestial way:
    Their pardon sure they vainly boast,
    In nature sunk, in darkness lost;
    Or if they of perfection dream,
    The light of grace is not in them.

No. 223   "Ms. Acts": Hymn on Acts 24:14
Believing all things which are written, . . .

1   The written word, entire and pure,
The word which always shall endure,
   My rule of faith and life I own;
Not reason or tradition vain,
Not the authority of man,
   Not an internal light *alone.*

2   Built, through the sacred oracles,
On Christ, the Rock that never fails,
   Religion from the fountain brought,
I find it in the heavenly book,
What *Moses* and the prophets spoke,
   What Christ and His apostles taught.

No. 224   Short Hymn on 1 Peter 4:11
If any man speak, let him speak as the oracles, . . .
(*Poetical Works,* XIII, 183)

1   Let all who speak in Jesu's name,
   To His submit their every word,
Implicit faith in them disclaim,
   And send the hearers to their Lord;
Who doth His Father's will reveal,
The only Guide infallible.

2   Jesus, to me Thy mind impart,
   Be Thou Thine own Interpreter,
Explain the Scripture to my heart,
   That when the church Thy servant hear,
Taught by the oracles Divine,
They all may own, the word is Thine.

No. 225   Short Hymn on Isa. 29:11
Read this: I cannot, for it is sealed.
(*Poetical Works,* IX, 395–396)

Proud learning boasts its skill in vain
The sacred oracles t' explain,
It may the literal surface show,
But not the precious mine below;
The saving sense remains conceal'd,

Till by the Spirit of faith reveal'd,
The book is still unread, unknown,
And open'd by the Lamb alone.

No. 226 "Ms. Matthew": Hymn on Matt. 9:20[5]
A woman, which was diseased with an issue, . . .

1 Unclean, of life and heart unclean,
   How shall I in His sight appear?
Conscious of my inveterate sin
   I blush and tremble to draw near;
Yet through the garment of His word
I humbly seek to touch my Lord.

2 The smallest things, the weakest means,
   The mournful fast, the plaintive prayer,
His sanctifying power dispense,
   His efficacious grace confer,
And through His sacramental clothes
The healing emanation flows.

3 Yet not in outward veils of grace,
   But in Himself the virtue lies,
Th' infusion of His righteousness
   This fountain of corruption dries;
And sure as I in Christ believe,
I shall a perfect cure receive.

No. 227 Short Hymn on Mark 12:24
Do ye not therefore err, . . .
(*Poetical Works*, XI, 55)

1 The Scriptures never can be known
But through the power of God alone;
The Spirit of power, and truth, and love
Doth first our unbelief remove,
Discovers the deep things of God,
And shows to me my Saviour's blood.

2 My Father's mind I then perceive,
And quicken'd by His Spirit live;
The Spirit doth His word reveal,
The Spirit teaches me His will,
And while into all truth He guides,
My Teacher in my heart resides.

SCRIPTURE HYMNS

No. 228   Short Hymn on Gen. 3:21
Unto Adam also, and to his wife, did the Lord God, . . .
(*Poetical Works*, IX, 10)

1   Clothed with the skins of victims slain,
Our parents turn'd on Christ their eyes,
The Lamb whom God did *then* ordain,
The grand vicarious Sacrifice:
By faith they knew the blood was shed,
For them, and all their race t' atone,
And trusting in His merits, made
His perfect righteousness their own.

2   O Thou slaughter'd Lamb of God,
From the world's foundations slain,
By Thy sacrificial blood
Wash out all my guilty stain,
Clothe my spirit's nakedness
With a covering from above,
Put me on my spotless dress,
Wrap me in heavenly love.

No. 229   Short Hymn on Gen. 28:12, 13
He dreamed, and behold a ladder, . . .
(*Poetical Works*, IX, 27)

1   What doth the ladder mean,
Sent down from the Most High?
Fasten'd to earth its foot is seen,
Its summit to the sky:
Lo! up and down the scale
The angels swiftly move,
And God, the great Invisible,
Himself appears above!

2   Jesus that ladder is,
Th' incarnate Deity,
Partaker of celestial bliss
And human misery;
Sent from His high abode,
To sleeping mortals given,
He stands, and man unites to God,
And earth connects with heaven.

No. 230   Short Hymn on Exod. 15:1
I will sing unto the Lord, . . .
(*Poetical Works*, IX, 46)

1   In *Moses'* song the Lamb we proclaim:
The praise doth belong To Jesus's name!
Triumphantly glorious Our Jesus hath been,
And more than victorious O'er hell, earth, and sin.

2   The world and its prince No longer are found;
Our tyrannous sins Are buried and drown'd,
O'erwhelm'd by a motion Of *Moses's* rod,
And plunged in the ocean Of Jesus's blood!

No. 231   Short Hymn on Lev. 8:35
Keep the charge of the Lord, that ye die not.
(*Poetical Works*, IX, 60–61)

1   A charge to keep I have,
            A God to glorify,
A never-dying soul to save,
            And fit it for the sky;
            To serve the present age,
            My calling to fulfill:
O may it all my powers engage
            To do my Master's will!

2   Arm me with jealous care,
            As in Thy sight to live,
And O! Thy servant, Lord, prepare
            A strict account to give:
            Help me to watch and pray,
            And on Thyself rely,
Assured, if I my trust betray,
            I shall for ever die.

No. 232   Short Hymn on Lev. 26:13
I have broken the bands of your yoke, . . .
(*Poetical Works*, IX, 64)

            Lord, if Thou from me has broke
            The power of outward sin,
            Burst this *Babylonish* yoke,
            And make me free within;

Bid mine inbred sin depart,
And I Thine utmost word shall prove,
Upright both in life and heart,
And perfected in love.

No. 233   Short Hymn on Num. 13:30
Caleb stilled the people, and said, Let us go up, . . .
(*Poetical Works*, IX, 73)

1   Silence, ye unbelieving fears,
Who clamorously deny the word!
The promise on our side appears,
The power and goodness of our Lord:
Let us go up in Jesus' name:
Our sin shall all to Christ submit,
And who for us the world o'ercame,
Shall bruise the fiend beneath our feet.

2   Is anything too hard for God?
Through Jesus we can all things do;
Who Satan and his works destroy'd,
Shall make us more than conquerors too:
Let us at once the land possess,
And taste the blessings from above,
The milk sincere of pardoning grace,
The honey of His perfect love.

No. 234   Short Hymn on Deut. 9:7
"From the day that thou didst depart, &c."
(*Poetical Works*, IX, 100)

The hymn reveals the emergence of Charles's theology of suffering that saw in his own pain a purifying effect. John Wesley marked the manuscript with his protest.

1   I now reflect with grief and shame,
That since I out of *Egypt* came,
I have rebellious been,
Provoked Thee in the wilderness,
And wearied out Thy patient grace
By adding sin to sin:

2   A rebel to this present hour!
Yet now for all Thy mercy's power
I ask with contrite sighs

To end my sin, but not my pain:
I would lament till death,[a] and then
   Rejoice in paradise.

No. 235   Short Hymn on Josh. 11:21
At that time came Joshua, and cut off the Anakims.
(*Poetical Works*, IX, 126)

Come, victorious Captain, come
   In Thine appointed day,
Execute their righteous doom,
   The sons of *Anak* slay;
Now these tallest giants kill,
Who longest in the land abide,
   All my stubborness of will,
     And all my strength of pride.

No. 236   Short Hymn on Judg. 16:16, 17
When she pressed him daily with her words, . . .
(*Poetical Works*, IX, 139)

Samson the strong, the weak, we blame,
And all in him ourselves condemn,
Who vanquish'd by the foe within,
The importunity of sin,
Yield to our bosom-*Delilah*,
Yet know, she flatters to betray,
To bind our souls in slavish bands,
And give us up to Satan's hands.

No. 237   Short Hymn on Judg. 16:3
Samson arose at midnight, and took the doors, . . .
(*Poetical Works*, IX, 139)

1 See the great Antitype arise,
   While darkness yet involves the skies,
   His *Israel* from their foes to save,
   He bursts the barriers of the grave,
   Puts forth His strength invincible,
   And tears up all the gates of hell!

---

[a]J.W.: God Forbid!

2 Triumphant o'er His baffled foes,
   The trophies openly He shows:
   And daily, in His people's cause,
   He spreads the victory of His cross,
   And still He takes the spoils, and still
   He bears them up the heavenly hill!

No. 238 Short Hymn on Judg. 16:29, 30
Samson took hold of the two pillars, . . .
(*Poetical Works*, IX, 142)

1 Samson the theatre o'threw,
   And thousands at his death he slew:
   But lo! our *Samson* from the skies
   A more triumphant conqueror dies,
   A nobler victory obtains,
   And heaven for all His *Israel* gains.

2 He by the pangs of death oppress'd
   With outstretch'd hands the pillars seized,
   Compass'd with foes He bow'd His head,
   For mercy, not for vengeance, pray'd,
   And groan'd His last expiring groan,
   And pull'd th' infernal kingdom down.

3 The author dire of sin and death
   He slew by yielding up His breath,
   The powers of darkness He destroy'd,
   And made their hellish boastings void,
   Died with the *Philistines*—but rose
   Triumphant o'er His slaughtered foes.

No. 239 Short Hymn on 1 Sam. 22:2
Every one that was in distress, and every one, . . .
(*Poetical Works*, IX 161–162)

1 In want and murmuring distress,
   In debt to sovereign righteousness,
   A wretched, desperate outcast, I
   To *David* for protection fly.

2 Jesus, the Antitype Thou art,
   The *David* after God's own heart,
   Commander of the helpless band,
   Enlist me under Thy command.

3   Assure me, Thou my debt hast paid,
    Hast for my sins atonement made,
    And on Thyself my burden take,
    And save me for Thy mercy's sake.

4   Captain of my salvation, show
    Thy strength against my threefold foe,
    And, sure of final victory,
    In life and death, I follow Thee.

No. 240   Short Hymn on 2 Chron. 32:31
God let him, to try him, that he might, . . .
(*Poetical Works*, IX, 217)

A few of Charles's latter hymns suggest that God withdraws His comfort from the
believer in order to purge inward sin; this view was strenuously opposed by John
Wesley. He reacted to this particular hymn at the indicated place. Charles's interest
in the "dark night of the soul" suggests something of his own religious experience
and the enduring impact the mystical divines had upon him.

1   May'st Thou not still conceal Thy face,
    Withdraw the sweet delights of grace,
        And from Thine own depart,[a]
    To try, and seal them for Thine own,
    To show the sin which lurk'd unknown
        In my deceitful heart?

2   Surely, before my Lord withdrew,
    Hid from myself I never knew
        What now I groan to feel:
    Thy absence hath my pride betray'd,
    And thus convinced, I see display'd
        The depths of my own hell.

3   Left to myself, I now confess,
    My heart is desperate wickedness,
        But trust Thy gracious power
    To make an utter end of sin,
    Thou wilt at last appear within,
        And never leave me more.

---

[a]J.W.: No, not unprovoked!

No. 241   Short Hymn on Job 9:13

If the scourge slay suddenly, He will laugh, . . .
(*Poetical Works*, IX, 239)

1   Shall man direct the sovereign God,
    Say, "He cannot use His rod
        But for some fresh offense?[a]
  From saints He never hides His face,
  Or suddenly their comfort slays,
        To prove their innocence."

2   Nay, but He casts the righteous down,
    Seems on His beloved to frown;
        Yet smiles their fears to see:[b]
  He hears the oft-repeated cry,
  "Why, O my God, my Father, why
        Hast Thou forsaken me?"

3   Then let the patient, perfect man
    His integrity maintain;
        But not before his God:
  The Lord may crush a sinless saint,
  As once He left His Son to faint,[c]
        And die beneath His load.

No. 242   Short Hymn on Job 9:33

Neither is there any daysman betwixt us, . . .
(*Poetical Works*, IX, 239–240)

1   But *we* a mighty Daysman know,
    By love Divine to sinners given,
  The Lord of all who dwelt below,
    And mediates betwixt earth and heaven.
  Of both the nature He partakes,
    United in Himself alone,
  An end of all the difference makes,
    For God and man in Christ are one.

2   Thou, Jesus, Thou that Umpire art,
    Whose hand on man and God is laid:
  Assure a trembling sinner's heart,
    My sin is purged, my peace is made:

---

[a]J.W.: True.
[b]J.W.: No.
[c]J.W.: No parallel case.

Thou who hast apprehended me,
  Give me Thyself to apprehend:
My peace, my sole perfection be,
  My present and eternal Friend.

No. 243   Short Hymn on Job 23:3
  O that I knew where I might find Him
(*Poetical Works*, IX, 257)

        Where but on yonder tree?
Or if too rich thou art,
      Sink into poverty,
And find Him in thine heart.

No. 244   Short Hymn on Ps. 34:8
  O taste, and see that the Lord is good!
(*Poetical Works*, IX, 290)

        Taste Him in Christ, and see
        Th' abundance of His grace,
Experience God so good to me,
        So good to all our race!
        Celestial sweetness prove
        Through Jesu's grace forgiven,
And then enjoy in perfect love
        The largest taste of heaven.

No. 245   Short Hymn on Ps. 51:10 (Prayer Book Version)
  Make me a clean heart, O God, and renew, . . .
(*Poetical Works*, IX, 299–300)

Jesu, Thy work begin
By cancelling my sin;
Thy cleansing blood impart,
To purify my heart;
Its utmost virtue show,
My spirit to renew,
And wholly sanctified
Take home Thy happy bride.

No. 246   Short Hymn on Ps. 62:10
If riches increase, set not your heart upon them
(*Poetical Works*, IX, 302)

Who of the rich hath ears to hear,
Divinely warn'd of danger near,
Or fears to find his wealth increase,
The mammon of unrighteousness?
Yet if on wealth ye set your heart,
Ye from the living God depart,
Your souls for nought to Satan sell,
And wisely barter heaven for hell.

No. 247   Short Hymn on Ps. 71:4
(Prayer Book Version)
Thou, O Lord God, art the thing that I long for.
(*Poetical Works*, IX, 307)

1   My longing heart's desire
      Is to its Maker known;
    Thou seest it now aspire,
      Jesus, to Thee alone.
    The one thing necessary,
      For Thee alone I pine:
    On earth I only tarry
      To know that Thou art mine.

2   More than the consolation,
      The Comforter I want;
    O God of my salvation,
      In me Thyself implant.
    With infinite expansion,
      My spirit pants for Thee,
    And swells to be Thy mansion
      Through all eternity.

No. 248   Short Hymn on Ps. 71:14
(Prayer Book Version)
I will make mention of Thy righteousness only.
(*Poetical Works*, IX, 309)

Let others of their virtue boast,
  And call it all their own,
I in the only merit trust
  Of God's most holy Son:

The righteousness by Jesus wrought
    Shall all my evil hide,
Till deep into my Spirit brought
    It shows me sanctified.

No. 249   Short Hymn on Prov. 18:10
The name of the Lord is a strong tower, . . .
(*Poetical Works*, IX, 351–352)

1 Jesus, Thy name is my strong tower,
    To which I still in danger run,
Thy name is Love, and Truth, and Power
    To all Thy faithful people known:
Salvation in Thy name I find,
And leave the world and sin behind.

2 Less than Thy least of mercies I
    A grain of faith from Thee receive,
And while I on Thy name rely,
    Beyond the reach of hell I live:
My strength, the joy Thy smiles impart,
Thy peace doth garrison my heart.

3 To this stronghold whoever turn,
    Within salvation's walls they dwell:
Their castle laughs a siege to scorn,
    And from *my* tower impregnable
I mark the alien host beneath,
I mock the darts of hell and death.

4 The Truth determined to obey,
    Continuing steadfast in the Word,
I in my rock and fortress stay
    (My rock and fortress is the Lord),
And feel my life secured above,
And rest in Thy almighty love.

No. 250   Short Hymn on Isa. 53:5
With His stripes we are healed.
(*Poetical Works*, IX, 439)

Pardon through Thy wounds I have:
    But is pardon all the cure?
Thou wilt to the utmost save,
    Make mine inmost nature pure,

Me to perfect health restore:
Then I shall relapse no more.

No. 251   Short Hymn on Jer. 32:39
I will give them one heart, and one way, . . .
(*Poetical Works*, X, 43)

1 No, they cry, it cannot be!
   Christians never will agree!
   All the world Thy word deny,
   Yet we on the truth rely,
   Sure, in that appointed day,
   Thou wilt give us all one way,
   Show us each to other join'd,
   One in heart, and one in mind.

2 Hasten then the general peace,
   Bid Thy people's discord cease,
   All united in Thy name,
   Let us think, and speak the same:
   Then the world shall know and own
   God Himself hath made us one,
   Thee their Lord with us embrace,
   Sing Thine everlasting praise.

No. 252   Short Hymn on Lam. 1:12
Is it nothing to you, all that pass by?
(*Poetical Works*, X, 48)

Oft have I unconcern'd pass'd by,
   Nor stopp'd on *Calvary*,
So small a thing, that Thou shouldst die,
   Or nothing, Lord, to me!
But now I see, the bleeding cross
   Is all in all to man,
To me Thy death is life, Thy loss
   Is mine eternal gain.

No. 253   Short Hymn on Ezek. 18:1
Make you a new heart
(*Poetical Works*, X, 53)

How can I my own heart renew?
The word confers the power to do:

      The word I now embrace,
I yield to be renew'd by Thee,
Accepting first the pardon free,
      And then the perfect grace.

No. 254   Short Hymn on Hos. 14:4
I will heal their backsliding.
(*Poetical Works*, X, 84–85)

1 How am I heal'd, if still again
    I *must* relapse with grief and pain
        Into my old disease?
    If Christ, with all His power and love,
    Can never *perfectly* remove
        My desperate wickedness?

2 But Lord, I trust, Thy gracious skill
    Shall thoroughly my backslidings heal,
        My sinfulness of soul,
    Destroy the bent to sin in me,
    Cure my original malady,
        And make, and keep me whole.

No. 255   Short Hymn on Zech. 13:9
I will bring the third part through the fire, . . .
(*Poetical Works*, X, 124)

    Tried is every faithful man,
      As gold and silver tried,
    Purged by grief, and purged by pain,
      And seven times purified:
    All who stand the fiery test,
Receive Thine image from above,
      Bear Thy favourite name impress'd,
      Thy favourite name of Love.

No. 256   Short Hymn on Matt. 1:23
They shall call His name Immanuel.
("Ms. Matthew")

1   Celebrate *Immanuel's* name,
      The Prince of life and peace;
    God with us, our lips proclaim,
      Our faithful hearts confess:

God is in our flesh reveal'd;
Heaven and earth in Jesus join;
Mortal with immortal fill'd,
And human with Divine.

2   Fullness of the Deity
In Jesu's body dwells,
Dwells in all His saints and me,
When God His Son reveals:
Father, manifest Thy Son,
And, conscious of th' incarnate Word,
In our inmost souls make known
The presence of the Lord.

3   Let the Spirit of our Head
Through every member flow;
By our Lord inhabited,
We then *Immanuel* know:
Then He doth His name express,
And God in us we truly prove,
Fill'd with all the life of grace,
And all the power of love.

No. 257   Short Hymn on Matt. 2:2
We have seen His star in the east, and are come, . . .
("Ms. Matthew")

1   Mine eyes have seen His orient star,
And sweetly drawn I come from afar,
Leaving the world behind;
His Spirit gently leads me on
A stranger in a land unknown,
The new-born King to find.

2   The word of all-preventing grace
Marks out the Saviour's natal place;
And follower of the word,
I keep His glimmering star in sight,
Which by its sure unerring light
Conducts me to my Lord.

No. 258   Short Hymn on Matt. 3:3
The voice of one crying in the wilderness, . . .
("Ms. Matthew")

1   Far from a world of noisy care,
I to the wilderness repair.

    In silence and retreat
Rous'd by the soul-awakening cry,
I hear the news of Jesus nigh,
    And His forerunner meet.

2 I feel the voice that cries "Repent,"
And struck with conscious grief, lament
    The sins which I confess,
In hope to find at last restored
The kingdom of my heavenly Lord,
    The justice, joy, and peace.

3 Allured and strengthen'd from above
I every obstacle remove,
    With every idol part;
The Spirit is His Harbinger,
And Jesus doth Himself prepare
    His way into my heart.

4 Repentance is His work before,
And wrought to this I wait the power
    Of faith and love Divine:
Come Lord, and bring Thy kingdom in,
Destroy the tyranny of sin,
    And reign for ever mine.

No. 259 Short Hymn on Matt. 3:11
He shall baptize you with the Holy Ghost, . . .
("Ms. Matthew")

1 Pure baptismal fire Divine,
    All Thy heavenly powers exert,
In my deepest darkness shine,
    Spread Thy warmth throughout my heart;
Come, seraphic Spirit, come,
    Comforter through Jesus given,
All my earthly dross consume,
    Fill my soul with love from heaven.

2 Love in me intensely burn,
    Love mine inmost essence seize,
All into Thy nature turn,
    All into Thy holiness;
Spark of Thy celestial flame,
    Then my soul shall upward move,
Trembling on with steady aim
    Seek, and join its Source above.

No. 260   Short Hymn on Matt. 5:3
Blessed are the poor in spirit: . . .
("Ms. Matthew")

> Jesus, on me the want bestow,
> Which all who feel shall surely know
>   Their sins on earth forgiven;
> Give me to prove the kingdom mine,
> And taste in holiness Divine
>   The happiness of heaven.

No. 261   Short Hymn on Matt. 5:24
First be reconciled to thy brother, and then come, . . .
("Ms. Matthew")

> In vain with angry hearts we dare
>   Nigh to Thine altar move,
> Since neither sacrifice, nor prayer
>   Atones for want of love:
> O may we each with each agree
>   Through Thine uniting grace,
> Our gift shall then accepted be,
>   Our life of love and praise.

No. 262   Short Hymn on Matt. 6:9–13
Our Father which art in heaven, . . .
("Ms. Matthew")

1
>   Father of earth and sky,
>   Thy name we magnify:
>   O that earth and heaven might join
>   Thy perfections to proclaim,
>   Praise the attributes Divine,
>   Fear, and love Thy awful name!

2
>   When shall Thy Spirit reign
>   In every heart of man?
>   Father, bring the kingdom near,
>   Honour Thy triumphant Son,
>   God of heaven, on earth appear,
>   Fix with us Thy glorious throne.

3
>   Thy good and holy will,
>   Let all on earth fulfill:

Men with minds angelic vie,
   Saints below with saints above,
Thee to praise and glorify,
   Thee to serve with perfect love.

4   This day with this day's bread
         Thy hungry children feed,
Fountain of all blessings, grant
   Now the manna from above,
Now supply our bodies' want,
   Now sustain our souls with love.

5   Our trespasses forgive;
         And when absolved we live,
Thou our life of grace maintain;
   Lest we from our God depart,
Lose Thy pardoning love again,
   Grant us a forgiving heart.

6   In every fiery hour
         Display Thy guardian power,
Near in our temptation stay,
   With sufficient grace defend,
Bring us through the evil day,
   Make us faithful to the end.

7   Father, by right Divine,
         Assert the kingdom Thine;
Jesus, Power of God, subdue
   Thine own universe to Thee;
Spirit of grace and glory too,
   Reign through all eternity.

No. 263   Short Hymn on Matt. 13:33
The kingdom of heaven is like unto leaven.
("Ms. Matthew")

That heavenly principle within,
   Doth it at once its power exert,
At once root out the seed of sin,
   And spread perfection through the heart?
No; but a gradual life it sends,
   Diffuse through the faithful soul,
To actions, words, and thoughts extends,
   And slowly sanctifies the whole.

No. 264   Short Hymn on Matt. 13:46
He . . . sold all that he had, and bought it.
("Ms. Matthew")

Have I not found that pearl Divine,
   That treasure in the field?
Yet still it is not surely mine,
   My pardon is not seal'd:
The ascertaining terms I know,
   And would with joy approve,
Sell all; myself, my life forego,
   To buy Thy perfect love.

No. 265   Short Hymn on Matt. 19:13
Then were there brought unto Him little children, . . .
(*Poetical Works*, X, 322)

1   Jesus in earth in heaven the same
      Accept a parent's vow,
   To Thee, baptized into Thy name
      I bring my children now:
   Thy love permits, invites, commands
      My offspring to be bless'd:
   Lay on them, Lord, Thy gracious hands,
      And hide them in Thy breast.

2   To each the hallowing spirit give
      Even from their infancy,
   And pure into Thy church receive
      Whom I devote to Thee:
   Committed to Thy faithful care,
      Protected by Thy blood,
   Preserve by Thine unceasing prayer,
      And bring them all to God.

No. 266   Short Hymn on Matt. 20:28
And to give His life a ransom for many.
(*Poetical Works*, X, 337)

As many as in *Adam* fell,
   And wander'd from salvation wide,
To ransom from sin, death, and hell,
   For them the Second *Adam* died;
Even those unhappy souls He bought
   Who their redeeming Lord deny,

Will not by Him to life be brought
But self-destroy'd resolve to die.

No. 267 Short Hymn on Matt. 25:40
Ye have done it unto Me.
(*Poetical Works*, X, 395)

To Christ who would not gladly give
   Raiment, or food, or ease,
And in His substitutes relieve
   His Saviour in distress?
Saviour, where'r conceal'd Thou art,
   Thee may I plainly see,
And always bear it on my heart,
   "Ye did it unto Me!"

No. 268 Short Hymn on Matt. 27:25
Then answered all the people, and said, . . .
(*Poetical Works*, X, 423)

1 Horrible wish! Thy murderers dare
   The blessing to curse pervert:
We turn the curse into a prayer;
   To cleanse our lives, and purge our heart,
In all its hallowing, blissful powers
Thy blood be, Lord, on us and ours!

2 On me, Thou bleeding Lamb, on me
   Be pour'd the consecrating stream,
From all, from all iniquity
   My life, my nature to redeem,
To fill with purity Divine,
And sign my soul for ever Thine.

No. 269 Short Hymn on Luke 2:46
They found him in the temple.
("Ms. Luke")[6]

Jesus whom once I knew,
   But lost out of my sight,
I come determin'd to pursue
   To seek by day and by night,
   I follow hard and fast
   To all his paths repair,
And look to meet my God at last
   In His own house of prayer.

No. 270   Short Hymn on Luke 3:8
Bring forth fruits worthy of repentance. . . .
("Ms. Luke")

> Repentance is a grace
> Which flows from Christ alone,
>   We cannot change the sinful race,
> Or nullify the stone:
> But if our God ordain,
> The rebels reconcil'd;
>   Turn'd into flesh the harden'd man,
> The stone into a child.

No. 271   Short Hymn on Luke 3:16
He shall baptize you with the Holy Ghost.
("Ms. Luke")

1   Holy, hallowing Spirit, come,
      Cleanse my life's impurity,
    All my nature's filth consume,
      Make an end of sin in me,
    Spread the pure baptismal flame
    Plunge me deep in Jesus' name.

2   Jesus, Thou that Spirit art,
      Thou the sinner dost baptize,
    Purify by faith my heart,
      Bid the fire of love arise,
    Consecrate the human shrine,
    Fill the earthly house Divine.

No. 272   Short Hymn on Luke 4:1
Led by the Spirit into the wilderness.
("Ms. Luke")

1   'Tis now the woman's heavenly Seed
    Begins to bruise the serpent's head, [Gen. iii.15]
          T' avenge us of our foe;
    But Jesus bleeding on the tree
    Completes His glorious victory,
          And gives the mortal blow.

2   Full of the Holy Ghost He comes,
    Provokes the fiend, nor yet presumes
          Who in Himself confides,
    By the almighty Spirit led:

Who all that in His footsteps tread
To certain conquest guides.

No. 273   Short Hymn on Luke 5:3
He entered into one of the ships, . . .
("Ms. Luke")

1   That apostolic ship,
           That church where Christ abides,
Loosed from the earth, while in the deep,
           Above the deep it rides.
           Of unity the school,
           Of truth the sacred chair!
Jesus delights to sit and rule,
           And teach His people there.

2   He at the helm appears,
           Directs by his command,
Cooperates with his ministers,
           And bids them leave the land.
           Themselves from sins secure
           From worldly things remove,
And keep their life and conscience pure,
           And work for Him they love.

No. 274   Short Hymn on Luke 7:22
The blind see, the lame walk, . . .
("Ms. Luke")

On us, O Christ, thy mission prove,
    Thy full authority to heal,
The blindness of our hearts remove,
    The lameness of our feeble will,
Open our faith's obedient ear,
    Our filthy, leprous nature cure,
Call us out of the sepulchre,
    And preach Perfection to the poor.

No. 275   Short Hymn on Luke 7:50
. . . And he said to the woman, Thy faith hath sav'd thee, go in peace.
("Ms. Luke")

1 Saving faith is not alone:
   All who savingly believe

Make their true affection known,
　To their dear Redeemer cleave;
Humbly at his feet they mourn,
　All his benefits restore,
Never to the world return,
　Walk in Christ, and sin no more.

2　Sav'd by faith from sin and fear,
　　Bright they in his image rise,
Must before his face t' appear,
　Sinners still in their own eyes;
Lord, on me the grace bestow,
　Pardon on my heart impress;
Sav'd by faith I then shall go,
　Go to God in perfect peace.

No. 276　Short Hymn on Luke 9:27
　. . . there be some standing here, which shall not see
　death, till they see the Kingdom of God.
("Ms. Luke")

1　O Wen [sic] it in my heart be made known,
Before I lay this body down,
　That I shall surely see
The power of thy victorious grace,
The joy, and praise, and righteousness,
　The kingdom fixt in me!

2　How gladly then should I resign
My soul into the hands Divine,
　To meet my Lord again,
To see the God of boundless love
And worship at thy throne above,
　And triumph in thy train.

No. 277　Short Hymn on Luke 15:8
　. . . what woman having ten pieces of silver . . .
("Ms. Luke")

1　Pure the soul at first was made,
　Mark'd with God's authentic sign,
But the image is decay'd,
　Wholly lost the stamp Divine:
Lost himself the sinner lies,
　Sunk in sin and trampled down,
Till the Lord of earth and skies,
　Finds and claims him for His own.

2   Then the sinner seeks thy grace,
        By the candle of the Word,
    Sweeps the house, th' untighten'd place
        Waiting to receive his Lord:
    Still he searches after Thee,
        And when Thou discover'd art,
    Feels the joyful ecstasy,
        Finds the image in his heart.

No. 278   Short Hymn on Luke 17:21
. . . the Kingdom of God is within you.
("Ms. Luke")

    Love, the power of humble love
        Constitutes thy kingdom here:
    Never, never to remove[,]
        Let it, Lord, in me appear,
    Let the pure, internal grace
        Fill my new-created soul,
    Peace, and joy, and righteousness,
        While eternal ages roll.

No. 279   Short Hymn on Luke 19:11
. . . the kingdom of God should immediately appear.
("Ms. Luke")

1   NOW, e'en now the Kingdom 's near,
        Peace, and joy, and righteousness,
    Soon it shall in us appear:
        Reverent joy, victorious peace,
    Real righteousness brought in
        Roots out selfishness and pride,
    Finishes the inbred sin,
        Makes us like the Crucified.

2   Nature cannot comprehend
        Jesus reigning on the Cross,
    That we may on Him depend,
        Suffering, dying in his cause;
    Nature would in pomp and state
        High at his right-hand sit down,
    Suddenly by rich and great,
        Shun the cross, but snatch the crown.

No. 280   Short Hymn on Luke 24:10
. . . the other women were with them. . . .
("Ms. Luke")

More courageous than the men,
   When Christ his breath resign'd,
Women first the grace obtain
   Their living Lord to find,
Women first the news proclaim,
   Know his resurrection's power
Teach th' Apostles of the Lamb
   Who lives to die no more.

No. 281   Short Hymn on John 1:18
No man hath seen God at any time, . . .
("Ms. John")[7]

1   Thee, Son of the Most High,
          Jesus we glorify
In Thy Father's bosom laid,
        Thou dost all His secrets know,
Partner of our nature made
        Dost declare His name below.

2   With eyes of faith we see
          Th' Invisible in Thee,
When Thou dost Thy Sire reveal,
        Then I know Thee who Thou art,
Find the great Unsearchable,
        God residing in my heart.

3   Thou dost the Spirit confer,
          The heavenly Comforter;
Thus the triune God of love
        God of glory we receive,
Antedate the joys above,
        Here the life eternal live.

No. 282   Short Hymn on John 5:1
There is at Jerusalem a pool which is called
Bethesda, . . .
("Ms. John")

O Jesus I see
My Bethesda in Thee;

Thou art full of compassion and mercy for me;
> Thy blood is the pool,
> Both for body and soul,
And whoever steps in, is made perfectly whole.

No. 283   Short Hymn on John 6:53
Except ye eat the flesh of the Son of God, and drink
his blood, ye have no life in you.
("Ms. John")

1   How blind the misconceiving crowd,
> Who in the literal substance dream
They eat Thy flesh and drink Thy blood!
> Alas there is no life in them:
And who partake of th' external sign,
> Without the hidden mystery,
They eat the bread, and drink the wine,
> But never feed, O Lord, on Thee.

2   What is it then, Thy flesh to eat?
> O give mine inmost soul to know
The nature of that heavenly meat,
> Ordain'd to quicken all below:
What is it, Lord, to drink Thy blood?
> Explain it to this heart of mine,
And fill me with the life of God,
> The Love, the holiness Divine.

No. 284   Short Hymn on John 9:2
Who did sin, this man, or his parents, . . .
("Ms. John")

Let every child of *Adam* own
> The cause of all his sufferings here:
The cause is sin and sin alone,
> And death and hell are in the rear!
My parents' sins engender'd pain,
> Entail'd eternal death on me;
Who still in misery bound remain,
> Till Christ appears to set me free.

No. 285   Short Hymn on John 18:38
Pilate saith unto Him, What is truth?
("Ms. John")

1   The men who human praise desire
    Who set their heart on things below,
Like *Pilate* carelessly inquire,
    But will not wait the truth to know,
But soon their slighted Lord forsake,
And cast His words behind their back.

2   Not with a cold or double heart
    But faith's sincerity unfeign'd
We ask Thee Saviour to impart
    The knowledge in Thyself contain'd,
And give our ~~hallow'd~~ new-born souls to prove,
~~The Truth of purity and Love~~
The Truth, the Life of perfect Love.

No. 286   Short Hymn on John 19:30
It is finish'd!
(*Poetical Works*, XII, 99)

1   'Tis finish'd! The *Messia[h]* dies,
    Cut off for sins, but not His own!
Accomplish'd is the sacrifice,
    The great redeeming work is done.

2   'Tis finish'd! all the debt is paid;
    Justice Divine is satisfied;
The grand and full atonement made;
    God for a guilty world hath died.

3   The veil is rent in Christ alone;
    The living way to heaven is seen;
The middle wall is broken down,
    And all mankind may enter in.

4   The types and figures are fulfill'd;
    Exacted is the legal pain;
The precious promises are seal'd;
    The spotless Lamb of God is slain.

5   The reign of sin and death is o'er,
    And all may live from sin set free;
Satan hath lost his mortal power;
    'Tis swallow'd up in victory.

6 Saved from the legal curse I am,
    My Saviour hangs on yonder tree:
See there the meek, expiring Lamb!
    'Tis finish'd! He expires for me.

7 Accepted in the Well-beloved,
    And clothed in righteousness Divine,
I see the bar to heaven removed;
    And all Thy merits, Lord, are mine.

8 Death, hell, and sin are now subdued;
    All grace is now to sinners given;
And lo, I plead th' atoning blood,
    And in Thy right I claim Thy heaven.

No. 287 Short Hymn on John 21:18
He saith unto him, Feed my Lambs.
("Ms. John")

Help me[,] Lord, to find and keep
First the Lambs and then the Sheep
Lambs to make my tenderest care,
Lambs within my arms to bear;
Both my happy charge I make,
Both I cherish for Thy sake,
Thus in life and death to prove
Lov'd of Thee that I Thee love.

No. 288 Short Hymn on Acts 11:8
Not so Lord; for nothing common or unclean. . . .
("Ms. Acts")

I want the gospel purity,
    Th' implanted righteousness of God:
Jesus reveal thyself to me,
    And wash me in thy hallowing blood;
Enter, thyself, and cast out sin,
    Thy nature spread thro' every part,
And nothing common or unclean
    Shall ever more pollute my heart.

No. 289   Short Hymn on Rom. 1:16
For I am not ashamed of the gospel of Christ: . . .
(*Poetical Works*, XIII, 3)

1   Superior to all fear and shame,
        Entrusted with the gospel-word,
    Through earth I glory to proclaim
        The love of my redeeming Lord,
    Which could so strange a method find
    To save our lost, apostate kind.

2   Jehovah's co-eternal Son
        Did in our flesh appear beneath,
    He laid His life a ransom down,
        For every man He tasted death,
    To justify us by His blood,
    And bring the sprinkled world to God.

3   Whoe'er the joyful news believes,
        Pardon'd through instantaneous grace,
    The saving power Divine receives;
        And while on Christ his soul he stays,
    He gains at last the perfect love,
    And mingles with the saints above.

No. 290   Short Hymn on Rom. 8:24
We are saved by hope.
(*Poetical Works*, XIII, 13)

    Saved by faith we once have been
    From the guilt and power of sin,
    But while the dire root remains,
    Hope our fainting soul sustains:
    Tempted to give up our shield,
    Saved by hope we cannot yield,
    Saved by hope, we wait to prove.
    All the holiness of love.

No. 291   Short Hymn on 1 Thes. 5:17
Pray without ceasing.
(*Poetical Works*, XIII, 93)

    Father, into my heart convey
    The power incessantly to pray,

> Or Thy command is void:
> But when the Power inhabits there,
> My heart shall be a house of prayer,
> Emptied, and fill'd with God.

No. 292   Short Hymn on Heb. 12:14
Follow . . . holiness.
(*Poetical Works*, XIII, 159)

1   That finish'd holiness,
   My calling's prize I see,
Consummate love, and perfect peace,
   And spotless purity,
   The nature and the mind,
   And image of my Lord,
I follow on with Christ to find,
   With paradise restored.

2   In all the works of faith
   My object I pursue,
   And strive in duty's narrow path,
   To keep the prize in view,
   I grasp the crown above,
   In sure and patient hope
And strain to reach the mountain top
   In all the toils of love.

3   I urge the race begun,
   The cross of Jesus bear,
And fight, and strive, and wrestle on
   In agony of prayer;
   In Jesu's footsteps tread,
   Hard following after God,
Partake the travail of my Head,
   And sweat His sweat of blood.

4   A thousand times I faint,
   Yet rise with spirit new,
With warmer zeal, and keener want,
   My Saviour to pursue.
   Saviour, my all Thou art,
   Enter this struggling breast,
And bid me now in peace depart
   To love's eternal rest.

No. 293   Short Hymn on James 2:14 [Greek text]
Can that faith save him.
(*Poetical Works*, XIII, 168)

> In vain thou say'st in words alone
>   Unproved by works, that "faith I have!"
> The faith by works which is not shown,
>   From sin[,] from hell can never save,
> Unprofitable all and void,
> The faith of man, and not of God.

No. 294   Short Hymn on James 2:15, 16
If a brother . . . be naked and destitute. . . .
(*Poetical Works*, XIII, 168)

> What doth thy *Gnostic* faith avail,
>   Who seest thy brother in distress,
> With ruthless heart insensible,
>   And bidd'st the poor depart in peace,
> Yet dost not his distress relieve,
> But words without assistance give!

NOTES

1. *JW Journal*, IV, p. 361, discusses Charles's editorial role in the preparation of John's famous *Notes Upon the New Testament*.

2. *P.W.*, I, p. 148, a hymn that Charles called "Hymn on the Titles of Christ," appeared in more recent hymnals in an altered form and headed "Arise My Soul Arise." The Authorized Version rendered the Phil. 2:7 passage as "he made himself of no reputation, and took the form of a servant." The translation studiously avoided the startling impact of the Greek word *ekenose*, "he emptied." Wesley's poetic rendition offered no evasion, and prefigured more modern readings of the passage:

> He left His throne above,
> *Emptied of all but love,*
> Whom the heavens cannot contain,
> God vouchsafed a worm t' appear,
> Poor, and vile, and abject here.

3. Charles's "Preface" to the *Short Hymns on Select Passages of Scripture* reported several of the sources he utilized in that project, and others emerged throughout the hymnological corpus. Among the commentators Wesley scrutinized were Robert Gell (1595–1695), who wrote a commentary *On the Pentateuch*, Matthew Henry's *Exposition of the Old and New Testament* (1708–1710), Johann Albrecht Bengel's *Gnomon Novi Testamenti* (1742), and the (then) recent work of William Jones of Nayland, *The Catholic Doctrine of the Trinity Proved by a Hundred Short and Clear Arguments Expressed in the term of the Holy Scriptures in a manner Entirely New* (1756). He was also quite familiar with brother John's *Notes upon the Old Testament* (1765) and *Notes upon the New Testament* (1754). Cf. *P.W.*, VII, p. 204; *P.W.*, IX, p. viii; Jackson, *CW Journal*, I, p. 285.

4. "Ms. Acts" located in the Methodist Archives and Research Centre, The John Rylands University Library of Manchester, Manchester, England. The manuscript was prepared between 1764 and 1765. It carries nearly one thousand short hymns, approximately one third of which remain unpublished. This hymn and others from this manuscript source are printed by permission of the Methodist Church Archives and History Committee, England.

5. "Ms. Matthew" contains nearly eight hundred poems on Matthew's gospel, almost all of which were published either in Charles Wesley's *Short Hymns* of 1762 or in *P.W.* Charles's note at the end of the volume indicated that "Ms. Matthew" was completed March 8, 1766. This hymn and others from the same source are printed with permission of the Methodist Church Archives and History Committee, England.

6. "Ms. Luke" contains nearly eight hundred hymns based on Luke's gospel, less than half of which have never been published. Charles's notation indicated that the collection was completed April 29, 1766. The manuscript is housed in the Methodist Archives and Research Centre, The John Rylands University Library of Manchester, Manchester, England. This hymn and others from "Ms. Luke" are printed here by permission of the Methodist Church Archives and History Committee, England.

7. "Ms. John" contains almost eight hundred hymns based on the Fourth Gospel, one fifth of which have never been published. Charles's record indicates that the volume was completed April 30, 1764. The manuscript is located in the Methodist Archives and Research Centre, The John Rylands University Library of Manchester, Manchester, England. Hymns from "Ms. John" are printed here by permission of the Methodist Church Archives and History Committee, England.

13 / The Final Days

Charles Wesley's declining years were punctuated by bouts of serious illness and flurries of ministerial activity. A hymn, one of his most autobiographical, reveals his state of mind during this final period. Written between December 3, 1763, and April 30, 1764, the following unpublished hymn revealed Charles's growing sense of physical frailty and increasing resignation of himself to the will of God. The text under consideration was John 21:18, in which Jesus told Peter: "When thou wast young, thou girdest thyself, and walkest whither thou wouldst: but when thou shalt be old, thou shalt stretch forth thy hands, and another shall gird thee, and carry thee whither thou wouldst not." (KJV)[1]

No. 295   Short Hymn on John 21:18
("Ms. John")

1 When young, and full of sanguine hope,
    And warm in my first love,
My spirit's loins I girded up,
    And sought the things above,
Swift on the wings of active zeal
    With Jesu's message flew,
O'erjoy'd with all my heart and will
    My Master's work to do.

2 Freely where'er I would, I went
    Through Wisdom's pleasant ways,
Happy to spend and to be spent
    In minist'ring his grace:
I found no want of will or power,
    In love's sweet task employ'd,
And put forth every day and hour
    My utmost strength for God.

3   As strong, and glorying in my might,
        I drew the two-edged sword,
    Valiant against a troop to fight
        The battles of the Lord;
    I scorn'd the multitude to dread,
        Rush'd on with full career,
    And aim'd at each opposer's head,
        And smote off many an ear.

4   But now, enervated by age,
        I feel my fierceness gone,
    And nature's powers no more engage
        To prop the Saviour's throne:
    My total impotence I see,
        For help on Jesus call,
    And stretch my feeble hands to thee,
        Who workest all in all.

5   Thy captive, Lord, myself I yield,
        As purely passive clay;
    Thy holy will be all fulfill'd,
        Constraining mine t' obey:
    My passions by thy Spirit bind,
        And, govern'd by thy word,
    I'll suffer all the woes design'd
        To make me like my Lord.

6   Wholly at thy dispose I am,
        No longer at my own,
    All self-activity disclaim,
        And move in God alone;
    Transport, do what thou wilt with me,
        A few more evil days,
    But bear me safe through all to see
        My dear Redeemer's face.

Charles's final illness began in February 1788. Brother John's letters from that spring are full of folk remedies he was certain would restore Charles's health.[2] By mid-March he was unable to take nourishment, or keep anything in his stomach. The family sent for Dr. Whitehead, whom John Wesley's letter of March 7 recommended as the finest physician in England.[3] Whitehead visited Charles several times and has left a recollection of Wesley's final days.[4]

The doctor remembered that Charles wrote the following hymn "a little before his death." It was probably the last poem he actually wrote, though at least one other was dictated to his wife.[5]

No. 296   Short Hymn on Hos. 14:2
Take away all iniquity, and give good
(*Poetical Works* VIII, 431–432)

1   How long, how often shall I pray,
    Take all iniquity away,
    And give the plenitude of good,
    The blessing bought by Jesus' blood,
    Concupiscence and pride remove,
    And fill me, Lord, with humble love.

2   Again I take the words to me
    Prescribed, and offer them to Thee,
    Thy kingdom come to root out sin,
    And perfect holiness bring in,
    And swallow up my will in Thine,
    And human change into Divine.

3   So shall I render Thee Thine own,
    And tell the wonders Thou hast done,
    The power and faithfulness declare
    Of God who hears and answers prayer,
    Extol the riches of Thy grace
    And spend my latest breath in praise.

4   O that the joyful hour was come
    Which calls Thy ready servant home,
    Unite me to the church above,
    Where angels chant the song of love,
    And saints eternally proclaim
    The glories of the heavenly Lamb!

No. 297   Dr. Whitehead's Account of Charles Wesley's Death[6]

Mr. Charles Wesley had a weak body, and a poor state of health, during the greater part of his life. I believe he laid the foundation of both, at Oxford, by too close application to study, and abstinence from food. He rode much on horse back, which probably contributed to lengthen out life to a good old age. I visited him several times in his last sickness, and his body was indeed reduced to the most extreme state of weakness. He possessed that state of mind which he had always been pleased to see in others—unaffected humility, and holy resignation to the will of God. He had no transports of joy, but solid hope and unshaken confidence in Christ, which kept his mind in perfect peace. A few days before his death he composed the following lines. Having been quiet for some time, he called Mrs. Wesley to him, and bid her write as he dictated:

No. 298   "Lines Dictated on His Death Bed"

In age and feebleness extreme,
Who shall a helpless worm redeem?
Jesus! my only hope Thou art,
Strength of my failing flesh and heart;
Oh! could I catch one smile from Thee
And drop into eternity!

The following account of Charles's death was composed by his daughter, Sarah
Wesley, and mailed to her uncle John, April 4, 1788.[7]

No. 299   Sarah Wesley's Account of Her Father's Death

Dear honoured Uncle,—We were all present when my dear, respected
father departed this life. His end was, what he particularly wished it might
be, peace!

For some months past he seemed totally detached from earth. He spoke
very little, nor wished to hear anything read but the Scriptures.

He took a solemn leave of all his friends. I once asked if he had any
presages that he should die. He said, "No," but his weakness was such,
that he thought it impossible he "should live through March." He kindly
bade me remember him, and seemed to have no doubt but I should meet
him in heaven.

All his prayer was, "Patience, and an easy death!" He bade every one
who visited him to supplicate for these; often repeating, "An easy death!"

He told my mother, the week before he departed, that no fiend [i.e.,
doubt] was permitted to approach him; and said to us all, "I have a *good
hope!*"

When we asked if he wanted anything, he frequently answered, "Nothing but Christ!"

Some person observed, that the valley of the shadow of death was hard
to be passed. "Not with Christ," replied he.

On March 27th, after a most uneasy night, he prayed, as in an agony,
that he might not have many such nights. "O my God," said he, "*not
many!*"

It was with great difficulty he seemed to speak. About ten days before,
on my brother Samuel's entering the room, he took hold of his hand, and
pronounced, with a voice of faith, "I shall bless God to all eternity, that
ever you were born. I am persuaded I shall!"

My brother Charles [Jr.] also seemed much upon his mind. "That dear
boy!" said he, "God bless him!"

He spoke less to me than to the rest, which has since given me some pain. However, he bade me trust in God, and never forsake Him; and then he assured me, that He would never forsake me.

The 28th my mother asked if he had anything to say to us. Raising his eyes, he said, "Only thanks! love! blessing!"

Tuesday and Wednesday he was not entirely sensible. He slept much, without refreshment, and had the restlessness of death, for I think, the whole week.

He was eager to depart; and if we moved him, or spoke to him, he answered, "Let me die! let me die!"

A fortnight before he prayed, with many tears, for all his enemies, naming Miss Freeman. "I beseech thee, O Lord, by Thine agony and bloody sweat," said he, "that she may never feel the pangs of eternal death."

When your kind letter to my brother came (in which you affectionately tell him, that you will be a father to him and to my brother Samuel), I read it to our father. "He will *be kind to you*," said he, "when I am gone. I am certain your uncle *will be kind* to all of you."

The last morning, which was the 29th of March, being unable to speak, my mother entreated him to press her hand, if he knew her; which he feebly did.

His last words which I could hear were, "Lord—my heart,—my God!" He then drew his breath short, and the last so gently, that we knew not exactly the moment in which his happy spirit fled.

His dear hand was in mine for five minutes before, and at the awful period of, his dissolution.

It had often been his desire that we should attend him to the grave; and though he did not mention it again (which he did the place of his burial) during his illness, we all mean to fulfill his wish; trusting we shall be supported, as we have been hitherto, in our afflicting situations.

My dear, honoured uncle, my mother presents you her respectful love, and my brothers join me in duty, begging your prayers for the widow and the fatherless! I am

Your afflicted and dutiful niece.

No. 300   Dr. Whitehead's Testimonial[8]

Five years after Charles's death, his physician and friend John Whitehead also composed a short summary of his life. The recollection closed with an advertisement for the projected publication of Charles Wesley's sermons, which were not published, however, until 1816.

Mr. Wesley was of a warm and lively disposition; of great frankness and integrity, and generous and steady in his friendships. His love of simplicity, and utter abhorrence of hypocrisy, and even of affectation in the professions of religion, made him sometimes appear severe on those who assumed a consequence, on account of their experience, or were pert and forward in talking of themselves and others. These persons were sure of meeting with a reproof from him, which some, perhaps, might call precipitate and imprudent, though it was evidently founded on a knowledge of the human heart. In conversation he was pleasing, instructive, and cheerful; and his observations were often seasoned with wit and humour. His religion was genuine and unaffected. As a minister, he was familiarly acquainted with every part of divinity [theology]; and his mind was furnished with an uncommon knowledge of the Scriptures. His discourses from the pulpit were not dry and systematic, but flowed from the present views and feelings of his own mind. He had a remarkable talent of expressing the most important truths with simplicity and energy; and his discourses were sometimes truly apostolic, forcing conviction on the hearers in spite of the most determined opposition. As a husband, a father, and a friend, his character was amiable. Mrs. Wesley brought him five children, of whom two sons and a daughter are still living. The sons discovered a taste for music, and a fine musical ear, at an early period of infancy, which excited general amazement; and are now justly admired by the best judges for their talent in that pleasing art.

From a review of the life of Mr. Charles Wesley, as delineated in the preceding sheets, it will appear evident, that the Methodists are greatly indebted to him for his unwearied labours and great usefulness at the first formation of the societies, when every step was attended with difficulty and danger. And being dead he yet speaketh, by his numerous and excellent hymns, written for the use of the societies, which still continue to be the means of daily edification to thousands. It had been proposed to publish a volume of his sermons, selected from his manuscripts, for the benefit of his widow: if this should be done, it is hoped the Methodists will show their gratitude to his memory, and that they are not unworthy of the benefits they have received from him.

No. 301   Death Notice from the Minutes of Methodist Conference: 1788[9]

Mr. Charles Wesley, who, after spending fourscore years with much sorrow and pain, quietly retired into Abraham's bosom. He had no disease; but after a gradual decay of some months,

> The weary wheels of life stood still at last.

His least praise was, his talent for poetry; although Dr. Watts did not scruple to say, that "that single poem Wrestling Jacob, is worth all the verses which I have ever written."

No. 302   Charles Wesley's Epitaph (from Memorial Plaque in Wesley's Chapel, City Road, London)

God buries his workmen, but carries on his work.

SACRED TO THE MEMORY
of
THE REV. CHARLES WESLEY, M.A.

Educated at Westminster School,
And Sometime Student at Christ-Church, Oxford.
As a Preacher,
He was eminent for ability, zeal, and usefulness
Being learned without pride,
And pious without ostentation;
To the sincere, diffident Christian,
A Son of Consolation;
But to the vain boaster, the hypocrite, and the profane,
A Son of Thunder.

He was the first who received The Name of Methodist;
And, uniting with his brother, The Rev. John Wesley,
In the plan of Itinerant Preaching,
Endured hardship, persecution, and disgrace,
As a good Soldier of Jesus Christ;
Contributing largely, by the usefulness of his labours,
To the first formation of the Methodist Societies
In these Kingdoms.

As a Christian Poet He Stood Unrivaled;
And his hymns will convey instruction and consolation
To the faithful in Christ Jesus,
As long as the English language shall be understood.

He Was Born the XVIII of December, MDCCVIII,
And Died the XXIX of March, MDCCLXXXVIII,
A firm and pious believer in the doctrines of the Gospel,
And a sincere friend to the Church of England.

NOTES

1. "Ms. John," pp. 461–462, *op. cit.* Printed by permission of the Methodist Church Archives and History Committee, England.

2. *JW Letters*, VIII, pp. 42, 43, 45, 49, 51; the last reports John Wesley's reaction to the news of Charles's death.

3. *Ibid.*, VIII, p. 43. Letter to Sarah Wesley, Charles's daughter, John's niece, dated March 7, 1788.

4. John Whitehead, M.D., ed., *The Life of the Rev. John Wesley, M.A. Some Time Fellow of Lincoln College, Oxford, Collected From His Private Papers, and Printed Works; and Written at the Request of His Executors. To Which is Prefixed Some Account of His Ancestors and Relations; with The Life of the Rev. Charles Wesley, M.A., Collected from His Private Journal, and Never Before Published. The Whole Forming a History of Methodism, in Which the Principles and Economy of the Methodists are Unfolded* (London: Stephen Couchman, 1793).

5. The Methodists' *Arminian Magazine* carried this hymn on page 446 of its 1788 edition. It was described as being "written a little before the author's death." George Osborn, editor of the massive *Poetical Works of John and Charles Wesley,* suggests that it was Charles's last written hymn (*P.W.,* VIII, pp. 431–432).

6. Whitehead, *Life of John and Charles Wesley, op, cit.,* pp. 209ff.

7. Jackson, *Life of Charles Wesley, op. cit.,* II, pp. 442–444.

8. Whitehead, *op. cit.*

9. *JW Works,* XIII, p. 514.

Appendix A / Charles Wesley's Favorite Sermon Texts

TEXT		PASSAGE	OCCURRENCES
John	1:36	"Behold the Lamb of God"	22
Luke	10:29	"The Good Samaritan"	18
Mark	1:15	"Repent Ye and Believe"	15
Matt.	11:28	"Come all Ye that are weak . . ."	15
Luke	15:11	"The Prodigal Son"	14
Isa.	35	"Expounded"	12
John	7:37	"Everyone that thirsteth . . ."	12
Lam.	1:12	"All ye who pass by . . ."	10
Luke	10:42	"One Thing Necessary"	9
Gal.	3:22	"All under sin . . ."	9

EIGHT OCCURRENCES

Matt.	1:21	"Call him Jesus . . ."
John	11	"Expounded"
Isa.	53	"Expounded"
Gen.	32:24	"Wrestling Jacob"
Isa.	40:1	"Comfort ye my people"
Rev.	7:14	"Out of the tribulation"

SEVEN OCCURRENCES

Matt.	10:46	"Blind Bartimaeus"
Eph.	6:10	"The Whole Armour of God"
Zech.	13:9	"The third part through fire . . ."

SIX OCCURRENCES

John	3:16	"For God so loved the world"
John	5:2	"The Pool of Bethesda"
Matt.	10:22	"Endureth to the End"
Isa.	64:5	"Thou meetest him . . ."

TEXT   PASSAGE

FIVE OCCURRENCES

1 John	3:14	"The Threefold State"
Eph.	2:8	"By grace ye are saved"
John	3:5	"Whatsoever he saith . . . do it"
Rom.	7	"Expounded"
Mark	7:24	"The Syro-Phoenician Woman"
Matt.	11:5	"The Blind receive their sight . . ."
Matt.	5:1–11	"The Beatitudes"

FOUR OCCURRENCES

Ezek.	37	"The Dry Bones"
Mark	5:25	"The Bloody Issue"
Titus	2:11	"I shall go away . . ."
[various]		"The Seven Last Words of Jesus"
Rev.	22:17	"The Spirit and the Bride . . ."
Rev.	2:10	"Fear none of these things . . ."
John	10:10	"I come that they might have life"
Luke	21:34	"Take heed to yourselves"
Acts	2:42	"They continued . . ."
Rev.	3:20	"I stand at the door"
1 Tim.	1:15	"A faithful saying"

THREE OCCURRENCES

John	4	"Expounded"
1 Cor.	1:30	"Wisdom, righteousness . . ."
2 Cor.	5:19	"God was in Christ reconciling . . ."
John	1	"Expounded"
Rom.	8	"Expounded"
Luke	14:7	"The Great Supper"
Rom.	8:31	"If God be for you . . ."
Isa.	58	"Expounded"
Acts	16:30	"What must I do to be saved?"
Ezek.	16	"Expounded"
Num.	14	"Expounded"
Rom.	8:32	"He spared not His own Son"
Luke	7:22	"Go tell John . . ."
Luke	19:10	"For the Son of Man is come . . ."
Luke	4:18	"The Spirit of the Lord . . ."
Heb.	13:8	"Jesus Christ the same . . ."
John	17	"Expounded"
Matt.	9:12	"The Physician"
Luke	7:36	"Into the Pharisee's house . . ."
Luke	21:28	"Lift up your hands . . ."

TEXT		PASSAGE

TWO OCCURRENCES

Rom.	5	"Expounded"
John	14:25	"These things . . ."
John	16	"The Comforter"
1 Cor.	6:9	"The Unrighteous . . ."
Mark	2:10	"The Son of Man . . ."
Rom.	9	"Expounded"
Rom.	12	"Expounded"
John	1:12	"As many as received Him . . ."
Matt.	5:11	"Blessed are ye . . ."
2 Cor.	5:17	"New Creatures"
Isa.	45:8	"Drop down ye heavens . . ."
Luke	4:8	"Prophet, Priest, and King"
Isa.	1	"Expounded"
Acts	2	"Expounded"
Isa.	63:1,2	"Preached Christ . . ."
Rev.	2:24	"As many that have not . . ."
Luke	2:25	"Simeon's Song"
1 Kings	19:11	"Go forth and stand . . ."
1 Cor.	10	"Expounded"
Acts	14:22	"Through much tribulation"
Acts	22:19	"And Saul said . . ."
Isa.	54	"Expounded"
Matt.	21:28	"A certain man had two sons . . ."
Acts	20:32	"An inheritance . . ."
Rev.	3:14	"The Laodicean Spirit"
Lam.	3:22	"The Lord's Army"
Matt.	21:19	"The Fig Tree"
Mark	4:3f	"The Sower"
Isa.	51	"Expounded"
Luke	12:32	"Greater than Jonas . . ."
Isa.	2:10	"Enter into the Rock . . ."
Luke	12:31	"Seek ye the kingdom . . ."
1 John	5:6	"Came by water and by blood"
John	19:30	"It is finished . . ."
Rev.	21	"Expounded"
1 Pet.	2:12	"The eyes of the Lord . . ."
Ps.	46	"Expounded"
Zech.	4:7	"Who art thou . . . ?"
1 Pet.	4:7	"The end of all things . . ."
Acts	26:18	"From darkness to light"
Matt.	27:25	"His blood be upon us"
Rev.	3:2,3	"Be watchful . . ."
Zech.	13:6	"What are these wounds . . ."
Isa.	35:10	"The ransomed of the Lord"
Matt.	7:7	"Ask and it shall be given"

TEXT		PASSAGE
Hos.	11:8	"How shall I give thee up"
Heb.	4:16	"Let us . . . come boldly"
Acts	3:19	"Repent ye . . ."
Gen.	22:18	"In thy seed . . ."
Luke	14:15	"Blessed is he . . ."
Col.	3:1	"If ye be risen with Christ"
Zech.	12:10	"I will pour . . ."
Luke	2:11	"Unto you is born this day"
Rev.	1:7	"He cometh with clouds"
Matt.	6:10	"Thy Kingdom come . . ."
Matt.	25:1	"Ten Virgins"
Zech.	3:9	"Behold the stone . . ."

Appendix B / Christological Titles in Wesley's Later Hymns

TITLE	H.S.P. (1749)	P.W. 9	P.W. 10	P.W. 11	P.W. 12	P.W. 13
Lord	379	112	242	276	205	80
Saviour	122	109	113	133	107	65
Lamb	113	23	26	27	34	21
Christ	38	78	124	175	120	67
Friend[1]	34	21	24	17	21	9
Judge	33	6	17	21	8	4
Prince[2]	24	6	9	7	10	1
Redeemer	31	20	18	19	28	16
Head	15	5	14	21	25	27
Captain	13	9	0	4	1	1
King	14	19	21	24	5	16
Shepherd	13	3	9	13	2	4
Master	12	5	26	36	24	4
Physician	12	3	19	10	4	0
Hope	11	21	1	3	1	0
Comforter	13	5	2	2	0	0
Bridegroom	7	0	1	2	1	1
Advocate	0	12	4	8	0	1
Rock	7	13	1	0	2	3
Immanuel	6	2	2	2	0	1
Brother	6	2	2	0	0	0
Husband	6	2	1	1	0	0
Conqueror	6	1	1	3	0	3
Man of Griefs	5	3	6	6	6	2
The Crucified	5	3	5	5	3	6
Son of Man	4	5	10	5	5	0

[1] As in the phrase "Jesus, Friend of sinners."
[2] Chiefly referring to the title "Prince of Peace."

Selected Bibliography

PRIMARY SOURCES

*Charles Wesley's Manuscripts**

Ms. Acts.
Ms. Brothers.
Ms. Cheshunt, held by the Cheshunt Foundation, Westminster College, Cambridge, England.
Ms. Clark.
Ms. John.
Ms. Luke.
Ms. Matthew.
Ms. Miscellaneous Hymns.
Ms. Ordinations.
Ms. Preparation for Death.
Ms. Scripture Hymns.

Published Primary Sources

Albin, Thomas A., and Oliver A. Beckerlegge, eds. *Charles Wesley's Earliest Sermons: Six Manuscript Shorthand Sermons Hitherto Unpublished.* A forthcoming occasional publication of the Wesley Historical Society (England).
Baker, Frank. *Charles Wesley as Revealed by His Letters.* London: Epworth Press, 1948.
Baker, Frank, ed. *The Representative Verse of Charles Wesley.* London: Epworth Press, 1962.
Curnock, Nehemiah, ed. *The Journal of John Wesley,* Standard Edition, 8 vols. London: Epworth Press, 1909–16.
Heitzenrater, Richard. *The Elusive Mr. Wesley,* 2 vols. Nashville: Abingdon Press, 1984.
Jackson, Thomas, ed. *The Journal of Charles Wesley,* 2 vols. London: John Mason Publisher, 1849. Reprinted by Baker Book House, 1980.
Osborn, George, ed. *The Poetical Works of John and Charles Wesley,* 13 vols. London: Wesleyan-Methodist Conference, 1868–1872.

---

*All of these manuscripts, unless otherwise indicated, are located in the Methodist Archives and Research Centre, The John Rylands University Library of Manchester, Manchester, England.

Telford, John, ed. *The Letters of John Wesley,* Standard Edition, 8 vols. London: Epworth Press, 1931.

Wesley, Charles. *Sermons by the Late Rev. Charles Wesley.* London: J. Baldwin, Craddock, and Joy, 1816.

Wesley, John, ed. *A Collection of Hymns for the use of the People called Methodists.* London: J. Paramore, 1780.

SECONDARY SOURCES

Baker, Frank. *Charles Wesley's Verse: An Introduction.* London: Epworth Press, 1964.

Bett, Henry. *The Hymns of Methodism in Their Literary Relations.* London: Epworth Press, 1912 (third edition, 1956).

Brailsford, Mabel Richmond. *A Tale of Two Brothers.* London: Hart-Davis, 1954.

Church, Leslie F. "Charles Wesley—the Man." *London Quarterly and Holborn Review* 182, no. 4 (Oct. 1957): 247–53.

Dale, James. "The Theological and Literary Qualities of the Poetry of Charles Wesley in Relation to the Standards of His Age." Ph.D. dissertation, Cambridge University, 1960.

Dixon, Neil. "The Wesleys' Conversion Hymn." *Proceedings of the Wesley Historical Society* 37, no. 1 (Feb. 1969–1970): 43–47.

Doughty, W. L. "Charles Wesley, Preacher." *London Quarterly and Holborn Review* 182 (1957): 263–67.

Edwards, Maldwyn. *Family Circle.* London: Epworth Press, 1949.

Edwards, Maldwyn. *Sons to Samuel.* London: Epworth Press, 1961.

England, Martha Winburn, and John Sparrow. *Hymns Unbidden.* New York: New York Public Library, 1966.

Findlay, George. *Christ's Standard Bearer.* London: Epworth Press, 1956.

Gill, Frederick. *Charles Wesley, the First Methodist.* Nashville: Abingdon Press, 1964.

Green, Richard. *The Works of John and Charles Wesley—A Bibliography.* London: C. H. Kelley, 1896.

Heitzenrater, Richard. "John Wesley's Early Sermons." *The Proceedings of the Wesley Historical Society* 37, no. 4 (Feb. 1970): 110–28.

Hildebrandt, Franz. *I offered Christ.* London: Epworth Press, 1967.

Hodgson, E. M. "John or Charles?" *Proceedings of the Wesley Historical Society* 41, no. 3 (Oct. 1977): 73–76.

Holland, Bernard. "The Conversions of John and Charles Wesley." *Proceedings of the Wesley Historical Society* 38, no. 2 (1971–1972): 46–53, 51–65.

Jackson, Thomas. *The Life of the Rev. Charles Wesley,* 2 vols. London: J. Mason, 1841.

Jones, D. M. *Charles Wesley, a Study.* London: Epworth, n.d.

Langford, Thomas. *Practical Divinity: Theology in the Wesleyan Tradition.* Nashville: Abingdon Press, 1983.

Lindstrom, Harold. *Wesley and Sanctification.* Grand Rapids: Francis Asbury Press, n.d.

Manning, Bernard. *The Hymns of Wesley and Watts.* London: Epworth Press, 1943.

Mitchell, T. Crichton. "Response to Dr. Timothy Smith on the Wesley Hymns." *Wesleyan Theological Journal* 16, no. 2 (Fall 1981): 48–58.

Noll, Mark, A. "Romanticism and the Hymns of Charles Wesley." *Evangelical Quarterly* 46, no. 2 (April–June 1974): 195–223.

Nuelson, John Louis. *John Wesley and the German Hymns.* Claverly, England: A. S. Holbrook, 1977.

Outler, Albert C., ed. *John Wesley.* New York: Oxford University Press, 1964.

Rattenbury, John Earnest. *The Conversions of the Wesleys.* London: Epworth Press, 1938.

Rattenbury, John Earnest. *The Eucharist Hymns of John and Charles Wesley*. London: Epworth Press, 1948.

Rattenbury, John Earnest. *The Evangelical Doctrines of Charles Wesley's Hymns*. London: Epworth Press, 1941.

Routley, Erik. *The Musical Wesleys*. London: Jenkins, 1968.

Rowe, Kenneth, ed. *The Place of Wesley in the Christian Tradition*. Metuchen, New Jersey: Scarecrow Press, 1976.

Runyon, Theodore, ed. *Sanctification and Liberation: Liberation Theologies in Light of the Wesleyan Tradition*. Nashville: Abingdon, 1981.

Smith, Timothy. "The Holy Spirit in the Hymns of the Wesleys." *Wesleyan Theological Journal* 16, no. 2 (Fall 1981): 20–48.

Swift, Wesley. "Brothers Charles and John." *London Quarterly and Holborn Review* 182, no. 4 (Oct. 1957): 275–80.

Telford, John. *The Life of Charles Wesley*. London: Wesleyan Book Room, 1900.

Townsend, James A. "Feelings Related to Assurance in Charles Wesley's Hymns." Ph.D. dissertation, Fuller Theological Seminary, Pasadena, California, 1979.

Tyerman, Luke. *The Life and Times of Rev. John Wesley, A. M.*, 3 vols. New York: Harper and Brothers, 1872.

Tyson, John R. "Charles Wesley and the German Hymns." *The Hymn* 35, no. 3 (July 1984): 153–58.

Tyson, John R. *Charles Wesley on Sanctification: A Biographical and Theological Study*. Grand Rapids: Francis Asbury Press, 1986.

Tyson, John R. "John Wesley and William Law: A Reappraisal." *Wesleyan Theological Journal* 17, no. 2 (Fall 1982): 58–79.

Tyson, John R., with Douglas Lister. "Charles Wesley, Pastor: A Glimpse Inside His Shorthand Journal." *Quarterly Review* 4, no. 1 (Spring 1984): 9–22.

Watson, Philip. *The Message of the Wesleys*. New York: Macmillan, 1954.

Welch, Barbara Ann. "Charles Wesley and the Celebrations of Evangelical Experience." Ph.D. dissertation, University of Michigan, Ann Arbor, 1971.

Whitefield, George. *George Whitefield's Journals*. London: Banner of Truth Trust, n.d.

Whitehead, John. *The Life of the Rev. Charles Wesley*. Dublin: J. Jones, 1805.

Wiseman, Frederick Luke. *Charles Wesley, Evangelist and Poet*. New York: Abingdon, 1932.

General Index

Index of Selections

Index of Hymns by First Line